Contemporary British Society

A New Introduction to Sociology

Nicholas Abercrombie and Alan Warde

with

Keith Soothill, John Urry and Sylvia Walby
of the Department of Sociology, University of Lancaster

Polity Press

First published 1988 by Polity Press
in association with Basil Blackwell
Reprinted 1988, 1989 (twice), 1990

Editorial office:
Polity Press
65 Bridge Street, Cambridge CB2 1UR, UK

Marketing and production:
Basil Blackwell Ltd
108 Cowley Road, Oxford OX4 1JF, UK

Cataloguing in Publication Data is available
from the British Library
   ISBN 0–7456–0224–X
   ISBN 0–7456–0225–8 Pbk

Typeset in 10 on 11pt Times
by Columns of Reading

Printed in Great Britain by
Billing & Sons Ltd, Worcester

Contemporary British Society

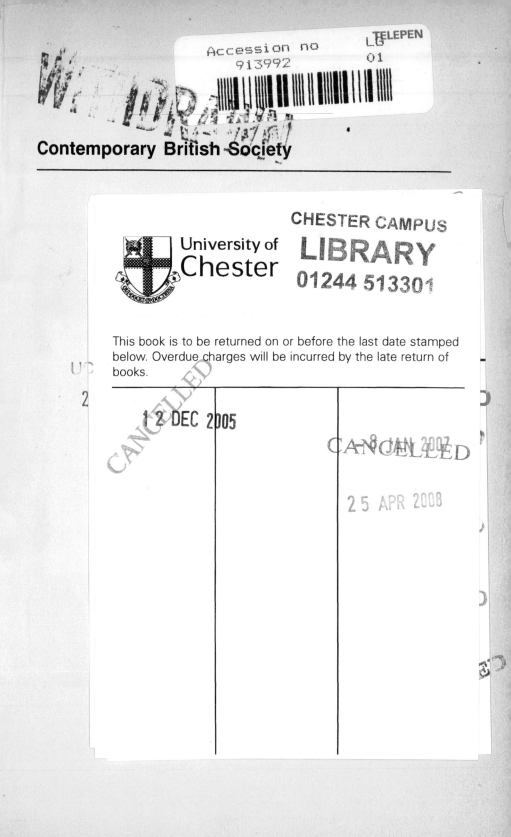

Contents

Acknowledgements

The authors wish to thank those people who helped to devise this book, advised on its contents, or who read sections of it: Tony Giddens, David Hill, Brian Longhurst, Jane Mark-Lawson, the anonymous readers of Polity Press and long-suffering students in the sociology department at Lancaster University. Maeve Conolly and Heather Salt were very patient in typing a long manuscript and we owe them a special vote of thanks. Finally, the staff of Polity Press, Jane Katjavivi, Anna Oxbury and Helen Pilgrim, have been extraordinarily helpful.

How to Use this Book

We have tried to write an approachable and accessible textbook on contemporary British society that looks at the society, rather than debates within sociology, and reviews relatively recent work rather than sociological classics. The following points may help you to get the best out of this book.

1 The book is divided into *chapters*, which are further subdivided into *sections*. We have assumed that many people will read only one section of the book at a time. Each section is therefore designed to stand on its own as a review of a particular topic, although in many chapters there is also an argument that connects sections.

2 In general we have avoided cluttering up the text with academic references. Where we do refer to a book or article we use the author-date system, that is, the reference appears as the name of the author or authors, followed by a date. You can find the full details of the reference by looking in the bibliography at the back of the book under the author and date.

3 At the end of each section you will find a summary of the topic and, often, a list of other sections which contain other relevant material. You will also come across references in the text to other parts of the book which are especially relevant.

4 At the end of each chapter, there is a brief list of books (further reading) that explore in more detail the issues raised in the chapter.

5 There are illustrations of various kinds throughout the book. Courses in sociology now often include exercises in interpreting social statistics presented in various ways. We suggest that you use our tables, diagrams and graphs to find out information that is not discussed in the text; a close reading of a table can often tell you more, or suggest more interesting problems, than pages and pages of text.

6 We have found that people often have a very hazy idea of the geography of the British Isles. To help all our readers we have included maps of Britain and London, with all the places mentioned in the book marked on them.

7   Lastly, enjoy reading our book!

Maps

Map 1 Britain, showing places mentioned in the text

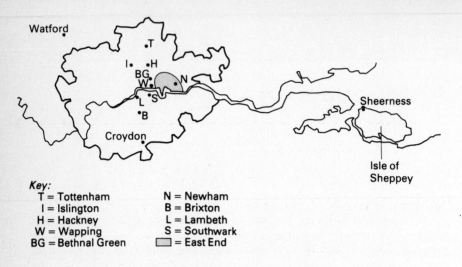

Key:

T = Tottenham	N = Newham
I = Islington	B = Brixton
H = Hackney	L = Lambeth
W = Wapping	S = Southwark
BG = Bethnal Green	▨ = East End

Map 2   London, showing places mentioned in the text

1 Introduction

This book is both an introduction to sociology and an outline of the structure of contemporary British society. Our approach to introducing sociology is through a detailed analysis of one society. Its principal message is that Britain is an extremely complex society, its various social groups having very different social experiences. Our sociological description and explanation seek to portray the extent of this social diversity, and to respect the complexity of social life. At the same time, we try to account for its distinctive features in terms of underlying social-structural mechanisms which produce experiences in the social world. What any individual experiences, and what any social group shares, are significantly constrained by the way in which the society as a whole is *structured*. There is *both* diversity *and* structure.

Approaching Sociology

There are many ways in which sociology may be introduced. One way is via the grand questions of how societies in general cohere or change, questions classically addressed by social theorists such as Marx, Durkheim, Weber and Parsons. A second way is by examining and defining concepts that belong to the sociological vocabulary – concepts like *role*, *status*, *network*, *authority*, *community* – which are related to one another and have more specialized and restricted meanings than they do in ordinary language, and through which it becomes easier to talk about and understand social processes. Or, one could show what sociologists do, the methods they use to discover the social world and the problems that arise in interpreting the data they collect. Yet another way is to present some of the findings about social practices and social relations in particular societies. This is the approach we adopt.

Runciman (1983) claims that sociology, and all other social sciences, consist of four distinct and separable activities: reportage, explanation, description and evaluation. Sociologists, first, report on what happened, on the events, processes or situations. Second, they try to explain *why* those events or processes happened, what were the reasons or causes for their occurrence. Third, sociologists attempt to describe what it was like for people who experienced these events or processes; How did it feel? How did the participants understand and interpret what was going on? Finally, sociologists may evaluate events or processes, declaring them to be good or bad, desirable or not. In practice these four activities tend to become intertwined, but in principle they are separate and different. Thus a reader is able, say, to accept explanations for gender inequalities offered in this book without sharing the evaluations; or the facts reported may be seen as accurate without the reader necessarily agreeing with the descriptions of what it is like to be a woman in contemporary Britain. As Runciman (1983, p. 38) puts it:

> It takes little familiarity with the writings of sociologists, anthro-pologists and historians to be aware how often and how intricately the four are intertwined. In any full-length account of a complex event, process or state of affairs, the writer's purpose is likely to encompass reportage, explanation, description and evaluation alike. He is likely, that is, to want not only to persuade the reader that the events, processes or states of affairs which he has chosen to report came about as he reports them and for the reasons or causes which he has put forward, but at the same time to convey to the reader his idea of what it was like for the participants and to bring the reader round to his view of them as good or bad. But however intricately the four are connected in his account, it will always be possible in principle for the reader to disentangle them. In practice, the disentanglement is often made more difficult than it need be by the language and style in which the work is couched. But the dinstinction between them is no less fundamental to the method-ology of social theory simply because a particular author obscures it, whether deliberately or not.

Sociologists, of course, disagree among themselves and all the elements of sociological inquiry are open to controversy. One sociologist can dispute the accuracy of another's *report* or offer a different *explanation*. But this is a feature of all kinds of knowledge: debate and argument, trying out competing explanations, confronting one report with another are, it is often said, the basis for the development of knowledge. It is not only in sociological knowledge that there is sharp disagreement over facts or theories. Yet in recent times text-books of sociology have tended to introduce sociology in terms of apparently mutually exclusive theoretical 'traditions' – functionalist, structuralist, interactionist, Marxist, or what-ever. There are, of course, theoretical disagreements among sociologists, and theories affect explanations, descriptions and evaluations. But the significance of such theoretical disputes for understanding change in contemporary Britain is easily exaggerated. *In practice*, sociologists tend to use techniques, concepts, explanations and interpretations which draw on many, if not all, theoretical traditions. Sociologists often use concepts from a number of competing theoretical positions, referring to action, meaning, structure and function when discussing social relations and social change. They make such references because of the complexity of today's societies. Sometimes from reading text-books one gets the impression that understanding and analysing the social world is complicated because sociologists make it so, unnecessarily, by adopting obscure and mutually exclusive theoretical positions. Rather, to our way of thinking, the difficulties of sociological analysis arise *because the social world is extremely complex*. We have, therefore, set about giving a concrete sociological analysis of one society, Great Britain, respecting its complexity rather than focusing on sociologists' perceptions of societies. We have tried to write a book about British society, not about sociologists.

Modern Societies

Modern industrial societies are probably the most complex of those known in human history. This is partly reflected in their *density*: relatively large populations are maintained in a comparatively limited space. What is now Britain supported a population of around 3 million in 1600, 6 million in 1800, but 56 million in 1984. This expansion of population was made possible by two developments: an increasing division of labour, and urban growth. The division of labour, through which more specialized work tasks were divided between different firms and individuals, increased the efficiency with which those things necessary to support the growing population could be produced (food, clothes, tools, houses, etc.). The expansion of cities provided a physical environment which helped the organization of the division of labour in production and a new social environment for the larger population. Perhaps the major cause of the complexity of contemporary British society is, however, the speed of social change: Britain (like all modern societies) is a *dynamic* society. This dynamism originated from and is sustained by *capitalist social relations*.

  Britain is fundamentally a capitalist society. By this we mean that:

1 there is private ownership of the 'means of production' (property, plant, machinery, etc.);
2 economic activity is geared to making profits;
3 profits go to the owners of the means of production;
4 workers generally do not own productive property but work for wages;
5 the processes of production and sale of goods and services are organized into markets; everything is *commodified*.

These economic processes produce a social structure, one of whose main characteristics is a division between the owners of the means of production and the waged workers.

To define capitalism in such a way does not, of course, mean that it has remained unaltered since its origins in the seventeenth and eighteenth centuries. Quite the contrary, as we show in this book there have been drastic changes in capitalism. The pattern of ownership of the means of production, changes in the distribution of income and wealth, the increasing complexity and fragmentation of the class structure, and the growth of the welfare state are but a few of the changes that have radically altered capitalist society. Indeed, capitalism by its very nature is an economic system that produces changes and diversity and this is one of its main features. It produces a self-propelling, ever-accelerating sort of society.

Max Weber, among many others, noted how early capitalists of the seventeenth and eighteenth centuries used what he considered a peculiar logic – devoting their lives to accumulating wealth, or capital, but without spending it. He described this as the development of a 'Protestant ethic' which forebade the use of wealth and encouraged 'asceticism'. At the same time, the Protestant ethic encouraged hard work and made worldly success a positive religious virtue. Manufacturers, farmers and merchants of the Protestant faith thus sought business success which was then, as now, measured by profit-making, but had no way of spending their increasing wealth other than reinvesting in their businesses. This process of profit-making and reinvestment, when seen in the light of competition between manufacturers, farmers and merchants, is a source of economic dynamism and growth in itself. It was Marx, among the classical theorists, who most clearly observed the way in which competition between private enterprises led to constant innovation. Firms cannot stand still. They must reinvest and reorganize their operations continually, otherwise their competitors will put them out of business.

The most simple example of this process is that of the introduction of new machinery. If firm A buys machines which make it possible to produce goods more cheaply than firm B, then B will be unable to sell its products and will go out of business, unless it responds. To purchase the same, or better, machinery is one response, but there are others – getting workers to work harder, producing new products, or buying out firm A, for instance. The point, however, is that this innovation and change is self-perpetuating, inevitably built into an economic system where individuals and firms are free to produce any goods they choose, how they choose, constrained only by profitable competition. This 'logic' can be seen quite clearly in contemporary economic life: machinery becomes obsolete very quickly; there are frequent mergers, take-overs, and closures; new firms are continually being set up, and new generations of products appear increasingly rapidly.

Rapid economic change, inherent in capitalist social relations, is closely linked to cultural change. Partly because of continual economic development, British people are used to change. Though not always welcoming it, many people positively *seek* change. This may occur at the personal and individual level (moving to another town, joining a new religious movement, buying new types of goods, taking a different job). It also occurs collectively, in the political sphere and in the neighbourhood: radical political parties and new social movements are associations of people who collectively set about changing the social world. Britain is an 'active' society: people act as if they can alter the conditions under which they live out their lives, to improve their own conditions and those of others.

This constant change and innovation generates a distinctive kind of social experience which some contemporary sociologists refer to as 'the experience of modernity'. Rapid change leads to uncertainty about the future, feelings of insecurity and anxiety, a sense of lost bearings in negotiating everyday life. Yet, at the same time, it brings a restlessness with permanence, a seeking after new experiences in pursuit of self-development, and selfish concern with personal well-being. The 'modern experience' generates particular personality types. At the same time, it threatens social instability as norms and behaviour change, old values and practices are discarded, new kinds of fads and fashions emerge, and traditional institutions become obsolete or are transformed. The experience of modernity is, thus, contradictory. On the one hand, it is exciting, bringing new and diverse experiences and fresh horizons. On the other hand, it removes all certainties, leaving people groping around in a social world without any established norms or guide-lines. This, the paradox of modernity, is neatly summed up by Berman (1983, p. 1):

> There is a mode of vital experience – experience of space and time, of the self and others, of life's possibilities and perils – that is shared by men and women all over the world today. I will call this body of experience 'modernity'. To be modern is to find ourselves in an environment that promises us adventure, power, joy, growth, transformation of ourselves and the world – and, at the same time, that threatens to destroy everything we have, everything we know, everything we are. Modern environments and experiences cut across all boundaries of geography and ethnicity, of class and nationality, of religion and ideology: in this sense, modernity can be said to unite all mankind. But it is a paradoxical unity, a unity of disunity: it pours us all into a maelstrom of perpetual disintegration and renewal, of struggle and contradiction, of ambiguity and anguish. To be modern is to be part of a universe in which, as Marx said, 'all that is solid melts into air'.

Britain is a capitalist society with a 'modern' culture. It has the 'paradoxical unity' Berman describes. Some of the possibilities for new experience and social experimentation are to be welcomed, others not;

the paradox is that we tend to get both the beneficial and the detrimental consequences at the same time. For example, family relationships are changing: new laws and new attitudes to divorce permit women, especially, to escape miserable marriages, but that often leaves them in situations of social and economic insecurity, with heavy responsibilities for their children. The growth of youth sub-cultures – punks, mods, and the like – is equally typical of modernity. Unconventional styles of dress, language, music, and entertainment, alter frequently as young people pursue distinctive, and new, group identities. Such styles are tied up with a capitalist commercialism which, in seeking to persuade people to buy more, encourages changes of fashion.

In an important sense the experience of modernity is an *urban* phenomenon, an experience that is strongest in the largest of cities. In the city, social relations are relatively impersonal, impermanent, varied and unpredictable. Of course, not all social relations are like that. There are urban communities that are tightly knit and long established, where everyone knows everybody else and where there are collectively enforced rules of behaviour. A sense of community survives within a more general culture of modernity, and this shows the complexity of modern social experience. Complexity involves a multiplicity of experiences, and an enormous diversity.

Diversity can also generate inequality and, thus, possibly, conflict. Key themes of sociological inquiry concern inequalities between classes, between the sexes, ethnic groups, status- and age-groups. Such differences need not produce conflict but they often do, particularly when difference is *interpreted* as inequality. The pursuit of equality, along with the pursuit of liberty, have been fundamental bases of actions to promote social change in Britain throughout the capitalist era. Social groups seeing themselves as unequally treated have organized together to improve their position. The struggle over the franchise (who should be able to vote), waged first by middle-class men, then working-class men, followed by women, is a well-known example of the pursuit of one aspect of political equality – the right of equal citizenship.

The mechanisms of capitalist social relations and the division of labour combine to reproduce economic inequalities. Some employers make more profit than others, and some people, having no capital, make no profit at all but work for wages. And the circumstances under which people work for wages vary widely too: some employees have well-paid, secure jobs, a lot of control over what they do, and work in pleasant conditions, but for others the experience of work is quite different. These inequalities, between employers, between employers and employees, and between different groups of workers, are perpetual sources of conflict in capitalist societies. In most cases, though, conflict is *institutionalized*, that is to say there are channels or institutions which resolve conflicts peacefully, by negotiation, without recourse to the use of force or violence. Thus, parliamentary democratic procedure, bargaining procedures in industrial relations or regulation of competition between firms, are all ways of institutionalizing conflict. Of course, these are not always effective: internal war in Northern Ireland, riots in the inner-city, policemen confronting striking miners, are all contemporary instances of conflict escaping from institutional regulation. But the point is, diversity generates conflict, fuelling experiences of instability, encouraging people to act to re-establish stability, which in turn produces further change.

Diversity, complexity and change are, then, features of contemporary British society. Any individual will know of, or share, only a very small proportion of the variety of experiences that make up the social mosaic of the modern society. That, indeed, is one of the fascinations of reading good sociological reportage and description – it allows some access to the range and pattern of the experiences of social groups other than those to which the reader belongs. Sociology, however, also seeks to connect together context and experience, to show how certain social mechanisms or structures constrain and shape experiences. For all the diversity and complexity of everyday life, there are patterns to social action and interaction. The social world is *structured*. Just as the mosaics of the floors of Roman houses are made up of hundreds of pieces which, nevertheless, make a complete design, the patterning of social relations cannot be seen by looking at the individual elements. The mosaic has to be examined in terms of the *relative* positions of its different pieces, how they stand in relation to one another.

One of the outstanding features of societies is the way in which component parts are highly interrelated, or *interdependent*. This inter-dependence is often expressed in technical language in terms of a social *system*. Or, sometimes, the social system is described as an 'organism', societies being likened to animal bodies in which the various organs – heart, liver, lungs – all work together to keep the animal alive. Like most analogies, the model of the organism can be misleading if used too literally. There *is*, however, something system-like about social organiz-ation, with one institution affecting many of the others. Thus, for instance, the social organization of work affects the way education is organized, changes the role of the family in bringing up children, and results in the unequal distribution of income and wealth. It is this, the interdependence of social institutions, which makes sociological explan-ation so difficult and complicated. If one part of the mosaic changes then the whole pattern is altered, making it difficult to pin-point a single cause of any particular event, process or change.

The concepts that we have discussed above are ones which we will use in our analysis of change in British society. We stress that Britain is a diverse, changing and complex society. At the root of that diversity is a capitalist economic system and a 'modern' culture. These are funda-mental bases of social change, sometimes generating order and harmony, at other times disorder and conflict. They are the structures behind everyday life with all its variety, ambiguity and contradiction.

Contemporary Britain

Some of the implications of the preceding remarks on the sociological interpretation of modern capitalist societies are briefly illustrated in the following thumb-nail sketch of key structures and changes of contemporary British society which we discuss in greater detail in the chapters that follow.

Our understanding of contemporary Britain begins by recognizing the process of industrial change which the country has experienced over the last decade or so. In the context of an international recession, the British economy has declined more than most other nations in a comparable position in the world economic system. Many British firms have lost out in competition with foreign equivalents, though it has to be recognized that, increasingly, the most important firms are multinational corporations anyway. In response to this harsh external environment many firms have undergone restructuring, with changes in ownership as a result of takeovers, and changes in their internal organization. This restructuring has serious effects upon employees, partly as new machinery is introduced making workers redundant, and partly as jobs are redesigned so as to save money by making each worker more productive. In fact, British workers have increased their productivity very considerably in the last decade, but this has not improved the relative competitiveness of British industry. One of the most significant effects of the general restructuring of British industry has been the decline of employment in manufacturing industry. Though some of the workers who have been displaced from traditional manufacturing industries have found jobs in the so-called 'service sector', many have joined the expanding ranks of the unemployed. The British state has, in the 1980s, been either unwilling or incapable of improving the situation, preferring to allow the cold winds of capitalist competition to reshape the economy rather than intervening directly.

Another effect of industrial change has been to moderate industrial conflict. Industrial disputes reached a post-war high in 1979 but, since then, with the marked exception of the bitter miners' strike in 1984-5, industrial conflict has been muted. A number of factors account for this. High levels of unemployment, the decline of the traditional heavy manufacturing industries such as shipbuilding and steel, which were bastions of trade unionism, and more determined anti-unionism by government and employers, have combined to weaken the trade-union movement. Changes in the division of labour and the industrial structure thus have contained conflict in the workplace, though there is no reason to imagine that the workers feel any less resentment about pay and working conditions.

Industrial change inevitably affects class relations and the class structure, because occupation is a fundamental basis of class position.

The shape of the occupational structure has been changing in recent years, the numbers of manual workers declining, and the numbers of professional and semi-professional jobs increasing. A debate rages about the effects of this on class relations. In the past, class conflict has been a major source of social change. In the twentieth century, the working class, through the organizations of the labour movement (primarily trade unions and the Labour Party), has exerted much political pressure for social reform. The main supporters of the labour movement were, however, manual workers, who were the majority of the working population and whose social situation was visibly distinct from that of the upper and upper-middle class.

The changing size and composition of British classes has, arguably, reduced the strength of the working class as a force for change. The future of class conflicts depend also on classes other than the workers. In many respects the income and work-situation of routine clerical workers is no longer different from that of manual workers, though in the past they have often had distinct political commitments. Other elements of the middle classes are also experiencing change and the future of British political life will be strongly affected by their reactions. Despite the flux at these lower levels of the class structure, there is very great continuity and permanence among the upper class, that network of property-owning families whose power and influence continues to structure social life in Britain. The upper class remains exclusive, as studies of the social origins of people in top positions show. Despite much upward social mobility in Britain in recent times, the very top positions remain within the grasp of hereditary upper-class families.

Women have played a critically important part in the redefinition of the social division of labour in the last 20 years. For instance, there are more married women in paid work today than there have been at any time in the last 100 years. However, the jobs women have tend to be ones which are relatively poorly paid and carry little authority. The segregation of men's work from women's work, which is the way that gender differentials are maintained, is increasingly a source of frustration and annoyance to women, who are currently organizing to improve their position. This is to be expected since, apart from education where opportunities for girls and women have been improving in recent years, the inequalities between men and women have not been reduced. The disadvantages women face cannot be entirely explained by the mechanisms of capitalist social relations. Because of this we have to look for different mechanisms and different sets of relations in order to explain the position of women. These *patriarchal* relations coexist with the logic of capitalist inequalities, producing the particular structure of inequalities between men and women in Britain.

Patriarchy is a concept which recognizes inequalities of power between men and women, inequalities which can be seen, for instance, in the unequal distribution of housework, stereotypes of femininity which describe women as helpless and passive, and in male violence against women. One of the more significant new developments of the last decade or so has been the revival of a feminist movement trying actively to promote change in the typical forms of gender relations in our society. Women have become more aware of their oppression; sexism and male chauvinism are expressions which have entered everyday language; groups of women have organized themselves to contest political issues which particularly affect women.

In a similar way, we can see the intersection of capitalist social relations and cultural stereotypes creating a further social division which is a source of social conflict – that between ethnic groups. Many members of ethnic groups, particularly those of Caribbean and Asian descent, even if many of them have been born in Britain, suffer social and material deprivation when compared with white people. The very presence in Britain of many different ethnic groups is one mark of the diversity of culture and experience among different sections of the population. Family forms and religious experience distinguish ethnic groups, and some of the most vital of contemporary cultural products – food, music, oriental religions – are the result of the presence of people with different cultural traditions. These differences are, however, frequently turned into bases for much-resented inequalities. There can be no doubt that black people tend to get poorer jobs than do whites. What is more, they tend to suffer the consequences of white racism, hostile or deprecatory attitudes and behaviours, which are directed at them merely on the basis of their skin colour. Again, one can see an intersection of the mechanism of the labour market, in which black people get the poorest of working-class jobs and suffer the highest rates of unemployment. And, once again, we see signs of active resistance, of attempts by the disadvantaged groups to express their dissatisfaction and collectively to alter their circumstances.

This discussion of the generation of inequalities between classes, genders and ethnic groups in terms of income and employment has mainly been concerned with the impact of capitalist relations of production on different sections of the population. We should emphasize yet again that this is insufficient, on its own, as an explanation of why such inequalities exist. There are many features of the particular inequalities between the sexes and between ethnic groups that are not satisfactorily explained by economic processes alone. We need to refer, in addition, to both the existence of patriarchal relations of male domination, and racial prejudice and discrimination (racism) in addition in order to explain how it is that women and ethnic minorities find themselves in a disadvantaged position. Separating out these mechanisms and weighing them against one another is extremely difficult but absolutely essential in the course of sociological explanation.

The next aspect of the contemporary social structure and change that we deal with is more directly concerned with the cultural experience of modernity. The family is one institution which, perhaps, exemplifies the degree of variety and complexity that characterizes social experience in Britain, and one which illustrates the insecurity and instability of social relations in the contemporary world.

One of the most striking features of the contemporary British family is the variety of forms it assumes. Besides distinctive household patterns of ethnic minorities, which are often adapted from their particular religious and cultural traditions or the need to provide accommodation for newly arrived immigrant kinsfolk, there are a remarkable diversity of household forms among other sections of the population too. There is a dominant image of what a 'normal' family is in contemporary Britain – a small, nuclear family of parents and dependent children. In reality, this is not normal at all, and only a small proportion of households are like this. Various social changes, including the facts that people live longer than they used to, that many more people are getting divorced, and that people expect more from marriage than before, have meant a rise in the numbers of single-person households, one-parent families and of families formed by remarriage and step-parenting. Such changes may produce stress and anxiety within marriage as well as satisfactions.

Many of the contradictions of contemporary British society, and some of the points of tension between the organization of economic life and the culture of modernity, are reflected within the education system. Educational institutions both express and create social divisions. Current emphasis upon making education relevant for work – training for economic life – typifies these contradictions. On the one hand, educating people for future work roles always entails selection and differentiation: some people are made into successes, others into failures. Schools create inequalities between individuals by preparing their pupils for different places in the division of labour. They treat their pupils differently by class, gender and ethnic group. On the other hand, schools are expected to transmit a common or dominant culture – to educate young people for citizenship and to be full members of a national community. To what extent schools actually do either of these things very effectively is open to debate. However, the complexity of the role that educational institutions play gives some indication of the complex interdependencies between institutions in British society: educational institutions are intended to fit in with the entire industrial and occupational complex, with the family, and with the dominant political institutions. What schools do is relevant to, and interdependent with, all other major institutions in contemporary Britain. Small wonder, then, that schools fail in some respects to satisfy the demand of all the groups who have an interest in their activities.

We have talked about the way that people in a modern, diverse, and rapidly changing world may set about trying to change it. To do this, people have to have a way of seeing the world, a way of understanding both what is wrong with it from their point of view and what is needed to effect a change. These ways of seeing we call *culture*. The modern world has an enormous diversity of cultures, each appropriate to the multiplicity of social groups we described earlier. So, the working-class way of looking at the world is different from that of the middle class; the culture of women, very different from that of men. However, there also exists a general set of cultural themes, perhaps to do with morality, the importance of nation and so on, that prevail in modern Britain. These are dominant, both in the sense that they are the themes most available in the educational system and the mass media, and in that they reflect the interests of dominant social groups. The intriguing sociological question concerns the relationship of the multiplicity of cultures to the dominant one. Are the many cultures subordinate or resistant to the dominant one? Is the dominant culture effectively transmitted through the mass media, for instance?

The same sorts of questions, concerning diversity and change in modern society and domination and resistance, also arise when considering politics. They are, indeed, the very stuff of politics. In parliamentary democracies people have the power, even if it is rather restricted, to change things. The most obvious way is through voting. Here too the social world is becoming more diverse and complex. Generally speaking, voters seem to be abandoning their traditional political loyalties, especially those formed along class lines. Also the *means* by which people seek to change their situation have become more diverse. Voting is, after all, only a periodic expression of opinion. British society is also characterized by a multiplicity of social movements and pressure groups. Again, many of these represent a new diversity of political mobilization. Women, ethnic groups and the peace and ecology movements are but four voices represented in new social movements which express their specific grievances and wishes.

It has, however, to be recognized that the capacity to change society, either by voting or by involvement in pressure groups, is limited. The powers of the state have very greatly increased in the twentieth century, especially since the Second World War. This is partly because the state has come to intervene in citizens' lives in a number of different ways, and partly a result of the vast resources the state can deploy. It is also a matter of the ultimate capacity to control. In this last respect, the growth in numbers of the police in Britain and of their powers, is of significance. The character of the police force is changing: it is becoming more professional and technologically sophisticated. Some of these changes have been brought about in response to the fear of a rising rate of crime. Others are introduced because of the civil disturbances which, as we indicated earlier, have to be seen as elements of a rapidly changing society showing symptoms of strain.

Contemporary British society, as we have argued, is increasingly diverse and complex and is, furthermore, changing very quickly. Underlying this complexity are some basic structuring elements, two of the most important of which are capitalist social relations and a culture of modernity. The rest of this book looks at these issues in much greater depth.

2 Work

2.1 Introduction

> To get the whole world out of bed
> And washed, and dressed, and warmed, and fed,
> To work, and back to bed again,
> Believe me, Saul, costs worlds of pain.
> John Masefield, *The Everlasting Mercy*

> Which of us . . . is to do the hard and dirty work for the rest – and for
> what pay? Who is to do the pleasant and clean work, and for what pay?
> John Ruskin, *Sesame and Lilies*

The organization of work is the basic element of modern social structure.
Many of the most important institutions in British society – the education
system, the family, the law, and politics – are tailored to meet the
requirements of work. Work is also a fundamental determinant of the
experience of individuals. There is a strong connection between the kind
of work a person does and many other aspects of their existence. How
long you live, whom you marry, how much money you have, where you
live, and how your children will fare, are all affected by your work.

Work is central to social existence because of the intensive division of
labour in modern societies. Labour, or work, is a feature of all human
societies. Personal survival and the reproduction of the species requires
always that work is done to provide food, shelter, security, and the like.
That work is always *socially organized*, though the pattern of organization
varies enormously between societies. Peasant households typically
produce for themselves most of what they need. Most modern Britons, by
contrast, do very specialized jobs, for which they receive wages, with
which in turn they buy most of the things they need. This specialization,
this complex division of labour, requires a very high degree of social
organization. Just think of how many people are required to behave
regularly and reliably in a huge range of different tasks in order to
operate British Rail, for example. The degree of coordination required

between BR's 180,000 men and women employees is immense, though we now take it for granted.

In capitalist societies, the way the division of labour is organized derives from the pursuit of profit by those who own the means to produce things – commodities that can be sold, usually to satisfy people's needs. Workers are paid wages to bring them to work to produce commodities. The parts played by individual workers in the production process are very varied and the rewards and satisfactions obtained from work are correspondingly different. From this phenomenon of differentation, social inequalities, social divisions and social conflicts are derived.

Examples of the inequalities deriving from work are well-known. In 1983 weekly earned incomes for workers in full-time employment ranged from £67 per week on average for women manual workers in clothing manufacture, to £2,275 per week for the chairman of Barclays Bank. The very rich, like the very poor, do not have earnings, but unearned incomes. Some jobs have more prestige than others: prestige is usually related to income and to the nature of the work done. Some jobs offer more freedom than others. Some work is creative, much more is very routine. Perhaps most important, some jobs give authority to their occupants: managerial and supervisory positions carry with them some degree of power. In all these respects, the division of labour produces social inequality.

Unsurprisingly, then, conflict arises. Individuals and social groups attempt to alter the social organization of work to their own benefit. The owners and managers of firms try to organize work to pursue the goals of profit, growth, efficiency and control. This generates competition between firms and conflict with workers. Recently, the reassertion of managerial prerogatives – the so-called 'right of management to manage' – has been a central strategic objective of these groups. This implies the existence of other groups who contest those goals and whose interests are served by a different manner of work organization. Both trade unions and professional associations are bodies that seek to influence rewards and working practices. Thus, we have the conditions for industrial conflict, primarily between workers and management, but also between groups of workers. Sometimes these conflicts become generalized: class struggles are those based on the shared interests of many groups of workers against many managements; gender struggles are those based upon a recognition of generalized, antagonistic interests between women and men. Gender struggles also appear in other spheres of work apart from employment.

Money mediates between capital and labour: employees get paid. But it must be recognized that much work is unpaid. Housework is the most outstanding example of this. A sample of housewives with children, interviewed by Oakley (1974), did an *average* of 77 hours of *domestic* work per week (i.e. routine household tasks and child-care). That is surely work, but not employment. The distinction is very important.

Employment is the kind of work classified as an occupation and paid for in wages. It is employment which produces the inequalities of power and income which are part of the sphere of industrial relations. Trades unions and professional associations, wage negotiations and job-demarcation disputes are expressions of employment relationships.

Other kinds of work are subject to different principles of organization. Domestic work is divided up between people, usually so that women do more than men. This unequal distribution of tasks is underpinned by the institutions of marriage and the family, producing conflicts between men and women (gender divisions). The link between these two different ways of organizing work is a matter of great dispute (dealt with at length in chapter 4).

The division of labour in society as a whole is constantly changing. Some industries expand while others contract. Within industries the nature of tasks changes, as new machinery is introduced and new working practices are imposed. The spread of occupations is altered at the same time: currently, for instance, the proportion of manual workers in the labour force is declining. Demarcations between men's and women's jobs change too. There is also a geographical aspect to the division of labour, in the sense that where firms choose to locate their factories and offices has significant social consequences. Increasingly, the largest international corporations are locating their factories in the developing countries where labour is cheap, and their headquarters, when in Britain, in the South East of England. Divisions of labour outside formal, paid employment also alter. The domestic division of labour is changing. The availability of domestic machinery and the virtual disappearance of domestic servants have changed tasks and social relationships within households.

Changes in the division of labour have consequences for many other aspects of life. For instance, educational reforms since the mid-1970s have been directed towards preparing children better for new employment opportunities. Vocational training, youth-training schemes, the expansion of engineering and information technology in universities, are all justified in terms of providing a more efficient social organization of work (see chapter 8, section 8.3).

Some of the effects of a changing division of labour are illustrated in figure 2.1. This diagram does not exhaust all the effects but, nevertheless, suggests that the division of labour has consequences for everyday life, family structure, community, class and politics. The connection between changes in the division of labour and other aspects of social life are not, however, necessarily direct or simple. The division of labour is not the only cause of, for example, political change and, indeed, political action in turn reacts to change the division of labour. The connections are complex.

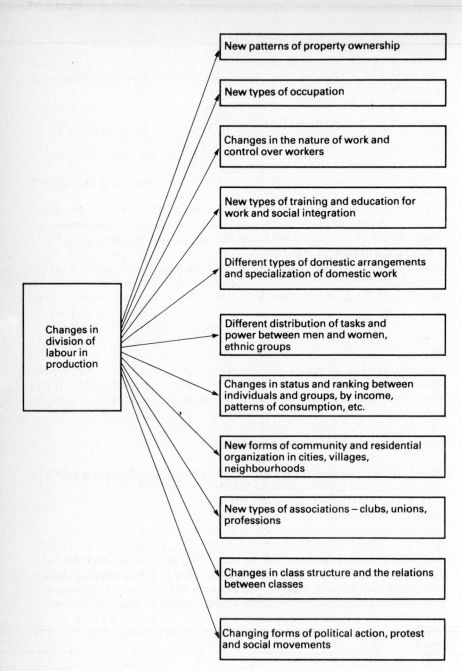

New patterns of property ownership

New types of occupation

Changes in the nature of work and control over workers

New types of training and education for work and social integration

Different types of domestic arrangements and specialization of domestic work

Different distribution of tasks and power between men and women, ethnic groups

Changes in status and ranking between individuals and groups, by income, patterns of consumption, etc.

New forms of community and residential organization in cities, villages, neighbourhoods

New types of associations – clubs, unions, professions

Changes in class structure and the relations between classes

Changing forms of political action, protest and social movements

Changes in division of labour in production

Figure 2.1 Some social effects of changes in the division of labour in modern Britain

2.2 Ownership and Control

> Economic power, in terms of control over physical aspects, is apparently responding to a centripetal force, tending more and more to concentrate in the hands of a few corporate managements. At the same time, beneficial ownership is centrifugal, tending to divide and sub-divide, to split into even smaller units and to pass freely from hand to hand. In other words, ownership continually becomes more dispersed; the power formerly joined to it becomes increasingly concentrated; and the corporate system is thereby more securely estabished.
>
> Berle and Means (1932)

It is a familiar argument that, in the twentieth century, the whole structure of the ownership and control of British industry has changed. A series of factors contribute to this: firms have grown larger by merger and take-over; increasingly, businesses are not owned by single entrepreneurs or their families but by many shareholders; and large financial institutions have gradually assumed ownership of significant sectors of British industry. These changes and others, raise the question of ownership and control which is posed in the quotation above from Berle and Means. If ownership is no longer concentrated in the hands of a single entrepreneur, but is spread among a number of shareholders who may have different interests, where does control of the enterprise lie? Do shareholders get together to dictate decisions? Or do professional managers take effective control? There are, in fact, a number of different issues raised by these questions and we start by considering the way in which the ownership of firms has become more concentrated.

Concentration and control

British industry might appear to be composed of a mass of competing firms. As consumers, when we wish to buy something, we are often faced with a welter of brand names. In the supermarket, for instance, a large number of manufacturers are represented, offering a wide range of different types of product. On the other hand, newspapers, radio and television in 1986 were full of reports of a 'merger boom' – of attempts by one large company to take over another. This led to take-over battles in which large companies struggled with each other to gain control of another firm which was often in a quite different area of business. These take-over battles were often very public as the advertisement in figure 2.2 shows.

Are firms typically independent or are they, perhaps, linked together? What then are the relationships of ownership *between* firms? Do the many apparently competing brands, for example, conceal the fact that a few firms manufacture them all? The general answer to these questions is that in the twentieth century, there has been a concentration of ownership in British industry.

Figure 2.2   Take-over battles, with large companies competing with each other to gain control of another firm, were often quite public
Source: Imperial Tobacco Limited.

Concentration and the corporate economy

In Britain today, there are fewer and larger firms taking a larger proportion of sales. The British economy is increasingly dominated by large corporations; it has become a 'corporate economy'. As Hannah (1976, p. 1) says in a recent study:

> It is a commonplace that in the course of the present century British industry has witnessed a transformation from a disaggregated structure of predominantly small, competing firms to a concentrated structure dominated by large, and often monopolistic, corporations. The 100 corporations which now occupy the dominant position account for something approaching one half of total manufacturing output, whilst at the turn of the century the largest 100 firms accounted for barely 15 per cent of output.

The rise of the corporate economy can be investigated in a number of ways. An initial approach is to look at the degree to which a few large firms dominate particular industries. The conventional way of measuring this is by the 'concentration ratio'.

The increasing concentration ratio: The concentration ratio usually refers to the proportion of sales in any particular industry accounted for by the five largest firms in that industry. Aaronovitch and Sawyer (1975) show substantial degrees of concentration in 1968 in a whole range of industries (table 2.1).

The table shows that in cigarettes, coal and petroleum almost all the sales are taken by the five largest firms, and in food the proportion is 70 per cent. Even in the industry group with the lowest concentration

Table 2.1   Five-firm concentration ratios in a number of manufacturing industries

Industry	Concentration ratio (%)
Cigarettes	99.7
Coal and petroleum	93.7
Metal manufacture	74.9
Vehicles	90.8
Beer, spirits	69.8
Food	70.4
Clothing and footwear	33.0
Timber, furniture	23.6

Source: Adapted from Aaronovitch and Sawyer (1975) *Big Business* (London and Basingstoke, Macmillan), table 4.8, p. 99, with permission.

ratio – timber and furniture – the five largest firms account for almost one-quarter of the sales.

The degree of concentration in manufacturing also shows a steady increase with the largest five firms taking a larger and larger proportion of sales. In the period 1963-8, for example, the concentration ratios rose about 1 per cent in food, 6.5 per cent in timber and furniture and about 10 per cent in metal manufacture.

Evidence of the degree of concentration in non-manufacturing industries is less easy to come by. In the financial sector in 1971 the four largest banks controlled 92 per cent of total deposits, while the four largest life insurance companies took 31 per cent of their market. At the other end of the scale there are service industries that are localized and segmented. The three largest hotel groups, for instance, control only 8 per cent of the total number of beds available.

The way in which a few firms dominate particular industries of markets is not necessarily the most sociologically interesting thing about the concentration of British industry. We also need to look at the economy as a whole and the way in which relatively few firms dominate it. This is particularly important as businesses have grown larger by absorbing other firms that operate in quite different areas of industry. The result is the increased importance of conglomerates with diversified interests in a very wide range of products.

The growth of conglomerate enterprises: In figure 2.3 we show what share of output in manufacturing industry is taken by the 100 largest firms.

In the early part of this century the largest 100 firms produced about 16 per cent of output, but the proportion had jumped to some 45 per cent in 1970 and it is still rising. Figure 2.3 also makes clear that there have been two spurts of concentration, from 1910 to 1930, and from the later 1940s onwards. An alternative way of showing concentration is to consider the proportion of assets held by the largest manufacturing firms. Table 2.2 shows that even in the short period from 1957 to 1965 there were substantial increases in the proportion of assets owned by larger firms. In 1969 the largest 200 firms had 86 per cent of assets, an increase of 13 per cent over 1957. The five largest firms own one-fifth of manufacturing industry.

Another sign that British manufacturing industry is becoming more concentrated with fewer and larger firms taking an increasing share of assets, sales, profits, investment and employment, lies in the declining significance of small firms. The share of manufacturing output taken by small firms (defined as those employing fewer than 200 people) declined from 20 per cent of the total in 1958 to only 16 per cent in 1963.

The most important single cause of concentration in the British economy is merger, or the acquisition of one firm by another. During the 1960s and 1970s most of the disappearances of firms quoted on the Stock

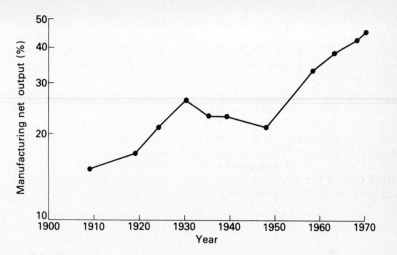

Figure 2.3 The share of the 100 largest firms in manufacturing net output, 1909–70 (log scale)

Source: Hannah (1976) *The Rise of the Corporate Economy* (London, Methuen & Co.), figure 7.1, p. 105. Reproduced with permission.

Table 2.2 Proportion of assets in UK manufacturing held by large firms

	1957	1965
Share of largest 5 firms	17.0	20.1
Share of largest 50 firms	48.4	60.9
Share of largest 100 firms	60.1	74.9
Share of largest 200 firms	73.0	86.2

Source: Hannah (1976) *The Rise of the Corporate Economy* (London, Methuen & Co.), p. 166. Reproduced with permission.

Exchange were due to mergers with other firms. One index of the importance of concentration by acquisition is the rising proportion of investment in the acquisition of other companies. In the past, the bulk of investment by a manufacturing company would be in the purchase of plant, machinery or the expansion of its work-force. More recently, the greatest proportion of investment finance goes to the purchase of other firms. The expenditure on mergers as a proportion of investment in manufacturing has increased from 17 per cent in 1957/9, to 30 per cent in 1963/5, and to 58 per cent in 1966/8 (Campbell, 1981).

We have been using manufacturing industry as the main example in the discussion so far. Indeed, it is this sector that has led concentration, although other sectors, in finance and property for example, are following suit. Related to this is a point that we made earlier about the diversification of large firms. Firms grow bigger often by the acquisition of other firms not trading in their sector of the economy. In 1955 only 12 per cent of all mergers were of this diversified or 'conglomerate' type, while by 1972 over half were (Campbell, 1981).

In sum, there is an increasing domination of the British economy by large firms, many of which are growing larger by extending their interests into new and different areas of the economy. As the take-over battles of 1986 seem to indicate, it is the already-large firms that are most involved in merger activity, giving themselves an ever-faster rate of growth.

Interlocking directorships

This process of concentration, the rise of the corporate economy, gives a certain unity to the British economy. Industry and commerce are no longer made up of a multiplicity of competing firms with little connection with each other but are dominated by relatively few firms. The evidence that we have presented so far actually rather understates the degree of unity. This partly arises from the fact that firms may own only relatively small parts of other firms, less than that required to give total control. These smaller overlaps in ownership do not count as a merger, yet they clearly do represent a considerable degree of cooperation and inter-dependence between firms. Equally as significant is the phenomenon of interlocking directorships. The ease of communication between firms is very much enhanced by the fairly common practice of having directors of one large company sitting on the boards of other similarly powerful firms. As Scott (1985, p. 44) says: 'These "interlocking directorships" tie together the diverse capitalist interests and provide a basis for some degree of coordination in their activities.'

Figure 2.4 shows part of the network of interlocking directorships by portraying the directorships held by a small number of people. In the study from which this illustration is taken, 11 people had a total of 57 directorships in the top 250 companies, and many others in subsidiaries of these companies and in smaller companies. The directorships of 9 of these 11 can be linked together in the chain shown. Thus, a mere 9 people link together 39 very large companies. This is clearly only a section of a large network but one which is, nevertheless, held together nationally, at least in the larger firms, by a remarkably small number of people. Scott (1985) argues that at the heart of this network are those companies which dominate the capital market and are able to provide finance for investment. The banks, particularly, are organized into cliques and clusters which occupy a central position. But this centrality should not be seen as bank *control* over the non-financial sector as a whole, rather it simply reflects the banks' importance as providers of capital. Besides providing capital, the network of interlocking directorships also makes for a more efficient flow of information between firms. The coordination and

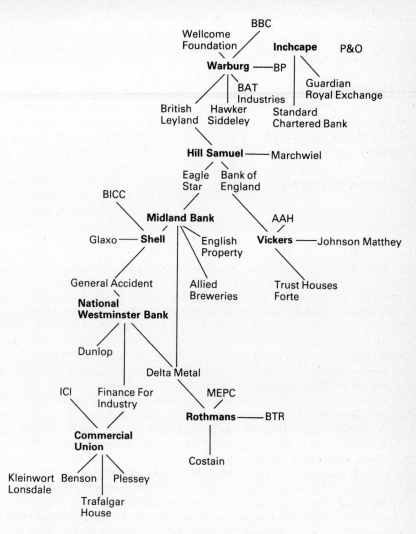

Figure 2.4 Networks of interconnecting shareholdings in a number of large companies, 1976
Source: Scott (1985), p. 45.

unity of the economic system which, we have agreed, is a characteristic much more pronounced now than even 50 years ago, is thus partly facilitated by the *personal* contacts between directors. Interlocking directorships are, however, not the only vehicle by which personal relationships unify British industry. Of some continuing importance is the persistence of family and kinship relationships – an issue we take up in more detail in chapter 3, section 3.6, on the upper class. Kinship connections are important because of the continuing significance of the personal ownership of shares, and it is to this issue that we now turn.

Ownership and control

The quotation from Berle and Means on page 17 argues that there has been a progressive separation of legal ownership from effective control. The discussion here applies mostly to large companies with multiple shareholdings; in small firms there may be no separation of ownership and control, but, as we saw in the previous section, the British economy is increasingly dominated by large firms. In such companies, shareholders each own only a relatively small proportion of the shares. With ownership diversified in this way, real control passes to the professional managers who, working in the company full-time, have a much better idea of the company's business than do shareholders. However, we should, perhaps, distinguish operational from strategic control. By the former, we mean those decisions that affect the day-to-day conduct of a company. Strategic control, on the other hand, refers to those large-scale decisions that are vital to the firms' future. Examples of strategic decisions would be what level of investment to aim for in which areas of the company, how to finance investment, or what new markets to develop. As a rule, strategic control will be exercised by the board of directors, while operational matters will be handled by the professional management. Essentially, then, the question is: what is the relationship of the board of directors to the owners of the company?

The first point to decide here is who does actually own shares in British companies. Table 2.3 presents some data on this issue. In 1975, the proportion of shares held by individual persons, or bodies acting on behalf of persons, amounted to 42 per cent while financial interests (insurance companies, pension funds, investment trusts, unit trusts and banks) held a further 40 per cent. The balance between these two kinds of shareholder has been shifting. In 1963, personal shareholders held 54 per cent of all shares while the financial institutions held only 30 per cent.

There has, therefore, been a move away from the personal ownership of shares towards ownership by large financial institutions. This is a *depersonalization* of ownership, in that individual people no longer own companies. It is worth noting that this depersonalization does not mean that *wealth* in the form of company shares is more evenly spread among the population. What has happened is only that the minority of wealthy families no longer hold their wealth in a single company but spread it more widely by buying shares in a number of companies (see chapter 3, section 3.3 for a discussion of the distribution of wealth).

The depersonalization of wealth might, however, seem to imply a separation of ownership and control. If individual persons are less

Table 2.3 Share ownership in British companies (1963-70)

Category of owner	% of shares held		
	1963 (all cos.)	1969 (all cos.)	1975 (all cos.)
Persons, executors, trustees	54.0	47.4	42.1
Insurance companies	10.0	12.2	14.9
Pension funds	6.4	9.0	15.2
Investment trusts	7.4	7.6	4.7
Unit trusts	1.3	2.9	2.0
Banks	1.3	1.7	2.1
Stock exchange	1.4	1.4	0.1
Other financial cos.	2.6	1.1	0.5
Non-financial cos.	5.1	5.4	2.2
Public sector	1.5	2.6	0.8
Charities	2.1	2.1	4.2
Overseas	7.0	6.6	3.5
Totals	100.0	100.0	92.3

Source: Diamond Report (1975), pp. 9 and 13. Crown copyright.

involved in ownership, perhaps managers can acquire more influence? One way to approach this question is to ask how *concentrated* ownership is, for it might be the case that a *single* institution owns a substantial, controlling proportion of a company's shares; shareholdings may be concentrated into relatively few hands.

Nyman and Silbertson (1978) carried out an investigation of how far large firms were, in fact, controlled by their owners. They concluded that a firm *was* effectively owner-controlled (i.e. there was no separation between ownership and control) if more than 5 per cent of the shares were owned by a single institution or by the board of directors and their families. By that criterion, 56 per cent of the largest 250 companies were owner-controlled in 1975.

Non-manufacturing industries tended to have a higher proportion of owner-controlled firms than manufacturing firms. This does not mean to say, however, that the remaining 44 per cent of firms were controlled by their management and able to act independently of the owners. The main reason for this is that a group of shareholders may be able to act together so that they function as a cohesive entity. Scott (1979) refers to such an arrangement as a *constellation of interests* and concludes that there is evidence that a large number of companies that are not directly owner-controlled may, in fact, be controlled by these groups of owners. One way in which a constellation of interests may be formed is by the mechanism of interlocking directorships and of mutual shareholdings. For example, a study of Burmah Oil showed that no single investor held a substantial proportion of the shares. Yet six of the largest institutional shareholders were, on more detailed examination, closely linked via the holding of shares in each others' companies and interlocking directorships. Burmah's six non-executive directors, for example, held six other directorships in four of the institutional shareholding companies.

The argument so far points to the importance of financial institutions in the ownership and control of large British firms, particularly where they are able to form alliances with each other in a constellation of interests. (It has been suggested that they may be less important in the 56 per cent of large firms categorized as owner-controlled). How then are the financial institutions – banks, pension funds, unit trusts and insurance companies – themselves owned and controlled? The short answer to this question is that the process of the depersonalization of ownership applies to financial companies as well as to other branches of the economy. Banks, for example, have substantial shareholdings in each other. Institutions like pension funds, unit trusts, building societies and insurance companies are in rather a different position, however, for they are not 'owned' by shareholders but by the very large number of individuals who have pension rights, insurance policies and unit trusts. This form of ownership seems to approximate much more to the Berle and Means model for it is impossible for, say, holders of insurance policies to control the policy of even small insurance companies, and this would appear to leave strategic control in the hands of management. In a sense this is correct. There is a divorce between ownership and control in these so-called 'mutual' companies. However, the evidence does not show that the managers of these mutual companies have a free hand. Their boards of directors contain the directors of other mutual companies and financial institutions. In other words, there is, here too, a substantial degree of interlocking directorships. The result is that *control* of these companies may well pass to constellations of interests represented by the directors of other companies, although, importantly, these interests are not those of *ownership*.

Summary

1   The British economy is dominated by relatively few large companies whose dominance is becoming more pronounced as firms merge with one another.

2   Not only is there a concentration of ownership by merger and take-over, but companies are also bound together in a network of interlocking directorships. The banks are located at the heart of this network.

3 There has been a depersonalization of ownership of British companies, with the financial institutions taking a larger proportion of the shares of large companies.

4 The bulk of British companies are still effectively controlled by owners, often through a 'constellation of interests'.

5 The mutual institutions have increasing importance and they tend to be controlled by boards of directors that overlap with one another.

Related topics

All these elements give a certain unity to the British economy. Large companies are bound together in a network of greater coherence than, say, 50 years ago. One question raised by this is whether the coherence of the network also gives a coherence to an upper class which is centred around the people who control British industry and commerce. This question is explored in chapter 3, section 3.6. Another question, dealt with in the following section 2.3, is how operational rather than strategic management is accomplished, and what effect that has on the structure of economic organizations.

2.3   Economic Organizations and Management

In the previous section we presented evidence showing that *strategic* control of the major, privately owned economic enterprises in Britain is concentrated in the hands of a relatively small number of socially interconnected people – the large shareholders, directors and top executives. The principal goal of strategic control in private enterprises, which is also a condition of the enterprises' survival, is the making of profit. Achieving that goal is not automatic: firms go bankrupt, unprofitable ventures close down, boards of directors get removed. There are real problems in transforming the decisions and directives of strategic controllers into the efficient, profitable production of goods and services for which there is a demand. The difficulties include adequate use of financial resources, the coordination of many different stages in the design, production and sale of commodities, and the integration of supervision of the varied activities of often thousands of employees. The various ways of linking strategic objectives with the daily operations of production is studied by organization theory.

  Organizations are concerned with the coordination of human efforts, on a regular basis, through the deliberate and formal establishment of a set of positions, with a view to achieving certain specified goals. Parties, trade unions and churches, as well as armies, hospitals and firms, are organizations. Economic organizations are those concerned with the production of goods and services. There are many types of economic organization, each with different goals: besides privately owned capitalist enterprises there are state agencies, cooperatives, charitable bodies, etc. In contemporary Britain, most production of goods and services, and most paid employment, is achieved through private enterprise, though state agencies also play a very significant role.

In this section, we first examine some features of the internal organizational structures common to both private enterprises and state agencies. *Organizational structures* are deliberately created with a view to achieving the specified goals of the people exercising strategic control. Organizational structure has been defined by Child (1972, p. 2) as 'the formal allocation of work roles and the administrative mechanisms to control and integrate work activities'. The structure of organizations has been a focus of attention (for the sociology of organizations and organization theory) because it is believed that this partly determines their effectiveness.

Next, we examine *management*. Management is part of the organizational structure and at the same time is responsible for the maintenance and operation of that structure. In the classic small firm, management is nothing other than the directives of the owner: the owner will personally supervise the implementation of his or her own strategic decisions. In the large economic organizations of contemporary Britain, whether private enterprises or public agencies, management is a complex network of interdependent roles and activities, hierarchically structured and itself requiring coordination.

In the final part of this section we look at the operations of multinational corporations because they are the most powerful and complex of private capitalist enterprises.

The internal structure of economic organizations

The sheer scale of the activities of large corporations creates enormous organizational problems. To plan, coordinate and control on a global scale, as do the multinational corporations, is a remarkable achievement and raises questions about how strategic control (discussed in section 2.2) is exercised and is transformed into the everyday operations of making and selling commodities. However, similar problems, even if on a smaller scale, face any economic organization. Large corporations are, increasingly, adopting a multi-division pattern of organization, in which a head office takes strategic decisions but control over everyday matters is decentralized to smaller operational units and their managements.

Strategic control is secured through strict and centralized financial discipline exercised at head office, the 'independent' plants being monitored closely in terms of their financial performance. The essence of this relationship, which is a fairly recent development in Britain, is clearly described in a book on the Vickers Company (Beynon and Wainwright, 1979, pp. 36-8):

1 'no large expenditures can be made without central vetting';
2 'each division is required to make detailed monthly reports (to Headquarters). In this way loss makers became quickly visible and, given the divisions of the company into the smallest possible viable units, responsibility for that loss is easily identifiable . . . It is centralized financial control with sophisticated budgetary information systems – allied with stress on decentralized responsibility for pro- fits – which provides the mechanism that determines the company's development.'

Practices of this kind have replaced more bureaucratic channels of strategic control in many of Britain's larger capitalist enterprises.

There are, however, alternative ways of structuring organizations. The design of organizational structure depends partly on the overall purpose or goal of the organization. Not all economic organizations are primarily oriented towards profit-making. The National Health Service, for instance does not sell its services to its clients, rather its clients have a *right* to treatment. This means that hospitals and clinics must provide *satisfactory* service on a *fair* basis (i.e. to all citizens who are entitled to it, without discrimination by class, gender or ethnicity) rather than on a commercial basis. These goals constrain the choice of organizational structure.

Another type of economic organization, the cooperative, seeks to be democratic as well as to produce goods for the market. The internal organizational arrangements have to be consistent with the fact that all workers share in ownership and have collective control over the policy and practices of their cooperative. It remains the case, however, that the majority of British economic organizations have primarily commercial goals – to sell goods or services for more than they cost to produce.

Bureaucratic organization

Fundamentally, organizational structure is a concept of describing *the exercise of authority associated with the coordination of (work) tasks*. It is no accident that the founding father of the sociology of organizations, Max Weber, began from a theoretical concern with power and authority. Weber analysed the most widely recognized, and most commonly maligned, form of organizational structure – the bureaucracy. The key characteristics of Weber's *ideal type* of bureaucracy are listed in box 1.

In reality, almost all complex organizations are to *some degree* bureaucratic, but few approach the 'pure' type. Most important in

---

Box 1   Key features of bureaucratic organization

1. A specialized division of tasks, undertaken by officials, each with his or her own duties.
2. A hierarchy of authority – 'a clearly established system of super- and sub-ordination in which there is a supervision of the lower offices by the higher ones' (Weber) – and a clearly demarcated system of command and responsibilities.
3. A formal set of rules governing operations and activities which coordinates behaviour in a predictable, uniform and impersonal fashion.
4. A body of officials who are permanent, full-time workers, appointed by superiors, trained in a specialized task, paid a salary according to rank in the hierarchy, and to whom a career is open on the basis of ability and seniority.

---

considering contemporary economic organizations are two features, hierarchy of authority and formal rules.

1 *Authority* in the ideal type of bureaucracy can be represented as a pyramid. Higher offices have authority over lower offices: subordinate officials are directly responsible to the official immediately above in the hierarchy. The result, in principle, is a single line of authority (see figure 2.5). This provides an integrated vertical chain of command, but prohibits horizontal communication between officials of the same rank.
2 The tasks and the decisions made in the course of operations are *rule-governed* in the sense that officials have limited discretion in dealing with cases – their activities are closely prescribed, which encourages predictability and impartiality.

Such a bureaucratic organization thus has a highly *centralized* structure of authority and a highly *regulated* set of activities.

Weber thought the bureaucracy was a more technically efficient mode of organization than any other previously developed. Its virtues, relative to earlier modes, included 'precision, speed, unambiguity, knowledge, continuity, discretion, unity, strict subordination, reduction of friction and of material personal costs' (Weber, 1968, p. 973). However, bureaucratic organizations also have widely acknowledged potential disadvantages for clients, officials and organizational efficiency alike. Clients, for example of the Department of Health and Social Security (DHSS) frequently complain of impersonality, inflexibility, the incapacity of officials to make firm decisions, and excessive rule-following. Studies of the behaviour of officials in such organizations tend to show either creeping timidity in decision-making by officials closely bound by both formal rules and responsibility to higher authority, or a tendency to

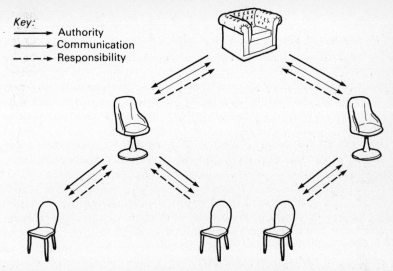

Key:
⟶ Authority
⟵⟶ Communication
- - - → Responsibility

Figure 2.5   Authority, responsibility and communication in a bureaucracy

subvert the organizational structure by developing informal and un-
authorized practices. The difficulties experienced by the people involved
with bureaucracies *under certain circumstances* may reduce the effectiveness of the organization. Hence some organizations are designed to be
less centralized than these.

Decentralized organizations still have some bureaucratic features, but
they are more flexible and less hierarchical. In such firms, rules are less
formal and less encompassing, authority and responsibility are less direct,
jobs and tasks are less tightly defined, communication is more varied and
not restricted to hierarchical channels. Such organizational structures
demand more initiative and personal responsibility from officials.
Outcomes are less predictable but may be more inventive and problem-
oriented. Such arrangements reduce central and direct control by higher
officials.

Contingent factors affecting organizational structure

Sociologists have tried to isolate what affects the degree of centralization
in organizational structures. A number of factors contingently influence
centralization, but none determine it. It partly depends on the purposes
and the circumstances of the particular organization. State agencies – the
DHSS, the army, the Inland Revenue – tend to be more bureaucratic.
They value the predictability of their officials' behaviour and impartiality
in treatment of clients, which bureaucratic forms sustain. It is considered
important that soldiers *obey* orders, and that supplementary benefit
claimants are treated *fairly* (i.e. get those benefits to which they are

entitled, but none other). Private manufacturing firms, being concerned with profitable production, are less likely to put up with the inefficiencies of bureaucracies, which tend to be slow in decision-making, rather rigid, etc. Nevertheless, where production processes are highly mechanized – in assembly-line production for instance – predictability and obedience are considered of the highest value and may support bureaucratic forms. But, for many firms, the dysfunctions of the bureaucratic mode are considered too great and they have, thus, developed less-centralized organizational structures.

Three contingent factors in particular constrain the selection of organizational structure: the *size*, the *technology* and the external *environment* of the enterprise.

Size: It is generally agreed that there is a statistical correlation between size and bureaucratization. With small firms there is scarcely a problem of organization. Coordination is maintained through face-to-face contacts, and control is likely to be exercised directly by an owner-manager. Very large units, by contrast, require methods of *impersonal* coordination and control, which is a key aspect of the bureaucratic mode. There is currently some tendency among business organizations towards reducing the size of working units by decentralizing activities both within and between firms. Factories etc. become smaller as their functions are divided among one or more separate plants. Equally, within individual plants there is a tendency to designate semi-autonomous operating units or profit centres: the design department may 'sell' its designs to the production department, which will in turn charge the sales department for the finished goods, so that each department has a separate measure of its performance. In other words, the size of operating units may be reduced if it is felt that this will benefit performance.

Technology: Machinery and equipment also set limits to alternative organizational structures. Mass production on the assembly-line involves a different form of supervision to homeworkers on piece-rates. Where mass production occurs in large factories, thus benefiting from economies of scale, there is usually a very specialized and standardized division of labour and, thus, a tendency to be bureaucratically organized. In this sense, technology and size are related.

Environment: Firms do not exist in a vacuum, they are affected by competition, by markets, by the state, etc. Certain environmental conditions dispose firms to adopt different structures. One outstanding example of this concerns adaptation to rapid *change*. In a classic study of electronics firms in Britain in the 1950s, Burns and Stalker (1961) argued that decentralized structures (they called them *organic* management systems) were more amenable to changing external circumstances. In the electronics industry, knowledge, techniques, design and products were all changing quickly. Those firms in which responsibilities and tasks were not rigidly defined, and where information passed openly regardless of status in the organization, tended to be more effective at innovation (at solving new problems). More centralized and bureaucratic organizations seemed to work best in stable environmental circumstances.

The complexity of the environment, particularly with respect to information, also affects structure. The more sources of information, and the more difficult the information is to interpret, the more likely is decentralization. This happens because of increased specialization in the process of handling information, people with specialized knowledge often being able to obtain some degree of independence from their superiors. (This is one basis of the power of the professions – see section 2.6.)

One other feature of the environment, the presence of a serious threat to the organization, also has consequences for structure. In periods of crisis, strategic controllers tend to centralize decision-making and exert tighter controls.

In conclusion, it should be noted that the factors of size, technology and environment do not *determine* organizational structure. One of the powers of people exercising strategic control is that of making choices about organizational form, and those choices are elements in the processes of competition between firms and of conflict between controllers and their staff.

Management

'Management' is a rather loose concept. At its broadest, it refers to all people in positions of authority over others within a firm – from the managing director at the top to the supervisor on the shop floor. It is, therefore, essential to distinguish between different types of managerial position: executives, who exercise *strategic* control, should be distinguished from middle management with *operational* control, and also from supervisory workers. Though these categories are blurred at the edges they reflect important differences in power, prestige and function. In this section we are primarily interested in 'middle management' – managers who are neither in position of strategic control nor directly supervising workers on the shop-floor. They are employees of the firm, but they exercise *authority* and discretion at plant or office level.

The purposes of management

Management has a number of purposes or functions which include liaison, filtering and transmitting information, allocating resources, directing subordinates, planning and handling disruptions of work. Managers generally combine some specialist, technical activities and some general, administrative work, the proportion varying considerably from one manager to another.

For example, an accounts manager may well work more or less alone on the specialized activity of accountancy, while some other managers, so-called line-management, are largely concerned with directing and monitoring the performance of other workers. The principal purpose of modern middle management is to plan, coordinate and control operations in the everyday running of the firm.

Management practices

As in many social processes, the fit is weak between the formal aims of roles like management and the actual behaviour of the people who fill those roles. Studies of what managers actually do when at work suggest that, with the exception of some specialist functions, the job of manager is a very fluid and indefinite one. The daily activities of management seem eccentric, disorganized and unpredictable. Thus Hales (1986), summarizing the literature on managers' behaviour, isolated ten widely agreed attributes of managerial work (see box 2).

One interesting feature is the diversity of activities of management and the fact that 'little time is spent on any one particular activity'. Nor does managerial work seem to entail a lot of decision-taking. This is probably particularly the case at the lower levels where the degree of discretion is very limited. Thus, for example, Crompton and Jones (1984), in their study of white-collar workers in a bank, an insurance company and a local county council, observed that there were a considerable number of people who were described as having managerial or administrative jobs who exercised very little control or discretion in their own work. Moreover, they had no power with respect to the recruitment and disciplining of workers or to the organization of work. In many cases these people, better described as supervisory workers, did the same kind of work as their subordinates, though they would be called in to sort out practical problems or advise on difficult cases.

The study of such 'white-collar proletarians' reminds us that managers are not a uniform or unified group of workers. A sample survey of 1,058 currently practising members of the British Institute of Management in 1980 (Poole et al., 1981) confirms this. The managers contacted were found in a wide variety of different circumstances, with different degrees of seniority, a wide range of incomes, and in different types of organization. They were also a heterogeneous category with respect to their social backgrounds and their qualifications. Managers are not from especially privileged backgrounds, and nor are they necessarily highly educated. Of this particular sample, one-third had a degree and another third had a technical qualification (e.g. OND or HND). So, managers are not a socially distinct group, but do they constitute a social class, as has sometimes been suggested?

Box 2 Key features of managerial work

1 It combines a specialist/professional element and a general, 'managerial' element.
2 The substantive elements involve, essentially, liaison, man-management and responsibility for a work process, beneath which are subsumed more detailed work elements.
3 The character of work elements varies by duration, time span, recurrence, unexpectedness and source.
4 Much time is spent in day-to-day trouble shooting and *ad hoc* problems of organization and regulation.
5 Much managerial activity consists of asking or persuading others to do things, involving the manager in face-to-face verbal communication of limited duration.
6 Patterns of communication vary in terms of *what* the communication is about and with *whom* the communication is made.
7 Little time is spent on any one particular activity and, in particular, on the conscious, systematic formulation of plans. Planning and decision-making, tend to take place in the course of other activity.
8 Managers spend a lot of time accounting for and explaining what they do, in informal relationships and in 'politicking'.
9 Managerial activities are riven by contradictions, cross-pressures and conflicts. Much managerial work involves coping with and reconciling social and technical conflict.
10 There is considerable choice in terms of *what* is done and *how*: part of managerial work is setting the boundaries of negotiating that work itself. (Hales (1986) What do managers do? *Journal of Management Studies*, 23 (1), p. 104. Reproduced with permission)

Some people argue that there has been a 'managerial revolution' in recent decades. The suggestion is that the expansion of management jobs has entailed a shift of power to middle management (sometimes called the 'technostructure') and the emergence of a new set of managerial objectives in which profit is of little importance. This argument is firmly rejected in Nichols and Beynon's (1977) study of middle management in a chemicals plant in South-West England. The managers there, despite their personal diversity, were jointly 'driven by the impersonal force of capital'. They were nothing more than '(relatively highly paid) labour', their decisions constrained and judged by the criterion of profit. Of the thesis of the managerial revolution, Nichols and Beynon observe (p. 31):

Somewhere there might just be a middle manager who believes it. But if there is, he isn't to be found at Riverside. None of the managers we talked to there was in any doubt that his job was to make profit and that if he failed in this his future with ChemCo was in jeopardy.

As a 48-year-old, middle manager at ChemCo's Riverside plant said at the end of a discussion about various experiments with new human-relations techniques for dealing with workers on the shop-floor (p. 41):

> Sometimes you do have the impression that we are not here to make fertiliser or chemical or cement at all but to be experimenting with new types of human relation techniques. The first thing to remember is that we are in business to make money and that management's job is basically production. If all these techniques help then well and good.

Multinational corporations

Among the most complex and powerful economic organizations now are the multinational corporations (MNCs). They are increasingly involved in coordinating production on a global scale. A firm like ICI had, for example, plant and offices in more than 60 countries in 1980. As table 2.4 shows, some of these corporations have enormous turnovers – much greater in fact than those of many *countries*. Because they have become so powerful in the last 20 years, it is necessary to appreciate the character of these organizations and their effects on economic life in Britain.

MNCs control considerable proportions of the world's production capacity and account for a considerable amount of employment. They are both 'multi-plant' and 'multi-product' organizations. That is to say, they have many factories and offices in different places around the world, and they operate in many different industrial sectors producing a vast range of commodities. One key feature is that they operate on an international scale. This gives great flexibility. In the first place, they are able to benefit from the different social and economic conditions in different nation-states. For example, analyses of the so-called 'new international division of labour' have shown how the MNCs make use of differential wage-rates. Operations which are labour-intensive (i.e. wages rather than machines or raw materials are the major cost to the enterprise) tend to be undertaken in Third World countries where wages are very low. Thus, electronics assembly work and textile manufacture take place in plants located in the Far East – Malaysia, Sri Lanka, Korea, etc. But there is no tendency for MNCs to shift their headquarters to the Third World, nor their research and development outfits.

The result is that the MNCs are altering the geography of industry on a world scale in the competitive pursuit of profit. Routine manual jobs are, in a sense, being exported to countries with cheap labour. In a less spectacular way, something similar is happening within Britain, where the 'higher-order functions' of research, finance and corporate planning in the

Table 2.4 Annual turnovers of some of the world's largest multinational corporations

	Country of origin	1976 turnover (US $ million)	1978 turnover (US $ million)
Mitsubishi Group	Japan	75,000	106,400
DKB Group	Japan	54,500	79,300
Sumitomo Group	Japan	51,200	78,100
Mitsui Group	Japan	48,800	76,500
Fuyo Group	Japan	57,000	71,200
Sanwa Group	Japan	46,100	64,500
General Motors	USA	47,200	63,200
Exxon	USA	48,600	60,300
Royal Dutch-Shell	Netherlands/Britain	36,100	44,000
Ford	USA	28,800	42,800
IBM	USA	16,300	21,100
General Electric	USA	15,700	19,700
Unilever	Netherlands/Britain	15,800	18,900
ITT	USA	11,800	15,300
Philips	Netherlands	11,500	15,100
Hoechst	W. Germany	9,300	12,100
US Steel	USA	8,600	11,100
Nestlé	Switzerland	7,600	11,000
EI du Pont	USA	8,400	10,600
Thyssen	W. Germany	7,900	9,200
ICI	Britain	7,500	8,700
British Steel	Britain	5,000	5,700

Source: From Nakase (1981), p. 86.

big corporations are being shifted to the South East of England, with lower-level managerial work and routine branch-plant production being concentrated in the North and West of Britain.

A second source of flexibility arises from MNCs being free from the control of the government of any single nation-state. It is possible to evade pollution-control laws, which may be very expensive to accommodate, by locating dirty processes in countries with no environmental legislation. It is possible to reduce tax-liability by shifting financial assets from country to country, but still keeping them internal to the corporation. Moreover, governments give concessions and privileges to MNCs to persuade them to invest and, thus, to bring employment and money to their countries. Such incentives include tax concessions, rent-free premises, grants towards installing new machinery, etc. Recent

British experience includes some well-publicized deals attracting Japanese car manufacturers to Wales and North-East England. These relationships are signs of the power of these global corporations and the impossibility of individual governments exercising control over them. The decisions of the corporations, made with a view to their own profitability, profoundly affect local, regional and national economies without any popular recourse being possible. When it is no longer profitable to produce motor vehicles in Britain, the MNC cannot be prevented either from moving car production to, say, West Germany, or from redirecting its investments to one of its other products – televisions, cardboard boxes, or whatever. This flexibility, and some of its consequences, can be observed in the brief case-study below of the British multinational, ICI.

Imperial Chemical Industries Ltd: a case-study of a global corporation

ICI was created by the merger of four British companies in 1926. It always operated abroad to some degree, though in its early days primarily in the countries of the British Empire – thus the title 'imperial'. By the 1980s it was a massive corporation, though it is still much smaller than some other international companies (see table 2.3). The size of ICI operations is, however, clarified by comparison with, say, a university: Lancaster University's turnover in 1978 was about £8 million compared with ICI's £5,000 million.

ICI's operations are truly global, having factories in more than forty countries and offices in more than sixty (Clarke, 1982). The phenomenal geographical span of ICI is illustrated in the maps in figure 2.6. Its dispersion is reflected in the firm's internal organization, it having separate divisions for different areas of the globe. Its factories produce a vast range of products which fall under 10 separate business categories – agriculture, organic chemicals, fibres, general chemicals, industrial explosives, oil, paints, petrochemicals, pharmaceuticals and plastics. It is notable how unsuccessful sections get abandoned or absorbed into others. This process of 'restructuring' has been rapid and extensive in response to the world recessions of the 1970s and 1980s, with the company rationalizing in response to adverse economic conditions.

Rationalization entails closing some plants and expanding production at others. For example, in 1980 in the man-made fibres division, ICI closed plants at Ardeer in Scotland and Kilroot in Northern Ireland. Production has been concentrated at other sites (e.g. Teesside), though not necessarily thereby increasing employment, since *technical changes* introduced simultaneously have had the effect of increasing output with a smaller work-force. The impact on employment is critical. Figure 2.7 shows both how the number of workers in ICI has fallen since 1971 and also how the proportion working in Britain has declined. Whereas, in 1971, 72 per cent of ICI employees were in Britain, by 1984 it was a mere 51 per cent. To take just one example of the way this happens, ICI in

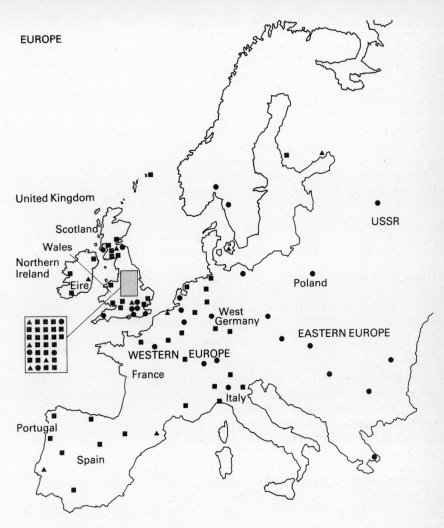

Figure 2.6 The world-wide distribution of ICI's factories and offices, 1980
Source: Adapted from Clarke (1982), The changing international division of labour within
ICI, in M. Taylor and N. Thrift (eds) *The Geography of Multinationals* (London, Croom
Helm), pp. 95-8. Reproduced with permission.

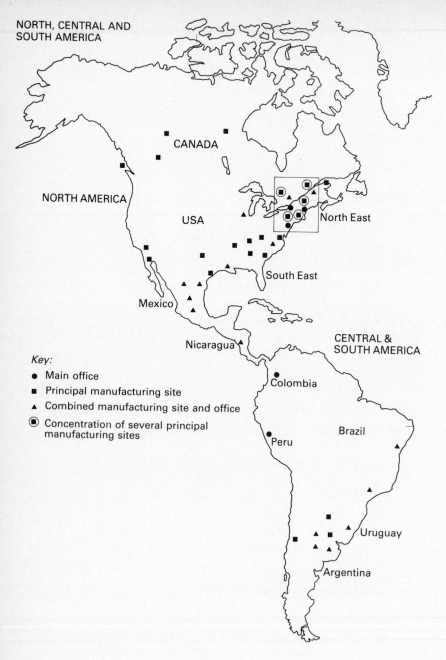

NORTH, CENTRAL AND
SOUTH AMERICA

NORTH AMERICA

CANADA

USA

North East

South East

Mexico

Nicaragua

CENTRAL &
SOUTH AMERICA

Colombia

Peru

Brazil

Uruguay

Argentina

Key:
● Main office
■ Principal manufacturing site
▲ Combined manufacturing site and office
◉ Concentration of several principal
    manufacturing sites

Figure 2.6   *continued*

THE MIDDLE EAST AND AFRICA

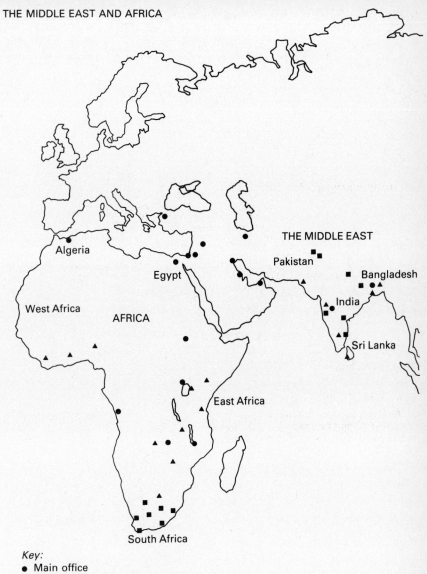

Figure 2.6 *continued*

THE FAR EAST AND AUSTRALASIA

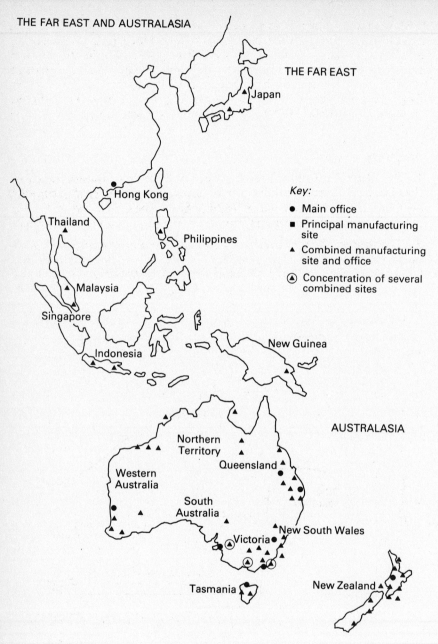

Figure 2.6   *continued*

1981 opened a new plant in Wilhelmshaven in West Germany, manufacturing exactly the same product (chlorine) which it was already producing in Cheshire and on Teesside. This was done primarily because electricity, which accounted for 80 per cent of the cost of producing chlorine, was cheaper by half in Germany (Clarke, 1982). It is clear, therefore, that what is economically rational for ICI is ominous for the employment prospects of the population of northern England.

Summary

1 The internal organizational structures of firms vary. Bureaucracies are characterized by the centralization of authority and the rigid application of rules that govern activities within the organization. Many modern private firms have a comparatively more *decentralized* power structure.

2 The degree of centralization of authority in an organization depends on contingent factors, among which are the size of the enterprise, the technology it uses, and the economic environment in which it operates.

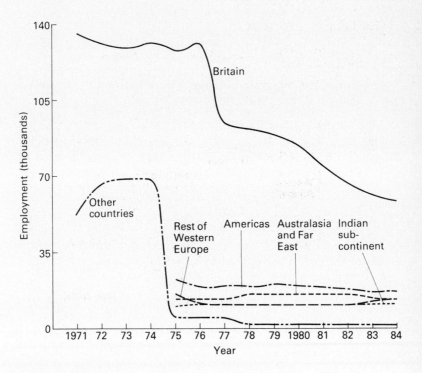

Figure 2.7 Employment, in thousands, in ICI world-wide, 1971–84
Source: Beynon et al. (1986), p. 72.

3 Management is a rather loose concept which refers both to the exercise of strategic control and to the supervision of routine activities. Most managers have very limited powers.

4 Multinational corporations are the most powerful and complex of modern capitalist organizations.

Related topics

Questions of authority and control at work are dealt with in other sections. In section 2.2 strategic control is discussed. In section 2.4 the methods of control by managers and supervisors over other workers is analysed in terms of managerial strategies. The class position of managers is explored further in chapter 3, section 3.5, on the middle classes. The tendency for men rather than women to be in positions of authority at work is examined in chapter 4, section 4.2. Industrial change, in international perspective, is referred to in section 2.7 and chapter 7, section 7.3.

2.4   The Labour Process

The experience of work

Consider this description, given by a man who works on the assembly line at Ford's, fixing the trim on to motor cars:

> 'It's the most boring job in the world. It's the same thing over and over again. There's no change in it, it wears you out. It makes you awful tired. It slows your thinking right down. There's no need to think. It's just a formality. You just carry on. You just endure it for the money. That's what we're paid for – to endure the boredom of it.
>
> If I had the chance to move I'd leave right away. It's the conditions here. Ford class you more as a machine than men. They're on top of you all the time. They expect you to work every minute of the day. The atmosphere you get in here is so completely false. Everyone is downcast and fed up.' (Beynon, 1973, p. 118)

Not every one finds work as unpleasant as this. Some people derive intrinsic satisfaction from their work. A recent study by Newby (1979) of agricultural labouring, hardly a glamorous occupation, found that 93 per cent of those interviewed in East Anglia considered their job either 'mostly interesting' or 'interesting all the time'. This perhaps represents the other extreme in work satisfaction among manual workers. Most workers like some parts of their work and dislike others. This was true of the sample of agricultural workers who appreciated the variety of their jobs, enjoyed using farm machinery, and liked seeing crops and animals grow, but disliked aspects of the hours and conditions under which they had to labour.

Worker's reactions to their jobs are understandably mixed. The deprivations resulting from not having a job – poverty, social isolation and low social status (see section 2.8 on unemployment) – are sufficiently severe to persuade people that any work is better than none. In this sense people want to work. Similarly, many people say when asked, that they are satisfied with their job because the realistic alternatives are not much better. Previous experience, qualifications and the local availability of other employment all severely limit any individual's choice of work. Thus a recent inquiry by Brown et al. (1983) found a large proportion of workers claiming to be satisfied (see box 3). On the other hand, employees usually feel that their talents and skills are poorly utilized in work which is often dull and monotonous. As one study of unskilled work in Peterborough observed, 95 per cent of the workers used more skill driving a car to work than they exercised on the job. This seems to be increasingly true of many clerical jobs as well.

Work absorbs a very substantial amount of most adults' time. The average working week for male manual workers in 1983 was 44.6 hours; and the working life of men stretches from age 16 to 65. The obligation for women to be in paid employment is somewhat different, since if they are married they may work only in the home – at housework. But, increasingly, this occurs for only a short period in a woman's life. In 1983 half of married women were in paid employment and, of course, they continued to do a disproportionate amount of housework at the same time. Since people typically spend such a lot of time working, the actual quality of the experience of work deeply affects both personal and social relationships. Sociologists have, therefore, closely examined the precise content of jobs and the kind of relationships established between employers, supervisors and employees. These are elements of the so-called labour process.

In order to show how the experience of work affects other aspects of social and political activity, it is necessary to compare the quality of jobs. Since there are thousands of jobs, each distinctive, we need to reduce differences to a few, important dimensions. For sociological purposes, jobs may be grouped in terms of:

1 the range of tasks involved;
2 the degree of discretion given to the worker to decide how to accomplish those tasks; and
3 the mode of control used by managers and supervisors to try to ensure that those tasks are completed satisfactorily.

In these respects, the workers in the Ford assembly plant of Halewood

Box 3   Job satisfaction

Brown et al. (1983, pp. 28–9) observe:

> Direct questions about the level of job satisfaction yield results which indicate a very high degree of satisfaction. As the *General Household Survey (GHS)* acknowledges 'The overall ratio of nine out of ten people saying they were either very satisfied or fairly satisfied with their jobs may seem to be unrealistically high: it may result from a general reluctance to admit dissatisfaction because to do so may be thought an admission of failure; or it may be that "satisfaction" is no more than an acceptance of the status quo' (GHS 1973, p. 188).
>
> Despite these reservations the *General Household Survey* includes, each year, a question about job satisfaction. In the years from 1971 to 1977 there was some indication of a slight overall reduction in job satisfaction both in terms of the mean satisfaction score and the proportion of respondents who gave neutral or dissatisfied responses, but this trend appears to have reversed since 1977.

In 1979, people responded as follows to the question, 'Which of these statements on this card comes nearest, on the whole to what you think about your present (main) job?'

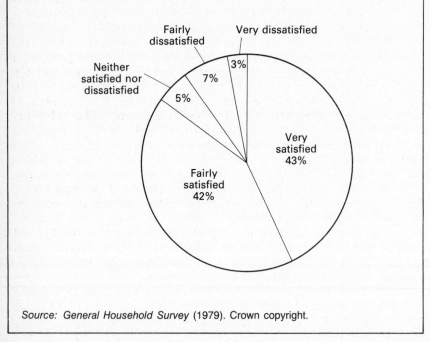

Source: General Household Survey (1979). Crown copyright.

and a schoolteacher are involved in very different types of labour process. Assembly work in car production entails that a single task be repeated, in a tightly prescribed manner, under the close surveillance of a foreman. The schoolteacher, by contrast, undertakes a wide range of tasks; the way of working is left to the teacher's initiative – *how* teachers teach varies from one person to the next; and supervision is distant, headteachers virtually never interfering in what happens in the classroom. Sociologists have spent much time exploring what determines the quality of different labour processes. Why is it that, for example, schoolteachers are given more control over their work than assembly-line workers? The answer currently offered in response to such a question is usually framed in terms of whether there has been any significant overall *change* in the nature of the modern labour process, an issue brought to light in the debate on 'deskilling'.

Deskilling

Recent sociological analysis of the quality of work has been inspired by a very influential book by Braverman (1974), which examined work in the USA. It was stated here that the labour process had become more fragmented and specialized since the 1890s, and the skill required at work was reduced for most jobs: a process of 'deskilling' had occurred. Braverman argued that this was the consequence not of technological innovation but of a conscious managerial strategy to increase control over workers' behaviour. Control was achieved by widespread introduction of the techniques of scientific management of the kind advocated by F. W. Taylor. 'Taylorism', as it came to be known, sought to break production tasks into their smallest possible units, to control the fashion and the speed with which each separate operation was completed, and to coordinate these operations as efficiently as possible. Characteristic of Taylorism is the 'time and motion study' and the assembly line. Wherever possible, the workers' autonomy was restricted and jobs were redesigned to transfer discretion and control from workers to management. As a result, according to Braverman, old political distinctions between skilled and unskilled workers, and between manual and non-manual workers, would disappear. The real nature of work for almost all the labour force would become similarly routine, fragmented, deskilled and controlled by management. This would happen in offices as much as in factories. Braverman saw this as the basis for the development of the kind of working-class political consciousness anticipated by Marx. This argument has been extensively criticized and, as a result of the ensuing debate, we are clearer about the changes in work in Britain.

One pertinent line of criticism of Braverman is that his analysis is not readily applicable to countries other than the USA. In Britain, it is clear that the transition to modern management occurred much later than in the USA, not happening here until the mid-1920s. Moreover, it had less of an impact in Britain. In this respect, Braverman ignores the considerable range of stratetgies employed by managements in order to control their workers. Taylorism is but one possible strategy.

The extent of deskilling is also disputed. Undoubtedly some jobs, like those of the workers at Fords mentioned earlier, are as Braverman describes. But it is debatable whether the number of jobs which have disappeared or been degraded in the last fifty years outnumbers those new skilled and professional jobs that have been created. The expansion of the welfare state has increased professional and semi-professional occupations, and new technology certainly generates some jobs for highly skilled technicians. Indeed, the uncertainty of the consequences of the introduction of new technology is underlined by Roberts (1982), who examined the effects of the introduction of numerical control on engineering workers in South Wales and South-West England. He found no consistent effect resulting from the implementation of identical computer-assisted techniques in different factories: whether the machine operators' job improved or deteriorated appeared to depend on other factors.

Resolving the question of the degree of deskilling partly depends upon obtaining an acceptable measure of skill. This is however, difficult. All occupational groups would like to be called skilled, since that is grounds for demanding high wages and is a source of social status. The very label 'skill' is a valuable resource which does not necessarily reflect the technical difficulty of a given job. It is significant that few occupations filled predominantly by women are called 'skilled'. For example, some of the intricate and dextrous work done by women in electronics assembly or in the garment-making trades clearly requires special aptitudes and a lengthy learning process, but is not considered as skilled and is poorly paid. This suggests that trade-union organization is at least as important as knowledge or aptitude in establishing work as skilled. If this is the case, if skill is primarily socially constructed, then evaluation of Braverman's thesis becomes impossible. It is for this reason that earlier we described jobs not in terms of the skill required, but in terms of tasks, discretion and control.

Furthermore, the political consequences anticipated by Braverman have not transpired. Even accepting that there has been a general tendency for workers to become deskilled, it does not follow that they will act as a politically united class. It seems that workers are today no less divided and fragmented than at other times in the last half century. In fact, Braverman paid little attention to the political consciousness of workers. This omission led him to underestimate the importance of workers' resistance to deskilling. Workers struggle against losing control over the labour process, against management intervention, and against new technologies. These struggles must be borne in mind when assessing changes in the nature of work.

In conclusion, Braverman probably generalized too widely from one kind of transition which occurred in the USA. He also focused his attention rather too narrowly on the process of production, without sufficient consideration of other political and economic constraints that also determine the quality of work. Subsequent reflection suggests that an adequate explanation of the quality of work experience requires that we look more carefully at individual enterprises and at particular occupations. The place of the firm in a market for its products affects both the kind of managerial strategy it can employ and the kind of technology it can use. Management's control over workers is maintained by wage payments as well as by control on the shop floor. The level and method of payment is itself constrained by the place of a firm in the market for its products. The quality of work seems to be the effect of a number of forces, none of which *alone* determine the nature of work, but which together, in different combinations, account for much of the variety of work. The most important factor is, as Braverman argued, the kind of managerial strategy used, but also important are the nature of the organization, the kind of technology employed, and the capacity of the work-force to resist management.

Organizations, technology and the quality of work

The nature of work is partly dependent upon the organization of the enterprise providing employment. Generally, large firms are more complex, rules and procedures are formally specified, and the element of administrative authority is more prominent. Thus there is a tendency for work to be more specialized and authority relations more impersonal than in small firms. Work may then be more fragmented, with less discretion left to the worker. However, the effect of size should not be exaggerated, for, as we saw in section 2.3, there are differences between large firms, some being more bureaucratic, others more flexible, depending upon the economic environment in which they operate.

The type of technology (equipment and machinery) used by an enterprise is obviously one important cause of the quality of work experience. A teacher's work might be much altered by the introduction of new electronic technology. In higher education, the Open University offers an instructive example. The use of television means that proportionately little of the teachers' time is spent personally teaching students. The same lesson can be broadcast to thousands of students simultaneously. Teachers thus become relatively specialized: as writers of the course materials, presenters of programmes, or as tutors corresponding with students about their work. Indeed, it is conceivable, with developments in communication technology, that in the near future people will be educated mostly at home, using televisions, micro-computers and direct-link telephones. Under such circumstances, the

Figure 2.8   A typing pool
Source: Network.

Figure 2.9   A production line in a chocolate factory
Source: Michael Ann Mullen/Format.

work of teachers would be transformed. Similarly, the tedium of assembly work in automobile manufacturing is a direct result of a decision to use production-line techniques to make cars. There are, however, other ways of manufacturing cars: some are still effectively hand-built by craft workers. But, among mass-manufacturers, Volvo, for example, launched a well-publicized and successful experiment in the 1970s to abandon assembly-line production. Instead, flexible work-groups were created, each collectively responsible for a wide range of tasks, which were rotated frequently among members of the group. The result, according to the firm, was lower levels of turnover and absenteeism, reflecting greater work satisfaction, without any loss of efficiency.

It is important to realize that enterprises have a degree of choice about what technology to use. Such choices are not purely technical matters. Of course, there are economic constraints over the choice: goods have to be sold at competitive prices, privately owned firms insist on making profits, and workers demand adequate wages. Nevertheless, as the Volvo example illustrated, there is often a choice. What determines the decision? Many sociologists now argue that employers and managers, when selecting technology, are especially concerned with establishing and maintaining *control* over the work-force. Decisions about technology are an aspect of so-called managerial *strategies*.

The effects of technology should not be exaggerated. It used to be thought that work satisfaction was directly determined by the technology used: manual workers on assembly lines were likely to be bored and discontented, while those involved in craft work, or in automated-process production would derive more satisfaction from their work. In turn, it was argued, greater work satisfaction would lead directly to a reduction in industrial and political conflict. Reality, however, is more complicated. Not merely the machinery, but also the social organization of the workplace and the general political culture beyond the factory strongly affect workers' attitudes.

One analysis which demonstrates that technology itself does not determine peoples' experience of work or their political attitudes is that of Gallie (1978 and 1983). Gallie compared the attitudes of workers in four oil refineries, two in France and two in Britain. All the refineries used advanced, automated, continuous-process technology; to all intents and purposes the technological situation was identical in each. But the industrial and political responses of the British and French workers differed sharply. The French workers identified strongly with the working class, expressed greater resentment of class inequality, were more hostile towards the management and believed that redress of their industrial grievances required political action. The British workers, by contrast, whilst recognizing the existence of class inequalities, showed significantly less resentment about it, were much more accommodative towards the management, and were more likely to seek remedies for their dissatisfactions at the local level, within the plant, through trade-union representation. This shows that the same technology can have quite different effects on workers in different contexts. The greater radicalism of the French workers, Gallie thought, derived from the interaction of a high level of work grievance and exposure over time to the radical messages of the parties of the French left. It was particularly important that trade unions were unable to effectively express the channel grievances in France, collective bargaining procedures being very weakly developed. As Gallie (1983, pp. 258-9) says:

> The most striking difference in the work situation of French and British workers lay in the structure of managerial power. French employers had retained virtually intact their traditional rights to determine unilaterally both the terms of payment and the organisation of work with the firm. It was an institutionalised system in which the representatives of the work-force were given minimal influence over decision-making. In other terms, it was a system in which there was a very low level of institutionalisation of industrial conflict. In Britain, on the other hand, the employers had made much more substantial concessions to the trade unions. Traditional conceptions of managerial prerogative had been considerably eroded and issues relating to both salaries and work organisation had become subject to procedures for joint regulation . . . The British cases had seen a deliberate attempt on the part of employers to develop procedures for institutionalising industrial conflict.

Gallie, then, demonstrated that technology alone determines neither the nature of the experience of work nor the character of workers' responses. Rather, national political culture is important, as are, especially, the strategies which managers use to control their work-force.

Managerial strategies and control at work

Managerial strategies are ways of getting workers to spend their hours at work in a fashion which advances the economic goals of management. Given that much work is unpleasant, management has a problem of motivating workers to complete their allotted tasks quickly and effectively. Care and effort on the part of workers is not guaranteed merely by their presence at work. A major source of industrial conflict is the so-called 'effort bargain', the negotiable definition of what constitutes a 'fair day's work'. Management has two, intertwined, resources at its command – payment and authority.

Management's control is based ultimately on the threat to stop paying wages to ineffective workers, i.e. if the worker's effort falls beneath a certain acceptable minimum he or she can be sacked. There are, however, more subtle ways in which payment can be used to generate effort. Payment by piece rates, for example, whereby a worker gets a certain amount for each article completed, means that wages are directly related to work effort. The productivity deal is the equivalent system in large-scale manufacturing industry where, since no individual completes any particular product, collective financial incentives are provided to encourage high output. The other main way of regulating effort by financial incentive is by constructing promotion ladders within companies. If promotion can be made to depend upon performance then workers have an incentive to work hard and obediently.

The other major managerial resource is authority, which is exercised in association with payment. By and large, workers accept that management has some right to instruct workers what to do. The presence of managers and supervisors watching over workers is, thus, legitimate. At the same time, though, in practice, that authority is frequently resented and challenged by workers. The concept of managerial strategies refers to the various ways of exercising authority at work, of making managerial control effective in the face of resistance. A considerable number of strategies have been identified. Here we will consider four pure (or 'ideal') types of strategy – those based upon direct control, technical control, bureaucratic control and responsible autonomy. These rarely exist in pure form: in practice, in most firms, elements of more than one strategy coexist.

Direct control

The employer or manager in small establishments, and the supervisor in larger enterprises, may watch over the worker, threatening to stop part of the worker's payment, or dismiss the worker, if he or she is not working sufficiently quickly or accurately. This is a method of direct control, sometimes called 'simple control' because it is the most basic way to ensure effort. Such a method unsurprisingly tends to cause extensive resentment on the part of workers. This strategy is probably used less than it used to be, though it still characterizes small firms and firms where workers are relatively poorly organized. It is less effective in large establishments, partly because workers organize collectively to resist the authority of supervisors, and partly because supervisory workers and lower-level managers are not necessarily as enthusiastic about disciplining workers as an owner might be. Many occupational groups – dockers, some engineers, etc. – succeed in regulating their own work effort by taming supervisors.

Technical control

This is associated with scientific management and Taylorism. Taylorism maintains that, for industrial efficiency, jobs should be broken down into the smallest possible component tasks and the labour process redesigned so that each task is completed in the fastest possible way. This has often involved time-and-motion studies, the time taken for each element of a task being precisely measured in order to specify a minimum rate of working for each task. This has had three distinctive consequences.

1 Jobs have been fragmented into a very narrow range of tasks or, ultimately, a single, simple task.
2 The appropriate way of doing that task has been decided by the work-study consultant on behalf of management, so that workers have no longer had any discretion over how to go about their work. (This principle is often called the separation of conception from execution.)
3 The design of the job, and the speed at which it has to be done, have been justified as 'scientific' because they are the result of the application of standardized measurement techniques.

These principles of Taylorism are widely applicable. The classic example still remains the operation of the assembly line, where tasks are few, discretion absent, and the speed of work is determined by the assembly line itself. The worker on the line is compelled to keep up the same pace of work as the machine. The rate of work is determined directly by the technology – thus the term 'technical control'. Of course, management chooses the machinery and the speed at which it operates. The attraction for management of technical control is great. Partly, it defuses interpersonal conflict between supervisor and worker because the process is deemed 'scientific'. Partly, it makes output predictable and, hopefully, quick. But technical control also generates worker resistance. Since such methods are generally only applicable in large enterprises, lots of workers, equally bored, are likely to be gathered together. Such workers are relatively easy to organize in unions and are likely to refuse to cooperate willingly with management. The kinds of resistance offered in such situations vary from 'soldiering' – working slowly when the work-study expert comes to assess the rate for individual tasks – to sabotage – throwing a spanner in the works to gain a rest. Managerial control is often strongly contested in such situations.

Bureaucratic control

This is the normal staple form of control in the civil service, though it is becoming increasingly common in advanced sectors of industry, especially among multinational corporations. Basically, the worker's approach to the job is governed by formal rules and policed by a minutely differentiated hierarchy of authority. From one angle this hinders solidarity among workers: resentment is dispersed as each rank complains about its immediate superiors rather than about the organization as a whole. Furthermore, because it is hierarchical, a bureaucracy offers promotion prospects. Promotion is used as a reward to obedience and loyalty, thus suppressing resistance. This strategy is used to control manual workers in manufacturing industry through the operation of 'internal labour markets'. Companies recruit new workers from the outside only at a very few levels and always promote workers from inside the company. Thus a worker's future depends upon satisfactory performance within that company, which may make him or her reluctant to oppose management. Work in a modern bank is a good example of bureaucratic control. The cashier does a fairly wide range of tasks – dealing with customers, checking records, exchanging money, etc. – but has little discretion in the design of the work and, being at the bottom of a hierarchy, has no authority.

Responsible autonomy

Under this mode of control, the worker is given a much greater degree of discretion and is less subject to supervisory authority. The classic case is the craft worker – skilled engineers, printers, and the like. Such workers are typically left to design and organize their own working time, largely because they have more knowledge than management about the work itself. Craft workers are trained apprentices, who build up a knowledge of tools and techniques, and apply that knowledge and experience in the course of work. This raises problems of control for management, since the quality of work and effort expended lies largely in the hands of the workers themselves. This may often not matter, since such workers frequently develop a kind of self-policing system whereby standards of work are collectively guaranteed. Besides, craft workers usually work efficiently because they derive satisfaction from the use of their skills, which are a source of personal pride. Nonetheless, management have to pay relatively high wages as part of the bargain to persuade craft workers to be 'responsible', and discontented craft workers can easily reduce the quality and quantity of their labour because it is not kept under close surveillance. There is, thus, a strong temptation for management to try to reorganize work to by-pass such crafts. This is, of course, a principal objective of Taylorism. If a craft task can be broken into simple operations, or machines can be introduced to replace craft workers, then management can wrest control from labour. It is Braverman's argument that jobs characterized by responsible autonomy are increasingly being replaced by ones subject to technical control.

The labour process in printing: a case-study

The combined role of technology, managerial strategy and worker resistance in the determination of the nature of work has been demonstrated by Cockburn (1983) in her excellent study of compositors in the British printing industry. The section of the printing industry involved in the production of newspapers underwent rapid change in the late 1970s. Industrial disputes between the National Graphical Association (NGA) – the union of the most 'skilled' printing operatives – and the newspaper proprietors were one consequence. *The Times*, for example, traditionally the newspaper of the establishment in Britain, ceased publication for eleven months in 1979 due to a strike by workers and a lock-out by employers. The principal issue at stake was the introduction of new technology.

The machinery used to produce newsprint – the linotype machine – had not changed since the 1890s. This technology was worked by a compositor. Having been given the journalist's written copy, compositors used the machine to select metal letters, which were formed into words and lines of print, mounted in a large frame. Completed frames were carried off to be copied. This 'hot-metal' technology provided a varied, challenging occupation for compositors. The machines themselves were quite complex, using a distinctive keyboard with 90 features. The compositor was responsible for basic maintenance tasks. Literacy in general, and spelling in particular, were essential to the job, as was a knowledge of the systems of symbols used in the printing industry to indicate the intended layout of the final printed page. The linotype machine also required considerable discretion on the part of the compositor in the process of layout since he had to make decisions, at high speed, about how many words should be put in each line in order to make the columns in the paper regular. Finally, the compositor was responsible for humping the heavy, completed frames of type to the press. The job thus required, in the view of the workers themselves, agility, literacy, some artistic appreciation and brute strength. The job entailed a wide range of tasks and considerable degrees of discretion.

New technology threatened to transform, even completely abolish, compositing. Photo-lithographic and offset-lithographic techniques had been in use in the USA for nearly 25 years and British management began to try to implement these techniques in the mid-1970s. Instead of using hot-metal techniques these new methods use photographic techniques for copying pages of print. The setting up of those pages can then be simplified. Indeed, typewriters, visual-display units and computers can replace the linotype machine. The setting out of pages then becomes indistinct from routine office work. A typist, using an ordinary typewriter, can print the journalist's copy (indeed, the journalist *could* do this). The computer justifies the margins and reproduces the images of complete pages of the newspaper on-screen. The layout can then be adjusted simply. New technology seems capable of making the compositor's job obsolete.

The British compositors, however, tried to resist the introduction of new technology in order to protect their trade. Their success in this depended partly on the nature of the firm in which they were employed. Cockburn compared the situation of two national dailies and two provincial newspaper firms. The dailies were located in Fleet Street, in central London. The others, producing local papers, were on the outskirts

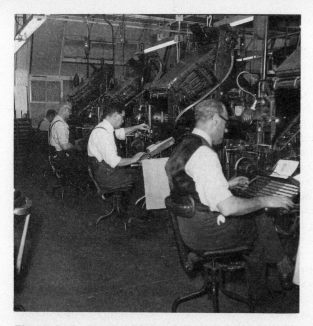

Figure 2.10 Printing before the new technology
Source: Syndication International.

of Greater London. Management in the provincial firms introduced the new technology quite quickly and with limited resistance. The two dailies – the *Mirror* and *The Times* – experienced protracted disputes. The differences are partly to do with the firms involved and their different 'environments'. The provincial papers were smaller firms, employing fewer compositors, and had fostered harmonious industrial relations. The compositors were not an especially privileged group and they were not likely to be made redundant by the new technology, because the firms involved were expanding. The situation on the dailies was different. The dailies are big enterprises, employing large numbers of very highly paid and very well-organized compositors. Competition for sales between dailies is intense. Employers and management had much to gain, compositors a lot to lose, from the introduction of new technology. The firms, however, were tied to central London. To ensure speed in distribution, the dailies have to be printed very close to the main London railway stations. Management, therefore, find it difficult simply to close down these particular operations and start up again elsewhere, which is what firms in other industries (i.e. in different commercial environments) often do.

In Fleet Street, the hot-metal compositors not only undertook varied tasks and used their own discretion in the job, but they also effectively controlled the compositing room: managers and supervisors were excluded. The 'father' of the 'chapel' of the firm's branch of the NGA – the equivalent of a shop-steward in other unions – took responsibility for the organization and completion of the work. In consultation with the workers, he was responsible for the delegation and rotation of tasks, for recruiting new workers and for communication with higher management. This degree of workplace control derived partly from knowing more about the job than management, and partly from effective union organization. These two things go together. Compositors underwent lengthy apprenticeships, and recruitment to apprenticeships was controlled by the NGA which operated a pre-entry closed shop. Their specialized knowledge was, thus, restricted to exclude both managers and all other workers. Compositors jealously protected their privileges against other workers in the printing industry, particularly against women. The benefits for compositors were considerable. They were well rewarded – earning £500 per week in 1982 for a 32-hour week, with 8 weeks' holiday a year. They were not troubled with surveillance by supervisors, which workers are inclined to resent. And they also derived a good deal of satisfaction from the work itself, as their comments to Cockburn indicated.

The compositors were afraid that the new technology would reduce their income, self-respect and job satisfaction. Some of the men on the provincial papers who were interviewed by Cockburn were already working with the new technology and they tended to be nostalgic for their old jobs. The men had been retrained to use ordinary typewriters instead of linotype keyboards. Many had found the learning process difficult and after a considerable length of time were less adept than office typists. The new jobs were, effectively, office jobs. The transition challenged the men's masculine identity. Hot-metal work had been both dirty and physical, as well as requiring specific skills, such that compositors thought of their work as 'man's work'. (As Cockburn demonstrated, it was man's work because the men and the union made sure that women could not obtain jobs as compositiors.) The new job had no such masculine characteristics and, indeed, working with women as colleagues was seen as a source of shame or embarrassment to former hot-metal compositors.

The challenge of the new work to the compositor's patriarchal assumptions about male superiority was one consequence of the change. However, they also missed the variety of tasks and discretion in work that the linotype machine had allowed. They were explicitly aware of having been deskilled, and were distressed, if not angry, about it. Previously, many of the compositors had enjoyed a sense of superiority over the mass of manual workers because of their skill. Taking less skilled work upset them: it was a traumatic decision, though many had volunteered for retraining, reasoning that they had better learn to use the new technology quickly in case they found themselves redundant otherwise. So, some accepted new work out of a sense of inevitability. A depleted task-range and little discretion or control was the outcome for the ex-compositor in the provincial firms.

The workers on the dailies, who were in a better tactical position, continued to resist their management's wish to deploy new technology, which in the case of *The Times* had been installed much earlier but not brought into use. Even so, by the time Cockburn was writing up her research material, the position of the compositors was becoming weaker. There was little doubt that the new machinery would come into service. Negotiations concerning the conditions under which that would occur were prolonged. The strength of the NGA allowed it temporarily to insist that *only* compositors should do typesetting on the new machines, and that there should be no redundancies.

In the long run, however, it seems that the employers have got their way, introducing new technology, thereby deskilling compositors, weakening the union and establishing managerial control of the workplace. This happened during 1986 at Times Newspapers, causing a bitter industrial dispute. The management finally dismissed its printers, shifted production to a new site at Wapping equipped with new technology, and engaged a new workforce consisting of members of the electricians' union (EEPTU). There were large demonstrations and months of picketing by the printers who demanded their jobs back. But, despite their resistance, the attempt to preserve their old jobs failed, thus allowing other newspaper firms to follow the example of *The Times*.

Summary

1 Different jobs give different rewards and satisfactions. Jobs in which the worker does a variety of tasks and has discretion over how to carry out those tasks tend to give most satisfaction.

2 Many jobs have been deskilled in the twentieth century as work has been reorganized to give management more control by reducing the workers' range of tasks and degree of discretion. At the same time, however, new occupations requiring technical capacities and specialized knowledge have emerged. Whether there has been an overall trend towards deskilling is disputed.

3 Too much emphasis should not be placed on technological innovation in explaining changes in work, because technology can be used in many different ways. The manner in which technology is deployed reflects power relations between management and workers.

4 The experience of work is strongly affected by the way in which management tries to control workers in the process of production. There are many types of managerial strategy of which direct control, technical control, bureaucratic control and relative autonomy are important variants.

Related topics

Some discussion of the effects of new technology on work patterns occur in section 2.8. A study of women's factory work, in a multi-ethnic setting, is reported in chapter 4, section 4.6. The characteristics of modern office work are discussed in chapter 3, section 3.5; and managers' work is examined in section 2.3 and chapter 3, section 3.5. Aspects of worker organization and consciousness are dealt with in the following section, 2.5, and at length in chapter 3, section 3.4.

2.5　Trade Unions and Industrial Relations

Trade unions are the most important and visible organizations of employee resistance in the workplace. The study of industrial relations is primarily devoted to the relationship between unions and management.

According to the opinion polls, a majority of British adults in the 1980s think that trade unions have too much power. Many of these people, expressing more-or-less hostile views towards unions, are themselves members of a union and tend to approve of their own union. (Consider, for example, the opinion-poll survey data in figure 2.11 to see if you think much sense can be made of such findings.)

The inconsistency of popular attitudes towards unions is perhaps to be explained by the gulf between the presentation of unions in the mass media and people's personal experience of relationships at work. In most workplaces, neither workers nor their union representatives can exercise much power or control and union membership seems a valuable, if weak, form of protection against the employer. When the media report a national strike, on the other hand, unions seem powerful institutions. Given that the presentation of such events is biased against unions (straightforwardly in the press, with more subtlety on television – see chapter 10, section 10.2), they are made to appear wicked too. It is, thus, instructive that a major recent survey, which asked *management* at 2,000 establishments in Britain in 1979-80, for their 'opinion of the general state of relations between management and workers at this establishment', got the following responses: first rate, 48 per cent; good, 34 per cent; fairly good, 15 per cent; not bad, 1 per cent; fairly poor or worse, 2 per cent (Daniel and Millward, 1983, p. 255).

The image of the unions, and the popular ambivalence towards them, results from their structural role. Unions are well-established. Together they have a vast membership. And, generally, they are organizations that support and protect their members against powerful adversaries – employers. This inevitably involves them in a degree of conflict with

Questions and answers	% Today	Questions and answers	% Today
1 I'm going to read you a few statements. For each, please tell me if you tend to agree or disagree with it.		f) Trade unions improve wages, working conditions and job security for workers	
		Agree	65
a) It is true in this country that if you work hard, eventually you will get ahead		Disagree	28
		Don't know	7
		g) Trade unions control, dominate or run business	
Agree	51	Agree	53
Disagree	43	Disagree	35
Don't know	6	Don't know	12
b) Wages and working conditions would have reached today's level even without the efforts of trade unions		h) Trade unions ensure fair treatment for workers	
		Agree	62
		Disagree	29
Agree	26	Don't know	10
Disagree	64	i) Trade unions get power or money for union leaders	
Don't know	9		
c) Trade-union leaders are out of touch with the workers they represent		Agree	73
		Disagree	13
		Don't know	14
Agree	72	2 Which of these two statements do you tend to agree with more?	
Disagree	20		
Don't know	9		
d) Most workers who are not in management jobs would be better off belonging to a union than not belonging to one		a) because of a few rotten apples among them, trade unions have tended to get a bad reputation	77
Agree	55	b) Most trade unions deserve to have a bad reputation	15
Disagree	30		
Don't know	14	c) Don't know	8
e) Trade unions may have been needed at one time in Britain, but not any longer			
Agree	32		
Disagree	61		
Don't know	7		

Figure 2.11   Attitudes towards trade unions, 1984, from a sample of 1,000 adults, nation-wide

Source: From *Gallup Political Index Report No. 285* (May 1984), table 12. Reproduced with permission.

management. There is a general conflict of interests between employer and employee concerning both control at work and payment. At the same time, however, that conflict is usually covert and limited. Mostly, in practice, unions accept private ownership, profit-making, managerial authority and market mechanisms. They seek not to undermine employers so much as to secure, within the existing framework, a 'fair' deal for their members – a customary and adequate wage, some security and some dignity. For their part, employers seek usually not to destroy unions but to secure satisfactory levels of output and profit. Employers and unions, therefore, struggle persistently over the terms of a bargain whereby the former buys and the latter sells labour power.

Bargaining and negotiation are the normal forms that the relationship between unions and management takes. Workers' representatives negotiate with management about the so-called 'wage-effort bargain'. Occasionally, negotiation breaks down and open conflict emerges. Strikes and lock-outs are the most publicized forms of conflict, but there are other forms of industrial action by means of which workers collectively resist managerial authority. Overtime bans and working to rule are common forms of industrial action. Workers may, alternatively, organize politically to reduce the power of management generally as, for example, by implementing wider consultation procedures or workers' control. Another important mode of resistance is individual: sabotage, work limitation and absenteeism may all be used by individual workers as ways of expressing hostility towards management. Such means may be the only ones available for non-unionized workers, but they are not restricted to such workers.

Being based upon an inequality of power between management and workers, industrial relations are always areas of potential conflict. As Fox described it, industrial relations are relations of 'low trust'. There are, however, considerable costs for both sides in engaging in sustained, open conflict. Management generally seeks a cooperative work-force, for strikes, work limitation, sabotage, and the like, reduce productivity and income to the enterprise. Management, therefore, tends to seek to reduce the arena of mutual conflict. This may be achieved in a number of ways: refusing to recognize trade unions, persuading employees that there are no grounds for hostility, and establishing procedures for negotiations over issues which cause grievance to workers, are alternative ways of handling potential conflict. Trade unions usually have no wish to escalate conflict either. They exist primarily to protect the economic interests of their members by securing satisfactory conditions for workers within a firm or industry. They are, thus, concerned with the exchange bargain under which workers sell their labour power – pay, hours, security or employment and safety at work are their immediate concerns.

Over a long period of time, a range of procedures have developed in many industries whereby such matters are negotiated routinely by union officials. Often these officials are as committed as management to those peaceful and routine procedures: unions themselves play a central part in what is referred to as the *institutionalization of industrial conflict*. Most industrial relations activity is institutionalized. Unions rarely use the ultimate sanction at their disposal – the strike. The point at which unions are prepared to cease negotiating and call upon their members to withdraw their labour depends on a number of factors – the strength of the union, the economic position of affected firms, the rate of unemployment, the law, etc. Given popular prejudices, it is worth recording that most workers have never been on strike and that, on average in 1983, only 3.8 million days were lost through disputes, an average of 0.1 days per worker. Even in 1979, the year in which days were lost through strikes since the Second World War, only 1.2 days per worker were lost through industrial disputes. In any year, many more days per worker are lost through illness.

Trade-union membership

Despite their unpopular public image, trade unions in Britain are highly successful in recruiting members. Over half the British work-force is unionized. In 1979, 55 per cent of the working population were members of a trade union or a professional association. That figure, referred to as union *density* (i.e. the proportion of people eligible for membership who actually join), was higher than at any time in British history. Statistics of union membership and density are presented in table 2.5. This shows that the number of union members increased slowly between 1949–69, whilst density remained constant at about 44 per cent. In the next decade, 1969-79, membership and density increased significantly. Since 1979 there has been a fall in membership which seems likely to continue for some time: in 1979 there were about 13.25 million members; by 1984 the number had fallen to just over 11 million.

Table 2.5 Union membership (in thousands) and union density (percentages) since the Second World War

	Union members (000)	Potential union members (000)	Union density level (%)
1949	9,318	20,782	44.8
1959	9,623	21,866	44.0
1969	10,479	23,153	45.3
1974	11,764	23,229	50.4
1979	13,447	24,264	55.4
1981	12,182	23,879	51.0
1984	11,086	—	—

Source: from Price and Bain (1983) *Industrial Relations* (Oxford, Basil Blackwell), table 1, pp. 46-7, with permission of the authors; and *Employment Gazette* (Jan. 1986), p. 17. Crown copyright.

Density of union membership varies between industries, between occupational groups, and between men and women. In 1979, for example, only 8 per cent of workers in the hotel and catering industry were unionized, compared with 99 per cent of post and telecommunication workers. Variations in density by industry are shown in figure 2.12. This figure demonstrates that employees in the public sector are generally more highly unionized than those in the private sector. In all, in 1979, 85 per cent of workers in public employment were in unions, compared with only 42 per cent in the private sector. This is partly because governments in the 1960s and 1970s encouraged their employees to join unions; in the private sector, many employers have resisted unionization. Workers in manufacturing industries are also better unionized than those in services. Thus, in the private manufacturing sector, density is around 70 per cent whilst in private services it is a mere 16 per cent (*Social Trends*, 1982, table 11.17, p. 196). These industrial variations account for some of the other differences in density of unionization. For instance, 66 per cent of manual workers but only 45 per cent of non-manual workers were unionized in 1979. Also, 65 per cent of men, but only 41 per cent of women were then in unions.

Explanation of the varying density of union membership may be considered from two points of view. First, why in general do people join unions? Second, what factors operate to produce variations in density for different groups of workers?

1 *People join unions primarily because collective action is the most effective way for workers to defend and promote their occupational interests.* Unions try to modify and regulate the conditions under which labour is sold by using their collective organizational strength to offset the power of employers. Individual workers have no effective sanctions at their disposal: when faced by an employer one worker alone cannot prevent wages falling, insist on improving working conditions, or protect jobs during an economic recession. The market situation of most occupational groups depends upon collective solidarity.

Strength of numbers is important, since the larger the organization of workers the more difficult it is for employers to replace the labour force: unions are generally weak in small firms because, unless very highly skilled, the replacement of a handful of workers is relatively easy.

The union's desire for a closed shop also follows. The closed shop is the logical end-point in union organization, since if all persons with available skills are members of the union their bargaining position *vis-à-vis* employers is greatly enhanced. In 1980, about 27 per cent of workers were subject to closed-shop arrangements. Unusually, these were 'post-entry' closed shops, that is if you took a particular job you had to become a member of a certain trade union. Closed shops were fairly rare among non-manual workers but quite common among manual workers. The larger the establishment, the more likely there was to be a closed shop.

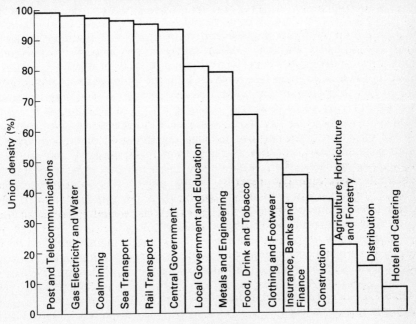

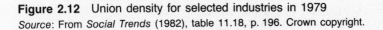

Figure 2.12 Union density for selected industries in 1979
Source: From *Social Trends* (1982), table 11.18, p. 196. Crown copyright.

A tendency of union organization toward centralization also follows. National bargaining replaced local and workshop bargaining between 1920 and 1970, both increasing the sense of solidarity of union members (because the outcome of a wage-claim is binding for workers in London, Lancaster and Llandudno), and preventing employers deserting high-wage regions for lower-wage regions. Centralized bargaining is almost universal in state administration and services. Pay and conditions are the same in all schools and hospitals, for example. However, one of the main trends in the last 20 years has been the re-emergence of workplace bargaining in manufacturing industry, especially in private firms. Localized agreements between management and work-force, concerning productivity and bonus payments, for instance, have become increasingly prominent. This, in turn has made union representation *in the workplace* more necessary – a development which led to the recent enormous increase in the numbers of shop stewards (see below).

Unionization is effective in the sense that better-paid employees are generally well organized. Organization does not guarantee high rewards, but is an important contributory factor. This can be seen by comparing average wages by industry with union density. Precise comparison is impossible, but if we consider average male manual wages by industry in 1981, eight out of the ten highest paid industries had a union density of 80 per cent or more. Printers (94 per cent density), miners (97 per cent and air transport (85 per cent) were three of the four best-paid industries; the other was oil refining (see table 2.6). Of the 10 lowest-paid industries, 8 had less than 50 per cent union density. The worst-paid – agricultural workers (23 per cent), catering (8 per cent), retail distribution (15 per cent) – are among the five most poorly paid industries.

Not only do unions improve the financial situation of their members among other things, but they also help to maintain workers' control over the labour process. This is sometimes part of the same process as obtaining high financial rewards: in the engineering industry and in printing (as we say in section 2.4), control over the job strengthened the union's bargaining position. On other occasions, though, the search for control at work is an end in itself for unions.

2 If it benefits workers to be union members, it might be asked why there are so many occupations with very low levels of unionization. There are several factors which contribute to levels of unionization: *the size,*

Table 2.6 Industrial wages[a] and union density[b] for manual men, an approximate comparison

| MLH[c] | Pay by industry | | Unionization | |
	Industry	Pay as % of all industries & services	Union density (%)	Industry
	HIGHEST 10 INDUSTRIES			
485	Newspaper printing	157.8	94	Printing and publishing
262	Mineral oil refining	143.2	59	Chemicals
101	Coal mining (underground)	133.6 (145.9)	97	Coal mining
708	Air transport	130.8	85	Air transport
601–2	Electricity & gas	122.9	95	Electricity and gas
489	Other printing and publishing	120.7	94	Printing and publishing
706	Port and inland water	119.8	83	Port and inland water transport
271	General chemicals	117.5	59	Chemicals
383	Aerospace equipment manufacturer	117.3	80	Metals and engineering
311	Iron and steel (general)	113.9	80	Metals and engineering

ownership and economic position of the employing establishment, the employers' and the government's attitudes to unionization, and the typical social characteristics of the labour force, may all affect levels of unionization.

This size of an enterprise is important. Small firms are weakly unionized; large, bureaucratically organized firms, especially those with centralized personnel management, can scarcely function in the absence of unions to transmit grievances and bargain on behalf of employees. This size-cum-organization effect is one reason why state-owned industry has higher levels of unionization – most public employment is in large organizations with centralized management and centralized bargaining procedures. Large firms in the private manufacturing sector are also subject to this pressure. In private services, by contrast, firms are smaller and employers are more reluctant to recognize unions, in part because such firms operate in a more competitive environment where wages are a relatively more important cost. Lower rates of female membership are one consequence of this. As will be shown in chapter 3, section 3.2, and chapter 4, section 4.2, women crowd into certain occupations, and many

Table 2.6 *continued*

LOWEST 10 INDUSTRIES

812	Wholesale distribution (excluding food & drink)	86.7	15	Distribution
XIII	Textiles (excluding synthetic fibres	86.2	99	Cotton and man-made fibres
894	Motor repairs and distribution	85.5		Distribution
831–2	Dealing in industrial materials	85.3	15	Distribution
441–9	Clothing	84.0	42	Clothing
820–1	Retail distribution	83.6	15	Distribution
414	Woollen worsted	82.3	47	Other textiles
872	Educational services	80.6	78	Local government and education
884–8	Catering	77.9	8	Miscellaneous services
001	Agriculture	72.4	23	Agriculture

Notes: [a]April 1981, highest and lowest paid adult manual men, average gross hourly earnings.

[b]Union density in 1979 is not always strictly comparable.

[c]MLH: Minimum List Heading number – the way in which official statistics group industries for purpose of analysis.

Source: Price and Bain (1983) *Industrial Relations* (Oxford, Basil Blackwell), table 6, pp. 54-5, with permission of the authors; Department of Employment (1981), table 54, pp. C6-9. Crown copyright.

of them are employed in private services. Only in one sector of manufacturing industry – textiles – do women comprise a majority of the work-force, and there union density is high.

Similar forces operate on white-collar workers. By 1979, 40 per cent of all union members were non-manual workers. Union density was, of course, still lower among white-collar workers than among manual worker – see chapter 3, section 3.5. (Figure 2.13 shows the rate of growth of white-collar unionism.) This is, however, less because of the attitudes of the workers, than because of greater employer resistance to recognizing white-collar unions, and because white-collar workers are typically found in smaller work units. Thus, public employees, who usually work for larger concerns, are increasingly well unionized; their counterparts in privately owned enterprises are less so.

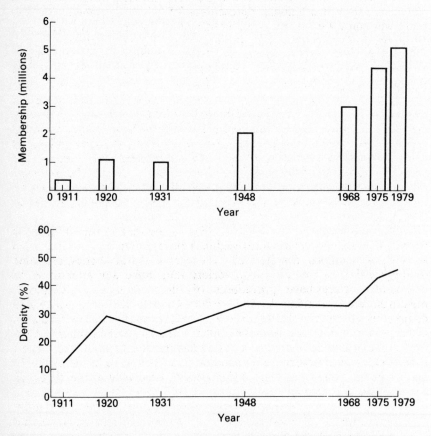

Figure 2.13 White-collar union membership and density, selected years
Source: From Price and Bain (1983) *Industrial Relations* (Oxford, Basil Blackwell), table 4, with permission of the authors.

If these determinants of union membership continue in force, then union density will tend to fall in the immediate future. Rising unemployment itself is one reason for falling membership in the 1980s. But, more important, employment has contracted most sharply in manufacturing industry and public services since 1979, which means that jobs in enterprises with high levels of unionization are disappearing fastest. To the extent that a larger proportion of remaining available jobs are in privately owned firms in the service sector of the economy, union density will decline.

The organization of trade unions

Mergers have resulted in unions being fewer, and larger, than before. In 1960 there were 650 unions, representing 9.8 million members. By 1980 there were only 438 unions, representing 13 million members. The largest 10 unions in 1980 represented 60 per cent of all union members.

Problems arise in attempting to organize large numbers of people. Unions are basically voluntary associations which seek to *democratically* represent their membership. Most officials, especially senior ones, are elected and the policies of unions are determined at conferences of delegates. However, some characteristics of bureaucratic organization (see section 2.3) emerge: large unions are staffed by permanent, salaried officials, who are distributed in a hierarchy of posts, the most influential of which are located at central headquarters. Because officials are supposed to represent the membership, tension may develop between the central officials and members. Conflicts may also arise over issues of union policy. Thus, it is often claimed that union leaders fail to represent their members.

Writing as long ago as 1915, Michels noted that it was difficult to maintain democratic procedures within a bureaucratic organization. On the face of it, unions, despite their bureaucratic characteristics, are some of the few institutions in British society that make any attempt to be democratic. They have procedures of direct democracy (elections, meetings, etc.), making leaders responsive to members, which are completely absent in schools, the army, the monarchy, or the House of Lords. Some unions are, however, more democratic than others. Also, the extent of democratic control varies historically. Overall, the biggest British unions are now more democratic than they were in the 1950s. In many unions, power has been decentralized, especially in the 1970s. In some cases, for example the Transport and General Workers Union (TGWU) and the National Union of Public Employees (NUPE), decentralization was sponsored by permanent officials. Recognizing that participation by lay members in union affairs was essential to a thriving and effective organization, powers were intentionally devolved to the workplace. In other instances, local rank-and-file pressure persuaded officials that they must take more notice of their lay members. The strike at Pilkingtons in St Helens, studied by Lane and Roberts (1971), where workers left the General and Municipal Workers' Union (GMWU) to set up a break-away organization because the national executive would not make their strike official, is but one example of such pressure.

The rapid expansion of the shop-steward system in the 1970s was another aspect of decentralization. Estimates of the number of shop-stewards put the figure at 90,000 in 1961, 175,000 in 1968 and over 250,000 by 1978. In 1961, shop-stewards had barely existed outside heavy manufacturing industry. By 1978, there were shop-stewards in the health services and local government, among white-collar workers and even in private services. Shop-stewards provide an accessible link, at the workplace, between paid officials and union members. In those firms and industries where bargaining is localized – predominantly in manufacturing industries – stewards have a central role to play in determining pay and conditions. In all circumstances, stewards provide a channel for the expression of workers' grievances. It may be, however, that shop-stewards simultaneously also reduce conflict in the workplace by helping to avoid disputes and smooth out problems.

The 1970s also witnessed a change in the ways union policy was made. There was greater competition in union elections between candidates advocating different policies for the union. Sometimes this competition developed from the same workplace pressures which led to the devolution of powers. In other cases, internal divisions were expressed more loudly and openly than before. The National Union of Mineworkers (NUM), for example, has always exhibited political and regional divisions. This was merely magnified in the 1984 coal strike, where miners from some regions continued to work despite picketing by miners from other regions.

The growth of democratic control within unions was, however, limited; some unions actually became more tightly controlled from the centre. Where there was no tradition of workplace organization, decentralization often proved temporary. As the recession worsened in the early 1980s and unions were forced into very defensive postures, rank-and-file movements declined. So too did the shop-stewards movement. Moreover, some of the changes in unions never became well established. For example, one way in which unions are unrepresentative of their membership lies in their behaviour to women. Though the number of women officials has increased and some unions have adopted policies to improve the conditions of women, achievements have been limited. The gap in earnings between men and women, after closing a little in the early 1970s, is widening again (see chapter 4, section 4.2). Very few senior posts in the unions are filled by women (e.g. the TUC General Council elected in 1984 had 5 women out of 55 members). The interests of women are weakly represented by unions, despite the fact that about 30 per cent of union members are female. Women who work part-time are particularly badly served as they are least likely to become members, as table 2.7 shows.

Table 2.7 Trade union membership by gender and age, 1983

		% who are trade union members	
	Males	Females	
Age	Full-time	Full-time	Part-time
16–19	21	24	5
20–4	47	45	21
25–34	56	52	29
35–44	59	56	33
45–64	67	58	38
65+	4	3	8
Total	57	50	33

Source: General Household Survey (1983), p. 100. Crown copyright.

Industrial conflict

Strikes are the aspect of industrial conflict which receives most publicity. But because strikes make for dramatic news stories, their frequency and importance to trade unionism are easily overestimated. Of course, the strike is the ultimate sanction available to a union in a dispute with an employer; the possibility of workers collectively withdrawing their labour is fundamental if unions are to have any influence over the behaviour of employers. But remember that, for much more of the time, unions are engaged in peaceful, routine, institutionalized/regularized bargaining.

One important source of information on patterns of industrial conflict is a survey undertaken in 1980, of management and employee representatives at some 2,000 establishments, the results of which are reported in Daniel and Millward (1983). The survey covered the whole range of workplaces–small and large, manufacturing and service sectors, public and private enterprises. It inquired about the frequency and type of industrial action which occurred in each establishment during a 12-month period between mid-1979 and mid-1980. This was a period of intense industrial conflict, as is shown in figure 2.14, which shows the number of days lost by strikes each year from 1961 to 1984. The survey suggested that only about one-quarter of establishments experienced any industrial action. Of these, manual workers were more likely to take strike action, non-manual workers taking other industrial action, i.e. overtime ban, work to rule, or blacking of work. (Establishments affected could, and often did, experience *both* strike and non-strike action.)

Daniel and Millward tried to isolate the factors associated with different types of industrial action. They found that, where no trade

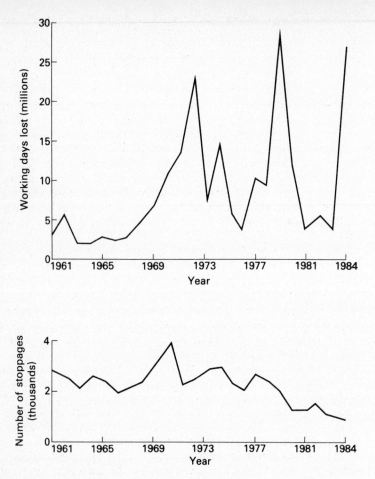

Figure 2.14   Days lost by strike action 1961–84
Source: Employment Gazette and *Social Trends* (various years).

union existed, industrial action was, unsurprisingly, rare. In establishments which were unionized, the likelihood of industrial action grew under the following five conditions:

1   the more manual workers there were at the establishment;
2   the higher the density of union membership;
3   the greater the proportion of workers who were men;
4   the greater the proportion of workers employed full-time;
5   the more the establishment itself was the main place of collective bargaining.

The final condition is important. One thing the survey showed was the variety of levels at which bargaining occurred in Britain. In some cases, bargaining over pay and other matters takes place at *national level*. Conditions are negotiated between all employers and relevant unions for all workers in a given industry throughout Britain. This occurs most commonly in state-owned industries (workers in education and on British Rail have the same contracts wherever they work). In other cases, bargaining occurs at the *company level*: all people employed by the same company in the same job have identical conditions. Alternatively, bargaining may occur at *plant level*, that is negotiations occurring between management and unions cover only those people working on a single site. Where bargaining has been decentralized to this extent, industrial action is more likely to occur. This is partly because this degree of decentralization often coincides with the use of a system of payment-by-results (PBR). Almost half the manual work-force is on some kind of piece-work system or productivity–bonus scheme: they get paid according to output. This, however, gives considerable scope for conflict at the workplace over the price paid per item, the speed at which tasks have to be accomplished in order to get a bonus, etc. This perhaps also accounts for the fact that, in about 60 per cent of cases in the survey, wages and earnings were reported by managers and workers as the reason for industrial action. The other most important causes were 'the duration and pattern of working hours' and 'manning and work allocation'. The latter was unlikely to cause a strike, however.

Resistance may take forms other than strikes. Industrial conflict occurs also in less-newsworthy ways. Absenteeism, quitting a job, withdrawing cooperation with management, sabotage, and working slowly, are all ways in which employees can express discontent by adversely affecting production. High rates of absenteeism and lack of effort, for example, both present themselves as problems for management, and thus may be used by workers as ploys in negotiation. Especially in establishments where unions are not recognized, these may be the only possible ways of registering dissatisfaction. At the same time, it cannot be assumed that every instance of, say, absenteeism amounts to workers' resistance. Moreover, it should be realized that some of these practices are much less effective in applying pressure upon management than others. Although high rates of labour turnover may create difficulties for management – new workers have to be trained, worker morale is likely to be low, etc. – quitting a job is a weak form of 'resistance'. Striking and quitting are now equivalents.

Unions, politics and the law

Trade unions have always caused political controversy and the recent period has been no exception. Political intervention in economic affairs has increased in the last 50 years. Nationalization of industry contributed to the rapid growth of state employees – in 1981, 31 per cent of all employees. Governments have acknowledged general responsibility for economic prosperity. This has entailed supervision of prices and incomes, selective state subsidies for private industry, control over money supply and exchange rates, manipulation of public expenditure, etc. (see also chapter 12, section 12.5). Economic policy has thus directed governments' attention towards industrial relations and the role of trade unions.

At a rather different level, political parties and governments have a stake in industrial relations because the balance of power between employers and workers is a pivot of British political life. Trade unions are connected to the Labour Party, through direct affiliation of members and, indirectly, through the Trade Union Congress (TUC). Employers individually, and through their collective organizations like the Confederation of British Industry (CBI), are closely identified with the Conservative Party. Because this political alignment exists, economic policy and the laws concerning industrial relations alter with changes of government.

Most recently, Conservative governments since 1979 have attempted to alter the balance of industrial power in favour of employers. These governments have tried to reduce direct state involvement in industrial relations, both refusing to intervene or mediate in serious disputes and rejecting the use of incomes policies. The determination of wages and conditions has been left to negotiation between managers and their employees. Simultaneously, however, the government introduced legislation which makes unions less powerful when bargaining. The Employment Acts of 1980 and 1982 made it more difficult for unions to organize or to take industrial action. New restraints were introduced on picketing and secondary picketing, and it became more difficult to maintain a closed shop. Further legislation in 1984 for compulsory ballots before strikes and concerning political funds, incidents like the banning of the union at the Government Communications Headquarters (GCHQ), and the stance of the government in the miners' strike of 1984–5, are additional signs of the government's aim to curtail the power of unions. The effects of these measures remain uncertain for, in the past, state intervention to reduce the unions' freedom of action has tended to provoke solidarity and concerted resistance. However, present economic conditions – high unemployment and continuing recession – are so unfavourable to workers that even if the new legislation was completely ineffective unions would still remain in a fairly weak position.

Summary

1 Industrial relations are mostly a matter of routine negotiation and bargaining between trade-union representatives and management: industrial conflict in Britain is *institutionalized*.

2 Currently, about 50 per cent of all workers are members of a union,

membership density having fallen from a peak of 55 per cent in 1979. People join a union because collective organization is necessary to protect their occupational interests. The rate at which workers join unions is affected by a number of factors, including the nature of the workplace, the employer's attitude towards unions and the social characteristics of the work-force.

3 Unions, as organizations, have experienced some decentralization of power in the last twenty years – local bargaining has increased, as has the number of shop-stewards – which is associated with problems of preserving democratic procedures in large organizations.

4 Conflict between workers and management is endemic to industrial relations, taking many forms and occurring unevenly in time and across industries. Among the factors which affect strike rates, for example, are the level of union organization, the social characteristics of the work-force, the bargaining system in operation, as well as the general economic and political climate.

Related topics

One important issue concerns the links between industrial behaviour and class formation. Material on the industrial and class attitudes and behaviour can be found in chapter 3, sections 3.5 (for routine white-collar workers) and 3.4 (for manual workers). Further information on women workers is in chapter 4, section 4.2. Material on media presentation of unions and industrial relations can be found in chapter 10, section 10.2. Further discussion of government economic policy and its connections with class conflict appears in chapter 12, sections 12.3 and 12. 5.

2.6 Professional Occupations and Associations

> All professions are conspiracies against the laity.
> George Bernard Shaw, *The Doctor's Dilemma*

Government statistics refer to some occupations as professional. Among the 'higher' professions are included doctors, solicitors, judges, university teachers, architects and top-ranking civil servants. The 'lower' professions include schoolteachers, nurses, librarians, physiotherapists and social workers. People in these occupations are relatively privileged. Professionals on average earn more than most other groups of employees. Professional jobs also carry a considerable degree of prestige: people may scorn bureaucrats, trade unionists and shopkeepers, but professionals are rarely considered anything but worthy. Given the financial and status rewards associated with being a 'professional', it is unsurprising that many occupational groups attempt to get themselves recognized as professional.

(There are parallels here with the strategies of manual workers to have their jobs described as 'skilled'.) Since practising a profession is merely taking part in some of the tasks generated by the complex, modern, division of labour, the question arises, what is distinctive about these jobs which makes them so well rewarded?

It is impossible to list a set of characteristics which will determine unambiguously whether or not an occupation is a profession. Various sociologists have tried to identify the distinctive 'traits' of a profession. But they have neither agreed upon what should be included, nor have such approaches helped in the explanation of professional privileges. This is partly because professions, like other occupations, change over time. The classic model of a profession is an ideal type based on the nature of a few elite occupations in the nineteenth century. The 'classic' model, contrasted with the model of proletarian occupations, is illustrated in box 4.

It should be stressed that box 4 shows ideal types and that rarely has any occupation had all these characteristics. Moreover, today, very few professionals work under the conditions described by the ideal type. People at the higher levels of legal, medical and architectural occupations, approximate most closely to this type – barristers and consultant doctors in private medical practice, for example.

Occupational control

The basis of professional privilege is the power to shape and influence the social organization of work. That power is maintained through collective organization in professional associations. Power derives from high degrees of *occupational control*, control by practitioners themselves over various aspects of the occupation, including payment, recruitment and working practices.

Consider, for example, doctors. Medical doctors are one of the highest-paid occupational groups in Britain. They derive their income from two sources – salaries paid by the National Health Service and fees paid by private patients. Though some doctors are entirely reliant on one of these sources, most have some income from both sources. Private practice is more lucrative, NHS work more secure.

The main professional association for doctors is the British Medical Association (BMA). It had 78,000 members in 1985. Specialists – surgeons, physicians and the like – have their own associations – the Royal Colleges. The professional associations negotiate salaries with the state and establish levels of fees. They are in a powerful position regarding levels of payment because entry into the profession is highly restricted. All doctors have to be registered with the General Medical Council (GMC). The GMC officially licences doctors on behalf of the state: it is illegal to practise medicine unless you are on the register of the

Box 4 Two ideal types of occupations: proletarian and professional

	Classical model of a proletarian	Classic model of a (collegiate) profession
System of reward	Wages paid by employer: workers are wage-labourers	Paid fees, by a client, in exchange for services; are self-employed
Training and recruit-ment	No credentials required and very limited training	Has higher-education qualifi-cations (usually a degree) and special practical training
Content of work	Routine, mindless and frag-mented work	Specialized theoretical know-ledge: combines 'conception and execution'
Authority relations at work	Most subordinate in a hierarchy of authority: no control over work	Self-regulating and self-directing: controls own work.
Occupa-tional organiz-ation	Organized, if at all, by a trade union that bargains with employers on behalf of members	Organized by professional association, membership of which is compulsory, which regulates entry and standards of practice and is a body of equals
Status situation	Low	High
Ideological image	Casual, irresponsible	Expert, responsible, altruistic

1 These are *ideal types*, artificial constructions of characteristics that do not always occur together in reality.
2 The classic professional model finds its closest approximation in reality among lawyers, doctors and the clergy in the later nineteenth century.

GMC. While some members of the GMC are lay people nominated by the state, the majority are doctors. The GMC, thus, maintains a monopoly in the market for medical services and monopolies, of course, can easily inflate charges. In order to become a doctor it is necessary to obtain certain qualifications – a degree and a period of practice in hospital are required, taking seven years' training in all. Medical education is largely controlled by the GMC and the Royal Colleges which decide on the content of education and on how many doctors should be trained in any given year. The GMC and the professional associations are also responsible for controlling working practices. The GMC and the BMA discipline doctors, dealing with complaints about malpractice. So groups of doctors effectively decide among themselves both what is good and what is bad medicine. The professional associations are thus very powerful, being exclusive, self-recruiting and self-policing. The professional associations exercise a high degree of control over the occupation on behalf of their membership.

Doctors as individuals in the work situation also exercise control, both over patients and over other workers in health services. Doctors lay claim to expert knowledge, which is inaccessible to patients, and they decide on treatment. Both of these conditions give doctors considerable power over their patients. In hospitals, doctors also exercise power over other workers. Nursing staff, radiographers, pharmacists, etc. themselves lower professionals, are subordinate in the hierarchy of authority to doctors. The question this raises is, How, or why, have doctors achieved such a powerful occupational position, from which their privileges flow?

Doctors themselves would probably justify their own privileges in terms of training, knowledge, responsibility, the importance to their client of good health, the inconveniences of the job or the public service which they provide. Some would argue, however, that these are merely self-legitimating reasons, a claim supported by the fact that other, far less-privileged occupations, have these qualities too. Rather, the doctors' advantages derive from their overall high degree of occupational control. That control is achieved by collectively exploiting, through an effective association (the BMA), favourable aspects of the work-situation and market position which, in turn, reinforce the power of the association. In other words, market position, work-situation and collective organization are the mutually supporting props of occupational control.

Professionalization as an occupational strategy

> Professionalism . . . [is] an occupational strategy which is chiefly directed towards the achievement of upward collective social mobility and, once achieved it is concerned with the maintenance of superior remuneration and status.
>
> Parry and Parry (1976)

The rewards are such that many occupational groups aspire to be recognized as professional. Implicit in the medical model is a lesson for other occupations: professionalization is an *occupational group strategy*, a way of achieving collective upward social mobility, as Parry and Parry (1976) describe it. If successful, all workers in a particular occupation improve their social and material positions.

This strategy has been attempted by many groups. Its key elements include setting up an association, getting universities to provide courses which all practitioners must attend and pass, and establishing a set of tasks unique to the occupational group and from which all other workers are excluded. The degree of success of such strategies is one thing which separates the lower from the higher professionals.

A number of factors determine the success of professionalization strategies.

1 It depends when, historically, the strategy is embarked upon. Because exclusiveness is a basis of control, professionalization is competitive between different occupational groups. If doctors have exclusive rights to sign death certificates or sick notes, (both important prerogatives), then nurses are barred from those tasks. Indeed, the rise of the modern medical profession was at the expense of groups like nurses and midwives whose opportunities for collective upward social mobility were blocked.

2 The origins and characteristics of the personnel of occupational groups is important. One reason why the older professions were invested with considerable exclusive powers (like the GMC monopoly) was because they were originally recruited from among the sons of the upper and upper-middle class. Such men were considered reliable and could be given state-guaranteed powers. The higher-class origins of judges, army officers and doctors remain strongly visible even today. Similarly, it is not accidental that many of the lower professions are staffed by women. In 1981, there were 12 male, self-employed professionals for every 1 woman. Patriarchal power is used to exclude women.

3 Professionalization strategies are likely to meet with resistance from potential customers. Generally speaking, professional occupational control is against the interests of the purchasers of services. Where there are few potential customers, or where the customers are organized, professionalization is difficult to secure. For example, as almost the only employer of teachers, the state has the power to oppose the extension of occupational control. Indeed, many of the lower professions are almost entirely dependent upon the state for employment – social workers, nurses, executive-grade civil servants, etc. By contrast, the higher professions are generally those where potential customers are many and there are opportunities for the professional to be self-employed in private practice. Generally, being an employee, whether of the state or a large corporation (company lawyers and accountants, etc.), tends to reduce the professional's control.

Professional knowledge

In many respects, then, both established and aspiring professions behave like most other occupational groups. They organize to promote their members' interests regarding pay and control at work in the same way as do trade unions. Similar processes produce a hierarchy of rewards among all occupational groups: professions are closed-shop occupations, with effective organization and control at work. There does, however, seem to be one distinctive feature of existing professions which marks them out from other occupational groups, and that is the role of their special knowledge in securing occupational control.

It has often been pointed out that professions try to prevent the general public gaining access to their expert knowledge by making it incomprehensible to an outsider. This is partly achieved through universities which give qualifications on the basis of the student's receptivity to a theoretical knowledge which is not made available to anyone else. But, while protected knowledge is undeniably part of professional strategies of exclusivity, that knowledge is also necessary for successfully carrying out the job. Where there is no need for the flexible use of expert knowledge in the course of doing the job, workers are unlikely to be able to maintain high levels of occupational control. Where work can be sub-divided or routinized, professionals, like skilled manual workers and managers (see section 2.4), must expect that employers *will* rationalize their activities. But the one feature which survives in common among the occupations described as professions today is the high degree of discretion and control over work tasks retained by the worker. It is the mixture of expert, abstract knowledge and practical experience that can neither be rationalized nor quickly acquired, which protects 'educated workers' from proletarianization.

The body of knowledge upon which a profession is based tends to have several distinct characteristics.

1 Professional knowledge must generally be considered true, which today usually means that it has scientific legitimation. The status of the clergy in twentieth-century Britain has fallen as theological knowledge has become less credible.
2 That knowledge can be applied successfully to practical problems and is useful to some substantial section of the community.
3 Professional knowledge must not be too narrow nor be too easily expressed as practical rules. This is because the exclusiveness of the occupational group is hard to maintain if untrained people can quickly master the techniques involved. At the same time, however, professional knowledge has to be specialized and coherent in order to be accepted as true, effective and capable of being transmitted during a professional training course.
4 The key feature of professional knowledge, perhaps, is that it allows

the professional to exercise his or her judgement in applying abstract knowledge to the client's particular case. The services of the higher professionals usually take the form of giving advice to clients in a situation of *uncertainty*, where the professional's knowledge and experience gives his or her judgment an authority which can scarcely be challenged by the client. Judgment in circumstances of uncertainty cannot be routinized or expressed as rules, thus providing an exclusive knowledge-base for the professional's control in work. Occupational control is extended by preserving space for informed judgment. One of the principal reasons why many occupations fail to achieve professional status is because they cannot carve out an exclusive sphere of activity in which they make important judgments.

The dividing line between trade unions and professional associations is now difficult to draw. Once there was a difference based upon the ways in which each sought to promote their members' interests – professions, for instance, rejecting tactics like going on strike. In recent years, however, professionals working in the state sector – doctors, university teachers, school teachers, nurses, etc. – have held strikes to support demands made to their employers for improved conditions. It also used to be the case that the social-class background of recruits to the higher professions was very exclusive, though that too is less marked now. In general, for sociological purposes, it is sufficient to note that occupational groups exert different degrees of *occupational control*, and that professions have high degrees of control.

Summary

1 Professions are relatively privileged occupations, being well-rewarded, prestigious and having autonomy at work.

2 Professions exercise high degrees of occupational control through exclusive, professional associations. In the higher professions, the extent of occupational control is very considerable, the members setting the level of their fees, being subject only to internal discipline, controlling recruitment, etc.

3 Many occupational groups seek to be recognized as professions though this is not easy to achieve. Other groups of workers and clients usually try to prevent this. Furthermore, only certain sorts of occupations – partly characterized by the giving of advice on the basis of knowledge inaccessible to the client – seem able to establish claims to professional status.

Related topics

Fruitful comparison can be made with the work situation of other kinds of employees (section 2.4) and their mode of organization in trade unions (section 2.5). The class position of professionals is discussed in chapter 3, section 3.5 on the middle classes. The role of the medical profession is further examined in chapter 9, sections 9.2 and 9.8.

2.7   Deindustrialization

Britain's changing industrial structure

In the nineteenth century, Britain acquired the reputation of being 'the workshop of the world'. The growth of Britain's manufacturing industries was the basis of the world's first 'industrial revolution'. Today, relatively few people are employed in these manufacturing industries. Vast numbers of jobs in textile manufacture, shipbuilding, steel production and the like, have disappeared recently. Greater numbers of people now are working in shops, financial services (banking, insurance, etc.) and in the provision of services like health care and education (see also chapter 3 section 3.2).

The decline of employment in manufacture has been an issue of great concern over the last decade. Decline has been rapid and dramatic, as figure 2.15 shows. In 1966, 8.6 million people were employed in manufacturing industry; by 1985 there were only 5.4 million. One reason

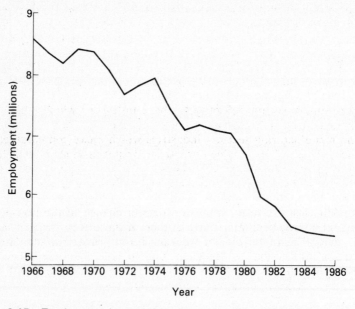

Figure 2.15   Employment in manufacturing industries, 1966–86
Source: Employment Gazette (various years).

for this has been the replacement of human labour by machines. The production of goods for mass consumption is particularly susceptible to mechanization and automation. In such cases, like motor vehicles, output may increase while the number of jobs falls due to the replacement of people by robots. Another reason is the declining demand for some manufactured products, like cargo ships and steel, during the world recessions of the 1970s and 1980s. A further reason is the declining competitiveness of some British manufacturing industries in the world market. This has affected both labour-intensive industries like textiles, where low wages in Third World countries reduce costs, and capital-intensive industries like motor manufacturing, where other advanced economies display higher rates of capital investment. (Labour-intensive industries are ones where labour is a high proportion of the cost of production. Expensive, physical assets – plant and machinery – are the major proportion of costs in capital-intensive industries.) The overall process of falling employment in the manufacturing sector is called 'deindustrialization'.

Deindustrialization describes a particular shift in the *industrial structure*. Industrial structure refers to all businesses engaged in producing or selling goods or services in the formal economy. The nature of what is for sale obviously changes over time, as does the amount of labour needed in the production of goods or delivery of services. Thus, for example, until 1851 over 50 per cent of the British working population was engaged in agriculture. By 1981, however, only 2 per cent of the work-force were either farmers or agricultural labourers. Improved transport facilities permitting more important food and an increased productivity of labour has meant that far fewer workers are required to feed a much larger population in 1981 than in 1851. One way in which the general shift in the industrial structure has been described is in terms of three *sectors*:

1 the primary sector, referring to those industries which either extract minerals from the ground or grow and harvest food;
2 the manufacturing sector – industries which *make* commodities;
3 the service sector, in which industries do not produce a final, tangible product, but either *circulate* commodities, as in retailing, or provide a service to clients, as in education and personal services.

Over the last 200 years there has been a change in the proportion of people who have been employed in each of these sectors, as is shown in figure 2.16. The proportion of workers in the primary sector diminished steadily as more people entered manufacturing employment. Thereafter, the tertiary sector started to increase its share so that in the 1980s around 65 per cent of all workers are now in service industries.

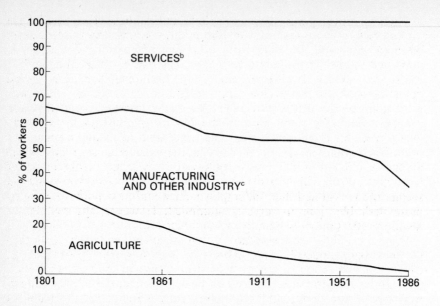

Figure 2.16   Approximate[a] proportions of workers in different economic sectors, 1801–1986

Notes: [a]Estimates of proportion vary considerably: this figure gives only a rough and rather unreliable impression of the situation, especially in the nineteenth century.
[b]Refers to transport, distribution, commerce, professional, personal and government services.
[c]Includes mining, construction and utilities (gas, electricity, etc.).

Source: Lee (1984); Deane and Cole (1967); Rowthorn (1986).

Social consequences: a post-industrial society?

There is considerable disagreement about the importance of this process of industrial-sector shift. Economists argue over whether deindustrialization is a cause or an effect of Britain's poor economic performance. Sociologists are uncertain about the social consequences. Clearly, such a change will affect the nature of work and the institutions and activities we have been considering in this chapter. For example, it has consequences for the membership of trade unions because heavy manufacturing industries typically had high degrees of union density. By comparison, service industries in the private sector (though not in the public sector) tend to have low rates of union membership. Again, the service sector has absorbed an increasing number of professional workers over the last few decades. Jobs in state welfare services, and in professional services to private-sector firms, have increased the proportion of professional workers in British society. Some people think that these changes will have important consequences for British politics because they affect class relations and, especially, the social base of the labour movement.

It used to be thought that as manufacturing employment disappeared, more jobs in services would emerge to replace them. Indeed, this happened for a period of time in the 1960s and 1970s. Daniel Bell, and other exponents of the 'post-industrial society thesis' argued that this process would generally improve the quality of life and work in the Western world. It was anticipated that unpleasant, dirty and routine jobs in factories would be eliminated. Instead, a greater proportion of workers would be dealing with people, doing more rewarding work, in better surroundings, providing assorted services to clients. The post-industrial society thesis assumed that full employment would be maintained as new, more desirable, jobs in services multiplied. However, the realities of deindustrialization in Britain are rather different.

First, as we have seen in section 2.4 above, many service occupations – clerical work, especially – are subject to deskilling and rationalization; others, like cleaning, never were any more attractive than traditional, manual, factory jobs. Second, as we will see in detail in section 2.8 below, the main recent effect in Britain of the decline of employment in manufacturing industry has been exceptionally high levels of *un*employment. New jobs have not emerged in sufficient quantity to replace those

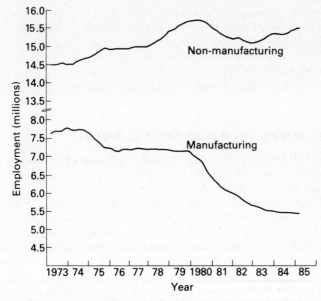

Figure 2.17 Employment in the manufacturing and non-manufacturing sectors 1973–85 seasonally adjusted
Source: Employment Gazette (August 1985), p. 56. Crown copyright.

lost in manufacturing (see figure 2.17). This may, partly, be due to the economic recession of the last ten years but it is also, importantly, a consequence of changes in people's patterns of consumption since the early 1960s.

Services and employment

Since it is unlikely that employment in manufacturing industries will ever again grow substantially, the future pattern of employment in the service sector is of critical importance. The concept of 'services' is difficult to define precisely, there being many kinds of services that appear to have little in common. For present purposes we can, however, say that service industries are those which do not produce a final, tangible product, and that there are two types of service industry. Intermediate-service industries are involved in circulating money, commodities or information. Banking, retailing, goods haulage and telecommunications are all intermediate services. These services may be rendered to firms (including those in the manufacturing and primary sectors) or to individuals. Human-service industries (sometimes called personal- and social-service industries) are involved in giving a service direct to a consumer. Hospitals, restaurants and laundries are all enterprises which provide a service to individuals which is consumed at the same time as it is provided.

Predicting future employment is difficult because service industries tend to grow at different rates. In recent years, intermediate services dealing with money and informaton provided to other industries (so-called producer services) have expanded quite rapidly as big manufacturing firms, for example, have found need for specialized financial, legal and administrative expertise. Those intermediate services more concerned with the distribution of goods – shops, warehouses, etc. – have also increased their turnover, but they have not generated much new employment. This is because the rationalization which affected employment levels in manufacturing industry has also had an impact on distribution. So, for example, big shops have reduced the number of shop assistants and, instead, employ staff mainly to stack shelves or collect money at check-outs.

The human services have been a principal source of new employment since the Second World War. The expansion of health, education, and social services provided many new jobs, a significant proportion of which have been professional and semi-professional positions. However, some personal services contracted during the same period, as cinemas have closed, laundries have shut, and the public transport system has contracted. Some commentators, notably Gershuny (1978), have argued that the contraction of these personal services is especially significant.

One reason why cinemas, laundries and passenger transport have declined is because many people now have personal access to machines which provide the same service, i.e. TV and video, washing machines and motor cars. It used to be the case that as people's incomes increased they spent more money on services and less on basic necessities, like food. (This observed regularity is usually called Engel's Law.) Gershuny (1978) noted that, in Britain, although people had become better-off since the 1950s and spent less on food, they did not tend to spend more on purchasing services. Rather, he claimed, they tended to buy the machinery with which they could service themselves: a 'self-service' economy was emerging. A clear instance of this is the proportion of average income spent on transport goods (cars, bikes, etc.) as opposed to transport services (trains and buses) over the last quarter century. As table 2.8 shows clearly, people are spending their money on goods. The economic impact of this is to boost the car-manufacturing industry, but to reduce employment in public transport. Since the manufacture of cars is less labour intensive than public transport, jobs have been lost overall. The preference for self-servicing is itself partly due to cost – labour-intensive services are expensive – but is also a matter of personal convenience and new life-styles based on aspirations to own mass-consumption goods.

Table 2.8 Buying goods rather than services; shifts in household expenditure on transport, 1954–83 as percentage of total household expenditure

	Purchase and maintenance of vehicles	Fares
1953/4	3.5	3.5
1958	5.1	2.9
1963	8.6	2.6
1968	10.5	2.1
1973	11.2	1.9
1978	11.0	1.8
1983	12.6	1.3

Source: Gershuny (1978); *Family Expenditure Survey* (various years).

The post-industrial society will experience very extensive unemployment. Gershuny, however, envisages that a range of new products made possible by advances in micro-electronics will emerge to provide back-up to more widespread use of domestic machines (for instance, cable television, shopping by computer, education through TV, etc.). Taken together, the manufacture of the new machines, the design of computer software for those machines, and the construction of a national infrastructure for a communication network could provide a whole galaxy of new employment opportunities. We consider Gershuny wildly optimistic. Current trends in employ-

	Manner of obtaining service	Who does work	Who pays (if anyone)	Principle upon which service is obtained	Mode of provision
i	Commercial purchase	Paid employees	Consumer	Market exchange	**Market**
ii	State provision	Paid employees	State	Citizenship right	**State**
iii	Personal connections	Neighbours or acquaintances	No money involved	Reciprocal obligation	**Communal**
iv	Household do-it-yourself	Members of household	No money involved	Family obligation	**Domestic**

Figure 2.18 Four ways in which services may be obtained

ment in service industries are not comforting, as an examination of the modes of service provision shows.

Modes of service provision

There are several ways in which services can be obtained. For example, if the interior of your house gets painted, you have consumed a human service. The painting could be done: (i) by paying a decorating firm; (ii) by getting the state to provide a decorating service; (iii) by arranging for a friend or neighbour to do it; (iv) by you or another member of your household, doing it yourself. In each case someone does the *work* of painting, but only under modes (i) and (ii) will someone be *employed* as a painter. This repeats the distinction made in section 2.1 between employment and work: employment is paid activity registered in the formal economy, but much work is done outside the formal economy. There is some evidence that the proportion of services produced outside the formal economy is growing. This would prevent the benign process anticipated by Bell of deindustrialization leading to more employment in services.

Figure 2.18 illustrates four different means of obtaining a service. In the past, there have been significant shifts in the type and quantity of services obtained in different modes. The balance in the quantity of services provided in each mode will affect both employment oppor-tunities and social life. The prospects for the expansion of those modes generating employment are not very encouraging. We will examine each in turn.

The market mode of provision

Many human services, and virtually all intermediate services, are bought in the market place. A meal in a restaurant, a visit to the cinema, attendance at a private school, are all bought at a price set by the market. Access to such services depends upon income: you can buy only those services you can afford. Money is the medium of exchange. Most workers in the market sector are in paid employment, though some transactions occur in what is called the 'black economy' (see below). Demand for many marketed services has, as Gershuny noted, remained stable over time, partly as a result of the growth of self-servicing. Use of marketed services is severely restricted among poorer households. Expansion of these services may be expected to continue increasing slowly.

The state mode of provision

Many human services are provided by the state. Access to state services is a matter of rights, established through political channels and exercised by virtue of being an eligible citizen. All citizens have a right to state health care at no (or minimal) cost; all citizens with appropriate qualifications are entitled to free higher education. A large number of people are employed to provide education, health and social services. Since the Second World War, state services have been responsible for the growth of professional and administrative jobs. Such services are paid for ultimately from taxation. Conservative governments since 1979 have been particularly concerned to reduce the cost of state-provided services, to cut public expenditure (see also chapter 12, section 12.5). The consequences of this are both a reduction in state employment and a reduction in services. In the 1980s, jobs have been lost in the areas of education, health, social services and public administration. Deterioration in the quality and quantity of services is more difficult to estimate, but if this trend continues (and it seems likely that it will due to the problem of financing state services from a declining tax-base), then this will become a less important source of human services. Demand may, perhaps, increase in other modes of service provision in response. Those who can afford to may buy private health care, for example. Those who cannot will suffer.

The communal mode

An alternative way to obtain a service is by exchanging services. A baby-sitting circle is arranged on the basis that if you look after my children I will do the same for you another time. But equally you might baby-sit for me and in exchange I will mend your car. Significantly, money is not involved. Access to these services is through personal contacts and social networks. Evidence suggests that not much work gets done this way, but it remains an alternative mode, though one which does not entail employment.

The domestic mode

The fourth alternative is to provide services yourself, for your own household's consumption. Such domestic services range from repairing your own house, through child-care, to cooking and cleaning. All are services you could obtain in other ways – by employing domestic servants, for instance – but which many people do themselves. No money is involved. This sector accounts for a considerable amount of all work done. It is this, the domestic provision of services, which Gershuny believes is increasing and which may prevent any great expansion in the market mode. Growth in the domestic mode of provisioning is a major source of sociological interest, affecting as it does employment opportunities, life-styles and gender relations.

Service provision on the Isle of Sheppey: a case-study

Gershuny is an optimist regarding the long-term economic consequence of deindustrialization. A recent investigation by Pahl and Wallace (1985), of the Isle of Sheppey on the north-Kent coast, gives reason for deep concern about the social implications of the decline in manufacturing employment. Pahl (1984) explores the ways in which households organize their time and resources in order to 'get by' in present economic circumstances. The central question he examined was, What services did households consume and by what means were those services provided?

The Isle of Sheppey has a population of about 33,000. Most jobs on the island used to be in the Admirality dockyard at Sheerness until it was closed in 1960. Between 1960 and 1981 there was work in the private docks (used for importing cars), in some manufacturing industries (steel and pharmaceuticals), and in the holiday trade. Wages were mostly low and opportunities for women were very limited. Jobs were also precarious and unemployment was above 20 per cent by 1983. The island is rather isolated, which partly accounts for the existence of relatively cheap owner-occupied housing. Although most households were working class, 77 per cent were owner-occupiers.

Pahl (1984) started his study with a concern for how people adapted to recession and unemployment. There has been considerable speculation about the extent of the 'black economy'. Some people work for money but without declaring their earnings to the Inland Revenue, in order to evade tax. Estimates of the value of such 'informal paid' (and illegal) activity are as high as 7.5 per cent of the national income. It is imagined that the unemployed are specially prone to such behaviour, using their 'free' time to work for an undeclared income. The availability of domestic durable goods like power drills, paint brushes, aluminium ladders, etc. were thought to be a factor permitting people to make a partial or total livelihood from doing odd jobs for neighbours, outside the formal economy. Pahl explored these issues and found these popular beliefs to be almost entirely unfounded. There was very little evidence of the existence of a 'black economy'. What there was, however, was an enormous amount of work being done in the *domestic* mode of provision. To his surprise, he found that it was not the unemployed who did a lot of domestic self-provisioning, despite the time they had available. Rather, the more people in a household who were in formal, paid employment, the more work they did at home. This was the basis of a social *polarization*. Households with more than one wage-earner had relatively high incomes but they also produced more services for themselves – house maintenance, car repairs, home cooking, etc. As a result their standard of living was substantially higher than that of households with little or no paid employment. In other words, extra time available because of unemployment was not used to improve living standards.

The evidence for Pahl's argument came from asking people about the

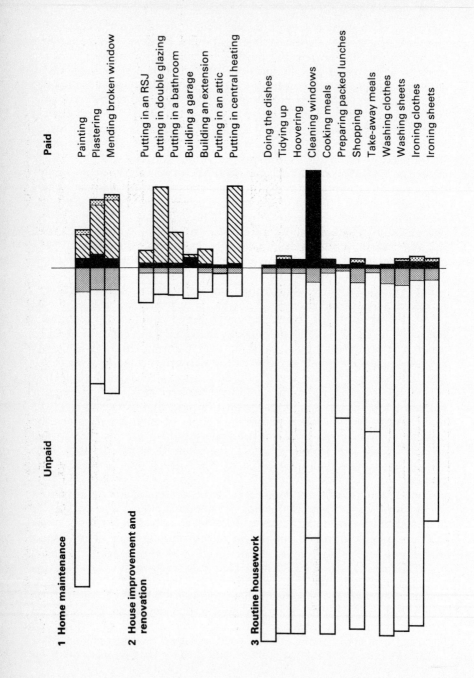

Unpaid   **Paid**

1 Home maintenance
Painting
Plastering
Mending broken window

2 House improvement and renovation
Putting in an RSJ
Putting in double glazing
Putting in a bathroom
Building a garage
Building an extension
Putting in an attic
Putting in central heating

3 Routine housework
Doing the dishes
Tidying up
Hoovering
Cleaning windows
Cooking meals
Preparing packed lunches
Shopping
Take-away meals
Washing clothes
Washing sheets
Ironing clothes
Ironing sheets

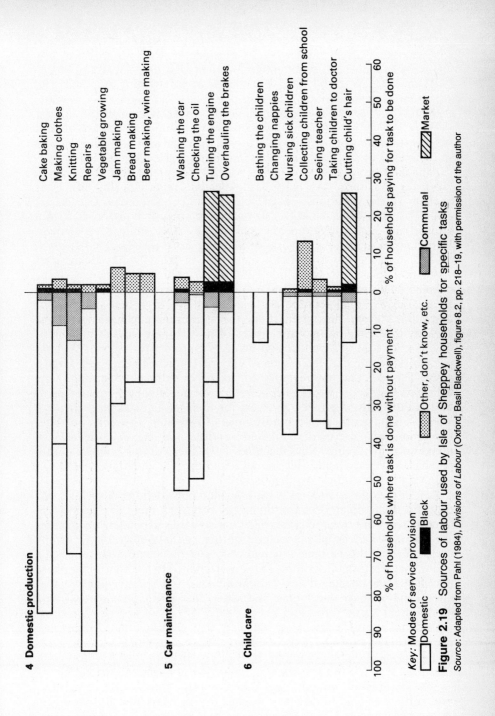

Figure 2.19 Sources of labour used by Isle of Sheppey households for specific tasks

Source: Adapted from Pahl (1984), *Divisions of Labour* (Oxford, Basil Blackwell), figure 8.2, pp. 218–19, with permission of the author

4 Domestic production

Cake baking
Making clothes
Knitting
Repairs
Vegetable growing
Jam making
Bread making
Beer making, wine making

5 Car maintenance

Washing the car
Checking the oil
Tuning the engine
Overhauling the brakes

6 Child care

Bathing the children
Changing nappies
Nursing sick children
Collecting children from school
Seeing teacher
Taking children to doctor
Cutting child's hair

% of households paying for task to be done

% of households where task is done without payment

Key: Modes of service provision

Domestic
Black
Other, don't know, etc.
Communal
Market

services their household consumed and who did the work to provide those services. He asked his sample of 730 respondents which, from a list of 41 services, their household obtained, and then who did that work. Figure 2.19 shows the list of tasks and which mode of provisioning was used. The only service widely obtained from the black economy was window cleaning. Neither the communal mode of provisioning, nor the market mode was much used (supporting Gershuny's argument). But households did a vast amount of work themselves, in car repairs, house maintenance and domestic production, as well as in routine housework and child-care.

Pahl then proceeded to examine which types of household did which tasks. The pattern was partly as expected. Stages of the life cycle explained some variations – households without children obviously do not change nappies. Income was also important: poorer households cannot afford cars and therefore do not need car-maintenance services. Variations in income on the Isle of Sheppey were very largely the result of the number of household members in paid work: social-class differences mattered very little. Being in employment increased the degree of self-provisioning even among those activities that might appear to be available to all households regardless of age or income – baking, or decorating. From this, Pahl drew the important conclusion that the capacity to engage in domestic modes of provisioning (and communal or 'black' ones too) is dependent on being in employment as well. Without paid work people lack the resources and the contacts to engage in unpaid work. The idea that the unemployed can get by through substituting time for money is simply wrong, because they cannot obtain the materials or tools with which to provide services, for themselves or anyone else.

Pahl's inquiries then corroborate some of Gershuny's speculation about the limited expansion of marketed services and the extensiveness of domestic provisioning. New machines – whether cars or hoovers – were purchased by households which could afford them to undertake more tasks in the home more efficiently than before.

Pahl also explored how tasks were divided up within the household. He confirms that women do more domestic work than men. The proportion of domestic work done by a married woman varies depending on whether she also has paid employment and by her age and stage of the family cycle. Women do the most unequal proportion of domestic labour when young and with small children. (This corresponds to the time when there are most tasks needing doing!) Domestic tasks are less unequally shared after children have left home and when the wife is in full-time paid employment.

Pahl, then, gives reasons for believing that recession and deindustrial-ization will have socially divisive effects. Those households with members in paid employment do relatively well, particularly as they use their resources through self-provisioning to further enhance their standards of living. Households without employment subside into a state of depriva-tion and are unable to do much to improve their position. Both kinds of households spend lots of time at home, the former vigorously pursuing a comfortable domestic life-style, the latter virtually imprisoned in a deteriorating domestic environment. Domestication and home-ownership is highly unattractive without the resources which are still only obtainable at a satisfactory level through regular employment. Thus life without employment, or a society 'beyond employment', looks bleak. Pahl and Wallace (1985, p. 224) sum the situation up:

> On the Isle of Sheppey, beyond employment most likely means poverty, isolation, little opportunity for informal work, involuntarily home-centred, with deteriorating dwellings and capital goods. Multiple earners bring prosperity, however short-lived: no earner brings a downward spiral of economic and social detachment.

Summary

1 A growth of employment in service industries has partially compensated for severe job-loss in British manufacturing since the mid-1960s, but there is a considerable short-fall which is registered in increasing rates of unemployment.

2 There is considerable debate over the implications of the increased proportion of workers in the service sector.

3 There are several ways in which people may obtain services: we have distinguished the market, the state, the communal and the domestic modes of service provision. The social relations involved in each are different. Only the first two provide employment.

4 There may be a tendency for more work to be done in the domestic mode, especially as part of a move to *self*-servicing. Since domestic- and informal-service provision require resources – materials, tools, etc – households without one or more members in paid employment are prevented from engaging in such 'do-it-yourself' work and, hence, tend to grow relatively more poor.

Related topics

More material on occupational change can be found in chapter 3, section 3.2. Regarding the domestic mode of service provision, discussion of gender differences occurs in chapter 4, section 4.3 and chapter 6, section 6.4, on households and housework, respectively. The state's role in providing services is discussed in chapter 12 section 12.4 and, especially, 12.5. A more detailed study of one largely state-provided service – health-care – is to be found in chapter 9, section 9.3.

2.8   Unemployment

What would you say is the most urgent problem facing the country at the present time? (September, 1985)

Unemployment	78%
Cost of living	2%
Other	19%
Don't know	1%

Gallup Political Index Report No. 301, September 1985

Unemployment is a condition suffered by an increasing proportion of the British population. It is an unenviable condition because it entails both material hardship and loss of social status. Despite popular belief to the countrary, to be unemployed is to be poor. Box 5 gives some information about the material circumstances of the unemployed. Lack of money is one reason why people seek to avoid unemployment, but there remains a motivation to work beyond mere income, as evidence from various recent surveys shows. Current trends in unemployment are, therefore, most disturbing. There seems little likelihood of the unemployment rate falling in the foreseeable future. Both demographic change and technological innovation will keep unemployment high. New technology is a particular source of concern, some commentators believing it heralds a future in which there will be steadily contracting employment opportunities. Gorz (1985), for example, believes that the demand for labour in the formal economy will decline rapidly given developments in electronics, robotics, etc. He argues that this could be used to improve the quality of social life. Since much work is unpleasant, would it not be preferable if necessary work was shared out equally and the working week reduced to 15 or 20 hours? There are, however, many obstacles to this rational response to a declining demand for labour. Under present circumstances those with full-time jobs cling to them tightly and often do overtime too.

The rate of unemployment

Official statistics showed that in April 1986, 3.3 million people were registered unemployed, 2.3 million men and 1.0 million women. This represented a rate of 16.5 per cent for men, 10 per cent for women, and 13.7 per cent overall.

These figures are conservative estimates. In May 1982, the government changed the basis for counting the unemployed, so that only people claiming social-security benefit were included. This had the effect of excluding among others, the formerly self-employed and married women.

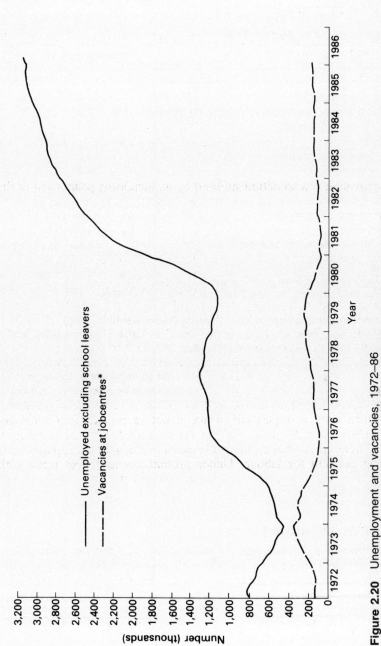

Figure 2.20 Unemployment and vacancies, 1972–86

Note: *Vacancies at job centres are only about a third of total vacancies.

Source: Employment Gazette (May 1986). Crown copyright.

Box 5   The material circumstances of the unemployed

1   Benefits, as at August 1986

	Weekly rate (£)
Unemployment benefit (if under state pension age)	
Single person	30.80
Extra for spouse or person caring for children	19.00
Supplementary benefit	
Ordinary rate	
Person living alone	29.80
Couple	48.40
Non-householder age 16 or 17	18.40
Long-term rate	
Person living alone	37.90
Couple	60.65
Non-householder age 16 or 17	23.25

Notes:
(i) Average male manual weekly wage in 1984 was £160.
(ii) The Youth Training Scheme pays its trainees £23 per week.

2   Consumption patterns of unemployed households, 1983
Average household expenditure per week on various commodities and services among unemployed households[a]

	£	As percentage of average household with someone in work
Housing	21.47	78
Fuel, light and power	8.49	88
Food	27.12	78
Alcoholic drink	5.90	66
Tobacco	5.79	122
Clothing and footwear	8.11	62
Durable household goods	7.37	54
Other goods	9.45	70
Transport and vehicles	21.55	75
Services	10.70	53
Miscellaneous	0.36	44
Total	126.32	72

Note: [a]Defined as households where the head had been unemployed for less than 12 months.
Source: Family Expenditure Survey (1983), table 16.

continues

Box 5 *continued*

3 People and poverty
Categories of people in poverty, as percentage of all poverty in 1984

	Total number	% of all persons dependent on supplementary benefit
Unemployed	3,704,000	48
Pensioners	1,944,000	25
Sick and disabled	403,000	5
Lone parents	1,325,000	17
Widows	36,000	1
Others	317,000	4
Total	7,729,000	100

Note: Poverty defined as people dependent on supplementary benefit.
Source: Hansard 23 and 24 July 1986.

There are many people wanting and seeking a job who are not counted as unemployed. The real figure is, thus, considerably higher than official statistics admit. But, even on official statistics, the extent of unemployment is enormous. The absolute number registered is higher now than it has been since figures were published; and the percentage rate is higher than all but the three worst years of the 1930s slump (see figures 2.21 and 2.22, pp. 100–1).

Who becomes unemployed?

The chances of certain categories of people becoming unemployed are higher than for others. Risk of unemployment varies with age, previous employment and gender.

The young and older men are most likely to be unemployed. Figure 2.23 (p. 102) shows the rate of unemployment among different age groups in January 1986. One in four young people aged 18–19 were unemployed; and the rates for all those under 25 were higher than for any other age group. The group next most at risk are those aged 55–9. At this age, however, it is necessary to consider men and women separately. There were more than three times as many men aged 55–9 unemployed than women in 1986. This difference reflects the fact that women of this age are unlikely to be counted in the statistics, as they will be mostly married

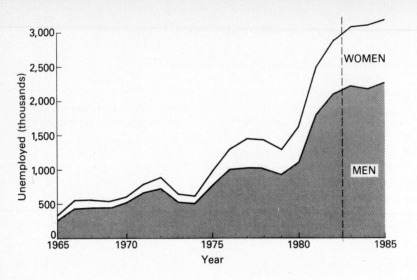

Figure 2.21   Numbers unemployed, 1965–85, official statistics
Note: The method of calculation was seriously altered in April 1982.
Source: Social Trends (various years).

and hence ineligible to claim benefit. The same age groups are also the most likely to be unemployed for a long time.

The risk of unemployment also varied depending on previous job. The chances of unskilled manual workers being unemployed at any time, or for long periods of time, are greater than for any other group. Unemployed rates among this group are around 35 per cent at present. In fact, unskilled workers tend to be out of work repeatedly throughout their lives. Unskilled jobs offer very little security. By contrast, professional, managerial and supervisory workers are relatively unlikely to be unemployed.

Finally, there is variation by gender. This variation is, however, largely artificial, a result of refusing to count married women as unemployed. Despite the difference suggested by the official statistics, there is reason to believe that women suffer from enforced unemployment just as badly, though no worse, than men.

Personal and social consequences of unemployment

The unpleasant consequences of unemployment have been demonstrated in many studies. A very substantial proportion of the unemployed live in poverty, surviving only on supplementary benefit. The longer unemploy-

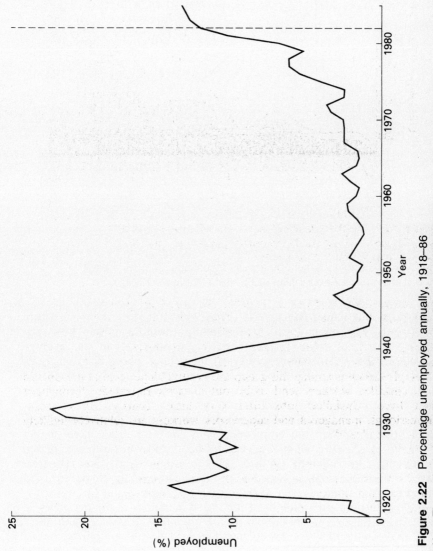

Figure 2.22 Percentage unemployed annually, 1918–86

Note: The method of calculation was seriously altered in April 1982.

Source: From Bain and Elsheikh (1976), pp. 134–5 and *Social Trends* (various years).

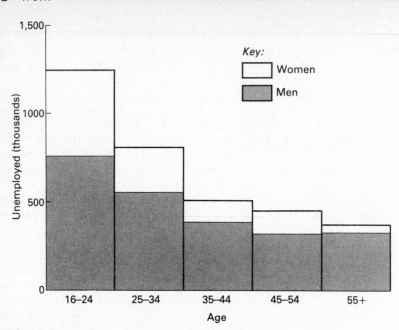

Figure 2.23   Unemployment by age, in thousands, January 1986
Source: Employment Gazette (May 1986), table 2.7. Crown copyright.

ment lasts, the deeper the poverty. This is illustrated by the expenditure patterns of the unemployed. Households whose head has been un- employed for less than a year are clearly poorer than the average household, but a fair amount better-off than those whose head has been out of work for a longer period. Since the number of people unemployed for more than 12 months has increased sharply in the early 1980s many households *are suffering severe poverty*.

The unemployed are also likely to suffer many other misfortunes. They are less healthy than the employed. They are also more likely to get divorced: increased conflicts between husband and wife, often expressed in violence, are regularly reported by the unemployed. Quarrels arise partly because of financial worries, partly because of the demoralization of unemployed men.

A cycle of demoralization has been noted in studies of the unemployed throughout the twentieth century. Being unemployed is acceptable for a few weeks but quickly leads to personal troubles. Boredom, sickness, sleeplessness, isolation, anxiety and loss of self-confidence are among the main complaints normally associated with any extended period of unemployment. The intensity of these complaints varies. As Hakim (1982, p. 449) notes, 'the severity of the psychological consequences of job loss is determined by the degree of attachment to paid employment and/or occupation as a central focus of personal identity.' The impact is greater for men than women, greater for married than single men, but greater for single than married women. Unemployment is least distressing to the young and to those almost having reached retirement age.

A very recent study by Platt has shown something that has been consistently denied – but often anticipated – that unemployed men are more likely than others to attempt suicide. Platt claims that men in Edinburgh who had been unemployed for more than one year were 19 times more likely than employed men to commit 'parasuicide' (deliberate physical self-harm). The work also claims that 1 in 50 men without a job for over a year committed parasuicide. Of course, the connection may not be a direct one – it may be the poverty caused by unemployment, or domestic stress, which induces parasuicide – but there is little doubt that the social stigma attached to being unemployed is implicated. It remains a source of dishonour for married men especially, to be unemployed. Even though there were, in September 1985, 20 people unemployed for each vacancy notified to job centres, the stigma remains. Thus, consider two men made redundant in Newcastle-upon-Tyne, talking about the experience of unemployment (box 6).

The social costs of high unemployment are, not surprisingly, considerable. Besides the case of unemployment benefits and the wasting of people's skills, illness, crime and family breakdown create severe and expensive social problems. Given how unpleasant it is to be unemployed, more resistance to the rapid increase in unemployment in the late 1970s might have been anticipated. After 1945, it was believed that no government could survive with employment rates much above 3 per cent because neither the electorate, nor the unemployed themselves, would tolerate mass unemployment. Yet, despite the great concern expressed about unemployment as a political problem, and notwithstanding the inner-city riots of 1981 and 1985, the political response has been muted.

Political consequences of unemployment

The absence of political unrest may be attributed to a number of factors, which themselves tell us more about unemployment.

First, there has been a significant, and apparently successful, campaign by government to reduce popular expectations about what can be done to change the situation. Unemployment has been presented as an inevitable outcome of recession and industrial change. Opinion polls suggest that many people, though deeply concerned about unemployment, believe no government policy can make any difference. Fatalism prevails.

Box 6   The experience of unemployment

A man, in his fifties, reflecting on his experience of unemployment after having been made redundant said:

> It affected me a lot when I was unemployed. I didn't think I was going to get another job. It was very depressing and got worse the longer I was unemployed. It wasn't so much the money or the way I felt. It was degrading – in the dole office or when people asked me what I was doing. People would say – 'are you still unemployed?' 'Are you not looking for work?' I was looking. It was very degrading. I have worked all my life and got angry. People who have never been unemployed don't know what it is like; they have never experienced it . . . When you are unemployed you are bored, frustrated, and worried, worried sick: at least I was. Of course it is worse for the man who has got a family: he has got responsibilities. So you worry for the wife and the bairns. (Sinfield, 1981, p. 41)

Another man in similar circumstances, who had later found himself another, but inferior, job:

> When I was unemployed I was very worried: I thought that was it, I didn't expect to get another job. I slept in late until about 11 a.m. I got very bored. Hours in the early afternoon were the worst – hours when I thought that I used to be working. I wasn't ready for retiring yet: I can still work, I wanted to work. I got very jealous of those who were working. My wife is right when she said it affects me *as a man*: it isn't the money so much as the feeling men have. (Sinfield, 1981, p. 41)

Second, the impact of unemployment is uneven. Those who suffer from unemployment are likely to have done so fairly regularly – especially among less-skilled workers – so the current crisis may only have exacerbated the problem. Furthermore, unemployment is regionally and locally unevenly distributed. As the map in figure 2.24 shows, the unemployment rate in South-East England is less than half that of Northern Ireland. There are even more extreme variations *within* regions. In Scotland, Aberdeen has a rate of 6.6 per cent whereas in Forres it is 27.9 per cent. In Wales, Carmarthen has a rate of 9.7 per cent, Cardigan one of 27.2 per cent. Within England, the rate in Winchester and Eastleigh is 5.3 per cent, that in Newquay 28.4 per cent. The worst area of all in Britain is Strabane, in Northern Ireland, where 38.9 per cent of

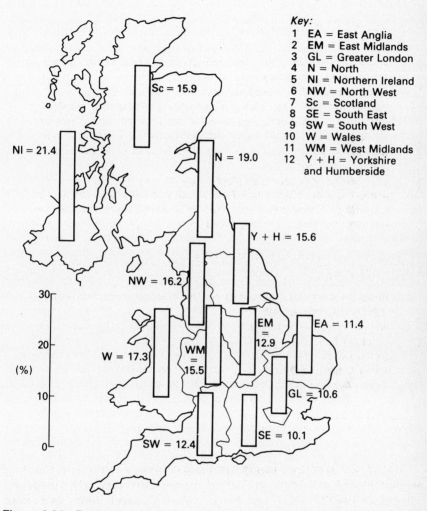

Figure 2.24   Regional* variations in unemployment, March 1986 (percentages)

Note: *For purposes of official data collection and planning, Britain is divided into 12 'standard planning regions'. They are varied in their demographic, economic, social and political characteristics.

Source: Employment Gazette (May 1986), table 2.3. Crown copyright.

the work-force is without a job. These local variations are partly a consequence of the established patterns of the location of industries: the North East of England, one of the worst affected regions, has been dependent upon shipbuilding and coalmining, which are declining industries. The geographical concentration of unemployment does have some political expression, in that areas of high unemployment tended to elect Labour MPs in 1983, but it clearly insulates many other people from the experience of unemployment.

Regional differences illustrate one aspect of the way in which unemployment is divisive. Those who remain in employment may *either* be comparatively well off, *or* may be so pressed that they are less prepared to support the unemployed, politically or financially.

The end of work?

Many writers doubt that unemployment can be reduced in the foreseeable future. By 1991 there will be 35.5 million people of working age, one million more than there were in 1981. There will be no change thereafter in the decade up to 2001. At the same time, many technological developments already underway are designed to reduce labour requirements. The gap between the demand for labour and its supply which has increased in recent years (see figure 2.20) may get even greater. Whether this will be the case depends partly on the effects of new technology, and partly on political decisions.

New technology

Micro-electronics is one, though perhaps the most spectacular, area of technological development at present. Its potential capacity is enormous for creating new products, changing production techniques and altering employment patterns. The development of 'microchips' – pieces of silicon, the size of fingernails, onto which are imprinted very complex electrical circuits – has reduced the size and price of electronic equipment, at the same time increasing its flexibility and power. The home computer is just one, rather mundane, example. Today's desk-top computer costing £500 has greater computational power than mainframe machines from 20 years ago which cost a thousand times more and required a room the size of a gymnasium to house. The possibilities in the field of, say, communications of the new cheap machines are remarkable: shopping from home, individualized, packaged educational programmes, programmes for medical self-diagnosis, electronic postal services, and participation in political decisions by computer, are but some of the uses envisaged today. We can do no more than guess about the likely social consequences. For example, it might make for yet more home-centred life-styles, with clerical, technical and managerial work being done in the front room and the output being transmitted as computerized messages to co-workers and customers. The consequence which is probably most debated, is its effect on employment.

Pessimistic interpretations observe the many current jobs which are threatened by the new technology. Robots in factories, stock-control systems in warehousing, computerization in the office, can all be expected to replace considerable quantities of human labour. In many cases, human skills will be rendered obsolete and work will be further degraded. Optimists point to the creation of new skilled jobs and the abolition of old, routine, unpleasant work. They also argue that technological innovation in the past has not reduced employment overall, because new and previously unimagined products and processes get developed. To date, microtechnology has probably had a limited impact on available employment; it has, in the short-run, created as many jobs as it has destroyed. Current unemployment rates are, primarily, due to other causes. However, little of this technology is yet in use in Britain, partly due to low levels of investment and partly to work resistance. When it becomes widespread – which may take a few years yet – it might be expected to have a massive impact. Because it tends toward greater ease of centralized control through improved communication then it will almost certainly reduce discretion at work, even where it does not abolish jobs altogether. We tend to be pessimistic, but it seems entirely safe to predict that the new technology will not *reduce* unemployment.

Political remedies

It is equally difficult to predict the direction of political interventions. It would seem, however, that new radical policies are necessary if unemployment is to be reduced. Recovery by private industry after economic recession alone will have little effect, since increased competitiveness probably entails less, rather than more, employment. Changes in people's patterns of work seem essential. Shorter hours, fewer working weeks per year, etc. could share available work out more evenly but, since this too would entail lower wages, it is unlikely to be welcomed in the absence of a sharp change in attitudes to work. The outlook is bleak for those unable to get a job in society where paid employment remains the basis of a tolerable standard of living. For, even if the unemployed were treated more generously, and there is some evidence that there would be more popular support for this now than in the 1970s, their situation would only improve in the context of other broad social changes.

Recent policies for dealing with youth unemployment indicate the nature of the problem. In April 1986, 187,000 young people, age 16–18, were unemployed. An additional 265,000 were in places on the Youth Training Scheme (YTS). YTS offers to school-leavers a mixture of work experience and further education for which minimal wages are paid – £28.50 per week for the first year in 1987. YTS has only been operating a short time and it is too soon to evaluate it properly. However, it will probably have rather similar effects to its predecessor, the Youth Opportunities Programme (YOPs), which was run by the state from 1978–83. Assessments of YOPs suggest that the main effect was political, keeping unemployment figures down and acting as a means of social control over restless youth. The problem is that training schemes cannot compensate for the lack of available jobs. Completing the year improved a trainees' chances of getting a job, but many failed to find employment afterwards. YOPs made no perceptible contribution to creating new, permanent jobs. This is not to say that government schemes for unemployed youth are a bad thing; rather, that such policies are not a solution to high levels of unemployment.

Summary

1   Unemployment is a major social and political problem, the numbers registered being greater than at any period in the past.

2   Unemployment is unevenly spread. Age, class, previous occupation, gender and region are all bases of variation in unemployment rates.

3   The personal and social consequences of long term unemployment are distressing and wasteful.

4   There is a debate about likely future levels of unemployment. The effects of technological change and political intervention are unpredictable, but do not seem likely to reduce unemployment levels in the near future.

Related topics

Material on the incidence of unemployment among women can be found in chapter 4, section 4.2 and, among ethnic groups, in chapter 5, section 5.4. Some of the problems faced by young people in gaining access to employment are discussed in chapter 8, section 8.3. On the relationship between unemployment and poverty see chapter 3, section 3.3, and the relationship between unemployment and health, see chapter 9, section 9.7.

Further Reading

The topic of ownership and control is surveyed by Scott (1979), while a more recent book of his (Scott and Griff, 1984) is a study of the networks of directorship. A good summary of the labour process debate is Thompson (1983). Another good book, with a wider scope, is Hill (1981), and this also reviews the literature on management. Littler (1982) provides a clear and original account of the development of the labour process in Britain.

A major survey giving general information about industrial relations is reported in Daniel and Millward (1983). Bain (1983) is a useful collection of essays giving detailed, up-to-date information about more specialized aspects of the subject. Johnson (1972) remains the best short overview of professions. For a brief review of the debate about professions and a discussion of the general link between knowledge and control, see Turner (1985).

Kumar (1978) and Gershuny (1978) offer good critical appraisals of versions of the post-industrial society thesis. Gershuny (1978) and Pahl (1984) both contribute considerably to understanding what kinds of services people produce and consume. A good, short survey of sociological issues surrounding unemployment, is Hakim (1982).

3 Class

3.1 Introduction

Social class must be the most debated concept in sociology. There are two important issues with regard to class that will concern us in this chapter. First, there is the problem as to whether the class structure is simple or complex. Are there two classes or several? Are the boundaries between classes fuzzy or sharp? Does our society consist of a number of discrete, separate classes or is it just a set of continuously graded layers? Second, we have to ask if social class is as important in social life as it once was. Have other forms of social differentiation, like gender or ethnicity, become as important as class or, perhaps, even more important?

Class structure – simple or complex?

One way of illuminating this first issue is to consider two extreme models of the class structure. Although it is actually a very misleading account of his work, Marx is often credited with the idea that modern, capitalist societies have two social classes – a large proletariat or working class, and a small bourgeoisie or capitalist class. Some of Marx's followers may have adopted a theory like this, although even they generally argue that the two significant classes have smaller groups between them that do not properly belong either to the proletariat or the bourgeoisie. More recent sociologists working within a Marxist framework have suggested that there is a fairly large, permanent, and socially significant middle class between the working and capitalist classes. Even with the recognition of a middle class, however, most Marxist theories propose relatively simple models of the class structure with a few, fairly well-defined classes organized around the antagonistic relationship between capital and labour.

In terms of simplicity or complexity, the opposite of Marxist theories are those accounts that argue that there are a multiplicity of social classes. A theory of this kind is proposed by Roberts et al. (1977). Here the class structure is seen, not as a set of relatively few, coherent, groupings but rather as a collection of fragments. The authors argue that the middle-class/working-class, manual/white-collar divide does represent a significant break in the class structure. But this does not mean that one can treat either class as a unified block. The middle class, especially, is much more fragmented than unified and it is difficult to speak of it as a class at all.

Most sociological theories of class fall somewhere between a simple two-class model and a multi-class or fragmentary model. It is usually argued that there are three classes, the middle class being created by the growth in new white-collar occupations since the beginning of the century. These classes are, however, not coherent entities but are themselves divided. It is conventional for example, to see the distinction between skilled and non-skilled workers as representing an important division within the working class.

The salience of class divisions

Sociologists usually understand the class structure as a system of inequality. In Britain, people in the working class tend to earn less money than those in the middle class, for example. However, class is not the only source of inequality between people. Gender or ethnic differences also provide a basis for unequal access to resources, or unequal treatment. We demonstrate in other chapters in this book, for example, that women are paid less than men, even for the same kind of work. Women also suffer other disadvantages. They are, for instance, treated radically differently from men in public places. It seems very likely that factors such as gender have become more important. They are certainly more significant as sources of social conflict; women are more aware of their inequality of condition and opportunity. Our argument in this book is, however, that social class membership remains an important determinant of life chances, that is the benefits of all kinds that an individual may have in life. For example, chapter 9 shows that the chances of remaining in good health vary with social class. Social class also remains a good predictor of success at school.

One's view of the complexity of the class structure or the significance of class clearly depends partly on what definition of social class is adopted. In this chapter we will largely follow Lockwood's (1958) celebrated definition of class membership in terms of market and work situation. Market situation refers to 'the economic position narrowly conceived, consisting of source and size of income, degree of job security, and opportunity for upward mobility' (p. 15). Work situation comprises 'the set of social relationships in which the individual is involved at work by virtue of his position in the division of labour' (p. 15) and refers to such matters as the degree of independence or control that a worker has over his or her work or the degree of skill that is deployed. Lockwood also mentions status situation, or position in the hierarchy of prestige, in connection with the determination of class. Although we will discuss questions of status, we do not see them as entering into the determination of class but rather simply as effects of class position. People do, or do not, have status *because* they occupy particular class positions.

The most obvious characteristic of Lockwood's definition is that it refers to *occupations*; class position is dependent on the market and work situations of occupations. We start this chapter, therefore, with an account of the occupational structure. The next section, on the distribution of income and wealth, discusses the most important element of market situation, namely income. The following three sections deal with the three major social classes and we conclude with a discussion of social mobility – the movement of people from one class to another.

3.2 Occupational Structure

> Occupational position does not encompass all aspects of the concept of class, but it is probably the best indicator of it. . . The hierarchy of prestige strata and the hierarchy of economic classes have their roots in the occupational structure; so does the hierarchy of political power and authority. . . The occupational structure also is the link between the economy and the family, through which the economy affects the family's status and the family supplies manpower to the economy. . .
>
> Blau and Duncan (1967)

For most people in modern Britain their occupation, and the occupations of other members of their household or family, determine the resources available to them. Occupational position is a central determinant of inequalities in income and life-style. For example, patterns of consumption vary: people live in the houses they can afford, producing 'residential segregation', whereby households with similar standards of living cluster in the same area. For sociologists, interest in occupations is great because of the connection between occupation and many aspects of social relations, especially class relations.

Problems of definition arise regarding the terms 'occupation' and 'class'. Occupation is what a worker does and is identified by the label given to a particular job: radiographer, crane driver, typist, etc. There are thousands of such jobs. Notice that the occupation refers to what a person is described as doing at work; no reference is made to the 'industrial sector' in which the person is employed. One can be a crane driver at the docks, or in the construction industry, for example. ('Industry' is defined by the final product or service.) For most purposes of sociological analysis, it is desirable to group occupations together to talk about aggregates of people who have roughly similar occupations, and thus similar material resources and working conditions. This can be done in several different ways. The most easily accessible, reliable

Table 3.1 Economically active men and women in occupation orders in Britain, 1981 (percentages)

Occupation order	Men	Women	Total
1 Professional and related supporting management; senior national and local government managers	5.0	2.0	3.9
2 Professional and related education, welfare and health	4.3	12.8	7.6
3 Library, artistic and sports	1.0	0.9	1.0
4 Professional and related in science, engineering, technology and similar fields	6.0	0.9	4.0
5 Managerial	11.6	5.4	9.2
6 Clerical and related	6.7	30.2	15.8
7 Selling	3.9	8.7	5.7
8 Security and protective service	3.2	0.6	2.2
9 Catering, cleaning, hairdressing and other personal service	3.6	20.6	10.2
10 Farming, fishing and related	2.1	0.6	1.5
11 Materials processing; making and repairing (excluding metal and electrical)	7.9	5.8	7.1
12 Processing, making, repairing and related (metal and electrical)	18.1	1.6	11.7
13 Painting, repetitive assembling, product inspecting, packaging and related	3.8	4.2	3.9
14 Construction, mining and related not identified elsewhere	6.0	0.1	3.7
15 Transport operating, materials moving and storing and related	10.0	1.0	6.5
16 Miscellaneous	3.1	0.5	2.1
17 Inadequately described and not stated	3.5	4.2	3.8
Total	99.8	100.1	99.9
Total number	15,527,000	9,879,000	25,406,000

Note: Numbers have been rounded.
Source: Census (1981), *Economic Activity in Great Britain*, table 8. Crown copyright.

information about occupations in Britain comes from official sources – the census and the Department of Employment. They use four categories: *occupation order, employment status, socio-economic group* and social classes. We, more precisely, call this last category *occupational classes*. We use these various categories to describe the occupational structure as it was at the time of the last census in 1981.

The occupational structure, 1981

Occupation orders

The basic unit of analysis in official data on employment is the *occupational unit group*. In the 'Classification of Occupations' used in the 1981 census, there were 549 units, which were amalgamated to form 17 *occupation orders*. The percentage of persons in each occupation order can be seen in table 3.1. Perhaps the most interesting feature of this table is the extent to which women are crowded into a very few occupation orders: 63.6 per cent of all economically active women were in orders 2, 6 and 9 – welfare, clerical and personal-service occupations.

Employment status

Classification by occupation order ignores the employment status of workers. This refers to two conditions. On the one hand, it denotes whether a person is an employer, self-employed, or an employee. On the other hand, it distinguishes between people with authority (i.e. managerial and supervisory positions) and those who are in a subordinate position. Data on employment status tell us about features of the labour force relevant to issues of ownership, managerial control and authority at work (see chapter 2, sections 2.2 and 2.4).

Table 3.2 describes employment status in 1981. Column B shows the percentage of people in employment at the time of the 1981 census by differing employment statuses. It shows that, in all, 8.3 per cent of people were self-employed. The majority (about two-thirds) of the self-employed are without employees. Working on their own account, without paid help, this proportion of the population might properly be termed *petit-bourgeois*. They are workers in very small businesses, a group which Marxists thought would disappear with the growth of organized capitalism, and the same group which recent governments have encouraged to expand in the hope that they would generate economic growth and reduce unemployment. In fact this group seems to change little in size. In 1911, there were 1,207,000 self-employed, 6.2 per cent of those in employment; by 1981 there were 1,212,000 or 5.3 per cent.

In 1981, the remaining 91.7 per cent of workers were employees, selling their labour power for wages. There are, however, distinctions within the category of employees. A substantial proportion of people

Table 3.2 Population in employment, activities by employment status, by gender, 1981 (percentages)

Employment status A	All B	Men C	Women D
Self-employed			
Without employees	5.3	7.1	2.6
With employees	3.0	4.1	1.6
Large establishments		0.1	0.02
Small establishments		4.0	1.6
Total self-employed	8.3	11.1	4.2
Employees		38.9	
Managers			
Large establishments		6.1	2.2
Small establishments		7.0	3.2
Total managers	10.0	13.1	5.4
Foremen and supervisors			
Manual		4.1	1.2
Non-manual		1.3	2.3
Total supervisors	4.6	5.3	3.5
Professional	3.2	4.7	0.8
Apprentices	2.6	3.3	1.4
Others	71.3	62.4	84.6
Total	100.0	99.9	99.9
Total number	22,916,190	13,764,720	7,151,470

Source: Census (1981), *Economic Activity in Great Britain*, table 9. Crown copyright.

were in managerial, supervisory or professional roles, thus exercising some authority or control at work. While most such people are far from being powerful, they are above the bottom rank in hierarchies of authority at work. In total, 74 per cent of all workers were without any degree of authority, though this does not necessarily mean that they were without discretion at work (see chapter 2, section 2.4).

Columns C and D of table 3.2 show quite significant differences between men and women with respect to employment status. 11 per cent of men, but only 4 per cent of women were self-employed. More striking still, only 66 per cent of men were in positions without *any* authority attached, whereas 86 per cent of women were in such a situation. The general point that women tend not to get positions of authority is borne out strongly by these figures. In fact, of some 6 million occupational

Table 3.3 Persons economically active, by socio-economic group, 1981 (percentages)

Socio-economic group (SEG)	Men	Women	Total
1 Employers and managers in central and local government, industry, commerce, etc.: large establishments	5.5	2.1	4.1
2 Employers and managers in industry, commerce, etc.: small establishments	8.7	4.3	7.0
3 Professional workers: self-employed	0.9	0.1	0.6
4 Professional workers: employees	4.5	0.9	3.1
5 Intermediate non-manual workers	7.3	14.4	10.1
6 Junior non-manual workers	9.5	37.3	20.3
7 Personal-service workers	1.1	12.2	5.4
8 Foremen and supervisors: manual	3.6	0.7	2.5
9 Skilled manual workers	26.3	4.0	17.6
10 Semi-skilled manual workers	13.6	10.4	12.3
11 Unskilled manual workers	5.8	6.7	6.2
12 Own account workers (other than professional)	5.3	1.8	4.0
13 Farmers: employers and managers	0.7	0.1	0.5
14 Farmers: own account	0.7	0.1	0.5
15 Agricultural workers	1.2	0.5	1.0
16 Members of armed forces	1.6	0.2	1.0
17 Inadequately described and not stated occupations	3.5	4.2	3.8
Total	99.8	100	100
Total number	15,527,000	9,879,000	25,406,000

Source: Census (1981), *Economic Activity in Great Britain*, table 17. Crown copyright.

positions which had some degree of control or authority, only 1.3 million (21 per cent) were filled by women.

Socio-economic groups (SEGs)

For sociological purposes, perhaps the most meaningful picture of the occupational structure is obtained from classification of people by socio-economic group (SEG). As the Office for Population Censuses and Surveys puts it, a socio-economic group 'brings together people with jobs of similar social and economic status. The allocation of occupied persons to socio-economic groups is determined by considering their employment status and occupation' (OPCS, 1980, p. xi). Table 3.3 shows the distribution of the economically active in 1981 by SEG.

Among the interesting features of table 3.3 is the fact that the proportion of persons in managerial positions (SEGs 1, 2 and 13) are clearly identified – 11.5 per cent of the total work-force. So too are the proportions of junior non-manual and personal-service workers. Again, the contrast between men and women is significant. Women comprise a small proportion of workers in the most prestigious SEGs – there are far fewer in managerial and professional groups, in skilled manual work and running their own businesses.

Occupational classes

It has frequently been thought that the most significant division among occupations is between manual and non-manual jobs. An estimate of the proportion of the work-force in manual occupations can be got from table 3.4, which is the 1981 census etimate of 'occupational class' distribution. It shows that 49 per cent of the work-force was in manual work in 1981. There were sharp gender differences, 57 per cent of men but only 36 per cent of women were in manual work. There were slightly more people in manual work than in non-manual work, 49 per cent as opposed to 47 per cent (the total is not 100 per cent because some occupations were inadequately decribed on census returns and members of the armed forces are considered neither manual nor non-manual workers).

The analysis of occupational class is useful, especially for purposes of historical comparison. It gives a brief guide to the occupation structure. It is not, however, the same thing as social class. Social class refers to the existence of common interests among social groupings which tend to generate common social and political practices. The occupation classes distinguished here do not necessarily produce similar social and political behaviour. For example, it is debatable whether the condition of people in occupational class III (N) is in any way distinct from those in the manual categories. Supporters of the thesis of the 'proletarianization of white-collar work' (see section 3.5) see no real differences. Identifying social classes requires a consideration of other things besides occupation.

Table 3.4 Occupational class structure, 1981 (percentages)

Occupational class	Men	Women	Total
I Professional etc. occupations	5.5	1.0	3.7
II Intermediate occupations	21.4	20.2	20.9
III (N) Skilled occupations: non-manual	11.2	38.6	21.9
All non-manual	38.1	59.8	46.5
III (M) Skilled occupations: manual	34.6	8.1	24.3
IV Partly skilled occupations	16.1	21.0	18.0
V Unskilled occupations	6.1	6.8	6.4
All manual	56.8	35.9	48.7
Armed forces and inadequately described	5.1	4.3	4.8
Total	100.0	100.0	100.0
Total number	15,526,710	9,878,880	25,405,590

Source: Census (1981), *Economic Activity in Great Britain*, table 17. Crown copyright.

Occupational change

Over the 10 years between 1971 and 1981, principal changes in the occupation structure in Britain were as follows:

1 There was an increase in the number of professional and managerial jobs for both men and women, overall by about 1 million. There were substantial increases in professional and semi-professional occupations in the health and education services, especially for women. Over 300,000 more women were employed – mostly as teachers, welfare workers and nurses. For men, there was significant growth in managerial and in scientific jobs.

2 Routine clerical work saw a continuing change. By 1981, there were 170,000 fewer men in office work, but 250,000 more women. 32 per cent (2.6 million) of all employed women were in clerical and related jobs by 1981.

3 There was a substantial decline in the number of people involved in manual work in manufacturing (see chapter 2, section 2.7 on de-

industrialization). The occupation orders covering manufacture (11, 12 and 13 in table 3.1) saw severe drops in employment – there were 700,000 fewer men and 420,000 fewer women in such jobs. (Proportionately, women suffered more severely: among men these groups provided 2.5 per cent less employment, among women 6 per cent.) There were also fewer jobs for women in textiles, garment-making, repetitive assembly and packaging work.
4 Large numbers of jobs for men were also lost in general (unskilled) labouring and in transport.

Many of these changes are the continuation of longer-run trends which have been apparent throughout the twentieth century. Professional and managerial positions have been expanding steadily since the late nineteenth century. So too has clerical work, especially for women. Meanwhile, manual employment has remained about constant in absolute numbers, whilst declining as a *proportion* of all jobs. Agricultural employment has declined both absolutely and proportionately. The broad pattern of change from 1911 to 1971 is shown in table 3.5.

The most widespread trend over this 60-year period was the general growth of white-collar work. In 1911, 20 per cent of workers were non-manuals, 4 per cent were in professional occupations and 5 per cent in clerical and related jobs. By 1971, these figures were 41, 11 and 14 per cent, respectively. This has entailed the gradual reduction in the size of the manual working class, which has led to widespread speculation about consequent changes in British politics, especially the decline of a social base for the Labour Party.

The four-fold increase in the number of professionals has several causes. The most prominent cause since the Second World War has been the expansion (until the late 1970s) of welfare services. There are many more teachers, doctors, nurses and social workers than before. There has also, though, been a growth in the numbers of scientists and engineers. The growing number of managers also is a consequence of changes in the division of labour and in economic organizations. As firms and plants have got bigger, more managerial staff have been recruited to coordinate operations, buy and sell, deal with workers, plan production, etc. The growth of professional and managerial occupations gave increased opportunity for upward social mobility (see section 3.7).

The key long-term trend in clerical work, besides its growth, has been its *feminization*. Intermediate and routine office jobs have grown at a great rate, increasing four-fold between 1911 and 1971. Whereas the proportion of all higher professionals who are women has remained more or less constant, at 5 per cent (see table 3.16, p. 171), the proportion in clerical work has increased. In 1911, there were 4 men for every woman in clerical work; by 1971, the ratio was 4 men to every 20 women. In parallel with feminization, there has been a decline in the rewards and the

Table 3.5 Occupational class and industrial status of the gainfully occupied population, 1911–71 (thousands)

		All					Males					Females				
		1911	1921	1931	1951	1971	1911	1921	1931	1951	1971	1911	1921	1931	1951	1971
1 Professional																
A Higher	Employers		25	38	34	79		25	37	33	75			—	1	4
	Own account		36	44	44	59		35	41	40	53		2	3	4	7
	Employees		134	158	356	687	173	126	144	326	646	11	8	15	31	40
	All	184	195	240	434	824	173	186	222	399	774	11	10	18	36	50
	%	1.00	1.01	1.14	1.93	3.29	1.34	1.36	1.50	2.56	4.87	0.20	0.18	0.29	0.52	0.55
B Lower	Employers		18	15	10	25		14	8	7	17		4	7	3	7
	Own account		62	70	42	59		20	22	22	37		42	48	20	22
	Employees		600	643	1007	1863	208	242	270	463	892	352	357	373	544	971
	All	560	680	728	1059	1946	208	276	300	492	946	352	403	428	567	1000
	%	3.05	3.52	3.46	4.70	7.78	1.61	2.02	2.03	3.16	5.95	6.49	7.07	6.83	8.18	10.95
2 Employers, administrators, managers																
A Employers and proprietors	Employers	763	692	727	457	621	661	613	646	400	485	102	79	82	56	136
	Own account	469	626	682	661	435	339	435	483	494	320	130	191	196	167	115
	All	1232	1318	1409	1118	1056	1000	1048	1129	894	805	232	270	278	223	251
	%	6.71	6.82	6.70	4.97	4.22	7.74	7.69	7.65	5.74	5.07	4.28	4.74	4.44	3.22	2.75
B Managers and administrators	Own account	21	29	30	31	46	20	27	28	27	35	2	2	2	3	11
	Employees	608	675	740	1215	2008	486	557	642	1029	1698	123	118	98	186	310
	All	629	704	770	1246	2054	506	584	670	1056	1733	125	120	100	189	321
	%	3.43	3.64	3.66	5.53	8.21	3.91	4.28	4.54	6.78	10.91	2.30	2.11	1.60	2.73	3.51

3 Clerical workers	Own account	—	1	2	3	22	—	1	2	2	5	—	—	—	1	17
	Employees	887	1299	1463	2401	3457	708	735	815	988	1008	179	564	648	1413	2249
	All	887	1300	1465	2404	3479	708	736	817	990	1013	179	564	648	1414	2466
	%	4.84	6.72	6.97	10.68	13.90	5.48	5.40	5.53	6.35	6.38	3.30	9.90	10.34	20.41	27.00
4 Foremen, inspectors supervisors	Employees	236	279	323	590	968	227	261	295	511	801	10	18	28	79	168
	%	1.29	1.44	1.54	2.62	3.87	1.75	1.91	2.00	3.28	5.04	0.18	0.32	0.45	1.14	1.84
Manual workers																
5 Skilled	Own account	329	293	268	251	349	170	205	200	214	324	159	88	68	37	25
	Employees	5279	5280	5351	5365	5045	4094	4200	4223	4519	4295	1185	1080	1128	847	750
	All	5608	5573	5619	5616	5394	4264	4405	4423	4733	4619	1344	1168	1196	884	775
	%	30.56	28.83	26.72	24.95	21.56	32.99	32.30	29.96	30.36	29.08	24.78	20.50	19.09	12.75	8.48
6 Semi-skilled	Own account	71	98	96	82	53	41	70	78	73	35	30	28	17	10	18
	Employees	7173	6446	7264	7256	6258	4305	3789	4181	4279	3272	2868	2656	3084	2978	2986
	All	7244	6544	7360	7338	6312	4346	3859	4259	4352	3307	2898	2684	3101	2988	3005
	%	39.48	33.85	35.00	32.60	25.23	33.63	28.30	28.85	27.92	20.82	53.42	47.11	49.51	43.12	32.90
7 Unskilled	Own account	47	62	78	33	92	38	48	65	29	86	9	14	13	3	6
	Employees	1720	2678	3034	2676	2895	1455	2232	2580	2129	1803	265	446	454	547	1092
	All	1767	2740	3115	2709	2987	1493	2280	2645	2158	1889	274	460	467	550	1098
	%	9.63	14.17	14.81	12.03	11.94	11.55	16.72	17.92	13.84	11.89	5.05	8.07	7.45	7.94	12.02
All	All	18,347	19,333	21,029	22,514	25,021	12,925	13,636	14,761	15,584	15,884	5425	5697	6264	6930	9138
	%	100.00	100.00	100.00	100.00	100.00	100.00	100.00	100.00	100.00	100.00	100.00	100.00	100.00	100.00	100.00

Note: Because numbers are rounded to the nearest thousand, totals may not equal the sum of their parts.
Source: Routh (1980) *Occupation and Pay in Great Britain* (London and Basingstoke, Macmillan and Atlantic Highlands, NJ, Humanities Press International, Inc.), p. 6. Reproduced with permission.

status of office work. Besides having filled lower-grade, non-manual work, women have also been increasingly concentrated in semi- and unskilled manual work.

The pattern of segregation between men and women suggests that women have not improved their position in the occupational structure since 1911 (see also chapter 4, section 4.2). Although there are far more women in employment now, a great many are in part-time work. (42 per cent of women employees were part-timers, compared with 2 per cent of men in 1981.) There was very little part-time work before the Second World War. Also of course, in an important respect, different women are in paid employment: a much greater proportion of women workers now are married.

Causes of occupational change

The causes of change in the occupational structure are more the province of the discipline of economics than of sociology. Clearly, available occupations are a result of, amongst other things, the demand for goods, the technological capacity to produce goods, and the availability of wealth to set up the production process. However, these economic conditions are themselves partly the consequence of a given set of social relations and social arrangements; for much of the time in the modern world, what is produced, and what people wish to and can afford to buy, is the result of *social* choices. For instance, the section concerned with work (chapter 2, section 2.4) made it clear that employers and managers chose between available technologies partly on the grounds of cost, but also partly on grounds of the capacity of different kinds of machines to afford social control over workers.

The process of occupational change is partly the result of constant restructuring of industry. Job opportunities alter as firms open and close and as new products emerge and others become obsolete. Restructuring in Britain today is the result of two, interrelated logics, one of the capitalist market, the other of state intervention in the economy. Market logic is based upon companies competing with each other in the pursuit of profit: decisions about what should be produced, how and where, are subject to a calculation about the profitability of production. By contrast, state-owned industrial enterprises (and the state administrative and welfare sectors of the economy) are subject to a political logic. Subsidies for state-owned industry in order to preserve jobs, and the level of provision of public services like health care, are issues for political decision. In Britain, however, the state sector is less important for employment than the private sector, providing rather fewer than a third of all jobs (see figure 3.1).

The restructuring of the private sector in recent years has had important implications for the occupational structure. One of the greatest

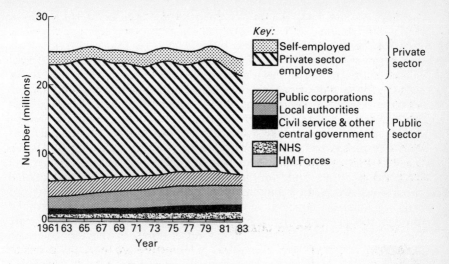

Figure 3.1 People in employment, by sector
Source: Social Trends (1985). Crown copyright.

areas of change in occupations since 1971 has been the decline of manual work in manufacturing industry. Some of this is the result of British firms, or sections of multinational firms, becoming uncompetitive within the world market. One area of declining jobs was routine assembly work. This is a result of what is known as the 'new international division of labour'. Increasingly, multinational corporations have located labour-intensive parts of their operations in the Third World, where wages are much lower and workers much less well organized than in Europe or America. The assembly of microcircuits for the electronics industry, and large parts of textile manufacture, are undertaken in places like Singapore, Taiwan and Hong Kong for just this reason (see also chapter 2, section 2.3). As a result, some kinds of jobs which previously would have been available in Britain are now absent. In other industrial sectors, the introduction of labour-saving machinery has reduced the number of jobs. Farming might be an example where the size of the agricultural labour force has steadily declined throughout the twentieth century, workers being replaced by machinery. In the past, job loss through technological development has mostly affected manual labour. However, there is a strong likelihood that many aspects of routine white-collar occupations will go through a similar process of mechanization in the near future.

One aspect of the pursuit of profit is the search for cheaper kinds of labour. The shift of some jobs to the Third World is paralleled, to a lesser degree, within Britain, as firms locate different parts of their operations in different parts of the country. Two important trends can be discerned. One is the tendency for firms, especially in private-sector manufacturing, to move their routine operations out of the cities into semi-rural areas (see chapter 7, section 7.1). This allows them to take advantage of less-well-organized labour forces who are prepared to accept somewhat lower wages. At the same time, there is a movement of the higher jobs – in scientific research, management, etc. – to the South East. This tends to produce regional inequalities in wealth and, of course, makes for locally varied occupation and class structure. The fact that the South East was relatively prosperous, even during the very severe recession of 1973–6 and 1979–85, is a result of the way in which regional differences are exploited by firms and, in turn, regional differences in occupational opportunity are created and sustained. Some governments have tried to make regional employment more even. Regional policy, which worked through subsidies to private firms and through the relocation of state employment to depressed areas, has offset some of the tendencies to imbalance.

Places and persons in the occupational structure

By occupational structure what is meant is the pattern of occupational places (or jobs) at any point in time. In order to understand the situation of, for example, women in paid employment, it is necessary to distinguish between *places* in the occupational structure and *persons* who fill those places. This is because the kind of person who typically holds a job actually affects the conditions associated with that place. Thus the rewards and the status of jobs typically filled by women, or by blacks, are comparatively low (see chapter 4, section 4.2 and chapter 5, section 5.3). This has little to do with the intrinsic nature of the jobs, much more to do with the characteristic *social evaluation* of women and blacks. This phenomenon is called *occupational segregation*, and is examined in detail in chapter 4, section 4.2.

Let us take the case of gender as an example. Women get different jobs from men. As was seen in table 3.1, almost two-thirds of women in paid employment are crowded into just three occupation orders – welfare, clerical and personal-service occupations. The work involved tends to duplicate the low-status, non-specialized, 'caring', domestic tasks which are typically allocated to housewives within the family. These jobs, usually filled by women, are paid at lower rates than those of men. In addition, women tend to cluster in the least prestigious places in any given occupational order or class. They fill the positions at the bottom of the hierarchy in the office and they fill the subordinate teaching posts. Overall, women get a systematically bad deal from paid employment. So too do black people. This implies that to understand the occupational structure we must *consider both places and persons because they are interdependent*.

The effects of occupational change

The social and political consequences of occupational change are very varied. When old jobs disappear and new ones are created, the effects on the life of different social groups may be very significant. Deskilling and unemployment are direct, adverse effects on individual workers. But occupational change also affects, more indirectly, educational institutions, urban development, family life and so on.

Take, for example, education. Recent governments have wanted education to be more 'vocational', more closely tied to the 'needs of industry'. This is partly inspired by the belief that new skills are required for jobs which are likely to emerge in the near future. New training arrangements have been introduced, the Youth Training Scheme being the most prominent at present. As jobs change, so does the content and form of education (see also chapter 8, section 8.2).

Occupational change also affects the built environment of villages and cities. One of the issues of the miners' strike in 1984–5 was the extent to which the plans of the National Coal Board for pit closures would destroy mining communities. Often, the pit is the only reason for the existence of a mining village. If the pit closes the village withers away. Equally, the geographical concentration of new employment opportunities creates some prosperous and expanding towns, but leaves others in serious decline.

Occupational change also affects relationships within families. For example, the rapid contraction of employment for men in manufacturing industry has altered the relative earning power of some men and women. If firms prefer to employ women because they cost less, and if they define new jobs as women's work, this could have profound implications for domestic arrangements. Some writers have speculated that by the year 2000 it could be normal for wives to be in paid employment while husbands are primarily engaged in household tasks. This seems unlikely but, nevertheless, the notorious aversion of men to housework is likely to be a greater cause of domestic conflict where wives have equal or better employment prospects than their husbands.

Occupational structure and class structure

> The backbone of the class structure, and indeed of the entire reward system of modern Western society, is the occupational order. Other sources of economic and symbolic advantage do coexist alongside the occupational order, but for the vast majority of the population these tend, at best, to be secondary to those deriving from the division of labour.
>
> Parkin (1971)

Sociologists have been interested in the occupational structure because it underpins the class structure and, in Western societies, class differences are very important in explaining social and political action. Occupation is not, however, directly and exclusively correlated with social and political action. Not all coal miners vote in the same way, nor do they share equally a disposition towards industrial militancy; and clerical workers show even greater differences in individual political responses. Class position should be thought of as related to, but not the same as, occupation. Social-class position refers to both the ownership of property and authority relations. There are several reasons why occupation is unsatisfactory as a sole indicator of class position.

1   Not all persons have occupations. If you consider the number of people too young and too old to hold jobs in the formal economy, the number of unemployed, and the number of full-time housewives, probably more than half the population is without an occupation. These different groups of the 'non-employed' are, nevertheless, normally considered as being in the class structure.

2   Common occupation does not itself produce a common consciousness or perceived common interests. Although trade unions and professional associations are organized on the basis of shared, *occupational* interests, people in identical occupations have differing values, attitudes, loyalties and allegiances. Some occupations generate more of a common outlook than others, though it is hard to decide whether it is aspects of the labour process, or of trade union organization, or the kind of communities in which they live that make miners more uniform in their political behaviour than clerks.

3   A person's present occupational place does not sum up their entire work experience. Some people experience mobility between occupations during their own lifetime. The term *career* refers to the way in which people often pass through several different occupations in their lifetimes. Where these are structured or predictable (as in the transition from apprentice to journeyman to master-craftsman; or from junior hospital doctor, through registrar to consultant), reactions to work and politics are often conditioned more by *expectations* of the final position to be reached than the more lowly, menial, or exploited, position taken up on entry to the career. The importance of this is shown by recent findings on male clerks discussed at length in section 3.5. Young male clerks tend to get promoted into managerial occupations, whereas the prospects of promotion for a female clerk are extremely poor. Hence, though male and female clerks share the same 'occupation', it is not clear that the political and class interests of women in clerical work coincide with those of their male colleagues.

Summary

1   There are various different measures used to describe the occupational structure which should not be confused.

2 The most important changes in the occupational structure in the last 20 years have been the growth of professional and managerial jobs, the decline of manual work and the feminization of clerical work. The increase in part-time work, mostly for women, is also important.

3 Occupations are segregated so that certain categories of person – women and ethnic minorities especially – obtain inferior rewards from their jobs.

4 The occupational structure is the backbone of the class structure and thus very important in understanding the formation of social class. However, a social class is more than a mere category of people in similar occupations. Members of a social class take part in common cultural activities and political organizations as well as having similar jobs.

Related topics

The ways in which people experience work and organize together on the basis of their occupations are examined in chapter 2, sections 2.4, 2.5 and 2.6. More on deindustrialization and the decline of manual work in manufacturing industry can be found in chapter 2, section 2.7. Employment for women is surveyed in much greater detail in chapter 4, section 4.2. The employment prospects of ethnic groups are explored in chapter 5, section 5.2. Links between education and occupation are examined in chapter 8, section 8.3.

Further Reading

The best account of occupational change in twentieth-century Britain is Routh (1980).

3.3 Income, Wealth and Poverty

As we indicated in section 3.1, part of what we mean by class involves the dividing up of the population into large categories based initially on occupational characteristics. As we noted in that section, a number of criteria are used in the identification of classes and we will be using these criteria in the next sections. However, a prior step in an examination of the class structure is a consideration of how income and wealth are distributed in the population.

The distribution of income

Although it might seem a relatively straightforward matter to measure an individual's income, it is not so by any means. Do we, for example, count individual or household income? Is it to be measured before or after tax?

Is it just that derived from a job or should it include welfare payments of various kinds? One solution to these problems of measurement is simply to present data on income calculated in different ways. We can, for example, differentiate original, disposable and final income. *Original* income comes from various sources including employment, occupational pensions, investment and from other households (as gifts or alimony payments, for instance). Adding to the figure for original income any cash benefits paid by the state, such as retirement pensions and welfare payments, and subtracting income tax and national insurance contributions produces *disposable* income. *Final* income reflects more concealed additions to, or subtractions from, disposable income. Thus households have to pay rates and VAT on goods that they buy but they also receive various benefits from the state, in the form of health and education services for example, which have a cash value. We should note that we are talking of household incomes here, for household rather than individual income is a more significant indicator of the benefits that individuals ultimately receive.

Distribution of income today

Box 7 shows how the three types of income are distributed in the population and how that distribution has changed in the period 1976–83. Between 1976 and 1983, the distribution of original income became rather more unequal, with the share of the bottom fifth (or 'quintile') of households falling to 0.3 per cent of the total while that of the top quintile rose from 44.4 to 48.0 per cent. In 1983, the top 20 per cent of households therefore received almost as much original income as the rest of the population put together. The inequality in the increase in disposable and final income is less marked, although the top quintile still took almost 40 per cent of all disposable income in 1983. Inequality in disposable and final incomes has also increased rather more slowly than that in original incomes. The fact that disposable income is a little bit more evenly spread compared with original income is, of course, due to the activities of the state in taxing the richer households more heavily and redistributing proportionately more in various kinds of benefits to the poorer households. It is notable, however, that the distribution of *final* income is not greatly different from that of *disposable* income. This is partly because indirect taxes like VAT or duty on tobacco and alcohol, which form part of final income, bear on all groups and do not tend to reduce income inequality. It is also because the benefits in kind from the state go to different groups differently. The main beneficiaries of education expenditure, for example, are households in the top half of the income distribution because they have more children who tend to stay in the education system longer. Health expenditure, on the other hand, goes disproportionately to those lower down the income distribution, partly because so many elderly persons have relatively low incomes.

Box 7   Distribution of income (percentages)

| | Quintile groups of households | | | | |
	Bottom fifth	Next fifth	Middle fifth	Next fifth	Top fifth
Original income					
1976	0.8	9.4	18.8	26.6	44.4
1981	0.6	8.1	18.0	26.9	46.4
1982	0.4	7.1	18.2	27.2	47.1
1983	0.3	6.7	17.7	27.2	48.0
Disposable income					
1976	7.0	12.6	18.2	24.1	38.1
1981	6.7	12.1	17.7	24.1	39.4
1982	6.8	11.8	17.6	24.2	39.6
1983	6.9	11.9	17.6	24.0	39.6
Final income					
1976	7.4	12.7	18.0	24.0	37.9
1981	7.1	12.4	17.9	24.0	38.6
1982	6.9	12.0	17.6	24.1	39.4
1983	6.9	12.2	17.6	24.0	39.3

Source: Social Trends (1986). Crown copyright.

This table uses a method of showing how any quality is distributed through-out a population. In this case, the population (of households) is divided into five equal groups called quintiles, starting with those households with the highest income and going down to those with the lowest. It's like arranging all the households in order of their income and then drawing lines at one-fifth, two-fifths, three-fifths, and so on, down the distribution. You can then see how much of the total national income goes to any one quintile. So, the richest quintile, or 20 percent of households, had almost half of the total amount of original income in 1983.

The various taxes and benefits, although acting in different directions, have the next effect of reducing the inequality of original incomes. It is worth noting that it is not just inequality by income quintile that is noticeable. There are also substantial inequalities over the life cycle as figure 3.2 shows. Household income rises sharply for married couples before they have children, falls while they have young children, and rises to its peak when the children are between 16 and 24. From that peak, income falls steeply towards retirement. Taxes keep final income below original income until just before retirement.

So far we have been discussing relatively recent and short-term movements in the distribution which show an increase in inequality. What of longer-term trends?

Changes in distribution of income since 1949

The Royal Commission on the Distribution of Income and Wealth (1979) showed an apparent increase in the equality of the distribution of pre-tax *personal* income in the years 1949–77. The share taken by the top 1 per cent was more than halved and that accruing to the top 10 per cent was also reduced. This was not, however, reflected in any significant increase in the share taken by the bottom 50 per cent. What has happened, therefore, is that there has simply been a redistribution amongst those individuals in the top 20 or 30 per cent of income earners. As a whole the income distribution showed a remarkable stability from year to year. As far as personal income *after* tax is concerned, there has been a small increase in the degree of equalization in the late 1960s and early 1970s (see figure 3.3). However, there are small movements in both directions from year to year and, as we have seen, there has been, if anything, a reverse in the process of equalization in the 1980s.

In sum, the distribution of income has, since the Second World War at least, remained fairly stable. There has been a degree of redistribution within the top half of income earners but little gain to the bottom half. There are small changes from year to year which can run in either direction and hence very short-run trends should be looked at with caution. With this qualification in mind, incomes have become more unequal in the 1980s.

The distribution of wealth

In many ways, wealth is more important than income from employment. Wealth often includes assets which can yield income in the future and it can be a more secure form of income than that which is earned. Even more than income, however, wealth is difficult to measure.

Problems of measurement

One may readily think of someone's wealth as comprising stocks and shares or building-society accounts. But should one include their house or valuable personal possessions, or even the capital value of their occupational pension scheme? The best way of dealing with these difficulties is to investigate the distribution of the different kinds of

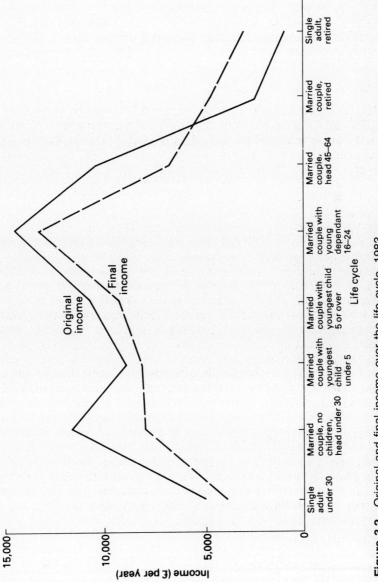

Figure 3.2 Original and final income over the life cycle, 1983

Source: Social Trends (1986), p. 91. Crown copyright.

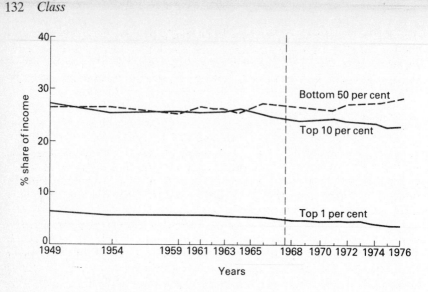

Figure 3.3   Distribution of personal income after tax
Source: Royal Commission on the Distribution of Income and Wealth (1979), p. 76. Crown copyright.

wealth. In particular, we should distinguish marketable from non-marketable wealth. The first refers to those assets that could potentially be sold, like houses or shares. The second includes assets such as pension schemes, that cannot be sold but which represent significant future income.

Another difficulty in measurement is that wealth is rather more concealed than income. People do, after all, have their income assessed on a regular basis by the Inland Revenue, but there is no equivalent set of procedures for wealth in whatever form it is held. There are, then, two main methods for determining how much wealth someone holds. First, the size of an individual's estate may be estimated from the account of their assets that has to be made for probate purposes when they die. Second, one can conduct a survey and determine the distribution of wealth simply by asking a randomly chosen set of people what they own. There are clear difficulties with both of these methods. The first, in that it only deals with wealth left behind by individuals when they die, tells us nothing directly about the distribution of wealth amongst the living. Furthermore, rich individuals tend to distribute their assets among members of their families precisely to avoid the higher taxes payable on death. The estates method may thus seriously underestimate the extent of the weath of the rich. Lastly, many people do not leave enough to qualify for taxation at probate and the Inland Revenue does not therefore provide very good data on the poorer members of the community. The second method, which depends on questionnaire survey, also has its drawbacks. Most importantly, many people will refuse to reveal details of their wealth to interviewers and this level of non-response calls the representatives of such a survey into question. It is also, clearly, very difficult to check that answers to a questionnaire of this kind are accurate.

The changing distribution of wealth

It is important to bear these difficulties of measurement in mind when assessing the evidence of the distribution of wealth. In presenting data, we will try to show the effects of different assumptions about what wealth is and different ways of measuring it. Some recent figures are presented in table 3.6. These are derived from the estate-duty method and show distributions for different types of wealth.

Looking at marketable wealth, the proportion owned by the richest 1 per cent has declined since 1971, although there has been little change in the 1980s. However, the top 50 per cent of the population still owns much the same proportion of the nation's wealth as it did in 1971. What redistribution there has been from the most wealthy has, therefore, not benefited the poorer half of the country. We should also note that, whatever small redistribution has taken place, the wealthiest 10 per cent still owned more than half of the marketable property in 1983. There is, therefore, a certain circulation of wealth among the wealthiest as measured by property possessed at death. As we have already pointed out, there is also a circulation of wealth before death, away from individuals to members of their families, a process which may be accelerating but which is not shown up in these figures.

If one defines wealth as including occupational pension schemes which cannot be sold but which do constitute an asset of a kind, then the inequalities of wealth distribution are less sharp, with the top 1 per cent and top 50 per cent taking less than they did when only marketable assets were counted. The inclusion of state pension rights makes for even greater equality, although only relatively so since the wealthiest 50 per cent still have a minimum of 80 per cent of all assets, including pension rights. What view one takes of these data depends at least partly on the definition of wealth and, specifically, whether or not pension rights are included. Townsend (1979) for example, argues that occupational pensions should be included, on the grounds that they usually have some cash value, but state pensions should not since they cannot be cashed. However one defines wealth, it is very unevenly distributed, and more so than income. Trends in distribution are also very similar for the different types of wealth showing some increase in equality, at least amongst the top 50 per cent, during the 1970s, followed by a flattening out in the 1980s. These conclusions reached by the estates method are roughly confirmed by studies based on the survey method (Townsend, 1979).

These are, of course, relatively recent changes. A more long-run perspective is provided by table 3.7. This does not include any

Table 3.6 Distribution of wealth in Britain, adults over 18 (percentages)

	1971	1976	1979	1980	1981	1982	1983
Marketable wealth							
Percentage of wealth owned by:							
Most wealthy 1 per cent of population	31	24	22	20	22	20	20
Most wealthy 2 per cent of population	39	32	28	27	29	27	27
Most wealthy 5 per cent of population	52	45	40	39	42	40	40
Most wealthy 10 per cent of population	65	60	54	52	56	55	54
Most wealthy 25 per cent of population	86	84	77	75	80	78	78
Most wealthy 50 per cent of population	97	95	95	94	96	96	96
Total marketable wealth (£s billion)	140	263	453	529	546	602	745
Marketable wealth plus occupational pension rights							
Percentage of wealth owned by:							
Most wealthy 1 per cent of population	27	21	19	17	18	17	18
Most wealthy 2 per cent of population	34	27	24	23	24	23	23
Most wealthy 5 per cent of population	46	40	34	33	35	34	34
Most wealthy 10 per cent of population	59	53	45	46	48	47	46
Most wealthy 25 per cent of population	78–83	75–81	70–4	69–73	71–5	70–4	69–73
Most wealthy 50 per cent of population	90–6	89–93	88–92	90–4	89–93	89–93	89–93

Marketable wealth plus occupational and state pension rights

Percentage of wealth owned by:

Most wealthy 1 per cent of population	21	14	13	12	12	11	12
Most wealthy 2 per cent of population	27	18	17	16	16	16	16
Most wealthy 5 per cent of population	37	27	25	24	25	25	25
Most wealthy 10 per cent of population	49	37	35	35	36	35	35
Most wealthy 25 per cent of population	69–72	58–61	56–9	55–8	56–9	55–8	57–60
Most wealthy 50 per cent of population	85–9	80–5	79–83	79–83	79–83	79–83	80–4

Note: Between 1979 and 1980 there was a change in methodology as described in *Inland Revenue Statistics* (1985).
Source: *Social Trends* (1986). Crown copyright.

adjustments for difficulties of valuation or of wealth understated in estate-duty returns and it is very difficult to allow for changes in the way that people give away their property before they die. Inclusion of these would increase the share taken by the richer groups. Since 1923, the share of the top 1 per cent has declined significantly from about 61 per cent to about 32 per cent. As we have noticed before, greater equality of this kind does not necessarily mean greater equality throughout the whole population, for wealth is largely being realiocated from the very richest to the not-quite-so rich. Thus, the share in total wealth of the top 20 per cent has

Table 3.7   Shares in total wealth 1938–72 (percentages)

	England and Wales				Britain			
	Top 1%	Top 5%	Top 10%	Top 20%	Top 1%	Top 5%	Top 10%	Top 20%
1938	55.0	76.9	85.0	91.2	55.0	77.2	85.4	91.6
1950	47.2	74.3	—	—	47.2	74.4	—	—
1951	45.8	73.6	—	—	45.9	73.8	—	—
1952	43.0	70.2	—	—	42.9	70.3	—	—
1953	43.6	71.1	—	—	43.5	71.2	—	—
1954	45.3	71.8	—	—	45.3	72.0	—	—
1955	44.5	71.1	—	—	43.8	70.8	—	—
1956	44.5	71.3	—	—	44.0	71.1	—	—
1957	43.4	68.7	—	—	42.9	68.6	—	—
1958	41.4	67.8	—	—	40.9	67.7	—	—
1959	41.4	67.6	—	—	41.8	67.9	—	—
1960	33.9	59.4	71.5	83.1	34.4	60.0	72.1	83.6
1961	36.5	60.6	71.7	83.3	36.5	60.8	72.1	83.6
1962	31.4	54.8	67.3	80.2	31.9	55.4	67.9	80.7
1963		not available*				not available*		
1964	34.5	58.6	71.4	84.3	34.7	59.2	72.0	85.2
1965	33.0	58.1	71.7	85.5	33.3	58.7	72.3	85.8
1966	30.6	55.5	69.2	83.8	31.0	56.1	69.9	84.2
1967	31.4	56.0	70.0	84.5	31.5	56.4	70.5	84.9
1968	33.6	58.3	71.6	85.1	33.6	58.6	72.0	85.4
1969	31.1	56.1	67.7	83.3	31.3	56.6	68.6	84.1
1970	29.7	53.6	68.7	84.5	30.1	54.3	69.4	84.9
1971	28.4	52.3	67.6	84.2	28.8	53.0	68.3	84.0
1972	31.7	56.0	70.4	84.9	32.0	57.2	71.7	85.3

Notes: Dashes denote that the information is outside the range of estate data.
　　*The estate data were not available by country for 1963: this means that we could not calculate a figure for Britain comparable with those for other years.
Source: From Atkinson and Harrison (1978), *Distribution of Personal Wealth in Britain* (Cambridge University Press), p. 218. Reproduced with permission.

only declined 10 per cent in the same period. The diffusion of wealth does not, in other words, extend very far.

,The twentieth century has been a period when there have been attempts to redistribute both income and wealth. The evidence that we have presented in this section does not suggest that these attempts have been very successful. Wealth is still very concentrated and it is still relatively easy, especially with good professional advice, for a wealthy person to pass it on to other members of his or her family. An unequal distribution of income and wealth is not achieved by accident; it requires active social processes to create and maintain it. As Townsend (1979, p. 365) argues:

> Riches are not only inherited or made: to be riches, they have to be unavailable to the vast majority of the population. A theory of riches depends not only on theories of acquisition – how much wealth is inherited, accumulated by entrepreneurial effort or by the exercise of scarce skills. It depends also on theories of denial of access to wealth – through selective succession, testamentary concentration, limitation of entry to the professions, monopolization of capital and property or at least severe restriction on the opportunity to acquire land and property.

Poverty

So far we have argued that changes in the distribution of income and wealth are confined largely to the richest 20 per cent. We turn now to look at what that might mean for the bottom 50 per cent and, specifically, at the incidence of poverty in contemporary Britain. It seems reasonable to say that there is a difference between being relatively deprived by being in the lower half of the income distribution, and being in actual poverty. There is an apparent distinction, in other words, between being relatively badly-off and having a standard of living below some fixed level. Most studies of poverty adopt the second of these as the basis for investigation; they have a 'Plimsoll line' conception of poverty. The difficulty with this lies in establishing where the Plimsoll line is to be drawn. How does one decide when somebody is in poverty if it is not simply that they are worse off than the average? The first point to make here is that there is no absolute poverty line which is assessable against objective standards. Any definition of poverty depends on the values of the society concerned and on its view as to what counts as the necessities of life. That means that there is a great deal of room for disagreement about where to put the poverty line. Government ministers, especially those of recent Conservative governments, have a tendency to put the line very much lower down than do, say, ministers in the Church of England.

Bearing the possibility of such disagreements in mind, it is still obviously vital to have some notion of a poverty line in order to produce an estimate of the numbers of people who need help. One widely used poverty line, employed because it has official sanction, is the supplementary-benefit level. The state recognizes that people need help when their incomes fall below this level because it then pays them supplementary benefit.

By the supplementary-benefit measure, there has been a sharp rise in poverty in very recent times. From 1960 to 1977, the estimated numbers of people living *below* the level of supplementary benefit remained more or less constant at 2 million. By 1981, this had risen to 2.6 million. However, one also has to consider those with incomes *equal* to the supplementary-benefit level. Mack and Lansley (1985) estimate that in 1983 there were 8.6 million people living at or below the supplementary-benefit level, an increase of 43 per cent over the figure for 1979.

The supplementary-benefit level, though in some sense official, is still not a very good guide to the level of poverty because it is more closely related to what governments can afford than to what people need by the standards of their society. One response to this is to draw up an index of items of what the researcher thinks is needed by people for a minimum ordinary existence in any society. This was the basis for Townsend's (1979) major survey, which estimated that, by his definition of poverty, some one-quarter of the households in Britain were in poverty. There is another approach, however, which takes even more seriously the notion that poverty has to be related to the standards of a reasonable existence that prevail in a society. This approach takes not the poverty line judged by researchers and experts, but that established by surveying the opinions of ordinary people about the necessities for living. This is the method adopted by a recent study which we are going to consider in rather more detail.

Breadline Britain: a case study

The study by Mack and Lansley (1985) aims to 'measure the extent of poverty not in terms of some arbitrary income level but in terms of the extent to which the poor are excluded from the way of living that is expected and customary in society today. This requires a survey not just of the poor but of the rest of society as well' (p. 9). Their sample survey was intended, simultaneously, to elicit views about what counts as poverty *and* to find out people's actual situation. First, then, they used the opinions that they obtained to construct a concept of those things that are minimally necessary for a customary way of life – a poverty line. A list of items such as heating, indoor toilet, warm coat, meat or fish every other day, dressing gown, etc. was shown to a sample drawn from the population and the respondents were asked to say which were necessary for an acceptable standard of living. The results of this inquiry are shown in table 3.8. Nine-tenths of the sample thought that heating, an indoor toilet, a damp-free home, a bath, and beds for everyone were necessary. Other items did not command this overwhelming support. However, two-thirds of respondents held that such things as a warm coat, toys for children, and a washing machine were necessary for a decent life. The authors found widespread agreement between all groups of society about items classified as necessities. Of course there are differences between say, Conservative voters and Labour voters or between the old and the young but, compared with differences in opinions that obtain on other issues, there was remarkable homogeneity. As the authors say of their respondents, 'their views are based, it seems, on a general cultural ethos of what is decent and proper' (p. 86). Furthermore, these views are deeply held, for the bulk of the sample was perfectly happy to see their taxes raised in order to finance the provision of certain necessities by the state.

This part of the survey, then, provides a yardstick, a measure of a minimum standard of living that is widely agreed among the population. The next question is, What proportion of the population fall below this minimum standard in that they say they cannot afford some of the necessities? On this basis, some 3 million people in Britain cannot afford to heat the living areas of their home, some 1.5 million children go without toys, and 5.5 million people are unable to afford basic items of food, such as meat or fish every other day, or two hot meals a day. There are two difficulties with this, however. First, people may well *choose* to go without some of the things that the population in general think are necessary. Second, those who go without may simply be incompetent at managing what money they do have.

Mack and Lansley address these questions by relating the lack of necessities to household income. Some people were found who went without some of these necessities by choice, in that they probably had sufficient income to afford them. In general, however, those people who did not reach the minimum level had incomes which did not allow the purchase of these necessities. They did not, in other words, have the ability to choose. Relating income to necessities gives a more accurate view of deprivation. Box 8 provides a way of seeing how many households miss how many necessities of each kind. About 20 per cent of the population lack one or two necessities, 5 per cent are without three or four, a further 4 per cent lack five or six and, finally, 5 per cent of the population live in the most intense deprivation, being unable to afford seven or more necessities.

In Mack and Lansley's view, vulnerability to *deprivation* extends throughout the bottom half and particularly, the bottom 30–40 per cent of society. It could be argued that this deprivation is the result of fecklessness or incompetence. This seems unlikely to be true, however, since the income of the deprived leaves little scope for fecklessness. However, in addition, Mack and Lansley showed that the deprived were not, on the whole, spending money on luxuries and neglecting necessities. On the contrary, their survey indicated that the more a household goes without necessities, the more it goes without other less-essential goods as well.

Table 3.8 The public's perception of necessities

Standard-of-living items in rank order	% classing item as necessity	Standard-of-living items in rank order	% classing item as necessity
1 Heating to warm living areas of the home if it's cold	97	18 New, not second-hand, clothes	64
2 Indoor toilet (not shared with another household)	96	19 A hobby or leisure activity	64
3 Damp-free home	96	20 Two hot meals a day (for adults)	64
4 Bath (not shared with another household)	94	21 Meat or fish every other day	63
5 Beds for everyone in the household	94	22 Presents for friends or family once a year	63
6 Public transport for one's needs	88	23 A holiday away from home for one week a year, not with relatives	63
7 A warm waterproof coat	87	24 Leisure equipment for children, e.g. sports equipment or a bicycle[a]	57
8 Three meals a day for children[a]	82	25 A garden	55
9 Self-contained accommodation	79	26 A television	51
10 Two pairs of all-weather shoes	78	27 A 'best outfit' for special occasions	48
11 Enough bedrooms for every child over 10 of different sex to have his/her own[a]	77	28 A telephone	43
12 Refrigerator	77	29 An outing for children once a week[a]	40
13 Toys for children[a]	71	30 A dressing gown	38
14 Carpets in living rooms and bedrooms	70	31 Children's friends round for tea / a snack once a fortnight[a]	37
15 Celebrations on special occasions such as Christmas	69	32 A night out once a fortnight (adults)	36
16 A roast meat joint or its equivalent once a week	67	33 Friends/family round for a meal once a month	32
17 A washing machine	67	34 A car	22
		35 A packet of cigarettes every other day	14

Average of all 35 items = 64.1 per cent classing them as necessities

Note: [a]For families with children only.
Source: Mack and Lansley (1985) *Poor Britain* (London, George Allen and Unwin), p. 54. Reproduced with permission.

Box 8 The living standards of the deprived

	Lack[a] of necessities % of households facing each deprivation			
Deprivations	1 or 2	3 or 4	5 or 6	7 or more
Inadequate heating	6	20	35	46
No unshared indoor toilet	1	4	17	13
Damp home	9	16	51	42
No unshared bath	1	4	15	15
Not enough beds	1	5	9	4
No warm waterproof coat	5	20	45	65
Less than two pairs of all-weather shoes	9	26	37	88
No refrigerator	2	5	9	13
Not enough carpets	2	7	2	31
No celebrations on special occasions	4	9	13	53
No roast joint each week	8	29	44	48
No washing machine	10	22	25	31
Second-hand clothes	4	13	46	66
No hobby or leisure activity	6	36	35	61
Less than two hot meals a day	3	11	28	28
Meat/fish less than every other day	10	27	33	88
Not enough money to give presents once a year	4	24	18	55
No holiday	47	65	76	96

Note: [a]Throughout, 'lack' is taken as those who do not have an item because they cannot afford it and excludes those who do not have it because they do not want it.
Source: Mack and Lansley (1985), table 5.1, p. 135.

One way of estimating poverty is simply to count the number of necessities that households do without. By this measure, households which go without seven necessities are clearly worse off than those which lack only one. However, it is also important to show *which* necessities are forgone by households in different degrees of deprivation. For example, of households lacking 'only' one or two necessities, 10 per cent have meat or fish less than every other day. Of those in intense poverty (lacking more than seven necessities), 65 per cent do not have a warm, waterproof coat.

Deprivation, for Mack and Lansley, is not, however, the same as poverty; people are in poverty when their *enforced* lack of necessities affects their way of living. This means that one has to decide when a lack of necessities is enforced and what level of deprivation will be defined as putting someone in poverty. The authors start by taking, as an indication of poverty, all those unable to afford three or more necessities. On this measure, around one person in seven in Britain (almost 8 million people) is in poverty. A number of adjustments have to be made to this figure. An allowance has to be made for those who have high incomes and whose lack of necessities seems to be voluntary. Similarly, a deduction has to be made for those who would appear to have enough money for necessities if only they did not smoke. Some people may also have their lives less seriously affected by the *kind* of necessities that they lack, even if they do not have three of them. These qualifications would have the effect of reducing the number in poverty to some 6 million. However, other adjustments would increase the number. For example, people may not agree that they need certain things because their poverty gives them such low expectations. In addition, some people who lack only one or two necessities may find their lives more seriously affected than those who lack three or more. If one took simply these additions, the number in poverty rises to 12 million.

Mack and Lansley therefore estimate that between 6 and 12 million people are poor in Britain in the 1980s: 'there are about 12 million people who are struggling by the standards of today; among this group, living standards gradually deteriorate so that somewhat over half of this group face wide-ranging and serious problems' (p. 183). Among the 6 million there will, of course, be those who face intense poverty and cannot afford seven or more necessities. Mack and Lansley estimate this group at 2.6 million people, including 1 million children, or about 1 in 20 people in Britain. As one of their respondents said (p. 275):

> The future for me doesn't hold much hope for me or my family – there's no prospects really that I can see of a better job, though I might get one if I'm lucky. I don't see any prospect for my children 'cos the way things are it looks as though there's gonna be a lot more people out of work and – I just don't feel right about it. You know, I feel as though I've brought my children into a world that's just dying.

Who is poor?

Some sections of the population are much more vulnerable to poverty than others, in particular, the low-paid, the unemployed, the disabled, one-parent families and the elderly retired. These minorities are represented in the population in poverty out of all proportion to their numbers in the general population. Clearly, these groups are vulnerable simply because they have low incomes and are largely dependent on benefit payments of various kinds from the state. Furthermore, various social trends and aspects of government policy are likely both to increase the numbers of people in poverty and to alter the distribution between the various groups at risk. For example, the age structure is changing in such a way that there is not only an increasing proportion of the population aged 65 or over, but also the numbers over 85 are increasing rapidly (see chapter 6, section 6.3). Government policy clearly affects the rates of benefit, which in turn affects the standard of living of vulnerable groups. Economic and industrial policy also significantly affects the numbers of people in poverty. For example, the abolition of wage councils is likely to increase the numbers of people who are in very low-paid jobs. The recent, very steep, increase in unemployment is also mostly attributable to government economic policy.

The *distribution* of poverty among the vulnerable groups is also changing. Figure 3.4 gives some indication of this. Although in 1971, pensioners made up over half of those in the bottom 20 per cent of the income distribution, in 1982 they were responsible for just over one-quarter. As we have seen, this is not because the *numbers* of pensioners have fallen. It is, instead, largely becaue there has been a relatively greater increase in the numbers of persons unemployed in all family types.

Poverty is a function of the distribution of income. As common sense would indicate, people are in poverty because they have a low income. The distribution of poverty is, therefore, explained by reference to those groups that are most likely to have low incomes. Any overall account of poverty, however, is dependent, in turn, on an explanation of how a particular distribution of income and wealth is created and maintained. One way of considering this issue is to see how society is divided into *social classes* and how the mechanisms that sustain class divisions keep a large number of adults and children below an acceptable standard of living.

Summary

1 Since the beginning of the twentieth century, there has been some redistribution of income in Britain, but the distribution has not changed much since the Second World War. In the period from 1945 to the present, there has been a small degree of equalization, but this appears to have involved only those households in the top half of incomes distribution. In the 1980s, the process of equalization has been reversed.

2 Wealth is more unequally distributed than income. As with income, what redistribution there has been has involved only the more wealthy half of the population.

3 However one measures poverty, a substantial proportion of the

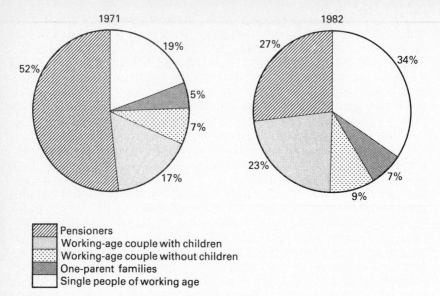

Pensioners
Working-age couple with children
Working-age couple without children
One-parent families
Single people of working age

Figure 3.4   Composition of the lowest quintile group of income by family type
Source: Social Trends (1986), p. 88. Crown copyright.

population are in poverty. The bottom 30–40 per cent of the income range are vulnerable and the bottom 5–10 per cent live in intense poverty.

Related topics

Questions of poverty are discussed at a number of points in this book. Chapter 6, section 6.3 on the elderly and 6.5 on single-parent families, are especially relevant. Chapter 2, section 2.8 discusses poverty in connection with unemployment, and the following section in this chapter, section 3.4, deals with poverty in connection with the working class. The rest of this chapter contains data on comparisons of income and wage rates. Section 3.6 gives some account of how the upper class have preserved their favoured situation.

3.4   The Working Class

Debates about the working class

The future of the working class is one of the most contentious issues in contemporary sociology. The debate is hard to appreciate without recalling Marx's view of the revolutionary role of the working class in capitalist society. Marx thought that the logic of capitalist accumulation would turn the vast majority of the population into proletarians, i.e. workers who relied on wages for their subsistence because they lacked my other means of livelihood. Lacking property and increasingly deprived of control over their own labour, the working class would come to share a common (homogeneous) economic position. Uniformly degraded work and poor pay would characterize the workers and distinguish them from a small, privileged social class of property owners. In such circumstances, Marx expected the workers to unite politically, on the basis of their common class position, to abolish capitalist domination.

The working classes of the Western world have rarely been revolutionary. For the last 150 years, however, the main force behind social and political change has come from organizations of the working class – trade unions and socialist parties. Such organizations have been 'reformist': they have pressed successfully for improvements in pay and working conditions, for the extension of political rights like the vote, and for social rights like health care, education and social-security benefits. These are achievements of labour movements on behalf of the working class, but they have not undermined capitalist economic relations. Since this reformist politics is universal in Western societies, except where it has been suppressed by dictatorships, it might be anticipated that it will continue as a form of working-class opposition to capitalism.

Some commentators believe, however, that the British working class is beginning to abandon even its reformism. They suggest that the working class is no longer an oppositional, never mind a revolutionary, force. It is argued that, since the Second World War, the working class has become thoroughly integrated into society. Standards of living have risen, welfare services have expanded, trade unions and the Labour Party have become accepted parts of the political system, with the result that the working class is no longer a marginal, excluded or deprived class. There is now one nation rather than two, with the working class committed to the perpetuation of welfare capitalism.

Differences over the way in which class conflict might be expected to develop have formed the background to sociological debates in the last 25 years, and have revolved around interpretations of how social changes have affected manual workers. Two issues have been central. The first is whether the position of the working class has changed relative to other classes, and particularly whether manual workers remain a distinctive class. The second concerns changes in the internal structure of the working class, especially whether or not it is becoming more *internally divided* and hence less prone to acting politically in a united, or 'solidaristic', way.

Sociological interpretations

A distinctive class?

Two main positions exist concerning the distinctiveness of the working class. One says that there has been a *convergence* between manual and other workers and that there is no longer a perceptible difference between the working class and the middle class. The other asserts that the boundary remains significant; the working class remains distinct even though some of its characteristics may have altered to such an extent that it constitutes a *new working class*.

These two positions were clearly presented in the famous debate about the effect of affluence on the working class. Proponents of the 'embourgeoisement thesis' detected convergence; their critics – Goldthorpe, Lockwood, Bechhofer and Platt (1968a, 1968b and 1969), – denied convergence, but identified a class of workers with new characteristics.

The embourgeoisement thesis, crudely stated, maintained that since workers had become better-off during the post-war boom, and their patterns of consumption altered, they had begun to adopt the life-style and social values of the middle class. Convergence was occurring between manual and non-manual workers; it was to be expected that manual workers would become 'bourgeois'. Thus, the working class would become indistinguishable from other classes.

Goldthorpe et al. tested this thesis on some well-paid manual workers in mass-production industries in Luton. These workers were prosperous but were not becoming middle class. They did not aspire to become middle class; they did not associate socially with white-collar workers; they were not involved in their work; they were trade unionists; and they voted very solidly for the Labour Party. Therefore, it was concluded, the embourgeoisement thesis was inaccurate. However, these affluent workers were different from earlier generations of manual workers. Their behaviour of work, their social lives, and their reasons for supporting labour organizations were not like those of traditional workers. The new worker was *instrumental* in attitude to work, unions and politics, and *privatized* in social life. The new worker worked purely for money and was concerned with unions only because collective action was essential for an increased income. That income was, in turn, increasingly devoted to improving the material circumstances of the worker's immediate family. New workers were very family-centred and were not involved in neighbourhood or community life. So, Goldthorpe concluded, a boundary remained between the working and the middle class, but the working class itself was changing from its traditional form.

The case for the emergence of a 'new', privatized and instrumentalist working class depended itself on a model of what the working class used to be like. Indeed, all questions concerning the extent and direction of change depend on some comparison with a previous condition. Goldthorpe et al. used a model of the *traditional proletarian*, and many other sociologists have done the same.

The traditional proletarian is attributed with various characteristics. Workers were often impoverished, but not obsessed by money or their lack of it. Poverty was partly compensated for by work, which was more skilled than today and which tended to foster more cohesive work-groups. Poor housing conditions were offset by the existence of close-knit communities where bonds of kinship and neighbourliness prevailed. A distinctive style of life supported a vibrant class culture. This culture included a consciousness of class divisions and a political commitment to the labour movement (unions and the Labour Party, mostly). Workers acted as a fairly homogenous political force in opposition to capitalist social relations. A contrast between proletarian and new workers is drawn in figure 3.5.

This model of the traditional working class was typical of some, though probably never the majority, of workers in the past. Using it as a device for comparison does, however, tend to exaggerate the differences between the past and the present. Workers have always found themselves in varied circumstances, with different jobs, in different industries and in different regions of the country, which have prevented the working class from ever being a homogeneous traditional proletariat.

A divided class?

The same model of the traditional proletarian plays a major role in sociological analysis of the internal homogeneity of the contemporary working class. It is generally accepted, after Marx, that the more homogenous the class, the more capable it would be of united political action. The traditional proletarian had a propensity for class solidarity. Close cooperation with workmates and neighbours encouraged an awareness of class interests and, thus, industrial and political solidarity in situations of conflict with other classes. The sociological debate concerns whether workers still experience conditions sufficiently similar to sustain such class awareness and solidarity. Some authors claim that the working class is now hopelessly divided, others argue the contrary.

Assessing this argument is difficult because while there can be no doubt that *differences* exist among manual workers (the working class is 'internally differentiated'), deciding whether these differences are deep enough to constitute structural *divisions* is a matter of interpretation.

The highly controversial subject of the modern working class can be approached by examining sociological evidence. We look at these issues with respect to various aspects of working-class experience in contemporary Britain: class position (market situation, work situation and status situation), life-style and culture (consumption and social participation)

	Traditional proletarian worker	Instrumental-privatized worker
Image of society	'Us' versus 'them': an oppositional and dichotomous view of centring on power inequality	A 'pecuniary' or money model; class differences seen in terms of income and possessions
Involvement in job	High	Low
Social interaction with workmates	High	Low
Community involvement	Extensive; social life often gender segregated, but public	Very limited; spends non-work time in the home with spouse and family
Salience of class	Identifies with class and recognizes class distinctions	Scarcely aware of belonging to a social class
Reason for joining trade union or voting	Class solidarity and communalism	Instrumental; concern with private goal of improving material condition of family

Figure 3.5   Ideal-typical characteristics of traditional proletarian and instrumental-privatized workers.
Source: Adapted from Lockwood (1966).

and political practices (class consciousness, voting, and membership of political organizations). In each case, we look at changes in circumstances and assess (a) whether those changes make the working class less distinctive, and (b) whether they affect the internal unity of the working class. Throughout the rest of this section we provide evidence and argument to help resolve the two main issues – the distinctiveness of the class and its internal divisions. We argue that recent changes have not greatly reduced the distinctiveness of the working class, but that divisions within the class (its internal differentiation) have altered and may affect its political actions.

Class position

When British sociologists talk of the working class they are usually referring to people currently or formerly employed in manual occupations, and to their dependants. Thus, heads of households in manual jobs, retired or unemployed ex-manual workers, and housewives and children not in employment, are considered members of the working class. This definition is problematic. It is not always easy to decide whether a particular job is 'manual' or 'non-manual'. As the discussion of the proletarianization of office work (section 3.5) indicates, the work and market situations of many non-manual jobs are developing characteristics very like those of traditional manual occupations. Furthermore, there are a substantial number of households in which the husband is a manual worker and his wife is in non-manual employment, which makes it difficult to attribute a class position to the *household*. Nevertheless, despite these difficulties, most sociologists have considered the distinction between manual and non-manual workers important because the work experience and social lives of these two groups have differed significantly in the past.

One important aspect of change has been the declining size of the manual work-force. Table 3.9 shows that there were 15.25 million manual workers in 1951, but only 12.4 million by 1981. Consequently, as the number of white-collar jobs has increased, the proportion of employees doing manual work has declined, from about 70 per cent in 1951 to less than 50 per cent in 1981 (see table 3.5 above). The manual working class is no longer a majority of the population.

Table 3.9 Number of manual workers and gender composition of manual labour force, 1951, 1971 and 1981

	1951	1971	1981
Total number of manual employees (including unemployed)	15,297,000	14,198,000	12,343,000
Male % of all manual workers	69	66	61

Source: Calculated from Routh (1980), p. 6, reproduced as table 3.5 in this volume (pp. 120–1); and Census (1981), *Economic Activity in Great Britain*, table 17.

We examine the class position of the British working class in terms of three main elements outlined in section 3.1: market, work and status situations.

Market situation

> Market situation . . . the economic position narrowly conceived, consisting of source and size of income, degree of job security, and opportunity for upward occupational mobility.
>
> Lockwood (1958)

Manual workers are better off than ever before. Real wages have risen over time, which is to say that the actual purchasing power of the average wage is greater than it used to be. Also, various Acts of Parliament have improved some of the fringe benefits of manual work. Longer, statutory holidays are an improvement; so too is the introduction of redundancy payments to remove some financial insecurities. On the other hand, the source of manual workers' incomes and their opportunities for promotion are probably the same as they were 50 years ago. However, the general improvements in market situation alone are insufficient for us to resolve either of our two controversial issues, whether the working class remains distinct from other social classes or if the working class is internally divided.

The distinctiveness of the market situation of the working class: Advocates of the convergence thesis point to changes which tend to reduce the differences in the market situation between manual and other workers. During the twentieth century, the average male manual wage, especially of semi- and unskilled workers, has increased relative to that for routine white-collar work. The 1984 New Earnings Survey showed that the average full-time male manual wage was £153 per week, whilst the average for clerical and related work was £148 per week. The average non-manual wage was much higher, £209 per week. The convergence of the weekly wage of clerks and manual workers obscures many differences.

First, manual workers work longer hours. The average working week for a British male manual worker in 1984 was 44.3 hours; non-manuals worked 38.5 hours. (Incidentally, working hours are significantly longer in Britain than in other major European countries.) This follows from the fact that high earnings from manual work usually depend upon lots of overtime: on average overtime was 5 hours per week, and 14 per cent of gross weekly earnings derived from overtime.

Second, manual workers have a less attractive profile of earnings over their lifetime. Manual workers earn most between the ages of 30–9, and tend to fall thereafter. In terms of family life cycles, wages start to fall as dependent children become most expensive. Most non-manual workers have career structures whereby promotion and/or salary increments increase income until fairly late in their working lives. Indeed, as Stewart et al. (1980) showed (see below, section 3.5), the relatively poor pay of male clerical workers was a statistical artefact, since very few men remained as clerks for their entire working lives. Male clerks are poorly paid, but they either get promoted or change to another occupation. Thus it is that the earnings over an entire lifetime for non-manual workers is considerably greater than that of manual workers.

Third, manual workers suffer from greater insecurity of employment. They are more frequently unemployed (see chapter 2, section 2.8). They may experience short-time working and temporary lay-offs. Manual workers are rarely entitled to sickness pay, are unable to take time off with pay to deal with family emergencies, and usually have pay deducted for lateness. Office workers suffer few of these indignities and insecurities; and the higher up the managerial hierarchy one goes, the better are fringe benefits and conditions of employment. It is, probably, in the end, the degree of insecurity which most strongly distinguishes manual work. Periods of life without a wage are the norm for manual workers, making periods of considerable hardship part of the normal life experience.

Fourth, some manual workers are very poorly paid indeed. A significant proportion of people in poverty are in work, but are paid an insufficient amount to bring them above the poverty line.

Thus, the market situation of manual workers is distinctive and inferior in certain respects even when compared with the most routine white-collar occupations.

Internal differentiation in the market situation of the working class: There is considerable variation in market situation among manual workers. Different jobs in different industries pay different wages. The best-paid manual workers in 1984 were in the newspaper printing and publishing industry, where the average male wage was £278 per week. By contrast, men in agriculture earned only £124 per week on average.

The most systematic difference, perhaps, was the gap between pay for men and women. One in three full-time women manual workers earned less than £80 per week; only one in four women earned more than £115. Although there has been some slight improvement over the last decade, women manual workers earn only 62 per cent of men even when employed full-time. Many women are part-timers and are even less well-paid.

The inferior position of women is often analysed in terms of 'dual labour markets' (for an extended discussion see chapter 4, section 4.2). Women, and to an extent men of ethnic minorities, cluster in the secondary, lower, sector of the labour market, where wages are poorer, jobs less secure, firms smaller and more precarious, and conditions worse. The market situation of women is one source of division among manual workers. It is also more prevalent than before, for as table 3.9 shows, whereas women used to comprise less than 30 per cent of manual workers, now they are 40 per cent.

On the other hand, however, wage differentials between skilled and less-skilled manual workers have declined. Both for men and women, unskilled and semi-skilled workers have caught up. Though differentials continue to cause conflict between unions, with skilled workers seeking to maintain their relative privileges, the range of incomes within the class has narrowed.

Probably, then, the market situation of the working class is no more differentiated than it used to be. However, differences along the dimensions of gender – or ethnicity – are ones which are readily identifiable and which might, therefore, create deeper political divisions, especially where the trade unions protecting white males can be seen as contributing to the inferior position of women and black people.

Work situation

> Work situation, the set of social relationships in which the individual is involved at work by virtue of . . . position in the division of labour.
>
> Lockwood (1958)

The work situation – or the relationships of authority in the labour process – of manual workers has been discussed at length in chapter 2.4. It was concluded that many workers had little control over their work, as control had been wrested from them by management. This was the essence of the process of deskilling, one which had had a very considerable impact on manual work and was also spreading to routine clerical work.

Most manual workers, other than craftsmen, have little discretion over their own working practices. Equally, manual workers, except for a small percentage of foremen and supervisors, exercise no authority over other workers. Rather, in general, they are in the most subordinate occupational positions. (In section 3.2 and table 3.2 we noted that even fewer women than men held positions of authority.) Consequently, most manual workers have an 'instrumental' or 'economistic' attitude towards work: their principal concerns are with pay and job security rather than with intrinsic features of the work. These attitudes often foster cooperative, or solidaristic, relationships among manual workers themselves.

The work situation of routine white-collar workers, and increasingly too of lower and middle managers, is developing many similar, proletarianized features (see section 3.5). Even among these jobs, however, conditions of work are usually more pleasant: they are less dangerous and less noisy, for instance. Nevertheless, in respect of work situation, the argument about the convergence between manual and non-manual workers is correct. The main contrast in work situations between classes lies in the superior conditions experienced by professionals, senior managers and owners of businesses.

There remains considerable variation within the manual working class in work situation, depending upon the type of industry, the nature of managerial control, and the degree of discretion which the worker has over the work process. This is not, however, a feature of working-class experience which in itself creates serious internal divisions. A man who is a process worker is not likely to feel hostile towards a worker on an assembly line or a farm worker just because of the difference in work situation.

Status situation

> Status situation . . . the position of the individual in the hierarchy of prestige in the society at large.
>
> Lockwood (1958)

The degree of prestige attached to manual jobs, and the social status of the incumbents of those jobs, suggest that manual employment is generally held in low esteem. When people are asked to rank occupations in terms of their desirability, there is a fair degree of consensus among people. In that hierarchy, manual jobs come at the bottom, though there is some degree of overlap between white- and blue-collar occupations. This suggests a fairly strong separation in most people's minds between manual and non-manual employment.

Another indication of the prestige of manual occupations, which also shows continued separation between manual workers and others, is given by patterns of sociability and friendship. Almost all studies show that the friends and acquaintances of manual workers are themselves predominantly working class. Patterns of sociability continue to be class-bound, which contributes to the separation of one class from another.

Again, there is little reason to think that differences of prestige attached to manual jobs cause serious internal divisions. Even supervisory workers in manual occupations, like foremen in the London docks, associate more with manual than non-manual workers.

Working-class culture and life-styles

Experiences outside work affect class solidarity and political action. For example, the nature of the community to which a worker belongs affects his or her voting behaviour. Two aspects of the changing life-style of the working class have attracted special attention recently – consumption patterns and privatization. Consumption patterns emerge from the choices made about how money is spent. Privatization refers to the use of time outside work, particularly the amounts of time spent at home with the family rather than in public and communal activities. Both changed consumption patterns and privatization have been said to reduce working-class identity and solidarity.

Consumption

Although poverty has remained widespread (see section 3.3), most workers in Britain have a better standard of living than fifty years ago. Average real incomes have risen, and manual workers now possess consumer goods which were previously only accessible to a small minority of the population. Working-class households are increasingly likely to own durable goods like cars, fridges and washing machines, and to have a telephone and central heating in their dwellings. Perhaps the most remarked-upon change is, however, the growth of working-class house ownership. In 1983, 65 per cent of skilled manual households, 48 per cent of semi-skilled and 34 per cent of unskilled either owned outright the house in which they were living, or were in the process of purchasing it on a mortgage. This represents a considerable expansion of owner-occupation for, except in a few regions of Britain, manual workers usually used to rent housing from private landlords or the council. It has frequently been assumed that these new consumption patterns would have lasting structural effects on the working class. Indeed, the embourgeoisement thesis was based on observing the spread of the goods associated with a middle class life-style.

The consumption patterns of different classes: One weakness of the argument that affluence leads to assimilation of workers to a middle class life-style is the fact that consumption patterns remain markedly unequal between classes. Table 3.10, taken from the *Family Expenditure Survey*, shows that, in 1984, household spending varied depending on the occupational class of heads of households. Administrative and managerial workers' households spent on average £50 per week more than skilled manual workers, and £90 per week more than non-skilled manual workers. Clerical workers' households spend marginally less than skilled manual workers. However, when expenditure *per person* is calculated, a different, and more pertinent, impression is obtained. Clerical workers' households are smaller than those of manual workers, so that the level of consumption of each member is considerably higher. Considered in this way, the expenditure of clerical (i.e. routine non-manual) workers is more like that of other non-manual households. That impression is reinforced by examining differences in what exactly is purchased.

Table 3.11 shows expenditure per head of households of different employment status and occupation, expressed in relation to the pattern of a skilled manual worker. A number of points emerge.

1 Expenditure on food and alcohol varies least across households;

Table 3.10 Expenditure of household by occupation and employment status of head of household, 1983 (£).

	Employees in work						Self-employed	Out of work			All households
	Occupation of head of household										
	Professional & technical	Administrative & managerial	Clerical	Skilled manual	Semi-skilled manual	Unskilled manual		Unemployed manual[a]	Unoccupied seeking work[b]	Retired	
Average weekly household expenditure	201	216	160	162	143	124	180	117	102	83	143
Average weekly expenditure per person	68	70	63	49	50	41	52	37	33	52	54

Notes: Although the first 6 columns are headed 'Employees in work', the figures from table 15 of the *Family Expenditure Survey* include some employees out of work, so that households in column 8 'Unemployed manual' appear twice. Similarly, while column 11 'All households' includes all households in the 1983 sample, not all are shown separately in the table.

[a] Employees whose last job was not more than twelve months ago, and who were seeking work.
[b] Employees whose last job was more than twelve months before survey, and persons who had never worked.

Source: Family Expenditure Survey (1983), tables 15 and 16. Crown copyright.

expenditure on services and consumer durables varies most.

2   Non-manual-household members consume considerably more than manual-household members, this applying to clerks as well as professionals and managers.

3   The unemployed and unoccupied are relatively deprived especially with respect to services and consumer durables. Spending on anything other than the necessities of food and shelter declines in the absence of a job.

4   Non-manual workers are most distinctive in the extent of which they purchase services, consumer durables and housing: in real (money) terms, professionals spend about four times as much per person as do their unemployed counterparts.

This evidence gives some support to the view that there are quite significant differences between manual and non-manual consumption patterns. Of course, it must be recognized that expenditure varies very much *within* each group. These are average figures. Levels of household expenditure depend crucially on the number of people in employment in the household, and the number of dependants. Nevertheless, class differences are still significant and to be expected given the weaker market situation of manual workers.

Internal differences: consumption cleavages?   Although class differences in consumption remain, many writers continue to see the *absolute* improvement in workers' living standards as of wider significance. Some, like Seabrook (1978), consider that the *aspirations* of the working class towards higher levels of consumption corrode values of solidarity. In a world where 'we are invited to define ourselves by what we can buy rather than what we can create,' workers become dehumanized, obsessed with an individualistic urge to consume, and are increasingly money-centred. Such concerns draw workers so heavily into the capitalist order that the values the labour movement embodied – cooperation, mutual support, care for the underprivileged, hope of a more creative way of life – get completely smothered.

Other authors argue that new patterns of consumption, especially of houses, divide the working class internally. *Consumption cleavages* have arisen between households with predominantely *private* access to housing and transport and those which depend on public provision (i.e. council housing and public transport). Consumption cleavages cut across classes: in 1979, 39 per cent of manual workers were owner-occupiers and 48 per cent owned a car. House ownership, in particular, may create differences of status and of material interests within the working class. Owner-occupiers have benefited financially since the 1960s because house prices have risen faster than inflation and because of tax relief on mortgages. The gains are, relatively, at the expense of tenants in rented housing. There has also been a certain prestige attached to owner-occupation, and perhaps some sense of greater control over one's life arising from ownership of property. Evidence for consumption cleavages comes from

Table 3.11 Expenditure per person on various services and commodities for certain occupational groupings of head of household in 1983 as proportion of skilled manual households (= 100)

	Occupation of head of household			
Commodity or service	Professional & technical employees	Clerical & related employees	Skilled manual workers	Unemployed manual workers
Housing	154	140	100	87
Food	113	114	100	78
Alcohol	98	99	100	59
Consumer durables	189	144	100	65
Transport	150	120	100	66
Services	195	161	100	66
Total expenditure per person (£s)	68.33	63.12	48.97	36.52
Total household expenditure (£s)	200.75	159.94	162.23	116.62

Source: Family Expenditure Survey (1983). Crown copyright.
Note: Expenditure per person has been derived by dividing the household expenditure for each commodity or service by the average number of persons per household. These figures have then been expressed as proportions of the equivalent figures for households whose head was a skilled manual worker.

analyses of voting behavior, which shows that manual workers who are home owners have been considerably more likely to vote Conservative than those who are council tenants. (See table 3.12 for a breakdown of housing tenure by socio-economic group.)

Privatization

The process of privatization: Privatization has been defined as 'a process . . . manifested in a pattern of social life which is centred on and, indeed, largely restricted to, the home and the conjugal family' (Goldthorpe et al., 1969, p. 97). This process was identified in the study of Luton in the 1960s. The social contacts of Luton manual workers were restricted to immediate kin (parents, spouse and children). They rarely

Table 3.12 Housing tenure of households, by socio-economic group of head of household, 1982 (percentages)

Socio-economic group of head of household[a]	Owner-occupied			Rented				Total number of households in sample[c] (thousands)
	Owned outright	Owned with mortgage	Local authority/ new town	Unfurnished private[b]	Furnished private	Rented with job or business		
Economically active heads								
Professional, employers and managers	19	68	5	2	2	4		1,536
Intermediate non-manual	17	60	10	6	4	2		696
Junior non-manual	17	46	21	7	5	3		607
Skilled manual and own account non-professional	15	41	35	6	1	2		2,343
Semi-skilled manual and personal service	11	24	48	8	3	6		1,025
Unskilled manual	15	12	60	8	4	1		272
Economically inactive heads	39	4	44	12	1	—		3,350
All heads of household	24	32	33	8	2	2		9,829

Notes: [a]Excludes households headed by members of the armed forces, full-time students, and those who have never worked.
[b]Includes those renting from a housing association.
[c]Excludes those living in caravans or houseboats, and cases where tenure is not known.

Source: Social Trends (1985), table 8.7. Crown copyright.

met workmates or neighbours. Most of their spare time was spent at home. The same patterns have been observed in other studies, by Young and Willmott (1973), in Greater London, Pahl (1984) on the Isle of Sheppey and Hill (1976) in the East End of London among dockers (see table 3.13). It remains possible that privatization is a localized phenomenon: all these studies were conducted in the South East of England. Moreover, the strength of the case for change again depends on the contrast with the traditional proletarian who spent non-work time in communal activities with neighbours and workmates. But even if the sociability of the traditional proletarian was exaggerated, and even if that sociability survives in the North, Wales and Scotland, there can be little doubt that many workers are 'privatized'.

The possible reasons for privatism are many. Most homes are more attractive places than they once were: they are less crowded and have more amenities for amusement and communication (televisions, videos, phones, etc.). They also absorb a large portion of most household budgets, which may encourage greater usage (or remove alternative possibilities). But, probably more important, are structural changes in industry and residence.

The disintegration of working-class communities has been a subject of much discussion because traditional proletarian political opposition tends to be community-based. Occupational communities develop where people working in the same industry live near one another, close to their place of work. A mining village is a classic case of an occupational community: pit-men who worked together were neighbours and also spent their non-work time in village institutions – clubs, churches, football teams, etc. (see the discussion of mining communities in chapter 7, section 7.3). Such settings have provided conditions for working-class solidarity. Solidarities emerging from conflicts with employers were reinforced outside work through overlapping loyalties of kinship, neighbourhood and friendship. Such places exhibited dense social networks and created strong group identities.

Such communities have become less common. Industrial change, urban 'renewal' and geographical mobility have combined together to destroy many such communities. Those industries which tended to generate occupational communities (coal-mining, shipbuilding, textiles, the railways) have declined considerably. New industries tend to be located long distances away from where their workers live. The geographical separation of workplace from residence is illustrated by comparing the picture of Preston in the 1930s with the ground-plan of Stevenage New Town (figure 3.6). In Preston, the cotton mills (see the chimneys) are spread evenly across the working-class districts of the town, each surrounded by closely packed terraced houses which would be occupied by the mill workers. Work and non-work were closely knit. The plan of Stevenage shows a sharp separation of industrial areas from commercial or residential areas. Workers in any one factory would be likely to be distributed thinly across the different housing estates (and beyond).

Table 3.13   Leisure activities and husband–wife segregation

Hill asked his sample of East London dockworkers and foremen how often in the past seven evenings they had spent more than one hour in any of these activities and how often they were accompanied by their wives.

| | DOCKWORKERS | | | | | |
| | Visit pub % | Stay home % | Outside entertain- ment % | Visit relatives % | Relatives visiting % | Visit friends % |
Frequency						
0	30	0	70	54	39	71
1	22	5	23	32	37	21
2	24	7	5	9	14	7
3	14	17	1	3	6	1
4	6	22	0	1	3	0
5	1	23	0	0	0	0
6	1	17	0	0	0	0
7	0	9	0	0	0	0
NA	1	1	1	1	1	1
Proportion of occasions when wife was present	41	89	89	63	99	66

| | FOREMEN | | | | | |
| | Visit pub % | Stay home % | Outside entertain- ment % | Visit relatives % | Relatives visiting % | Visit friends % |
Frequency						
0	52	3	61	46	58	61
1	17	3	28	36	28	24
2	13	11	5	13	9	11
3	9	8	2	2	2	1
4	3	26	0	0	0	0
5	0	20	0	0	0	0
6	0	11	0	0	0	0
7	0	15	0	0	0	0
NA	3	3	3	3	3	3
Proportion of occasions when wife was present	47	95	98	97	100	91

Source: Hill (1976) *The Dockers: class and tradition in London* (London, Heinemann), p. 228. Reproduced with permission of the author.

Figure 3.6 (a)   Aerial photograph of Preston in the 1930s. This demonstrates the high density and closely built-up nature of the early industrial town. Though open space is lacking, the town is small and open countryside is not far away (though not visible here); and, with factories scattered among houses, the journey to work is short.
Source: Aerofilms.

The same urban-planning policies have resulted in enforced geographical mobility. Although most manual workers have strongly preferred to stay near their place of birth, because kin and friends are there, as jobs are moved to new towns and away from the old cities they find little alternative but to follow the work. Even where work remains available in the cities, slum clearance and road building destroy communities. Social bonds of neighbourhood, which take a long time to develop, are upturned and cannot quickly be replaced. Residential mobility (moving house) also reduces the frequency of contact with kin, especially parents, which increases the social isolation of the conjugal family.

Privatization and class characteristics: Privatization is a process which tends to make manual workers more like clerical workers, but distinguishes them from professional and managerial workers. The latter groups of the service class are more involved in associations and have

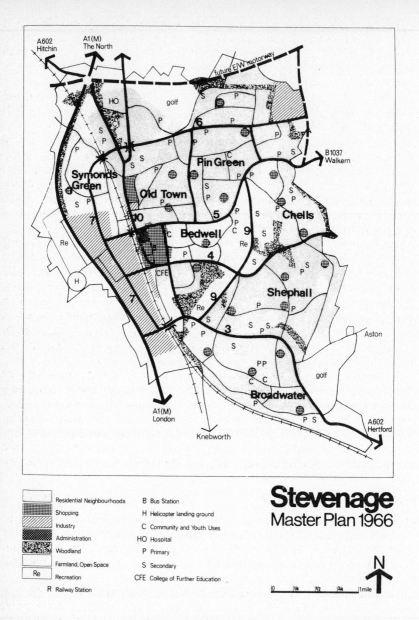

Residential Neighbourhoods
Shopping
Industry
Administration
Woodland
Farmland, Open Space
Re Recreation
R Railway Station

B Bus Station
H Helicopter landing ground
C Community and Youth Uses
HO Hospital
P Primary
S Secondary
CFE College of Further Education

Stevenage
Master Plan 1966

Figure 3.6 (b) The master plan for Stevenage, the first new town to be designated (in 1946). Built for London overspill and sited 30 miles north of the metropolis, in Hertfordshire, Stevenage is a good example of the 'Mark One' new town of the 1940s, designed on neighbourhood unit principles.
Source: The commission for the New Towns (1966). Reproduced with permission.

more dispersed networks of friends than do the former. The social life of manual workers has usually revolved around kin and, to a lesser degree, around neighbours. Residential mobility reduces the frequency of both these kinds of contacts.

Privatization probably has little effect on the homogeneity of the working class because it affects most manual workers. The privatized worker is *not* a distinctive type of worker, as Goldthorpe et al. (1969) suggested. The privatized worker cannot be usefully contrasted empirically with the proletarian because there is no such animal. Studies of traditional proletarians – of dockers and shipbuilders – show that privatization is affecting those workers. And studies of working-class norms and values have never uncovered a syndrome of practices or ideology which are specific to privatized workers. Some workers live more privatized lifestyles than others, but no-one has yet demonstrated that there is a systematic structural basis for this, or that it undermines traditionalism.

Privatization, however, probably reduces the capacity for collective solidarity from which political unity might be fashioned. Community solidarity has been one basis for the oppositional politics of labour. If the social circumstances for face-to-face interaction which reproduce communal solidarity are reduced, as they have been by urban change, then communal solidarity will weaken. (This process is largely independent of workplace solidarity, where one must anticipate the perpetuation of industrial class conflict.) Privatization might produce greater atomization and isolation among workers.

It remains possible, however, that the effect of privatization may be restricted to, or may be greatest, among owner-occupiers. There may yet be a link between consumption, privatization and divisions within the working class. There is some evidence that manual owner-occupiers develop some middle-class traits, both in voting behaviour and in patterns of sociability. So, perhaps consumption cleavages are developing and altering social life-styles as well. But this is not yet a very strong tendency.

Working-class politics

In many respects, the debates about the working class are aimed at resolving questions about political consciousness and action. Do workers identify themselves as a class with shared class interests? To what extent does this lead them to support membership of particular political organizations?

Class awareness and identification do not seem to have altered much in recent times. It continues to be the case that the 'subjective' class position of many manual workers (i.e. which class they consider themselves as belonging to) does not correspond with their 'objective' class position. Those manual workers who *do* consider themselves 'middle class' tend to be those with extensive social contacts with non-manual workers and/or those who live in predominantly middle-class areas.

The vast majority of British people (in most surveys about 90 per cent) recognize the existence of social classes and will see themselves as belonging to one of those classes. There is a good deal of variation in the way people describe those classes, and little consensus on how many classes there are or what it is that determines which class a person belongs to. Attempts to explain how different 'images of society' (as popular conceptions of class structure are often called) arise and are adopted have mostly failed. It is probably the case, however, that the more a manual worker shares the attributes of the traditional proletarian, the more likely she or he will see workers as a class. There is no reliable evidence that demonstrates that new images are emerging or spreading.

Distinctiveness: proletarians or citizens?

It used to be argued that the working class had a distinctive conception of social and political conflict which sustained its support for the labour movement. Thus, traditional proletarians had a dichotomous image of society, distinguishing sharply between 'them' (the rich, the owners, the bosses) and 'us' (the workers). From this arose both a class identity and a sense of politics as class conflict. For example, it was frequently reported in the 1960s that manual workers voted consistently for the Labour Party because it was the party of the workers, of 'people like us'.

Despite many claims to the contrary, recent sociological evidence suggests that this imagery and awareness remains predominant and is the only pattern consistently found among manual workers. Moorhouse (1976) pointed out that, despite there being considerable variation in workers' images of society, evidence from sociological surveys did show some considerable agreement that there was a small group of persons – aristocrats, owners or bosses – who had substantially more wealth and power than the majority of the population. He contested the significance of evidence showing that workers think of class in terms of monetary resources and that they are instrumental about improving their financial position. First, he suggested that workers had always been instrumental in that sense. Second, he argued that most responses in terms of the 'pecuniary' model of class (attributed to the 'new' workers) identified considerable differences in power between the minority and the majority – money was merely a way of symbolizing power differences. If this were the case, and Moorhouse corroborated it in some degree with evidence from a small survey of workers from Barking in 1972, then Lockwood and Goldthorpe's 'new working class' was actually very like their forebears.

A similar conclusion might be drawn from Roberts et al. (1977) study of class images in Liverpool in the early 1970s. They suggested that there was only one coherent image of society prevalent among the working class, and that was the proletarian image. This was held in different degrees of intensity and consistency: often it was so ill-formed and faint that it seemed unlikely to affect workers' political behaviour. The main exception was a group of manual workers whose attitudes were indistinguishable from those of the lower ranks of the middle class. There was no evidence for the existence of a new privatized/instrumental working class with a distinctive image of society.

It does not appear that respondents to questionnaires are showing any less awareness of class. Class remains something which they can observe and which they experience, and through which they view aspects of both politics and everyday life. Consider, for example, table 3.14. Every so often Gallup Polls, in their regular monthly opinion polls, ask a question about the importance of 'class struggle'. The answers to the same question posed at different times since 1964 show a very substantial increase in the percentage of respondents who consider there to be a class struggle. In March 1984, 74 per cent said there was one. Although the validity of the exact figures may be questioned, the trend in answers to the question is remarkable.

Table 3.14   Class struggle

Replies to the question, 'There used to be a lot of talk in politics about the "class struggle". Do you think there is a class struggle in this country or not?' (percentages)

	July 1964	June 1972	Jan. 1973	Feb. 1974	April 1975	April 1981	March 1984
Is	48	58	53	62	60	66	74
Is not	39	29	33	27	29	25	20
Don't know	13	13	14	11	11	9	6
Total	100	100	100	100	100	100	100

Source: Gallup Political Index (various years); and Moorhouse (1976).

The evidence from this poll suggests that working-class people do still feel some sense of class identity and consider that it affects their lives. This is probably the result both of living in a political environment which is structured by class interests, and by the experience of class in everyday life. However, the awareness of class only sustains a radical, alternative, political value-system among a minority of manual workers and is not often translated into class-based political action.

Perhaps the most distinctive feature of the working class in action is its lack of political participation. Although there are no accurate figures, individual membership of the Labour Party fell from about 1 million to a quarter of a million between 1950 and 1980 and in the process, the *proportion* of members who are manual workers has almost certainly been reduced. Parallel to that is the fall in the proportion of manual workers who are selected as candidates for the Labour Party at elections. The working class has become less involved in Labour Party politics, but has not replaced that by participation in other parties of the left or right. Although workers in 1983 voted for the Conservative Party and the

Alliance they are not joining them, nor the Communist Party either. The indications are that, as involvement in Labour politics declines, working-class people cease to participate in party politics, except to vote. Disillusionment with party politics and with governments among the working class is a process identified by opinion polls. Although other social classes express disillusionment with party politics, they have tended to participate through other channels: the campaigns of pressure groups and social movements, like the Campaign for Nuclear Disarmament (CND) are mostly run and supported by middle-class personnel. Increasingly, working-class political activity is restricted to voting and to industrial activity, where membership and support for trade unions remains extensive.

Voting behaviour is discussed in chapter 12, section 12.2. Briefly, the Labour Party remains dependent on manual workers for votes: of all those who voted Labour in 1983, 55 per cent were manual working class, the same proportion as in previous elections. However, only 20 per cent of manual workers who were eligible to vote, and only 38 per cent of those who actually *did* vote, chose Labour. Working-class support was, though, highly concentrated geographically, in the largest cities, in the North, South Wales and Scotland. Only in those areas can it be said that the working class exhibits distinctive, class-like, voting behaviour.

In most respects, the working class has become integrated into the dominant, national political institutions. This is true of both workers themselves and even more so of their principal political organization, the Labour Party.

Most workers accept the political order in Britain. They accept parliamentary institutions (including the House of Lords), the monarchy, the civil service, and law-enforcement agencies. They also accept the inequalities that arise from both the market and from political decisions. It is debatable to what extent this acceptance is based on a belief in the positive desirability of these institutions. Probably, acceptance is, 'pragmatic': because people believe that things are difficult if not impossible to change, and because it is unclear what might be better, no one puts up opposition. Pragmatic acceptance probably fades into a weak endorsement of the legitimacy of those institutions.

The low level of political class conflict in Britain is partly the result of the Labour Party's success. When in government, Labour has pursued egalitarian policies. Having aimed to extend political and social rights to all citizens equally, it has necessarily reduced some of the basis of class resentment. Comprehensive education, the National Health Service and economic planning procedures, have been justified in terms of their potential for removing class distinctions. When the Labour Party points to its achievements it legitimizes the mixed economy and the welfare state, encouraging workers to see themselves as *equal citizens* rather than as a deprived social class. In this way, the Labour Party, itself an organization deeply involved in the established political system, incorporates or integrates the working class into society.

The incorporation process is, however, never likely to be complete, largely because of the experience of work. It is ironic that the popularity of accounts bidding farewell to the working class should coincide with the miners' strike of 1984–5, the longest and one of the most bitter conflicts in the history of British industrial relations. The strike, lasting twelve months, was characterized, on the one hand, by intense solidarity and commitment by men and women in the communities on strike but, on the other hand, by divisions within the National Union of Mineworkers which led to the Nottinghamshire miners continuing to work. The state has become more involved in regulating industrial relations since the 1960s, so the boundary between industrial and political conflict has become hard to draw. In this way industrial action by workers such as the 1984–5 miners' strike, increasingly appears to be political action.

For these reasons, it is unwise to anticipate the end of working-class politics. It is true that worker opposition has moderated in recent years. But this is, importantly, because the conditions for the mobilization of opposition are unfavourable. First, deep economic recession does not provide fruitful circumstances for industrial conflict: unions are weakened by high levels of unemployment, redundancies and company bankruptcy. Also, the party political balance has lain with the Conservative Party for the last few years. The failure of the Labour Party to make much impact upon either the government or upon potential supporters among the working class is also part of the adverse current political climate. A second main reason for the relative political passivity of workers in current conditions probably derives from a lack of unity within the working class. The situation has been described by some authors as the *fragmentation* of the working class.

The politics of a fragmented working class?

As we have seen, the working class *is* internally differentiated. Never has there been a homogeneous working class in Britain but, arguably, it is more fragmented now than in the past, and this may account for the declining fortunes of the Labour Party. There are three main accounts of this fragmentation.

1 The main body of politically active workers used to be white males. Today, not only is the number of white, male, manual workers declining, but a larger proportion of all manual workers (close to 50 per cent) are either women or black people. Gender and ethnic differences create some distinctive political interests which have recently been the focus of political action. To the extent that these interests are in competition with those of white men, disunity follows.
2 The existence of many trade unions gives rise to another fragmenting force. Unions are run for their members. Often, this results in competition between unions: demarcation disputes are an example whereby one group of workers tries to exclude other groups from, usually

highly paid, tasks. This kind of competition frequently occurs between men and women too. Thus unions become 'sectionalist', that is putting the interests of the section of the class which they represent, before the interest of the class as a whole.

3 Differences within the class also occur between those organized in trade unions and those who are not. The organized tend to be better-off because they can exercise some power. However, their gains may be at the expense of the unorganized, which will again include many women and people from ethnic minorities, but also the unemployed and the retired. This is interpreted by, for example, Gorz (1985) as a process of polarization, whereby the organized perceive their interests to be served by the existing political system and, thus, become directly opposed to the remainder of workers. The working class is thus fundamentally divided with the minority of organized workers exercising its power at the expense of the rest.

All three of these accounts contain some truth. Whether any of these divisions justify bidding 'farewell to the working class' is largely a matter of judgment. We deal with some evidence for each account in turn.

1 Racist and sexist behaviour, common to all social classes in Britain (see chapters 4 and 5), is sometimes especially apparent in working-class environments. For instance, black people are disproportionately clustered in manual occupations and are likely to live in working-class residential areas. They may, thus, experience racism directly at the hands of working-class whites, a situation hardly likely to encourage class solidarity. The experiences of women in paid employment are somewhat similar. Some work cultures are aggressively masculine (see chapter 8, section 8.2), exhibiting hostility or contempt towards women. Trade unions often appear as organizations of men and for men, excluding women from participation and defending men's occupational interests. In many workplaces, supervisory workers are men and they use strategies of control which express male power (see chapter 4, section 4.6). Hence, ethnic and gender identities may inhibit class solidarity.

2 Union organizations open up other sectionalist divisions besides those based on ethnicity and gender. A union exists primarily to further the interests of its members (see chapter 2, section 2.5). In the process, unions come into conflict with one another: they compete for members and they try to give their own members a better deal than other unions can achieve. As bargaining has become more decentralized recently, with agreements made at plant rather than national level, wage differentials between workers in the same occupation have increased. Unions also fight about rights over particular jobs: a notorious incident of the 1980s concerns the dispute over newspaper production at Times Newspapers (see chapter 2, section 2.4) where one union permitted its members to operate new technology which another union had refused to use. So, there are bases for sectionalism among unions. But at the same time it

must be recognized that most unions still cooperate at plant, local, national and international levels. There have always been episodes of sectionalism, but allegiance to the trade-union movement has not been undermined.

3 Perhaps the most widely voiced argument is the third, concerning polarization. Organized workers in paid employment are generally better-off than the unorganized, not to mention the unemployed and other welfare recipients. Organized workers have benefited from their improved representation in the corridors of power over the last 50 years. The so-called 'corporatism thesis' (see also chapter 12.4) is one indication of this. Corporatism refers to the presence of institutionalized bargaining between the central organizations of capital and labour (in Britain, the Confederation of British Industry, CBI, and the Trades Union Congress, TUC), coordinated by the state, with a view to planning the economy and regulating wages. In such a system the interests of the most powerful groups among the working class are represented, but the unorganized are ignored. The weakness of the corporatism thesis is that it overestimates the power of the trade unions and fails to recognize the role that the TUC plays in pressing for social reforms which benefit other, weaker, social groups.

We are inclined to believe that all these divisions are old and persistent and do not imply a qualitatively new type of politics.

Summary

There are no simple and unambiguous solutions to the question of the condition of the contemporary working class. However, the following points may be made.

1 Manual workers are a declining proportion of all workers; and an increasing proportion of manual workers are either female and/or from ethnic minorities.

2 Manual workers in aggregate remain socially distinctive, particularly in respect of their market situation, their status situation, consumption patterns and political imagery. However, there is overlap, especially with workers in routine non-manual occupations.

3 In some respects, especially in work situation and privatized life-style, manual workers are indistinguishable from routine non-manual workers; but they still remain distinct from professional and managerial workers in these respects.

4 There is considerable internal differentiation within the manual working class. This has always been the case, but it may be increasing, creating political divisions within the working class along lines of ethnicity, gender, region and union membership.

5 The effects of these divisions on working-class political movements for social change (socialism) are uncertain, but quite clearly dependent upon

the relations established between manual workers and other non-manual employees.

Related topics

The material dealt with in this section appears in many other places in the book. A few of the more important sections which give greater understanding of the circumstances of the working class are as follows: chapter 2, sections 2.4 on work, 2.5 on trades unions and industrial relations, 2.8 on unemployment; chapter 3, section 3.7 on social mobility; chapter 4, section 4.2 on women and employment; chapter 5, section 5.3 on ethnic disadvantage; chapter 8, section 8.4 on inequalities in education; chapter 10, sections 10.3 on leisure and 10.4 on working-class youth cultures; and chapter 12, section 12.2 on voting.

3.5 The Middle Classes

The growth of the middle class

The starting point of any sociological analysis of the middle-class is the growth of certain kinds of occupations in the twentieth century (see table 3.15). The most noticeable shift in the period 1911–71 was the steep decline in classes 5–7 (manual workers) and the growth of the number of foremen and supervisory positions and the three white-collar categories, of clerks, employers and managers, and professionals. Over the years 1911–71, classes 5–7 lost over 21 per cent of the total employed population, made up of 6.5 per cent to professionals, over 2 per cent to managers and employers, 9 per cent to clerks, and over 2.5 per cent to foremen. The white-collar categories themselves did not all gain equally. The higher professional group more than tripled in size, managers more than doubled, while the size of the employer group declined. The *rate* of growth of white-collar occupations has also varied over time. The growth in the clerical grade, for example, was at its highest in the years 1911–21, while the higher professional category increased most quickly between 1951 and 1971.

For both men and women, there has been a shift out of manual work into white-collar occupations. However, the movement out of manual work has been greater for women (30 per cent) than for men (16 per cent). Significantly, disproportionate numbers of women have moved into clerical work and, indeed, the proportion of men employed as clerks has hardly increased between 1911 and 1971. As far as the other categories of non-manual work are concerned, however, the increase in the numbers of male managers, and of higher and lower professionals, is considerably greater than for their female equivalents. In moving out of manual work in the twentieth century, therefore, men have tended to go into the higher white-collar jobs and women into the more routine ones.

Table 3.15 Occupational class of the gainfully employed population of Britain, 1911–71 (percentages)

	All					Men					Women				
	1911	1921	1931	1951	1971	1911	1921	1931	1951	1971	1911	1921	1931	1951	1971
1 Professional															
A Higher	1.00	1.01	1.14	1.93	3.29	1.34	1.36	1.50	2.56	4.87	0.20	0.18	0.29	0.52	0.55
B Lower	3.05	3.52	4.46	4.70	7.78	1.61	2.02	2.03	3.16	5.95	6.49	7.07	6.83	8.18	10.95
2 Employers and managers															
A Employers	6.71	6.82	6.70	4.97	4.22	7.74	7.69	7.65	5.74	5.07	4.28	4.74	4.44	3.22	2.75
B Managers	3.43	3.64	3.66	5.53	8.21	3.91	4.28	4.54	6.78	10.91	2.30	2.11	1.60	2.73	3.51
3 Clerical workers	4.84	6.72	6.97	10.68	13.90	5.48	5.40	5.53	6.35	6.38	3.30	9.90	10.34	20.41	27.00
4 Foremen	1.29	1.44	1.54	2.62	3.87	1.75	1.91	2.00	3.28	5.04	0.18	1.32	0.45	1.14	1.84
5–7 Manual workers	79.67	76.85	76.53	69.58	58.23	78.17	77.32	76.73	72.12	61.79	83.25	75.68	76.05	63.81	53.40

Source: Adapted from Routh (1980) Occupation and Pay in Great Britain (London and Basingstoke, Macmillan, and Atlantic Highlands, NJ, Humanities Press International, Inc.), p. 6, table 1.1, with permission.

Some further light on these differences is thrown by table 3.16, which shows the gender composition of white-collar occupational groupings. The higher professional category is overwhelmingly male, and there was less change in this area of employment than in any other. In the lower professions, an initial preponderance of women in 1911 was turned into a position of more or less equality by 1971, largely through the heavy recruitment of male teachers. Similarly, the proportion of women managers also declined over the period. The sex composition of the clerical grade, on the other hand, was almost reversed. While almost 80 per cent of clerks were men in 1911, 70 per cent of them were women in 1971.

Table 3.16   Gender composition of certain occupations, 1911–71 (percentages)

	Men					Women				
	1911	1921	1931	1951	1971	1911	1921	1931	1951	1971
1 Professional										
A Higher	94.02	95.54	92.50	91.94	93.93	5.97	5.13	7.50	8.29	6.07
B Lower	37.14	40.59	41.21	46.46	48.61	62.86	59.26	58.79	53.54	51.39
2 Employers and managers										
A Employers	81.17	79.51	80.13	79.96	76.23	18.83	20.49	19.73	19.95	23.77
B Managers	80.45	82.95	87.01	84.75	84.37	19.87	17.05	12.99	15.17	15.63
3 Clerical workers	79.82	56.62	55.77	41.18	29.12	20.18	43.38	44.23	58.82	70.88

Source: Calculated from Routh (1980), p. 6, table 1.1.

Not only have there been significant movements between classes, there have also been important changes within them. Within the higher professions for example, the numbers of engineers increased by 17 times from 1911, to 1971, while scientists were 15 times as strongly represented, and accountants 7 times as numerous. The traditional professions – law, medicine, and the military – only doubled their numbers, while the numbers of clergy actually declined. The lower professions are dominated by government service. Teachers and nurses alone accounted for 57 per cent in this category in 1911 and 58 per cent in 1971. Social-welfare workers and laboratory technicians increased some 20-fold in the same 60 years, while the numbers of teachers and nurses only quadrupled, an increase which included a striking growth in the numbers of male teachers and nurses.

There has, thus, been an impressive growth in the numbers of persons employed in white-collar tasks, a growth concentrated in newer occupations rather than in traditional middle-class occupations such as lawyers, doctors or clergymen. How do we interpret these changes? Does the occupational shift from manual to white-collar employment represent a significant alteration in the class structure towards the creation of a larger and more solid middle class? Three different solutions are offered in the sociological literature to this question.

1   It is argued that there are only two main classes with, perhaps, an intermediate stratum which does not, however, really constitute a middle class. Such a position is usually, though not invariably, informed by Marxist arguments. Critical here is the idea that large sections of the middle class are becoming *proletarianized*, that is, are becoming more and more like the working class in their conditions of life or 'life-chances'.
2   A number of writers suggest that, even if a two-class model might be appropriate to the nineteenth century, contemporary societies have a three-class structure with a prominent middle class. Giddens (1973) is a well-known exponent of such a position.
3   A third view is that the middle class actually comprises a number of very different elements which makes it difficult to see it as a coherent class. Indeed, in this view the class structure as a whole is so fragmented into different groups that it hardly makes sense to think in terms of discrete social classes.

Routine white-collar workers

As we have already implied, one critical issue in deciding between these three theories of the middle class is that of proletarianization. If it can be shown that much white-collar work is, in most respects, similar to manual work, then the idea that there is a large and significant middle class is greatly undermined. However, this is a complex question. Firstly, we cannot necessarily assume that there is one single *working* class, which parts of the middle class are said to resemble (see section 3.4). Second, the criteria of proletarianization are not that clear. Lockwood's (1958) classical study gives us some guidance, in distinguishing *market* (pay, hours of work, promotion prospects), *work* (social relationships at work) and *status* (prestige and political inclinations) aspects of the clerk's position. If, in these three respects, the routine white-collar worker's position is like that of the manual worker, then one might reasonably speak of his or her proletarianization.

Market situation

Earnings: There is widespread agreement that there is a fairly well-marked gap between average manual and non-manual earnings, a gap which has, furthermore, remained remarkably constant over the last 70 years or so. This apparently persistent difference is reinforced by continuing differences in earnings over the career as a whole, fringe benefits of different kinds, and job security (see above, section 3.4). However comparisons of this kind can be misleading, for there are substantial overlaps between non-manual and manual occupations if one breaks down the larger categories. In other words, the market situation of *some* non-manual occupations resembles that of manual occupations. Kelly (1980), for example, in his study of civil servants, found that there had been a decline nationally in the manual/non-manual differential which was reflected in civil-service salaries. Management grades had, more or less, held their own, but among clerks 'a very definite decline in salaries *vis-à-vis* manual workers has occurred and civil service clerks have done even less well than clerks in other occupations' (p. 131). Nor had clerks actually preserved an advantage in their career earnings which followed a similar pattern to those of manual workers. In respect of hours of work, fringe benefits, pension schemes, sick-pay schemes and job security, routine white-collar workers may be better placed, although the evidence does not allow very precise discriminations within the non-manual sector. There is some evidence, however, that the traditional resistance of clerical grades to unemployment, when compared with manual workers, is being eroded.

Promotion: A more subtle way in which the market situation of routine white-collar workers may differ from that of manual workers is in the greater promotion prospects enjoyed by non-manual workers in general. The recent study of Stewart et al. (1980) offers data which bears on this question, arguing that proletarianization has not occurred. The authors' starting point is a consideration of the age structure of the occupation 'clerk' (see figure 3.7). There are two age peaks which seem to represent two distinct elements, ex-manual workers moving into clerical work with advancing age, and those starting as clerks who will mostly move out of the occupation as they get older (see figure 3.8). The age distribution of clerks is presumptive evidence that clerical work represents a route of upward mobility. Further evidence is provided by examining the promotion prospects and histories of clerks. If the age 30 is taken as the watershed in a clerical career, only 19 per cent of current clerks over 30 started their careers as clerks; 73 per cent of all those who began as clerks, *and* are still in white-collar occupations, have been promoted. In fact, 30 per cent of those starting as clerks leave white-collar work altogether but that still means that half of all those starting as clerks will be promoted. Of course, in considering promotion and mobility one must consider not only the chances of promotion but also the distance travelled. Stewart et al. (1980) believe, for various reasons, that promotion is likely to be long-range: once started in the hierarchy, clerks can travel far.

Stewart et al. argue that, because of the way that clerks move over their work life, one cannot talk sensibly about the proletarianization of white-collar workers of this type. Since, over their career, most clerks will be promoted, they cannot be proletarianized. In sum, while clerical work may have become more routine, no *people* have been proletarianized, therefore there is no proletarianization.

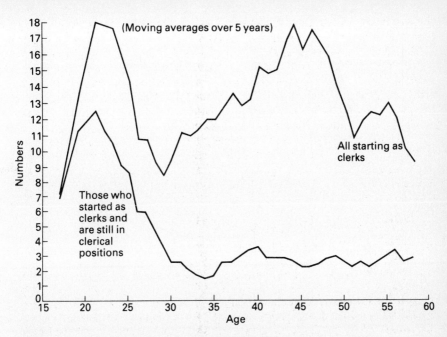

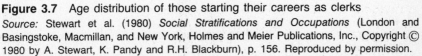

Figure 3.7 Age distribution of those starting their careers as clerks

Source: Stewart et al. (1980) *Social Stratifications and Occupations* (London and Basingstoke, Macmillan, and New York, Holmes and Meier Publications, Inc., Copyright © 1980 by A. Stewart, K. Pandy and R.H. Blackburn), p. 156. Reproduced by permission.

The argument of Stewart et al., that clerical work represents an occupational category through which people pass on their way to management positions, is given some support by the data from the Nuffield Mobility Study (see section 3.7). However, as Crompton and Jones (1984) point out, the relatively good promotion chances of male clerks are dependent on two factors that may depend on a relatively favourable economic situation. First, there has to be a continuing supply of managerial positions for clerks to be promoted to. Second, the high *proportion* of junior clerks being promoted will only be possible if a substantial minority leave clerical work for other occupations, but other work may be hard to find in a changed economic environment. In addition, Crompton and Jones criticize these recent studies of social mobility because they are based on the mobility experiences of *male* employees. But since these occupations are largely female, a study of male clerical workers can say little about clerical workers as a whole.

Gender differences: As we showed at the beginning of this chapter, one of the most striking features of the white-collar occupations is the way in which women have moved into the routine jobs, while not greatly improving their position in the higher reaches. In 1911, 11 per cent of

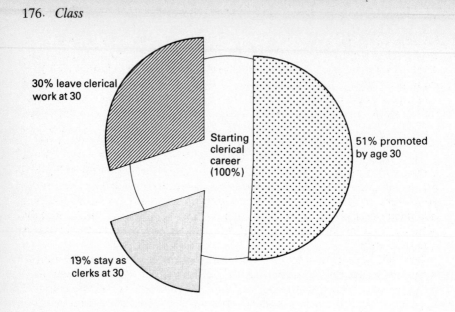

Figure 3.8 The promotion chances of male clerks
Source: From Stewart et al. (1980).

clerks were women; in 1921, 44 per cent; in 1951, 59 per cent; and in 1971, the proportion had risen to 71 per cent. In some occupations, the proportion is even higher. Almost 99 per cent of secretaries and 83 per cent of telephone operators, for example, are women. Office employment has, of course, attracted women for some considerable time and women formed the bulk of office labour well before office work became noticeably automated. Furthermore, other white-collar employments, such as that of shop assistant, have been female preserves for some time. This heavy, and increasing, concentration of women in routine white-collar work is reflected in their lower rates of pay. The New Earnings Survey of 1985, for example, showed that the average hourly earnings of adult male clerical workers was 396 pence while their female counterparts only earned 318 pence.

Promotion prospects for women in routine white-collar jobs are also limited, certainly more limited than those for young men in the same occupations. This is partly because of the way that women's work lives are structured. Generally speaking, in white-collar work, women enter employment directly from school, continue working when they marry, but stop when they start a family. When their children have left home they will go back to work. This break in the career has a number of consequences. First, employers do not believe that younger women will be with them long enough to be promoted. Second, the women themselves do not think it worthwhile undertaking further training which might qualify them for promotion. Women, in other words, have low expectations of their work and employers respond to those expectations. That is, however, only part of the story. Crompton and Jones (1984), in their study of female white-collar workers, concluded that a number of employers (or their managers) actively discriminate against women by, for example, dissuading them from taking examinations which are necessary for promotion. That generates resentment. As one of Crompton and Jones's respondents said: 'Well men get priority, they're looked after first, they move on quicker even when they're not as efficient. The bank say they're not biased but they are. We're not dim, we can see it around us. But when you get passed over you lose interest in your work' (p. 155). Interestingly, Crompton and Jones also found that qualifications did not seem to have much to do with the kinds of skills actually used in work; unqualified women are doing work as skilled as qualified men.

It would be dangerous to assume that the career patterns of women in white-collar work will continue to take this form. The expectations held by women may well change, in that they may actively seek promotion and adjust their child-rearing patterns accordingly. Similarly, women may seek the qualifications previously largely reserved by men. There are signs that this is already taking place with increasing numbers of women taking banking and accountancy examinations.

Work situation

A number of features including mechanization, bureaucratization, and changing relations of authority, have an impact on the work situation of routine white-collar workers. The computer may represent a particularly dramatic way of reorganizing office work but other machines have also replaced particular traditional skills. Duplicators, photocopiers, dictating and addressing machines and, more recently, word processors, have all had a large and growing impact in large offices. Within the period 1956–66 in the civil service, there was a 400 per cent increase in duplicators and photocopiers. Some indication of the extent of office mechanization can also be gauged from the numbers of persons employed in various branches of office work. Routh (1980), for example, shows that the number of typists increased much faster than the rest of the clerical group between 1931 and 1951. In the next 20 years, however, the number of office machine operators rapidly increased, while typists just about kept pace with the group as a whole. There are indications that, since 1971, the proportional rate of decline in the typist category accelerated. In a further index of office mechanization Crompton and Jones (1984) found that 89 per cent of the white-collar workers they interviewed in banking, life-insurance and local authorities worked with computers.

The introduction of computers usually means a centralization of activities, a tendency also produced by the introduction of other machines. These are all so expensive that it only makes economic sense to have them concentrated on one place, in a 'word processing centre', for example, to benefit from economies of scale. Centralization of this kind will clearly have implications for the conditions of work of white-collar employees, but it would be misleading to attribute these effects entirely to the machines themselves. It is the way that machines are allied to new ways of organizing *human* labour that will have the most significant impact on the work situation. Indeed, in the literature designed to help management with the introduction of computers, it is constantly emphasized that mere mechanization is insufficient. Machines are only efficient to the extent that they are incorporated into a reorganized labour process. Early failures in the use of office automation have been attributed to a mistaken emphasis on hardware, and the slow speed of introduction of word processors to an inability to reorganize the flow of work – an inability often due to the resistance of both management and workers. What is required, and what is happening to a great extent, is the introduction of a much greater division of labour into white-collar work. By breaking up the work into more separate stages, specialized machines can be introduced which require less-skilled workers, thus lowering the costs of production. One incidental benefit of this process, as far as management is concerned, is that the supervision of white-collar work is made more effective.

Automation embedded in these changed methods of work can produce conditions of work that approximate to those enjoyed (or rather not enjoyed) by manual workers. Office work becomes more routine, involves a smaller sphere of decision and responsibility, is more subject to managerial control, involves less skill, and takes place in organizations that are larger, more bureaucratized, and characterized by a minute division of labour. Downing (1980), for example, argues 'the move to word processing effectively transfers the control which the typist has over a conventional typewriter on to the machine itself. Word processors are designed with supervisory and monitoring elements built into them. In addition, the word processor can perform all the elementary functions of typing which take a person years to perfect' (p. 283). The introduction of the word processor thus takes away a substantial degree of control over the typist's work, permits a lower level of skill, fragments the labour process, for example by having printing done elsewhere, and lessens personal contact between typists, and between typists and principals. McNally (1979) distinguishes the secretary from the routine office worker. Her analysis of the latter is similar to Downing's in that the worker is seen as being machine-paced, performing entirely routine work, and separated from management. However, in her view, even the personal secretary's position is being undermined by office reorganization, since mechanization has made typing and shorthand obsolete skills. In conclusion, white-collar work, especially in offices but also, for example, in shops, is becoming characterized by a greater and greater division of labour and is making the work situation of this section of the middle class very much like that of substantial parts of the working class.

Status situation

The third criterion of proletarianization provided by Lockwood (1958) is that of status or style of life.

If middle-class people see themselves as middle class, or are seen by others as middle class, or behave differently from the working class, then it might be more difficult to speak of middle class occupations as being proletarianized. There is some evidence that, if one takes the middle classes as a whole, there are differences between the middle and working classes in their styles of life. Other chapters in this book show some of these differences in education, family life, voting, and residential areas, for example. Evidence on the status and style of life of *routine* white-collar workers is, however, much more sketchy. One study, however, found a substantial section of the middle class who placed themselves in the same class as manual workers (Roberts et al., 1977).

Despite these considerations, we would argue that the notions of status and style of life should not be criteria of class membership. These do not enter into the *determination* of class but are best seen as crucial *effects* of class position, that can, in turn, serve as partial explanations of action by middle class groups. The most important way in which action by the middle class is researched is in the many investigations of white-collar trade unions (discussed also in chapter 2, section 2.5). The critical issue is whether white-collar trade unions are different from manual trade unions, reflecting a different class basis of membership.

To summarize much of the literature, the prevailing view is that, as white-collar occupations become more mechanized and bureaucratized, so white-collar unions become, in their industrial policies, more like manual unions. For example, in his recent study of British civil servants, Kelly (1980) suggests that three groups of workers – managers, scientists and clerks – have responded very differently to changes within the civil service. The clerical group have become more like a manual trade union, with a strike policy, the use of militant action, and close links with the TUC. The scientists, on the other hand, have behaved more like a professional association. The activities of the managerial association have been something of a compromise between these two positions, although more recently it has taken up a more militant posture. In Kelly's view, these differences in union militancy are to be explained in terms of the degree to which the particular occupations have been bureaucratized, mechanized and feminized. In conclusion, the evidence suggests that in *certain* respects, some routine white-collar workers have styles of life and take political actions not unlike those of manual workers, a convergence that is in part due to change in the *working* class (see section 3.4).

Managers and professionals – the service class

So far we have argued that there is a substantial section of the middle class which, chiefly in its work situation but also in its market situation,

Box 9   Gender differences in white-collar unionism in Britain, 1948–74

Membership of white-collar unions (000s)

Male				% increase		Female				% increase
1948	1964	1970	1974	1948–74	1970–4	1948	1964	1970	1974	1948–74
1267	1681	2143	2593	+104.7	+21.0	697	1003	1447	1629	+133.7

Union density (%)

Male				% increase		Female				% increase
1948	1964	1970	1974	1948–74	1970–4	1948	1964	1970	1974	1948–74
33.8	33.4	40.0	44.5	+10.7	+4.5	25.4	24.9	30.7	32.6	+7.2

Source: From *Women for Hire: a study of the female office worker* by Fiona McNally. © Fiona McNally 1979, p. 48, and reprinted by permission of Macmillan London and Basingstoke and St. Martin's Press, Inc.

This table shows that men and women white-collar workers do not join unions to the same extent. The top part of the table gives information about the numbers of men and women joining unions in the period 1948–74. The increase in women union members is 133.7 per cent, while that for men is 104.7 per cent. However, these figures can be misleading, for the proportions of men and women in white-collar work have also been changing over that period: white-collar work is now overwhelmingly female. A more reliable measure of unionization is, therefore, the *proportion* of people in any occupation who are unionized. This is usually called union density. The table shows that union density for both men and women has increased between 1948 and 1970; a higher proportion of white-collar workers are unionized. However, the growth in union density for women is less than that for men, even though the *numbers* of women show a greater increase.

has a class position increasingly resembling that of the working class. The corollary of this is that the category of routine white-collar workers is also sharply distinct from the 'upper' part of the middle class – the managers, higher professionals, businessmen – and even from some sections of the 'lower' professionals including teachers and nurses. The market and work situation of these categories is much better than that of routine white-collar workers.

Thus, average earnings of the 'upper' part of the middle class are considerably higher than those of routine white-collar workers. In 1978, for example, higher professionals earned an average of £8,286, managers £8,050, lower professionals £5,435 and clerical workers £3,701 (Routh, 1980). In addition, there are sharp differences in holiday entitlements, sick pay and pension arrangements. Perhaps equally as important, the higher middle-class occupations can expect steady promotion through a *career* – or at least the men can. In a large number of cases this is because these occupations are found in large bureaucracies, whether in private companies or state agencies. Bureaucracies of this kind function as 'internal labour markets', giving many employees relatively stable expectations about opportunities that will be open to them. They expect career rewards, having fulfilled specific and known requirements.

Careers within bureaucracies do not only involve steadily improving pay and conditions. They also imply changes in work situation. Professionals and managers, unlike routine white-collar workers, enjoy considerable freedom from control. Indeed it is more usually they who do the controlling (see chapter 2, section 2.6, on the occupational control exercised by professionals). This provides a sphere of autonomy within which it is possible to organize and pace work as one likes, taking responsibility for the work done. Professional and managerial work is also relatively more skilled, less sub-divided and mechanized. An illustration of the greater skill and control exercised by managerial grades is given in box 10. Technical staff also tend to have greater autonomy and skill. Computer programmers and systems analysts, partly because of the technical nature of their work, have considerable freedom from supervision. As Hales (1980) says of his work as a systems analyst: 'At the most basic level of the apparatus of work – time economy – my activity is more or less self structure. This derives partly from managerial recognition that "problem solving" is an open-ended process and partly from the status of a "responsible" employee who is not expected to need close supervision' (p. 35).

To set against this superior work and market situations, there is some evidence that the processes of mechanization and division of labour affecting routine white-collar work are also having an impact on middle management, professional occupations and, especially, the lower professions. For example, after mechanization and reorganization of offices, the power to make decisions, often offered as the definition of management, passes up the hierarchy to top management or to the new specialist groups. Computers, for instance, can make many of the more routine decisions previously made by bank managers. Computer programming, which originally included the whole process of software preparation and demanded the involvement of highly skilled professionals, has become subdivided and rationalized into sets of less-skilled tasks. Leggatt (1970) points to the manner in which the work situation of teachers is degraded by employment in bureaucratic institutions which more minutely control what is done in the classroom. Freeman (in Fraser,

Box 10 Work description (degree of control) by grade level[a] (percentages)

	Cohall		Lifeco		Southbank		All[c]	
	Clerical[b] grades	Administra-tive[b] and supervisory grades	Clerical grades	Administra-tive and supervisory grades	Clerical grades	Administra-tive and supervisory grades	Clerical grades	Administra-tive and supervisory grades
No control, simple rules	39	0	32	23	79	5	50	13
No control, medium complex rules	41	33	60	50	21	26	41	37
Self control	20	67	8	20	0	68	10	50
Total	100	100	100	100	100	99[d]	100	100
Total number	64	15	60	20	58	19	182	54

Notes: [a] Programmers and systems analysts have been excluded from this table.

[b] We have standardized grade levels across the three organizations to allow for comparison. Thus, in this table, 'clerical grades' includes grades 1–4 in Lifeco, and clerical grades 1–3 on the local authority scale for Cohall, but only grades 1 and 2 for Southbank. Administrative and supervisory grades include APT local-authority grades, executive officer 1 and 2 at Lifeco, and clerical grades 3 and 4 at Southbank.

[c] Higher-grade levels have been excluded (they amounted to 16.6% of our interviews), that is, grades of PO and above at Cohall, E3 and above at Lifeco, and Appointed Officer and above at Southbank.

[d] Because of rounding, percentages may not add to 100.

Source: Crompton and Jones (1984), *White-Collar Proletariat: deskilling and gender in clerical work* (Macmillan, London and Basingstoke and Temple University Press), p. 62. Reproduced with permission.

Crompton and Jones's study is of white-collar workers in three organizations, a local authority (Cohall), an insurance company (Lifeco) and a bank (Southbank). The data is presented for clerical grades and for administrative grades by the kind of task that each grade performed. The authors distinguished tasks that required the worker:

1 to exercise no control and were governed by simple rules such as data punching;

2 to exercise no control but where the rules were quite complex, like checking errors; and

3 to exercise discretion and self-control, for example writing non-standard letters.

Clearly, administrative personnel tended to perform the third kind of task and clerical workers the first or second. Only 10 per cent of clerks had self-control in their work, while only 13 per cent of administrators had jobs dominated by simple rules. There were, however, substantial differences between the organizations, differences that reflect the degree of mechanization and division of labour. In the bank, for example, three-quarters of the clerks worked at the lowest level of skill. Supervisors were most self-directed in the bank and the local authority. In general, then, the more mechanized and rationalized the organization, the greater is the difference between clerks and managers.

1968) shows how journalistic work is subdivided with each journalist producing a small proportion of each story. In a more general way, Crompton and Jones (1984) present evidence which suggests that the content of some junior managerial work has become more 'proletarian' over time. Many middle- to lower-level managers spend very little of their time exercising what are commonly thought of as managerial functions. Indeed, the content of their job may differ little from that of their alleged subordinates (see also chapter 2, section 2.3). Deskilling, therefore, increasingly affects the lower reachers of the upper-middle class, especially junior management and the 'lower' professions such as nurses, teachers and social workers.

Conclusion: the divisions in the middle class

We conclude that the occupational category usually referred to as the middle class is, in reality, divided into two unequal sections with some intermediate strata in between. The larger part has a market and work situation not dissimilar to large sections of the working class. The smaller part has a much more advantageous situation. In between these two sections is a further set of occupations largely composed of lower management, parts of the lower professions, and technicians, who may have better market and work conditions than clerks or shop assistants, but who do not have the control over their work and the rewards of higher managers and professionals. These groups are also particularly vulnerable to the rationalizing and deskilling processes described earlier.

There is one other group, not so far mentioned, which does to some extent also fit in between the service class and routine white-collar workers. These are small businessmen, shopkeepers and traders, or people working on their own account. Many of these people are in a paradoxical position for their market and work situations diverge. On the one hand, they have some control over their work lives, being able to regulate and pace their tasks and deploy considerable skill. On the other hand, their pay and conditions often approximate to that of clerks or skilled manual workers. For example in 1968, many of the small shopkeepers studied by Bechofer et al. (1968) were earning little more than many manual workers. This relatively low income was earned by very long hours of work in poor conditions. The average working day was 10.5 hours, with the two most numerous groups – grocers and news-agents – exceeding this figure.

Summary

1 There has been a substantial growth in the proportion of people employed in middle-class occupations. Women now occupy some three-quarters of the positions in clerical work.

2 The middle class can be divided into two major sections, the 'upper' middle class and routine white-collar workers, with certain occupational groupings, for example, junior management and some of the lower professions, ranged in between.

3 Routine white-collar workers have very much poorer work and market situations than upper-middle-class workers. Their pay, hours of work, holidays and pension arrangements compare unfavourably. The promotion possibilities for male clerks are, on the other hand, fairly good, although for women, who form the bulk of the occupation, they are not. The white-collar work situation is increasingly mechanized and deskilled and lacks autonomy.

4 Upper-middle-class occupations, on the other hand, have a good market situation and work situation over which they have considerable control and can deploy their skill.

5 Junior management and the lower professions have a generally better market situation than routine white-collar workers but their work situations are continually threatened by mechanization and greater bureaucratic control.

Related topics

Chapter 2, section 2.3 gives detailed consideration to the nature of managerial occupations. Further discussion of professionals is to be found in section 2.6.

3.6 The Upper Class

In the previous section on the middle class, we distinguished an upper-middle class from a routine middle class which is becoming proletarianized. Although the upper-middle *appears* to merge with the upper class, actually the latter is separated by a number of important features which may be summarized as property, networks, and power.

Property and wealth

The most obvious point to make is that the upper class is wealthy. In section 3.3 we have shown how unequal is the distribution of income in Britain and how even more unequal is the distribution of wealth. Atkinson and Harrison (1978) estimate that, during the past 20 years, the top 1 per cent of wealth-holders owned about one-third of the country's wealth, although the exact porportion has fluctuated somewhat. Taking a longer-term perspective, this proportion has fallen considerably from an estimated two-thirds immediately before the First World War. Income appears to be more equally distributed. Townsend (1979), for example, estimates that the top 1 per cent of income earners took only 6.2 per cent of total income. Part of the reason for this discrepancy is that the wealth of the upper classes is not necessarily used to produce income which would only be liable to high rates of tax. (For more detailed treatment of the distribution of income and wealth see section 3.3.)

Since wealth is at least *potential* income, its concentration is the key to the market situation of the upper class. Changes in the way that wealth is taxed in this century may have led wealthy individuals to disperse their wealth more widely in their family during their lifetime. Very import- antly, therefore, we are not talking of wealthy individuals in the upper class but wealthy *families*. In this context, inheritance is of great significance. In general, individuals or families are wealthy because their fathers were also. As one detailed study concluded 'inheritance is the major determinant of wealth inequality. The regression analysis attri- buted some two-thirds of the inequality in the distribution of wealth in 1973 to inheritance. The proportions of top wealth leavers since the mid- fifties who were preceded by rich fathers was shown . . . to be in excess of 60 per cent' (Harbury and Hitchens, 1979, p. 136).

In referring to the upper class as propertied, we do not only mean to say that individuals and families in that class are wealthy. Property confers income and a favourable market situation. It also gives control. The upper class, in other words, are not merely passive in the luxurious enjoyment of continuous leisure. It is also a question of how property is *used*.

In chapter 2, section 2.2 we reviewed changes in the pattern of ownership and control in Britain. The most important conclusions are:

1   the ownership of land is more dispersed;
2   through take-overs and mergers, many businesses have grown larger;
3   ownership of business no longer typically lies in the hands of families but is relatively more dispersed via share ownership, particularly to various financial institutions;
4   wealthy families no longer have their assets concentrated in particular areas such as land but have them dispersed over various fields of activity.

One of the consequences of these changes is, as Scott (1982) points out, the creation of a unified propertied class in the twentieth century, a class, moreover, which had to *use* its capital actively to perpetuate its privileged position. As Scott says: 'the core of the class consists of those who are actively involved in the strategic control of the major units of capital of which the modern economy is formed . . . the class of property-owners is transformed into a business class' (p. 114). The upper class as a whole depends on the activities of this core which is extremely small, estimated by Scott as about 0.1 per cent of the population, or between 25,000 and 50,000 people. The members of this core occupy positions of leadership in

Figure 3.9 A scene from upper-class English life
Source: BBC Hulton Picture Library.

the large businesses in Britain whether those businesses are largely in manufacturing or banking and finance. Scott points out that, although small, the core of the upper class is not homogeneous. There are three important groups – entrepreneurial capitalists, internal capitalists and finance capitalists. The first of these will own a substantial part of the enterprise which may well have been founded by the entrepreneur or his family. Internal capitalists also have a main interest in one particular company although they will not have a substantial shareholding. They are the senior executives heading the extensive bureaucracies that run large companies. Finance capitalists, on the other hand, do not have an interest in any one company but are essentially concerned with the performance of the large company sector as a whole, often through the medium of financial institutions. The relationship between these three groups determines the pattern of control of business in Britain.

In sum, the upper class consists of wealthy families rather than individuals. Wealth is not passively enjoyed but is actively used. In this process, a small core of the upper class involved in the strategic control of large business is crucial to the continued privileges of the upper class. This mention of strategic control, incidentally, shows how the upper class's work situation differs from that of the upper-middle class discussed in section 3.5. Members of the upper-middle class are essentially managers who carry out day-to-day technical, professional and administrative functions. Although their role in modern businesses is clearly important, they do not have overall strategic control over the enterprise. That control – decisions over investment, new markets, relations with other companies, for instance – lies with the senior executives who belong to the core of the upper class. It is that capacity for control that differentiates the upper class from the middle classes.

Networks

We have already argued that discussion of the upper class should focus on families rather than individuals and that the relationships between entrepreneurial, internal and finance capitalists are important in the strategic control of large British business. These points imply that the *networks* of relationships between members of this very small class will be significant.

There are different kinds of networks, different kinds of relationships, between members of the upper class. There are marriage or kinship relations, friendship or the 'old boy network', business and financial relationships, and the whole area of common background formed, amongst other things, by school and university. We have already referred to the way that the wealth of upper-class individuals largely derives, by inheritance, from family connections. Members of the upper class also tend to marry other upper-class individuals, giving the class a unity based on kinship and marriage. This has, of course, always been the case. In the nineteenth century, when individual families controlled large businesses, there was extensive intermarriage, as for example between the Quaker families which owned large food firms.

Connections of kinship and marriage are further extended by the ties of friendship and acquaintance which are often summarized in the phrase 'old boy network'. To a large extent, this network is social. It is based on individuals seeing each other regularly, not only in the way of business but also socially.

Social contacts of this kind are possible partly because of common background. Members of the upper class associate together easily because they have the same tastes, attitudes and inclinations formed by being brought up in the same kinds of family and going to the same kinds of school and university. As Scott (1982) argues: 'The integrative role of the public schools concerns their ability to mould the ideas and outlook of their pupils and to ensure frequent and easy interaction among them' (p. 160). Members of the business core of the upper class do, indeed, have a public school background. For example, three-quarters of clearing bank directors studied in 1970 were from public schools, and one in three were from Eton. In addition, between half and three-quarters of these directors had been to either Oxford or Cambridge Universities. Or, to take a different case, Otley (1973) found that, in 1971, 75 per cent of senior army officers (lieutenant-general and above) had been to *major* public schools.

A common background in family, school and university gives a common culture to members of the upper class which enables them to

Box 11 Trends in elite recruitment

Author	Group studied	Time period	Results
Boyd (1973)	Higher civil servants; ambassadors, judges, admirals, generals, air marshals, bishops and bank directors	1939–70	A slight increase over time in the openness of the higher civil service, but no change recorded with any of the other groups.
Kelsall (1974)	Higher civil servants	1929–67	'A certain, if not spectacular, broadening of the band of types of social and educational background from which top civil servants were drawn over this period of nearly 40 years' (Kelsall, 1974, p. 174), the proportion with fathers in routine non-manual or in manual work increasing from 12 per cent in 1929 to 31 per cent in 1967.
Morgan (1969), Thompson (1974)	English diocesan bishops	1860–1960	'[A] decline in landed and peer-age connections, and [a] shift in terms of parental occupation from old landed ruling class to a more professional background (especially worthy of note being the increase in the number of bishops whose fathers were themselves clergymen)' (Thompson, 1974; p. 200).
Harbury and Hitchens (1979)	Wealth-leavers	1924–73	'The importance of fathers' wealth for substantial wealth-leavers (those leaving over £50,000 in 1956–7 prices) did not appear to change greatly between the mid-1920s and the mid–1950s. Thereafter a decline was observable in 1965, which appeared to continue in 1973' (Harbury and Hitchens, 1978, p. 67).
Stanworth and Giddens (1974)	Chairmen of major corporations and banks	1900–72	'Our data do not indicate that there has occurred a process of increasing "openness" of recruitment to the Chairs of the largest corporations but, if anything, something the contrary of this. . . But these phenomena vary to some degree according

continues

Box 11 *continued*

			to the type of economic sector in question. Banking is clearly shown to be the most fixed and unchanging' (Stanworth and Giddens, 1974, p. 89).
Erickson (1959)	Executive directors in steel manufacturing	1865–1953	No change during the nineteenth century but an increasing proportion with fathers in routine non-manual and manual occupations in the first half of the twentieth century.
Erickson (1959)	Executive directors in hosiery	1844–1952	Fluctuations in recruitment throughout the period, with the twentieth century slightly more open than the nineteenth.
Otley (1970)	Entrants to Sandhurst, entrants to Woolwich, lieutenant-generals and above	1810–1939 1880–1939 1913–59	'There seems to have been a "democratisation" of recruitment, but it was only really during war-time that the lower social strata sent really substantial numbers of boys to Sandhurst and Woolwich.' (Otley, 1970, p. 231–2.) 'Open competitive entry undoubtedly helped to break the stranglehold the upper class had on the officer corps, but it also helped to establish, in its turn, a new stranglehold – that of the upper middle class' (Otley, 1970, p. 234).
Razzell (1963)	Officers in the Indian army	1758–1834	'The purchase system ensured that the British army was never closed to the wealthy middle classes – the Indian army allowed lesser lights to quench their thirst for social status' (Razzell, 1963, p. 259).
Razzell (1963)	Officers in the British home army	1780–1952	'Perhaps the most surprising finding of the study was the way the landed upper classes maintained their position within the army throughout the nineteenth century and even into the twentieth. The great watershed was of course the First World War. After this war members of the landed classes were remnants; although very important remnants' (Razzell, 1963, p. 259).

continues

Box 11 *continued*

Compton (1968)	Entrants to the Indian civil service	1854–76	'Those who profited most from the abolition of patronage were the clergy and the professional classes whose sons together made up nearly a half of the "new competitives". Represen-tation of the landed interest was cut from a quarter to a tenth whilst Indian civilians who might formerly have pushed their sons in as "hard bargains" found such a channel of automatic employment blocked' (Compton, 1968, p. 283).

Source: Heath (1981) *Social Mobility* (London, Collins), pp. 90–2. Reproduced with permission.

interact freely. It also serves as the path of recruitment into the upper class by giving the required qualifications. The result is that the class has a high degree of self-recruitment and social closure. What this means is that current members of the upper class are likely to be the offspring of wealthy individuals and their sons and daughters are also likely to remain in the same social position.

The Nuffield Mobility Study gives some evidence which bears on this question (see section 3.7 for further discussion). This study found that class I, the higher level of the 'service' class, is the most self-recruiting class. 45 per cent of the sons of class I fathers had secured places in the same class, while only 14 per cent would have done so if social background has played no part. If one looks in detail at class I, there seem to be differences between various groups within it. Heath (1981) shows that large proprietors and self-employed professionals (doctors, lawyers, accountants) are heavily self-recruiting, while administrators and managers are less so. 40 per cent of self-employed professionals had fathers in the service class and 47 per cent of large proprietors were themselves sons of proprietors. At the other end of the scale, only 19 per cent of industrial managers were sons of class I fathers. Where people are part of a bureaucracy, therefore, there is a good chance of upward mobility. Where this career structure is lacking, occupations are much more closed.

Part of the difficulty in using the Nuffield Mobility Study data is that class I is very much larger than what we have called the upper class. A few people in Nuffield class I are more properly considered members of the upper class. Many self-employed professionals depend on the business core and are often related by ties of family and common background to members of this core. Townsend's (1979) study of income distribution, for example, found a surprisingly high proportion of professionals among the very rich in Britain. Studies have investigated the social origins of those in 'elite' positions not only of the business core, but in the civil service, the army, the judiciary, and the church. Boyd (1973), for example, found that no fewer than 45 per cent of bank directors and 30 per cent of judges listed in *Who's Who* also had fathers listed (Heath 1981). We have to conclude that entry to the upper-class is 'sponsored' in the sense that upper-class individuals have to have the 'right' sort of background; it is not a competitive process. The upper class is relatively closed to outsiders.

One last issue in the formation of the upper class as a network deserves mention. We have referred to the way in which the business core of the upper class can mix its business and social contacts. Business relationships may, however, be cemented in a much more solid way via the networks of interlocking directorships. This is an issue discussed in more detail in chapter 2, section 2.2, but an illustration is provided by Scott (1985) in a study of the directorships of large companies. In 1976, 11 people had a total of 57 directorships in the top 250 companies and had many others in smaller companies. The directorships of 9 of these 11 can be linked together in the chain shown in figure 2.4 on page 23: a mere 9 people linked together 39 very large companies. Interlocking directorships provide a powerful network linking firms, but they also cement the connections of members of the upper class.

Prestige and power

So far we have argued that the upper class and, especially, its business core forms a relatively closed, coherent and self-recruiting elite. That sort of coherence combined with great wealth and the effective control of very large business gives great power. However, that represents only a part of the upper class's influence. The primary point is, perhaps, that the business core is connected with other members of the upper class at the top of *other* fields like politics, the civil service, and the professions.

We have already looked at the recruitment patterns of certain upper-class occupations. There is overwhelming evidence that those in such positions come disproportionately from upper-class families and from public schools and Oxford and Cambridge Universities. They have, in other words, common backgrounds and a common process of education and training. In 1974, for example, three-quarters of Conservative MPs had been to public school, including 17 per cent to Eton, and 54 per cent had received an education at Oxford or Cambridge. The same pattern of education predominates in the higher reaches of the civil service, two-thirds of whom in 1970 had attended public schools. Senior churchmen and members of the judiciary are also recruited disproportionately from public schools and Oxbridge and, in addition, have a strong tendency to come from families also in high-ranking positions in the church and the law.

The common origins, common education and common experiences of

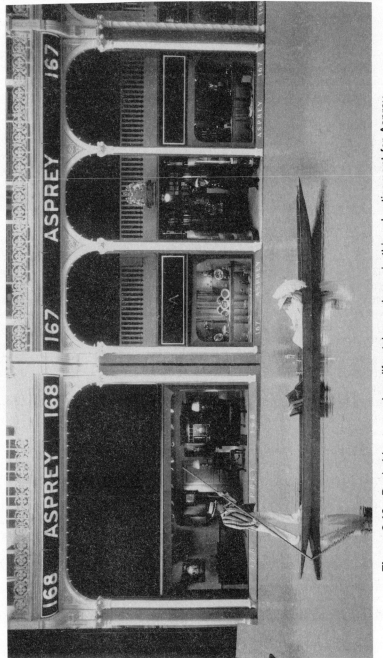

Figure 3.10 Desirable upper-class life-style as shown in this advertisement for Asprey
Source: Asprey plc, London.

the holders of a variety of elite positions leads many commentators to refer to the 'establishment'. The members of the establishment constitute a coherent and self-recruiting body of men who are able to wield immense power. A similarity of outlook and day-to-day contact between civil servants, politicians, businessmen, churchmen, professionals and the military, gives the upper class political power to add to the power given by wealth. This argument carries a great deal of conviction. However, common origins and common education do not of themselves necessarily mean common interests or common action and little is known about how holders of elite positions *actually* do interact.

The coherence, wealth and power of the upper class is reflected in its prestige. Doubtless, in the past, some of the prestige of the upper class derived from a flamboyant and luxurious life-style conspicious to all. To some extent, this life-style continues to exist; it is, after all, one of the privileges of wealth. The doings of the rich continue to be displayed and even celebrated in the press and television. It could also be argued that an upper-class life-style is frequently presented as desirable, as in the advert in figure 3.10, and as something that everybody should seek. *The Official Sloane Ranger Handbook* (Barr and York, 1982), for example, purported, humorously, to give guidance on the upper-class life-style appropriate to Sloane Rangers. As the jacket of the book announces: 'This is the handbook of the Sloane's style, the eternal stream of English Life, an invaluable reference for a lifetime of decisions about What Really Matters in Life. You can't go wrong.' Despite this, however, upper-class people probably display their lives less conspicuously than they used to; in this sense the class is becoming more invisible. It may also be that rank and title command less respect than they once did. New hereditary peerages are not now generally created. However, periodically, an Honours List is announced which will include knighthoods and life-peerages as well as hosts of lesser awards. These higher honours largely go to those who have rendered 'public service'. This public service is defined in such a way that honours will be given to individuals who are, in our sense, upper class. Apart from anything else, the system of nomination for honours ensures that only those who are relatively well connected in public life are likely to be nominated. There are, however, some indications that the Honours List is losing its prestige in the wider community. The appearance of each list is almost routinely greeted by a chorus of disapproval, based largely on the notion that the ideal of public service is being debased.

Summary

1   The upper class is distinguished by its wealth, its coherence, and its power.

2   Members of the upper class are very wealthy. The top 1 per cent of wealth holders own one-third of the nation's wealth.

3 We should see the upper class as much in terms of families as individuals. Wealth is distributed widely in families and family origin and influence is important in gaining upper-class occupations.

4 The core of the class consists in those actively involved in the control of large businesses.

5 The upper class is very coherent, being bound together in a network of kinship, similar education, friendship and business contacts.

6 This coherence gives power which is reinforced by the fact that those of upper-class origin occupy powerful positions, not only in the business world, but also in politics, the civil service, the military, the church and the judiciary.

7 An upper-class style of life still carries a certain prestige, though that may be declining.

Related topics

Chapter 2, section 2.2 presents some arguments about ownership and control and the question of interlocking shareholdings amongst the upper class; the social position of managers is discussed in section 2.3. Section 3.3, reviewing income and wealth distributions, gives some account of upper-class wealth, while section 3.7 presents some data on elite recruitment.

3.7 Social Mobility

Social mobility is the process by which people move from one class to another. *Social* mobility should not be confused with *geographical* mobility, which refers to people moving their place of residence. In modern society, nobody is prevented by religious, political or legal regulations from moving between classes: entry to classes is not closed. At the same time, though, there are barriers to movement into some class positions. In practice, entry into the upper class is limited either by birth or access to wealth. There are also effective limits on access to the more prestigious positions in the professional middle class. To be a doctor requires a degree in medicine, and only a small proportion of the working population have that qualification. More interesting, though, is what kind of people are allowed into medical school to get that qualification. Most are the children of higher professionals; few are from unskilled, manual backgrounds. This raises the question of fairness, usually as an issue of equality of opportunity. Since some groups of occupations provide better rewards, better conditions and more work satisfaction than others, it is a matter of concern on what grounds those positions are filled and whether most citizens have a reasonable chance of obtaining such posts. Studies of social mobility assess those chances.

Social mobility bears upon another central social process – that of class formation and class solidarity. It has usually been thought that high degrees of social mobility would reduce class conflict. There are several plausible reasons for this. People believing that they have a fair chance of joining the higher social classes may feel little resentment on the ground that privileges are deserved: talent is being rewarded. If there is a lot of movement between classes then solidarity and common identity will be hard to sustain. People may pursue individual rather than collective solutions to their discontents, preferring further education to trades-union meetings. Also, the cross-class contacts built up by socially mobile people might reduce the sense of the exclusiveness of social classes and the hostility between them. Indeed, ultimately, if there was perfect fluidity between positions, social background having no influence on occupational success, one key basis for identifying social classes – common life chances – would be removed. The nature and degree of social mobility in Britain is, therefore, interesting from the point of view of class politics.

The concept of social mobility

Social mobility concerns movements between social classes. It is usually estimated by reference to occupational positions. Movement may happen within an individual's lifetime, called *intra-generational* mobility, as for example the cases of the promotion of a clerk to a manager or a manual worker obtaining qualifications permitting access to a profession. Or, the movement may occur between generations, children coming to fill places in a different occupational class to their parents, which is called *inter-generational* mobility. Examples would be the child of an engine-driver who becomes a solicitor, or the child of a solicitor who becomes an engine driver. The former would be an example of *upward* social mobility, the latter of *downward* social mobility. It is assumed that occupational classes can be graded in a hierarchy of prestige, and that the criterion of mobility is to shift across a class boundary. It should be noted that people also obtain new jobs without crossing a class boundary, moving sideways so to speak.

Deciding what are *relevant* class boundaries is bound to be contentious. For many people, upward mobility used to be associated with a move from blue-collar to white-collar occupations. However, since many routine white-collar jobs now pay less well and are less satisfying than skilled manual jobs, that boundary may well be thought less meaningful. The most authoritative recent study of mobility in Britain concentrates on movement into and out of the service class (composed largely of professional and managerial occupations), on the grounds that for most people upward mobility is achieved by entering professional and managerial occupations. It is to the finding of this study, the Nuffield Mobility Study, reported by Goldthorpe, Llewellyn and Payne (1980), that we will turn next. To make sense of the findings of this study, however, it is necessary to be familiar with the class categories being used.

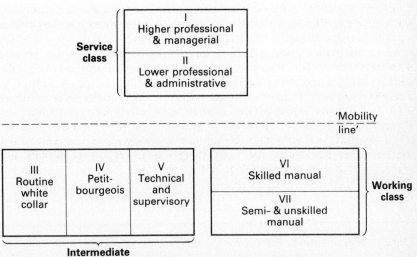

Key:
'Occupational' class (with roman numerals). Contain the following types
of occupation:

I Higher-grade professionals; higher-grade administrators and officials;
managers in large establishments; large proprietors.

II Lower-grade professionals and higher-grade technicians; lower-grade
administrators; managers in small establishments; supervisors of non-
manual workers.

III Routine non-manual workers (largely clerical) in administration and commerce;
sales personnel; other rank-and-file employees in services.

IV Small proprietors, including farmers and small-holders; self-employed
artisans; other 'own account' workers (except professionals).

V Lower-grade technicians; supervisors of manual workers.

VI Skilled manual wage-workers.

VII All manual wage-workers in industry in semi and unskilled grades;
agricultural workers.

Figure 3.11 Goldthorpe et al.'s (1980) model of the British class structure
(Nuffield Mobility Study)
Source: From Goldthorpe, Llewellyn and Payne (1980) *Social Mobility and Class Structure
in Modern Britain* (Oxford, Oxford University Press), pp. 39–41. Reproduced with
permission.

The definitions of the seven occupational classes used by Goldthorpe et al. are listed in figure 3.11. For many purposes, these seven classes are grouped into three – the service class, the intermediate class and the working class. For Goldthorpe et al., the 'service class' includes higher and lower professionals and middle management (a broader definition than we used in section 3.5); the intermediate class comprises routine white-collar workers, small proprietors and supervisory workers; the working class is defined as manual workers without positions of authority. Their conception of class structure is shown diagrammatically in figure 3.12. Importantly, although Goldthorpe et al. study movement between all seven occupational classes, they consider *only movement into and out of the service class* as socially meaningful mobility.

Contemporary social mobility

Goldthorpe et al. (1980) discovered more inter-generational mass social mobility in Britain since the Second World War than might have been expected. Previous studies had suggested that classes in Britain were largely self-recruiting. Sons would usually end up in the same class as their fathers. (Regrettably, almost all mobility studies, including the Nuffield one, only analyse the movement of men.) It was believed, on the basis of a survey in 1949, that there was a lot of short-distance but little long-distance movement, that the elite was highly self-recruiting, and that the blue/white collar boundary was a major barrier. Goldthorpe et al. paint a different picture.

Consider table 3.17. This is an 'outflow' table, showing the class *destination* of sons, which indicates the extent to which opportunities are equal. If classes were perfectly self-recruiting, every son would be in the same class as his father and the diagonal boxes would all register 100. What we observe is, rather, much movement between classes. Consider, for example, the row of fathers in class VII – semi-skilled and unskilled manual workers and agricultural labourers. 6.5 per cent of sons of such fathers were in class I occupations (higher managerial and professional) in 1972; another 7.8 per cent were in the lower professional grade, class II. However, 34.9 per cent of such sons were, like their fathers, in class VII; and a further 23.5 per cent were in the other class of manual workers – class VI, skilled manuals. In effect, then, about 6 out of 10 became white-collar workers.

It is in some degree a matter of judgment whether you will be impressed by the number of sons who were upwardly mobile, or by the number who remained in class VII. But, whatever your judgment, the table does show different degrees of self-recruitment. Looking at the diagonal boxes you can see that only one in eight of sons of routine white-collar workers (class III) were to be found in that class in 1972. The sons of such workers were, in fact, fairly evenly distributed across all occupational classes. By contrast, class I fathers were the most likely to pass on their 'class position' to their sons. Nearly one in two class I sons

Table 3.17 Intergenerational occupational mobility of men aged 20–84 in England and Wales, 1972, outflow[a] (percentages, by row)

		Son's class[b] (1972)							Number (of fathers in sample)	%
		I	II	III	IV	V	VI	VII		
Father's class	I	45.2	18.9	11.5	7.7	4.8	5.4	6.5	688	7.3
when son	II	29.1	23.1	11.9	7.0	9.6	106	8.7	554	5.9
aged 14	III	18.4	15.7	12.8	7.8	12.8	15.6	16.9	694	7.3
years	IV	12.6	11.4	8.0	24.8	8.7	14.4	20.5	1,329	14.1
	V	14.2	13.6	10.1	7.7	15.7	21.2	17.6	1,082	11.5
	VI	7.8	8.8	8.3	6.6	12.3	30.4	25.9	2,594	27.5
	VII	6.5	7.8	8.2	6.6	12.5	23.5	34.9	2,493	24.6

Notes: [a] i.e. class distribution of sons by the class of their father when son was aged 14 (a measure of equality of opportunity).
[b] For definitions of classes see figure 3.11.
Total number of respondents = 9,434.
Source: From Goldthorpe, Llewellyn and Payne (1980) *Social Mobility and Class Structure in Modern Britain* (Cambridge, Cambridge University Press), p. 48. Reproduced with permission.

had class I jobs. It is this capacity for privilege to be transmitted inter-generationally that arouses suspicion about the social significance of the, undeniably large, absolute amounts of mobility. Clearly, the class into which a man was born did not *determine* his class destination; lots of men were upwardly mobile in the period 1928–72. But the chances of ending up in class I were weighted heavily in favour of those with fathers there already.

Issues relating to class formation are best illustrated by considering an 'inflow' table, table 3.18. Based on exactly the same data as the previous table, this shows the *composition of social classes* in 1972, in terms of the class origins of sons. Reading down the columns you can see who has arrived in which classes. Compare class I and class VII. Class I, which comprised about one worker in eight (13.6 per cent) in 1972, had drawn its members from all social classes. Although one in four members also had fathers in class I, the rest came more or less equally from the six other classes in Goldthorpe et al.'s classification. Class I in 1972 was, then, very heterogeneous (i.e. of very mixed origin). 28.3 per cent of class I were sons of manual workers. Class VII, by contrast, was largely composed of sons of manual workers (69.6 per cent). Only 2 per cent of class VII had fathers in class I. Skilled manual workers had similar origins. Thus Goldthorpe et al. propose that Britain now has a 'mature' working class, alike in its origins, and therefore capable of exhibiting

Table 3.18 Intergenerational occupational mobility of men aged 20–64 in England and Wales, 1972, inflow[a] (percentages, by column)

		Son's class[b] (1972)						
		I	II	III	IV	V	VI	VII
	I	24.2	12.0	9.1	6.0	3.0	1.9	2.0
Father's	II	12.5	11.8	7.6	4.4	4.9	3.0	2.2
class when	III	12.0	10.0	10.2	6.1	8.3	5.4	5.3
son was	IV	13.0	13.9	12.2	36.5	10.6	9.6	12.3
aged 14	V	12.0	13.5	12.5	9.4	15.6	11.4	8.6
	VI	15.7	21.0	24.8	19.2	29.2	39.4	30.3
	VII	12.6	17.8	23.6	18.5	28.5	29.4	39.3
Number (of sons		1,285	1,087	870	887	1,091	2,000	2,214
% in sample)		13.6	11.5	9.2	9.4	11.6	21.2	23.5

Notes: [a] i.e. class composition, by class of father when son was aged 14 (a measure of class formation).
[b] For definitions of classes see figure 3.11.
Total number of respondents = 9,434.
Source: Goldthorpe, Llewellyn and Payne (1980) *Social Mobility and Class Structure in Modern Britain* (Oxford, Oxford University Press), p. 44. Reproduced with permission.

considerable solidarity. If they are correct, and being in the same class for two or more generations does increase solidarity, then their study does suggest the existence of a solidaristic working class and considerable fragmentation among the other occupational classes.

Given the very considerable movement between classes, it might be imagined that Britain had become a fairer, more open, society, opportunity becoming less and less dependent on class origins. In an important sense, though, this is a misleading impression. Much of the upward mobility into the service class is merely a consequence of changes in the occupational structure. The number of positions in the service class increased sharply in the period examined by Goldthorpe et al. Men occupied in service class occupations rose from around 1.2 million in 1931 to 3.5 million in 1971. Compare the proportions of *fathers* in the service class (classes I and II) in Goldthorpe's et al. sample – 13.1 per cent (see table 3.17 – and the proportion of *sons* – 25.1 per cent (see table 3.18). What Goldthorpe et al. point out is that the service class increased in size to such an extent that, even if every son of a service-class father had obtained a service-class job, there would still have been more men with origins in other classes in the service class in 1972. This can be seen in table 3.19 with summarizes information on movement across the boundary of the service class. Boxes A and D are percentages of men

Table 3.19 Intergenerational social mobility into and out of the service class, men aged 20–64, in England and Wales, 1972 (percentages)

		Sons' social class in 1972		
		Service (I-II)	Other (III-VII)	All
Fathers' social class when son aged 14	Service (I-II)	**A** 7.7	**B** 5.4	13.1
	Other (III-VII)	**C** 17.4	**D** 69.5	86.9
	All	25.1	74.9	100.0

Note: Total number of respondents = 9,434.
Source: From tables 3.17 and 3.18 above.

inter-generationally stable; Box B is the percentage downwardly mobile; box C is the percentage of men upwardly mobile. The upwardly mobile vastly outnumbered the downwardly mobile. Put another way, the service class of the previous generation did not breed fast enough to fill all the new service-class occupations made available in the long boom after the Second World War. A large amount of upward social mobility was inevitable.

This fact led Goldthorpe et al. to try to separate out *absolute* mobility, of which we have seen there is a great deal, from *relative* mobility, which is a measure of whether class differentials have narrowed. In other words, if there had been no change in the occupational structure would there still have been an expansion of opportunities for the lower classes? Answering such a question is fraught with difficulty, not least because the occupational structure is always changing. However, it is an important question because it is unlikely that we will see, during the rest of the twentieth century, further 'upgrading' of the occupational structure which would allow the service class to continue to expand. It will, then, matter to what extent exclusive class privileges can be maintained from generation to generation. Goldthorpe et al. suggest that, relatively speaking, the capacity of service-class fathers to transmit privilege did *not* decline between 1928 and 1972. The simplest indication of this is the low rate of downward mobility from, especially, class I. Look at table 3.17 again. 64.1 per cent of class I sons ended up in the service class; only one in three moved down: and this may be an underestimate given the nature of *intra*-generational mobility. It seems, then, that a use of material resources accumulated by fathers in lucrative careers and a capacity to secure high educational qualifications for their children has ensured that sons of the service class are heavily protected against downward mobility.

The importance of the mobility data for understanding class relationships is harder to interpret. Only the working class is inter-generationally stable, being composed predominantly of sons of manual workers, in a ratio of 30.9 per cent with fathers from classes VI-VII to 13.8 per cent with fathers from classes I-V (see table 3.20). Whether that 30 per cent, or 3 men in 10, do constitute a 'mature' working class in the political arena remains to be seen. Voting behaviour until 1979 bore this out to some extent. Heath (1981) shows that working-class men with working-class fathers and working-class fathers-in-law are more likely than any other category to vote Labour. He, indeed, shows that men with working-class connections at any level of the class hierarchy were more likely to vote Labour than those without. This corresponds to information on the friendship and leisure patterns of the upwardly mobile. Such patterns provide strong evidence that men who are inter-generationally stable, whether in the service class or the working class, mostly have social contact with people of their own class. As might be expected, a man upwardly mobile is more likely to have working-class friends and associates than a man born into the service class. However, there seem to be few problems for the upwardly mobile in becoming assimilated into their new class position. (It used to be thought that such men might be isolated or unwelcome, but such problems have probably been overcome through the sheer volume of the upwardly mobile.) The upwardly mobile have sociable relations across classes.

The third, intermediate, class seems to have relatively little identity, either over time or internally. With the exception of sons of men in class IV, the *petite bourgeoisie*, who because they inherit property are relatively likely to continue in the same line of business as their fathers (see table 3.18), the other intermediate classes spread out across the class structure almost at random. This is, in important part, due to the typical patterns of *intra*-generational mobility in the period. Men tend to pass through jobs in the intermediate classes. Hardly any men spend their entire working life in occupational classes III-V. Stewart et al. (1980) showed that young men who were routine white-collar workers would, before they reached 35 years of age, either be promoted into managerial occupations or would leave to try other jobs, usually manual ones. The other main group of male, routine white-collar workers were older men, over 50, who had been promoted from the shop-floor, often because they were no longer physically capable of manual tasks. These are both instances of changes which can be understood in terms of *careers*. (It is important to bear in mind that many people's social and political behaviour may be oriented to their anticipated future rather than to their current situation). People may be mobile during their life-time, *intra*-generationally.

Again, Goldthorpe et al. demonstrate a considerable amount of *intra*-generational mobility among men. In their survey, they asked for a man's

Table 3.20 Intergenerational social mobility into and out of the manual working class, men aged 20–64, in England and Wales, 1972 (percentages)

		Sons' class (1972)		
		Other (I-V)	Working (VI-VII)	All
Father's social class when son aged 14	Other (I-V)	34.1	13.8	47.8
	Working (VI-VII)	21.2	30.9	52.1
	All	55.3	44.7	100.0

Note: Total number of respondents = 9,434.
Source: Calculated from table 3.17 (p. 199) and table 3.18 (p. 200).

first full-time job and for the job he held after 10 years of working life. A very considerable proportion (73 per cent) of those aged 35 and over in the service class in 1972 had had first jobs in other classes. Moreover, there was no evidence that this route into the service class was closing up. (It used to be thought that increased numbers of people getting qualifications in higher education would block channels of upward mobility within firms and organizations.) Another interesting feature of intra-generational mobility is that, while sons of service-class fathers often have first jobs in other social classes, after 10 years of working life they have secured service-class posts. Only 27 per cent of service-class sons were direct entrants into service-class occupations, while a further 36 per cent had first jobs elsewhere.

There are two major limitations of existing survey-based studies of social mobility, and the Nuffield study in particular. First, the greatest exclusiveness of social groups is at the very top of the occupational hierarchy, the elite being more highly self-recruiting than any other. Second, the mobility experiences of women are ignored.

The elite and mobility

The Nuffield Mobility Study examined *mass* mobility. It would be false to imagine that the existence of considerable mobility into the service class meant that *all* top positions were equally accessible. While the son of a manual worker may become a solicitor, he is very unlikely indeed to become a High-Court judge. The evidence concerning recruitment to the upper class is considered in detail in section 3.6 above. People at the very top of the hierarchy tend to have impeccable upper-class backgrounds. To take just a single example, of those bank directors listed in *Who's Who* in

1970/1, 45 per cent also had fathers listed in earlier editions of *Who's Who*. This is 300 times greater than chance. It does not leave much space for others to be upwardly mobile into top banking jobs! Of course, sample surveys like the Nuffield one could never pick up sufficient of these kind of people to allow effective analysis. These elites are too small for that. But, at the same time, they are exceptionally powerful, very important persons. No complete understanding of social mobility can afford to ignore this upper class.

Women and mobility

The Nuffield study examined only men, as have other studies of mass mobility. It is very doubtful whether the same kind of study could be undertaken if it included women, because women's experience of social mobility is so different from men's. Men move from one occupational class to another fairly infrequently during their life-time and are unaffected by marriage and divorce. Women's intra-generational experience is likely to be much more varied and hard to capture with orthodox sociological categories. Most women work full-time as housewives for part of their life, but that work is not included in occupational classifications. Then, the jobs available to women are more restricted, there being few women in class I, while a great many shift in and out of white-collar and manual work. Women's economic position is, as chapter 4, section 4.2 demonstrates, much more precarious than that of men, and much less well-paid. We have seen that two jobs with the same name may be of a different nature for women; young male clerks tend to be promoted to become managers, women clerks rarely are.

It is equally problematic to analyse women's inter-generational mobility. Should a daughter's occupation be compared with that of her mother, rather than her father, for instance? Should we take account of the occupation of a woman's husband when considering her work experiences, or not? Our present state of knowledge allows us to say very little about women and mobility. That implies, however, that we do not understand a major experience of one half of the British population.

Summary

1 There have been relatively high levels of absolute, inter-generational social mobility in Britain since the Second World War, much of it being upward mobility into an expanded service class. As a result, the service class consists of men of mixed-class origins.

2 The high rate of mobility can be attributed to the upgrading of the occupational structure – rapid growth in service class positions has occurred. This has permitted low levels of downward mobility. Thus, sons of service-class fathers have usually secured service-class positions for themselves. It also follows that most of today's manual workers had working-class fathers.

3 The degree of self-recruitment is highest in the upper class, elite positions being filled by men of exclusive social-class background.

Related topics

The Nuffield study included an examination of the relationship between education and mobility, which is examined at length in chapter 8 section 8.4. On elite recruitment, see section 3.6. Further discussion of the careers of clerical workers is to be found in section 3.5.

Further Reading

The best account of occupational change in Britain in the twentieth century is Routh (1980). As far as poverty is concerned, the two most useful studies are Townsend (1979) and Mack and Lansley (1985), although the former is based on fieldwork carried out in the late 1960s. Atkinson (1979) has undertaken a series of investigations of the distribution of income and wealth in Britain. On the class structure of capitalist societies in general, the best text is Giddens (1980). A short introduction to the British working class is Roberts (1978). For discussion of the fragmentation of the working class see Roberts et al. (1977). King and Raynor (1981) is a useful introductory book in the middle class in general. Abercrombie and Urry (1983), while also discussing various theories of the middle class, formulate a particular argument about the position of middle-class occupations. Hyman and Price (1983) is a collection of readings on the subject. On the upper class, the best available source is Scott (1982). Heath (1981) is an accessible and interesting analysis of social mobility.

4 Gender

4.1 Introduction

This chapter will examine the state of social relations between men and women in contemporary Britain. These are usually called gender relations, gender being the social aspect of the differentiation of the sexes. Sociological discussion in this area recognizes that social rather than biological processes are the key to the understanding of the position of women (and of men) in society. Old-fashioned notions that a woman's anatomy, through her capacity to bear children, determined the shape of her entire life have been replaced by complex debates as to how different social structures have interacted to produce the variety of patterns of gender relations which are to be found across different societies and over time. The nature of sociological discussion on gender has been transformed by the impact of the contemporary women's movement; no longer are issues concerning gender subsumed under 'the family' with its connotation of a happy haven of consensus. Instead, we find separate chapters on gender, in which the inequality between women and men has a central place.

The position of women is often considered to have improved during the last few decades. There is, however, considerable debate as to the extent of change, and the reasons for it. Some writers, pointing, for instance, to the formal legal equality that women have with men, suggest that women are now fully emancipated, and have no need for any further changes. Others, focusing on issues such as the inequality in the wages paid to men and women or the violence that women receive at men's hands, argue that women still have a long way to go before they are fully liberated.

One of the major tasks of this chapter, then, will be to examine the different aspects of gender relations in contemporary Britain in some detail, to see if the conditions under which women live are as rosy as the first set of writers suggest, as unchanged as the second school of thought has argued, or some complex mixture of change and continuity.

Some theories of the position of women in society

These debates have taken place in sociology in the context of discussions of the best way to explain patterns of gender relations. Some *mainstream stratification theorists* have suggested that gender inequality is not particularly important for understanding the unequal distribution of resources in society, or the causes of political change. They assert that this is because women's position is determined by the position of the family in which they live, and that this is determined by that of the male breadwinner. This notion, that gender inequality is thus almost irrelevant for mainstream sociological theorizing, has met with an onslaught of criticism by writers who have argued that it is inappropriate to take the family as the unit of analysis in such a way. These criticisms include the points that:

1 there is inequality between men and women within the family;
2 women's earnings are important in the standard of living and position of the household; and
3 not all people live in households in which there is a male wage earner, let alone one in which such a man brings in all the family income.

That is, the critics assert that there is significant inequality between men and women, and that for a woman to be married to a man does not mean that she gains all the privileges that he has access to.

Functionalists have provided one of the more optimistic accounts of the nature of gender relations in modern society. These writers considered the relations between the sexes to be different but equal. They focus on the family, analysing both its internal structure and its functions for the wider society. They suggest that, within the family, women take on the expressive role of nurturing the other family members, while men take on the instrumental role and go into the outside world to earn the family's wage. Women's relative absence from paid work was considered necessary by many, but not all functionalist writers, for both her expressive role as housewife and full-time mother, and also to prevent strains which competition with the male breadwinner might create. The family as a whole was considered essential to the carrying out of certain necessary societal functions – for the rearing of children, the regulation of sexuality and as a unit of consumption. The functionalist view of the family as a haven of consensus and fulfilment has been challenged from several directions. The main criticisms are:

1 that functionalism incorrectly ignores the power inequality between men and women:
2 that men and women are not different and equal, rather, different and unequal; and

3 that women's paid work is both important and a long-term
   phenomenon.

These types of criticism have led some to reject the functionalist
framework altogether, especially since there have been parallel criticisms
of functionalist explanation in other areas of sociology. However, others
have tried to modify and develop some of the early functionalist ideas, for
instance in the examination of the development of paid work among
married women. Its implications for women and families have been
explored, rather than dismissed as marginal phenomena. These writers
have sometimes been called the '*dual-role*' *theorists* because of their focus
on the double work of women as simultaneously housewives and paid
workers.

Most contemporary writers on gender relations today recognize that
there are important aspects of inequality between men and women and
that these have a broad social significance. There are now many
sociological studies of the disadvantages women face in particular
situations, from problems in particular places of employment, to seeking
health care, or trying to participate in party politics. Some writers have
kept their analyses at the level of specific situations. For instance, one
problem not entirely trivial for women pursuing careers, is their exclusion
from male gatherings in bars, which are important channels for passing on
information. Or consider the problem of becoming an MP when the
House of Commons starts its sitting in the middle of the afternoon and
continues into the evening, which cuts across any conventional domestic
commitments. While this small-scale level of analysis has its place, it is
severely limited by focusing so much on the detail that it fails to deal
adequately with the wider structures which generate these situations. The
detailed studies are useful in helping to build up the data necessary for a
wider picture, but a full explanation requires a broader view.

A more structural view is that of *Marxist feminist* writers who have
argued that the family exists, not for the harmonious delight of its
members, but rather because it is a source of benefit to capital, since
women can be made to labour for free in the reproduction of wage-
labourers. In this perspective, the work which housewives do – housework, child-care, and so on – is called domestic labour, which results in
the production of children and well-fed, cleansed and cared-for husbands
who go to work for wages. That is, housewives produce or reproduce
both the next generation of labourers and the current one. This is much
cheaper when done by housewives in nuclear families than any other way,
since these women do not get paid for the work, obtaining only their
maintenance. The Marxist feminists argue that it is capital which gains the
benefit from this exploitative form of labour, since it means that they can
pay these women's husbands lower wages than would be the case if male
workers had to buy these services, for instance meals in cafes, laundries
for clothes-washing, and nannies for their children. A further con-

sequence of benefit to employers of this nuclear-family form, is that it places women in a weak position when competing on the labour market.

Women's weak labour-market position is a source of disadvantage to women from which only employers benefit, since it enables them to pay women workers less than they would men. Marxist writers vary quite substantially in their interpretations of the reason for women's oppression. Many (such as Beechey, 1978) place great emphasis upon the advantage to capital of women's position in the family in order to explain their subordination in other many spheres in society. Others, such as Engels (1972), have argued that this particular form of domestic oppression exists in order that men may be sure that they pass such property as they possess to their heirs without fear of it going to the sons of other men. Still others have argued that women's oppression in capitalist societies is to be explained primarily at the ideological level as a result of the prevailing conceptions of passive and dependent femininity.

An even stronger attack on the view that harmony and equality characterize the relations between men and women arises within the *radical feminist* school of thought. These writers argue that the oppression of women by men is the most important aspect of social inequality in society, and that men's exploitation of women is not a by-product of any other form of inequality. The term *patriarchy* is used to describe this system. They disagree with the Marxist view that women's oppression stems ultimately from capitalism, but disagree with each other in what they see as the basis of women's oppression. Some have tended to concentrate on the problem of men's systematic violence towards women and on the power relations involved in contemporary forms of heterosexuality. Other radical feminists have focused on the problems to women of men's control over their work, especially in the home as unpaid housewives. Others have focused on the socialization process through which girls are brought up to be gentle, passive people who will do as they are told, while boys are brought up to be bolder and more aggressive.

More recently, some writers have tried to combine elements from various of these approaches, so as to be able to explain both class and gender inequality. In particular, there are those who have sought to combine an analysis of gender inequality as a system of patriarchy together with an analysis of the changing nature of capitalist relations. Because these writers have tried to combine an understanding of two systems, those of patriarchy and capitalism, they are sometimes known as *dualists*. One of the leading writers taking this approach is Hartmann. Hartmann (1979) argues that male workers are able to keep women out of the better jobs because of their organization, and that as a consequence women are obliged to marry on unfavourable terms, such that they have to do most of the housework. Hartmann argues that there is a vicious circle in which partriarchy and capitalism tend to maintain each other.

So, what is the actual position of women in modern Britain? The following sections will examine gender relations in paid employment, politics and public life, sexuality, male violence, welfare and housing, and in the household.

4.2   Women's Employment

Wages

One of the most obvious places to start looking for the existence or not of inequality between different social groups is the amount of income that people earn, since money is so important in our society. Do women earn significantly less than men? The New Earnings Survey shows that in 1984 women earned only 74 per cent of men's hourly rate, and only 66 per cent of men's gross weekly earnings. This proportion has remained around this figure since 1975, with only minor fluctuations. In 1975, women earned 72 per cent of men's hourly rate, and 62 per cent of men's gross weekly earnings. This represents an improvement over the situation a few years earlier, since in 1970 women earned only 63 per cent of men's hourly rate, and only 55 per cent of men's gross weekly pay. Table 4.1 and figure 4.1 show these percentages. They represent a serious degree of inequality in the earned income of men and women and, while the 1984 figures show a marked improvement over the figures for 1970, there still remains a serious gap in the earnings of men and women.

Since statistics rarely mean what they appear to at first glance, we should, however, look at these figures with caution. Women work slightly fewer hours than men on average, even when we are only comparing full-time workers, so we should expect that women would earn less than men. While this may account for part of the gap in the gross weekly earnings of men and women, however, it cannot account for the difference in hourly *rates* of pay. Again, part of men's extra earnings comes from their greater tendency to work shifts for which they get paid extra, and overtime which gets paid at premium rates. But this still leaves the question of why men do more of the higher-paid jobs.

There are significant differences in the degree of inequality between men's and women's earnings within the same occupation. For instance, among police officers (below the rank of sergeant) women earn 93 per cent of men's hourly earnings, and women who work as registered and enrolled nurses and midwives earn 90 per cent of the hourly rates of men in this occupation. However, among footwear workers women earn only 71 per cent of men's hourly rates and women sales supervisors earn only 66 per cent of the hourly rates of men in the same occupation.

One of the most important features of the pattern of women's lower wages is that of the occupational distribution of men and women workers.

Women typically get paid less than men because of their concentration in low-paying occupations.

Some writers have suggested that men get paid more than women because women can neither work the hours necessary to earn the higher rates, nor do they possess the skills to get the better jobs because of the time and effort they expend on the care of home and children. This is the argument that women's domestic responsibilities get in the way of their paid work, and prevent them from taking the opportunities for higher-paid work. Women, according to this view, are too busy looking after children (and their husbands and elderly parents) to participate as fully as men in the labour market. If we agree with this view, then women's lower wages may be seen as either their just reward or, alternatively, as the result of a most unjust family system.

This argument may be assessed by examining patterns in women's paid work. The results of a large-scale survey by Martin and Roberts (1984) of 6,000 women may be used to explore some of these issues. They interviewed this large sample of women about their work histories, current employment and current domestic position. They found that when women spent time out of paid work bringing up their children they were placed at a disadvantage on the labour market. However, this survey also found that women spent less time out of the labour market rearing children than is often believed. Women on average spend only five years out of paid work when they are having children, although there are wide variations in this. They also found that on their return many women were unable to utilize the skills that they had acquired before having children. That is, women had felt obliged to take less-well-paid and less-skilled jobs than those for which they were actually qualified. Not only lack of skill, but lack of opportunity to utilize those skills, depressed women's rate of pay. Since, women's break in labour-market experience constitutes only a small part of their life-spans, other factors must help account for their disadvantaged position.

Are women discriminated against simply because they are women? Women are certainly found in a very narrow range of jobs, that is they are *segregated* from men in the labour market. The Martin and Roberts (1984) survey found all manner of weird and wonderful reasons given by husbands as to why they thought women could not do their jobs. It is still popularly held, in the face of all the evidence, that women are incapable of doing certain forms of work.

Access to paid employment

Participation rates

The explanation of the inequality in the wages of women and men is closely related to the explanation of women's more restricted access to paid employment compared with that of men. Women have difficulty

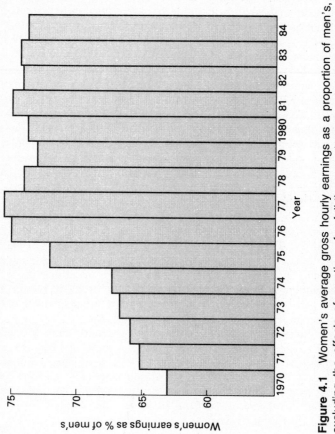

Figure 4.1 Women's average gross hourly earnings as a proportion of men's, excluding the effects of overtime, for full-time employees aged 18 and over, 1970–84

Source: *New Earnings Survey* (1970–84), part A, tables 10 and 11. Crown copyright.

Table 4.1 Average gross hourly earnings excluding the effects of overtime, full-time employees aged 18 and over, 1970–83 (pence per hour)

	1970	1974	1975	1976	1977	1978	1979	1980	1981	1982	1983	1984
Men	67.4	104.8	136.3	162.9	177.4	200.3	226.9	280.7	322.5	354.8	387.6	417.3
Women	42.5	70.6	98.3	122.4	133.9	148.0	165.7	206.4	241.2	261.2	287.5	306.8
Differential	24.9	34.2	38.0	39.5	43.5	52.3	61.2	74.3	81.3	92.7	100.1	110.5
Women's earnings as a % of men's	63.1	67.4	72.1	75.1	75.5	73.9	73.0	73.5	74.8	73.9	74.2	73.5

Source: New Earnings Survey (1970–84), part A, tables 10 and 11. Crown copyright.

obtaining paid employment, not only of a high level of skill and wages, but of any sort at all. They are much more likely than men to be confined to housework within the household for which no wages at all are paid. Further, they are much more likely to be engaged in part-time work, or homeworking.

In Britain in 1983, 47 per cent of women aged over 16 were in paid employment, compared with 76 per cent of men. Among women who were not married (single, widowed, divorced or separated), the percentage was 44 per cent, while among married women it was 49 per cent.

There is a pattern in which women are likely to leave the labour market at the birth of their first child, and to return a few years later, typically when the last child has entered school. The period that women spend out of the labour force for child-care has been steadily reducing over the post-war period. Martin and Roberts (1984) show that, among women whose first child was born between 1970 and 1974, 51 per cent had returned to paid employment within 5 years, and that the median period before return to work for this group was 4.8 years. The median years for return to work for the next cohort, who had their first birth between 1975 and 1979, is estimated to be only 3.7 years. However, the group which had their first babies between 1950 and 1954 had a median of 9.7 years before they returned to paid employment. Before the Second World War the pattern was somewhat different since women were, typically, sacked by their employers when they married. In this earlier period, married women found it hard to get employment, except in exceptional industries, such as cotton textiles, or as casual employees.

Part-time work

Women are far more likely than men to work part-time, as table 4.2 shows. After a period of full-time child-care, many women return to paid employment on a part-time basis. The General Household Survey shows that, in 1982, 44 per cent of women in paid employment worked part-time, and 70 per cent of part-time women workers had dependent children. The number of part-time women workers has continued to increase in recent years despite the recession, growing steadily from 2.8 million in 1971 to 4.2 million in 1984. Since conditions of part-time work are usually poor, this concentration of women in part-time time employment represents their segregation into the worst part of the labour market. Part-time workers who work only a very few hours do not benefit from many of the forms of employment protection introduced by legislation over the last decade or so, although those part-time workers who work at least half the usual hours are covered on some items. Married women with dependent children are especially likely to work part-time (see figure 4.2).

Table 4.2 Part-time working, spring 1984 (millions)

Employees in employment	Males	Females	Total
Full-time	11.1	5.0	16.1
Part-time	0.5	4.0	4.4

Source: Employment Gazette (May 1985). Crown copyright.

Homeworking, (paid work done in the home, for example, sewing garments) is another form of work almost exclusively performed by women and usually entails poor rates of pay and insecure forms of labour contract.

Unemployment

The question whether women or men are worst affected by the current high rates of unemployment is an important issue. According to the official figures, in 1984, 1 million women were registered unemployed, compared with 2.3 million men. However, these figures are often held to underestimate the true amount of unemployment, especially among women, because of the way in which they are collected. The figures are based on the number of people claiming state benefits because they are unemployed, thus excluding those people who are unemployed and yet

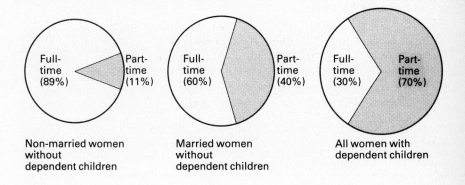

Figure 4.2 Working women by family status and whether working full-time or part-time, 1982.
Source: General Household Survey (1982), table 6.9. Crown copyright.

not claiming such social-security or unemployment-benefit payments. More women than men are excluded on this basis because of the rule which states that men should normally claim benefit on behalf of the women they are living with (whether they are married or not). Thus, many women who are living with or married to a man cannot claim benefits on their own behalf, and, thus, do not appear in the unemployment figures.

An alternative way of measuring unemployment is by asking a sample of the population whether they are unemployed. In surveys of this type, such as the General Household Survey and the EEC Labour Force Survey, about the same proportion of women as men claim to be unemployed.

Ethnicity

There are some significant differences between ethnic groups in the extent and level of women's participation in paid employment. The 1981, EEC Labour Force Survey showed that Afro-Caribbean women were most economically active (i.e. in paid employment or looking for it) at 67.6 per cent, followed by 48.1 per cent among women of Indian origin, by white women at 47.2 per cent, and 15.5 per cent among women of Pakistani or Bangladeshi origin. Yet Afro-Caribbean women have substantially higher rates of unemployment than white women: 20 per cent compared with 13 per cent for white women (according to figures for the PSI survey (Brown 1984)).

Occupational segregation

Restrictions on women within paid employment are further evidenced by the extreme concentration of women within a very narrow range of occupational groups. As figure 4.3 shows, in 1984, 41.5 per cent of full-time women workers were to be found in clerical employment, while a very few further occupational groups account for the rest of most women in paid work. In contrast, men are spread through a much wider range of occupations. This segregation of the sexes in paid employment may be considered to have both a vertical and a horizontal component. Women are confined both to lower-grade jobs (vertical segregation), and to different jobs (horizontal segregation).

Vertical segregation: This is illustrated by figure 4.4 which shows the percentage of women in different grades of the civil service. Women are to be found in the lower grades in large numbers but are much less common as the grades go up, until at the highest grade of all there are no women at all.

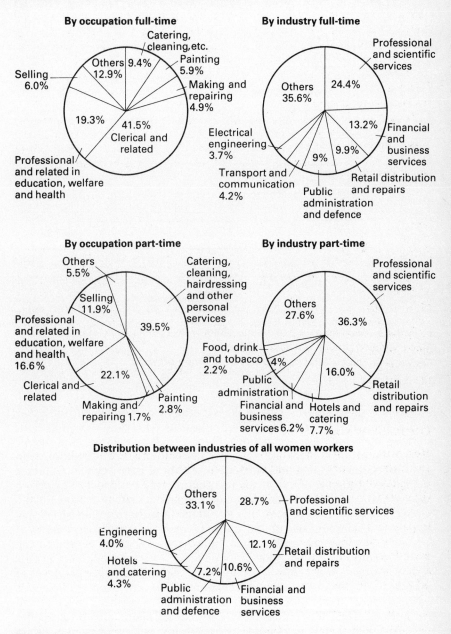

Figure 4.3 Distribution of female workers, 1984
Source: New Earnings Survey (1984), part E, table 138. Crown copyright.

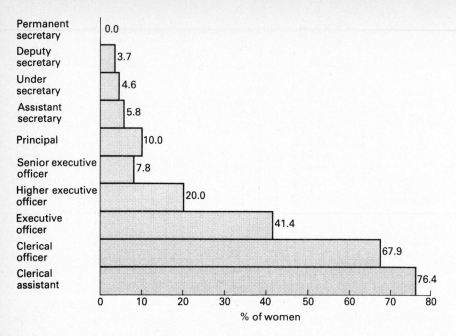

Figure 4.4   Women as a percentage of home civil servants, by selected grades (administration group), January 1984
Source: Civil Service Statistics (1984), table 4. Crown copyright.

Horizontal segregation: This is the separation of women into different occupations from men. Figure 4.5 illustrates horizontal segregation, showing that in most occupations there is either a clear majority of women or of men; there are very few occupations in which there is an even proportion of men and women. While there have been some minor reductions of segregation over the last century, the basic fact of extensive segregation by gender in employment remains a striking feature of the labour market. Further, part of the reduction in horizontal segregation has been a consequence of the entry of men into traditional areas of women's employment, rather than of women into those higher-paying sectors traditionally monopolized by men.

The segregation becomes more marked, the more detailed the level of investigation. This is because segregation within any given workplace is more severe than that shown by national statistics covering all workplaces. The study reported by Martin and Roberts (1984) found that over half their female respondents worked only with other women, while of their sample of men (these women's husbands), 81 per cent worked only with men.

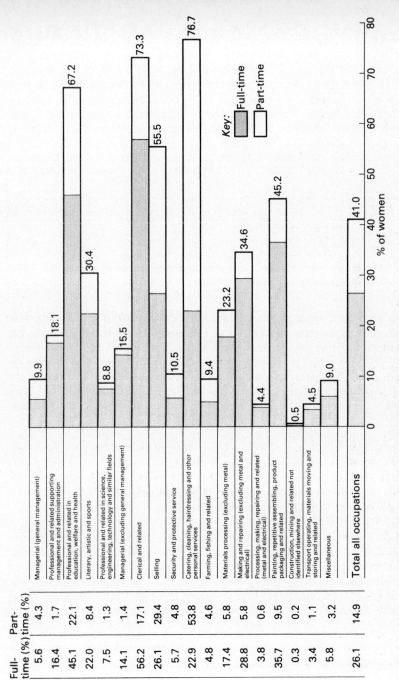

Occupation	Full-time (%)	Part-time (%)
Managerial (general management)	5.6	4.3
Professional and related supporting management and administration	16.4	1.7
Professional and related in education, welfare and health	45.1	22.1
Literary, artistic and sports	22.0	8.4
Professional and related in science, engineering, technology and similar fields	7.5	1.3
Managerial (excluding general management)	14.1	1.4
Clerical and related	56.2	17.1
Selling	26.1	29.4
Security and protective service	5.7	4.8
Catering, cleaning, hairdressing and other personal services	22.9	53.8
Farming, fishing and related	4.8	4.6
Materials processing (excluding metal)	17.4	5.8
Making and repairing (excluding metal and electrical)	28.8	5.8
Processing, making, repairing and related (metal and electrical)	3.8	0.6
Painting, repetitive assembling, product packaging and related	35.7	9.5
Construction, mining and related not identified elsewhere	0.3	0.2
Transport operating, materials moving and storing and related	3.4	1.1
Miscellaneous	5.8	3.2
Total all occupations	26.1	14.9

Key:
Full-time
Part-time

% of women

Figure 4.5 Women as a percentage of occupational labour force, 1984
Source: New Earnings Survey (1984), part E, table 138. Crown copyright.

It is the segregation of employment by gender which gives the best clues as to why women generally earn less than men. Women are confined to those sectors of the job market which pay the least, no matter whether or not they are skilled. One of the main problems for women's pay is that women are in occupations which are badly paid, rather than that women are poor workers. If women were evenly distributed across the spectrum of employment, their pay levels would be much closer to those of men.

	Pay	Security	Promotion prospects
Primary sector	High	High	Good
Secondary sector	Low	Low	Poor

Figure 4.6 The dual labour market

This pattern of segregation is sometimes characterized as that of a dual labour market. Barron and Norris (1976) suggest that the labour market is divided into two segments – a primary sector which provides skilled, secure work at good levels of pay which is reached by long promotion ladders, and a secondary sector characterized by unskilled, insecure work with few promotion prospects and low levels of pay (see figure 4.6). They suggest that women fit into the secondary labour market for five reasons:

1 they are less economistic than men, that is they do not only seek more rewards;
2 they do not seek training as much as men;
3 they are less solidaristic, that is less likely to organize, than men;
4 they may be clearly demarcated from men; and
5 they are more easily dispensable than men.

While the complexity of the patterns of segregation suggest that Barron and Norris' work is oversimplified, their focus on processes in the labour market is of great value. However, they underestimate the amount of opposition there is from some groups of men to women getting good jobs. The work of Hartmann (1979), referred to in the introduction to this chapter, demonstrates the importance of patriarchal structures in the labour market for an understanding of the sexual divisions of labour.

Paradoxes and implications

There is a curious paradox in these patterns of women's paid employment. While the number and proportion of women in paid employment has increased significantly since the Second World War, there has been only a very small improvement in women's wages compared with those of men, and little growth in the range of occupations in which women are able to gain employment. Thus we have a picture of constancy in change.

This contradicts certain of the assumptions and theories which are popular in explaining patterns of inequality in employment. Increasing labour-market experience does not appear to improve women's position in the way that, for instance, 'human-capital' theory would predict. Women's increasing commitment to the labour market does not appear to pay off in the way that would be expected if people were actually rewarded according to their ability and effort. Women's move away from full-time housework does not improve their labour-market position in a manner consistent with the theory that their disadvantaged position in the labour market is due solely to their domestic responsibilities.

Summary

1 Women earn less than men, have lower hourly rates of pay even in the same occupation, are more likely to be employed part-time or in homeworking, and are more vulnerable to unemployment.

2 The market position of women is related to the period that they may withdraw from the labour market to have children. The length of this period has been declining, partly because people are choosing to have smaller families. Women returning to work may find that they cannot use the skills that they had acquired before having children.

3 Women tend to be concentrated in certain kinds of occupations and in the worst-paid levels of those occupations.

4.3 The Household

This section on the family should be read in conjunction with chapter 6, which is entirely on the family. Here we will focus on only those aspects of the family which are central to the issue of gender inequality, while chapter 6 is concerned with a wider range of issues.

Until recently, it was conventional in sociology to analyse the family in terms of norms and roles, and the relationship of family members to their wider kin network. This approach assumed a degree of consensus within the family which was not assumed to the same extent in any other social institution. Even people who wrote of conflict and struggle within the sphere of paid employment would rarely use the same set of concepts to analyse the family. Such a romantic view of the family has been demolished by the women's movement and by recent empirical work on domestic relations. Violence has been discovered to exist within the family, evidenced by the refuges for battered women provided to help women escape from violent men with whom they lived. The romanticized picture of housewives happy over their labour of love is also challenged by accounts of the higher rates of depression among women with small children who stay at home, by such eagerness to take paid work that they will accept rates of pay and conditions of employment that no man would tolerate, and by accounts of the slow hard slog and monotony of housework.

A recent account of the nature of housework is to be found in Ann Oakley's (1974) *The Sociology of Housework*, where she describes the character of this work as any industrial sociologist would describe paid work. She gives accounts of the long hours worked by women and the effort put into maintaining what were seen as adequate standards. She describes how women organized their time creating routines to give order to their days and set goals so as to be able to feel that they had achieved something with their labour. And while these women were not displeased with the *role* of housewife they did not like housework, despite the fact that this was what they spent most of their time doing.

Although it is more usual to think of it as a place of rest, a great deal of work is performed within the household. This includes not only the obvious tasks of cooking, cleaning and child-care, but many more besides. Within Marxist writings housework is usually termed 'domestic labour' in order to capture the full range of tasks involved. One of the issues for us here is who does this work and whether it is equitably distributed between different family members.

Changes in housework?

Some writers have suggested that the increase in the number of household gadgets such as washing machines, fridges, freezers, food mixers, vacuum cleaners and non-stick pans must have significantly reduced the amount of housework that women do. It is optimistically forecast that women will become freer from household burdens as a result of these technological innovations. It is further suggested that this will lead to women being able to take up paid work instead, further advancing their equality with men. Other writers, more pessimistically, have argued that as one household task is reduced or eliminated by advances in technology, then others are added to the list and standards are raised. Thus, it is suggested, the application of modern technology to housework merely changes the tasks a housewife has to do without significantly reducing her overall workload.

The investigation of this issue is quite problematic since it would obviously be rather awkward for a sociologist to hang around lots of families with a stop-watch! Further, it is unlikely that simply asking people whether they have an equal division of domestic labour would produce accurate results, given the obvious temptation to exaggerate one's own contribution to the household.

The most effective method is that of asking all members of a sample of households to keep diaries, noting what they are doing at all times of the day. These time-budget studies, as they are known, reveal that the amount of time that housewives spend on housework has not significantly changed for several decades. However, the proportion of women who are full-time housewives has significantly dropped during the post-war period and, since married women who have paid employment spend less time on housework than those without paid work, this means that overall, there has been a significant decline in the amount of time the average woman will spend doing housework. However, Gershuny's (1983) work has shown that married women typically spend more time on housework than their husbands, even if they also have paid employment. There are complex variations in this, women with young children putting in the largest number of hours of work and women with neither young children nor paid jobs the least.

Equality of consumption in the family?

The household is often treated as a unit of consumption, and it is frequently assumed that all members of a household have equal access to its resources. If this were true, then men and women who are married to each other could be assumed to have the same standard of living. While there is some obvious truth in this, there are also some ambiguities which need careful consideration. There is the issue of whether a household's resources really are shared equally between husbands and wives. Some writers have suggested that men have greater access to them than women. For instance, husbands are more likely than wives to have control over the use of the family car, if a car is shared by the household. Further, the husband is more likely to be able to use family income for his leisure pursuits (e.g. drinking) than the wife.

Summary

1 Domestic life cannot be seen as a balanced and equal relationship between men and women.

2 Women, even those in employment, do considerably more housework than men. The development of domestic gadgets has generally raised standards, not decreased the amount of housework done.

3 Domestic resources are not equally shared either, which suggests that men benefit from the division of domestic labour at the expense of women.

4.4   Culture, Sexuality and Welfare

Femininity and masculinity

That boys are supposed to be aggressive and outgoing, strong and demanding, while girls are neat and tidy, gentle and obedient is central to our stereotypes of masculinity and femininity. Such differences between the genders are encouraged from an early age by a variety of rewards and punishments. These patterns of behaviour are absorbed through the reading materials of children, the toys they play with and the roles they see played out in television programmes. While the 'Janet and John' type of book used to teach children to read portrays slightly less-stereotyped roles than 20 years ago, there is still a clear distinction between the activities of the males and females in the stories. Some people try to introduce toys that do not reinforce gender stereotypes but, nevertheless, girls are much more likely to get dolls to dress up in the latest fashion, boys more likely to get toys for military-type games. Again, while the emphasis in television has changed slightly from a few decades ago, for instance in the acceptance that women can be sufficiently authoritative to read news broadcasts, nevertheless we still have Westerns full of macho cowboys and soap operas with glamorous full-time housewives. Through all these processes, more people are socialized into the forms of behaviour deemed appropriate for their sex; in such a way people learn to become 'gendered subjects'.

Although femininity is often a problem for women seeking equal treatment with men – in that it is easier to take advantage of people who are gentle than those who are aggressive and pushy – its positive aspects in terms of openness, emotional expression and human warmth are also important. Indeed, this latter aspect of femininity is emphasized by some recent writers on masculinity who protest that men do not have such a wonderful deal in the world, since the social pressures on them to contain rather than express their emotions are oppressive and restrictive, stunting their full emotional development. However, while it is doubtless true that men pay an emotional price for the power they have, this should not blind us to the power and privileges from which they do benefit. For instance, while some men's sexual fulfilment is doubtless restricted by the narrow fantasy of sex as power contained in much of contemporary pornography, others enjoy acting out those fantasies of domination on women's bodies.

Much of the early writing on femininity and masculinity adopted a socialization perspective, in which the main question was how people learned gender stereotypes and internalized them. More recent work has shifted the question to that of understanding the varied content of femininities and masculinities, not simply how individuals learn to adopt these identities. Much of this latter perspective has developed through an

Figure 4.7 Contemporary images of masculinity
Source: Melanie Friend/Format and Geoff Franklin/Network.

analysis of media of various sorts, especially television, magazines and film.

Winship (1978) points to the contradictions in the ideology of femininity in magazines such as *Woman*. She shows that women's magazines recognize the experiences of women and, especially, the difficulties of balancing the expectations held by others – in particular husbands and boyfriends – with their own hopes and desires. She shows how stories in the magazines recreate the dilemmas that women face, exploring their various options but with a final resolution in a traditional direction. Here the notion of femininity is a more social one, rather than a matter of personality characteristics; it entails social actions of particular varieties which are not simply dependent upon the person being gentle rather than aggressive.

Comparisons between different women's magazines show the variety of forms of conduct which can be called feminine. The femininity of *Woman* with its emphasis on the role of wife and mother, is vastly different from that of *Cosmopolitan*, where the feminine woman is encouraged to be adventurous in catching the most sexually desirable man, retaining him for as long as he is interesting, and getting a super job into the bargain.

Figure 4.8 Contemporary image of femininity
Source: Roshini Kempadoo/Format.

Cosmopolitan is different from *Woman* yet it still clearly has a view of femininity that includes an emphasis on a sleek appearance, good make-up, and sexy dressing.

There is no one form of femininity but rather, several and the same applies to masculinities. They vary especially by age, marital status, class and ethnicity. For instance, the forms of masculinity among the working class lay more emphasis on physical prowess, than those of the middle classes, where appropriate career is more important because masculine status is limited to being successful as husband-father breadwinner.

Images of femininity and masculinity vary significantly by ethnicity; it would be a mistake to assume that the patterns among British whites are to be found among black people. At the most obvious level there are different dress codes to denote masculine and feminine genders. More significantly, the greater participation of Afro-Caribbean than white women in paid employment means that the cultural notion of the dependent domesticated housewife is a white rather than universal stereotype.

Westwood (1984) vividly captures the ethnic variety of femininity in her ethnography of factory life at Stitch Co. We see the different marriage customs for Indian and white women; the former with arranged marriages with complex, rich ceremonies; the latter marriages based on short-lived romance with white gowns instead of gold saris. Yet, despite the difference, the attractions of marriage for women in both groups comes through clearly; it both symbolizes and constitutes the movement from adolescence to full adulthood; it means independence from the family of origin; and it is hoped that it will be financially advantageous. Gender identities are ways of life, multi-faceted and sometimes contradictory. Yet they are perceived in terms of a fundamental dichotomy, an insuperable barrier between the life-styles of women and men.

Sexuality

It is in the area of sexuality that women are often supposed to have made great advances towards equality with men. We hear of the sexual revolution which is supposed to have happened sometime in the 1960s and liberated women from the constraints of Victorian ideology with its oppressive double standard in which non-marital sex is alright for men and not for women. So, do women have equal access to sexual pleasure with men? Is the double standard dead, and are women sexually liberated? There certainly have been many changes in both attitudes to women's sexuality and in women's sexual practices over the last few decades. But how many?

Equality and sexuality

First, is the double standard dead? While it does seem to be a little less pernicious, in that male respondents less often say that they want to marry only a woman who is a virgin than they used to, it is still alive and well in that women are more often criticized than men for engaging in non-marital sexual activity. This appears to be the case even in youth sub-cultures where one might have expected the greatest changes. Young women are still assessed as either 'slags' or 'drags'. That is, women are more narrowly constrained sexually than are men.

Second, there is the issue of the increase or decrease in overtly exploitative, degrading and violent forms of sexuality. Prostitution, in which men buy sexual access to women's bodies, has not been eradicated by changes in sexual mores. Some men still prefer to buy women's bodies rather than construct egalitarian sexual relationships. Women are not, however, forced into the worst aspects of this trade by their lack of money to the same extent as they used to be. Pornography, however, appears to be both growing in its availability, and in the violence of its content. Further, some men play out their fantasies of power over women through their sexuality in the form of rape, sexual harassment and other forms of sexual molestation of women. This is hardly the basis of a sexual revolution.

However, there is some evidence that women are more likely to engage in pre-marital sexual activity and that the negative sanctions on this are less than they used to be. The much greater availability of contraception and safe abortion has made the consequences of sexual intercourse for women, in terms of unwanted children, much less likely. Indeed, some writers have suggested that the development of cheap, fairly reliable and fairly safe forms of contraception, together with the liberalization of the laws on abortion, have been among the most important gains to women in recent decades. They have meant that women are no longer quite so much at the mercy of their biology and may engage in sexual intercourse free from the worry of unwanted pregnancy. The 1967 Abortion Act made it possible for women to get abortions if they were in the early stages of pregnancy and could persuade two doctors that they met certain criteria. These criteria were open to interpretation, but meant that a woman could get an abortion if either her physical or mental health were deemed to be at risk. Some doctors have interpreted this broadly, since an unwanted pregnancy can be catastrophic to the life of a woman, so that abortion is granted to any woman who considers this to be the case. Others stick to a narrower and more penal interpretation. The growth of non-profit-making abortion clinics since the act has meant that abortion is widely available.

Some writers have been sceptical of the advantages to women of these advances in contraceptive and abortion technology. They have suggested that the changes have simply meant that women are freer to be sexually exploited by men, and that greater sexual activity does not mean better sex. Others have pointed to the medical hazards of the new devices, and the deaths and illnesses of women which have resulted. Further, not all women feel free to use contraceptives such as the pill or diaphragm which require forethought, since 'nice girls' do not plan to have sex.

It is often considered that there is much greater sexual tolerance than used to be the case and the public response to homosexuality and lesbianism is sometimes cited as evidence for this. However, the extent of this new-found tolerance is shown to be limited by the hysteria generated by the disease AIDS against male homosexuals. In the case of female homosexuals, the difficulty lesbian mothers have in retaining the custody of their children when this is contested by the children's father is further evidence that lesbian sexuality is not accepted on a par with hetero-sexuality. Thus, over the area of sexuality as a whole we see some improvements in the lot of women, but not the great liberation that some writers have suggested.

A final point should be made: sexuality is learnt, rather than simply unfolding. Young people usually learn forms of sexuality which are considered appropriate to their gender. Hence men will typically learn more aggressive sexual scripts than women. Sexual orientation towards the same or different gender is similarly something which a person learns rather than is born with. Interactionists point to the fluidity of human sexual conduct; to the changes that can occur within an adult's lifetime; to the movement back and forth between different types of sexual conduct. For instance, interactionists point to the evidence in the Kinsey report on sexual behaviour that over one-third of male adults have had a homosexual experience to the point of orgasm, and that only one in twenty goes on to adopt a continuing homosexual role.

Inequality in housing, health and welfare

Housing

A house is one of the most prized possessions in our society. A home is both a material necessity and, if one is bought, it is usually a person's most expensive purchase. We might imagine that access to housing would be equal for men and women, since they most often share this in the marital home. However, while it is certainly true that many housing units are occupied by both men and women, there are still some issues at stake here.

Until very recently, it was usually the case that the ownership of a house in which a married couple lived was held by the husband, the woman having little direct legal claim to it. This is now less common since building societies, through which most homes are purchased, will now automatically register a property in the names of both spouses. Further, wives' legal access to the marital home has been improved by the recent practices of divorce courts which have more often allowed the wife to claim possession of a portion of the marital home even if her name did not appear on the title deeds.

The issue of access to the marital home at the end of a marriage is a very important one, since to lose one's home is a serious disincentive for a woman to leave an unhappy marriage. The same issue occurs in a slightly different form in rented property, since if the flat or house is registered in the husband's name, the woman can be disadvantaged in times of marital discord. There have been recent increases in the extent to which tenancies are registered in the names of both parties, again of benefit to the woman.

Nevertheless, there remain substantial inequalities in the relative access of women and men to housing because of the fact that men are more likely than women to have an income sufficient to support a mortgage or high rent. This places non-married (divorced, separated, widowed and single) women at a disadvantage on the housing market.

Welfare benefits

Welfare benefits currently form a higher proportion of many individuals' income that was formerly the case, because of the rise in unemployment to levels unheard of since the 1930s, and because of the increase in the number of old people who are dependent upon state pensions.

At first glance there appears to be substantial equality in the income maintenance payments made to men and women, in that the same rates apply to both, and there are no rules debarring women from access to benefits just because they are women. However, the detailed workings of the supplementary-benefit system give rise for concern.

In particular, there are complex rules which disadvantage married women. For instance, while a married woman may claim unemployment benefit, she is ineligible to claim supplementary benefit in her own right, but must be dependent upon her husband (or cohabitee) to do this on her behalf. While the same level of benefit may be claimed by the household, the wife must depend upon her husband for her share of it. There have been some minor revisions of these rules recently, since the European Court ruled that they were discriminatory against women, but this has not made much difference.

What are the implications of the structure of welfare benefits for women? Is it trivial and a result of the state simply being slow in adapting to contemporary patterns of gender relations, and new patterns of women's employment in particular? Or is it part of the systematic structural bias of the state, part of a policy to entrench the nuclear family? In fact, benefits are so low as to make it difficult for a woman and her children to live on them, which puts pressure on her to find another male supporter. Also the cohabitation ruling makes it difficult for a woman who is on supplementary benefit to have a relationship with a man without becoming financially dependent upon him, since her benefit will be stopped if they are deemed to be cohabiting.

Health

Regarding access to health care, we meet the fact that women usually live longer than men. This is one area of life in which women have a definite advantage! It would appear that access to the health service is reasonably equitable between men and women, and that women's longer lives should not be attributed to prejudice against men in the health sector! However, some writers have suggested that the diseases commonly found among men are treated with greater concern and more expensive medical treatment than those more commonly found among women. For instance, attention has recently been drawn to the inadequate provision of screening for cervical cancer despite the fact that this service could provide the means of identifying early forms of the disease before it reaches its incurable and lethal stage. (More discussion of women and health can be found in chapter 9, section 9.5.)

Education

Education is important in determining the place in the social hierarchy that an individual can assume (see chapter 8, section 8.4). Girls do not gain the same level of formal qualifications as do boys, and the gap is especially marked at the upper levels of education, in the universities. However, there has been a substantial diminution in the gap between the educational achievement of girls and boys in recent decades.

Statistics from the Department of Education and Science show that girls are now more likely than boys to gain 'O' levels, obtaining 51 per cent of 'O' level passes in 1983. Boys gain only very slightly more 'A' levels than girls, and the gap is still closing. In 1983, girls gained 47 per cent of the number of 'A' level passes.

In further and higher education, the gap has also been declining in recent years. In 1983, young women took up 53 per cent of the non-advanced places in further education, although only 38 per cent of the advanced further-education places. Also in 1983, young women constituted 38 per cent of the number of students in advanced-level courses in polytechnics. In universities, women took 41 per cent of the under-graduate places in 1983–4, a significant improvement over the 28 per cent of such places in 1965–6. This proportionate increase is still continuing, despite an overall reduction in the number of university undergraduate places (see table 4.3 below). The number of women postgraduate students has also substantially increased, from 21 per cent in 1965–6 to 32 per cent in 1983–4, although this is still significantly below the proportion of women undergraduates, and is far from an equitable distribution between the sexes.

This picture of increasing equality in the number and level of educational qualifications gained by women and men, should however, be

Table 4.3 Women as a percentage of full-time undergraduates and post-graduates in universities, 1965–6 to 1983–4

	Undergraduates				Postgraduates			
	Men	Women	Total	Women as % of total	Men	Women	Total	Women as % of total
1965–6	101,519	38,660	140,179	27.6	22,568	5,860	28,428	20.6
1970–1	129,533	56,339	185,872	30.3	32,592	9,492	42,084	22.5
1975–6	136,883	74,585	211,468	35.3	36,707	13,083	49,790	26.3
1976–7	142,665	78,820	221,485	35.6	36,631	13,663	50,294	27.2
1977–8	148,107	83,547	231,654	36.1	35,314	13,557	48,871	27.7
1978–9	151,079	88,144	239,193	36.8	35,131	14,065	49,196	28.6
1979–80	152,011	93,082	245,093	38.0	33,470	14,175	47,645	29.7
1980–1	153,284	97,870	251,154	39.0	33,013	14,513	47,526	30.5
1981–2	152,497	100,874	253,371	39.8	32,331	14,493	46,824	31.0
1982–3	148,574	101,450	250,024	40.6	31,159	14,211	45,370	31.3
1983–4	144,261	99,988	244,249	40.9	32,502	14,971	47,473	31.5

Source: Equal Opportunities Commission (1985), p. 15, from data in: *Hansard*, 13(18), 27 November 1981, column 488; University Grants Committee, *University Statistics*, 1981–3, 1983–4, 1, *Students and Staff*, table 1.

qualified by an assessment of the segregation of women into certain fields of educational endeavour. Women are much more likely to gain arts qualifications, while men are more likely to gain scientific ones. Further, women are more likely to gain craft qualifications in domestic subjects, while boys are more likely to gain craft qualifications in metalwork, woodwork and technical drawing. If we lived in a society where such specialization had little significance, this difference might not matter. However, this is not the case, since science and technical qualifications have some important occupational advantages over arts and domestic ones. In 1983, while girls gained 98 per cent of the 'O'-levels in domestic science, they gained only 5 per cent of those in technical drawing; girls gained 75 per cent of the 'A'-level passes in French, but only 21 per cent of those in physics. The same pattern is repeated in further education, with girls gaining only 4 per cent of the places on advanced further-education courses in engineering and technology, yet taking 70 per cent of those in medical, health and welfare courses at this level. Again, among undergraduates in universities we find only 9 per cent of the full-time places in engineering and technology taken by women, yet they fill 69 per cent of those in language, literature and area studies (as table 4.4 shows).

Education in schools, colleges and universities is only one part of the educational system in Britain. There are also a wide range of training schemes, run both by employers, often involving day-release schemes, and by the Manpower Services Commission. Only 5 per cent of girls attend day-release schemes in 1984, compared with 12 per cent of boys. These figures represent an increase in the number of girls on such courses, but a decline in the number of boys, in recent years. There has been a rapid increase in the number of young people on training schemes organized by the Manpower Services Commission (see also chapter 2, section 2.8, and chapter 8, section 8.3). With the high levels of unemployment among young people, these are beginning to form an increasingly important sector of activity. In February 1985, there were 162,148 male trainees on the Youth Training Scheme but only 121,215 girls. Among the girls, 81 per cent were on the Mode A employer-based schemes, as opposed to 72 per cent of the boys. On the Mode B schemes (which are in colleges and voluntary organizations), girls were significantly less well represented in the information-technology schemes and training workshops, as figure 4.9 demonstrates.

There are, thus, significant inequalities in the education of males and females in contemporary Britain. Nevertheless, education is one of the areas of our society in which the inequalities between men and women are at their least, and appear to be continuing to decrease.

Summary

1 Distinct images of masculinity and femininity are presented in the

Table 4.4 Women as a percentage of full-time undergraduates in universities by selected subjects, 1975–83

	Women as a percentage of all students								
	1975	1976	1977	1978	1979	1980	1981	1982	1983
Education	67.1	69.3	65.4	64.6	67.2	65.7	65.4	65.3	65.8
Medicine, dentistry and health	36.3	36.7	37.5	38.6	40.2	41.7	43.2	44.9	44.5
Engineering and technology	4.0	4.4	4.9	5.5	6.1	6.9	7.6	8.6	9.1
Agriculture, forestry and veterinary science	29.1	29.5	32.1	32.9	35.0	36.3	37.3	38.6	38.5
Science	29.6	29.9	30.1	30.5	31.4	32.2	32.7	33.3	33.2
Social, administrative and business studies	37.0	37.3	37.9	39.0	40.0	41.3	42.4	43.8	44.8
Architecture and other professional and vocational subjects	24.0	25.9	26.0	27.9	30.6	32.6	34.4	35.9	36.5
Language, literature and studies	62.4	62.8	63.9	65.0	66.7	67.8	68.5	69.2	69.0
Arts, other than languages	51.9	—	52.2	52.6	53.2	54.3	54.5	54.4	53.8

Source: Equal Opportunities Commission (1985), p. 15, from data in: Department of Education and Science, *Statistics of Education*, 6, *Universities*, 1970–9, table 1; University Grants Committee, *University Statistics*, 1980–2, 1983–4, 1, *Students and Staff*, table 1.

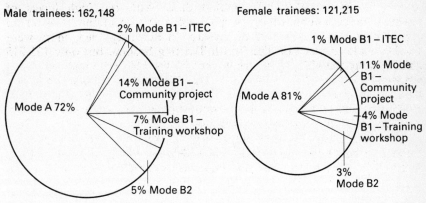

Figure 4.9 Distribution of trainees between modes of the Youth Training Scheme, February 1985

Source: Equal Opportunities Commission (1985), p. 11, from statistics provided by the Manpower Services Commission.

media and the educational system which have a profound effect in forming gender identities. There is, however, some variation in these images with different kinds of femininity being represented.

2 Women are still not permitted the same sexual freedom as men.

3 There are substantial inequalities between men and women in housing, welfare benefit and health.

4 Generally, girls do not achieve the same level of formal educational qualifications as boys, although the gap is narrowing. Girls also tend to take certain subjects at school or university in much the same way as they are segregated into particular jobs.

4.5   Politics, Power and Violence

This section looks at overt struggles over power. It will encompass issues of the force men use against women, gender relations in the formal political arena, and the variety of women's resistance to their subordination. It will ask why women put up with their subordinate position in society, or rather, examine the strength of the pressures which make it difficult for women to produce social change despite their continuing attempts to do so.

Male violence

The extent and significance of male violence against women is a contentious issue. The official statistics reveal only a relatively small amount of such violence, yet most women are sufficiently convinced of its prevalence to organize their lives quite carefully in order to protect themselves from being exposed to such violence. For instance, most women are reluctant to walk by themselves at night.

Sociologists have varied quite substantially in their assessment of the situation. Some have taken the official statistics at their face value and suggested that such violence is the infrequent action of a few psychologically disturbed men. Others have argued that the official statistics are grossly inadequate and seriously underestimate the extent of such violence, and hence its significance for women.

The official crime statistics show that, in 1980, 421 cases of rape were proved in the courts, out of a total of 1,225 cases recorded by the police, and that 2,423 cases of indecent (i.e. sexual) assault were proved out of 11,498 recorded by the police. (The British crime statistics do not make it possible to ascertain the number of convictions for non-sexual violence of men against women since they do not state the sex of the victim.) However, the statistics seriously underestimate the incidence of rape, since the majority of women do not report cases to the police, considering that they have faced quite enough distress without taking such a case through the courts.

A community study of violence by Hanmer and Saunders (1984) also shows that male violence against women is widespread and that the official figures are a gross underestimate. In their study, they interviewed women in one neighbourhood in depth about the violent experiences they had suffered. Rather than only recording those instances of violence that the women had reported to official agencies such as the police, they explored a wide range of violent incidents from the women's points of view. They concluded that the level of violence was high and reported that, in a period of only one year, 59 per cent of women had experiences of violence. These researchers divided this violence up into three categories: threats, violence and sexual harassment. They found that over the course of the year, two-thirds of the women interviewed reported experiences of sexual harassment, one-quarter of the women had experienced threats, and one-fifth, violence. In order to estimate the level of violence an average woman would experience in the course of her life, this figure would need to be multiplied by the number of years the average woman lives.

The conventional accounts of violence against women suggest that most men who are violent to women are mentally unstable in some way. They argue that these men have suffered bad childhood experiences which have prevented their normal development. These accounts imply that incidents of violence against women are few and far between; that they are products of a few sick individuals. However, these explanations of violence against women do not tally with the evidence of the extent of the violence nor its continuity with other forms of male conduct towards women.

Rape and battering are merely one end of a continuum of aggressive forms of behaviour of men to women. This continuum includes forms of behaviour such as flashing, sexual harassment and wolf whistles. It also has links with exploitative forms of sexuality such as prostitution and pornography. These forms of behaviour from men to women, while by no means universal, are sufficiently regularly repeated features to be considered institutionalized practices. Indeed, they are often considered to be so routine that they are taken to be 'normal'. The response of the law-enforcement agencies is taken by some writers as further evidence that this violence against women is considered legitimate and that the state should, therefore, be considered a patriarchal institution rather than a neutral body. The neglect by the police force of women's complaints of rape, domestic violence and other forms of physical abuse by men is now quite notorious (figure 4.10).

The lenient sentences handed down by judges, in those minority of incidences in which men are convicted of these crimes, is only slightly less so. Indeed, the study by Hanmer and Saunders (1984) suggested that women's low expectations of police assistance led them to become ever

Figure 4.10
Source: Idea from Hanmer and Saunders (1984), p. 46.

more dependent upon other men who were also untrustworthy. They suggest that this causes a vicious circle for women: the fear of violence leads women to greater dependency upon a known male; dependency makes the woman particularly vulnerable to attack from this male, because he has no fear of retaliation; when women go to the police about such attacks nothing is done; consequently many women consider that the police are unhelpful, and this reinforces women's fear of violence and dependence upon individual male protectors. This vicious circle is shown in figure 4.11.

Thus we see in sociology two strikingly different analyses of crimes of violence against women: one in which they are the infrequent consequence of a few mentally deranged men (which is supported by the low incidence of such crimes in the criminal statistics); and one in which they are an institutionalized set of practices which are part of an overarching system of gender inequality (in which the low number of convictions for such crimes is merely evidence of the state's collusion). The former, while fitting in with much of popular ideology, is contradicted by current sociological studies of men's violence; the latter is more consistent with the evidence of this research.

Formal politics

The public sphere and the political arena are important in determining aspects of social inequality. While women now have many of the formal

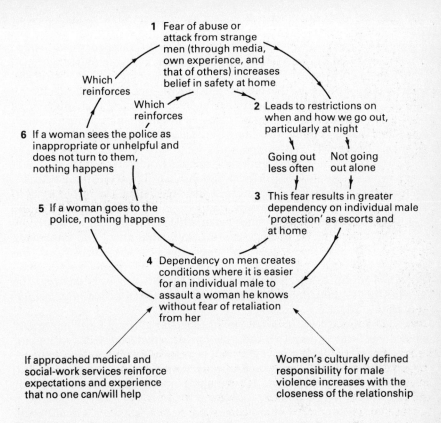

Figure 4.11 The perpetuation of the division between the public and private sphere of women's lives

Source: Hanmer and Saunders (1984) *Well Founded Fear* (London, Hutchinson), p. 66.

political and legal rights that men have, there is still a striking absence of women from positions of public power and authority.

Over the last hundred years, women have won most of the legal and political rights that men possess. All adult women won the vote in 1928, after partially winning it for women over 30 who possessed some property in 1918. This is the most important of the political rights and is the basis of women's claims to equal citizenship with men. Women are not debarred from any legal statuses which are held by men, as they were in the last century. Having won the vote, women were able to make good their claims to the right to sit on juries and to take up seats in Parliament and local government.

In the early 1970s, the government passed two acts of parliament which were supposed to make illegal certain forms of discrimination against women, especially in paid work. In 1970, the Equal Pay Act made it unlawful to pay women less than men for doing the same or similar work (although this was not to be implemented until 1975). In 1975, this legislation was further strengthened by the Sex Discrimination Act, which made it unlawful to discriminate against women in a wide range of fields, including employment. This legislation was the outcome of a struggle, primarily by women in the labour movement, since the late-nineteenth century. However, this legislation has been less effective than many of its supporters had wanted and most cases of discrimination against women which are taken before the industrial tribunals do not succeed. Two reasons explain this low success-rate. First, the tribunals to which the cases are taken are almost entirely composed of representatives of that group which benefits from discrimination against women, that is, men. Second, there are many loopholes in the legislation; for instance, until very recently a woman could only claim equal pay if she were doing the identical work of a man and, since occupations are typically segregated by sex, it is often difficult to find such a comparable man. The underlying problem is that the legislation only touches the surface of the disadvantages that women face, which are more deeply rooted than individual instances of overt discrimination. This can be seen from the way in which occupational segregation thwarts the effective implementation of the Equal Pay Act.

It is sometimes suggested that women's legal rights are fairly minor and have done little to improve the position of women in society. Yet for others, these rights demonstrate that women have now gained equality with men. Perhaps the most appropriate position is that these rights are necessary, but not sufficient for women's liberation, and that in their absence things would be a lot worse.

Another question is whether women do, in fact, have real equality with men in access to public positions, and how significant this is for gender inequality. Women MPs make up only a very small proportion of the total number of MPs. In the 1983 general election, only 23 women won seats in the House of Commons but out of a total of 635, so that only 3.5 per cent of MPs were female. The proportion has changed very little in the 50 or so years that women have had the vote, and the current number is actually one less than that in 1945. The high point was reached in 1964, when a grand total of 28 women were elected to the House of Commons. There are no substantial differences between the parties, although the Conservatives have usually had a slightly lower proportion than the Labour Party or the Alliance. The Cabinet formed in the reshuffle of Ministers in the autumn of 1985 was the first since the war to contain no women (apart from the Prime Minister herself). Britain has one of the lowest proportions of elected female representatives in the Western world.

There is a slightly higher proportion of elected women representatives in local government than in central government. In 1982, women formed 18 per cent of elected local-government members. This varied from 20

Table 4.5 Women as a proportion of local councillors, by type of authority, 1982

	Number of councils	Male councillors	Female councillors	Women as a % of total
London boroughs	32	1,534	391	20.3
Non-metropolitan districts	333	12,080	2,778	18.8
Non-metropolitan counties	47	2,991	677	18.5
Metropolitan districts	36	2,068	395	16.0
Scottish districts	53	957	166	14.8
Metropolitan counties	6	513	86	14.4
Greater London Council	1	79	13	14.1
Scottish regions	9	385	53	12.1
Scottish Islands	3	73	5	6.4
Total	520	20,680	4,564	18.1

Source: Equal Opportunities Commission (1985), p. 35, from data in *The Municipal Yearbook and Public Service Directory*, 1983.

per cent in the London boroughs to 6.4 per cent in the Scottish islands, as table 4.5 shows.

Women hold a very small proportion of other public offices. In 1984, the government appointed 31,172 men to public bodies, compared with only 7,233 women, that is, 19 per cent. The government departments varied widely in this, from only 3.5 per cent of employees in Agriculture, Fisheries and Food, to 32 per cent in the Home Office. There are very few women judges, and very few women on the boards of nationalized industries. Even the Equal Opportunities Commission appointed a male chief executive in 1985. There have never been any women chief constables, and women are in general at the lower levels of the police force. Women hold only subordinate positions in the military forces.

Among trade unions, the picture is little different. In the National Union of Tailoring and Garment Workers (NUTGW), there were only 8 women members of its 15 strong executive in 1984, despite the fact that 91 per cent of its members were female. Similarly, in the National Union of Public Employees (NUPE), one of the unions with the largest female membership, 10 out of 26 of its executive were women, despite women being 67 per cent of its membership. The situation is the same in the majority of trade unions. However, some trade unions now have special women's committees to assist the representation of the views of their women members in an effort to ameliorate the problem.

Women's representation in the European Parliament is somewhat better than in the British Parliament. After the 1984 elections, 17.5 per cent of. the total number of Euro-MPs were women and, even among the British members, 15.4 per cent were women. Indeed, the European Parliament has been an important source of pressure on the British government to improve its sex-equality legislation. The EEC declared that the 1975 Sex Discrimination Act (which incorporated the 1970 Equal Pay Act) did not come up to its standards, and that the British government had to make it stronger. This is the reason that the 'equal-value amendment' was passed, which means that a woman seeking equal pay can compare herself with a man doing work of similar value, and not the more stringent condition of a man who is actually doing exactly the same work. This has led, in 1985, to a series of significant equal-pay decisions to women's advantage.

Instances such as this support the question that a higher number of women in public positions would significantly improve the position of women in society. Indeed, there is a pressure group to get more women MPs, called the 300 Group, which seeks 300 out of the 600 or so seats in Parliament for women. However, others are more sceptical of the significance of merely more women in positions of influence in the state. This is partly because they fear women in such positions simply get incorporated into the structures as they exist, and merely reproduce the same decisions as the dominant male group. Some suggest that it is more important to be able to bring political pressure to bear, so that the elected representatives of whatever sex will pass legislation of benefit to women. Still others argue that Parliament is not the most important site of political struggle for women, and that women would be better spending their political energies at the level of local politics or in everyday struggle.

In short, women are relatively absent from the formal positions of power in contemporary British society. This is a problem both in its own right, and because it reflects the relative lack of all forms of power that women have in contemporary Britain.

Acceptance and resistance

In the face of the documentation of the unequal treatment women receive in contemporary Britain, one in tempted to ask why women put up with it. The insuperable difficulties of doing anything else is one answer often suggested. Women have difficulty organizing because of the isolation they experience in the home, combined with their socialization into passivity. Further, once women get themselves into the position of dependent housewives, they have a vested interest in the maintenance of the status quo since it is too late in their lives to think of independent careers, and sexual freedom merely means the freedom for their husbands to seek younger women. While these approaches may have a grain of truth in them, they founder in the evidence of women's actual political activity around their own demands. Women have long been politically active; it is not something confined to the present wave of feminism. The women's movement at the turn of the century raised and won a wide range of radical demands for women.

The contemporary women's movement has constructed a list of seven demands:

1 equal pay and job opportunities;
2 equal educational opportunities;
3 free contraception and abortion on demand;
4 24-hour child-care;
5 legal and financial independence;
6 an end to discrimination against lesbians and the right to an autonomous sexuality;
7 an end to male violence.

In pursuance of these demands there has been a lot of collective action. For instance, the campaign for equal pay has been continued by the trade-union movement, especially women trade unionists, after the passage of the Equal Pay Act, since the legislation was rather weak. In education, we have seen campaigns to allow girls to take crafts in school and to be given non-stereotyped jobs on the youth-training schemes. The abortion legislation of 1967 is regularly defended against attempts to restrict the relatively liberal access given to women within that Act of Parliament. Women still seek equal treatment under the social-security provisions, for instance in being allowed to claim benefit as individual persons, and not be treated as dependent on the men they live with. The actions around sexuality have included campaigns against the derogatory images of women in pornography. The problem of male violence against women has been attacked by the provision of refuges for battered women to facilitate their escape from violent men, and rape-crisis lines to help women who have been sexually attacked. Indeed, this chapter may also itself be seen as the result of feminist activity within sociology, in that analyses of the position of women in society are no longer confined to chapters on the family.

Summary

1 Official statistics understate the amount of male violence against women both in public places and in the home. Some of the lesser forms of violence are almost routine and tend to be ignored by the police.

2 Women have achieved some parity in legal and political rights, although some of the more recent equal-pay legislation is not very effective.

3 There are comparatively few women in public positions, in politics or the trade unions, for instance.

4 Although, for various reasons, women may have difficulty in organizing themselves, there is now a growing and influential women's movement.

4.6   Women's Position in British Society

This overview of the relations of the genders in contemporary British society has demonstrated the severe nature of the inequality between men and women today. While the situation has improved to some extent in recent years, especially in the field of education, nonetheless the basic pattern of inequality remains in all aspects of the social structure, from paid work to the household division of labour, from sexuality to violence.

This chapter has examined spheres in which the experiences of men and women diverge in modern Britain and differ in a way which is, typically, to the disadvantage of women. Gender is not the insignificant phenomenon that some class theorists have suggested. Nor is the allocation of rewards in contemporary Britain commensurate with skill, hard work and the importance of one's contribution to society, in the way that functionalist analyses of stratification would suggest. Neither is the rosy functionalist conception of the family based on complementary roles correct; some aspects of consumption might be shared, such as a common roof, but the unequal distribution of power, the prevalence of paid employment among married women, and the violence some women suffer from men they live with, precludes such an interpretation.

So far, we have given a view of the myriad ways in which women are disadvantaged. The next question is that of whether and how these are connected to each other, and also how they relate to inequalities of class and race.

The radical feminist analysis described at the beginning of this chapter would see these as aspects of men's patriarchal control over women; the Marxist feminists would see them as a result of capitalism; others would see them as the outcome of both systems, and indeed of racist systems too.

The life of women workers at Stitch Co.: a case-study

The practical interconnection between gender, ethnicity and class can be seen in some of the ethnographies of women's lives that have been recently produced. For instance, Westwood (1984) explores the lives of women factory workers. As is typical of most women's paid employment, this work is not considered particularly skilled and wages are low. The workers studied by Westwood made up clothes from pre-cut pieces of cloth, using sewing machines and presses to finish them. The work was less skilled than it had been formerly since no women made up a *whole* garment, but rather worked on one fragment of the process, for instance sewing up side-seams all day, every day. The women were segregated from the male workers in the factory, and the remaining skilled jobs – cutting the cloth and mending the machines – were retained by the men, despite the willingness of some of the women to learn these skills. The white, male mechanics thus had control over the women, since the female machinists were dependent upon the men to maintain and mend their machines. This segregation of men to skilled work and women to unskilled gave men control over women both in the factory and, as a consequence of their higher wages, in their homes as well.

The division of labour placed restrictions on the options open to women in all other aspects of their lives. While this took different forms for the Asian and white women involved, nontheless for all it was the only real economic option. Westwood describes the various forms of dependence of the women on their husbands and the control the husbands had over their wives. She tells how the women came to the factory beaten by their husbands and how some were scared to be downgraded in their work because they feared a beating from husbands who would think that they were holding some money back. Westwood also captures the women's simultaneous resistance and accommodation to their situation in the custom of making a fancy dress for women about to marry. These costumes were made in work-time, using work materials, and utilized the women's skills as clothing makers to the full. They were gaudy and sexually suggestive and each tailored to the individual characteristics of the woman to be wed. The women stole more work time in celebration of the marriage with much hilarity and sociability. Yet what were they celebrating? A woman's marriage. They hope that marriage will make life better for the woman.

Westwood offers an account of how the structures of gender, ethnicity and class fit together for a specific group of women workers. But what of a theoretical analysis of how these structures intersect?

Conclusions

One way in which gender, ethnicity and class have been seen to fit together is as a consequence of capitalist social relations: women are exploited in the workplace because of the benefit that employers derive from this, and in the home because employers need to have a new generation of workers produced as cheaply as possible. Some of the evidence of the earlier part of this chapter supports this view. Women are paid less than men, and employers do benefit from this. Women do a lot of unpaid work in the home – significantly more than men. However, other data presented here suggest that this is not an adequate explanation.

Within paid employment, male workers benefit from their ability to keep the best and most skilled jobs for themselves; they are beneficiaries of occupational segregation by gender. Men also gain from the unequal division of labour within the home, in which women do more than their fair share of housework. Further, the physical and sexual abuse of women, which the evidence shows is much more widespread than is popularly believed, cannot be understood in terms of anything other than patriarchal relations.

This suggests an analysis in terms of both capitalist and patriarchal relations. However, this is insufficient because by itself it does not enable us to understand the diverse experience of women of different ethnicities. Women of colour who face racist practices cannot be simply incorporated into models which assume white women as the norm. Hence, any adequate analysis must take into account the intersection of capitalist, patriarchal and racist structures in order to understand gender relations in contemporary British society.

Related topics

Since women constitute rather more than half of the population of Britain, discussions of their social position will be found in all of the other chapters of this book. Discussions of various aspects of women's work are to be found in chapter 3, sections 3.2, 3.4 and 3.5. The whole of chapter 6 is concerned with analysis of the household and women's place in it. The relationships of women to the health-care system and to the criminal law are dealt with in chapters 9 and 11 respectively. Chapter 8 treats the educational disadvantages of women amongst other topics. Femininity, masculinity and youth cultures are also discussed in chapter 10, sections 10.2 and 10.5.

Further Reading

For a general account of women in society, Oakley (1982) is easy to read. For a survey of key aspects of women's experience in the family, at work, in education and in health, in Britain now, see Beechey and Whitelegg (1986). For other collections of articles on women's position in society see Evans (1982), or Whitelegg et al. (1982). For more specific issues: on violence see Hanmer and Saunders (1984); on experiences of factory work see Westwood (1984). For a survey of theories of women's position see Barrett (1980).

5 Ethnicity and Racism

5.1 Introduction

A good deal of this book is about the inequality that exists in British society. Sociologists have often talked about this inequality in terms of differences in social class. However, recently, there has also been emphasis on inequalities that arise out of gender or ethnic differences. This is not simply a question of looking at the differences in income, wealth, or educational opportunities between men and women or between different ethnic groups. It also involves a consideration of the *interrelationships* of class, gender, and ethnic inequalities, of the way in which, for example, black people may tend to have working-class jobs.

Inequalities between the British white population and ethnic minorities of various kinds have not always been the focus of sociological interest. In the period 1955–70, a good deal of sociological work in ethnic relations was centred around a different, but related problem – that of the integration of black immigrants into British society. Actually of course, Britain is, in a sense, wholly an immigrant society, subject to successive waves of incomers of diverse origins in earlier centuries. More recently, it has been estimated that there were some 20,000 black people in Britain in the eighteenth century and, in the nineteenth century, substantial numbers of Irish entered the country, especially following the potato famine of the 1840s. Immigration is not a new phenomenon.

Current attention, public and sociological, has focused on immigration since the Second World War from the so-called New Commonwealth, chiefly from the Caribbean and the Indian sub-continent. Sociologists used to operate with a model which conceived of the problem here as being one of integration. How would numbers of black, culturally different, people be integrated into British society? The leading assumptions of this model are as follows (Richardson and Lambert, 1985).

1 The immigrants are strangers by virtue of their colour and culture.

2   The host society is confused and insecure and, as a result, reacts with both hostility and intolerance.
3   The host society is stable and does not have any fundamental conflicts within it.
4   This stability is temporarily disturbed by immigrants. Order is restored, however, when the immigrants adapt to British society and the white population accepts immigrants.
5   This process of adaptation and acceptance may be broken into several phases which can proceed at varying speeds and may be complete only after several generations have passed.

Such a scheme clearly directs attention to certain research problems, the presence of discriminatory or prejudicial attitudes amongst the white population, or the way in which the religious beliefs of ethnic minorities impede adaptation to the British education system. To a large extent, this 'integration' model is still present in sociological research and public concern. However as immigration, at least from the New Commonwealth, has been restricted by various Immigration Acts, so sociological interest has shifted to the inequalities of condition and opportunity of ethnic minorities resident in Britain, many members of which were born in the country. In addition, commentators record the persistent racism of British society, which impedes 'integration' and may function to perpetuate the inequalities suffered by black people. The integration model, in other words, is supplemented and, to some extent contradicted, by an inequality model. It is the latter which is the main focus of this chapter.

5.2   Immigration and the Structure of the Black Community

> Well, it's out of order, isn't it? Everyone's entitled to live, you know, there's a little bit of racial in everyone, but there you go. Especially if we're sort of, we're inundated with them, ain't we, it's getting overcrowded. I mean you've got to admit, even the housing problem's enough, isn't it?
>
> BBC radio *File on 4*, 25 February 1981

The changing pattern of immigration

For many people in Britain, ethnic relations means immigration and the apparent belief that large numbers of people are pouring into the country and making it overcrowded. Certainly that is how the press, with a few exceptions, has treated it. There are more stories about immigration and the alleged evasion of immigration control than about other aspects of race relations, with the possible exception of the recent riots which the media often interpret as caused by 'racial' tension. Furthermore, successive governments have appeared to accept this definition of ethnic relations as largely a question of immigration control. Since an expanding post-war economy stimulated immigration into Britain, governments have imposed more and more severe restrictions on entry.

After the Second World War, migration into Britain was regulated partly by a work-permit scheme which did not, however, apply to British Commonwealth citizens. The British economy was growing, providing an increased demand for labour. Both government agencies and large employers encouraged immigration from the Commonwealth to meet labour shortages throughout the 1950s. At this time, the largest numbers were coming from Caribbean countries, secondarily from the Indian subcontinent, with fairly small numbers from Africa and the Far East. By the early 1960s, however, there was increasing pressure for control over immigration. Acts of 1962, 1968 and 1971 restricted immigration from Commonwealth countries but, because the entry of dependent relatives of earlier immigrants was not restricted, the total numbers of migrants continued to grow throughout the 1960s. Since the 1971 Act, most immigrants have needed work permits and these have been granted mostly for work in those industries like the health service and hotels, where there is a shortage of domestic workers. The numbers of work permits issued have fallen as the British unemployment rate has risen. Furthermore, the proportion of work permits issued to inhabitants of Commonwealth countries has also fallen. It seems likely that permits are increasingly being given for non-manual occupations, which has tended to favour the white inhabitants of developed countries such as the USA and South Africa. The 1971 Act also effectively discriminated against black workers by the introduction of the concept of 'patrials', which was intended to distinguish persons with close ties to Britain from those without and give them the right to reside in Britain. In practice, the majority of overseas patrials have been found in the 'white' Commonwealth of Canada and Australasia.

Even if recent legislation and immigration control has limited the numbers of black *men* seeking work in this country, the wives and children of settled immigrants have maintained the proportion of black immigrants out of all immigrants during the 1970s. Table 5.1 demonstrates the changing pattern of immigration in this period, by showing the proportion of the total numbers of immigrants coming from each part of the world. The total numbers have been going down from 200,000 per year in 1971 to just over 150,000 in 1981. Within this number the balance is shifting towards those from the Indian subcontinent, the EEC and the rest of the world, and away from the Old Commonwealth (Canada, Australia and New Zealand). What these figures conceal, however, is the changing age and gender ratios of immigration, particularly from the Indian sub-continent. The proportion of married women and young people is much higher, as dependants follow the male head of household. In the 1950s, the bulk of immigration was from the Caribbean, the men coming first, followed by their families. Immigration from this area is now very small: in 1981, only 2 per cent of all immigrants were from the Caribbean. The same pattern is now being repeated for immigration from the Indian subcontinent. The number of men being admitted has declined as work permits become restricted, but there is a catching-up process as families come to join their menfolk.

Table 5.1   The origins of immigrants into Britain, 1971–81 (percentages)

	Old Commonwealth[a]	Indian subcontinent[b]	New Commonwealth[c]	EEC	USA	Rest of world	Total number, all countries (thousands)
1971	26.0	12.0	20.5	10.5	11.0	19.5	200
1976	20.9	14.1	20.9	13.1	8.4	22.5	191
1979	15.9	16.9	21.5	11.8	6.7	26.7	195
1980	13.2	14.4	19.5	13.2	9.8	29.3	174
1981	13.1	17.6	19.0	15.0	11.1	24.2	153

Notes: [a] Canada, Australia, New Zealand.
　　　　[b] India, Pakistan, Bangladesh, Sri Lanka.
　　　　[c] All New Commonwealth except Indian subcontinent.
Source: Calculated and adapted from *Social Trends* (1984).

Ethnic minorities in Britain

A concentration on immigration is misleading. It is politically misleading, in that it suggests that the source of the social problems of ethnic relations lies in immigration rather than, for example, in the discrimination and prejudice shown by white people. It is also sociologically misleading for it implies that the bulk of black people are new to this country. This is far from the case. In 1982, over 40 per cent of the people labelled as of Asian or West Indian origin were, in fact, born in this country although the proportion varies from group to group as can be seen from figure 5.1. The reason for these differences is perfectly straightforward. Since the peak of West Indian migration occurred well before that of Asian migration, West Indians have had more opportunity to form families and have children who are, of course, born in Britain. Among those aged 16–24, over 80 per cent of West Indians and 15 per cent of Asians were born in Britain, while of those *over* 25, only 3 per cent of West Indians and less than 1 per cent of Asians were born here. The different timing of migration also has an effect on the age and gender structure of the different ethnic groups. The balance of the sexes among the West Indian population is very similar to that of the white population, but among Asians there is a relatively high ratio of men to women as figure 5.2 shows.

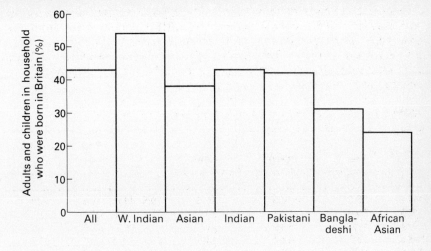

Figure 5.1 Birthplace of Asians and West Indians in Britain, 1982
Source: Adapted from Brown (1984) *Black and White Britain* (London, Heinemann), p. 25, with permission from Gower Press.

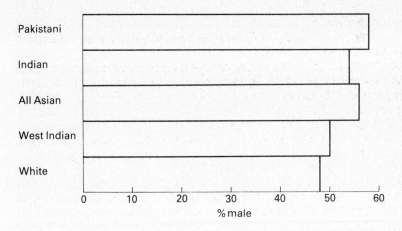

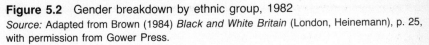

Figure 5.2 Gender breakdown by ethnic group, 1982
Source: Adapted from Brown (1984) *Black and White Britain* (London, Heinemann), p. 25, with permission from Gower Press.

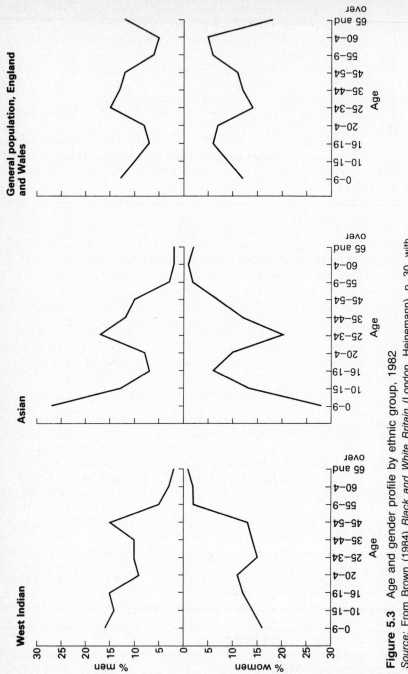

Figure 5.3 Age and gender profile by ethnic group, 1982

Source: From Brown (1984) *Black and White Britain* (London, Heinemann), p. 30, with permission from Gower Press.

The age structure of the West Indian and Asian communities differs not only from each other but also from the general population. Figure 5.3 shows the proportions of people of different ages of each sex in each ethnic group.

If one simply takes age and sex distributions, there are, therefore, substantial differences between various ethnic minorities. There are also differences of religion and of family structure, and quite different expectations about the possibility, or desirability, of returning 'home'. West Indians, for example, came to Britain with the intention of settling here, Pakistanis with the conviction that they would eventually return. This last point, and the more general issues of the adaptation of an ethnic community to British society, is discussed in the following case-study of Pakistani immigrants.

Pakistanis in Rochdale: a case-study of an ethnic group

Anwar's (1979) study is of the Pakistani community in Rochdale, Lancashire. Anwar suggests that immigration from Pakistan takes the form of a chain, with early settlers reporting back on their experiences and encouraging others, particularly family and friends, to follow them. A system of mutual support, very necessary in an alien and often hostile environment, results in the immigrant community being concentrated geographically in towns that offer jobs which white workers often will not take. In common with a number of other Lancashire textile towns, Rochdale attracted immigrants, especially from Pakistan and, according to the census, some 5 per cent of Rochdale's population in 1971 were born in New Commonwealth countries, with about 3 per cent coming from Pakistan.

Settled in a society whose way of life and language was strange and whose members were often openly hostile and abusive, Pakistani immigrants formed a tightly knit ethnic community, maintained by a number of factors. Most important of these is the existence of strong ties of family and friendship. In Pakistan, it is common to find three generations of a family living in the same house perhaps together with aunts, uncles and cousins. In addition, wider family loyalties are intense, extending even to those who share only a very remote common ancestor.

This intensity of family and kinship connections does, of necessity, break down as Pakistanis move to Britain. The extended families are split up as the men move first, to be followed only after a fairly long interval by wives and children and often never by other relatives. Nevertheless, by comparison with the host population, Pakistani immigrant families are very close-knit in several aspects. First, individual households will not be restricted to nuclear families, i.e. parents and their children. Frequently, unmarried brothers of the husband or wife may share the house, as might more distant relatives, or people from the same village in Pakistan may come as lodgers. Second, even if nuclear families do inhabit separate houses, they may be part of a joint family: 'A joint family may consist of several branches living as separate households in different residences but pooling their incomes, all the major decisions relating to finance, ceremony performances and marriages, etc. being taken jointly' (Anwar, 1979, p. 55). Third, most families maintain close relationships with their kin in Pakistan, consulting the head of the family about important decisions, sending money back for the purchase of land and visiting the home country as often as possible. The patriarchal structure of most families reinforces the integration of the whole unit. The father or elder brother makes important decisions for the whole extended family even if members are widely separated geographically.

In sum, Pakistani immigrants in Rochdale maintain very close links with members of their family, distant or near, through exchanges of goods and services, loans of money in times of need, active social contact and advice (or instruction) on important decisions.

The intensity of these family relationships, and the importance of maintaining family and wider connections in Pakistan, are shown in the continuance in Britain of the Pakistani institution of *Biraderi* which governs obligations to relatives and non-relatives outside the immediate family: 'Biraderi includes all the men who can trace their relationship to a common ancestor, no matter how remote' (Anwar, 1979, p. 62). In practice, men may treat even non-kin as members of their Biraderi. It functions as a network of contact and support. Members of a Biraderi who come to Britain act as informants, sponsors and contacts for newer migrants. They help with the provision of housing, food and employment and give continuing support with money, perhaps to set up a business, go on a visit to Pakistan or to cope with unforeseen disasters. Ceremonial occasions such as births, deaths, weddings or circumcisions, would involve the Biraderi. It is important to stress that Biraderi relationships amongst Pakistani immigrants are not restricted to Britain but serve to connect Britain with Pakistan. Obligations incurred by one member in Britain may be honoured by another in Pakistan.

Family, kin, and the more extensive institution of Biraderi therefore serve to help Pakistanis in Britain and to forge a strong sense of community. They also effectively isolate Pakistanis from the wider British community or, as Anwar puts it, the immigrant community is *encapsulated*. There are other factors which contribute to this. The range of occupations taken up is relatively narrow, concentrated in industries where the work is hard, dirty and poorly paid. In Rochdale, this has meant the textile industry, in which immigrants have jobs mostly because whites will not take them. As already indicated, the recruitment to these jobs is usually through the sponsorship of Pakistanis already employed in the industry. The result is the creation of work-groups that are exclusively Pakistani, especially where night-work is concerned. For whites, the night-shift is the least desirable and, as a result, many textile firms are dependent on Pakistanis to work it. In turn, they prefer it precisely because it enables them to be with fellow immigrants and avoid the hostility of white workers on the day-shift. Insulation of immigrant workers into ethnic work-groups is further reinforced by a fairly general lack of adequate spoken English.

Culture and religion also serve to integrate the immigrant community and to insulate it from wider society. The Pakistani parents in Rochdale were very anxious to bring up their children in an Islamic culture and regarded this as the key issue in decisions as to whether or not to stay in Britain. As Anwar says: 'the pattern of the religious activities in the community seemed to maintain a separate Pakistani cultural existence in Rochdale. As religion is the whole way of life so it affects individual social relationships across the ethnic boundaries thereby leading to Pakistanis' encapsulation' (pp. 168–9). Ethnic organizations also play a role in encapsulation by reinforcing loyalty to the community and to Pakistan.

In sum, a variety of processes contribute to the insulation of the Pakistani immigrant community in Rochdale. Not all immigrants are encapsulated to the same extent. Women are much more isolated, since their culture and religion control their public appearances. Amongst the men, different occupations will predispose to different degrees of encapsulation: professional employees, for example, have more contacts with the white community than industrial night-shift workers. Furthermore, encapsulation may only extend to first-generation immigrants who are sustained by the 'Myth of return', the belief that they will return to Pakistan eventually. The second generation may behave quite differently.

Summary

1 Immigration into Britain has been slowed down. There is also a decreasing proportion of men, as wives and children come to join men already in the country.

2 Over 40 per cent of people labelled as of Asian or West Indian origin were born in this country.

3 The balance of the sexes among the West Indian population is very similar to that in the white population. Among Asians there is a relatively high ratio of men to women.

5.3   Ethnic Disadvantage

As Anwar shows, Pakistanis in Rochdale tend to be concentrated in certain industries. The same is true of the male black population nationally which, as can be seen from table 5.2, is over-represented in manufacturing industry, especially vehicles and transport. Black people are relatively less well represented in service industries and in construction. There are also clear differences within the black population. For example, Asians, particularly Pakistanis, are more concentrated in manufacturing than West Indians, the ethnic balance being reversed for transport, and services more generally.

Table 5.2 Industrial sector by ethnic group (percentages)

	White	West Indian	Asian	Indian	Pakistani	Bangladeshi	African Asian
Mining, chemicals and metal manufacture	9	4	7	7	8	2	6
Engineering and metals	15	9	13	14	13	8	14
Vehicles and ship-building	5	12	11	13	10	9	7
Textiles, clothing and leather	2	3	13	8	20	32	7
All other manufacturing	10	14	14	13	19	7	10
All manufacturing and mining industries	41	41	57	55	70	59	45
Construction	8	7	3	3	2	—	4
Transport and communication	10	24	12	16	9	4	12
Distributive trades	8	6	6	4	3	2	13
All other service industries	23	14	17	16	13	31	18
All service industries	41	45	35	36	25	37	43
Public administration and defence	7	3	2	2	—	2	3

Source: Brown (1984) *Black and White Britain* (London, Heinemann), p. 202. Reproduced with permission from Gower Press.

The distribution is broadly similar for women workers, except that there is a heavy concentration of West Indians in the professional and scientific category which is simply due to the large numbers of West Indian women employed in the health services at fairly low levels.

In looking at the industries in which black workers work, we are only examining the kind of work they do – what industry they are employed in. Another way of considering the position of black workers is to consider their socio-economic group (see chapter 3, section 3.2 for discussion of this measure) for this will show what *level* of job black workers hold. *Generally* speaking, black people hold jobs lower down the socio-economic scale, being under-represented in comparison with whites in non-manual occupations, and over-represented in the less-skilled manual occupations. However, there are still differences within the black population. Table 5.3 shows differences between various categories of male worker. For example, a higher proportion of Asians than West Indians is found in the professional occupations. Indeed, the proportion of African Asians who are professionals is higher than that of the white population. A high proportion of West Indians are skilled manual workers. Interestingly, for women workers, there is rather less difference between the white population and ethnic minorities, the latter being relatively over-represented in semi-skilled occupations and under-represented in non-manual jobs as a whole.

Table 5.3 Socio-economic category by ethnic group, 1982 (percentages)

Job level	White	West Indian	Asian	Indian	Paki-stani	Bangla-deshi	African Asian	Muslim	Hindu	Sikh
Professional, employer, management	19	5	13	11	10	10	22	11	20	4
Other non-manual	23	10	13	13	8	7	21	8	26	8
Skilled manual and foreman	42	48	33	34	39	13	31	33	20	48
Semi-skilled manual	13	26	34	36	35	57	22	39	28	33
Unskilled manual	3	9	6	5	8	12	3	8	3	6

Source: Brown (1984) *Black and White Britain* (London, Heinemann), p. 197. Reproduced with permission from Gower Press.

As one might expect, the socio-economic position of black workers affects their earnings. White men on average earn a good deal more than black men, although the earnings differential between different groups of women is much less. A study conducted in the early 1970s found that non-manual ethnic minority workers earned 77 per cent of the earnings of their white colleagues, skilled manual 89 per cent, while for semi-skilled and unskilled manual workers the earnings were the same. However, in this last case, in order to achieve this equality of earnings, ethnic-minority workers have to do more shift-work because their jobs are intrinsically worse paid. These differences derive from a number of factors. For example, black workers are concentrated in certain industries which traditionally pay low wages. Again, it is the case that in certain occupations older people are paid more than younger ones. We have already seen earlier in this chapter that the black population is younger than the white and this will in itself depress wages. Further, within any broad socio-economic category, white workers tend to occupy more promoted positions. But lastly, having eliminated these factors, black workers are paid less than white ones simply because they are black.

So far, we have discussed the position of black people who are in employment. Particularly in times of high unemployment as in the 1980s, it is obviously also important to consider those who are unemployed. In the 1982 survey (Brown, 1984), the results of which provide much of the recent information about the black community in Britain, the unemployment rates are 13 per cent for whites, 25 per cent for West Indians, and 20 per cent for Asians, although there are large differences within the Asian group. When discussing differences in earnings between black and white workers, we noted that it was important to look at a number of factors, for example, the age structure of the two groups and the kind of industry in which they worked. The same is true of the differences in unemployment rates. A whole range of explanations might be available. Black workers may work in industries particularly hard-hit in the recession, or there may be a high proportion in particular age-groups (like the young or old) who are particularly prone to unemployment. One way of looking at the effects of the kind of industry they work in is to see whether black people and whites living in the same area – inner cities for example – have similar rates of unemployment. In fact, although the differences between black and white unemployment are much reduced in these areas, they do not disappear entirely. Similarly, if one compares blacks and whites *within* any age-group, there are still differences in vulnerability to unemployment.

In sum, as far as employment is concerned, ethnic minorities are disadvantaged even if there are differences between different minorities. They are heavily concentrated in particular industries, often those in relative decline; they occupy lower socio-economic positions; have lower earnings; work longer, and often unsocial, hours; and are more prone to unemployment. Further, this disadvantage extends to other areas of social life. For example, the quality of housing occupied by ethnic minorities is much lower than that occupied by whites (see chapter 7, section 7.3). Properties are older and more likely to be terraced houses or flats; they have fewer rooms but more people per room; and they are less likely to have a garden. As with other areas, global comparisons between black and white populations hide differences within the black population. Asians and West Indians, for example, favour very different types of accommodation. The proportion of the former who are owner-occupiers is higher than that amongst whites. West Indians, on the other hand, have a low rate of owner-occupancy and a high rate of tenancy of council accommodation compared with the white population. These different tenures mean that Asians and West Indians have different housing problems. It still remains true, however, that when compared with the white population, black people have worse housing conditions.

Summary

1 Ethnic minorities tend to be concentrated in certain industries, and in the less-skilled occupations with lower pay. They are more vulnerable to unemployment than white workers.

2 Ethnic minorities are also disadvantaged in other ways, e.g. housing.

5.4 Class and Racism

In the previous section, we sought to show that the black population suffers from a series of multiple disadvantages and is often, moreover, heavily geographically concentrated in inner-city areas. As Smith (1977, p. 292), says:

> There is overwhelming evidence from the PEP survey to show that local concentrations of the racial minority groups are associated with poor housing, poor jobs and low incomes, and among Asians with large and often extended families with a high ratio of dependants to wage earners and consisting of people who speak little or no English. Those Asians and West Indians who are more dispersed among the white population are far less likely to suffer every kind of disadvantage than those living in the areas of local concentration.

Explaining ethnic inequalities

The question remains, however, how to interpret these data of ethnically based inequality. What are the factors involved in producing this situation? The essential problem is whether the explanation of racial disadvantage lies in the nature of the British class structure or in the racism, and its associated practices of racial discrimination, which pervades British culture. We will first roughly contrast these explanations.

Class explanations of racial disadvantage

In terms of this approach ethnic disadvantage is essentially a function of the British class structure. British society is unequal, with those at the bottom of the hierarchy having many overlapping disadvantages, as described for black people. Black immigrants form part of this class structure, having jobs which tend to place them at the bottom. They, therefore, share class disadvantage with many white people. Although, as we saw for Pakistanis in Rochdale, the culture of immigrants may separate them out from the white community, the children of immigrants will gradually become assimilated into white society, into the wider working class and some, by upward mobility, into the middle classes. To the extent that black people are not assimilated into white society, the obstacle will be the way that they preserve a separate cultural identity. For example, if they refuse to allow their children to attend British schools, do not learn English, or insist on forming ethnically based work-groups, their assimilation will be impeded. The sociological question here, then, is the way that black people are integrated into white society and the effect that their separate cultural identity has on the rate of integration. Clearly there are policy implications of this view. The suggestion seems to be that integration is desirable and possible if the obstacles posed by black culture were removed. The problem, in other words, is caused by the ethnic minorities themselves. This is very much the view advanced in newspapers, and to some extent, on television.

White racism as an explanation of racial disadvantage

The other view essentially starts from the proposition that the problem is caused by whites, and the disadvantages suffered by black people are the result of white racism and the discriminatory practices of racial discrimination that flow from it. It is white racism that keeps ethnic minorities at the bottom of the hierarchy and separated from white society as a whole. In no meaningful sense are black people part of the British working class. This racism is very profound, going to the roots of British society. It is highly visible in racial attacks or the activities of the National Front, but it also exists in subtler forms at all levels of society in Britain. It is even there in much sociology which, so proponents of this view would claim, is implicitly racist in treating ethnic minorities as the deviants from the British norm. Indeed part of the prevalent culture is the belief that black people have no culture of their own or that what there is will impede their attempts to 'get on' in white society. The sociological implications of this view, that racism produces ethnic disadvantage, are that attention should focus on the history and mode of operation of racism rather than the ways in which ethnic minorities do or do not adapt to British society. The political implication is that blacks should be self-assertive and proud of their black identity and not rely on well-meaning attempts to assimilate them into white society.

The differences between these two ways of approaching ethnic disadvantage show most clearly in the case of education. The former view would see education as one of the most important means by which black people become integrated into the mainstream of white British life. As black children go through the education system, they not only learn to speak English, they also gain qualifications, which help them with jobs, and acquire British cultural values, which enable them to assimilate. It is, therefore, a question of black children *fitting into* the educational system and the sociological problem might be to explain why they fail to integrate. Thus, failure could be due to reluctance to speak English, to the way that black children are suspended between two worlds, or to the manner in which black, particularly West Indian, families do not encourage educational success. From the second point of view, the central issue would not be 'What is it about black children that causes them to fail?' but 'What is wrong with an educational system that produces failure and does not recognize the cultural distinctiveness of black people, whether West Indian or Asian?' In this view, the fault does not lie with black children or their families but with white teachers who label black children as educational failures. This debate over the education of black children is reminiscent of an earlier one over the failure of white working-class children in British schools (see chapter 8, section 8.2). This failure was attributed to defects of language or of home background rather than to an educational system that only valued one kind of language and actively discriminated against working-class culture.

We have presented two possible positions in the explanation of ethnic disadvantage. There is some truth in both positions. They are not irreconcilable and sociological analysis can only be frustrated by trying to make them so. To take the analysis further, we need to look in more detail at racist beliefs and discriminatory practices.

Racism and discrimination

It is quite clear that British society is racist. British culture can often be fiercely nationalistic, as we all saw at the time of the Falklands war. The British way of life is thought to be best and the ways of foreigners, inexplicable. Furthermore, this nationalism is *anxious*. We mean by this that alien or foreign ways of life are not only treated as odd, they are also very threatening, especially when actually present in the country. British history is littered with examples of violent reactions to anything foreign to British culture; such reactions indicate that some feeling of threat is being experienced.

Now, it is, of course, true that many countries exhibit fearful nationalistic reactions of this kind which appear as violent hostility to minority groups. The obvious example from recent times is the treatment of Jews in Germany in the 1930s. However, British people probably have reasons for reacting to *black* immigrants in this way. Britain, after all, was an imperial nation. Until relatively recently, the British benefited greatly from lordship over large numbers of people in many different countries, most of whom were black. For the past 300 years, first as travellers to places deemed exotic, and later as imperial masters, the British have learnt to identify blackness of skin with inferiority, strangeness, and allegedly repellent religious and cultural practices. The decline of empire has only made these deep-seated attitudes more pronounced. It means that the loss of the colonies and the consequent lessening of Britain's position in the world goes hand in hand with the independence of black nations. Immigrants from the New Commonwealth arrived at just the time that Britain lost an empire and with it her position in the world.

For various historical reasons, therefore, British culture is, in a very general sense, racist. Surveys of attitudes tend to confirm this. One recent study (Jowell and Airey, 1984) for example, found that rather more than one-third of the sample described themselves as racially prejudiced. Racism of this kind is constantly experienced by black people at all levels of society even if it takes the more subtle form of simply being treated differently. Here is a black middle-class man speaking:

> Professional blacks are treated as rare specimens by most of their white colleagues. I am no exception. Generally speaking, racist humour is used to make simple conversation and reactions to these generally leaves us, the black individuals, feeling guilty that we have challenged them. It is a continuous process that those blacks like myself, who have moved up (in a manner of speaking) in society, have very often to contend with the labels that not only do we

Figure 5.4   The decline of empire: a child surveys a statue of Queen Victoria, ruler of the largest empire in history, overturned shortly after the independence of Guyana from Britain
Source: The Scotsman Picture Collection.

carry 'chips on our shoulders', but we are over-sensitive to racial issues . . . Making it in Britain is simply a dream for many whites let alone blacks. My colour, my cultural norms and me – a person – will always be viewed through white coloured lenses with all its distortions. (Husband, 1982, p. 181)

Naturally, racism does not always take subtle or relatively gentle forms. Physical assaults on black people are common and there is some evidence that they are becoming more frequent. A Home Office report of 1981 on racial attacks estimated the rates of racially motivated incidents per 100,000 of the population at 1.4 for whites, 51.2 for West Indians and Africans, and 69.7 for Asians in a three-month period. This refers to all incidents, not just those involving offences against the person. These figures, however, certainly underestimate the true rates of racially motivated attacks for they are based on reports to the police and, as is well known, large numbers of incidents are not reported. Indeed a recent study (Brown, 1984) calculated that a more accurate estimate would be a figure at least 10 times the Home Office figure. The media are full of stories of attacks in which black people are assaulted by gangs of white youths in the street or in which black families have their houses regularly attacked. The evidence shows that these incidents reported in the media are merely the tip of the iceberg; for many black people in Britain, physical assault or violent verbal expressions of racial hatred are part of their daily life.

To a large extent, these racially motivated attacks will be random, spontaneous and unorganized. However, one should not underestimate the role played by anti-black organizations like the National Front. White attackers often claim to be members of organizations like this and to be acting on their behalf and, certainly, the National Front has contributed to an atmosphere in which some white people think it acceptable to assault blacks. Clearly, the possibility of being randomly assaulted is going to make black people feel very insecure and anxious, feelings which, in turn, promote the formation of black community and self-defence organizations.

Racism, then, may be subtle or overtly violent. It also permeates practices which discriminate against ethnic minorities and contribute to their unequal position in British society. There are many spheres of life where ethnic groups are faced by discriminatory practices, including recruitment to jobs, relationships with fellow workers, access to housing and contact with the police. We deal with each of these in turn.

Employers and recruitment

We have already seen in section 5.3 that the employment situation of black people is not nearly as good as that of whites; they are concentrated in declining and low-wage industries, work unsocial hours for low wages, have poor promotion prospects and are at greater risk of unemployment. A good deal of this position can be attributed to discrimination on the part of employers.

One standard way of establishing the degree of discrimination in employment is to arrange for equally qualified black and white workers to apply for the same job. The method is for, say, a West Indian to pretend to apply for an advertised job and then to be followed a little later by a white person applying for the same job. These experiments generally show that there is discrimination against black people in the sense that the black actor is not given the job, or is told that it is filled, while the similarly qualified white actor *is* given the job. As Smith (1977, p. 11) says of his tests:

> The results of the actor tests show that there are still substantial levels of discrimination against Asians and West Indians when applying for manual jobs; that the discrimination is stronger against applicants for non-skilled rather than for skilled jobs; that it is mainly based on colour prejudice rather than prejudice against foreigners; and that levels of discrimination against Indians, Pakistanis and West Indians are much the same.

Over all, the white actor was preferred ten times more often than the black one. Similar tests were devised for white-collar jobs by applying for advertised posts by letter in the name of fictitious black and white applicants, again with similar qualifications, but making clear what the applicants' ethnic origins were. In this case, the test of discrimination was whether the applicant was invited to interview. This is a weak test because an invitation to interview is only the first stage of selection. Discrimination is even more likely actually *at* interview. In the event, nearly one-third of black applicants failed to get to interview because of discrimination. Discrimination was highest for male, junior clerical jobs, management trainees and accountants, and lowest for female clerical jobs.

There is, therefore, active discrimination against black workers in both manual and non-manual occupations, being probably more pronounced in the latter. The net effect will be to push ethnic minorities into jobs that are low-paid, dirty, involve shift work, and are vulnerable in an economic recession. It is clearly very difficult to say how much of this discrimination is the result of policy decisions by employers. Many large firms will have official anti-discrimination policies, although the personnel management at local level may practice discrimination, perhaps avoiding hiring black workers or laying them off first in time of recession. Further, firms' employment policies may be discriminatory even when they appear not to be. Thus some northern textile firms set out to hire black workers because white workers will not work shifts for the kind of wages paid.

Relations with workmates

Employer discriminatory practices are often based on the belief that white workers will be opposed to the employment of blacks in any but the most menial of jobs. This belief is often well-founded. Black workers often report encountering overt hostility when they start work. Here is a West Indian talking about his fellow white workers:

> Soon their grumblings became open discontent and no amount of encouragement from the foreman or shop steward could quench the open hostility of the men around us; in fact I was forced to retaliate verbally. During which time I found that at the worst all Englishmen stuck together in regard to the West Indians . . . it was like a thorn in my heels to know that I was working in an atmosphere of hostility. It gave me an unwelcome feeling and a 'you're not wanted here, get out' complex, from which I became utterly pessimistic and a trifle hostile. In the end I lost interest in my job, and the work at hand, and fell down on my efficiency and aptitude as a skilled man. (Collins, 1981, p. 152)

Much of this sort of hostility can be expressed in the practices of trade unions. Again, officially, trade unions adopt anti-discrimination policies. However, these are often frustrated at branch level or by union officials in individual firms. Shop-stewards can fail to support black workers or can participate in employers' discrimination because they know the prejudiced opinions of their members and feel that they cannot afford to lose their support.

Housing

In housing, for example, similar tests using black and white actors to those described in the investigation of discrimination in employment, have also been utilized in studies of the private housing market. These experiments show that at least one-third of landlords discriminate against ethnic minorities on grounds of skin colour. However, as we show in chapter 7, section 7.3, the private renting of housing is no longer nearly as important as it once was; owner-occupancy and council renting are now the most significant forms of housing available. Evidence of discrimination in these sectors is less easy to obtain. However, it seems likely that there is little direct discrimination in the provision of finance for owner-occupation, from building societies and banks. There may be some degree of indirect discrimination in that building societies are sometimes reluctant to lend for houses in certain run-down areas of the city. These may be precisely the areas in which ethnic minorities may have to buy houses because they are cheap. In any event, as we have already seen, owner-occupancy among ethnic minorities, especially those of Asian origin, is higher even than that among whites and, on these grounds, discrimination in this sector is unlikely to be severe. However, a number of studies have shown that the allocation of council housing is likely to be discriminatory. Black people can be denied eligibility by rules which were originally drawn up for completely different purposes; property let to ethnic minorities tends to be of lower quality than that allocated to the white population; and black families, which tend to be larger, may not find council accommodation which is large enough for their needs (Brown, 1984).

The police

A question that has, from time to time, preoccupied newspapers and television in the last few years is the relationship between the police and black people, especially young black people. There is now a good deal of evidence of such discrimination. Thus, a recent survey of the Metropolitan Police suggested that the culture of the police was pervaded by racially abusive talk. A lecturer at a police training college published essays written by officers in training which showed them to be openly racist. Of course, studies of police attitudes or talk however racist, do not *necessarily* show the police to be discriminatory in practice. However, there is also evidence of active discrimination of this kind. A privileged account of racial prejudice in the police is provided by an interview with the first black policeman to join the Metropolitan Police, Sergeant Roberts, who is still a serving officer nineteen years later:

> While still a recruit at the Hendon police training centre, he began receiving notes that said 'Nigger go home' – on the kind of paper that only his fellow recruits were using . . . 'If anyone tells you that there isn't prejudice they have got to be lying' . . . 'If you were brought up in Brixton or Hackney, and have been stopped regularly for no reason by the police, you are bound to view them with a bit of hatred' . . . But Roberts discovered that it did not matter much where he grew up when he was driving through Southwark late one night on his way from work. He was pulled over by a policeman who verbally abused him after he had challenged the officer's authority.
> 'He said to me, "Look, you black bastard, I can do what I bloody well like",' Roberts says. 'I thought, bloody hell, it does really happen.' (The *Guardian*, 13 May 1986, with permission)

In discussing the prevalence of racism and discriminatory practices in British society, we have often drawn a distinction between the racism of lower levels of an organization and the official anti-discrimination policies of the organization itself. We can, therefore, distinguish the employment policies of the head office of a large firm from the activities of local personnel managers, the stand taken by unions from the racism of union branches, or the declaration of senior police officers from the practices of the individual junior officer. It is, similarly, often argued that the racism manifested by the central institutions of British society is actually due to the activities of a few individuals – the rotten apples. However, too much is made of the distinction between official policies and the lower levels of an organization, and the rotten-apple argument largely misses the point. The central issue is that racism is so widespread that it is institutionalized. As we have shown in employment, housing allocation and the police force, discriminatory attitudes and practices are so pervasive as to be part of the everyday, routine culture of the organizations concerned. To some extent, also, the very operating procedures of an organization may be discriminatory in practice even if they are not overtly intended to be. For example, in the late 1970s there were widespread reports in the press and on television of attacks on and thefts from innocent people in the street, attacks which subsequently became known as 'muggings'. It became widely accepted that the attackers were predominantly black, although there was little evidence for this belief. This effectively defined black people in the street, especially black youth, as potential criminals. Not surprisingly, in view of the public pressure, the police responded by adopting routine tactics of stopping and searching black people in the street, especially in areas where muggings were thought to be common-place. Not precisely by design then, racism and discriminatory practices become part of the institutional culture.

The underclass

At the beginning of this section, we distinguished two kinds of explanation of ethnic disadvantage; one concentrates on racism and discrimination and the other on the economic mechanisms of the British class structure. As we have said, these explanations are not inconsistent and both contain elements of the truth. The economic and social requirements of British society create disadvantaged positions in the class structure and it is the racism of British society that ensures that black people continue to fill them. A number of European countries are dependent on migrants from poorer European or Third World nations to make up a labour shortage in certain industries. Britain is, of course, one of them. Effectively, racist policies not only fill these jobs with black workers but then discriminate against them in a number of ways including, in the case of certain countries, the possibility of expulsion. One of the consequences of this is an ambivalent attitude to black immigrants. On the one hand, the white population needs them to work while, on the other, their presence is resented.

To show the unity of the two types of explanation, one using the analysis of class and the other the concept of racism, we turn to a study which proposes the concept of the *underclass*. Rex and Tomlinson's (1979) study of Handsworth in Birmingham was undertaken with the intention of discovering something of the relationship of Asian and West Indian immigrants and their children to the class structure of contemporary British society. Their essential conclusion is that the black population is not absorbed into the white working class and is unlikely to become so within the foreseeable future. Quite the reverse, ethnic minorities form an underclass, a class beneath the white working class, disadvantaged by jobs, housing, and education. Blacks and whites work in different labour markets. West Indian and Asian populations are more concentrated in labouring jobs in hot and dirty industries and are poorly represented in professional, scientific and administrative jobs. Of course there is some overlap between the two; there are some black people in professional work just as there are whites in unskilled labouring jobs. Nonetheless the situation is almost one of a 'dual labour market' (see chapter 4, section 4.2, p. 15): one set of jobs is reserved for one category of the population (blacks) and another for the other (whites). In housing, as the authors say 'The white authorities are torn between two discriminatory policies. One of these is the segregation of the black immigrant population in the least desirable housing, and here they are positively helped to find homes. The other is to disperse them so that their unwanted presence may be put more or less out of sight' (p. 280). Education provides a final measure of inequality. The inequality built into the education system simply reinforces the position of black children.

The black population, thus, effectively constitutes an underclass, placed in a structurally different location from the white working class. Their position is made the more disadvantaged because of the hostility directed at them by white society. Rex and Tomlinson (1979) are clear that the position of ethnic minorities and the conflicts that surround race and ethnicity in Britain can only be understood in the light of Britain's imperial past and the recent collapse of empire; 'a serious sociological analysis of race relations problems must rest upon a concept of the social structure of Empire and of the class formations which occur within it' (p. 286). The point is that the fact of empire affects both white and black communities. Much of Britain's prosperity is founded on exploitation of colonial territories, an exploitation based on the assumption that black people were inferior. That perception of inferiority in turn means that some sort of caste barrier is erected between black and white. For black people, similarly, colonialism has left its imprint. West Indians, for example, were, less than two hundred years ago, sold into slavery and separated from their African culture. They have, therefore, fewer cultural resources with which to resist the forces that place them in the underclass. For Rex and Tomlinson, the only way in which black people are likely to change their own situation is to develop forms of self-defence and self-help which are, in a sense, anti-colonialist, in that they are based on Third World models, 'looking to a change in the balance of power and resources between rich and poor nations as a means to their own liberation' (p. 293).

We have argued that one cannot counterpose the class and racism models of ethnic disadvantage. A proper explanation has to employ both even if there is room for argument about the weight to be placed on each factor. The mechanisms of the class structure create positions – jobs – which are filled by ethnic minorities, originally entering the country as migrant workers. Racism, and its associated discriminatory practices, are part of the explanation of the way in which black workers fill the worst-paid jobs. Any correction of ethnic disadvantage, therefore, has to focus both on racism and on the mechanisms of class disadvantage. The riots that occurred in the British cities in 1981 and in Brixton and Tottenham subsequently, were an expression of the double – class and racist – nature of ethnic disadvantage in Britain. For many black people, this is the only form of protest open to them in a society which is racist and discriminatory *and* which consigns them to the lowest positions in the class structure.

Summary

1 Ethnic minorities are disadvantaged both by white racism and by their position in the class structure.

2 The racism of British society is manifested in a number of ways including employment, housing, in treatment by the police, trade unions and physical assault.

Related topics

For some account of the way that newspapers and television discuss immigration issues, see chapter 10, section 10.2. The concept of a dual-labour market is discussed in chapter 4, section 4.2. Material on ethnic youth cultures can be found in chapter 10, section 10.4. More discussion of the interrelationship between gender, ethnicity and class is in chapter 4, section 4.6. Issues of health care are dealt with in chapter 9, section 9.6.

Further Reading

A recent source of data about the ethnic minorities in Britain that has been extensively used in this chapter is Brown (1984), which is based on a large-scale survey for the Policy Studies Institute. A useful collection of readings on various aspects of ethnicity has been brought together by Husband (1982). Cashmore and Troyna (1983) have written a general and basic introduction to the sociology of race relations (not just in Britain). Last, but by no means least, a book collectively written by members of the Centre for Contemporary Cultural Studies (1982) provides a strong critique of the state of the sociology of ethnicity in Britain, focusing on white racism.

6 Families and Households

6.1 Introduction

The family is a central institution of modern British society, at least in the sense that almost everybody has had experience of living in a family at some time in their lives. Most people also assume that their family experiences are normal and that all families resemble their own. This assumption is false, as this chapter will show. There is, in fact, an enormous diversity of family forms in modern Britain.

The fact that everybody has had experience of family life also means that families *appear* as natural and inevitable ways of organizing human social life. They seem built into human nature and it is often impossible to imagine a society without them. Thus, it seems natural to love one's children, to respect parents and to share a house with blood relations. These feelings are misplaced. Even if *some* form of family is natural or inevitable, that does not imply that any *particular* form is. Furthermore, people often associate the feeling that families are part of human nature with the further assumption that families are good for you. If we appear to be unable to do without families, then they must be beneficial for us. We cannot assume that. For many people their family life is positively harmful and, probably for the majority of people, their experiences with families bring a good deal of pain as well as pleasure.

All of us, then, tend to make a number of assumptions about the family based on our common-sense, everyday experiences, and these assumptions find their way into sociological research. This is particularly true of what has been called the functionalist theory of the family. This theory proposes that the family performs certain functions for society. A sophisticated variant of this view is offered by Parsons (1956). He argues that societies change by a process of structural differentiation. This means that, in simple societies, each institution performs several functions. As the society develops, these functions become separated out into different institutions. Thus, the pre-industrial family in Britain will not only have cared for its members but will also have educated them and been the focus of their work activities. As the society becomes industrialized, the family loses its education and work functions to other institutions which develop to cater for them; schools educate and factories provide a workplace. In Parsons' view, the modern family deals only with the socialization of children and gives stability to adult personalities.

In sum, as societies become industrialized, so the family loses its range of functions and comes to concentrate on only a few. The most significant implication of this idea of Parsons concerns family size and the connections the family has with the rest of society. Parsons' view is that the modern industrial family is relatively isolated from society, certainly more so than its pre-industrial predecessor. Concretely, modern families are *nuclear*, consisting only of parents and children, and *conjugal*, emphasizing the relationship between husband and wife rather than either of their relationships with their own families of origin. When a man and a woman marry they, typically, set up a new household independently of their relatives and their responsibilities are towards one another, not towards the wider family. Pre-industrial families tend, on the other hand, to be extended, that is to involve relatives more widely. Marriage partners will feel obligations to their wider kin which may even transcend those they feel towards each other. Parents and children will live near to other relatives or even share a house with them.

The idea that industrialization created the relatively isolated nuclear family has been very influential in the sociology of the family and has stimulated a wide range of studies, many of which have been critical. First, a number of historical studies have shown that the nuclear family was common before the industrial revolution, if only because people did not live long enough for older relatives to live near or with their younger kin. Furthermore, it seems doubtful if the pre-industrial family had the resources to serve the functions of education, medical care or support of the elderly. Perhaps even more striking, is the finding that the upheaval of the industrial revolution actually promoted the formation of extended family groups. In this period of rapid social change, involving families moving from the countryside to the town, the support given by the wider network of relatives was of great importance for individual families. For a short time at least families became relatively less isolated. Last, a good deal of research effort has been put into the study of families in contemporary society. One of the conclusions of this research is that nuclear families are not isolated but are actually placed in a network of relationships with kin and others. We will be looking at this issue later in the chapter.

So far, we have argued that much sociological research into the family has been influenced by functionalist theory which is, in turn, apparently dependent on some common-sense, everyday, beliefs about family life. We now look in more detail at these everyday images of families in Britain.

6.2 Of Cereal Packets and Nuclear Families

> The family is the fundamental unit of contemporary British Society. Judging by the critical reaction to certain passages in the third of my recent Reith Lectures this dogma is very widely held to be a self-evident truth. But what is it supposed to mean. We use the word family in so many different ways . . . but the standard stereotype seems to be provided by the jolly scenes on the back of a packet of breakfast cereal – a young married couple in their middle thirties with two or three pre-adolescent children.
>
> Dr Edmund Leach in the *Guardian*, 29 January 1986, with permission

Most societies have a prevailing image of what desirable family life would be like; modern Britain is no exception. In our everyday lives, we are constantly subjected to such images. The process of socialization involves forming ideas of family life in children by a variety of devices including the stories that children read. In the old card game 'Happy Families', every family involved is made up of a father, mother and two children. Mr Dose the doctor, for example, not only has a Mrs Dose but also a Master and a Miss Dose. In adult life, similar images are formed. The medium of advertising is one notorious example of this image-making as illustrated in figure 6.1 in an advertisement involving a 'typical' family.

What does the image of the typical, normal or conventional family consist of? There are two parents aged between twenty and forty-five, legally married to each other, and not having been married to anyone else previously. Two children, born of these parents (and not others), live with them. The husband is in full-time employment while the wife is not. The wife takes on the bulk of the household tasks even if the husband may help occasionally. The family itself is a self-contained, almost private, institution – a world to itself. Lastly, its members are happy.

This manner of thinking about the family is not just an image that can be presented in advertisements of childrens' stories. It is very widespread and can have real social consequences. For example, many of our social policies 'embody assumptions about the nature of families and thereby influence what families are expected to be' (Parker, 1982). The taxation and social-security systems, for instance, assume that the man is working and the wife is not; the wife is held to be financially dependent on her husband. Furthermore, couples are assumed to be legally married. So *married* men are paid a tax allowance (not unmarried, cohabiting men). Widows are given an allowance because they are deemed to have been financially dependent. Until very recently, married women were unable to draw the allowance for the care of invalid relatives because it was *assumed* that they would do that anyway as they were at home all the time, despite the fact that two-thirds of married women work.

It is doubtful if the image of the conventional family ever accurately

Figure 6.1   Advertising the nuclear family
Source: Axel Zajaczek/Camera Press.

described the majority of families in Britain. In this chapter, we will review a whole range of factors which affect family life and which produce a diversity of family forms often very different from the cereal-packet norm that we have described. The changing age structure, with people living longer, is producing an increasingly large proportion of elderly households often containing only one person. Earlier marriages with fewer children means that couples are together for a long time after their children have left home. Changing social values have increased the numbers of homosexual or unmarried households. The fact that a large proportion of women now work has potential implications for the balance of power and dependency within families and the way that domestic tasks are performed. Families are not necessarily self-contained or happy as the rising rate of divorce partly indicates. The diversity of family forms that have been produced by these changes amongst others is illustrated in figure 6.2.

Since the 1960s, there has been a significant rise in the proportions of households containing people living alone and single parents with dependent children. (The category 'Other households' includes households containing two or more unrelated people, lone parents with independent children, and more than one family.) The proportion of households consisting of a married couple with dependent children is

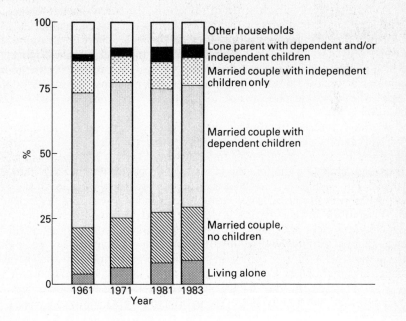

Figure 6.2 Types of household
Source: Social Trends (1985), p. 31. Crown copyright.

gradually declining; only about 4 in 10 people actually live in such households. However, the category 'married couples with dependent children' is not the same as the cereal-packet image. Some of these married couples will include partners who have been divorced, working wives, unemployed men, and children from previous marriages or adopted. The cereal-packet image represents, in sum, very much a minority phenomenon. In the rest of this chapter, we will look in more detail at the diversity of family life in Britain and at some of the factors that affect it.

6.3   The Family Life Cycle

In the previous section we argued that the cereal-packet image of family life in modern Britain was seriously misleading in that, at any one time, relatively few families conform to the image and many households never do. For example, at any one time, 1 household in every 3 contains a dependent child, 1 in 5 consists of a person living alone, 1 in 4 is a childless married couple, 3 in 10 are married couples with dependent children, and 1 in 10 contains one or more people over retirement age. Even if most people will at some time in their lives live in a family which *does* conform to the cereal-packet image, they will also necessarily spend much of their lives outside it. In other words, the cereal-packet image not only neglects the diversity of family forms at any one time, it also obscures the changes that all families go through. There is a family 'life cycle', only part of which is represented on the back of cereal packets, which is illustrated in figure 6.3. Again, we must stress that this is the life cycle of a 'typical' family. Many families will not have life cycles of this type. Many people choose not to marry, for instance, or not to have children.

We have referred to the life cycle depicted in figure 6.3 as that of a 'typical' family. We have to recognize, however, that what appears as typical will change greatly over time. A whole variety of factors will affect the cycle, changing the lengths of each stage or the relationship between stages. For example, people are living longer than they used to. The expectation of life at birth for women born in 1976 was 75.8 years, while for those born 50 years earlier it was 59.3 years. For men, the comparable expectations were 69.7 and 55.4 years. One of the implications of this is that married couples will be together for longer. It may also mean that there may be a sharper 'problem' of old age as people live longer after their retirement from work.

The centrality of the family as a social institution means that its structure and the family life cycle is affected by an enormous range of other changes. Demographic processes, not only concerning the expectation of life but also changes in the birth-rate for instance, economic change, including the increase in the numbers of married women

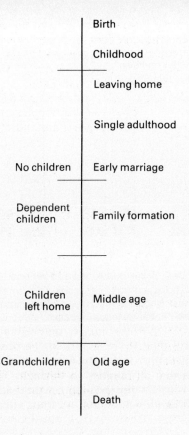

Figure 6.3 Life-cycle of 'typical' person

working, and even government policy, all affect the family. To illustrate these points we are going to consider two of the life-cycle stages identified in figure 6.3 – family formation and old age.

Having children

Marriage and child-bearing

For most people, though not all as we shall see, the whole process of beginning a family is started by marriage. There have, during the twentieth century, been considerable changes in the proportions of married people in the population, as can be seen from figure 6.4. At the beginning of the century, there were more single than married people. By 1974 this position has been reversed and, incidentally, single men outnumber single women, again the reverse of the position in 1901. These

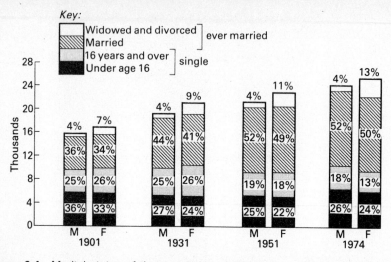

Figure 6.4 Marital status of the population of England and Wales, 1901–74
Source: Leete (1977) Changing patterns of marriage and remarriage, in R. Chester and J. Peel (eds) *Equalities and Inequalities in Family Life* (London, Academic Press), p. 3. Reproduced with permission of the Eugenics Society.

changes are not solely due to different marriage patterns but also to a change in the age structure which results from alterations in fertility, migration, and mortality. In looking at changes in marriage patterns alone, one finds that, generally speaking, people are marrying younger and a higher proportion of women are marrying. In 1931, 26 per cent of women aged 20–4 were married: in 1951, this figure had risen to 48 per cent and, in 1961, to 59 per cent (Leete, 1977). These figures are produced by a combination of younger marriages and a higher proportion of women marrying. Figure 6.5 shows movements in the average age at first marriage; women are marrying, on average, some three years younger than they did forty years ago. In turn, the propensity to marry can be measured by estimating the proportion of women still unmarried at ages 35–44. In 1931, this proportion stood at 14 per cent but by 1974 was only 6 per cent.

Although there is a general trend towards marriage, and towards marriage at a younger age, there is considerable variation between social classes. Men and women in the higher social classes, for example, tend to marry rather later than those in lower social classes. Women from the higher classes have a greater tendency to stay single. The reverse is true for men, however, with a smaller proportion of working-class men marrying than their upper-class contemporaries.

The main reason for the changing pattern of marriage is probably a rather different attitude to the starting of a family. As we shall see, families now are very much smaller than they were even at the beginning of the century. Couples do not, therefore, have to delay marriage in

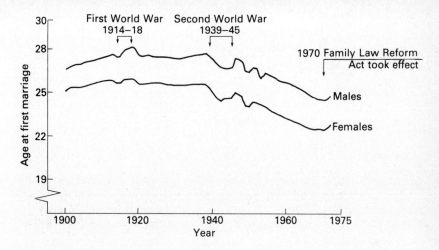

Figure 6.5 Mean age at first marriage, England and Wales 1900–75
Source: Leete (1977) Changing patterns of marriage and remarriage, in R. Chester and J. Peel (eds) *Equalities and Inequalities in Family Life* (London, Academic Press), p. 4. Reproduced with permission of the Eugenics Society.

order to ensure that they can adequately support a larger family. Other factors include the greater acceptability of contraception within marriage, the increased tendency for married women to go on working, and the reduced inclination to start a family immediately after marriage.

The custom of marriage has gained strength, in the sense that more people are entering into it and that it seems to be considered a necessary prelude to having children. Two qualifications have to be made, however, concerning 'cohabitation' and illegitimacy.

1 In the great amount of talk about the permissive society, it is sometimes claimed that marriage is losing its sanctity because couples live together without being married and the number of illegitimate babies (those born to unmarried mothers) is rising. These, then, are represented as symptoms of the moral decay of modern British society. There is, indeed, evidence that the practice of cohabitation (a man and a woman who are not kin living together without being married) is on the increase. To some extent, this may indicate a lessening preference for the institutions of marriage. It also, however, reflects a tendency for couples to live together before getting married. For example, one-quarter of women aged 16–34 getting married in the period 1979–82 lived with their husbands before marriage, while the corresponding proportion for those married between 1970 and 1974 was only 8 per cent. Where one or more of the partners had been married before, the proportions are even higher, 65 per cent of those married in 1979–82 and 42 per cent in 1970–4.

2 There are also indications of changing social attitudes as regards

legitimacy. In 1983, 16 per cent of all live births in England and Wales were illegitimate, 2.5 times the proportion in 1961. There is also some evidence that couples are living together in a stable relationship without being married, having a child, and then getting married later. There is, in other words, apparently less social pressure to legitimize the birth of a baby outside marriage. Whether these changing social attitudes to marriage indicate a decline in moral standards or a welcome moral flexibility is, of course, another matter.

Family size

Probably the most important factor affecting family formation is that people are choosing to have fewer children, although 9 out of 10 first marriages do have children. Thus, women of between 20 and 24 marrying in 1900 had an average family size of 4.0 children, while by 1950 the figure had dropped to 2.3.

During the twentieth century, married couples have not only reduced the size of their families, they have also completed their families much earlier in the marriage. In general, at the present time, married couples complete their families within ten years even though the intervals between the births of children are longer now than earlier in the century. However, it should also be noted that the interval between marriage and the birth of the first child has lengthened since the early seventies. Couples seem to be delaying the start of a family even though they then go on to complete it within the same time. These historical trends are summarized and commented upon in box 12.

New patterns and their consequences

We have argued in this section that there are a number of demographic changes in the period 1860–1980 affecting the family-formation part of the family life cycle, which also affect the life cycle as a whole. The most important of these are:

1   reduction in the age of marriage;
2   a lengthening of the expectation of life;
3   an increase in the proportion of the population getting married;
4   a decrease in family size.

Since the Second World War and, more especially, from the 1960s onwards, there have been other changes, some of which have appeared to reverse the general tendencies summarized above. There have, for example, been slight increases in average family size and in the average age at marriage. The rates of illegitimacy and of cohabitation are also rising. It is, however, too early to tell what the social significance of these changes might be and whether they indicate a further shift in the social institutions of marriage and the family.

Box 12 Length of stages in the family cycle for successive marriage cohorts, 1860–1950

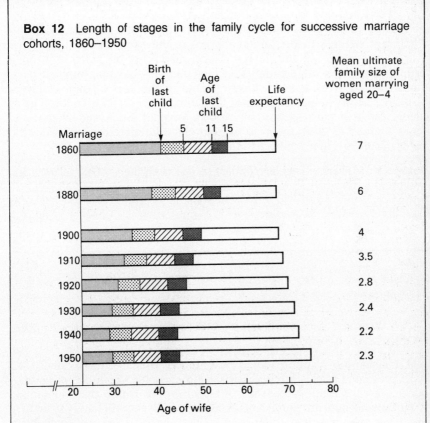

Figure B.12

Source: Hole and Pountney (1971) *Trends in Population, Housing and Occupancy Rates 1861–1961*, p. 15. Crown copyright.

This shows changes in the length of the family cycle and is based on the assumption that all the brides involved (in all of the periods) were aged 22.5 years at marriage. For a couple marrying in 1860, the wife was 40 before she had had her last child, while in 1930, the corresponding stage would have been reached before the wife was 30. This difference reflects changes in family size. The Victorian family would have had young children around until the parents were in their late middle age. If we take into account the fact that women are now marrying at a younger age as well, twentieth-century families will be completed even earlier than the chart indicates. One final point completes the picture. For families in the twentieth century, not only is middle age largely free of care for children, but old age is lengthened by an increased expectation of life. Married couples in the 1980s can expect to spend a much greater part of the later part of their lives together without their children.

The net effect of these changes is, of course, that women are relatively free of child-rearing for a much longer period of their active lives and are, therefore, more likely to seek paid employment. One of the most significant changes in the labour market in the twentieth century is the rising proportion of the labour force made up of married women returning to work after completing their families. As one might expect, women's paid work is very closely related to the *ages* of their children. Table 6.1 shows how women enter the labour force as their children grow older. Greater participation by women in paid work and changes in family structure thus seem to be closely related, although what the mechanisms are that connect the two changes is less clear.

Table 6.1   Mothers in paid employment by age of children, 1978 (percentages)

Mother's employment	Age of children				All ages 0–15
	0–2	3–4	5–9	10–15	
None	79	69	52	36	51
Part-time	16	25	37	42	35
Full-time	5	6	11	22	14

Source: Rapoport, Fogarty and Rapoport (1982) *Families in Britain* (London, Routledge and Kegan Paul), p. 101.

A final note of caution should be sounded. Much of the evidence we have presented in this section is based on *averages* which do, of course, conceal great variations between different groups within the population. In particular, there are significant social-class differences in family structure. We have already noted differences in the age of marriage. Even birth intervals are strongly class-related. For example, the interval between marriage and the birth of the first child for professional and managerial families is twice as long as that for the families of unskilled workers.

Old age

The number of people over 85 will rise by 54 per cent in the next 20 years, threatening a 'health care catastrophe,' the British Medical Association said yesterday . . . it adds: 'the general treatment of the frail elderly by the state is a scandal. Lack of money and bureaucratic confusion has left a legacy from the Victorian era with the state looking backwards, remodelling ancient buildings and patching up a system of care which is fragmentary, pitifully inadequate and increasingly inadequate to the elderly age group.'

At a press conference yesterday, Mr John Dawson, head of the B.M.A.'s professional and scientific division, said that if no action was taken, the elderly could be forced to rely on charity and 'could even be forced to beg.'

The *Guardian*, 13 March 1986, with permission

As this extract indicates, increasing attention is being paid in Britain to the problems of the elderly. The lengthening expectation of life and a changing age structure have produced a population with a rising proportion of people over 65. This rise is dramatic, as is illustrated in figure 6.6, which shows a steep rise in this age-group in the first half of the twentieth century and a levelling out at about 15 per cent from the 1980s well into the next century.

Figure 6.7 presents data for the age structure of the population in more detail. In 1983, the 65 and over age-group represented 15 per cent of the population, compared with 5 per cent in 1901. The proportion will not increase greatly towards the end of the century because of low birth-rates in the 1930s. However *within* this age-group there is a rising proportion of those over 75 and even more so of those over 85, who are projected to make up 12 per cent of the elderly in 2001, compared with less than 8 per cent in 1983. The figure also gives some idea of the changing size of the dependent population (those over 65 together with children under school-leaving age) which has to be supported by those of working age. This population reached its peak in 1974, although it has to be remembered that the ranks of the dependent could be greatly increased by even higher rates of unemployment.

At present, only some 5 per cent of the elderly population live in institutions. The remainder live in private households. Because they live longer, women over 65 are much less likely to be living with their spouse than men of a similar age. For example, 83 per cent of men aged between 65 and 70 live with their spouses, while the corresponding proportion for women is only 55 per cent. Again, as one would expect, the numbers of old people living alone increases with age. Although only 32 per cent of

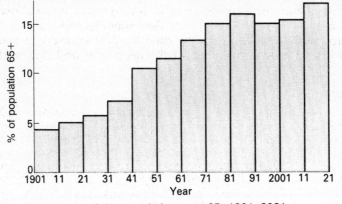

Figure 6.6 Percentage of the population over 65, 1901–2021
Source: Family Policy Studies Centre (1984) *An Ageing Population* (London, Family Policy Studies Centre), Fact sheet 2, p. 1. Reproduced with permission. Based on OPCS Census data 1901–81 and Government Actuary Projections mid-1983, OPCS. PP2, no. 13.

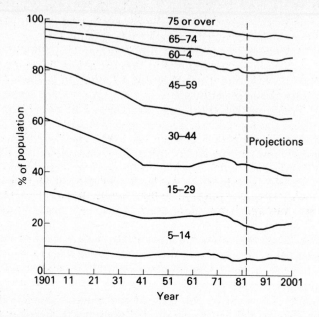

Figure 6.7 Population by age group
Source: Social Trends (1985), p. 21. Crown copyright.

women between 65 and 70 live alone, the proportion rises to 60 per cent for those over 80. Only 25 per cent of women over 80 who have no surviving spouse live with other members of their family.

The fact that the proportion of elderly people in our society has increased rapidly, together with an even greater increase in those aged 75 or over, creates a number of social problems. This is partly a question of the so-called 'burden of dependency'. Old people take up a disproportionate share of health and social-security resources and they are also a non-earning sector of the population, thus dependent on those at work. The most obvious factor here is health. Older people are prone to ill-health, which often confines them to their homes. Naturally enough, they make demands on the National Health Service. For example, those aged 65 and over accounted for one-third of all NHS prescriptions and about 40 per cent of acute hospital-bed occupation. The health problems of the elderly are compounded by their declining income. It has been estimated that three-quarters of the elderly, compared with one-fifth of the non-elderly, live on or below the poverty line. Part of this, clearly, is due to the loss of earned income. In fact, the proportion of men over 65 who are still working has declined from over half in 1931 to some 15 per cent in 1979. The result is that a large proportion of the elderly are solely dependent on the basic state pension, with supplementary benefit.

We have already noted that a substantial proportion of old people live alone; one-third of those over 65 do so and the proportion increases with age. Many of these people will feel lonely and socially isolated, especially if they are very old and, hence, relatively inactive. It is, perhaps, difficult to find a universally acceptable index of loneliness. One study (Hunt, 1978), however, found that one-quarter of the 65–75 age-group 'would like a relative to visit more often'. This response was given by 36 per cent of those over 85. One cannot, however, jump to the conclusion that, because many old people live alone, they have little support from their families. A government survey found that, of those elderly people who were having some difficulty in coping with the tasks of everyday life, about half were helped by members of their family who provided help with shopping, cleaning, the preparation of meals and laundry. In practice, family care of this kind is usually provided by women.

Although social isolation is undoubtedly a problem for many old people, many more do have an active family life. Furthermore, the lines of support do not always run in one direction. Elderly people are a source of child-care for the offspring of their own children. Men, for example, can be expected to live an average of 14 years after the birth of their first grandchild, and women 23 years. The elderly are, therefore, still involved in extended family relationships, a point taken up again in section 6.6.

Summary

1 The cereal-packet image assumes a static family structure, when clearly individual families change considerably as children are born, grow up and leave home.

2 The typical family life cycle has changed from the early years of this century.

3 As far as family formation is concerned, more people are marrying, they marry younger and there is more cohabitation before marriage. Families are smaller and are completed earlier. One major factor in all these changes is the great increase in the proportion of married women who take paid employment.

4 At the other end of the age range, there has been an increase in the proportion of the population over 65. This may create a 'burden of dependency' in that the elderly population makes a disproportionate claim on various services, particularly the National Health Service.

Related topics

The relationships between parents and children are dealt with in a general way in chapter 10, section 10.4.

6.4   The Division of Labour within Families

Part of the image of the family in our society depends on assumptions about the relationships of men and women *inside* the home. The cereal-packet image assumes that the man is the breadwinner and the woman is responsible for domestic tasks including child-care, cleaning and cooking. Men make the large-scale decisions affecting the family, while women only control those areas that are strictly 'domestic'. There is, in other words, a *division of labour* within the home.

This image may well have borne some relation to reality at one time in the first half of this century and the second half of the last, following the process of industrialization which took men out of the home to work in factories. But is it still the case?

The symmetrical family?

Young and Willmott (1973), argue that, in modern Britain, this is *not* the case; a new family form – the symmetrical family – which does not require a domestic division of labour, is slowly emerging, in which the roles of men and women are less differentiated. A whole series of factors have combined to produce the change from families with a high division of labour to those in which domestic tasks are more equally shared. These include the rise in the proportion of married women who work (see chapter 4, section 4.2), the trend towards smaller families (see section 6.2), the 'privatization' of the family (see section 6.6), and changing social attitudes about the proper role of men and women. It has also been argued that changes in patterns of work may alter the balance of domestic work. For example, if the male breadwinner is unemployed, more of the domestic tasks may fall to him.

For Young and Willmott, the symmetrical family has three main features. First, the married couple and their children are very much centred on the home, especially when the children are young. Second, the extended family counts for relatively less and the immediate nuclear family for relatively more. The third and 'most vital' characteristic is that the roles of men and women have become less segregated and more balanced. Young and Willmott's detailed empirical study found that in poorer and older families there was still a considerable domestic division of labour but that, nonetheless, the great majority of married people in their sample formed the newer symmetrical family (p. 94):

> Husbands also did a lot of work in the home, including many jobs which are not at all traditional men's ones . . . there is now no sort of work in the home strictly reserved for 'the wives'. Even clothes-washing and bed-making, still ordinarily thought of as women's

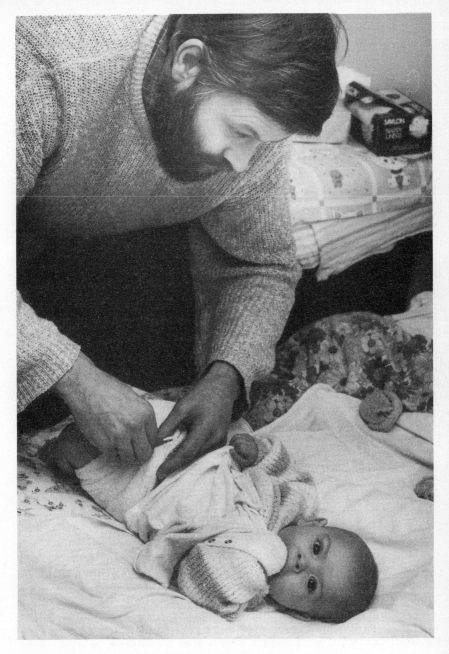

Figure 6.8   Contemporary divisions of labour
Source: Sheila Gray/Format.

Table 6.2 Social class and husband's help in the home – reported help to wife at least once a week (percentages)

	Professional and managerial	Clerical	Skilled	Semi-skilled and unskilled	All
None	14	13	14	24	15
Washing up only	16	7	13	12	13
Other tasks (cleaning, cooking, child-care etc.), with or without washing up	70	80	73	64	72
Total number	171	70	236	107	585

Source: Young and Willmott (1973) *The Symmetrical Family* (London, Routledge and Kegan Paul), table 8, p. 95. Reproduced with permission.

jobs, were frequently mentioned by husbands as things they did as well. The extent of the sharing is probably still increasing.

Table 6.2 shows the proportion of the sample of men in each social class who reported helping their wives in various tasks once a week. Only one in seven men did not help their wives at all in the professional/ managerial, clerical and skilled classes, although, for the semi-skilled and unskilled, the proportion rose to one in four.

From evidence of this kind, Young and Willmott conclude that there is a growing tendency for husbands and wives to share their lives together more symmetrically. One might expect that women's paid work would have the most profound effect on the domestic division of labour: the more work a women does outside the home, the less she is able to do within it. Some, though not unequivocal, support is given to this argument by a study of the Isle of Sheppey (Pahl, 1984). Pahl constructed an index of the division of domestic labour composed not only of 'female' tasks such as cooking, clothes washing or child-care but also 'male' jobs such as house repairs, car maintenance or beer making. One of his most striking findings was that the more a woman was employed the more domestic work was shared. However, it is not quite as simple as that. Although households in which both partners are employed do manifest a more equal division of domestic labour, women still do the bulk of the domestic work; more equal does not mean absolutely equal. Further- more, the balance of the domestic division of labour does not seem to be related to the work done by *men*. It does not matter if the man is full- time employed or unemployed, the balance of domestic work is still determined by the woman's employment status. Thus, in households where the woman is in full-time employment, unemployed men are likely to do just as much (or rather little) domestic work as those who are fully employed.

In our society, a woman's identity is still organized around the home, domestic work and child-rearing. These features of her life provide her identity, whereas a man's identity is given at least partly by his work. This has the further consequence that a woman's life is largely confined to *private* spaces – the home – while men dominate the public spaces outside the home. The result is that the majority of women are engaged at least for part of their lives in *full-time* domestic work, especially while their children are young. Such a position is very unusual for men.

Housewives and housework

What are the characteristics of the full-time housewife role? The most important point to stress here is that, as Oakley (1974) points out, housework is *work* and should be compared with paid jobs outside the home. There is, indeed, a good deal of work involved. The average working week in Oakley's sample was 77 hours, with a range from 48 to 105. It is demanding and monotonous work. Oakley compared housewives' feelings about the various domestic tasks with workers' feelings about their jobs as revealed in Goldthorpe et al.'s (1968a) study. The housewives were asked if they found housework monotonous, fragmented (composed of many, unconnected tasks) and too fast-paced.

Table 6.3 The experience of monotony, fragmentation and speed in work: housewives and factory workers compared (percentages)

Workers	Monotony	Fragmentation	Speed
Housewives	75	90	50
Factory workers	41	70	31
Assembly-line workers[a]	67	86	36

Note: [a]The assembly-line workers are a sub-sample of the factory workers.
Source: Oakley (1974) *The Sociology of Housework* (Oxford, Martin Robertson), table 5.1, p. 87. Reproduced with permission.

As table 6.3 shows, housewives experience more monotony, fragmentation and speed in their work than do workers in a factory. The gap is narrowed considerably when the comparison is with assembly-line workers, a comparison which reveals a great deal about the nature of housework. However domestic work is also *not* like paid work, especially factory employment, in a number of respects. Two of the most obvious differences are the degree of social isolation and the possibilities of autonomy. These cut in different directions. Many of Oakley's respondents complained about the loneliness of housework. As one of them said on being asked if she ever felt that she spent too much time on her own in the daytime:

> Yes. The last couple of months it's been dragging: you feel 'I wish I could talk to somebody' . . . not knowing anybody else you tend to get this feeling that unless you go out and talk to someone you'll go stark raving mad. (Oakley, 1974, p. 91)

On the other hand, housework offers the housewife considerable autonomy. She has a fair amount of control over her work; 'being one's own boss' was a phrase used by over half the sample. In this respect, housework contrasts favourably with many kinds of paid work. (For a further discussion of these aspects of domestic work, turn to chapter 4, section 4.3.)

The notion that domestic roles remain highly segregated while the wife is not in employment is widely confirmed. In a study of professional and managerial workers, Edgell (1980) concludes 'that marital relationships remain highly segregated, unequal and husband-dominated'. A majority of his sample reported that the wife typically performed a distinct range of domestic and child-rearing tasks considerably more often than the husband, and also that she deferred to the husband in more important areas of decision-making. Child-care was the only area in which husbands participated at all actively, and they saw that as helping with *her* job. The allocation of domestic work can obscure other areas of the gender segregation of domestic tasks, especially in the area of power and authority. This was an area specifically considered by Edgell. Table 6.4 gives some data concerning decision-making between husbands and wives.

Power and inequalities in marriage

At first sight, the data in table 6.4 seem to indicate that decision-making is roughly balanced. Some decisions are shared equally and the remainder are split between husband and wife. However, this does not take account of the *importance* of decisions and amongst the research families, there was widespread agreement about which decisions were important and which were not. Generally, the more-important though less-frequent decisions tend to be husband-dominated, whereas the less-important though more-frequent decisions are made by the wife. There is some evidence from studies of families in which both wife and husband have careers that even in these situations the husband dominates decision-making, partly because his job comes to be seen as more important.

As we have already argued from Pahl's (1984) study, even when women do paid work they still do the bulk of the domestic work,

Table 6.4 The importance, frequency and pattern of decision-making in different areas of family life

Decision area	Perceived importance	Frequency	Decision-maker (majority pattern)
Moving	Very important	Infrequent	Husband
Finance	Very important	Infrequent	Husband
Car	Important	Infrequent	Husband
House	Very important	Infrequent	Husband and wife
Children's education	Very important	Infrequent	Husband and wife
Holidays	Important	Infrequent	Husband and wife
Weekends	Not important	Frequent	Husband and wife
Other leisure activities	Not important	Frequent	Husband and wife
Furniture	Not important	Infrequent	Husband and wife
Interior decorations	Not important	Infrequent	Wife
Food and other domestic spending	Not important	Frequent	Wife
Children's clothes	Not important	Frequent	Wife

Source: Edgell (1980) *Middle Class Couples* (London, George Allen and Unwin), figure 5.1, p. 58. Reproduced with permission.

although it may be more equally distributed than it was when they were full-time housewives. Young and Willmott (1973), for example, (although they are generally trying to demonstrate the increasing symmetry of domestic relationships) show that married men spent some ten hours per week on domestic tasks, compared with 23 hours for full-time and 35 hours for part-time employed women. Men seem, furthermore, to spend their domestic hours in the more rewarding tasks, such as playing with children, rather than tedious and repetitive jobs, such as preparing meals or cleaning. In addition, husbands tend to see their participation in domestic work very much as helping their wife rather than the assumption of definite and perhaps permanent responsibility for some domestic duties.

We can conclude from this discussion that there is still a substantial and unequal division of labour between men and women in British families; the symmetrical family is not here yet. It should be noted that this is not an outright refutation of Young and Willmott's position as outlined at the beginning of this section, for they were arguing only that there is a *tendency* towards a less-gender-segregated division of labour. However, they also suggest that the symmetrical family form 'trickles down' from the middle classes to the working class. As we have said, there is little evidence for this, as professional families manifest considerable segregation of domestic tasks. Indeed, there is little differentiation by class at all in domestic divisions of labour. Pahl (1984) found that only women's employment and stage in the life cycle affected the extent to which domestic tasks were shared. When children are young and the wife is not employed, an asymmetrical division of labour is likely. However as she grows older, and perhaps re-enters the labour market, domestic tasks are shared more equitably.

Summary

1 It has been argued by some that families are becoming more symmetrical, with domestic work being more balanced between men and women. Recent evidence indicates that, although there may be such a tendency, it is still not very pronounced.

2 Even when women take paid employment, they still do the bulk of the domestic work and men take the important decisions.

3 The degree of sharing of domestic work depends on the amount of paid work taken on by the wife and the stage reached in the family life cycle. Social class seems to make little difference.

Related topics

Further discussion on the domestic division of labour can be found in chapter 4, section 4.3, especially as it affects the inequality between men and women. The background to Pahl's (1984) study can be found in the case-study in chapter 2, section 2.7.

6.5   Divorce, Single People and Alternative Households

In previous sections we have contrasted the cereal-packet image of the family in modern Britain with the different sorts of arrangements and structures that occur over the family life cycle. In this section, we look at another, and perhaps more-obvious way, in which the idealized image is misleading, namely family dissolution through divorce. Although, as we shall see, a large proportion of divorced people remarry, there are at any one time a good number of single-person households or single-parent households created by divorce. In addition, there are people who choose not to live in 'conventional families' but by themselves or with others in what we might call 'alternative households'. This section will also briefly consider these alternatives to the family.

Divorce and marriage breakdown

The rate of divorce

As newspapers and television are always telling us, divorce is more common than it was a generation ago. The *numbers* of divorces granted has risen dramatically: in the 20-year period 1961–81, the number granted in Britain jumped from 27,000 to 159,000. This should be compared with under 3,000 in 1921 and a mere 700 in 1911. These figures do indicate that divorce is more popular. However, the numbers of divorces could be slightly misleading in that, not only has the general population risen in numbers, but marriage itself is more popular, as we saw earlier in this chapter. A larger number of people are getting married, so a larger number of people will get divorced if the divorce-rate stays the same. The method of allowing for this is to show how many divorces there are per 1,000 of the married population. This gives a more accurate idea of the *rate* of divorce. Even expressed in this way, the rise in the divorce-rate has been striking. In 1961, just over 2 persons divorced per 1,000 married people in England and Wales, while in 1981 it was almost 12. In 1931, it was under one-half. An even more revealing way to consider the changes in the popularity of divorce would be to look at the proportion of each marriage cohort that divorces after a particular period of time. For example, one could compare the divorce-rate of those married in 1971 with those married in 1981, both after a period of, say, ten years. Detailed studies of this kind do, indeed, show that divorce is a more popular option for later marriage cohorts. Recent estimates are that one-third of current marriages are likely to end in divorce.

Causes of a rising divorce-rate

Why has the divorce-rate increased? Why do more-recently formed marriages have a higher risk of divorce? The most obvious initial explanation is that changes in legislation have made divorce easier. As marriage is a legal contract, divorce requires legal approval; if this approval becomes easier to obtain, then there will be more divorces. The assumption of this explanation is, of course, that there used to be many couples who wanted a divorce but could not have one because their case was not covered by any legislation. All that legislation does is to *permit* these marriage to end. It is true that there have been spurts in the divorce-rate as legislation becomes more and more permissive towards divorce. However, changes in the law cannot really be the only *cause* of increases in the rate of divorce. The law, rather, reflects social changes in that it permits marriages that have in practice effectively ended to be legally dissolved. We have, therefore, to consider why marriages effectively end, as well as why couples will go as far as to go to the courts to legally separate, and what social factors underlie the responses to changes in legislation.

One such factor is *the changing role of women in society*. The position of women has changed in a number of ways, such that a wife does not have to put up with an unsatisfactory marriage in the way that her mother might well have done. Women are not expected to be socially subservient to their husbands as was often the case even 50 years ago. The financial constraints on wives are also not so serious, as an increasing proportion of married women are in full-time work. One cannot press this argument too far. There are still inequalities within marriage, as are documented both in this chapter and in chapter 4. Women's work does not generally pay as well as that of men, which clearly gives wives less potential for financial independence than their husbands. Nevertheless, women have more independence than they had and that will influence their decision as to whether or not they wish to leave a marriage. Very relevant to the changing social role of women is the finding that women are, in general, less satisfied by their marriages than men. In their study of a sample of divorcees, Thornes and Collard (1979) found that wives tended to believe that there were marital problems much earlier on in the marriage. By the third wedding anniversary, 69 per cent of wives had concluded that there were problems, compared with 46 per cent of husbands.

In sum, any relaxation of marital constraints on women is likely to lead to a rise in the divorce-rate, whether these constraints are ones of tradition or custom or finance. Indeed, a further factor in the rise in divorce-rates is, precisely, *the relaxation of traditional attitudes to divorce*. Divorce is no longer so shameful and is popularly seen as a permissible solution to marital difficulties. The more common it is, the more people will know of others who have been divorced and they are correspondingly less likely to condemn this action. As Allan (1985) points out, contemporary attitudes to divorce are illustrated by the prevailing opinions as to the effect of divorce on children. While in former years parents were encouraged to stay together for the sake of their children, more recently emphasis has been put on the damage done to children by parents who *do* stay married but are in constant conflict. In these circumstances, divorce is often popularly thought to be the preferable alternative.

It is not only a question of social attitudes to divorce. The frequency with which marriages dissolve will also be related to the way married couples – and the family – are integrated socially. As Allan (1985) argues, within the last century, the *family has become increasingly defined as a private institution* in which people find a haven in a heartless world. The wider family, and society at large, do not have the right to interfere in family life. But, since the family unit is then not supported by its integration into a wider social network, family problems cannot be so easily shared. As a result, modern marriages are under a great deal of stress. On the one hand, a great deal is expected of them, particularly in the capacity to provide emotional and physical support for husband and wife. On the other hand, the marriage does not itself have support from wider society: 'There is less pressure for a couple to stay together because their break-up has little impact outside the domestic sphere and causes fewer ripples than it would in a society where kinship is more central to the wider social organization' (Allan, 1985, p. 104).

Who divorces?

These three factors – the position of women, moral attitudes to divorce and the involvement of the family in wider society – are important factors in explaining the rise in overall divorce rates. For a fuller understanding of the factors affecting divorce, we have to consider not only changes in rates over time but also differences between social groups in rates of divorce. For example, the age at marriage is strongly associated with the likelihood of divorce. Generally speaking, the older people are when they marry, the less chance they have of divorcing. Couples who marry in their teens are almost twice as likely to divorce as those who marry between the ages of 20 and 24. The divorce rate also varies by the amount of time the marriage has lasted. For example, in 1979 nearly half of all divorces occurred within the first 10 years. This may, however, underestimate the volume of marital breakdown in the earlier years of marriage, for several studies have shown that couples may split up, on average, five years before they actually divorce. One investigation (Thornes and Collard, 1979) found that of all marital separations (rather than legal divorces), 60 per cent occurred before the tenth year of marriage. Young spouses and young marriages are, therefore, most at risk.

Social class is also closely related to the incidence of divorce. As can be seen from table 6.5, the divorce-rate for unskilled husbands is more than four times that for professionals and for the unemployed, almost five times that for the professionals. These social-class differences are even

Table 6.5 Divorce rates by social class of husband, 1979, England and Wales

Social class of husband	Divorces per thousand husbands (aged 16 to 59)
Professional	7
Intermediate	12
Skilled non-manual	16
Skilled manual	14
Semi-skilled manual	15
Unskilled manual	30
Unemployed	34

Based on a sample of 2,164 divorces in 1979.
Source: J. Haskey, Social class and socio-economic differentials in England and Wales, *Population Studies* 38. Reproduced with permission.

more marked for younger husbands, where the unskilled manual rate is 5.5 times as great as the incidence in the professional category.

Divorce, remarriage and single parents

So far, we have shown that divorce is increasingly popular and more common in some social groups than in others. This does not mean however, that marriage as an institution is less popular, for substantial numbers of divorced people remarry. Present estimates are that some two-thirds of divorcees will eventually remarry. Of women who separated between 1970 and 1974 before the age of 35, nearly one-quarter had remarried within three years, while just over half had remarried within six years. Further, the fact that there has been such a steep rise in the number of divorces, combined with a fairly high rate of remarriage, means that a rising proportion of all marriages are of people marrying for at least the second time. In 1961, for example, 14 per cent of all marriages were remarriages but, by 1982, the proportion had risen to 34 per cent.

Reconstituted families

The frequency of remarriage after divorce must mean that so-called *reconstituted* families have become an increasingly significant social phenomenon. These are families, often with children, in which one or both of the parents have been married previously. The involvement of children is of particular importance. As we have seen, the younger the marriage and the younger the partners, the higher the rate of divorce. These marriages, of course, are also more likely to be childless since the couples will not have had time to have children. Nevertheless, the number of children involved in the divorce of their parents is considerable. Currently, the total number of children who experience divorce is about 160,000 per year in England and Wales. These children will also tend to be young. In 1982, two-thirds of the children in separated families were aged under 11 and one-quarter were under 5. Not a great deal is known about the numbers of these children who end up in remarriages, but Burgoyne and Clark (1982) estimate that 7 per cent of all children under 17 live with a step-parent.

Reconstituted families are clearly different from the cereal-packet norm. Most particularly, such families have, or are likely to have, close ties outside the family, through children, with the previous partners. Children will be pulled in two directions between their natural parents and may well have tense relationships with their step-parents. It is as if Snow White, living with her step-mother, also had her natural mother living in another part of the kingdom. These features make the life of reconstituted families very complex; they cannot be seen as enclosed entities in the same way as cereal-packet nuclear families are. This position is complicated by the fact that society has no established customs surrounding either the step-parent role or, perhaps even more acutely, the role of the divorced parent no longer living with his or her children but visiting them from time to time. Reconstituted families involving step-children may try to approach the conventional norm if the parents decide to have children of their own. This will, of course, only introduce a new level of complexity.

Reconstituted families are, therefore, of a different type. As Burgoyne and Clarke (1982, p. 290) say:

> It is clear that the warp and woof of everyday life in stepfamilies differs from that of unbroken families not merely because of external constraints which frustrate the efforts of those who may seek, as some do, to recast their family lives in the mould of the nuclear family, but that family norms themselves may also be markedly altered, tempered to fit the limits of the new situation and fabricated anew from the post-marital residue of family beliefs and sentiments.

Reconstituted families will become increasingly common but do not yet have a clear identity in British social life.

Single-parent families

In considering the impact of divorce on family life, popular attention to the mass-media probably focuses more on the situation of single-parent families than on reconstituted ones. As one might expect from the rise in the divorce rate, the proportion of single-parent families has been increasing. Divorce is, of course, not the only cause. Death of a spouse will also contribute to the numbers of one-parent families, as will the rising numbers of unmarried mothers. As can be seen from table 6.6, the proportion of all families with dependent children which are headed by a single parent increased from just over 8 per cent in 1971 to just under 12 per cent in 1981. The bulk of this increase comes from families headed by a lone *woman* and, most often, a divorced woman. Although single-parent families have, on average, fewer children than married couples, clearly a considerable number of children will be living in a one-parent family at any one time. The National Council for One Parent Families estimated that, in 1982, there were about one million one-parent families, containing 1.6 million children. Even this underestimates the numbers of children who will, at some time in their lives, experience living in such a family situation.

The social and economic situation of one-parent families is very disadvantageous. This is partly a consequence of the fact that the great majority of single parents are women and partly because such families are disproportionately working class. The Finer Report (1974) on one-parent

Table 6.6 Families with dependent children by marital status (percentages)

Family type	1971–3	1973–5	1975–7	1977–9	1979–81
Married couples	91.8	90.7	89.8	88.9	88.1
Lone parents					
（total）	8.3	9.3	10.1	11.0	11.9
Lone father	1.2	1.3	1.3	1.3	1.5
Lone mother	7.1	8.0	8.8	9.7	10.4
Single	1.2	1.3	1.5	1.7	2.2
Widowed	1.8	1.9	2.0	1.9	1.7
Divorced	1.9	2.5	3.2	3.8	4.1
Separated	2.1	2.2	2.1	2.3	2.5

Source: Popay, Rimmer and Rossiter (1983), p. 10.

families) found that only 1 child in 18 in social classes I and II lived in a simple-parent family, while in class V the proportion was almost 1 in 7. The combination of these two factors – social class and gender – means that many one-parent families live in poverty. As we have seen in chapter 4, women's work is generally less-well-paid than men's. In addition, married women may well have had their careers interrupted by child-rearing. Single-parent women can earn relatively little money out of which they will have to pay the expenses of child-minding. In these circumstances it is hardly surprising that many lone women parents do not work. Indeed, it is estimated that one-half of them have to depend on state benefits. Single-parent men are generally much better off financially. Not only do they have better-paid jobs, but society expects that they should work and, for this reason, they may receive more help with looking after children.

The social situation of single-parents is one of stress. They are poor and have to cope with young and demanding children on their own. They are also often isolated. The network of friends people built up when married often depends on their being part of a couple. Divorced and separated women often complain of the speed with which they lose contact with their married friends. New friendships tend to be formed with people who are also on their own, and this tends to reinforce the feeling of having lost the desirable married status. There is little social provision for single-parent families and, indeed, government policy is much more favourable to the widowed parent than to the divorced parent, even if their situations are very similar. There is, in sum, no socially recognized place for single-parent families in Britain.

Indeed, social attitudes to divorce, in general, and single parenthood, in particular, are still disapproving despite the changes noted earlier in this chapter. As the Finer Report (1974, p. 6) said:

To fail in marriage nowadays is to go bankrupt in a business of life in which everyone engages and in which the large majority at least appear to be successful. So it is likely that a family in which a mother or father has to bring up children single-handed will think of itself and be treated by others, as a little cluster of deviants from the marital norm. (Quoted in Popay, Rimmer and Rossiter, 1983, p. 18)

Single-mothers can often be the target of unfavourable press attention in which single-parenthood is associated with 'welfare-scrounging'.

In these circumstances of deprivation, stress and social disapproval, it is not surprising that the first priority of single parents is to get married and re-enter the 'secure' state. As we noted before, some two-thirds of divorcees can be expected to remarry. This has been used as evidence of the continuing popularity of marriage. Our discussion of single-parenthood, however, indicates that divorcees and single-parents do not remarry out of dedication to the institution. It is just that they have no other choice.

Table 6.6 shows one way in which the cereal-packet norm is becoming dented; single-parent families are becoming more common. However, it would be difficult to argue that single parents are rebelling against the conventional family form *in principle*. However, some people do strive after alternative ways of organizing 'family' life and it is to a brief examination of these that we now turn.

Alternative household forms

There have always been objections to the family structure of Western industrial societies. Families have been felt to be rigid, narrow, and highly constraining institutions which repress the individual and stop the development of his or her individuality. In contemporary Britain, a whole series of alternatives are offered. The way in which the conventional family depends on heterosexual relationships, for example, has inspired the open proclamation of the desirability of homosexual households. Some theorists, on the other hand, feel that the orthodox household confines heterosexual sexuality too much and that what is required are more 'open marriages' in which the partners are free to experiment sexually. Feminists often argue that marriage merely reproduces and reinforces the inequality between the sexes prevalent in wider society. Many of them, therefore, set up households composed solely of women – heterosexual or homosexual. A not uncommon solution to the feeling that the conventional family stunts the individuality of its members is for people to elect to live on their own. A contrary solution, to the same perceived problem, is to live in large households or communes.

Communal living has received a great deal of publicity during the last twenty years, partly as the result of the experiments with alternative life-styles widely advocated by members of the middle classes in the 1960s. As McCulloch (1982, p. 324) writes:

> The struggle systematically to open up the domestic and intimate relations of the normal kin-based nuclear household is premised on the belief that what is chiefly at fault with the conventional family household is that it is excessively closed and rigid. Furthermore, this isolation (of the nuclear family) is a threat to the very integrity and expression of the self.

It is very difficult to estimate the numbers of people living in communes; this is not an area recorded by government statistical surveys. A number of publications in the area suggest, however, that there are probably no more than 100 communes in Britain at any one time. Clearly, communes differ considerably from one another. They can be differentiated along a continuum, one end of which consists of a community of individuals sharing everything, while the other end is characterized by a number of family groups which share a house, and perhaps other things as well, but whose degree of involvement as individuals in the collective is limited. The first type could be called communal and the second collective (Lee, 1979). Many proponents of commune life would probably not regard the collective solution as a real commune but, in reality, most British communes are collections of couples living together. Communal arrangements tend to be very short-lived and are, ironically, often beset by the same problems as plague the cereal-packet family. For example, communes have difficulty in coping with adolescent children. Indeed, children only very rarely stay in communal arrangements as they grow up. Just as a crisis point for conventional families is the point at which children leave home, so also is it for communes.

Summary

1   When parents get divorced they, and their children, enter into new kinds of family arrangements which are becoming increasingly frequent in Britain.

2   Reconstituted families, formed by the remarriage of divorcees with children, are fairly common and may generate difficult and non-institutionalized relationships, (a) between step-parents and resident children, and (b) with the previous spouse and children.

3   Around 12 per cent of households with children contain only one parent. Single parents are most frequently women and they suffer from considerable social and economic stress.

4 Some people seek to avoid privatized or nuclear-family living and make alternative household arrangements.

6.6 Families and Others

> My own reading of the evidence is that the wide ranging family network (Rosser and Harris's 'extended family') is fast losing all functional significance and, that being so, the elementary family of conjugal pair and children is reverting to its original condition – once again it is a domestic group not a kinship group.
>
> Leach (1968)

Social attitudes and images of the relationship between the nuclear family and the wider kinship grouping of uncles, aunts, grandparents, cousins and in-laws are various and sometimes confusing. On the one hand, 'family life', by which is meant the life of the nuclear family, is much praised in government statements. On the other hand, the nuclear family is sometimes said to be selfish and inward-looking, failing in its wider duty, especially towards the elderly. The sociological debate about the relationship of the nuclear to the extended family has also swayed back and forth.

Extended families

One early sociological argument, now rejected, ran as follows. Before the industrial revolution in Europe, the predominant family form was extended; people had regular and extensive contact with their wider kin. Industrialization, however, changed that. With the requirement for greater geographical mobility, people lost contact with their extended family and families shrunk to the minimal, nuclear size. Emotional and personal needs are met within this smaller unit. So, the nuclear family 'fits' industrial society while the extended family is more characteristic of pre-industrial society.

A number of studies, both sociological and historical, carried out in the late 1950s and 1960s provided the basis for a critique of this position.

1 It was argued by historians (for example, Laslett, 1965) that the family in pre-industrial England was not extended. A low expectation of life, high infant mortality, relatively low fertility, and late marriage combined to produce small households which were not multi-generational. Grandparents were rare compared with the situation today and the population as a whole was relatively youthful. On Laslett's estimate, only one household in twenty contained more than two generations. Family structure, in other words, conformed more closely to the nuclear form.
2 A second line of argument maintained that the industrial revolution did not produce a nuclear family form through the disruption of rural

Figure 6.9 Forced to concentrate more and more on caring for children who are victims of divorce, the National Children's Home seeks to convey the distress divorce causes
Source: National Children's Home.

communities. Rather, the reverse was true. Anderson (1971), for example, suggests that there was actually an increase in extended households in this period. Parents lived with their working, married children and provided child-care while receiving support in their old age.
3   A number of sociological studies suggested that the isolated nuclear family is not the predominant family form in contemporary Britain. Nuclear families are deeply involved in a number of different ways with their wider kinship groupings. The classical study is that by Young and Willmott (1957). They found that families in the heart of London, in Bethnal Green, lived near their kin and had frequent contact with them. Of particular strength was the tie between mother and daughter. Bethnal Green was, at that time at least, an area of residential stability; a lot of the people interviewed by Young and Willmott had lived there all their lives. However, not all regions of the city have this kind of stability. Young and Willmott also investigated a new housing estate to which some East-Enders had moved. They found that the people living on the estate did not have such intimate contact with their extended kin network. The nuclear families were instead relatively enclosed and inward-looking. Successive studies of family and community life in different areas of the country found, as one might expect, different relationships between nuclear and extended family. Most of them suggest, however, that most members of families in Britain have *some* contact with their wider kin.

We cannot, therefore, draw too sharp a distinction between nuclear and extended family types. If there is *one* family type in contemporary Britain, it is one that is not isolated from wider family connections. However, the image of modern families as isolated and inward-looking does not only extend to relationships with kin. It is also often supposed that there is less contact these days with neighbours and friends; in Young and Willmott's (1957) telling phrase, modern life on council estates is not face-to-face but window-to-window. Family members become more interested in the home and more inclined to follow their leisure pursuits in the home rather than in the wider community. Modern families are, in other words, 'privatized' in a whole range of respects.

Privatization of the family

The argument that certain kinds of family are becoming privatized has been put by Goldthorpe et al. (1969) in their study of affluent workers in Luton. They define privatization as a process 'manifested in a pattern of social life which is centred on, and indeed largely restricted to, the home and the conjugal family' (p. 97). The primary reason for the adoption of this life-style is the attitude to the economic rewards of work. The Luton workers valued the high incomes that they could earn; they were involved in a 'quest for affluence'. This meant that they had often moved to their present jobs away from their previous connections of kin and friends. Furthermore, the jobs themselves left little time and energy for sociability outside the home because they involved both overtime and shift-work. The Luton families studied had relatively little free time left after work, given the multifarious activities required to keep a house, garden and car even minimally organized. What time there was free was devoted overwhelmingly to home and family life, including such home-based leisure pursuits as watching television. For example, of all the spare-time activities reported by affluent workers and their wives in the few days before being interviewed 62 per cent were in or about the home itself. Three-quarters of all activities were ones carried out by the husband or wife alone or together with other members of the household. Almost a quarter of the couples had engaged in *no* activity together with people from outside the household. Figure 6.10 indicates these points in recording how Luton families typically spent their weekends.

Although the main reason for this privatization of family life is the instrumental orientation to work, it is not the only one. Apart from the constraints of work life, many of the affluent workers studied actually appeared to prefer their home-centred lives. For example, even those who did live near their kin did not see them especially often. In interviews, respondents would emphasize the central place that their immediate family had in their lives. These 'familistic' values were demonstrated in other ways. For example, there was relatively little leisure-time involvement by husbands with their mates but considerable participation in what traditionally has been regarded as women's work, especially child-rearing.

Goldthorpe et al. (1969) were talking, of course, primarily about affluent workers, all of whom were married and between the ages of 25 and 45. They did, however, draw attention to a process of convergence, between affluent manual and white-collar workers, towards a more privatized family life-style. Privatization can, of course, mean many things, not all of which necessarily run together. It can, for example, refer to an increased interest in the home, or a conviction that families should be the main focus of interest, or a greater sharing of domestic and child-rearing tasks between husband and wife, or a generalized tendency to treat the home as the focus of leisure and consumption activity. There is some evidence, besides that offered by Goldthorpe et al., that many British families do exhibit these features. One obvious indicator is the extent of home ownership. In 1984, 61 per cent of households owned their own homes, the proportion in 1971 being only 49 per cent. The proportion of households owning domestic equipment of various kinds has also increased. There may well be a greater stress on family commitments and we reviewed some of the evidence on sharing of tasks in section 6.4. However three points of qualification should be made.

1   Comparative data is difficult to obtain. This should make one wary of talking about *changes* in family life as the evidence about the privatization of families even in the recent past is not available.

Couple A Migrated from Scotland seven years previously; husband a setter at Skefko; one daughter aged three, wife pregnant and not working; have recently bought a new semi-detached house.

	Husband	Wife
Week-day 1		
Evening	Worked on building a garage to adjoin house	Did housework
Week-day 2		
Evening	Fitted new cupboard and shelves in kitchen	Watched TV
Saturday		
Morning	[Worked overtime]	Went shopping in Luton with daughter
Afternoon	[Worked overtime]	Did housework
Evening	Drove to other side of Luton to collect cement for use on garage	Watched TV
Sunday		
Morning	[Worked overtime]	Did housework
Afternoon	Laid linoleum in kitchen	Played with daughter
Evening	Watched TV	Watched TV and knitted

Couple B Migrated from London area five years ago, wife Irish; husband an assembler at Vauxhall on shiftwork; two boys aged twelve and nine; wife working part-time as a shop assistant; live in a council house but are planning to buy their own shortly.

	Husband	Wife
Week-day 1		
Evening	[Worked overtime]	Went 'bulk' shopping in Luton
	Read stories to younger son	
	Played guitar with elder son	
Week-day 2		
Evening	Gardened with elder son	Knitted
	Played guitar with elder son	Wrote letters to relative in London
	Watched TV	
Saturday		
Morning	[Worked overtime after night shift]	Did housework
Afternoon	Went shopping for gardening supplies with sons	Did housework
Evening	Went to bed	Watched TV and knitted
Sunday		
Morning	Read papers	Went to Mass
		Did housework
Afternoon	Visited by wife's sister and husband (also living in Luton)	(as husband)
Evening	Went to 'local' for a drink with brother-in-law	Watched TV

Couple C Husband a Lutonian, wife from Lancashire; husband a craftsman at Skefko; three children, eldest twelve; wife not working at present; have bought their own house.

	Husband	Wife
Week-day 1		
Evening	Watched TV	Watched TV
Week-day 2		
Evening	Went shopping with wife and children in Luton	(as husband)
	Watched TV	Knitted
Saturday		
Morning	Went shopping with wife and children	(as husband)
Afternoon	Went for a car ride into country with wife and children	(as husband)
Evening	Went to 'local' for a drink with wife	(as husband)
Sunday		
Morning	[Worked overtime]	Did housework
Afternoon	Watched TV	Watched TV
Evening	Went to 'local' for a drink with wife	(as husband)

Couple D Have lived in Luton for seventeen years, originally from the Midlands; husband a process worker at Laporte on shiftwork; two teenage sons; wife works full-time at a dry cleaners, also on shifts; now buying their own home.

	Husband	Wife
Week-day 1		
Afternoon	Helped elder son paint his motor scooter	Did housework
Week-day 2		
Afternoon	Went shopping for provisions	Did housework
	Worked on repairs to car	
Saturday		
Morning	Did housework with wife	(as husband)
Afternoon	Went shopping in Luton with wife	(as husband)
Evening	Watched TV	Watched TV
Sunday		
Morning	Stayed in bed	Did housework
Afternoon	Visited for lunch by a couple of 'old friends'	(as husband)
Evening	Watched TV	Went to bed early

Figure 6.10 Use of 'leisure' time: four typical cases among affluent workers

Note: The actual questions were: 'Now I know it's difficult, but could you try to think back and tell me what were the main things you did in your spare time [last two week-days]?' It was explained that 'main' activities meant ones lasting roughly an hour or more. After respondents had given their accounts they were also asked: 'Would you say that is typical of the way you spend your spare time? Is there anything else that you usually do?' Over 80 per cent of both husbands and wives gave answers to these last two questions indicating that their accounts were typical, and in the remaining cases the tendency was, if anything, for accounts to be thought atypical in the direction of exaggerating the extent of respondents' spare-time activities and social contacts – as, for example, when the days in question fell in a holiday period.

Source: Goldthorpe, Lockwood, Bechofer and Platt (1969) *The Affluent Worker in the Class Structure* (Cambridge, Cambridge University Press), pp. 99–101. Reproduced with permission.

2   An interest in home and family does not *necessarily* imply that modern British families are inward-looking. Home-centredness can still go with a measure of sociability with family and friends.

3   Most importantly, the experience of privatization will vary considerably between social classes and even more significantly between men and women. We are now going to explore some of these variations, first in the context of contacts with family and friends and, second, in leisure pursuits.

Gender, class and the privatized family

So far, we have argued that people in modern Britain give great importance to their immediate family, that is their husband or wife and children living with them in the same house. Despite the image of the inward-turned family, however, wider kinship connections continue to be important, especially the relationship between parents and older children who no longer live with them. A range of studies have demonstrated the vitality of the parent–child tie, sustained not only by visiting but also by a flow of assistance of various kinds in both directions.

Kin as companions

The obligations felt towards kin, and the patterns of visiting and assistance that flow from them are characteristic of all social classes. Young and Willmott (1973) found, however, that those lower down the occupational scale were more family-centred than the professional and managerial classes. Table 6.7 shows the average number of friends and relatives seen in the week before the interview. The professional class saw fewer relatives but greatly more friends. Some care should be exercised, however, in interpreting these contact-rates. A lower contact-rate may say nothing about the quality or duration of the contact, but may be due to the physical separation from kin caused by the relatively greater mobility of the middle class. It should also be noted that Young and Willmott's data do not record the number of contacts with each relative, only the number of relatives contacted. This may well understate the extent of contact by the working class who may well see their relatives living nearby several times in one week.

Class and friendship

However one interprets the data, there is, therefore, good evidence that the working class have more frequent contact with a wider range of kin than do the professional and managerial class. The reverse is true for patterns of friendship, as table 6.7 shows. Professional men, for example, see half as many friends again as unskilled workers. Interestingly, however, clerical workers show least sociability in this respect.

Table 6.7 Average number of relatives and friends seen in previous week

	Professional and managerial	Clerical	Skilled	Semi-skilled and unskilled	All
Married men working full-time					
Local friends (living within ten minutes' walk)	2.8	1.8	2.8	3.8	2.9
Work friends	3.0	0.3	0.8	1.1	1.4
Other friends	5.2	2.1	2.7	2.2	3.3
Total friends	11.0	4.2	6.3	7.1	7.6
Total relatives	2.6	3.2	3.9	3.7	3.4
Total friends and relatives	13.6	7.4	10.2	10.8	11.0
Number of people in sample	168	69	238	107	582
Married women aged 64 or under					
Local friends (living within ten minutes' walk)	2.6	1.6	2.5	2.1	2.4
Work friends	0.3	0.3	0.3	0.1	0.3
Other friends	3.4	1.1	1.3	1.3	1.9
Total friends	6.3	3.0	4.1	3.5	4.6
Total relatives	2.9	3.8	3.8	3.3	3.5
Total friends and relatives	9.2	6.8	7.9	6.8	8.2
Number of people in sample	156	70	258	104	388

Note: If work friends lived within ten minutes they were counted in the category of local friends. There were in fact very few such people in any class.
Source: Young and Willmott (1973) *The Symmetrical Family* (London, Routledge and Kegan Paul), tables 46 and 47, p. 229. Reproduced with permission.

A number of studies confirm the differences between middle- and working-class people in their friendships. An investigation by Allan (1979), for instance, found that not only did the middle class have more friends, but they were also drawn from a greater variety of social settings and over a wider geographical area. Allan argues that these class differences are due to very different ways of organizing friendship (p. 49): 'Briefly, whereas the working-class respondents tended to restrict interaction with their friends (and with their other sociable companions) to particular social contexts, the middle class respondents developed their friendships by explicitly removing them from the constraints imposed by specific settings.' Middle-class friendships start in particular settings, such as work or a sports club. However, people only truly become friends when the interaction is continued outside that setting. So, for example, someone met initially at work may be brought home to a meal, or arrangements may be made to go out to the theatre, perhaps. The point is the transfer of friendship outside the original setting. The meaning of middle-class friendship is not given by the original place of meeting but by the individuality of the people concerned who can now interact in *any* situation. The same is not true of working-class people, whose social contacts tend to be confined within particular settings. In this case, people met at work or in the pub will not be asked home or invited to go out to a dance. The sociability is confined to the original setting. Allan's working-class respondents, therefore, experienced their social contacts in terms of their setting; there were workmates, people in the pub, or neighbours, but *not* friends whose relationship transcended the original setting. Part of the consequence of this was that working-class respondents were often unwilling to use the term 'friend', being unsure if they were using it appropriately. They preferred instead to use the designation related to the setting – neighbour, for example. They also tended to see their social contacts as unplanned. For example, although they might see the same people every night in the pub, that was not a planned attempt to see *those* people but an unplanned consequence of going to the pub. In sum, Allan suggests that middle-class sociability involves a 'flowering out' of friendship while, for the working class, there is a confinement of social contact to *particular* settings.

Gender and companionship

So far, we have dealt with class differences in patterns of contact with family and friends. Gender differences are equally as important, as table 6.7 shows. In all social classes, women have less social contact with friends than men do, the disparity being most marked in the case of professionals and managers. In all classes, however, women see more relatives than men, although the differences, interestingly, are not very great. Relatively speaking, women, therefore, tend to be involved with relatives, men with friends. As Young and Willmott (1973, p. 227) say 'there was still a women's world and a men's, in social contacts as in other ways.' There is a strong sense, therefore, in which women do not inhabit the public world where they might meet and develop friendships; men are evidently less privatized than women. This social position is clearly the outcome of women's confinement to the home by domestic and child-care responsibilities. This is made worse for working-class women by the convention, which we noted earlier, that working-class families do not, in general, see their friends in their homes. In these circumstances, it is not surprising that women turn to their close relatives. Working-class women, particularly, may see few relatives but they see them more often, a fact not revealed by the data in table 6.7. A young working-class woman's mother and, perhaps, sister, constitute her trade union – an essential circle of support and advice.

The relative isolation of women from the public world of their husbands does not just have an impact on their access to relatives and friends but also, not surprisingly, on their use of leisure facilities outside the home (see also chapter 10, section 10.3). Part of the reason for this is, again, the way in which women are effectively confined to the home at least for some part of their lives. Also relevant, however, is the manner in which leisure in our society is defined in opposition to work. Because work is still considered a male role, leisure, similarly, is thought to be a male preserve. For women, the social customs do not seem to permit such a clear distinction between work and leisure. The result is that men and women inhabit different leisure worlds; in access to leisure activities, class is very much less important a variable than gender.

Summary

1 Families in modern Britain are generally more privatized and inward-looking than they used to be, with a greater interest in the home and the immediate family of wife or husband and children.

2 Wider kinship relations are, however, still of great importance, particularly the ties between adult children and their parents, which are actively sustained by visiting and the exchange of support and help.

3 The relationships between members of the nuclear family and those outside the family are differentiated by class and gender. This is true for relations with wider kin but is also the case for friendships. Middle-class and working-class people and men and women have quite different patterns of friendship.

Related topics

Chapter 3, section 3.4 deals with some other aspects of privatization. The question of leisure and the family is discussed in chapter 10, section 10.3.

Further Reading

An excellent, recent, introductory book on the family is Allan (1985). Rapoport, Fogarty and Rapoport (1982) have edited a collection of essays on various aspects of family life. Barrett and McIntosh (1982) discusses the family from a feminist viewpoint.

7 Towns, Cities and the Countryside

7.1 Introduction

In this chapter we will consider how social inequalities occur not just between social groups in Britain but also between different areas. Particular regions, towns, areas of the countryside, are wealthier and more desirable to live in than others. Attention will be directed at these areas and the causes of some of these differences. We will also consider further aspects of living in different areas. What is it like to live in the countryside? How are cities organized? Why does one region appear to prosper, while another is highly depressed?

Up to the sixteenth century or so, most people in Britain lived in the countryside. Towns were relatively small and of little importance. At the end of the fifteenth century, the largest city, London, accounted for less than 2 per cent of the population in England. The second town at the time, York, only had a population of 11,000. All towns were primitive, and contained very few public buildings. They operated mainly as market centres for local areas and, as such, they were overwhelmingly dominated by the countryside, where wealth and power were concentrated.

This changed in the sixteenth century in the case of London which grew very rapidly (see figure 7.1). By 1600, its population had grown to 200,000 out of a national population of 3.5 million. James I declared that 'soon London will be all England.' By 1700, its population was over half a million and, by 1801, it was described by contemporaries as 'the metropolis of England, at once the Seat of Government, and the Greatest Emporium in the known World'. What had happened was an extraordinary growth of world trade which was controlled by merchants and financiers who lived and worked in London. Other towns were dominated by London's monopoly of trade and commerce. Also, the expanding production of agriculture, particularly of wool, came to be controlled by the same London merchants. London became much more the capital of England and a centre of culture, of elegant houses and 'conspicuous

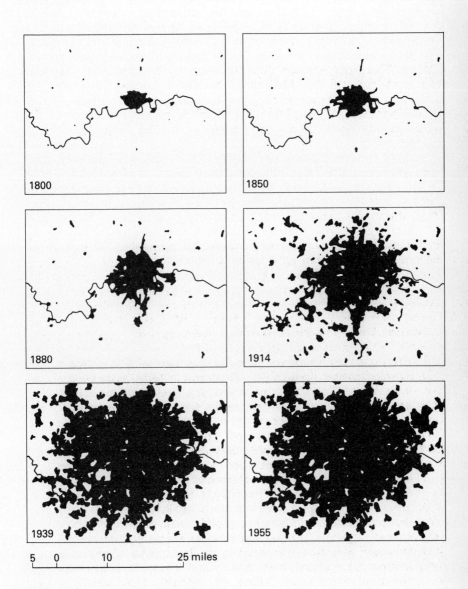

Figure 7.1 The growth of London

Source: Johnson (1972) *Urban Geography* (Oxford, Pergamon), p. 130. Reproduced with permission of Pergamon Books Ltd.

consumption'. In the time of the Tudors and Stuarts (the sixteenth and seventeenth centuries), London came to dominate the rest of the country, controlling and prospering at the expense of other towns and of villages.

Surprisingly, however, it was outside London, particularly in the north, that the great industrial towns and cities developed. Indeed, their growth generally occurred without direct funding by London financiers and merchants. Nevertheless, the size and wealth of London as a centre for consuming the products of the new industries was important. Daniel Defoe, for example, wrote in 1724 of the 'general dependence of the whole country upon the city of London . . . for the consumption of its produce'.

Much of the development of industry in the north was on a very small scale and occurred in large villages or small towns often very close to the areas where coal was mined. In 1801, only one-fifth of the population of England and Wales lived in towns. By 1911, this had increased to four-fifths. The towns and cities that particularly grew in the eighteenth and nineteenth centuries were those which were relatively free of controls by medieval guilds. One of the best-known descriptions of life in such an industrial town has been provided by Engels (1969).

Box 13   Life in a nineteenth-century northern city

Every great city has one or more slums, where the working-class is crowded together. True, poverty often dwells in hidden alleys close to the palaces of the rich; but, in general, a separate territory has been assigned to it, where, removed from the sight of the happier classes, it may struggle along as it can. The slums are pretty equally arranged in all the great towns of England, the worst houses in the worst quarters of the towns; usually one or two-storied cottages in long rows, perhaps with cellars used as dwellings, almost always irregularly built. These houses of three or four rooms and a kitchen form, throughout England, some parts of London excepted, the general dwellings of the working-class. The streets are generally unpaved, rough, dirty, filled with vegetable and animal refuse, without sewers or gutters, but supplied with foul stagnant pools instead. Moreover, ventilation is impeded by the bad, confused method of building of the whole quarter, and since many human beings here live crowded into a small space, the atmosphere that prevails in these working-men's quarters may readily be imagined. Further, the streets serve as drying grounds in fine weather; lines are stretched across from house to house, and hung with wet clothing. (Engels, 1969, p. 60)

The condition of London during the nineteenth century was particularly bad. It too had grown dramatically, having a population of over 6 million by the end of the century, and was easily the largest city in the world. Its wealth was largely non-industrial and it contained an enormous pool of underemployed and unemployed people. Particularly significant, was the fact that most workers were employed on a casual basis in very small workshops. It is surprising that London did not industrialize and that the population continued to grow at such a rate. Indeed, it is suggested that the very speed with which the population had grown acted as a disincentive to established large factories using the latest technology. There was a plentiful supply of cheap labour that could be easily employed in tiny sweatshops. The overall effect was that the world's largest and richest city of the time contained the world's most extensive slums.

In the twentieth century, there has been an accelerating physical expansion of large towns and their increasing influence over the countryside surrounding them. Over 4 million houses were built in Britain between the two world wars. By 1939, one-third of all British houses were less than 20 years old. At the same time, there was a slowdown in the increase of population in the industrial areas in the north of England, and in industrial Scotland and Wales. Towns and cities in the southern half of Britain increased in population, while many of the industrial towns outside that region lost people. This resulted partly from migration: between 1921 and 1951, for example, the South East gained more than 1 million people through migration from other parts of Britain. The areas around London grew in population throughout the inter-war period. They also acquired higher proportions of managerial and professional jobs than the other parts of the country. In this period, while suburbs grew greatly, most work remained concentrated in city centres. As a result, there was an increased separation between the place of work and the home. This led to the development of widespread commuting, the importance of improving public transport, and increased isolation for the housewife unable to escape from her suburban house.

Up to the Second World War, different industries in Britain were concentrated in different regions. Cotton textiles and textile machinery were produced in the North West of England, coalmining and steel-making were found in South Wales, agriculture in East Anglia, shipbuilding and related heavy industry in the North, and vehicle manufacture in the Midlands. The type of industry concentrated in a particular region affected the development of towns and cities in that area. In the post-war period, this regional specialization has decreased. Particular industries are no longer overwhelmingly concentrated in particular regions, and the character of the regions is 'not so directly related to the industries predominant within them. So there is a decline in *regions* as distinct units of economic and social organization.

There are still, however, very significant economic inequalities between different areas. Inequality exists:

1   between different towns and cities within the same administrative region (in the North West, between Crewe or Nantwich as relatively successful economically, Liverpool as very unsuccessful);
2   between declining centres (such as London, Liverpool, Tyneside and growing medium-sized towns (such as Milton Keynes, Cambridge, Peterborough, Rugby);
3   between older industrial areas that were once based on manufacturing industry (such as the North West, the North, the West Midlands) and those areas with a high concentration of newer services and high-technology employment (such as the South East, East Anglia);
4   between those mainly urban areas with declining manufacturing industry (such as the North West, the North, the West Midlands) and those mainly rural areas with considerable growth of manufacturing employment (such as East Anglia, the South West, North Wales); and
5   between those areas in which most industry is controlled by organizations based outside that area (such as Scotland, Wales, the North and those areas in which control is mainly found within that area (the South East).

One particularly important feature in recent years has been the growth of manufacturing employment within rural areas. This can be seen in figure 7.2, which shows how manufacturing employment in the 1960s and 1970s grew most dramatically in what were basically the more rural parts of the country. This development is, in turn, related to the growth of 'counter-urbanization' from the 1960s onwards. By this, is meant the failure of large cities to continue to grow in population and indeed, gradually, to lose population. The larger the city, the greater the decline in population. Between 1961 and 1981, the population of the six largest conurbations fell by 2 million. The longstanding drift of people to the south is now less important than the movement of population out from the cities to surrounding smaller towns and to rural areas. This decentralization of the British population out of the cities has been brought about by a number of factors.

1   The changes in the location of industry mentioned above.
2   The policy of 'urban containment' as found, for example, in the 1947 Town and Country Planning Act. Because towns and cities had grown too rapidly in the 1930s, it was decided to restrict the growth of cities and to disperse populations into new towns. At the same time, many inner-city slums were knocked down, so part of the growing post-war population was forced to move out of the central urban areas.
3   The Conservative Party placed a strong emphasis on developing owner-occupation. This resulted in the proportion of owner-occupiers increasing from 32 per cent in 1938 to 53 per cent in 1971 and 56 per cent in 1981 (table 7.1). At the same time, there was relatively little housing available for purchase within inner-city areas, especially as the desirable parts of the central areas of cities were generally 'redeveloped' for offices.

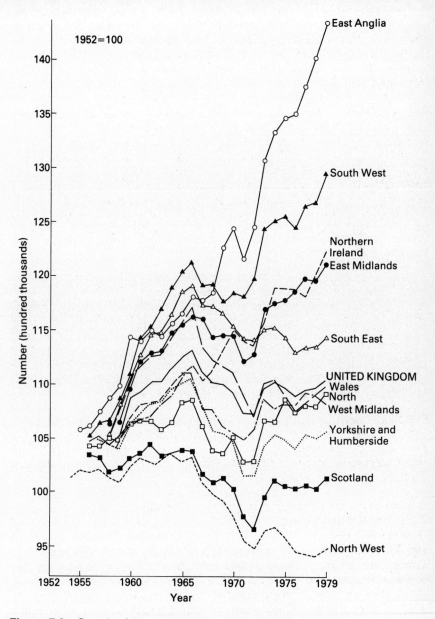

Figure 7.2 Growth of employment in manufacturing in hundred thousands
Source: Fothergill and Gudgin (1982) *Unequal Growth: urban and regional employment change in the UK* (London, Heinemann Educational Books).

4   The Labour Party's housing policy emphasized the development of council estates generally on the edge of cities or within the various new towns where land was much cheaper. The population of council housing in Britain rose from 18 per cent in 1950 to 32 per cent in 1982.

Table 7.1   Housing stock and tenure (percentages)

Housing	1914	1938	1960	1971	1980	1981
Privately rented	90	58	32	19	13	13
Local authority	negligible	10	25	29	32	31
Owner-occupied	10	32	44	53	55	56
Total stock (million)	7.9	11.4	14.6	17.1	21.0	21.1

Source: Ball (1983) *Housing Policy and Economic Power* (London, Methuen), p. 2. Reproduced with permission.

5   The widespread growth of car ownership enabled people to commute often substantial distances to their places of work.
6   A very strong emphasis has been placed upon the desirability of living in suburbs or in semi-rural areas. People felt that suburbs or semi-rural estates provide a better environment in which children could be brought up. This ideal of suburban or semi-rural living has been constructed around a 'cult of domesticity' which was particularly strongly held in the post-war period. This has been partly connected with a deep-seated hostility to cities and to urban living in general.

People in Britain tend to have strong feelings about what it is like to live in rural or urban areas. Sociologists have also devoted much attention to developing concepts that try to summarize the 'rural' and 'urban'. In the following sections we shall consider ideas of rural and urban life in more detail.

7.2   The Countryside

The ideas of 'town' and 'country' are peculiarly strong and seductive. Throughout British history, people have fought for, or fought against, powerful images of urban or rural life. Much of our literature and culture stems from or relates to attempts to represent conceptions of town or country, conceptions that invariably contrast the one with the other; town and country are always represented as opposites.

But these are deceptive contrasts. What is thought to be 'rural' has varied enormously. Indeed, it is a concept that is generally blind to the very people who have done most of the work in such areas – agricultural

Figure 7.3 Rural and urban environments

Source: Maggie Murray/Format and Janet and Colin Bord

workers. Moreover, the (olde) English village is a relatively recent creation, resulting from the eighteenth-century enclosure movement and improvements in agriculture. It had only just come to be important before the 'unnatural' town of the industrial revolution conjured up some of the most dramatic and 'romanticized' of contrasts. William Cobbett, the nineteenth-century essayist, perhaps has done more than anyone to influence our feelings about the rural. He described rural life in terms of a beneficent landowner, a sturdy peasantry and a village community – self-supporting and static. As the poet Gray said of Grasmere in the Lake District: 'This little unsuspected paradise, where all is peace, rusticity and happy poverty.'

Continuity is a particularly powerful image in Britain. Because the countryside involves working the land, and that land has in a sense been here forever, there appears to be something eternal about rural life, its rhythms and patterns, that city life can never reproduce. Indeed, because of its aesthetic claims – the lie of the land, the thatched cottages, the grazing livestock – there is a belief that life in the countryside must be meaningful, worthwhile, and able to support a socially desirable pattern of life for all people, whether rich or poor. This is, incidentally, one of the clearest messages from the radio programme, *The Archers*. Box 14 characterizes rural life.

Box 14   Patterns of rural life: ideal typical features

1 It is organized as a *community* with people frequently meeting together and being connected to each other in lots of different ways. People keep meeting each other as they take on different roles in relationship to each other.
2 People have close-knit social networks; in other words, your friends know each other, as well as knowing you.
3 Most inhabitants work on the *land* or in related industries. There is a high proportion of jobs that overlap and there is relatively simple division of labour. Most workers are relatively unspecialized farm labourers.
4 Most people possess an *ascribed* status fixed by their family origin. It is difficult to change your status through achievement. People are strongly constrained to behave in ways appropriate to their status. This status spreads from one situation to another, irrespective of the different activities in which people engage.
5 Economic class divisions are only one basis of social *conflict*. Various strategies are developed to handle potential conflicts that cannot be overcome because people keep meeting each other. Generally, social inequalities are presumed to be justified, often in terms of tradition.

Life in the East-Anglian countryside: a case-study

The model of life in rural society represented in box 14 undoubtedly fitted Britain in the early part of this century and fits some more remote rural communities in Britain today. Newby (1979, 1980) examines this in detail. He argues that, by contrast with urban-industrial areas where occupation structures a person's place in society, it is the ownership of land that shapes the rural social structure: the crucial consideration determining someone's place in rural society is whether he or she owns land, or rents land, or works for someone who owns or rents land. In the nineteenth century, most land in Britain was owned by very few landowners. This was then worked by tenant farmers, who in turn employed many agricultural labourers. In the twentieth century, three main changes have occurred in this ownership of agricultural land. First, there has been a large increase in owner-occupation so that about three-quarters of farmland is now farmed by its owners (see figure 7.4). Second, there has been a substantial increase in the ownership of agricultural land by large institutions, especially financial institutions from the City of London. And, third, there has been an irreversible 'rationalization' of agriculture: instead of farming being a 'way of life' as described by Newby (1980), it has become a business where farms are organized in terms of profitability. This has been particularly heightened by the growth of so-called agri-business, where large food-processing companies like Bird's Eye, Ross and Walls control and direct individual farmers. Agriculture has, thus, become 'industrialized', particularly with the growth of factory-farming.

One aspect of these developments has been the increased mechaniz-ation of farm work. This has had quite dramatic effects in reducing the work-force employed on farms. About one-half of all farms in Britain now employ only one farm-worker and quite a few, in fact, employ none at all (the work being done by family members). As a result of this reduction in the size of the labour force, the one or two farm-workers have to be skilled at most of the jobs that have to be done. In other words, mechanization has *increased* the variety of skills that must be mastered – it has reduced rather than increased the division of labour (see chapter 2, section 2.4 on contrasting patterns in other industries). The different tasks undertaken by each worker are organized in sequence throughout the agricultural year.

The reduction in the numbers of farm-workers has weakened the basis of agricultural trade unionism, the peak membership of the National Union of Agricultural and Allied Workers being in 1948. It has also partly reduced the bureaucratization of farms and lessened the social distance between farmers and their workers. This helps to sustain the 'deferential' relationship between farmer and farm-worker(s). Newby summarizes (1979, p. 434):

> the changes at work wrought by mechanisation and the decline of
> the village as an occupational community have brought the

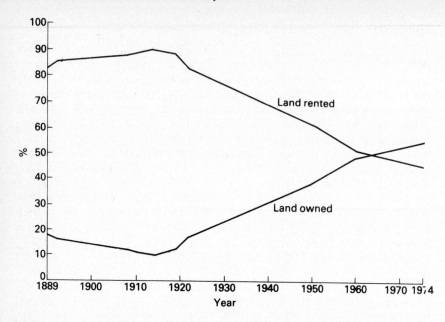

Figure 7.4   Proportion of farm land rented and owned in England and Wales, 1889–1974

Source: Newby et al. (1978) *Property, Paternalism and Power* (London, Hutchinson), p. 36. Reproduced with permission.

agricultural worker under the social influence of his employer. Today most workers are integrated neither into the oppositional rural working-class sub-culture of the occupational community nor into the predominantly traditional, middle-class culture of their employers.

The connections between farmers and their worker(s) have been strengthened by the influx of people from towns and cities. The rural community is now organized around the farm and farming and defined in opposition to the urban newcomers. Farmers and farm-workers form a community within a community. To some degree, this has reinforced a kind of 'nostalgia' for the past when rural societies were thought to be organized as relatively undivided 'communities'. The influx of urban newcomers has generated the feeling that the quality of relationships in rural communities is threatened by their arrival. It is thought that the newcomers bring their own interests and beliefs into the community, and they do not appreciate or recognize the value of agricultural work. Newcomers also seek to preserve aspects of rural charm, part of what has been called their 'village in the mind', which often involve opposing new shops or council houses of benefit, especially, to farm-workers.

Summary

1 The terms 'urban' and 'rural' are often contrasted with one another, the countryside being seen as a haven of peace.

2 In the twentieth century, a series of changes have transformed rural areas. These include the growth of owner-occupancy, the ownership by large financial institutions of agricultural land, the industrialization and mechanization of farming, and the appearance of 'newcomers' in the rural community.

7.3 Towns and Cities

Urban villages

We will now consider some research which explores the nature of social life in towns and cities. We will begin by considering whether 'communities' can also exist in urban areas.

Research in the 1950s showed that 'urban villages' (like 'Coronation Street') can exist in certain areas within large cities. The best-known study in this regard was that of Bethnal Green in the 1950s (see Young and Willmott, 1957). At the time, Bethnal Green was a relatively compact borough of about 50,000 people concentrated within a very small area (about 2 square miles), with no major roads running through it. Almost three-quarters of the male labour force were manual workers and most of the non-manual workers were shopkeepers and publicans. It was, thus, an overwhelmingly working-class locality, although there was no single dominant industry in the area. At the time of the research, children could generally find employment in the area without leaving home.

Box 15 Life in an urban village

One consequence of this immobility is that everyone is surrounded by people very like himself, most of whom he has always known. Bethnal Green has many points of similarity with a village, or rather with a whole series of overlapping and interlocking villages. The opportunities for close, long-term relationships are greater than is usually the case in a large, metropolitan, residential area. The likelihood of an inhabitant having neighbours who are strangers, or whose way of life is very different from his own has, until recently, been very slight. This immobility also makes it essential for him to be on good terms with his neighbours, as they are likely to be there, for better or worse, for most of his life. (Frankenberg, 1966, pp. 185–6)

Life in parts of some towns and cities in Britain is organized along the lines described in box 15. In the coal-miners' strike of 1984–5, it was clear that one of the social structures that reinforced the militancy of many strikers was the community within which each mine was located. It has been argued that in most mining areas the strong sense of 'community' stems from the overwhelming importance of the coal-mining industry in the area and from the shared experiences this produces for male miners. In particular, a strong sense of community is reinforced by the local nature of mining knowledge and experience. The colliers' skill, seniority and, even, knowledge of technical terms are often not transferable from pit to pit, let alone village to village, district to district, or coalfield to coalfield. This is a factor that binds miners to their home towns and their home collieries and is one important reason why they are generally unwilling to move elsewhere to work. Such a community spirit is also reinforced through the shared misfortune of mining disasters. Community here is, thus, based on the relations between male miners, a process which has meant that miners' wives, except, perhaps, until very recently, have been kept in a different and subordinated position within such communities.

The inner city

There are, however, large areas of Britain's cities which are different from either Bethnal Green in the 1950s or from these coal-mining areas. Many people living in 'inner cities' do not stay there because of the 'community' but because they cannot escape. They cannot afford to rent or buy a house elsewhere and they do not have the qualifications or skills to move, so they are, essentially, trapped. In some areas, a large proportion of the local population are in this position, reinforcing the

---

Box 16   Urban decay in the 1980s

So much of the inner city's essence was enacted here: two people, both, as it happened, with no work, imprisoned in squalid architecture, loudly destroying each other and their children. Apathy or passive withdrawal among neighbours. And the grand finale, the police acting as undertakers at the public burial of what, once upon a time, must have been a human relationship . . .

For the saddest aspect of such places is the way that they accentuate adversity, setting their inhabitants at each other's throats like rats in an overcrowded cage. (Harrison, 1983, p. 37)

sense of decay and despair now found in many city areas. Harrison (1983) has researched Hackney (which is close to Bethnal Green) in the 1980s. In box 16, he comments on a domestic argument between husband and wife in Hackney.

Hackney has not always been as Harrison describes it. In the eighteenth and early nineteenth centuries, it was an area of country houses, pleasure gardens and farms. During the later part of the nineteenth century, the landowners sold the land to developers in very small lots. At the same time, there was a rapidly expanding population, so house-builders constructed many small houses as cheaply and as quickly as they could (without proper foundations). It was then that Hackney's problem of sub-standard housing was begun. Charles Booth, who constructed a survey of London's poor in 1900, commented thus: 'Hackney is becoming poorer. The larger houses are turned into factories. The better-to-do residents are leaving or have left . . . Their places are taken . . . by a lower or middle grade. Each class as it moves away is replaced by one slightly poorer and lower' (Harrison, 1983, p. 41). These processes have continued to the present day. Those who can get out generally do; those who cannot, remain trapped by poor housing, declining job opportunities, inadequate public services, increasing crime and vandalism, worsening education, declining likelihood of new employment opportunities, increased likelihood of disturbances and riots, and so on. In other words, there is a 'vicious circle' found in some areas – in inner-city London, Birmingham (Handsworth), Bristol (St Paul's), Liverpool (Toxteth) and Manchester (Moss Side), for example.

The worsening of the conditions in inner cities have been caused by two recent developments:

1 There has been a marked reduction in expenditure on various social and welfare services, especially that on housing. Semi-skilled and unskilled workers are much less likely to be able to buy their own house (26 per cent of unskilled workers are owner-occupiers, compared with 87 per cent of professional workers). As a result, they need to rent accommodation. Yet this is becoming increasingly difficult as the numbers of new council houses being built have been greatly reduced in recent years, while many have been sold off by Conservative councils.

2 Major economic changes have recently occurred in the location of industry and employment. There has been a contraction and closure of plants, especially in the central urban areas, while there has been some expansion elsewhere. For example, manufacturing employment fell in London between 1960 and 1981 by 51 per cent, in Birmingham by 41 per cent, in Manchester by 46 per cent, while it expanded in rural areas by 24 per cent. A major factor that has contributed to this has been the process of acquisition, by which firms get taken over and merged into larger companies. These larger companies often own plants in different regions of Britain, as well as in other countries. They are able to pursue a 'global

strategy', and this has often involved the closure of older plants in inner-city areas, with large losses of employment and of income to the local population. Inner cities experience a high rate by which plants 'die' and a low 'birth'-rate of new plants. Plants in such areas tend to be less innovative, their technologies are older, and they employ less skilled labour. Inner cities generate lower levels of local rates and, hence, the social facilities and provisions (schools, parks, leisure facilities and so on) available are less developed than in other areas.

So far, then, we have seen that inner cities clearly suffer from very severe problems. However, it is interesting that poverty is, in fact, widely dispersed in Britain. Rich and poor people are found everywhere. Almost half of the poor people actually live in some of the richer areas of Britain. Hence, although there are areas with concentrations of poverty (as in Hackney), the majority of the poor do not live in these particularly deprived areas. Moreover, even these poor areas do, in fact, contain substantial numbers of moderately affluent people. Some recent government policy has been directed to certain inner-city areas as though these areas were in themselves the *cause* of poverty and deprivation. It was falsely believed that deprivation was a 'geographical' problem rather than a social and economic one, that particularly affected families in inner cities who passed multiple deprivations from generation to generation.

The suburbs

So far, we have considered what social life is like in the centres of large cities. However, many people living in towns and cities do, in fact, live in suburbs. The main pattern of suburban life is set out in box 17. Clearly, not all of these features will be found in all areas outside the inner cities. There is variation depending particularly on social class, household composition, and stage in the life cycle. Thus, households where one or both members are in manual jobs will place less emphasis on making and sustaining extensive friendship patterns and concentrate more on contact with relatives. Many working-class people living in suburban council estates will not have the resources (e.g. car) to make and keep such contacts. In the case of, say, a single person living in a suburb, however, a wide variety of types of social life is possible, including a strong concentration upon work-based friendship. And households where there are young children will, for example, engage less in the entertainment of friends, especially other couples, compared with when their children are older, or have left home.

Residential segregation

There are, therefore, different patterns of social life in urban areas and these, in part, reflect the availability of different kinds of housing. One

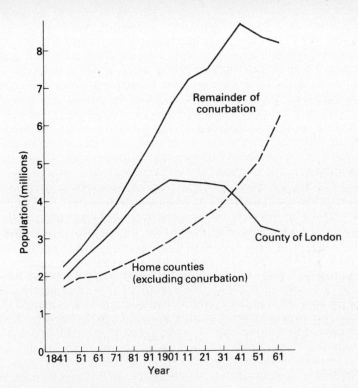

Figure 7.5   The suburbanization of London
Source: Johnson (1972) *Urban Geography* (Oxford, Pergamon), p. 135. Reproduced with permission of Pergamon Books Ltd.

Box 17   Suburban life

1   Life is centred not on the neighbourhood or the street but on the home.
2   This 'home-centredness' is reflected in a strong emphasis placed on obtaining consumer durables, on an orientation to consumption.
3   There is relatively less emphasis on contact with relatives and relatively more on choosing, making, and keeping friends, often from a fairly wide geographical area and not just from the neighbourhood or street.
4   Where households are made up of husbands and wives there is more emphasis (compared with say Bethnal Green) on sharing tasks *and* sharing friends.
5   There is fairly high participation in a variety of informal and formal organizations and the development of friendships out of this voluntary participation.

set of writers, the Chicago school of urban sociologists writing in the 1920s and 1930s, argued that, as the population of towns grows, there is an increased specialization of people into different economic positions, and that these different groups of people come to live in different sections of the town. In particular, the pressure for space at the centre creates an area of high land values, and this determines the cost of land and housing in the rest of the town. These differences in land values (which mean higher rents or higher prices for land or houses) provide the mechanism by which different groups are distributed throughout the urban area, often in the form of circles radiating out from the centre.

In Sunderland, for example, it was found that the northern part of the town shows this pattern of concentric circles, although in the south there was a wedge-shaped pattern of development (see figure 7.6). London and Huddersfield also illustrate the concentric pattern. However, patterns of segregation within towns also depend on the ways in which roads and railways have expanded, and on political decisions regarding the location of council housing and more general planning policies.

One important cause of residential segregation is competition for access to preferred forms of housing. This competition is often highly unequal. In a study conducted in the 1960s, Rex and Moore (1967) argued that the shared desire of people living in cities is to move to the suburbs. Different groups have different access to resources that may enable them to make such a move. These different groups, made up of all those who are in a similar position in the housing market, are called housing classes. There is, of necessity, competition and conflict between different housing classes for access to the generally preferred form of suburban housing. Rex and Moore point to two determinants of this competition: the size and security of income, and the need for housing and length of residence in the local area. Black immigrants to Britain in the 1960s were in the lowest housing class. This was because they generally had low and insecure incomes, so they could not obtain a mortgage for buying their own suburban house. Also, they generally had not been living in the city (in this case, in Birmingham) long enough (5 years) to obtain council housing and, if they had, they were generally offered sub-standard short-life housing in the inner city. Immigrants were, thus, forced to seek accommodation in the inner city, either renting privately or buying large deteriorating houses, usually with short-term loans at high rates of interest. This, in turn, encouraged multi-occupation as immigrant landlords sought to get some return from the purchase of these decaying properties. But the quality of the housing then further declined and indigenous families tended to move out of the area.

There was, therefore, a 'class struggle' within cities but not a struggle between classes as discussed in chapter 3. It was rather a struggle between *housing classes* for access to the central scarce resource, namely suburban housing. Moreover, this struggle was not simply determined by the market. This was because the state played a crucial role in segregating

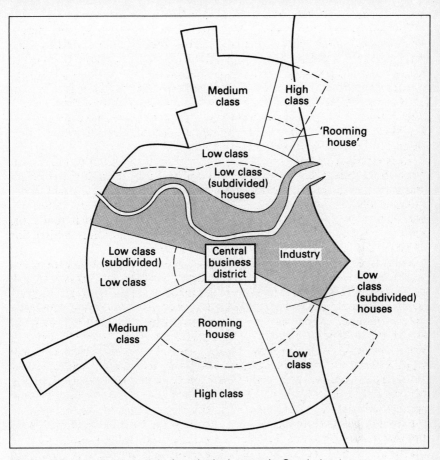

Figure 7.6 Idealized model of ecological areas in Sunderland
Source: Robson (1971) *Urban Analysis: a study of city structure* (Cambridge, Cambridge University Press), p. 128. Reproduced with permission.

immigrants into twilight zones as a result of its making council housing available mainly to the white working class. It also played an important role in preventing the expansion of immigrant landlordism into neighbouring districts – a policy that reinforced the central inner-city areas as immigrant ghettoes.

Thus, towns and cities are sources of major social inequalities over and above those generated within the world of work. There are, however, some further issues worth noting here.

1 Suburban housing is not, in fact, universally valued as the most desirable form of housing. In recent years, there has been a desire both to move into the countryside and, for many young professional people, to

Figure 7.7

Source: Posy Simmonds. Reprinted by permission of A.D. Peters & Co. Ltd.

move into areas fairly close to city centres. The latter has led to the tendency to 'gentrify' previously run-down areas, like Islington in London, and to establish the pattern of social life immortalized by Posy Simmonds in the *Guardian* (figure 7.7). Indeed, Rex and Moore largely concentrate upon housing classes as comprised of families with a male head. However, households comprised of single people, and especially single women (with or without children), do not value suburban housing so greatly. For them, access to other single people will be more significant and private renting will often be the preferred form of housing tenure.

2 Although these are described as classes with common interests, their members are also in direct competition with each other. Indeed, it is possible to divide up any given housing class into further categories, such as 'fatherless families' or 'tenants in slum stock'.

3 Housing classes cannot be separated from wider social processes, particularly the high rate of immigration into Britain during the 1950s and 1960s. Immigrants were drawn into semi- and unskilled work and their inadequate housing mainly stems from their weak labour-market position, their low status and the patterns of institutionalized racism that pervade British society. In 1981, 39 per cent of West Indians and 41 per cent of Pakistanis were in semi- and unskilled jobs, which were generally located in inner-city areas – the very areas that have suffered the most dramatic and sustained decline in employment in the past 20 years. It is more useful to talk of a black 'underclass' defined in terms of a whole variety of employment, housing and educational deprivations which are the bases for relatively unplanned spontaneous actions, as in the urban riots in 1981 and 1985 (see chapter 5).

Types of towns

It is obvious from the discussion so far that it is much more pleasant to live in some places than in others, although this will depend to a certain degree on the particular individuals and groups we are considering. Towns and cities vary, not only with respect to resources like housing but, more generally, with respect to the number and variety of jobs that are available, and to a wide range of educational, cultural and scenic facilities. Donnison and Soto (1980) explored 40 different aspects of 154 cities in Britain, including various indicators of social status, social deprivation, and educational provision. They concluded that there were a number of rather different sorts of town and city in Britain with dramatically varying levels of high-status jobs, social-welfare and educational provision. Box 18 gives some examples from the different categories.

Donnison and Soto go on to divide towns in Britain into three basic categories:

A Prosperous, white-collar towns and cities mainly in the South and

---

Box 18   Types of towns in Britain

1   Metropolitan centres: London, Cambridge.
2   Regional service centres: Reading, Bristol, Southampton, Brighton, Edinburgh.
3   Resorts: Southend, Blackpool, Southport.
4   Suburbs and new towns: Solihull, Watford, Hemel Hempstead.
5   Mining and engineering towns: Rhondda, Doncaster, Sheffield, Preston, Coventry, Barnsley;
6   Inner conurbations: Bootle, Salford, Nottingham.

---

dependent upon private-service industries and government employment. They include type 1, 2 and some of 3 identified in box 18.
B *Relatively deprived towns*, cities and conurbations based on declining manufacturing industry, mainly found in the North. They include types 6 and most of 5.
C *Relatively prosperous independent towns* and cities with considerable manufacturing industry generally located in 'Middle England' – prosperous but lacking the cultural facilities and scenic pleasantness of A. They include Slough, Coventry and Watford.

Donnison and Soto point out that the 'establishment' in Britain has always had a dismissive attitude to the third category. John Betjeman, the former Poet Laureate, wrote just before the Second World War ('Slough' in Skelton, 1964, p. 74):

> Come, friendly bombs, and fall on Slough
> It isn't fit for humans now
> There isn't grass to graze a cow
> Swarm over, Death.

To a significant extent, though, such towns have relatively low degrees of social inequality and have high levels of social provision, partly because of the particular policies pursued by the Labour Party controlled local councils. In the final section of this chapter, we will consider the issue of urban-based politics in more detail, having noted the considerable variation in the levels of public provision between different towns and cities in Britain.

Summary

1   'Urban villages' can still be found in some parts of Britain.

2 Generally, however, inner-city areas are very deprived, partly because of reductions in government welfare expenditure and, partly, because industrial employment is being relocated away from the inner city. Despite the concentration on the 'problems' of the inner city, the poor are actually quite widely dispersed geographically.

3 Different patterns of social life obtain in different areas of the city. Suburban styles of life are very different from those in the inner city.

4 Areas of residential segregation often develop roughly in the form of concentric rings. A major cause of such segregation is competition for land and for preferred forms of housing.

5 Towns vary widely, although it is possible to group them in various types.

Related topics

Ethnicity and housing is dealt with in chapter 5, section 5.3. Chapter 3, section 3.3 discusses poverty and the distribution of income. Relocation of industry is touched on in chapter 2, sections 2.3 and 2.7. Section 2.8 gives an account of research into unemployment.

7.4 Urban Politics

Urban managers

In our society, people have very different amounts of power. In addition, resources are very unevenly distributed. We can conceive of urban politics as the means by which power is exercised, or resisted, in the distribution of urban resources. We can begin here by noting how, in any town or city, there are a considerable number of important individuals and groups who control access to vital resources. In relation to access to housing, for example, some influential 'urban managers' are: the local authority (with respect to council housing and mortgage provision); housing associations; building societies; estate agents; finance houses; private landlords and property developers. Consider council-housing policy in Lambeth. Its aim was that of maximizing the provision of services in an area of acute housing shortage. However, the council was faced by a number of constraints, in particular, a shortage of building land, finance, and the attitudes of other boroughs. Given the shortage of land, the only option was to redevelop existing buildings while increasing the amount of housing on each site. The greatest gain in housing would come by redeveloping those areas of lowest housing density, in particular, those where there were small households, the retired and the old. These people had, however, to be rehoused when their homes were redeveloped. Paradoxically, therefore, in order to gain extra housing, the building programme had to be geared to the demands of smaller households needing rehousing, rather than to larger households which were those in greatest need of rehousing. These latter households would only be rehoused by moving to other boroughs which were reluctant to take them.

Clearly, the ideology and the constraints applicable to a manager in the public sector differ from those operating in the private sector. The allocation of housing for sale is a process of interaction between client, financier, solicitor and estate agent, each party having a range of values and beliefs which influence them in their interactions and the decisions they make. Local building-society managers exhibit values concerned with 'caution', 'least risk', 'privacy', and 'confidentiality'. These values are seen to be realized in the successful identification of good payers and the absence of defaulters. The manager's interaction with the client, on which this identification is based, is both an explicit and an implicit process of categorization, in which the values of the manager are important. Since it is often difficult to make a judgement, managers resort to various 'social' criteria like dress or manners. In the event, both economic criteria and social values influence the allocation of housing finance. Economic status alone may not be sufficient for one to be successful in gaining a mortgage.

Pressure groups

We can now consider the wider political processes in urban areas. We begin by looking at Newton's (1976) study of how decisions get made in Birmingham. Newton analysed the role of the 4,250 pressure groups and organizations that operate within Birmingham politics (see box 19). He showed that almost one-third of these had been politically active in the course of one year. These organizations were important in forming and regulating those issues which were to become matters for political decision.

Box 19   Some of 4,250 pressure groups in Birmingham

Birmingham Mouse Club
Forget-Me-Not Ex-Servicemen's Club
Birmingham Area Anti-Fluoridation Group
The Head Injuries Club
Midland Cold Rolled Steel Strip Club
Midland District of the Water Polo Referees' Association

Newton considers the issue of reform of education and notes that between 15 and 20 organizations were involved with this issue. This suggests that local politics involve a plurality of groups and are not decided by a single, cohesive, elite group. Education was, however, such a controversial issue in the city because of the question whether comprehensive schools should be developed, that it would have been rather surprising if a lot of groups had not been interested. Furthermore, the interests that were mobilized did not derive equally from all parts of the city. Thus, 'middle-class' areas were best represented while, of course, none of the children in the schools were represented at all. Some educational pressure groups were particularly important in effectively blocking certain proposals for educational change.

Newton also notes how the black population was largely outside the pressure-group system. It has been suggested that the urban riots in many of Britain's largest cities in 1980, 1981 and 1985, resulted partly from the fact that black people had few legitimate means to challenge the racism of British society. They lacked access both to trade unions in the workplace and to pressure groups in the towns and cities in which they lived.

Overall, Newton considers that the elites in Birmingham were forced to respond to the demands of certain pressure groups but could ignore others with impunity. He summarizes thus (p. 236):

> In the power struggle for scarce resources some publics are amply supplied with the political resources necessary to press their case while others have few resources. Some have powerful sanctions, others have weak ones, some are organized into cohesive and influential power blocks, others are isolated and atomized. The end result is that the system responds differentially to different interests according to the strength with which they can press their case.

Examples of groups which are very badly represented in local politics are housewives, battered women, immigrants, tenants of privately owned property, and users of public transport.

Urban politics in Croydon and Newham

Croydon

In another study, Saunders' (1979) investigation of Croydon, these issues are examined in the context of how and why politics centred on various social services like education come to be important. Saunders clearly shows the power of a relatively small group of councillors and local-government officers, whose overall judgement is generally seen to be neutral and objective. He also notes the conflicts caused by the election of many new Labour councillors who used the full council meetings to publicize their opposition to what they saw as top-level 'wheeler-dealing'.

But his main concern is to demonstrate the effects of middle-class urban protest, particularly in the south and east areas of Croydon (what he terms the 'Deep South'). What he finds is an extremely effective organization of the 'suburban middle class' whose interests are by no means congruent with other groups in Croydon (p. 239):

> The suburban middle class in the southern wards of the borough is generally very efficiently organized. Every ward in the area boasts at least one residents' association . . . one claimed a 95 per cent paid-up membership of all eligible households. Total memberships in excess of one thousand households are not uncommon . . . the Federation of Southern Croydon Residents' Associations . . . with a collective active membership of 17,000 families.

The overall effect of this organization has been to preserve low levels of rates in Croydon (and hence low levels of local-authority services), to preserve large areas of green-belt land in the south of the borough, and to maintain the low density of housing in the area. Thus, when new housing schemes have been approved in South Croydon, only three to five houses per acre have been allowed. In other parts of Croydon, housing has been built with up to five times that density of population. Saunders maintains that the southern residents have greatly benefited from the successful maintenance of these policies in the local council. There have, at the same time, been many losers, especially the low-income groups who live in the north and west of the borough. These groups lose out because of the relatively poor levels of local-authority services in the borough, the higher density of housing and the concentration of industry and office development in their areas of the town. Saunders puts this succinctly (p. 272): 'middle class amenity groups are nearly always willing to impose what they regard as disastrous proposals for their own districts on "soft" working class areas elsewhere.'

Saunders also notes the different ways in which various groups are treated within the political system. Even when 6,000 ratepayers refused to pay their rates and, hence, were breaking the law, they were still not regarded as 'irresponsible'. Likewise, a campaign to establish a nursery was successful, partly because the organizers came from a fairly wealthy suburban area and had considerable financial and other resources to bring the nursery to their area.

Newham

A similar kind of analysis has been developed by Dunleavy (1977), who investigated the development of high-rise flats in Britain during the 1960s. They rapidly became an extremely visible element in most large British cities. Almost 1.5 million people lived in such flats in the 1970s. Their development was enthusiastically encouraged by very large building firms

Figure 7.8 Different densities of housing: two parts of Croydon
Source: Malcolm Pendrill.

who had developed new techniques of industrialized house-building. Architects, too, during the boom period of the 1960s, encouraged high-rise development, and both Labour and Conservative Parties embraced the trend, locally and nationally. Dunleavy suggests that high-rise building programmes were successfully adopted because such housing could be represented as a technological short-cut to social change. In other words, inner-city housing could be apparently improved without diverting land resources from rural to urban use, without equalizing housing standards for all urban residents, and without building new working-class housing in middle-class suburbs and, hence, raising housing densities. The high-rise flats were not, however, cheap – they were between 50 and 80 per cent more expensive to build than conventional council housing. Moreover, they represented a massive decline in the standards of public housing provision. They were totally unsuitable for families with young children and for old people, the two groups who most lived in them. Many of them have deteriorated so rapidly that they can no longer be let or have even had to be knocked down. However, in general, most of the people who have been affected by these developments have not protested about the policy of building such high-rise flats. This is true both of the people whose older houses were knocked down in order to build tower blocks, and of those people who lived in the new blocks.

Dunleavy (1977) considers one particular area where there was urban protest about housing provision – in Newham, part of the working-class East End of London. The Labour council devoted itself to a massive programme of high-rise flat building in conjunction with Taylor Woodrow–Anglian, a subsidiary of Britain's third-largest building firm. Soon after the first tenants had moved in, a small explosion in one tower block, Ronan Point, caused a partial collapse of the block and five people were killed. As a result, a movement of urban protest began amongst the residents in the neighbourhood of Beckton against being moved into the blocks of flats still being completed. This was the first time that people in an area being cleared for rehousing had organized and protested in Newham: 700 out of 2,000 residents signed a petition stating 'under present conditions we will flatly refuse to leave our present slums to enter modern slums'. However, the Labour councillors refused to discuss this Beckton protest, the organizers of which then turned to the Conservatives for help. A central-government inquiry found that such blocks did, indeed, contain unacceptable weaknesses under certain conditions, but the Newham council did nothing to stop work on the contract for the nine blocks in question. Indeed, the company concerned received a contract for £1 million to strengthen the blocks and a further £5 million contract to build some new low-rise blocks. Yet, throughout, the Labour council refused to meet the Beckton protesters, who were being forced to engage in various forms of demonstration and publicity-seeking protest in order to get a hearing of any sort.

Within a few months this protest collapsed, partly because, in despair,

Figure 7.9 Different types of council housing
Source: Mike Abrahams/Network (bottom).

some people had left the area and others, including two of the protest committee, had been rehoused in other parts of the borough. At this point, the media coverage ceased. In short, the protest showed, first, that even a strong Labour council would not take the protest of its 'own' supports at all seriously and second, that people would, if given the chance, have adopted a quite different system of housing from the high-rise tower blocks they were offered. The normal lack of protest on such issues demonstrates that most people most of the time are in a 'powerless situation constantly reproduced by the routine exercise of power by the public housing apparatus' (Dunleavy, 1977, p. 215).

Finally, we should note that, in the early 1980s, urban politics resulted in rather different policies being developed in a limited number of areas. The provision of urban services has become an extremely significant political issue. Systematic attempts were made by the Conservative government to prevent left-wing councils from providing reasonably generous systems of collective provision of such services. Disputes revolved around public transport (cheap fares in South Yorkshire and London), council housing (cheap rents in Sheffield), new systems of social-service provision (as in parts of the West Midlands), and increased levels of council employment (in Liverpool). It is, thus, quite clear that towns and cities in Britain will continue to be the basis for a wide variety of major social conflicts centred upon control of these various urban resources.

Summary

1   Urban politics is the means by which power is exercised or resisted in the allocation of urban resources.

2   There are many agencies (or 'managers') involved in the distribution of urban resources.

3   There are also a large number of pressure groups seeking to influence policy at the local level.

4   Some pressure groups are a great deal more effective than others. Middle-class groups are much more likely to influence council policy than are working-class ones.

Related topics

Politics in modern Britain is discussed generally in chapter 12.

Further Reading

Useful books in urban sociology are Mellor (1977) and Saunders (1981). On rural life, see Newby (1980). On recent shifts in industry, see Massey (1984).

8　Education

8.1　Introduction

The amount of time children spend in formal education has increased enormously over the last 100 years. In the middle of the nineteenth century, most children attended primary schools for two or three years and that was all. Government legislation since then has *compelled* children to attend school for greater lengths of time. The 1902 Education Act made schooling compulsory from the age of 5 until 12. In 1918, the school-leaving age was raised to 14, in 1947 it was lifted to 15 and, in 1972, to 16. Moreover, a substantial minority of young adults have attended educational establishments after the minimum leaving age, in secondary schools, sixth forms, further-education colleges and in higher education (polytechnics, universities, etc.). The state provides most educational facilities; the main exception today is to be found in private schools (called independent or, rather misleadingly, public schools). The cost of educational provision is therefore, very considerable. In 1983, £15,000 million was spent, which comprised 5.3 per cent of Britain's Gross National Product (GNP). It has been one of the intentions of the Conservative government since 1979 to reduce this expenditure on education. In real terms, less is being spent and the quality of the service has deteriorated as a consequence.

Since it is publicly funded, the character of the education system is, in part, the direct result of political decision-making. In Britain, the broad outlines of the nature of provision are determined by central government – by Parliament and the Department of Education. Political parties, civil servants, and interest groups (like teachers and employers), all contribute to the formulation of education policy at this level. However, local and regional authorities actually have ultimate responsibility for the provision of schooling and much of higher education. At this level, local politicians, teachers and, to some degree, parents, influence the system. In fact, there is significant variation within Britain in the organization of education. Both Scotland and Northern Ireland have their own distinctive systems of education; and within England and Wales, some local authorities have never introduced comprehensive schools, despite pressure from the Department of Education ever since 1965 to do so.

Education has been an important issue in British politics. Social groups and political parties have persistently tried to change the nature of the education system to suit their various material interests and political beliefs. Some educational reformers have sought to reorganize schools and improve access to them so as to promote social equality between classes. Others, by contrast, have sought to segregate children in different kinds of schools on the basis of ability, or capacity of parents to pay for education. Much consideration has been given to what the schools should teach and in what ways they should try to influence their pupils. Some liberal educationalists believe that children should be treated as individuals and helped to develop their distinctive personal capacities and potentialities. Others think that the purpose of education should be to transmit basic skills – reading and writing, obedience and civility. Yet others aspire to make education vocational that is to say, schools should prepare their pupils for particular kinds of work. All these positions can be seen in on-going political debates about education.

People debate about education as if the education system could be quickly and effectively changed to fit political blueprints. In reality, although emphases may change, for example vocational relevance might be encouraged at the expense of the development of the individual's creative potential, there are great continuities in the educational system. The sociology of education has typically been concerned with those continuities, seeking to interpret the social effects, intended and unintended, of the ways in which education is organized.

8.2   Education and Society

Durkheim observed that education could play a central role in fostering social integration in societies with a complex division of labour. Following him, sociologists throughout the twentieth century have identified two basic functions of educational systems. Education is, on the one hand, an agency of socialization, transmitting social rules and values; on the other hand, it is a channel for selecting and training people to fill the many occupations of industrial economies. This dual function of socialization and selection *is* fulfilled to some degree by all educational systems. The ways in which this is done are, however, complex and not always successful.

It is very difficult to imagine an educational system which transmitted values seriously in conflict with those of government and the state, or which contributed nothing towards training young people for their future adult work-roles. Formal and publicly provided educational systems will necessarily *attempt* to socialize children into socially acceptable cultural behaviour and teach them useful skills. Schools which tried to do anything else would be looked upon with great suspicion by any state. However, educational systems are often only partially successful. This is partly because social classes, political parties, teachers and parents have different views of what elements of culture (norms and values) should be stressed, and what skills are useful. Such disagreement has a fundamental basis in the social structure of modern Britain, there often being a contradiction between the two functions of socialization and training. This is because the two functions are not easily separated in practice. The norms and values transmitted to any group of children have to be somehow related to the kinds of skills they are being taught. To take an extreme example, social problems would be likely to occur if schools taught the kinds of social behaviour appropriate to the aristocracy to children destined to become unskilled manual labourers. The culture of the aristocracy is not the same as that of working-class neighbourhoods in the inner cities. Similarly, training for different sorts of work needs to be different: to be proficient in Latin is not useful to the shop assistant, just as expertise in woodwork is irrelevant to a university teacher.

One response to this inevitable contradiction in a class society with a highly specialized division of labour is for policy-makers to educate different groups of children in different ways. This is common practice. As we will see below, schools treat girls differently from boys – they socialize them differently into gender roles and tend to train them for different kinds of jobs. Another example is the tripartite education system, introduced in Britain in 1944, which explicitly set about providing a different kind of education for children with 'different abilities and capacities'. Children were to be sent to grammar, technical or secondary-modern schools depending upon the aptitudes and levels of attainment they demonstrated in primary schools. Such an arrangement, however, caused a further set of problems. It tended to perpetuate class inequalities, because parents of the middle and upper-middle classes proved more able to get their children into the schools which produced the best results. In turn, this generated difficulties regarding the transmission of culture. These different types of schools tended to be 'class confirming', that is to say, schools ensured that children from a certain social-class background remained within that class and learned social behaviour suited to that class. Secondary-modern schools were institutions where the ambitions of children from working-class back-grounds were deflated, preparing them for low-status, manual labour, and powerlessness. It was argued that the secondary-modern school primarily taught discipline – punctuality, obedience to authority, and other things which made for a placid work-force for industry. Reality was more complex. Pupils often resented and resisted school and considered their schooling worthless. Moreover, the different cultures being imposed in the different schools tended to perpetuate class hostility rather than integrate children into a common national culture.

So, the intention that schooling should socialize children and foster social integration was undermined; different kinds of preparation for future working lives generated social conflict. It is in this sense, then, that we talk of contradictions between the functions of socialization and training. It is a far-from-simple task simultaneously to integrate children into society and to prepare them for their future work-roles.

Sociology and inequality in education

The sociology of education has explored in detail how this contradiction has affected behaviour in school and its consequences for the subsequent careers of children. One impetus for the development of the sociology of education in Britain came from a number of scholars in the 1950s who were concerned about class inequalities in education. Sympathetic to the Labour Party's professed aim to establish a system of equal educational opprtunity, these writers – Halsey, Floud, Banks, among others (for example, see Halsey, Floud and Anderson, 1961) – sought to document inequalities of achievement, explain their origins, and suggest remedial solutions. They recognized that there were inequalities in both *access* to education and educational *outcomes*. The desire for equal access to education was the primary concern of a Labour Party seeking to make entry to selective secondary schools and universities as easy for children of the working class as for those of the middle class. This was the aspiration towards *meritocracy*, where success, particularly in gaining entry to superior educational institutions, was to be made dependent on ability rather than social status or wealth. Equality of educational outcome remains a more radical aim, implying that schools themselves, and not just their selection procedures, need to be altered to prevent working-class children both leaving education at an earlier age and acquiring disproportionately fewer educational certificates. The sociology of education was spurred on by the fact of its having some influence on educational reform, during the campaign for comprehensive schooling for instance.

In the 1950s and 1960s, sociologists advanced several series of causes of educational inequality.

1   One explanation was that the organization of the schooling system was at fault. The system of competitive selection for secondary schools (the 11-plus examination), the continued existence of elite private schools, and the streaming of school classes, were identified for special criticism. It was hoped that the introduction of *comprehensive* secondary schools, to which entry was non-competitive, and which had more flexible internal arrangements for teaching, might solve the problem.

2   Another explanation was in terms of the teachers' differential expectations of the capacities of children from different social classes. Teachers were said to be inclined to reward and encourage middle-class children, with whom they had affinities in values and styles. This

Figure 8.1 Different types of schooling
Source: Raissa Page/Format and John Sturrock/Network.

explanation concentrated on the value-system of the school, the role of the teacher and the mechanism of the self-fulfilling prophecy, whereby educational outcomes were produced in accordance with the expectations of educationalists about class differences.

3   A further series of explanations emphasized the role of the family and home environment in determining educational success. Some such explanation emphasized the different extent to which parents of different classes encouraged their children to succeed; others stressed the particular attitudes of working-class communities and peer groups towards school; and the now-famous work of Bernstein (1971) identified variable linguistic capabilities among children from different class backgrounds.

The search for an adequate explanation of the correlation between a pupil's social class or origin and his/her educational attainment continues, though now in a more sophisticated form than before. Sociologists of education have become more careful in their discussions of social classes, no longer freely using the crude distinction between the middle and the working class. Sociologists are now less convinced that reforming educational institutions will readily produce a more equitable society, are more concerned in detail about what happens *within* schools, and are better informed about the relationship between increased educational provision and achievement.

Summary

1   It is difficult for education to simultaneously fulfil the dual function of socialization and training.

2   Sociological researchers in the 1950s and 1960s advanced several different explanations of class inequalities in education, among which were the organization of the system of schooling, the nature of teachers' expectations and differences of home environment.

8.3   Education and Economic Production

Economic production in contemporary Britain is characterized by a complex division of labour, a high degree of organization, advanced technology and a disciplined work-force. Sociologists argue about the precise contribution of educational institutions to economic production. However, broadly speaking, the education system has two important, related, economic effects – training and selection. Schools and colleges *train* students in two ways: by teaching useful skills, and by teaching the personal characteristics and social orientations required in work. From an employers point of view, skills – like literacy, numeracy, carpentry and cookery – are beneficial only if workers turn up regularly, on time and will do the tasks allotted to them when at work. The habits and motivations of *work-discipline* have to be instilled into each new generation of workers.

Educational institutions also perform a *selection* function: the very many positions produced by a highly specialized division of labour require some means of allocating people to positions. Schools are closely involved in this process, most obviously because they distribute qualifications, but also because there are differences in prestige and practice between schools. Selection procedures present pupils with different job opportunities and ensure that the economy gets the differentiated work-force it requires.

The positive economic contribution of the educational system stretches beyond training and selection: universities and polytechnics, in particular, play an important part in scientific and technological innovation, and educational institutions, themselves, provide a lot of jobs.

In this section, we will consider various aspects of training. In the next (8.4) we will consider selection. Remember, however, that training and selection are interrelated – schools select pupils for different kinds of training and the kinds of training offered limit occupational choice. Remember, also, that training and selection are often in a relationship of tension with the 'socialization function' of the school (considered in section 8.5).

Training

The main protagonists in recent debates on educational policy have recommended both that education should be more practically relevant to work and that new attitudes towards work and industry should be transmitted to students. There is said to be a shortage of skilled labour, even at a time when more than 3 million people are unemployed. It is also said that the antagonism of the landed aristocracy of the nineteenth century towards industry persists among the British population in general. These two conditions are thought to account for Britain's poor economic performance, and both are blamed in part on the educational system. Both technical competence and positive motivations towards work will, other things being equal, make a work-force more productive. The school probably has more impact on motivations and attitudes than on technical competence.

Technical and vocational training

Some politicians and industrialists advocate a more 'vocational' education, that is to say one better fitted to a child's future economic role. For a number of reasons this seems mistaken. Schools seem inappropriate places for transmitting specific occupational skills. Whereas literacy and numeracy are very generalized skills essential to an efficient industrial labour force and may best be taught in schools, specific skills are more easily taught on the job. Indeed, it is only relatively recently that educational policy-makers have thought it especially important to train young people in technical skills – in the nineteenth century it was thought far more important that a moral and religious education for 'citizenship' should be provided to the mass of the population.

It is difficult, even if it is thought desirable, to render the educational system vocational. It would require a very strong form of educational planning to make the supply of skills meet the demand. This is partly because the demand for skills in a capitalist, market economy is unpredictable. No one knows how many draughtsmen, for example, will be needed in ten years' time. New computing technology, new products, or changes in the world market, might make the skills of the British draughtsman obsolete. Even if one did know how many draughtsmen were to be required, there is no way of coordinating between different schools to make sure that the right number are trained. Only at the level of higher education are the number of places in different subjects controlled. At present, moreover, available skills are not fully utilized; most people do not use the training they have received. This occurs partly because of the deskilling of jobs (see chapter 2, section 2.4), and, partly, because, as educational provision expands and more people get qualifications, the minimum standard for entry into a job is raised: higher qualifications are demanded by employers for the *same* jobs. For example, to become a schoolteacher has required a degree since 1980; previously it required only a teaching certificate; in 1900 it required no qualifications at all. This represents an inflation of educational credentials but it does not guarantee better teaching.

In fact, some sceptics say that there is no relationship between worker productivity and educational attainment. Qualifications, whether 'A' levels or a university degree, are but a condition of entry to an occupation, future success being determined more by environmental situation or personal characteristics. This illustrates the important point that the demand for skilled workers is largely independent of their supply. Training schemes may increase your skill, but they will never change the number of types of jobs available in the labour market. This has consequences for recent educational policy: expanding or improving vocational-training schemes will not reduce unemployment, but merely raise the qualifications for entry to all jobs.

New policies for vocational training

The 1980s have seen fundamental changes in the organization of educational institutions, designed primarily to extend training with a view to improving Britain's economic performance. Significantly, this includes a shift in the control and provision of training away from the Department of Education towards the Manpower Services Commission (MSC), a branch of the Department of Employment. Through the Youth Training Scheme (YTS) and its predecessor, the Youth Opportunities Programme (YOP) (see chapter 2, section 2.8), the MSC provided trainees with both work experience and further education. The new, experimental, Training and Vocational Education Initiative (TVEI) is another channel through which the MSC is providing educational resources. This shift in responsibility between departments of state symbolizes a change in priorities: the intention is to overcome the resistance of defenders of liberal educational values in order to introduce more practical and relevant training.

The TVEI experiment is one example of the new policies. Introduced in 1984, TVEI invited schools to put forward schemes for new courses of instruction for students of all abilities in the 14–18 age-range. Courses designed for approval have to meet certain criteria which are over-whelmingly related to future employment. Courses must:

1 tie in with other training and job opportunities;
2 include a 'work experience' component;
3 be constructed in the light of local and national changes in employment opportunities; and
4 include technical education.

Successful schools are provided by MSC with the resources to mount these courses, which for those requiring 'hi-tech' equipment may be expensive. Although relatively few schools (in 1985) have been involved in the experimental stage, TVEI exemplifies the concern of government to try to make schools prepare pupils better for work.

Besides MSC involvement in education, there have been other significant changes. While in some respects, the role of schools in the education of pupils over 16 is being reduced, more young people are staying on at school than before. In 1976, 41 per cent of 16-year-olds remained in full-time education; in 1984, 45 per cent did (see table 8.1). This tendency is much greater in some regions of high unemployment. There is also a strong tendency towards more centralized control of education. Britain has had a wide variety of examination boards in the past (e.g. the Associated Examining Board, the Joint Matriculation Board, etc.), each independent, setting its own syllabus and giving its own qualifications. For all qualifications except A-level, this is to be ended. As O-level and CSE examinations are abolished in 1987, to be replaced by a single qualification – the General Certificate of Secondary Education (GCSE) – a common syllabus will be introduced for all students.

The hidden curriculum and work

While skill training in schools is necessarily quite limited, schools do seem

Table 8.1   Educational and economic activities of 16-year-olds (percentages)

Activity	1975/6			1982/3			1983/4		
	Boys	Girls	Total	Boys	Girls	Total	Boys	Girls	Total
In full-time education									
School	28	28	28	30	34	32	29	32	31
Further education	11	15	13	13	20	17	11	18	14
In employment (outside YTS)									
With part-time day study	19	6	12	10	4	7	8	4	6
Other[a]	32	43	39	10	12	11	10	13	11
On YTS/YOP[b]	—	—	—	20	18	19	28	22	25
Unemployed[c]	10	8	9	16	13	14	14	11	13
Total number of 16-year-olds (thousands)	428	406	834	467	443	909	461	438	899

Notes: [a] Included in 1975/6 the unregistered unemployed and those who were neither employed nor seeking work (e.g. because of domestic responsibilities) and in 1982/3, those who were seeking work but not claiming benefit and those who were neither employed nor seeking work.
[b] Included those in further-education establishments attending Youth Training Scheme/Youth Opportunities Programme courses.
[c] Registered unemployed in 1975/6 and claimant unemployed from 1982/3. (These are Department of Education and Science estimates.)
Source: Social Trends (1986), p. 50. Crown copyright.

in a position to teach attitudes and motivations towards work. Such teaching is part of what has become known as the 'hidden curriculum'. The concept of the hidden curriculum implies that social knowledge which is imparted as a by-product of schooling is more important than the content of the visible, 'formal' curriculum, i.e. geography, maths, technical drawing. The hidden curriculum teaches many things – from obedience and punctuality to gender identity and political awareness – which contribute to producing and reproducing a labour force.

One influential and controversial account of this process is given by Bowles and Gintis (1976). They argue that 'the US educational system works to justify economic inequality and to produce a labor force whose capacities, credentials, and consciousness are dictated by the requirements of profitable employment in the capitalist economy' (p. 151). In essence, schooling has to be understood in terms of the need for workers suited to a capitalist division of labour. This division of labour means that a small minority own and control production and that the remaining

Figure 8.2 The 'hidden curriculum' prepares children for working life
Source: R. Taylor/Camera Press and Jenny Matthews/Format.

majority of workers regularly and conscientiously complete the tasks allotted to them. For Bowles and Gintis, schools are vital in the teaching of regularity, conscientiousness and obedience. Instruction in technical skills associated with particular tasks is less important. The personal characteristics, attitudes and social behaviour of the ideal labourer are taught *in*directly in schools: the school timetable does not have slots called 'obedience' or 'conformity'! According to Bowles and Gintis, the personal qualities desired at work are developed because of the *form* of schooling rather than its overt content. They assert that there exists a correspondence between the organizational environment of the school and the workplace. Merely attending school, following its rules and routines, experiencing its hierarchial organization, instills into pupils attitudes and outlooks required later in the workplace. This is partly because of the kinds of behaviour that are rewarded and penalized at school. Bowles and Gintis's research showed that pupils with the characteristics of independence, creativity or aggressiveness were comparatively unsuccessful at school. Successful pupils exhibited traits of perseverance, consistency, dependability, loyalty to the school, obedience and punctuality. This second set of characteristics is, the authors demonstrated, almost identical with the ones sought by supervisory staff in industry when hiring new workers. In short, the principal contribution of schooling is that it prepares *obedient* workers. It does this by getting children accustomed to the behaviour demanded by hierarchical organizations. As they say (p. 131):

> The educational system helps integrate youth into the economic system, we believe, through a structural correspondence between its social relations and those of production. The structure of social relations in education not only inures the student to the discipline of the workplace, but develops the types of personal demeanour, modes of self-presentation, self-image, and social-class identifications which are the crucial ingredients of job adequacy. Specifically, the social relationships of education – the relationships between administrators and teachers, teachers and students, students and students, and students and their work – replicate the hierarchical division of labor.

This has come to be known as the 'correspondence principle' and has been subject to critical evaluation by other authors.

Resistance

One problem with the correspondence principle is that not all pupils are turned into disciplined, obedient workers by the education process. The simplest proof of this is that workers resist the control of employers. Workers fight against the established organization of work, using methods from strikes to industrial sabotage (see chapter 2, sections 2.4 and 2.5). In this sense, the hidden curriculum may be thought ineffective and the correspondence principle flawed.

In fact, though, the correspondence principle might be saved if it is interpreted more subtly. Just as workers resist, so, too, do pupils in school. In schools of all types, pupil sub-cultures, hostile to schooling, develop. Contesting the authority of teachers, disobeying rules, rejecting the values of the school, are characteristics of 'anti-school cultures' which flourish among groups of, usually academically unsuccessful, pupils. Such sub-cultures have been shown to exist in grammar schools and secondary-modern schools. A recent graphic account was given by Willis (1977).

Willis studied a group of working-class boys in a secondary modern school in the Midlands. The behaviour in and out of school of a group of friends, 'the lads', was documented by recording conversations and participating in their activities. The priorities of the lads were almost wholly opposed to those of the school, the teachers, and of other conformist pupils (whom they charmingly called 'ear 'oles'). The lads openly broke school rules about dress, smoking, etc. They played truant sometimes but, more imaginatively, they systematically avoided working whenever in school. Willis (p. 27) records one group discussion in which he asked, halfway through one term, 'When was the last time you've done some writing?'

Fuzz (one of the lads) Oh ah, last time was in careers, 'cos I writ 'yes' on a piece of paper, that broke my heart.
Willis Why did it break your heart?
Fuzz I mean to write, 'cos I was going to try and go through the term without writing anything. 'Cos since we've cum back, I ain't dun nothing.

Lack of involvement and commitment in the formal aspects of school life gave the lads time to 'have a laff'. The laff, Willis explains, was 'irreverant, marauding misbehaviour', ranging from joking to vandalism, which countered authority and relieved boredom.

The culture of the lads expressed their entrenched hostility to authority, though they avoided open confrontations. Their behaviour in school paralleled that outside. Masculinity was a particularly central value, and sexism was prevalent. Racism was also prominent. In an important way, the three characteristics Bowles and Gintis said were penalized in schools – independence, creativity and aggressiveness – find a strong presence in this anti-school sub-culture.

The lads' resistance to authority and rejection of some dominant values is typical of elements of working-class culture, especially of the factory shop-floor. Willis suggests that the messing about in school and the resisting of the teachers' authority actually prepared 'the lads', *culturally*, for life on the shop-floor. Willis interviewed some of the same boys again after they had been at work for six months. For the lads, mostly in general labouring jobs, there were cultural continuities between school and work. Toughness, masculinity, being able to stick up for yourself and enjoying a laugh are central to the way labouring men in non-skilled manual work come to terms with repetitive, but often hard, work. Officially denied any control over work, labourers fight back through attempts to recover some control from supervisors, by time-wasting, insubordination and pilfering. These were things that the lads' behaviour at school had prepared them for. Being paid for their time, they preferred work to school. 'Ear 'oles', on the other hand, when they took similar jobs, which many necessarily did, found themselves in a cultural situation that they experienced initially as alien and disturbing.

Willis's findings are paradoxical. Some pupils reject the discipline of the school, seeking gratification through informal groups. An independent, oppositional culture is actively created. Such behaviour leads to failure in academic terms but, in the end, it turns out to be 'vocationally relevant', even 'realistic' and it goes some way to explaining the problem with which Willis began (p. 1): 'The difficult thing to explain about how middle class kinds get middle class jobs is why others let them. The difficult thing to explain about how working class kids get working class jobs is why they let themselves.'

Varieties of the hidden curriculum?

Though resistance does arise in schools and in work, British, like American, schools still reward conformity. While the lads rebel, the ear 'oles conform. This raises the question of the degree to which schools present a *differentiated* hidden curriculum. Are different types of pupil exposed to different hidden curricula, just as the formal curriculum requires some pupils to take history and others domestic science?

It has been clearly demonstrated that the hidden curriculum is differentiated by gender: girls and boys are encouraged to behave in different ways and to develop different identities and aspirations. Sharpe (1976) documents how boys and girls are treated differently: boys' activities are granted higher status than girls', boisterous and aggressive behaviour is less tolerated in girls, etc. Teachers reinforce feminine stereotypes, expecting girls to be quiet and submissive, and assuming that the most central element of their future adult lives will be as wives and mothers rather than as employers in the formal economy. This is made clear from the quotations in box 20 about teachers expectations of their female students' situations.

There is Australian and American evidence to suggest that the hidden curriculum is also differentiated by social class. Anyon (1980) compared fifth-grade pupils (aged 10) in five elementary schools in the USA which enrolled children from different social-class backgrounds. In two schools, children came from families of the manual working class; in another, pupils were from routine white-collar backgrounds; the fourth school

Box 20   Teachers' expectations

The typical expectations held by teachers are documented by Stanworth (1983, pp. 30–1) when she asked staff teaching A-levels to predict what their female students would be doing five years on. Some of the responses are quoted below:

Of a girl believed capable of getting a university degree:

Female teacher: Well, I can see her having a family, and having them jolly well organised. They'll get up at the right time and go to school at the right time, wearing the right clothes. Meals will be ready when her husband gets home. She'll handle it jolly well.

Of a girl intending to qualify as a psychologist:

Female teacher: Obviously married. She's the sort of girl who could very easily be married in five years' time.

Interviewer: Would she be working then, do you think?

Teacher: She might. But she's the sort of girl, I think, to stay at home with the children. She's a caring person, as I said.

Of a girl with outstanding academic capacity:

Male teacher: Well, I'd be surprised if she wasn't married.

Interviewer: Is she the sort of person you would expect to marry young?

Teacher: Well, not necessarily marry young, but let's see . . . 16, 17, 18, 19 years old . . . somewhere along the line, certainly. I can't see what she'd be doing apart from that.

Of a girl of average ability:

Male teacher: Definitely married.

Stanworth notes that marriage was mentioned only once with respect to boys' futures and that on only one occasion did a teacher view early marriage for a girl as a potentially harmful interruption to her development.

Source: Stanworth (1983) *Gender and Schooling: a study of sexual divisions in the classroom* (London, Hutchinson). Reproduced with permission.

recruited from professional families; and the last from the rich business elite. (Remarkably, in the working-class schools, the average family income was US $12,000 per year, whilst in the fifth school all family incomes were greater than US $100,000.) Anyon sat in classrooms observing teachers and pupils. She was interested in how teachers related to their pupils, and what kinds of aptitudes they attempted to cultivate in lessons. She discovered great difference in hidden curricula. The working-class schools taught pupils to follow procedures, to copy notes and learn by rote. No decisions were taken by pupils. Little explanation was given as to why the work was important. Classroom discipline was strict and arbitrary, with teachers ordering pupils around. The professional school, by contrast, stressed creative and independent approaches to school work, asking children to think about what they were doing. Teachers exercised less *direct* control in the classroom and maintained order mostly by negotiation. Anyon suggests that these different styles of teaching prepare children for different occupational classes: labourers follow orders, professionals control their own work. She also shows that the routine white-collar school had styles suited to work in bureaucratic organizations, whilst the business-elite school emphasized decision-making and problem-solving. In this manner, schools help reproduce social classes. By offering different 'lessons' to each social class, schools prepare the children of labourers for labouring, of clerks for routine white-collar work, and of executives for business life. The hidden curriculum is class-confirming.

Anyon may have overstated the contrast between the schools. Possibly, too, differences may be less stark in Britain because pupils are less segregated by class background. Comprehensive secondary schools, especially, tend to enrol pupils from varied social backgrounds. But, nonetheless, it seems probable that the style of teaching in British schools varies (public schools teaching decision-making, secondary moderns, rule-following, for instance). In addition, within schools, as a result of putting children in different streams, sets or bands, teachers may transmit different 'hidden' curricula. Certainly, this suggests a more complex interpretation of the 'correspondence principle'. This itself may be assessed by considering the extent to which the children of manual workers do get manual jobs. How consistently does the education system transmit class privilege from one generation to the next? This raises the question of *selection*.

Summary

1 Schools and colleges train students by teaching both useful work skills and work discipline. They also perform a selection function.

2 In recent years, there has been much pressure from government to make schooling more technically and vocationally relevant and there has been significant recent reform in this area.

3 Schools have a hidden curriculum, inexplicitly teaching social attitudes which turn children into obedient employees. This hidden curriculum is differentiated by social class and gender, in that different types of student are encouraged to develop orientations which are specific to their likely future work-roles.

Related topics

Various sections of chapter 2 concern the nature of work in Britain and the kinds of qualifications and skills required in different occupations. Chapter 4, section 4.4 considers more evidence about gender inequalities in education.

8.4 Inequality and Selection in Education

Family, class and education

Educational facilities have expanded greatly during the twentieth century in Britain, as in other Western states. In England and Wales, one major landmark in this development was the 1944 Education Act, which required that all children be provided, free of charge, with a place at secondary school until they reached the age of fourteen. (Subsequently the minimum school-leaving age was advanced to 15 in 1947 and to 16 years in 1972.) Previously, most children had not attended a secondary school but had remained in elementary education throughout their schooldays; selective secondary schools, which charged fees, were available only to a minority. The 1944 Act reorganized schooling on the tripartite system: with the exception of those in private education, children were to be transferred at age 11 to either a grammar, technical or secondary-modern school, on the basis of their individual abilities and aptitudes. The expressed wish was that all three types of school should be accorded 'parity of prestige'; each should cater for different kinds of children by offering different training. It was imagined that this system would provide better, and more equal, educational opportunities, eradicating the waste of talent among working-class children. Halsey et al. (1980) studied the workings of the tripartite system, inquiring into the extent to which inequalities in education had been reduced for boys born between 1913 and 1952.

Halsey et al. examined the educational biographies of 8,526 men aged between 20 and 60 in 1972, a part of the national sample taken in the Nuffield Mobility Study. These men were assigned to groups by their *social class of origin* and by *age cohort*. The class categories used were the same as in Goldthorpe et al. (1980), described in chapter 3, section 3.7), based upon father's occupation when the respondent was 14 years' old. An age cohort is a group of people born between two given dates. Halsey et al. considered four separate cohorts, born in the years 1913–22, 1923–32, 1933–42 and 1943–52. Thereafter, the educational experiences of each cohort were compared to test whether equality of access and attainment had *changed over time*. This comparison was organized in order to assess the argument, advanced by Jencks et al. (1972) and Bowles and Gintis (1976), that the organization of schooling made little difference to the chances of success of working-class pupils. The cohorts were chosen so that all men in the last two cohorts (born between 1933 and 1952) would have experienced the tripartite system, since the men born earliest, in 1933, would have passed into the secondary system, at age 11, in the year of the introduction of the new Education Act. If educational institutions did affect social structure and social inequalities, Halsey et al. reasoned, then comparison between the first two and the last two cohorts should show this to be the case.

The findings of Halsey et al. suggest that the 1944 Act made very little difference to inequality between classes. Of course, the total number of places in educational establishments increased and this allowed many more children of all classes to attend selective schools and universities, with corresponding increases in the qualifications achieved. But the differentials between classes hardly changed. In general, the proportions of children from each class remained more or less the same. Among the 1913–22 cohort, 7.2 per cent of sons of the service class (classes I and II) attended university, whilst only 0.9 per cent of the working class (classes VI, VII and VIII) did. Of the 1943–52 cohort, who would have gone to university between 1961 and 1970, 26.4 per cent of the sons of the service class reached university, whilst 3.1 per cent of working-class boys did. The *rate* of increase is, thus, more or less the same for each class: the proportion of sons going to university grew 3.5 times for both classes. As with some of the other reforms associated with the growth of the welfare state after the Second World War, the dominant rather than the subordinate classes benefited most. Not *all* trends confirm the hypothesis of constant class differentials: the chances of working-class boys, relative to their service-class peers, staying at school a year beyond the minimum leaving age did improve substantially over time, for example. Nonetheless, in most respects, the service class maintained its educational advantages, relative to both intermediate and working classes, over the 40-year period examined. The disadvantages of the working class persist still, as can be seen from table 8.2, which shows that only 20 per cent of candidates accepted for university in 1984 came from manual-worker families.

Halsey et al. seek to show how, and to a lesser extent why, such unequal educational selection takes place. Dealing successively with the various 'choices' or transitions that define an educational career (private or state primary school; selective or modern, private or state secondary school; when to leave school; whether to enter higher or further education), they evaluate various explanations of educational inequality.

Despite much debate, it has never been conclusively established whether the cause of working class under-achievement is material poverty or the cultural attributes of typical working-class families. Halsey et al. approached this question by attempting to separate the effects of material circumstances and cultural background. They measured the former by family income, the latter by the cultural characteristics of parents (particularly their educational experiences). They found that cultural

Table 8.2 British candidates for university accepted in 1984, by social class

Social class		Percentage acceptances	Approximate percentage of total economically active population[a]
I	Professional, etc. occupations	22.1	6
II	Intermediate occupations	48.2	23
III(N)	Skilled occupations, non-manual	10.1	12
III(M)	Skilled occupations, manual	12.4	36
IV	Partly skilled occupations	6.2	17
V	Unskilled occupations	1.1	6
Total number of acceptances		65,829	
Number not classified by social class		5,939	

Note: [a]These figures are drawn from the 1981 Census and are based on economically active men. For technical reasons the occupational-class categories used in the census are not directly comparable with those used in the educational statistics.
Source: UCCA (1984) *Report 1984, Statistical Supplement*; Census (1981). Crown copyright.

background and, specifically, parental values, were of principal importance in determining the child's progress up to age 11. Whether a child went to a private primary school, and whether he subsequently entered a selective secondary school, were most clearly related to cultural background. After age 11, however, material circumstances became much more important in determining at what age, and with what qualifications, a boy was likely to leave school. This reflects the financial expense of keeping a child at school, a cost more difficult for working-class parents to bear. This discovery undermines arguments that working-class children have inadequate cultural preparation for engaging in the intellectual pursuits required of academically successful children.

Success in secondary schooling was, according to Halsey et al., most importantly determined by the school a pupil attended. Jencks et al. (1972) and Bowles and Gintis (1976) had argued that the type of school attended made no difference to achievement because all schools were merely 'class-confirming' institutions. Halsey et al. disagreed. They found that it did not matter whether a child went to a private or a state *primary* school. However, the kind of *secondary* school a boy attended was considerably more important than any other factor, including the material circumstances of the family. The chance of a boy in a secondary-modern school surviving past the minimum school-leaving age, or obtaining any certificates, of course, was much lower than for a boy at grammar school. What Halsey et al.'s analysis shows, however, is that this fact is not accounted for directly by social-class composition nor IQ: rather, it is an effect of the school itself. Under the tripartite system, survival past the minimum school-leaving age was usual if a child attended a selective secondary school. It was, thus, the case that the 'decision' made at age 11, by the 11-plus examination, was the critical point in determining whether children 'succeeded' or not. Incidentally, this does not imply that social class or IQ are irrelevant. What Halsey et al. did was to *standardize* for these variables, showing that if class and IQ were held constant for any two children there would still be a very significant difference in educational outcome depending upon which schools the children attended. Thus, for example, *holding social class constant*, the success of boys in gaining O-levels was the same in state-maintained grammar schools as in the leading public schools, but the *actual* proportion of boys gaining O-levels at these two types of school was quite different, since the public schools took in boys from higher-class backgrounds. Hence, Halsey et al. affirmed that schools *do* matter. Box 21 illustrates the main determinants of educational success according to Halsey et al.

Critics of Halsey et al. have tended to concentrate on whether the limited biographical information collected in the study was sufficient to test the theoretical positions they set out to evaluate. In particular, it is argued that their measures of cultural background were too crude for the purpose. Two other limitations are apparent: Halsey et al. have almost nothing to say about either comprehensive schools or girls. The first limitation was unavoidable: of the sample, only 121 boys attended comprehensives because such schools, having developed only recently, were unavailable to most men born between 1931 and 1952. The second ommission was disappointing.

There is other evidence to suggest that schools, and what goes on inside them, matter. Schools of the same type differ among themselves. Davis (1977) showed that within one English county, among comprehensive schools, the proportion of children obtaining six or more O-levels, ranged from 6 to 32 per cent, for example. Rutter et al.'s (1979) study showed that the internal organization of the school had an effect on academic outcome. Rates of exam success in a dozen inner-London, non-selective, secondary schools varied considerably even after having controlled for differences in social-class background and educational ability at the point of entry to secondary education. They suggested that various arrangements which are open to modification *within* the school make a difference to educational attainment. For instance, teachers' skills in classroom management, the degree of emphasis put on academic matters, good conditions for the students and the provision of encouragement and incentives, all combined to create a school 'ethos' conducive to exam success. Such evidence has a bearing on the current political debate on standards in schooling and the most effective modes of teaching.

Comprehensive schools

The idea of comprehensive schooling has a long ancestry in Britain, being forcefully advocated by some sections of the Labour Party since the

Box 21 Main determinants of the educational careers of men born 1933-52

Parental circumstances	Child's educational career through key thresholds by age

	5 Entry primary school (private/state)	11+ Entry secondary school (grammar/technical/modern)	15	16 Minimum leaving age O-level	18 A-level

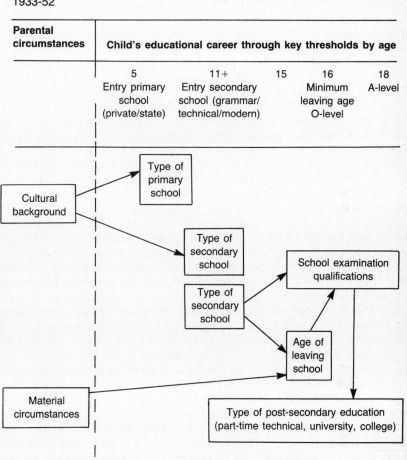

Source: Constructed from Halsey et al. (1980).

This model shows the *main* causal determinants only. It indicates that a child's cultural background is mainly relevant to explaining the nature of primary schooling and entry into secondary school. When considering qualifications, the material circumstances of the child's home become important, along with the type of secondary school attended. The qualifications obtained are the primary determinant of entry into the various forms of further and higher education.

1920s. It was not, however, until the later 1960s that significant numbers of pupils were educated at comprehensive secondary schools. The decision by the Labour government to promote comprehensive education was embodied in the circular 10/65, issued by the then Minister of Education Anthony Crosland, which instructed local education authorities to prepare plans for making secondary education comprehensive. The reasons for the introduction were partly that, as Halsey et al. (1980) conclusively demonstrated 15 years later, the tripartite system did not seem to ensure equal educational opportunity: the segregation of 11-year-olds into the three different types of school did not produce a meritocracy. But, also, the movement for comprehensive education had social objectives, particularly that class divisions and prejudices might be dissolved if there were greater mixing between social classes at school.

The success of the movement in getting institutional change in the secondary-school system may be seen from figure 8.3, which shows the rate of growth of comprehensive schools in England and Wales. In 1965, comprehensives accounted for only 4.5 per cent of secondary schools and 8.5 per cent of pupils. By 1973 half of all secondary-school pupils were being taught in comprehensives. By 1977, the proportion had reached almost 80 per cent. The most recent figures available (*Social Trends*, 1981) show the proportion to be 88.7 per cent in 1980.

The comprehensive education system has, thus, been working for a very few years and it will be a long time before we can be sure about its effect. Whether it is likely to achieve its meritocratic and social goals remains a matter of speculation, though informed opinion is currently pessimistic. It is often pointed out that the survival of selective schools, and private schools, is detrimental to the comprehensive project. (In Britain in 1980, 8.2 per cent of children were in independent schools and 3.2 per cent in state-maintained grammar schools. It has also frequently been observed that streaming and banding within comprehensive schools tend to segregate pupils within those schools, thereby replicating the old tripartite divisions. Most schools are internally organized in a way which facilitates differentiated treatment of pupils. Putting children into different streams, bands or sets, permits teachers to transmit different 'hidden' curricula. Beachside Comprehensive, a school studied by Ball (1981), had a policy of putting children into 'bands' on the basis of their performance at primary school. This resulted in the top band initially containing a disproportionate number of middle-class children. Because the two bands were taught different subjects (i.e. the formal curriculum was different) there was very little movement between bands. Thus, the bands tended to coincide with social-class differences and to generate different patterns of interaction between pupils and teachers as an oppositional culture emerged within the lower band. During the time Ball was examining Beachside, the school's policy changed to mixed-ability grouping. For the first three years in the school, pupils were put into

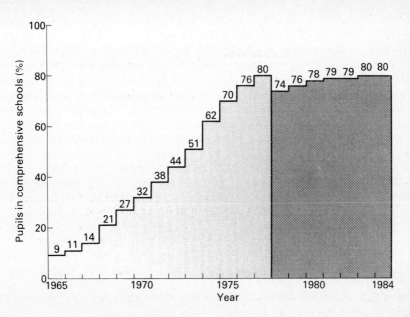

Figure 8.3 Proportion of pupils in comprehensive schools as a percentage of all pupils in maintained secondary schools in England and Wales,[a] 1965–84
Note: [a]Data is available only for England after 1978.
Source: Department of Education and Science (1978); and *Social Trends* (various years).

classes without reference to their academic abilities. This system seemed to prevent the emergence of an oppositional, 'anti-school' culture and to increase social interaction between pupils with different social-class backgrounds. However, at the time of entry into their fourth year, the pupils' friendship networks were sharply delimited by social class and academic attainment.

Recently, Hargreaves (1982) has pointed out that, since the curriculum of the new schools is modelled on that of the old grammar schools, comprehensives are increasing social divisions rather than reducing them. Hargreaves considers that comprehensives have adopted *too* meritocratic an ethos – they have become excessively concerned with examination results at 16-plus. Since many pupils fail competitive exams, antagonism toward the school, and boredom with irrelevant courses of instruction, increase among the less academic pupils. Finally, international comparisons also inspire pessimism because the relationship between social class and educational achievement does not disappear in other countries which operate systems like the British comprehensives.

Gender inequalities in education

Girls have better educational records than boys until adolescence; girls score higher on IQ tests, and they get more O-level and CSE passes. Thereafter, their advantage disappears; they have less chance of getting three A-levels or of attending university. Consequently, women have fewer of the qualifications necessary to obtain the most prestigious, professional jobs. The severe discrepancy between the sexes in higher education remains the most remarkable aspect of statistics about women's opportunities, though differences in attainment now seem to be decreasing. Figure 8.4 shows that the rate at which girls embark on A-level courses has become more like that for boys in the last decade: in 1969, 43.4 per cent of A-level registrations were for girls, whilst in 1979 the proportion was 46.9 per cent. Also, slowly, the proportion of mathematical and scientific subjects taken by girls is increasing, though it remains at a rate still *less than half* of that for boys. In the same period, as table 8.3 indicates, the proportion of women unversity undergraduates has increased, from a mere 29 per cent in 1968 to 41 per cent in 1983.

Table 8.3 Gender composition of university undergraduates 1967–8, 1973–4, 1978–9, 1983–4

	Total undergraduates	Women	Women as percentage of total
1967–8	169,610	49,598	29.2
1973–4	203,601	68,595	33.7
1978–9	245,933	90,937	37.0
1983–4	252,238	103,605	41.0

Source: Department of Education and Science (1981), table 1 (1); University Grants Commission, (1984), table 1.

These improvements are, so far, unexplained. It may be that changes in the schooling system have benefited girls, though some authors contend, on the contrary, that coeducational schooling actually hampers girls. In single-sex schools girls choose course options with less reference to gender stereotypes, see women teachers in powerful occupational positions and, perhaps, are less constrained to act in 'feminine' ways. Alternatively, it may be the result of political pressures which produced among other things, legislation promoting equal opportunities for women. Otherwise, it may be the effect of changes in occupational opportunities for women, more education reflecting the more intense involvement of women in paid employment in the post-war period.

Explanations of the continuing unequal educational opportunities for girls are various. Educational inequalities are related to other aspects of

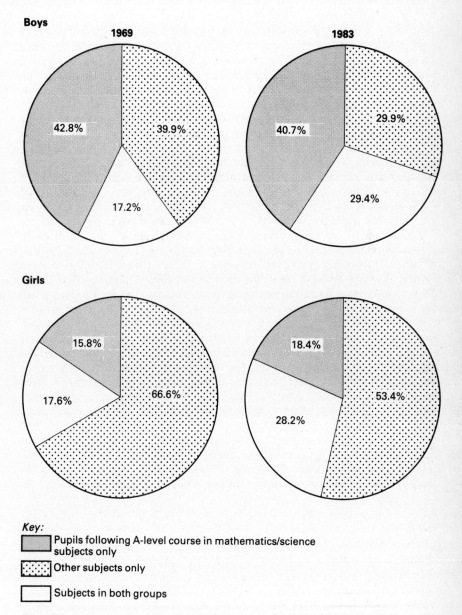

Boys

1969

42.8%

39.9%

17.2%

1983

40.7%

29.9%

29.4%

Girls

15.8%

17.6%

66.6%

18.4%

28.2%

53.4%

Key:

Pupils following A-level course in mathematics/science subjects only

Other subjects only

Subjects in both groups

Figure 8.4 A-level courses studied by boys and girls, 1969′ and 1983
Source: From Department of Education and Science (1985), pp. 41–2. Crown copyright.

gender inequality, but the precise nature of such a relationship is disputed. The various theoretical accounts of women's subordination have not yet been applied systematically to the sphere of education. Some of the best-documented accounts attribute under-achievement to sexist socialization processes within the school. Children learn to read from books which portray little girls in passive roles, helping mother in domestic tasks, etc. while more active and exciting roles are filled by boys. The formal curriculum often excludes girls from certain subjects – like technical drawing, physics and chemistry – directing them instead towards subjects considered more fitting for females. Perhaps more important is the extent to which the *hidden curriculum* (see section 8.3) is gender-specific. Schools not only make it likely that girls will be relatively unsuccessful at school, but also reinforce gender identities in other spheres of activity (see section 8.5).

Other accounts attribute educational disadvantage more directly to the sexual division of labour in society as a whole. On the one hand, girls are educated with a view to their adopting the domestic roles of housewife and mother, roles vital to the reproduction of the labour force from day to day and from generation to generation. On the other hand, as women comprise a large proportion of the paid labour force (40 per cent in 1981), school must play some part in preparation for such work though, since there is no close 'fit' between qualifications obtained and the actual jobs people do, this should not be overemphasized. Baron et al. (1981) argue that these two effects of schooling are interrelated. They assert that women constitute a 'reserve industrial army of labour', being drafted in and out of paid employment in accordance with fluctuations in the trade cycle. Such marginal and insecure employment is possible for women because they can return to the home in periods of high unemployment. Schools prepare women for this condition. This argument, however, attributes too much importance to the operation of the labour market and, therefore, gives an inadequate understanding of what precisely goes on in schools. This is because there is no very direct connection between educational opportunities, which can be expanded or contracted quite flexibly, and occupational opportunities, which are more rigid.

Summary

1 The recent study of education and social mobility suggests that although, in absolute terms, more working-class boys are going into the sixth form and on to college, their chances *relative to other classes* did not improve much in the last 50 years. It is shown that the kind of school a pupil attends is the main factor determining educational achievement.

2 It is too soon to know whether the spread of comprehensive schooling will reduce class inequalities in educational achievement, but it seems unlikely.

3 Girls are disadvantaged in educational opportunities compared with boys, but the inequalities have reduced recently.

In this section, and in the previous one (8.3), we have seen how complex is the relationship between schooling and economic life. The objectives schools set themselves are difficult, if not impossible, to achieve simultaneously. The conditions that promote equal opportunities are hard to reconcile with the school's role in social control and selection. From the process of schooling, certain unintended effects emerge which produce conflict both within the school and in the wider society. Figure 8.5 illustrates how the legitimate, economically relevant objectives of schools generate social divisions and conflicts.

Related topics

A detailed consideration of the other major part of the Nuffield Mobility Study can be found in chapter 3, section 3.7. Gender inequalities in education are discussed further in chapter 4, section 4.4.

8.5 Social and Cultural Reproduction

Schools do not merely prepare children for work. They also help reproduce social norms and cultural preferences. Intentionally or unintentionally, schools play a part in the creation of adults socialized to be consumers, Britons, decent citizens, spouses and the like. That people should accept such identities, and adopt corresponding patterns of behaviour, is just as important to the maintenance of society as is economic production.

Schools encourage their pupils to absorb social rules, manners and values – like those that mark out gender divisions in society. Boys and girls are treated differently by their teachers, who expect and encourage different behaviour from the two sexes. For instance, as box 20 showed (p. 351), a group of teachers at A-level, when asked what they imagined their students would be doing in five years' time, replied almost exclusively with reference to work in the case of boys, but marriage in the case of girls. Girls may 'learn to lose' through schools. When asked to rank fellow students in terms of academic performance, there is a strong tendency for girls to underestimate their own attainment when making comparisons with boys. Boys, on the other hand, overestimate their own attainment in comparison with girls. Images of superiority and inferiority abound. Teachers at all levels frequently highlight gender differences, whether by having competitions between the boys and the girls or by comparing the behaviour of one sex with the other for the purpose of maintaining discipline. Social norms regarding gender are rehearsed and performed in the classroom.

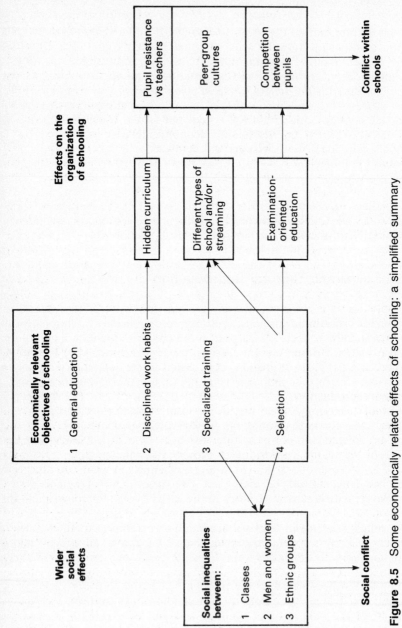

Figure 8.5 Some economically related effects of schooling: a simplified summary

A similar point, concerning a different aspect of social reproduction, was made by Rutter et al. (1979). They argue that 'to an appreciable extent children's behaviour and attitudes are shaped and influenced by their experiences at school and, in particular, by the qualities of the school as an institution' (p. 179). They advanced evidence for believing that the organization of the school was itself partly responsible for levels of delinquency. Delinquency (the measure of which was someone having been 'officially cautioned or found guilty of an offence in a Juvenile Court on at least one occasion') varied considerably among pupils at 12 non-selective secondary schools in inner London. For example, the rate for boys varied between 44 and 16 per cent, that for girls between 11 and 1 per cent. Other factors are important in predicting whether an individual is likely to be delinquent (academic attainment, parental background, etc.) but the secondary school itself has a independent influence. In this sense, schools make a difference to social reproduction.

Schools also familiarize students with a distinct British cultural tradition. Dickens and Shakespeare, Handel and hymns, and the history of the British Empire and the British Constitution seem to find prominent places in the school curriculum. Tolstoi, reggae and international communism are less common. What is worth knowing, which books are worth reading, and the like, are defined selectively, though not very systematically, by schools for their pupils. To some degree, a British culture is reproduced over time as generations of pupils are exposed to similar cultural themes.

While the educational experience certainly does include exposure to the values and beliefs that legitimate the social, economic and political arrangements of British society, the importance of the school in social and cultural reproduction is easily overestimated. Many writers on education have described this exposure as a process of the transmission of a 'dominant ideology'. Loosely, the 'dominant ideology' refers to a set of beliefs, attitudes and dispositions which presuppose that Britain is the best of all *possible* worlds. It is argued that the dominant ideology has the effect of persuading subordinate groups and classes that they owe allegiance to existing laws, institutions and practices. Put another way, schooling legitimates the existing social order and each individual's location within that social order. In this way, individuals come to 'fit in' with the social system, performing willingly the social roles into which they become inserted. Under such conditions, there would be a high degree of *social integration* based upon *consent*. Some authors see this as an ideal situation, consensus being the basis of an orderly society. Others see the dominant ideology as disguising or excusing unacceptable inequalities which benefit privileged classes. But there are a number of problems with either of these versions of 'the dominant-ideology thesis'. It is doubtful whether it adequately describes the condition of modern Britain. And it is doubtful whether schooling has this kind of effect.

1   It may never be possible to estimate to what extent a dominant ideology is transmitted through schools because of the methodological difficulty caused by the fact that other institutions and organizations also contribute to social and cultural reproduction. For instance, it would be difficult to tell whether girls learn the characteristics of the wife-mother role more from school than from within their own families, from reading newspapers and magazines, or from their peer groups. Social norms are reinforced by countless experiences and episodes, only some of which occur within th school. McRobbie's research on a group of schoolgirls reminds us how complex are the processes of social reproduction. The sub-culture of the group of working-class girls studied by McRobbie (1978) was one of resistance to the values of the school (just like Willis's 'lads' described in section 8.3). The resistance of these girls, however, revolved around an *exaggerated* model of femininity involving marriage, family life, fashion and beauty, which all contribute to the feminine anti-school culture. McRobbie points out that by paying attention to these interests, to an obsessive extent, the girls are 'doing exactly what is required of them'. Paradoxically, their own culture, created in resistance, becomes the most effective agent of social control over their adult roles. What McRobbie also shows, though, is that at least for these girls, the peer group is much more influential than the school in the process of social reproduction. The girls resisted the cultural and social models of behaviour preferred by the school, but the identity adopted instead was even more likely to reproduce working-class wives, with all the attendant disadvantages of that position.

2   A more substantial objection to the dominant-ideology thesis is the proposition that there is not one set of beliefs identifiable as a dominant ideology. There is little agreement as to the content of the dominant ideology in Britain. Evidence from attitude surveys regarding social and moral beliefs and political opinions shows widespread disagreement. One ambitious attempt to see if there was social consensus in Britain found that no value was shared by more than 75 per cent of the population, except for a vague nationalism. If there is a dominant ideology, a large proportion of the population has failed to 'internalize' it. The ideological role of the school, thus, can be little more than a negative one, excluding or dismissing unacceptable beliefs and values, preventing pupils being exposed to the unthinkable and the unspeakable.

3   The variety and inconsistency of most people's beliefs, the widely charted existence of sub-cultures, even the existence of different kinds of schools for different kinds of pupils, should make us sceptical of accepting any simple view of the process of the transmission of a dominant ideology. Indeed, it would be surprising if the educational system transmitted the same kind of knowledge and norms to all students when their future lives are likely to be widely different. It might, then, be argued that the most important ideological effect of the schooling system is to persuade people to accept their own place in the division of labour in

an unequal society. Schools and colleges sort people by giving them different qualifications or 'credentials'. Credentials are widely considered to justify why some people get better jobs than others. Somehow, possessors of credentials are thought to *deserve* their privileges. Credentials, obtained during formal edcuation, are usually justified in terms of *merit*. Students are said to succeed because of hard work and aptitude. Those who obtain well-paid jobs or positions of power, claim to deserve their privilege. This disguises the existence of social distinctions of class, gender and ethnicity, which lie behind examination performance.

Summary

1 Schools make a contribution, difficult to measure, towards social and cultural reproduction. This occurs in a more complex way than is suggested by the dominant-ideology thesis.

2 Perhaps the most important 'ideological effect' of schooling is that the distribution of qualifications is considered adequate justification of the allocation of people to positions, unequally rewarded, in the division of labour. The experience of compulsory educational competition serves to legitimate general social inequality.

Related topics

Issues of dominant and subordinate cultures are dealt with in chapter 10, especially sections 10.1, 10.2 and 10.4. More material on femininity and cultural stereotypes of women are to be found in chapter 4, section 4.4.

Further Reading

The best general introduction to the sociology of education remains Banks (1976); the most recent textbook by Burgess (1986) is also a useful, up-to-date survey of evidence about Britain. A brief introduction to the study of education and mobility is Heath (1980). Finch and Scrimshaw (1980) contains articles relevant to current political debates about education. A good short introduction to girls and schooling is Stanworth (1983).

9 Health

9.1 Introduction

'What does illness mean? Our level of "being well" is wrong. Most people are half not well most of the time. The thing is that so many people are not actually aware of it. It is the way that expectancies of what constitutes a healthy person are being lowered that I find so distressing. If we have a good year, or a good day, we think "Wow!", but it should not be like that. What makes us sick is the environment we live in . . .'

'Vera', in Mitchell (1984)

The political context of health care

In Britain today, problems of health care are on the political agenda, and the topic of health is an emotive one. The Conservative government's concern has been to reassure the public that health provision is being maintained and to argue that with greater efficiency the service could be improved, even without additional resources for the health service. The public has shown that it is rather less convinced, being concerned by the apparent decline of the National Health Service (NHS). At the same time, there is a growing awareness of new hazards, such as environmental dangers to health, as well as the increasing reality of links between unemployment and ill-health. Questions such as the dangers of radiation, which seemed rather academic just a few years' ago, or issues such as the debilitating consequences of long-term unemployment, which used to affect only a small proportion of the population, are now – more and more – occupying the centre of the political stage. Although many politicians may regret or even, for a while, ignore the fact, there is no doubt that questions of health are now firmly back on the political agenda.

We say the matter of health has *returned* to the agenda, for the setting up of the NHS in 1948 was one of the genuine accomplishments of the post-war Labour government (1945–51), as indeed was the introduction of a national health-insurance scheme by the Liberal government of a much earlier era (1906–15). The two legislative acts – the National Health Insurance Act of 1911 and the National Health Service Act of 1946 – are landmarks in the evolution of British health-care policy in the twentieth century.

The National Health Insurance Act of 1911 represented an incomplete revolution in British health-care policy. This scheme of Lloyd George's government covered only a small portion of the British people and, even by the 1940s, only about 40 per cent of the population was covered by national health insurance. By 1946, there was overwhelming popular, professional, and political enthusiasm for the notion that health care was a right for all people and an obligation of the state. Aneurin Bevan later described the NHS as 'the most civilised achievement of modern government'. Nearly four decades after its birth, many people remain more than willing to echo those sentiments. As figure 9.1 shows, over one-half of the population seem at least quite satisfied with the NHS, and this proportion is regardless of the social class of the respondent. It is largely for this kind of reason, of course, that the Conservative government of Mrs Thatcher has tried to keep a fairly low profile in the area of health and to make fundamental shifts in health care provision without any fanfare.

We should be aware of the similarities and differences between now and these earlier periods of the twentieth century when questions of health were also on the political agenda. Today, as before, there is increasing popular and professional dissatisfaction with the existing medical-care system; complaints arise from both the providers (doctors, nurses and ancillary workers) and the consumers (the patients). Also, change in party control in 1979 with the election of a Conservative government, was equal in significance to the Liberals coming to power in 1906 and the Labour Party in 1945. Undoubtedly, the Conservatives also have a mission to change the nature of health-care provision but there, perhaps, the similarities end. In the earlier periods, the inadequacies of the health-care system were highlighted by Britain's involvement in war – the Boer War at the turn of the century and then the Second World War. The low standards of health in Britain were vividly revealed as the population was mobilized into the war efforts. The Conservative's policy shift, in contrast, is more concerned to limit state involvement in health-care provision and argue for financial restraint. In fact, a government report which did reveal the shortcomings of the health care of the nation and which appeared in 1980 (*Inequalities in Health*, known as 'The Black Report' after the chairman of the working group, Sir Douglas Black) was released quietly in the hope that the contents and recommendations would go unnoticed. So, instead of the much-heralded government reports of the earlier eras – the Report of the Commission on the Poor Law (1909) and the Beveridge Report (1942) – which set the tone for the health reforms that followed, Mrs Thatcher's government has tried to muffle the most significant report on health to emerge in the present era.

Social class of respondent

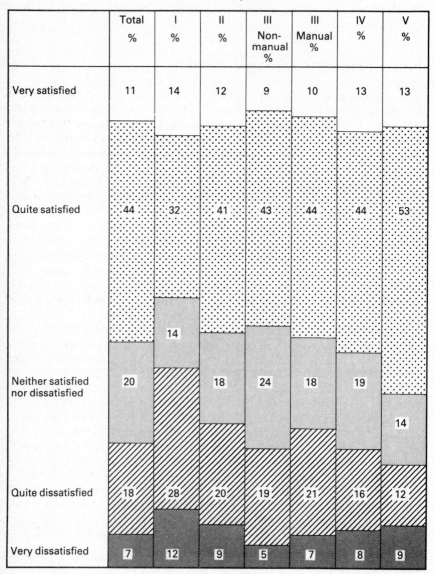

	Total %	I %	II %	III Non-manual %	III Manual %	IV %	V %
Very satisfied	11	14	12	9	10	13	13
Quite satisfied	44	32	41	43	44	44	53
Neither satisfied nor dissatisfied	20	14	18	24	18	19	14
Quite dissatisfied	18	28	20	19	21	16	12
Very dissatisfied	7	12	9	5	7	8	9

Figure 9.1 Overall satisfaction with the NHS
Source: Drawn from data supplied by Social and Community Planning Research.

While the increasing privatization of medicine and the accompanying demise of the NHS is likely to continue to arouse deep emotions within many sections of the electorate, we need to ask whether any of the political parties have really grasped the problems in the current provision of health care.

9.2 Sociological Interest in Medicine

Among sociologists, concern with health and illness is comparatively recent. Even after the Second World War, the sociology of medicine was very slow to develop. The important point to grasp is the tremendous feeling of satisfaction and accompanying complacency that followed the launching of the NHS in 1948. It raised all sorts of hopes that the benefits of health would be available to all, irrespective of wealth or position in society. The belief was that the health of all sections of the nation would now improve steadily. In short, unlike the early developments in the sociology of education, there was not the feeling that the health-care system was a major determinant of social stratification. In other words, nobody was really prepared to pose the question whether health determines your place in society. So questions posed in other fields decades earlier only really began to come to the fore in health in the early 1980s. With this background in mind, it is possible to recognize the importance of (and the potential political dynamite contained within) the Black Report when it was published in 1980.

The mid-1970s to mid-1980s have been an important period in the examination of health problems. Probably the most important contributions of sociologists in this field have been to provide fresh insights that implicitly challenge traditional medical assumptions.

The crucial shift, towards the end of the 1970s, was the recognition that sociologists should be concerned with issues of health and illness rather than of medicine. Stacey (1978) has emphasized that we should have a sociology surrounding the problems of health and illness and of suffering. Stacey suggested that the shift should be towards being more patient-oriented than doctor-oriented. In other words, we should not be too ready to assume that what is clearly in the interests of the doctor is equally in the interests of the patient. The wider implication of this message is that the medical profession may have a somewhat narrow or limited vision in terms of improving health.

More specifically, perhaps the most important recent sociological development has been the radical analyses of medical-care systems. Marxist approaches identify class as a factor in determining the division of labour in health-care institutions, and profit as a factor determining the activities or inactivity of the institutions and their personnel. Feminists have come to identify the health-care system as one of the major arenas of the subordination of women. Increasingly, the work of feminists has been crucial in one major respect – challenging the male-dominated professionalism of medicine, while re-creating or reasserting female self-confidence by 'demedicalizing' (that is, taking out of the direct medical sphere) such natural female functions as menstruation, conception, pregnancy and child-bearing.

One of the reasons why sociologists are not always popular is that they tend to challenge traditional ways of looking at issues and problems. This is often disturbing, as well as threatening to established interests. Perhaps the most fundamental challenge revolves around the definition of health and the treatment of illness.

Health and illness: medical or social conditions?

As Kelman (1975) has pointed out, 'perhaps the most perplexing and ambiguous issue in the study of health since its inception centuries or millenia ago, is its definition' (p. 625). Kelman argues that the definitional problem is crucial to the determination of health-care policy. Usually, the problem is dodged by assuming, implicitly or explicitly, that 'health' is the absence of illness. However, this evades the issue.

The first scientific approach to health originated with the development of the machine model of the human body. With this conception, 'health' came to be regarded as the perfect working order of the human organism. Kelman argues that the methodologies that developed from this view (and continue to dominate in the practice of medicine today) consider illness to be both *natural* (biological) and occurring on an *individual* basis. It then follows that treatment is pursued essentially on an individual basis, using surgical or chemical means of treatment. This approach relegates the recognition and implications of social causes of illness to secondary importance.

While an appreciation of the social basis of many diseases and ill-health has a long history, the great thrust in this direction came with the publication of the Chadwick Report in the mid-nineteenth century. The report showed that the gross inadequacy of water supplies, drainage and facilities for the disposal of refuse in big towns were the biggest sources of disease. The study of epidemics – or *epidemiology* – had begun in earnest. Since that time there has been a great deal of writing and research on social epidemiology and the *environmentalist* approach to health. However, this approach is clearly in conflict with the biological and individual orientation of the classical school which underpins most of modern medicine.

Some theorists take the argument one stage further by suggesting that health is primarily socially, rather than strictly biologically, determined. In short, we cannot view 'health' as independent of the form of society in which it is studied. This insight lays the foundation of a materialist or radical epidemiology which is developing support among some sociologists. They argue that, since the advent of capitalist industrialization, the primary determinants of death and illness in the West have shifted gradually from infectious and communicable disease – spread by unhealthy conditions such as malnutrition, overcrowding or inadequate sanitation – to a rather different set of problems, such as cancer, heart disease, hypertension, stroke, mental illness, drug addiction.

The total number of deaths in Britain in 1982 was about 663,000, nearly half of which were from circulatory disorders. The next largest cause of death was cancer, accounting for about 150,000 deaths. As figure 9.2 illustrates, there have been identifiable shifts over the last quarter of a century. The percentage of deaths due to cancer (especially among women) and circulatory diseases has increased. The most striking feature is the virtual disappearance of deaths due to infectious diseases (notably the disappearance of tuberculosis). Relatively, very few young people die, particularly those aged between 5 and 35, and a high proportion of the deaths in this age-group are caused by accidents and violence rather than disease.

The key claim of radical epidemiologists is that these new diseases have a similar chain of complex social factors. So, though their victims do not die in physical proximity to one another or in a socially concentrated space at a particular moment in time, these 'new' diseases are as much the epidemics of our century as tuberculosis was in the nineteenth century. In contrast to traditional medicine which looks to disease or illness as an individual problem, this new approach therefore emphasizes the fact that the victims of poor health share a common social history.

Sociologists differ in their emphasis but all probably recognize the dangers of being too complacent about the success of conventional medicine. We should recognize two features of Western society that are easily overlooked in this regard. First, the decline of death-rates due to the reduction of childhood and infectious diseases has slowly been by-passed by increased premature death, particularly among males, due to self-destructive behaviour – industrial cancers, diet and routinized stress. In fact, Stark (1977) has pointed out that the life-expectancy after the age of 15 for white males in England and the USA is approximately what it was in 1910! Second, and equally disturbing, is the fact that medicine is almost wholly ineffective against these new epidemics. So, given these facts, there is a danger of focusing entirely upon what doctors manage to accomplish. Stark goes further still, arguing that 'death is now socially constructed and distributed with barely any reference to nature or to disease in the traditional sense. It is endopolic, not endemic, the outcome of politics, not biology' (p. 686).

Even if one does not accept this kind of analysis, it certainly gives food for thought. So what alternative has radical epidemiology to offer? Essentially, it suggests that the prevailing mode of life may itself be sick. For example, one could argue that the nature of our current society produces the diseases of chronic stress. In other words, we have new

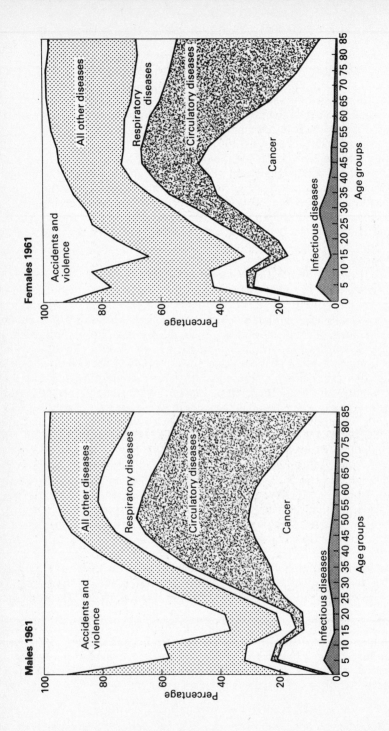

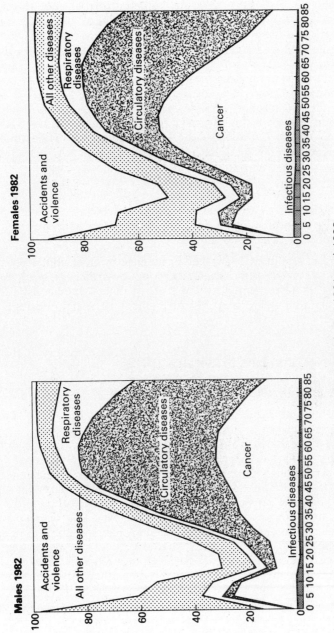

Figure 9.2 Selected causes of death by gender and age, 1961 and 1982

Note: Circulatory diseases includes heart attacks and strokes.

Source: Social Trends (1983) and (1985). Crown copyright.

kinds of epidemics which are masked behind a clinical medicine- and hospital-based technology.

This challenge to modern medicine is likely to be strongly resisted by the medical profession, in particular. Nevertheless, both the medical establishment and its critics agree that there is a crisis of medicine. The medical profession feels that it is being blocked from fulfilling its mission by being starved of resources. Its more radical critics maintain that the problem of modern medicine is not simply a question of resources because medicine cannot cure society's ills.

Against this background of fundamental challenge to the traditional medical approach, we will now consider the performance of the NHS, for inevitably its success or otherwise is central in discussing the health of the British people.

Summary

1　Sociological interest in this area was late to develop. Recently, it has moved its focus from studying doctors and medicine to consideration of the conditions for heatlh and illness.

2　There is an argument over whether medical or environmental models of health are most appropriate. Among environmentalists, radical epidemiologists have pointed to new sorts of illness characteristic of the twentieth century which may be attributable to social pressures and forces.

9.3　The National Health Service (NHS)

The success of the NHS

The apparently simple question, 'Has the NHS been a success?', needs a rather complex answer.

Spending on health care in Britain, as in other industrialized countries, has grown steadily since 1960, both in total and as a share of GNP. However, even though more resources than ever before are being used in the health sector, waiting lists still grow and the system shows increasing signs of strains. The pressure of spending seems to grow the more that is spent, yet those who established the NHS believed that demand would fall once a high standard of care was freely available to all. This, clearly, has not happened.

With the exception of maternity cases, all the trends in use of the NHS are upwards, as figure 9.3 shows. Does this mean that, as a nation, we are getting less healthy and so the NHS needs to cope with the increasing number of health problems? Or does it mean that people are getting more healthy but are wanting treatment for less-serious complaints which in previous times they may not have bothered about?

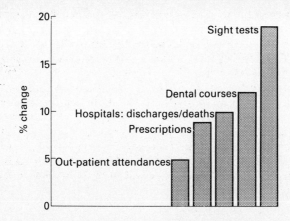

Figure 9.3 Percentage change in use of NHS facilities from 1974 to 1981
Source: Harrison and Gretton (1984) *Health Care UK 1984* (London, Chartered Institute for Public Finance and Accountancy), p. 14. Reproduced with permission of Policy Journals.

Harrison and Gretton (1985) point out that, while the use made of the NHS is increasing, it is not increasing as fast as the illnesses we report. The only evidence we have, on a national scale, for how healthy people feel, and what they do if they do not feel healthy, comes from the General Household Survey. Figure 9.4 shows the results of asking people a similar question at regular intervals over a number of years, both about their own state of health and their use of the NHS. Interestingly, the numbers of men and women reporting some form of serious complaint rose between one-third and a half between 1972 and 1980. In contrast, the numbers consulting their doctors or attending hospitals as out-patients rose only slightly or not at all.

How does one interpret this evidence? It could mean that we are getting less healthy as a whole, or we could simply be becoming more aware of health and our own lack of it. However, as Harrison and Gretton (1985) suggest, whether or not the population of Britain is getting less healthy, it is also increasingly reluctant to use the NHS facilities.

International comparisons

Leichter (1980) contrasts the health-care policy of four countries – West Germany, Britain, the Soviet Union and Japan. He stresses that 'the most obvious difficulty lies in the definition and measurement of the term success'. Leichter goes on to illustrate this difficulty. For him, one measure of the relative achievement of the NHS would be, to compare the intention and purposes of the original act with its actual accomplishments. The purpose of the National Health Service Act was 'the establishment in

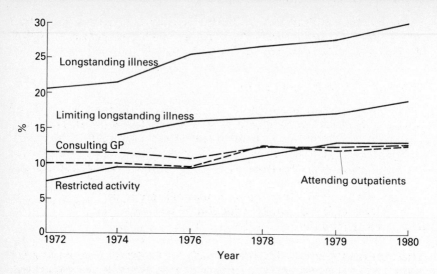

Figure 9.4　Trends in health as measured by self-reporting
Source: Harrison and Gretton (1984) *Health Care UK 1984* (London, Chartered Institute for Public Finance and Accountancy), p. ix. Reproduced with permission of Policy Journals.

England and Wales of a comprehensive health service, designed to secure improvement in the physical and mental health of the people in England and Wales, and the prevention, diagnosis, and treatment of illness'. Furthermore, it was the intention of the Act 'to divorce the care of health from questions of personal means or other factors irrelevant to it'.

Essentially – but we say this with increasing reservations – medical care is available to every resident of Britain, regardless of their ability to pay. In broad terms, therefore, the original objectives of the NHS have been achieved. But there are other questions that need to be asked. Are the British healthier under the NHS than before? Leichter (1980) notes that, compared with the period at the start of the NHS, people today are much less likely to die in infancy, and are less likely to die from diseases such as tuberculosis, influenza and pneumonia, appendicitis, or whooping cough. In contrast, as we have seen (figure 9.2), they are more likely to die from heart disease and cancer. However, Leichter stresses caution, for he notes that the general trends that appear in Britain are similar to those appearing in other economically developed countries such as the USA, France, West Germany, the Soviet Union and Japan over roughly the same period of time. The crucial point is that, as Leichter stresses, the explanation for the similarity of these trends lies less in the nature of their health-care delivery systems (that is, the way their health-care systems are organized) – which vary enormously in the different countries mentioned – than in the general socio-economic conditions in these countries.

So, while the overall health of the British people is better today than it was before the NHS was introduced, it would be unsafe to simply attribute these improvements in health to the NHS.

Unequal access to health care

Leichter (1980) usefully focuses on the question of the distribution of and access to the health-care system. Is there equal access, by all people, to the nation's health services? Is there reasonable uniformity in the quality and quantity of services available to all people? Leichter identifies three major problems of inequality from which the health service suffers:

1 a geographical maldistribution of medical resources;
2 a related social-class maldistribution of resources; and
3 irrational priorities within the medical community.

On all three counts, the NHS has failed, to the extent that one can say that the NHS does not provide all sections of the British population with equal health services. In short, we can summarize by saying that the regional and social-class variations inherited by the service in 1948, and which were part of the rationale for developing a national health service, have not really been remedied in the last three decades or so.

Regional variation

In the 1970s, there was considerable regional variation in the availability of medical personnel and services. Although there were exceptions, the general picture showed that the industrial areas of northern England and Wales had fewer and older hospitals, fewer hospital beds per population, higher patient/doctor ratios, and inadequate specialized medical personnel and facilities. One result of these regional differences is that there tend to be higher mortality-rates in the northern regions of the country than in southern regions. There have been attempts to remedy this situation, for instance by prohibiting general practitioners from starting new practices or taking over existing practices in over-doctored districts. However, there has always been a general tendency for the NHS, through its system of funding health facilities, to perpetuate these geographical inequalities. Those regions which were well off in terms of hospitals beds and doctors in 1948 have been given relatively more money, while those with fewer resources have been given less. There have been some recent attempts to move somewhat closer to a policy of reallocating resources to needy areas, but, when resources are limited, trying to make such shifts will inevitably result in some levelling-down rather than a general levelling-up of services.

In the first annual report of the NHS ordered by the Social Services Secretary (DHSS, 1984), there was a breakdown of finance for each of the 14 English health regions, showing whether their level of spending was within targets to meet the Conservative government's estimate of patients' needs in those areas. The figures showed that the government had succeeded in cutting back finance to three of the 'overprovided' regions: the North-West Thames, North-East Thames and South-East Thames regional health authorities. They provided extra resources for another three: the North-Western, Trent and Northern regional authorities. Certainly, this report indicates that the government remains aware of the problem of regional differences.

Variation by social class

There is, of course, a relationship between the health status of people from different social classes and the regional differences we have just discussed. Some of the geographical areas which have been proportionately starved of resources also contain a higher proportion of people from the lower social classes. While the social-class aspect has, until recently, been less talked about, the evidence has gradually built up suggesting that the differences in health-care provision for different social classes have *not* diminished since the introduction of the NHS. In some instances, the sad fact is that these differences have actually increased. The persistent efforts of Peter Townsend in particular, together with the work of pressure groups such as the Child Poverty Action Group, have meant that this point has not entirely been lost. In 1977, David Ennals, the Secretary of State for Social Services of the then Labour government, set up a Working Group on Inequalities in Health, under the chairmanship of Sir Douglas Black, to review information about differences in health status between the social classes, to consider possible causes of such differences and the implications for policy, and to suggest further research. The report of the working group was submitted to the Secretary of State of the new Conservative government in April 1980. As we discuss in the next section, the report received a chilly reception. But its findings are important. Its overall message was that the health problems of the British working class are probably more a function of their overall standard of living than of the health system itself. This has immense political implications for the Conservative government, whose economic policy – whether or not deliberately – is lowering the living standards of certain sections of British society. The last thing the government wishes to be told is that, while a better distribution of health facilities and personnel would have some impact on the health status of the poor and neglected, an improvement in their general standard of living would have a much greater impact.

Priorities in health care

Leichter (1980) also identified the problem of relative priorities, in the

NHS, as measured by the allocation of resources to different parts of the health-care system. In brief, there is a tendency for the less-glamorous medical-care problems to receive a disproportionately small share of the available resources. Although the 1984 NHS Report (DHSS, 1984) showed some improvement, the elderly, the mentally ill and the mentally retarded in long-stay institutions still tend to be neglected. In contrast, the medically more prestigious, acute, health-care problems attract both the more able physicians and more government resources than the areas of chronic illness. As private medicine increases, an extra ingredient will be that the more financially rewarding medical work will get increasing attention. However, with regard to the NHS, Leichter makes the macabre comment, 'The unfortunate result is that those who are neither quick to die nor quick to recover tend to be short-changed under the NHS' (p. 194).

Summary

1 The demand for health care continues to rise, though it is unclear whether this means that people are less healthy than before.

2 The new kind of illnesses from which Britons suffer are equally prevalent in other advanced industrial societies.

3 Access to health care in Britain is unequal. There are differences by region, by social class, and because of decisions about priorities in allocating resources between medical specialisms.

9.4 The Black Report

The Report of the Working Group on Inequalities in Health (known as the Black Report) was submitted to the Secretary of State in April 1980. Instead of being properly printed and published by the DHSS or HMSO, it was arranged that only 260 duplicated copies of the typescript be publicly made available, in the week of the August bank holiday. Major organizations within the NHS, including health authorities, did not receive copies. There was, in other words, an attempt by the government to bury the report. In most respects, this plan backfired, for the media, their curiosity aroused, became much more interested in the contents of the report than they might have been otherwise. With its subsequent publication (Townsend and Davidson, 1982), the Black Report has been brought to the attention of an even wider audience. Why is this report regarded as so alarming that the government tried to disown it?

The evidence of inequalities

In essence the Black Report stated that Britain's health service does not work, especially for the working classes. It provided evidence, only previously available in academic journals, that the lower down the social scale you are, the less healthy you are likely to be and the sooner you can expect to die. Furthermore, it also pointed out that if you are working class, then your children will also be at greater risk of injury, sickness and death. Using later statistics than those contained in the Black Report, figure 9.5 shows that this remains the case. Twice as many babies born to mothers in social class V (unskilled working class) die as those born to parents in social class I (professionals). The risk of a baby dying increases with declining social class. No other statistic more clearly illustrates the unequal level of health enjoyed by different sectors of the population. Over the years there have been improvements in these rates. However, the point to stress is that while the risk to babies has markedly declined, the difference in risk between social class I and V has actually *increased*.

More important than the findings, however, are the bold assertions which the Black Report makes regarding the implications of the evidence. The poorer health of the lower social classes, it says, is a result not just of failings in the NHS, but of glaring inequalities in income, education, nutrition, housing and working conditions, as well as cultural differences. Perhaps even more seriously and significantly, the report goes on to say, the gap in health standards between the upper and lower classes has actually increased steadily since 1949. Analysing a vast amount of data, the report shows that class divisions in Britain are, if anything, greater today than thirty years ago. The crucial conclusion is that quite drastic shifts in social policy are needed to establish equal health standards. As we shall see, the Conservative government has explicitly rejected the implications of this conclusion.

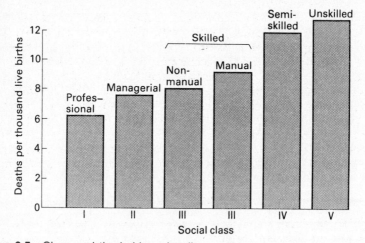

Figure 9.5 Class and the babies who die
Source: T. Garrett, *New Society* 28 March 1985. Reproduced with permission of the author.

Table 9.1 Mortality rates per 100,000 (1951–71), England and Wales, men and married women

Occupational class	Age	Men 1949–53	Men 1959–63	Men 1970–2	Married women 1949–53	Married women 1959–63	Married women 1970–2
I and II	25–34	124	81	72	85	51	42
III		148	100	90	114	64	51
IV and V		180	143	141	141	77	68
I and II	35–44	226	175	169	170	123	118
III		276	234	256	201	160	154
IV and V		331	300	305	226	186	193
I and II	45–54	712	544	554	427	323	337
III		812	708	733	480	402	431
IV and V		895	842	894	513	455	510
I and II	55–64	2,097	1,804	1,710	1,098	818	837
III		2,396	2,218	2,213	1,202	1,001	1,059
IV and V		2,339	2,433	2,409	1,226	1,129	1,131

Source: Townsend and Davidson (1982) *Inequalities in Health* (Harmondsworth, Penguin), p. 68. Black Report © DHSS 1980. Introduction © Peter Townsend and Nick Davidson. Reproduced by permission of Penguin Books Ltd.

It is, of course, impossible to do justice to the contents of the Black Report by quoting a couple of examples. However, these give at least a flavour of the type of statistical evidence it provides. Taking mortality-rates as an indicator of health, the report shows (see table 9.1) that over the last half century, men in occupational classes IV and V have made no improvements in their health, even in absolute terms. Between 1949 and 1972, the number of deaths per 100,000 working-class men in the 45–54 age-group dropped by only *one* from 895 to 894, while in the 55–64 age-group, the death-rate actually increased from 2,339 to 2,409.

In contrast, women seem to have fared better than men in these comparisons: their health has shown an improvement in all occupational and age-groups. But, again, there are differences between social classes. Upper-class women are getting healthier a lot more quickly than their lower-class contemporaries: also, their chances of surviving childbirth and producing healthy babies are greater. In 1972, the maternal mortality rate for class V women was nearly double that for women in classes I and II.

Problems of interpreting health statistics

As the Black Report itself makes clear, studies of patterns of ill-health are handicapped by the difficulty of obtaining information on sickness- and disease-rates. As a consequence, mortality-rates continue to be the main focus of attention. While these rates certainly do give some indication of inequalities, they may be of more limited value than is sometimes realized. The historical decline of infectious diseases and tuberculosis, and the increased incidence of chronic and degenerative diseases (like multiple sclerosis, cancers, strokes etc.), suggest that the relationship between mortality (i.e. death-rates) and morbidity (i.e. sickness-rates) has changed and may now be fairly weak. The point is, therefore, that the study of mortality-rates may not provide an adequate or accurate picture of patterns of ill-health; inequalities in death may not be similar to inequalities in health. This essentially methodological problem may be particularly serious in the case of mental illnesses, which rarely result in death but yet account at any one time for around one in four NHS patients. It is, of course, important to stress that the methodological weakness of using mortality-rates to estimate health does not undermine the evidence of the Black Report, but rather suggests that the work they cite seriously underestimates the differences between the social classes in the actual health they enjoy. Increasingly, for many in the working classes, to use the words of Sir Thomas Browne writing in the seventeenth century, 'life itself is but the shadow of death.'

There are, of course, other points to emphasize with regard to many of the statistics on health – the appropriate facts are often hard to measure and are difficult to interpret. For example, although the figures clearly show that working-class children are much more vulnerable to fatal injury and illness, their parents are less likely than those in the middle classes to take them to the doctor. This may in fact have much to do with the quality of the care and the inevitable cost (financial or otherwise) anticipated by the parents than with any unreasonable response to illness on the part of working-class parents. Health services in predominantly working-class areas are less accessible and of poorer quality. The report suggests that working-class adults may be typically more sick than are middle class ones before they seek help, so countering the stereotype of the working-class making unnecessary demands on the health service. One needs to recognize that middle-class patients tend to get better care from their GPs, not only because they live in areas which are better served, but also because they are more skilled at demanding and obtaining the care they need.

Comparing Britain's experience with other industrialized Western countries, the Black Report confirms that, while adult mortality patterns are about the same, infant mortality is worse in Britain than elsewhere. Using more recent figures than were available to the working group, British rates of improvement continue to be unimpressive when compared with, for example, France and Japan (see table 9.2).

The Black Report's recommendations and their reception

The chief causes of unequal health identified in the Black Report are poverty and the relatively poor access of low-income groups to the knowledge and facilities that help to maintain physical fitness. The main

Table 9.2 Infant mortality, 1960–80

	Deaths per 1,000 live births		
	1960	1970	1980
England and Wales	21.8	18.2	12.0
Australia	20.2	17.9	10.7
Canada	27.3	18.8	10.9[a]
France	27.4	18.2	10.0
West Germany	33.8	23.6	12.6
Italy	43.9	29.6	14.3
Japan	30.7	13.1	7.5
Netherlands	16.5	12.7	8.6
Sweden	16.6	11.0	6.9
USA	26.0	19.8	12.5

Note: [a] 1979.

Source: Harrison and Gretton (1984) *Health Care UK 1984* (London, Chartered Institute for Public Finance and Accountancy), p. 129. Reproduced with permission of Policy Journals.

recommendation followed from this, that a determined shift of resources should be regarded as a top priority, towards community care and greater provision for mothers, young children and the disabled. The report proposed free milk for infants without their parents undergoing means-tests, an enlarged programme of health education, better facilities for recreation in the inner cities, the establishment of 'National Health Goals' and strong anti-smoking measures. It recommended that child-benefit allowance be increased to 5.5 per cent of average gross male industrial earnings.

These were some of the recommendations, so what was the response? In a somewhat curt foreword to the report, Patrick Jenkin, the then Social Services Secretary, claimed that the report's 37 recommendations, if implemented in full, would cost upwards of £2 billion a year, and added that this was 'quite unrealistic in present or any foreseeable economic circumstances . . . I cannot, therefore, endorse the group's recommendations.'

It is very difficult, however, to challenge or contradict the conclusions of the Black Report, given the massive weight of evidence that systematic class-related differences in health experience do exist. Nevertheless, some commentators have argued that the discussion of the relationship between health and economic activity is not pursued in the report as far as it might have been. A more sociological approach looking to the sources of inequality might well have permitted the report to answer why inequalities have been so persistent and so difficult to reduce.

Rather paradoxically, then, the report is for some radical crictics as 'unrealistic' as it was for the Social Services Secretary of the Conservative

Box 22   Social class and the cost of health care

A recent report by Le Grand has stressed how using the NHS costs the poor more than it does the rich. The poor generally have further to travel to medical facilities and rely more on buses and trains, which cost more per mile than do private cars. They cannot, therefore, time their arrival exactly so, invariably, they have longer to wait. Those poor people in work are more likely to lose money for taking time off than are professionals and managers on annual salaries.

These factors, argues Le Grand, account in part for the fact that, when ill, the poor make less use of the NHS than do the rich. As the figure below shows, the NHS spends 40 per cent more on sick professionals, employers and managers than it does on manual workers.

One way to alleviate this inequality is to move hospitals, clinics and health centres closer to the poor in deprived areas.

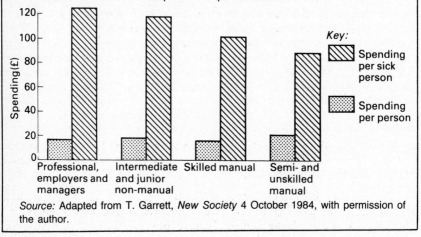

Source: Adapted from T. Garrett, *New Society* 4 October 1984, with permission of the author.

government. Gray (1982) points to a contradictions implicit in the report. In brief, the report notes the important role of 'economic and associated socio-structural factors', the persistent and deep-rooted nature of unequal income and wealth distribution, and the possibility that the present economic system may actually promote inequality. Yet, at the same time, the report assumes that a number of major changes are capable of being enacted to substantially reduce or eliminate inequality, whilst still leaving the framework of these 'economic and social-structural factors' unchanged.

Gray is not denying that there is scope for making changes that might help to reduce the severity of inequalities and their origins, but rather suggesting – quite rightly as it turned out – that such changes would be resisted. As Gray suggests, perhaps the authors of the report were the ones who were being 'unrealistic' in their assumption that a favourably inclined government initiating legislation would really go very far along this road.

The Black Report is too radical for some but not radical enough for others. Nevertheless, whatever view one takes, one must recognize that one of the particularly original contributions of the report is the willingness to see medical care as only one (perhaps not even a very efficient) way in which health can be influenced. It revives the possibility of focusing health programmes on other areas of social policy such as housing or income maintenance.

Many critics, including Gray (1982), stress that the Black Report understates the range of inequalities in health. Certainly, it fails to consider the many aspects of sexual inequalities in health that cannot be understood solely on the basis of sex-specific mortality-rates. As an example, Gray refers to the enormous variations in access to NHS abortion services across different regions; it is difficult to believe that such discrepancies would be tolerated in services that affected men more directly. More generally, many women are dissatisfied with the attitudes of the health service to their health problems and needs, particularly on consultations with doctors and in the tendency to treat pregnancy and childbirth as illnesses. There is a pattern of health experience based on gender which overlays the social-class patterns that the report primarily considers, and which is a further important dimension of inequality.

Summary

1 The Black Report demonstrated severe and persistent class inequalities in health and attributed this more to *social* causes than to restricted access to health-care facilities.

2 The report recommended a shift in resources. It declared that improvements in social conditions were essential to reduce the degree to which lower social classes suffered more illness. Nothing has changed however, since the publication of the report.

9.5 Health Care and the Subordination of Women

'Look, doctor, this is not ordinary menstrual pain. I am forty years of age. I have lived with menstrual pain all my life. I must know the difference between ordinary menstrual pain and what is happening to me.'

'Ruth', in Mitchell (1984)

Since the mid-1970s, the health-care system has become more and more an area of concern for feminists. There has been the spread of direct, collective action by women, reflecting and influenced by the Women's Health Movement in the USA. An increasing number of local women's health groups meet regularly in Britain. Indirectly stemming from this activity, there has been growing general recognition of the significance of medical care in women's everyday lives.

Medicine affects women to a much greater degree than it does men. The gender-role system, which relegates caring and nurturing duties to women, results in them being involved in the health-care system not only as workers but also from within the family, in a way in which most men are not involved.

While the vast majority of workers in the health-care system are women, they are concentrated at the bottom end of the medical hierarchy. Nearly 90 per cent of nurses are women, but only just over one-fifth of practising doctors are women. Few of those at the top of the profession are women: only 1 per cent of surgeons and 12 per cent of gynaecologists are women. In brief, males dominate the highly technical and skilled, responsible and dominant roles in the medical hierarchy – those, incidentally, which also provide the greatest status and salary. In contrast, these jobs involving the greatest contact with the patient and the most practical, day-to-day, caring functions are occupied by women (see also chapter 4, section 4.2).

The ambivalent relationship between women and medical care has a curiously long history. Before the rise of the modern medical profession, lay healers were traditionally female; midwives in local communities, for instance, were also skilled herbalists or 'wise women'. Gradually, during the Middle Ages, women began to be forced out of medical care by men. Eventually, women were left only midwifery, and even this came to be taken over in the seventeenth century by male barber-surgeons after the invention of forceps which women are not allowed to use. Certainly, by the eighteenth century, the medical profession had become completely male-dominated.

However, the outlawing of the traditional female healer that was associated with the rise of the medical profession, did not bring an end to women's traditional caring role. Women were simply relegated to the subordinate role of helpers and general dogsbodies in the increasingly technological, expanding, male medical profession.

Women are, however, the biggest users of health care facilities, which is largely due to their twin roles of child-bearers and child-rearers. The appropriateness of the intervention of the medical profession in women's lives is a facet of health care challenged by the women's health movement. Indeed, much of the feminist literature and practical action in the women's movement has focused, in a critical manner, on the medical control of reproduction through control of contraception, abortion and childbirth facilities, as well as the management of the supposed female 'disorders' such as the menopause. Giving birth, preventing birth, or even having an abortion, are not intrinsically the concern of the medical profession. Women are not necessarily, or even normally, ill in connection with these matters although, of course, they may be so. There is, naturally, tremendous resistance towards attempts to 'demedicalize' these matters, because it threatens medical specialities dealing specifically with women, for example gynaecology and obstetrics.

Feminists argue that the essentially male control over women's reproduction is central to the question of male domination and female subordination. Feminists want women to control their own health and fertility. Recent action towards this goal has taken the form of women's health groups, where women learn about their own bodies, and 'Well Woman Clinics', where women are able to consult other women about their health. It has led to calls for a woman's right to choose whether or not she gives birth at home with the help of a midwife, or in hospital. At present, something like 98 per cent of births in Britain take place in hospital and there is no doubt that home births are definitely discouraged. Furthermore, labour is often induced for the convenience of the hospital and women are forced to assume the delivery position which affords most ease to the doctor. The battle by feminists to regain control over women's reproduction, though not won, has certainly begun.

Summary

1 Women, especially because of their conventional role in the family, are likely to have more contact with the health services than men.

2 Women are poorly represented among the higher ranks of the medical profession and many feel that male medical control over women's health is unacceptable, and seek control for women themselves.

Related topics

Some further consideration of women's health and welfare can be found in chapter 4, section 4.4. On the position of women in medical occupations, see chapter 2, sections 2.6 and 4.2.

9.6 Race and Health

When considering the ethnic dimension of inequality in health there is a sparseness of statistical evidence. The Black Report met this problem. In fact, one curious feature of the Black Report was that in the poorer occupational classes, it seemed that men born in India, Pakistan or the West Indies tended to live longer than their British-born counterparts. There are a whole set of reasons to explain this apparent anomaly. Certainly, as the authors of the Black Report point out, men and women prepared to cross oceans and continents in order to seek new occupational opportunities in Britain do not represent a random cross-section of people, any more than did the Pilgrim Fathers who crossed from Britain to America in 1620. Nevertheless, this finding is in stark contrast to the stereotype of the black immigrant, which was widely circulated in the 1960s and early 1970s, as someone who brought disease into the country and who, once here, created a risk of epidemics because of origin and living conditions.

However, as McNaught (1984) shows, the present situation is more depressing. After noting the virtual absence of ethnically sensitive health statistics in Britain, he suggests there is little evidence to indicate that health authorities in areas where ethnic minorities live have developed adequate strategies to meet the needs of these groups.

From what data is available, the pattern of mortality and morbidity that emerges from a variety of small-scale studies is that, apart from those haemoglobinopathies such as sickle cell anaemia and thalassaemia that have a clear race/genetic link, the health conditions that affect ethnic minority groups in Britain are the same as for the population as a whole. However, McNaught notes that the incidence of certain conditions is much higher among ethnic minority groups and this can be linked to their socio-economic conditions in Britain (see chapter 5, section 5.3), including changing patterns of diet, increased smoking and urbanization. In short, McNaught stresses that the social consequences of racial inequality are much more powerful determinants of the health status of ethnic minority groups than genetic or racial susceptibilities.

Not only do ethnic minorities suffer problems that reflect their class position, but over and above these general difficulties, they experience difficulties because of language and cultural differences, or because of racial discrimination.

Many people from the ethnic minorities, particularly women, either speak no English or only know it poorly, as a second language. Consequently, they have difficulty in obtaining treatment, advice and guidance from health workers. Health authorities have developed a number of approaches to try to surmount this, but such initiatives have, in the main, been very patchy. Cultural barriers have also created problems for the NHS. Perhaps most well known in this regard is the desire of some black women to see only women doctors. McNaught (1984) reports that some health authorities have responded to this need, but many have not.

The extent to which racial discrimination occurs in the NHS is difficult to determine. A significant number of black people are convinced that it does and, as McNaught argues, this may be more important than attempting to demonstrate its actual incidence or volume. He goes on to suggest that (p. 26):

> What this issue does demonstrate is that interaction of poor professional standards and racial discrimination reduces access to services, causes unnecessary suffering, discomfort and probably deaths. This has a corrosive effect on the relationship of individual black and ethnic minority patients and health workers. Further it weakens these groups' support for the National Health Service.

Quite clearly, there is much work to do before we can say that the NHS is responding fully to the health needs of ethnic minorities.

Summary

1 Ethnic minorities tend to suffer from the same illnesses as the rest of the population.

2 Due to their class position and restrictions on access to health care, ethnic minorities are prone to relatively high levels of ill-health.

Related topics

On the social conditions of ethnic minorities in Britain, see chapter 5.

9.7 Unemployment and Ill-health

Recently, prompted by the economic recession, there have been inquiries into the links between unemployment and ill-health or early mortality. An American social scientist, Brenner (1972), comparing trends in the US economy and fluctuations in the rates of mortality, claimed to have demonstrated that recessions and wide-scale economic distress have an impact on a number of important health indicators. These included fetal, infant and maternal mortality, the national mortality-rate – especially of death ascribed to cardiovascular disease, cirrhosis of the liver, suicide and homicide rates – as well as rates of first admission to mental hospitals. While Brenner's work is both methodologically and theoretically controversial, it has sparked off further investigation in this field.

One relevant report which the Conservative government clearly did not want discussed extensively was the partially suppressed report by Leonard Fagin on unemployment and family health, which came out in 1981. As with the Black Report published the previous year, there was a clear attempt to dilute the impact of this study. Again, the DHSS published only a few, expensive, copies of the report and, again, released it without proper publicity (it was later published by Penguin – see Fagin, 1984).

Fagin's report illustrates that the use of unemployment as a tool to control inflation has far greater costs than simply the loss of production and tax revenues, the additional payments of supplementary benefits, and so on. He catalogues the severe consequences of long-term unemployment, echoing previous research that goes back to the recession of the 1930s. Significantly, Fagin concentrated on the family as a whole rather than simply the male 'breadwinner' and found that there was financial worry and family tension and that husband, wives and children all displayed signs of distress – depression headaches, asthmatic attacks, loss of appetite.

Some commentators have stressed that there are interesting parallels between the controversy over the impact of unemployment on health and the developing concern over the links between smoking and cancer. The early research that first proposed the relationship between smoking and cancer generated much academic debate on methodology and validity. Slowly (for some people, fatally slowly), the links became more widely accepted as the amount of research evidence grew. A crucial difference, however, is that those who most resisted the evidence in the smoking controversy were the tobacco manufacturers, while with unemployment it is the Conservative government that has the worst record of resisting the evidence.

Summary

1 Unemployment leads to additional ill-health for both the unemployed person and other members of the household.

Related topics

See chapter 2, section 2.8 on the personal and social consequences of unemployment.

9.8   Current Health Trends and Issues

Medical care is increasingly being provided in very large and complex settings, so that it is no longer based on a simple doctor–patient relationship. To take an extreme example, in the current enthusiasm for heart-transplant operations, it is the technological aspects that are emphasized and one almost expects one day to hear the announcement that 'it was a successful operation but the patient died.'

Prevention or cure?

Where there has been progress recently in improving health this has, perhaps, depended more upon the control of the physical environment than upon clinical medicine and the doctor–patient relationship. Pure water, improved nutrition and sanitary waste disposal, have probably contributed more to length of life than the clinical use of antibiotics. In turn, it is argued, antibiotics have contributed more than surgery; and surgery, Gallagher (1976) suggests, may well have contributed more than the inadequate efforts of doctors to have their patients alter dietary, smoking and drinking habits.

Gallagher argues that the training and general orientation of doctors is more attuned to coping with illness than towards the maintenance of health. This is particularly true of specialists but also true of general practitioners. Many doctors simply do not see health promotion as their job. In fact, many are not particularly in favour of mass screening for

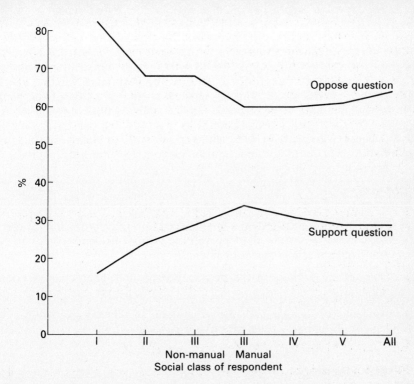

Figure 9.6   Should the NHS be available only to low income families?

Source: Drawn from data supplied by Social and Community Planning Research.

early disease, believing it a more efficient use of their time and skill to deal with definite pathology or illness. The reluctance of many doctors to engage in an active manner in health promotion apparently belies the argument that doctors are increasingly inclined to stray into areas where their competence is extremely limited.

Overall, there has been what has been termed an increasing medicalization of life, such that social problems become labelled as manifestations of illness. Some people look to doctors to solve problems of drug addiction, working conditions which produce industrial diseases and, perhaps, even riots. There are considerable dangers in believing that the expansion of medicine will provide a solution for social problems; medicine is a limited science.

Privatization of health care

A dominant feature of the early 1980s has been the Conservative government's commitment to privatization in the NHS, by contracting-out services like laundering and cleaning, by sharing resources (beds, equipment) with the private sector, and by encouraging more people to take out private health insurance. Any more changes are likely to be resisted. For most people, the NHS will remain the central plank of national health care. Interestingly, the British Attitudes Survey (Jowell and Airey, 1984) showed that any changes in the direction of the NHS being available only to low-income families is likely to be unpopular. As figure 9.6 shows, this proposition was opposed by two-thirds of the respondents in the survey. Nevertheless, attempts to change the face of the NHS are likely to continue and privatization of the health service is certainly on the political agenda.

Summary

1 There is a trend towards the 'medicalization' of everyday life. Surgery becomes more important than prevention; while medicine comes to be viewed as a solution to social problems.

2 There is an increase in the private provision of health-care services and facilities.

3 Concepts of health and the treatment of illness are subject to fundamentally political redefinition and revision.

Further Reading

A useful book which gives some interesting case-histories is Mitchell (1984). The Black Report, described as 'the most important single document on health since the war' has been published by Penguin and edited by Townsend and N. Davidson (1982). A provocative book presenting a more radical critique is Doyal (1979).

10 Culture and Media

10.1 Introduction

The term 'culture' is defined very broadly in sociology. It is most commonly used to delineate the *symbolic* aspects of human society so as to include beliefs, rituals, customs, conventions, ideals or artistic endeavours. In this usage, culture contrasts with the biological aspects of human behaviour, on the one hand, and society or social institutions, on the other.

Culture does, therefore, cover a very wide range of social phenomena and that is why so many varied topics are included in this chapter, each of which is a branch of sociology in its own right. We begin with a section on the media. Here the central sociological questions issues are: What sort of view of the world is portrayed by radio, television and the press? Why are some views excluded or included and what effect, if any, does the presentation of a particular view of the world have on the audience?

A somewhat different set of questions is raised by the study of leisure and popular culture. In this section, we look at the way social groups use their leisure time in different ways; women's leisure, for example, is much more home-based than that of men. Watching television is, itself, an exceptionally popular leisure activity and we consider whether audiences for popular television, for instance, are passive recipients of entertainment or whether they *actively* react to what they watch. Some of these issues arise again in a rather different form in the study of youth cultures. We show the way in which youth groups, whether based on class, gender or ethnic differences, have quite distinct cultures. We also discuss the way in which youth cultures acquiesce in, or are resistant to, parent cultures or the dominant culture in a society. In our discussion of religion in modern Britain, we pose a different set of questions, contrasting the decline of orthodox Christianity with the vitality of newer sects often inspired by Eastern faiths.

As we have said, each of these areas of culture raises its own questions. There is also, however, an important sociological problem common to them all, namely the relation of culture to power. Is there an overarching dominant culture which subordinates all other cultures and thereby helps to preserve existing social arrangements? Or, are there numerous, different cultures appropriate to different social groups which are not assimilated to a dominant culture, even if that exists?

A way to illustrate this problem is to consider two alternative models of the relationship between culture and power.

1 This model sees a culture common to most members of a society which effectively holds that society together. This culture is *dominant* in three senses. First, it is the culture that pervades all institutions in society and is transmitted by those institutions like the family, the school and the mass media. Second, the dominant culture is the culture of the dominant social groups in society. More accurately, we should say that the dominant culture helps to keep dominant groups in power. It is not the case, of course, that the upper class deliberately formulates such a culture as a kind of propaganda. It is, however, an unintended effect of the dominant culture that challenges to the dominant groups are not heard more often. Third, the very pervasiveness of a dominant culture suppresses alternative cultures, different ways of looking at the world. For all members of a society the dominant culture is so much part of everyday life that alternatives almost literally cannot be thought of. They certainly cannot be effective. This is not to say that alternatives do not exist at all; the dominant culture is not that powerful. However, it does mean that the alternatives are subordinate to the dominant culture and do not have the capacity to be actively resistant.

2 This model denies that there is a dominant culture linked to the powerful. Indeed, it may deny that there is any connection between power and culture at all. Rather, societies are seen as composed of a very large number of cultures which compete with one another. Each culture is an expression of the way of life of a particular social group. Some writers see this 'pluralization' as a special feature of modern societies. Older societies, of the last century or earlier, were organic wholes with a relatively static social structure, unified around some common system of beliefs and values, usually a religious one. Social changes since then have tended to produce a more fragmented social order. The class structure of modern Britain, for example, is more complex than that of Victorian Britain. Each class fraction, so the argument runs, will form its own culture, perhaps further complicated by ethnic or gender divisions.

These are, of course, extreme models of the relationship of culture and power. We do not claim that any sociologist holds either of them in a pure form. The more likely position, and one illustrated in this chapter, lies somewhere between these extremes. The diverse social groups in modern Britain do, indeed, formulate cultures expressing their own way of life – cultures which are often very different from each other. We show, for example, how male and female youth cultures differ from one another, and how different religious movements appeal to different sections of the population. At the same time, there is a rudimentary dominant culture centred on certain values and beliefs which is transmitted via the mass media and the education system. As we show particularly in the next section on the mass media, however, the dominant culture is rather fragmentary and not very coherent. The important sociological question raised in this chapter is the relationship between this dominant culture and diverse other cultures. In what ways does the dominant culture organize or subordinate other cultures? As we will argue, there is no single or straightforward answer to this question. There are conforming cultures (e.g. middle-class youth cultures) but there are also resistant cultures (e.g. working-class youth cultures). However, there are also cultures that effectively involve a withdrawal from society (e.g. some new religious movements) or in which there is a form of accommodation or negotiation with dominant culture. In modern Britain, much working-class culture takes this form, involving a capacity to live with dominant values while not embracing them fully.

10.2 The Mass Media: Radio, Television and the Press

Media content

> What the BBC and ITN present as news is not news at all: it is pure, unadulterated bias. News presents a 'digest' of what's going on. In order to achieve 'balance' it *must* reflect all the elements comprising that phenomenon called truth.
>
> Yet the truth about the miners' strike is absent from most television news broadcasts. The truth about Plan for Coal. The truth about Britain's energy needs. The truth about coal board and government plans to butcher our industry. We won't find them reported by the BBC or ITN.
>
> Arthur Scargill in *New Socialist* (1984)

> This, in our view, is the most serious charge we have to bring against the men who are now in control of the BBC – that they abandon its principles in the face of the onslaught of anti-God . . . At present the BBC seems to many people to be trying to lead the country in a very definite direction, and it is not towards a God-centred, but rather a man-centred society.
>
> Mrs Mary Whitehouse, *Cleaning Up TV*

One often hears accusations of bias directed against the media, accusations that can come from widely different political perspectives as these two quotations show. Yet social surveys also show that a large proportion of the population believe that radio and television objectively report the news, even if they also show that this proportion is declining.

What is the truth of the matter? This is a complicated question. There are a large variety of different communications media – newspapers, magazines, radio, film, television, books and advertisements, for example – and it might seem unlikely that all of these will be biased in the same direction and to the same extent. Furthermore, although all news broadcasts must involve the *selection* of newsworthy items from the events of the day, and hence give a partial view, that selection may not always be made according to the same principles. Similarly *Coronation Street* will not be a perfect mirror of everyday life in Salford, but neither will it *necessarily* be a mirror that always distorts in the same way.

The mass media, therefore, *cannot* give a flawlessly objective presentation of the world around us because they must select from the flow of events and they have to create dramas that will involve an audience. Media personnel, in other words, have to make choices, and the choices that they make are partly determined by social factors. To see whether or not this amounts to bias we have to investigate the principles on which choices are made. We have to try to find out what picture of the world is presented by the media if, indeed, any coherent picture is presented at all.

News and current affairs

The presentation of news and current affairs is a good place to start this investigation. If news presentation were biased, there might well be serious consequences because television broadcasts and newspapers are, for most people, the only source of information about events in the wider world. Newspapers, of course, often do not even claim to be unbiased and their proprietors sometimes freely admit that they use their newspapers or magazines for the purposes of propaganda. The broadcasting media – television and radio – claim greater objectivity, a characteristic actually demanded by the Charter of the BBC. The study of television, thus, provides a good test case of principles of selection. An additional reason for concentrating on television is its power and pervasiveness. In Britain, for example, some twenty million TV licences are issued every year and viewers spend an average of twenty hours per week watching broadcast television. Equally, television news is important. One survey showed that 58 per cent of the population rely on television as their principal source of news. Even more importantly, 68 per cent believed that television news reporting was the most objective available, while only 6 per cent believed this of the press.

Television and radio do not attempt to be unbiased about everything. It is, for example, official policy not to be impartial in the conflict between terrorism and ordered government. For some parts of the audience, this may make the broadcasting institutions suspect, as 'terrorism' may itself be difficult to define. Supporters of the Republican cause in Northern Ireland, for example, may well believe that the BBC is being improperly biased in its treatment of the Irish Republican Army (IRA). Of greater significance is the question of whether in general, the presentation of views on the television is dictated simply by the flow of events, as many

Figure 10.1 Television watching is the central family leisure activity

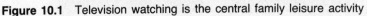

broadcasters claim, or whether some set of factors intervene to select certain events for particular treatment in particular ways.

Selectivity

The evidence overwhelmingly favours the second of these possibilities. A number of closely linked factors are involved.

1 News, and even current-affairs programmes, have a marked tendency to report events as they occur and not to discuss the background to these events; the opening of a new building may be news, but its construction is not. The result of this tendency is that peoples' actions, if reported in a strike for instance, will appear irrational and immoral because they have no *explanation*.
2 Journalists operate by a set of values about what is newsworthy, what events they think the audience will find interesting. Broadcasters have to imagine their audience and that constrains their presentation of news in much the same way as the producer of a drama series has to imagine the way in which dramas will appeal to viewers.
3 The most important factor however, is what has become known as

agenda-setting. This means that the broadcasting media effectively decide what are important issues, promoting some and leaving others out altogether.

For example, in the treatment of race relations in Britain, discussions in the media have tended to establish racial *conflict* as the central, newsworthy issue, leaving out factors that may explain such conflicts – the multiple disadvantages that black people experience in Britain, for example. Black people, therefore, become defined as a threat, an implicit assumption which structures news reports. Agenda are constructed using a variety of methods. Particular issues are taken up while others are ignored; one viewpoint is stressed while others receive less-extensive treatment; some sources are seen as authoritative and neutral while others appear as biased; participants in a story will be treated in different ways, some being subjected to hostile interviewing; particular words will come to be associated with particular issues (conflict with race for instance), while the language used in other issues will be more neutral; visual material is used as evidence for a spoken commentary when it does not provide relevant illustration.

The question remains, What sort of agenda is it that is set by the media? One common answer is that the media occupy a position in the centre of the social spectrum and that the news reflects that position, particularly in stressing social harmony. As Alastair Hetherington, former editor of the *Guardian*, said in a debate about media coverage of the miners' strike of 1984 (*New Socialist* 1984):

> the media tend to reflect the values of the society in which they live; that anything that threatens the peace, prosperity and harmony of that society is likely to attract headlines; and that the reaction of a large part of the audience is likely to be *unfavourable* to those who disturb social harmony – whether it is Mrs. Thatcher banning trade unions at GCHQ or Mr. Scargill contriving a national strike.

An alternative answer is that the agenda set by the broadcasting institutions reflect the interests of dominant groups in society. For an example of this viewpoint on the media and an illustration of the points about agenda-setting discussed above, we turn to a more detailed consideration of a recent and thorough analysis of television news undertaken by the Glasgow University Media Group (1976 and 1980).

Bad News and *More Bad News*: case-studies in selectivity

> The work reported in this volume reveals that 'facts' are situated in dominant story themes, that such themes build upon basic frames of reference – basic assumptions about society viewed in particular ways –

which often hinder the full and proper coverage of the events in question.
Glasgow University Media Group (1976)

For the Glasgow group of researchers, the media present certain issues for public attention and leave others out. In the coverage of industrial matters, for example, television news concentrates on strikes but rarely mentions industrial accidents. Again, strike behaviour in some industries, such as motor-vehicle manufacturing, receives more attention than in other industries in relation to the actual frequency of strikes. The point, however, is not only that an agenda is set but also that those issues that *are* dealt with on television are presented in a particular way. In their discussion of a strike by dust-cart drivers in Glasgow in 1975, the Glasgow University Media Group point to the very extensive television coverage of this action. They argue that this coverage presented the strike as being simply about pay. From the point of view of the strikers, however, the stoppage was about achieving *parity* in pay with other comparable groups of workers. This aspect of the strikers' case was hardly mentioned in the media, an omission reinforced by the fact that, during the course of the stoppage, not one striker was interviewed. The cause of the strike was thus obscured.

In a more extended case-study, *More Bad News*, the Glasgow University Media Group (1980) analysed the treatment of the economic situation in 1975, particularly the rapid rise in the rate of inflation. Television news and analysis presented this important issue in one particular way; the economic crisis was caused by inflation and inflation was caused by excessive wage demands. The crisis was, in other words, produced by workers. This framework was constructed in a number of ways. The 'official', government view, namely that wage demands produced inflation, was mentioned far more often than alternative views, for example that the crisis was produced by lack of investment. When so-called neutral or expert persons were interviewed – Bank of England representatives or stockbrokers' analysts for instance – they tended to confirm the official view. When people who put an alternative economic analysis *were* interviewed, they were much more likely to be challenged by the interviewer than were 'official' spokesmen. Uncritical use was made of government statistics as if these were neutral facts incapable of more than one interpretation. Even the numerical dominance of the official view of the crisis understated the role of this explanation in news coverage. Much of the news simply assumed that wages were a problem and this framework organized the coverage of even routine wage claims. By contrast, alternative interpretations appeared, not as central, but as marginal. A summary of the Glasgow University Media Group's argument is presented in box 23.

A whole range of studies of news and current affairs programmes confirm the basic finding of the *Bad News* and *More Bad News* investigations, namely, that the media set an agenda for the treatment of

Box 23   Bias in television news

In the period of our study, the news was organised and produced substantially around the views of the dominant political group in our society. We have shown how the views of those who disagree fundamentally with this position, or who offered alternative approaches, were downgraded and underrepresented in the news coverage. This is in stark comparison with the careful explanation and heavy emphasis given to the dominant analysis and the political policies which flowed from it.

The content of news and the manner in which it was organised embodied a specific way of understanding the social and industrial world. In essence our case is that the numerical repetition of certain themes and explanations, together with the embracing and under-lining of them by media personnel, are parts of a general process by which the news is produced from within a limited and partial world-view. This is reflected in the choice of material, the themes that are emphasized, the links that are made between these, and the final conclusions that are drawn. At times, as we have shown, fragments of alternative information appear which could be linked, developed and emphasized to produce a quite different body of explanations and policy conclusions. It is a measure of the strength of the dominant social and economic interpretation of the news that this was never done in the whole four-month period covered by our analysis.

At its most basic, the organising principle of this interpretation is that the normal workings of the particular economic system are never treated as if they might themselves generate serious problems. Rather, the causes of economic problems are sought largely in the activities of trade unionists who reject the priorities and purposes of the dominant group. The logic and priorities of the social and economic order, thus, remain unchallenged. Instead, what we have in the news is a partial diagnosis of what social problems are, and how they may be solved, which is facilitated by a highly selective account of the nature and workings of that economic order.

The importance of this 'world view', which is implicit in journalistic practices, is that it prestructures what the news is to consist of and, in a sense what the journalists themselves actually see as existing, or as being significant in the world. Thus information about the decline in investment, which would be a critical part of an alternative world view, is either not treated at all by news journalists, or occurs as a disparate fragment because it has no part in the 'normal' descriptions which they offer of the industrial crisis. (Glasgow University Media Group, 1980, *More Bad News* (London, Routledge and Kegan Paul), pp. 110–11. Reproduced with permission.)

news. An even more difficult question concerns the output of television as a whole. Is a particular view of the world also presented in drama, soap operas or documentaries? Does television as a whole present a coherent world-view?

Fictional programmes and social values

It is, in fact, very difficult to assess the output of television as a whole because of the enormous diversity of programmes on offer. It is impossible, at first glance, to see what quiz shows, *The Sweeney*, current-affairs programmes, *Coronation Street*, and *Life on Earth* have in common. The range of interest is so wide that it makes no sense to talk of television programmes as presenting a coherent view of the world. It might, however, be the case that certain kinds of programme have common themes. Take, for example, the representation of gender relations in the James Bond films (frequently shown on televsion) and *Dr Who*. Although the former are adventure films and the latter is a science fiction series largely aimed at children, they have some things in common. The central point is that men are active and women passive. Men make things happen and women stand and stare, or worse, positively get in the man's way. Both Bond and Dr Who have female helpers who are portrayed as essentially 'feminine'. They tend to be silly, irrational, prone to bouts of hysteria or panic, to make mistakes, or to get into situations from which they have to be rescued. At the same time, they are warm, loving and trusting and, in the case of James Bond films, desirable sexual objects as well. To emphasize the 'feminine' role of women, both Dr Who and James Bond films contrast the silly if faithful helper with evil women who are opponents. These women exemplify undesirable qualities, being cold, calculating, unsympathetic and, occasionally, sexually ambiguous. This contrast between 'good' and 'bad' femininity is further emphasized by styles of dress. The helpers adopt feminine styles, wearing dresses and skirts with lots of frills and colour. Opponents, on the other hand, affect a masculine appearance, wearing trousers, drab colours and harsh fabrics like leather.

Programmes of this kind may, therefore, convey a certain view of femininity and masculinity. Even in this area of drama, however, it would be difficult to find uniformity, let alone in other areas of television work such as news or current affairs. Women may be portrayed who break the stereotypes and who do not conform to either the helper or opponent model. Several recent series have tried to show women not as passive and dependent adjuncts to men but as active and forceful. To conclude, although there will be some coherence in some areas of television presentation, there is no sense in which television output as a whole is organized around one view of the world.

These conclusions raise two crucial further questions: *Why* do the media produce a particular view or views in some areas of their output,

Figure 10.2   Dr Who and his helper

Source: Peter Davison as the Doctor and Janet Fielding as Tegan from the Doctor Who story 'Warriors of the Deep'. Copyright BBC 1983.

especially news? Do these views influence the way in which people think about their world? We consider these questions in the following two sections.

Media productions: external and internal constraints

No one argues that the particular way in which television news is structured is the result of a conspiracy by television journalists. We have to look for other factors that account for the view (or views) of the world presented in the media. It is convenient to divide these into factors external and internal to the institutions in which media personnel work.

External factors

The state and the government: We have already implied that the institutions of the state can be something of a constraint on the media by saying that the BBC does not regard itself as impartial towards terrorism or any other force that might obviously threaten the stability of the state. Of course, governments of the day will seek to extend the definition of what threatens the state. In 1926, for instance, the government succeeded in making the BBC take its side in the General Strike against the labour movement. Furthermore, governments ultimately have financial control over the BBC, in that they can decide on the level of the licence fee. Ministers and government departments have access to broadcasting institutions through their public-relations agencies and the expression of ministerial displeasure and, hence, some measure of control can be very effectively conveyed. More subtly and, therefore, probably more efficiently, governments can make their influence felt by the way in which the media portray the institutions of state as neutral and as above political controversy. As indicated in our account of the *Bad News* study, government statistics and even some government spokesmen are treated as objective, impartial, observers on a particular news item when, say, trade-union or management representatives are not. Government *policy* can, therefore, seem beyond media comment. However, although governments do exercise some control, this is not very great. There are several instances of the BBC resisting ministerial interference. More importantly, we have to look elsewhere for an explanation of the way in which the media assume that the institutions of the state and of parliamentary democracy are neutral.

Ownership: In looking at newspapers one might easily think that their ownership had something to do with control of their content. Proprietors do interfere with editorial policy and it would be surprising if they did not. Lord Beaverbrook, for example, said that he only kept his newspapers (the *Daily Express*, for example) for the purposes of propaganda. Independent television and radio, since they are privately owned, are also *potentially* subject to influence from their owners. Even the BBC, though dependent on the state for its revenues, may be indirectly influenced by commercial interests since it has to compete with privately owned broadcasting institutions for a share of the audience. The ownership of broadcasting organizations, then, is another possible source of external control of the media.

As you will see from chapter 2, section 2.2, British industry has, especially since the Second World War, been characterized by a wave of mergers and take-overs which have resulted in the agglomeration of firms into much larger units. At the same time, the tendency for individual or family ownership of firms to be replaced by joint-stock or share ownership, has not in practice resulted in widening of ownership. Ownership of large firms tends to be relatively concentrated in the hands of individuals or institutions that hold large blocks of shares. All this is equally true of the communications industry. Firms have become larger, there are fewer of them, and most sectors of the industry are dominated by a handful of firms.

> In central sectors such as daily and Sunday newspapers, paperback books, records, and commercial television programming, two thirds or more of the total audience are reading, hearing, or looking at material produced by the top five firms in that sector. Other markets, notably cinema exhibition and women's and children's magazines are even more concentrated, with the lion's share of sales going to the top two companies in each. (Murdock, 1982, p. 118)

Furthermore, communications companies have become more diverse. Some have become part of holding companies with interests in several sectors of industry, while others have diversified inside the industry and have stakes in different media of communication. At the same time, ownership remains concentrated in relatively few hands, not only those of the investing institutions, but also unusually, families, particularly in the case of newspapers.

The ownership of television companies illustrates some of these points. Granada Television, for example, is owned by Granada Group Ltd, which is also involved in television-set rental, cinemas, motorway service areas and book publishing. ATV is owned by Associated Television Corporation Ltd, which also has a diverse range of interests in the music industry, film production and West-End theatres. Television companies are, therefore, involved with other companies in a wide range of often-related fields held together by common ownership. Perhaps even more important, however, is the fact that the different television companies, which may appear to compete with one another, are themselves joined together. This is achieved partly by overlapping ownership and partly by interlocking directorships (a concept discussed in more detail in chapter

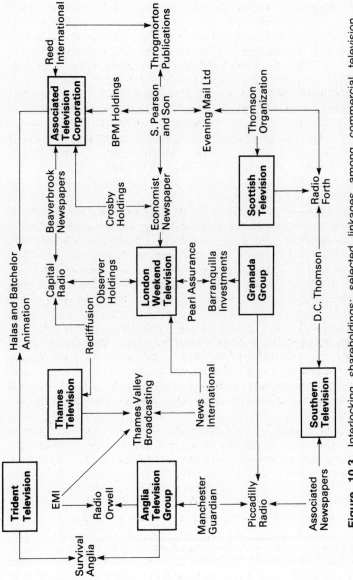

Figure 10.3 Interlocking shareholdings: selected linkages among commercial television companies and other communications and corporations (arrows indicate the direction of the holding).

Source: Open University (1977), DE353: Mass Communication and Society, Unit 10, Patterns of ownership; question of control, by G. Murdock, figure 3, p. 33. © 1977, The Open University Press. Reproduced with permission.

2, section 2.2). The way in which certain television companies are related to one another and to other companies in related fields is shown in figure 10.3.

External control over media content: Firms in the communications industry are, therefore, bigger, more diverse, fewer, and relatively concentrated in ownership. What consequences does this have for the control of the output of the media? There is little evidence of widespread direct proprietorial interference, where an owner will insist on having a story written in a particular way. There are, however, a number of well-known instances of commercial considerations overriding editoral ones, because a newspaper or television station is losing money. But this does not really represent continuous intervention by owners in the social or political policy of television, radio or newspapers. One other source of commercial intervention comes from advertising. Advertisers may well want to advertise their products together with programmes that offer a view of the world that favours those products. For example, after the war, US television drama was dominated by plays with working-class settings. Advertisers became worried by this emphasis, since it did not give the required glamour. As a result, they moved their advertising to adventure series slots that implied a fast-moving, affluent and glamorous world in which their products might well have a place (Murdock, 1982).

The values, themes and topics promoted by the media may well fit in with those espoused by owners. One might guess that, other things being equal, owners would like to see the media take a central position, leaning neither to the left or the right, which emphasizes consensus on common values, and sets the agenda on items of public debate, all features described in the first section of this chapter. Apart from the fact that this is assuming rather a lot about owners, and it ignores the diversity of the media, this does not, however, explain *why* there might be a coincidence between owners' interests and the content of media output. We know, especially in the case of radio and television, that this is not because owners *directly* control the media. The point may be that owners do not *need* to intervene because they already *share* social values with the people who produce newspapers and television and radio programmes; owners, producers and audiences are bound together in a set of social values that are continually reinforced in media content.

Internal factors

This last point draws attention to factors that may constrain media output that are internal to media institutions. These will, chiefly, be factors to do with the social characteristics of people working in these organizations or with the structure of media institutions. We have concluded earlier that media output is diverse, sometimes contradictory, and that it is difficult to describe the output of television as representing a *coherent* view of the world. Despite these qualifications, what appears on our television screens is not random or arbitrary. It is socially constructed, by which we mean that certain topics are excluded and certain themes, social myths or ways of life, receive undue and unrepresentative emphasis.

Organizations: The way in which media institutions are organized has an effect on the nature of their output. The BBC, for example, is organized as a bureaucracy in which the upper levels to some extent control the lower ones. Not unnaturally, media personnel feel some pressure to conform when their careers, or even their continued employment, might be at stake. Sensitivity to outside criticism can make the BBC exercise internal control. Burns (1977) points out, in a study of the BBC, that if producers feel in any way uncertain about a programme they are expected to refer the problem to their superior.

Media 'professionalism': In all occupations there is pressure to conform to the particular occupational culture. Where these occupations are professionalized, these pressures can take a distinct form. While there is no recognized profession of broadcasting in the sense that medicine is a recognized profession, several studies note the way in which people who work in the media stress the 'professionalism' of their work. This has become so pronounced that professional values appear to take precedence over all others. This attitude implies a view of the purpose of broadcasting very different from that of the early days of the BBC, when the role of broadcasting institutions in raising the British nation to new moral heights was stressed. As Kumar (1975, p. 232) says, 'To make professional presentation the goal of broadcasting, to elevate, so to speak, the means to the ends, is to indicate a very different reading both of the possibilities of broadcasting and of the social environment in which it operates.' In practice, an adherence to professional values means an emphasis on *methods of presentation* rather than content, skill in devising programmes, in being efficient and craftsmanlike, in imagining the audience and producing programmes to satisfy it, in achieving balance and impartiality. Television and radio are then, seen as the means by which the various voices or interests in a society may be heard and balanced. These voices, however, are not equally skilled, resourceful or, even, obvious and the professional's role in merely representing them will be to include some while leaving others out. In other words, the very professionalism of broadcasting and journalism, the dedication to methods rather than content, will have the agenda-setting consequences that we have already noted.

Professionalism, however, also has another consequence which might, under certain circumstances, run counter to this. The emphasis on skill, experience, and efficiency enables broadcasters to defend themselves from interference, either from management or from the outside world. They can present themselves as impartial professionals who do a good job and have no axe to grind. Here lies one of the sources of resistance to control by governments. Nonetheless, although professionalism might well act against *direct* control, it might still allow the indirect distortion associated with agenda-setting.

Class origins of personnel: One final, familiar, factor of constraint on the media should be noted. Journalists and broadcasters are recruited from a relatively narrow segment of the population. Their social origins will inevitably influence the way they look at the world. Some viewpoints will seem more important than others and some topics will be altogether lost to their sight. All social groups have some ways of looking at the world that differ from those held by other groups. The generally middle-class origins of most broadcasters and journalists will predispose them to respect expert opinion and to treat it as unbiased, to find it easier to talk to fellow members of the middle class than to the working-class population, and to seek out other middle-class opinion – that of management for instance. The middle-class experience of life often excludes the recognition of other experiences. It may, therefore, be quite natural for a broadcaster or journalist to be unaware of whole areas of working-class life, to believe that ranges of problems and difficulties do not exist and, therefore, not to represent certain voices or topics on programmes. Clearly, the professional training of media personnel must be partly designed to overcome this partiality of vision. It cannot, however, entirely succeed.

The impact on the audience

As McQuail (1977, p. 81) says: 'A long list of studies can be cited showing the media to have certain inbuilt tendencies to present a limited and recurring range of images and ideas which form rather special versions of reality.' The media *project* socially constructed images of the world, even if these can be confused and incoherent. The question remains as to *how the audience interprets* these 'media messages'. Does it, for example, uncritically accept them? Or does it evaluate and assess them in the light of its own experience?

One popular answer is that the media do, indeed, have a powerful effect on the audience, particularly when the medium is television and the audience concerned is made up of children. Thus, there have been several public debates about the exposure of children to violent scenes on television and 'video nasties'. These debates are often founded on the assumption that children are profoundly affected by what they see on television, even to the extent of being moved to commit acts of violence themselves. Similar feelings have been expressed about advertisements, which are thought to persuade people to buy things that they neither need nor really want. Again, there is an assumption that people cannot or do not react critically to the media of communication – the audience is seen as empty vessels into which media messages are poured. This actually seems unlikely, however, since people do not believe everything that they are told.

At the other extreme is the view that the media have no effect on the audience at all. People resort to radio and television for entertainment and any message merely washes over them. This view is also dubious, particularly when radio, television and newspapers may be the only source of information about those aspects of social life of which the audience has no direct experience.

Problems of method

It is notoriously difficult to say how audiences interpret the output of the media and many studies avoid it altogether simply by *assuming* that audiences are affected. There are substantial methodological problems in the way of any empirical investigation of the audience. Even if it is clear that people react to, and are influenced by, television programmes in the very short term, it is very difficult to measure long-term changes. Any long-term study will find it awkward to isolate changes in the audience due to the media, from those stemming from other social influences. It is not even obvious what is to be measured. Is one interested in the influence of the media on the attitudes that people have or on their knowledge of events?

For some time, research into these questions was dominated by laboratory and experimental methods, which took selected audiences, exposed them to some media experience, and then measured the changes in attitudes that might result. This method is unsatisfactory as a means of sociological analysis. It is too artificial, extracting audiences from their regular social settings; it concentrates exclusively on the concept of attitude; it focuses on short-term changes rather than more fundamental long-term influences; and it tends to treat audiences as unrelated individuals rather than collectivities involving relationships *between* individuals. In addition, laboratory studies cannot agree about the limited effects they measure. Some researchers believe that television violence encourages violent acts by children, others that violent programmes act as a safety-valve for children who would otherwise be violent in everyday situations.

Given all these difficulties, it is not surprising that we do not have any clear answer to questions about the way in which audiences interpret media messages. There is, however, a little evidence in certain areas. One investigation of the impact of the media on race relations showed, for example, that the media did not have any noticeable effect on the creation of attitudes in school children but did contribute to the definition of black people as creating problems for society, particularly in areas with *small* black populations. There is also some evidence that relates to the treatment of political questions by the media. That television should have more impact on voting seems more likely, given that the electorate is now less-firmly attached to political parties (see chapter 12, section 12.2) and that, with greater coverage, television has become an important source of information about politics. Blumler and McQuail (1968) found that during the 1964 election campaign, there was little evidence of media influence on adherents of the Labour and Conservative parties. With the Liberal Party, however, the position was rather different, at least amongst those who were not especially interested in politics. These people appeared to be influenced in favour of the Liberal Party by watching Liberal programmes. On other political issues, researchers have not found any evidence of media influence.

Audience differentiation

One of the implications of these studies is that, if the media do have an influence, the effect is different for different sections of the audience. Just as it is risky to see the output of media organizations as homogeneous, so it is even more dangerous to assume that the audience is monolithic. Even in such an apparently straightforward medium as advertising, particular advertisements may be interpreted in different ways by different groups of people, a factor which may, or may not, work to the advertisers' advantage. One study (Morley, 1980) shows up the differentiation of audience response particularly well.

In Morley's study, various different groups (28 in all), including black students in further education, shop-stewards and bank managers, were asked about their responses to the current-affairs programme *Nationwide*, by getting them together for group discussions of the programme. Different groups had very different reactions. Morley classifies these reactions into three types: dominant, negotiated and oppositional. If a section of the audience responds in the dominant mode, they are using the values, attitudes and beliefs that are dominant in society. If they use oppositional modes, they are, as the term implies, employing a way of thinking that contradicts the dominant mode. Other groups within the audience using the negotiated mode are neither oppositional nor dominant but have a meaning system that can live with dominant values without believing or accepting them. However, as box 24 (p. 414) indicates, the division of audience into these three blocks still oversimplifies the social structure of the audience. For example, both black students and shop-stewards had oppositional ways of thinking and saw *Nationwide* as biased against the working class. However, they were also very different from each other. The black students essentially withdrew, considering the programme as irrelevant to them. The shop-stewards, on the other hand, tended to be actively critical, seeing *Nationwide* from a radical working-class perspective. Similarly, amongst those adopting the dominant mode there are great differences. Bank managers were traditionally conservative.

Apprentices, on the other hand, tended to be much more cynical about people appearing on the programme, whoever they were, but at the same time held 'dominant' attitudes on the evils of trade unionism or of the social-security system. Audiences for television programmes cannot therefore, be seen as a solid block all reacting in the same way. They are comprised of different groups, all with different responses, partly based on their position in society.

One other feature of audience differentiation deserves mention. The media may work on sectors of the audience that are potentially powerful and, thus, have strong effects *through* them. There is considerable evidence that politicians, police, and judges, for example, are sensitive to media comment that affects them and may act accordingly, even if the comment is ill-informed.

The media, by concentrating on an issue, can create a 'moral panic', defining certain people or events as social problems. For example Cohen (1972) argues that the periodic visits by mods and rockers to seaside towns in the 1960s, which resulted in violent confrontation, received a great deal of newspaper and television coverage, probably out of all proportion to actual events. As a result, the original problem was amplified: the mods and rockers themselves tried to conform to their media image. Police and magistrates also reacted to the new definition of mods and rockers, as hooligans and a serious social problem, by making large numbers of arrests on vague charges and imposing relatively severe penalties.

Summary

1 The mass media are inevitably selective and partial. They have some tendency to reflect central political positions and certain social values, like those concerning gender. They do not, however, present anything like a coherent message and, for that reason alone, it is difficult to see the media as expressing the culture of a dominant class.

2 The kinds of television programme or newspaper story that appear are determined by a variety of factors, internal and external to media organization. Internal factors include bureaucratic organization, a sense of 'professionalism' and the class origins of media personnel. Among external factors, are pressures from the state and from the private owners of the mass media.

3 The audience for the mass media cannot be treated as a solid, coherent block, passively accepting all media output. Although the assessment of audience response is difficult, different sections of the audience react in very different ways.

Box 24 Audience responses to *Nationwide*, 19 May 1976

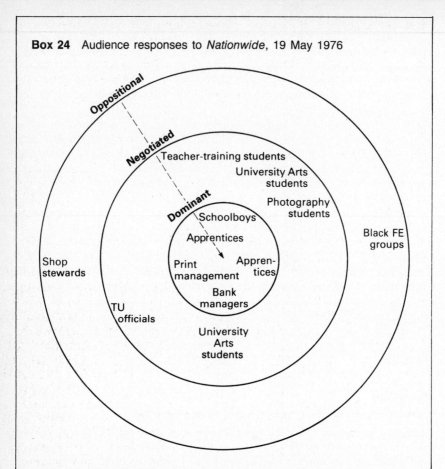

Source: Morley (1980), Television Monograph no. 11, *The 'Nationwide' Audience* (British Film Institute), p. 136. Reproduced with permission.

The figure shows three basic modes of audience response to a *Nationwide* programme. Dominant responses were those that adopted the prevailing or dominant values of society. People taking up oppositional responses, on the other hand, had opinions and beliefs opposed to the dominant values of society. Negotiated interpretations of *Nationwide* occupy an intermediate position, because people with this response have a system of values that partly reflects dominant conceptions but also incorporates values, perhaps based on their everyday experiences, that run counter to dominant conceptions.

The three sorts of response are presented as circles because there are differences *within* each response; they cannot be ranked along a single dimension of opposition or conformity.

Related topics

The issue of ownership and control in British industry as a whole is discussed in chapter 2, section 2.2. The next section, 10.3, touches on the audience for popular culture. Chapter 8 presents a discussion of the way in which the education system transmits cultural values.

10.3   Leisure

Since the Second World War, there has been a great deal of public discussion about the 'leisure society'. People have spent less time working and, consequently, have had more time to themselves and more time for leisure. Even more recently, the very rapid rise in unemployment in Western Europe and other parts of the world, combined with all sorts of new technologies which replace human labour, seems to mean that people's lives will in future be much less organized around work.

These statements imply that leisure is defined in terms of work. That is, indeed, how our society sees it. Leisure is the opposite of work. We will follow this concept and define leisure time as that which is left over after work. Perhaps partly because of the way that our society perceives work as a constraint and a limitation, the definition of leisure as non-work also includes the idea that leisure represents free time and activities that people have *chosen*. However, this definition is clearly problematic for those people who do not have work with which they can contrast leisure. The groups most notably affected are women at home, the retired, the unemployed and young people. For these sections of the population, leisure is still defined as comprising that time over which they have control. For women at home, for example, their leisure occupations are contrasted with domestic work. The same is true for large numbers of elderly and unemployed, although they will have more time for leisure and, to some extent, their lives are organized, not around work, but around what other groups of people would regard as leisure. As we shall see in the next section on youth culture, this is even more true of young people who will see their lives, not in terms of work, but of leisure – even if this perception only lasts a few years.

Our discussion so far suggests that, if we have a 'leisure society', it must have been created at least partly by a reorganization of *time*. Most obviously, the amount of time that people spend at work has been falling steadily. At the beginning of this century, manual workers normally worked a 52- to 54-hour week, reduced after the First World War to 48 hours. After the Second World War, there was a further reduction to 44 hours and the present standard working-week for industrial workers is now 40 hours. Non-manual workers tend to have a rather shorter week, averaging something like 37 hours. It seems possible, however, that any more extensive lessening of the time spent at work will come, not from a shortening of the working day or week, but from longer holidays. The custom of giving manual workers a paid holiday entitlement is actually comparatively recent but, by 1972, most such workers had been given three weeks' holiday a year. Much more recently, the practice of closing factories and offices for much longer periods than was usual at Christmas and Easter has been growing.

Table 10.1   Time use in a typical week, spring 1985

Weekly hours spent on	Full-time employees		Housewives	Retired people
	Males	Females		
Employment & travel	45.0	40.8	—	—
Essential domestic work and personal care	33.1	45.1	76.6	49.8
Sleep	56.4	57.5	59.2	60.2
Free time	33.5	24.6	32.2	58.0

Source: Henley Centre for Forecasting, *Leisure Futures*, autumn 1985. Reproduced with permission.

Opportunities for leisure may have been created by the greater availability of free time, at least to those groups of people who can actually work. Table 10.1 shows how free time varies between employed people, housewives and retired people. For fully employed men, available free time is equal to three-quarters of the time spent working and travelling to work. The manner in which people can avail themselves of leisure time, however, clearly depends on the money that they can spend. Since the Second World War, as people have become more affluent, their expenditure on leisure has increased. Between 1966 and 1976, for example, consumer expenditure of all kinds rose 21 per cent in real terms. There was a very slight increase in the *proportion* of the household budget that goes on leisure, as figure 10.4 shows, but the crucial point is simply that people have more to spend in their free time. Also of significance, is the fact that patterns of expenditure or leisure change. Spending on alcohol goes up, for example, while that on tobacco or going to the cinema goes down.

Obviously, there is an enormous variety of leisure pursuits. Generally, however, the greater part of most people's leisure is taken at home, watching television, listening to music, reading, knitting or doing house repairs or home improvements. Leisure activities outside the home come a very poor second, with the exception of going out for a drink or a meal. There are, however, great gender, life-cycle and class differences in

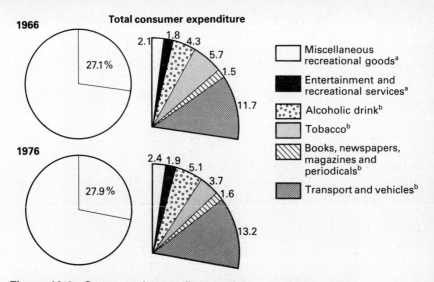

Figure 10.4 Consumers' expenditure on leisure, 1966 and 1976
Source: From Parker (1979), p. 118.

leisure patterns. The differences between men and women in access to leisure activities outside the home is particularly noticeable, which very much fits men's dominance of the public sphere. There are comparatively few leisure activities outside the home which are as open to women as they are to men. Voluntary associations of all kinds tend to be run by men for the benefit of men, whether they are charitable organizations, political parties or school governing boards. Sporting facilities are also used far less by women. As we have already said, the pub is still the most popular leisure destination outside the home, yet it is a strongly male institution. According to the 1983 General Household Survey, 64 per cent of men had been out for a drink in the preceding four weeks while only 46 per cent of women had and most of those, of course, would have been accompanied by men.

The gender imbalance in access to leisure is a function of the more general inequalities between men and women which we discussed in chapter 4. This is partly because leisure facilities are simply not provided for women or are not geared to their needs and demands. It is also because the home is still seen as the natural place for a woman to be; her domestic work may mean that there is literally less time for leisure beyond the front door. As table 10.2 shows, women full-time workers have considerably less free time than their male counterparts because they have domestic as well as paid work. Even housewives have less time to themselves than men in full-time work. Lack of opportunity, lack of

Figure 10.5 Men still largely dominate leisure pursuits outside the home

time and the customary restriction of the woman to the home, all play their part. The social definitions of the roles of men and women also contribute. As Allan (1985) points out, women are less likely to be able to drive – a very simple restriction. Deem (1985) also notes that many husbands are very reluctant to allow their wives to go out unaccompanied.

In many ways, gender differences in leisure activities are more obvious than class. A study by Young and Willmott (1973) showed surprisingly few marked class differences between married men, except in certain areas like active sports, reading or gardening (see table 10.3).

The sharpest class differences are between unskilled or semi-skilled men and the other classes taken together. In almost all areas of leisure, whether home-based, active or spectator sports, the professional and managerial classes do more than any other class. This is a finding very much in line with other evidence about non-work activity patterns, which are further discussed in chapter 6, section 6.6, and it must reflect, amongst other factors, the greater financial resources available to the professional and managerial classes. We should also note that, although table 10.3 does not show great class differences in most leisure activities, it may in some respects be misleading. For example, the 'quality' of leisure activities will vary across classes. So, even if people of all classes

Table 10.2 Average weekly hours spent in different ways (diary sample: married men and women aged 30 to 49)

	Men	Women working full-time	Women working part-time
Paid work and travel to work	49.5	40.2	26.3
Household tasks	9.9	23.1	35.3
Subsistence	73.9	76.1	72.5
Leisure	31.7	25.7	31.2
Non-work travel	3.0	2.9	2.7
Number of people	188	46	55

Source: From Young and Willmott (1973) *The Symmetrical Family* (London, Routledge and Kegan Paul), p. 113. Reproduced with permission.

Table 10.3 Selected leisure activities by socio-economic group, married men working full-time (percentages)

Proportion in class doing activity 12 times or more in previous year	Professional and management	Clerical	Skilled	Semi-skilled or Unskilled	All
Watching television	95	99	98	95	97
Gardening	70	62	66	50	64
Playing with children	59	63	66	59	62
House improvements	52	55	56	45	53
Car cleaning	55	44	51	35	48
Reading	67	63	33	28	46
Swimming	34	25	20	8	22
Golf	9	11	4	2	6
Table-tennis	10	10	4	2	6
Going to pub	51	42	54	58	52
Going for a walk	56	63	41	36	47
Dancing	12	14	10	12	11

Source: Adapted from Young and Willmott (1973) *The Symmetrical Family* (London, Routledge and Kegan Paul), pp. 212, 214, 216. Reproduced with permission.

go out occasionally for a meal, professionals may well eat better than the unskilled.

A person's age, or more accurately, stage, in the life cycle, also affects participation in leisure activities. The young and the elderly have more free time than other age-groups and, in a sense, the lives of both these groups are organized around leisure, although these are also times when income is at its lowest. This is especially true of young people whose leisure culture is discussed in the next section. Married couples with young children experience most constraints. They have less money and less time. As children grow up, household income is rising to its peak and husband and wife are beginning to have more free time, even if they are still involved with their children on a day-to-day basis. When children have left home, couples have more time available even if their income is no longer rising. For middle-class couples at least, this is a period when they return to a pattern of shared leisure pursuits that they may have followed when they were very much younger.

Families and the leisure industry

We have shown that the bulk of people's leisure activities take place within their home – some 70 per cent for men and 80 per cent for women. Many sociologists have seen this as a relatively new phenomenon, dating perhaps from the Second World War, part of a growing tendency to *privatization*, to the increasing involvement of people with their immediate family and their homes. (For further discussion of this issue see chapter 3, section 3.4, and chapter 6, section 6.6.) While the process of privatization probably has a longer history than this, there is some reason to think that leisure activities are more private than they used to be. There is, in other words, less involvement in 'public' spheres of recreation. It is not only that people participate less in public events such as carnivals, religious events, processions, and fairs (or 'public' holidays). It is also that there is relatively less involvement in leisure activities outside the home. So there are fewer visits to the pub or cinema in favour of more drinking at home and a greater dedication to watching television.

This privatization of leisure is connected with the growth of a commercial leisure industry. As we said earlier, although the proportion of income spent on leisure is not rising greatly, it does rise as consumer expenditure, as a whole, goes up. There is a flourishing industry providing goods and services for people's leisure. Very large firms like the Rank Organization, the Grand Metropolitan Group or the big brewing groups provide for leisure activities across the social spectrum. Furthermore, this commercialization of leisure provision does not extend only to activities outside the home. Many home-based forms of leisure are obviously commercialized – from video-recorders to home improvements.

These dual processes of privatization and commercialization have persuaded some sociologists that the appearance of a distinctive set of leisure activities can have some undesirable effects. The consumer, it is suggested, is fed with ready-made leisure – at a price and making a profit for someone – which serves to divert attention away from real problems by giving spurious pleasure. This cultural influence is all the more pervasive because it is brought right into the home. The most frequently cited culprit here is television.

It is often alleged that television provides programmes representing the lowest common denominator. These programmes provide a means of escape from a dull or threatening everyday life. Alternatively, they transmit a set of attitudes and beliefs about society that favour the position of the powerful. The television audience, on the other hand, is seen as largely passive, absorbing quiz shows or soap operas quite uncritically and, thereby, acquiring a false view of the world.

Television is, indeed, an important source of leisure interest. As we have seen, television-viewing takes up a great deal of our free time. Women watch more than men and the lower social classes more than the higher ones. In the winter of 1985, women watched an average of about 30 hours per week and men about 27 hours. Television is also commercial. ITV and Channel 4 depend, of course, on advertising and their programming is heavily constrained by this fact. The BBC does not have to operate directly by this kind of commercial logic but it has to compete with ITV and, therefore, tends to offer the same kind of programmes. There is, hence, a certain homogeneity of programming. But what of the model of the audience as passive, escaping, duped consumers of leisure and, more specifically, television programmes? To illuminate this question we turn to a recent study of television audiences.

Uninvited Guests: a case-study

'Passivity' is an odd term to describe the manner in which so many of these people watched their screens. In the early days of television, it may have been true, that the flickering box in the darkened room could actually 'entrance' its audience: nowadays this hardly fits any description of its use. But neither should we go to the opposite extreme and declare that people hardly watch it at all; that it flickers away unattended in the corner while they get on with making tea, hoovering the carpet and completing their aerobic workouts. Sometimes it is watched with great intensity and emotional involvement (quite enough to produce tears of sorrow or joy): at other moments, with an irreverent concern (in which actors and plot readily become mere laughing matters). In both cases it is likely to be a subject for conversation and comment among those present either during or after the specific programme. And whatever may have been the case in the past, nowadays, with at least four channels available and a prerecorded film for hire a few hundred yards down the road, choice is likely to be continually exercised.

Taylor and Mullan (1986)

Taylor and Mullan's (1986) book, from which this quotation is taken, is a report of a study of audience responses to television programmes of various kinds. It is based largely, though not completely, on tape-recorded transcripts of group discussions involving people who watched television. The groups were chosen from those sections of the population that tended to watch the shows in question. So, for example, discussions of game and quiz shows were held principally by people over forty in skilled and semi-skilled occupations.

The fundamental conclusion of the study is that television audiences can be deeply involved in what they watch though they are not passive spectators but are active, critical and creative. There is, therefore, a sense in which the audience is simultaneously involved and detached. Involvement is shown in the detailed conversations that people have about television programmes. For example, participants in the study talked about characters in soap operas as if they were real. *Coronation Street* and *Brookside* strike a chord because they are so realistic and the audience can respond to the problems or joys experienced by the characters. It is not, however, just that members of the audience acknowledge the reality of such soap operas by talking about the characters as real people. It is also that their involvement in the drama moves them deeply. As one of the (male) participants said of *Coronation Street*: 'I must be perfectly honest, I watched it when Stan died, I watched it and I cried. I sat down and watched it when Stan died because it was so real and I could relate to it. I just sat there and cried' (Taylor and Mullan, 1986, p. 45). The audience's involvement through the realism of television goes well beyond the presentation of drama. Even in chat shows, for example, audiences in this study greatly preferred hosts who were 'real', not apparently putting on an act. Thus, Terry Wogan was the most popular presenter because his television self was seen to be most like people thought he would be at home.

Despite these symptoms of involvement, audiences are also detached and critical. In general, people watching television are aware that, however 'real' the presentation, it is not *actually* real. They know, for example, that *Coronation Street* is a fiction. The groups in Taylor and Mullan's study were very quick to analyse programmes in terms of their realism. American soap operas were felt to be less realistic than British ones, at least partly because the range of human emotions is not realistically portrayed. Audiences analyse the performances and skills of the actors, well aware that these *are* actors playing a role, not real people. The tricks and techniques utilized by television are also noted and commented on. Viewers noticed stock film used over and over again, mistakes in the setting out of rooms in soap operas and unconvincing car crashes. Audiences, in other words, are quite clear that television events are not real and this very lack of reality is itself a topic of conversation. The offices in *Dallas* and *Dynasty* are not real offices because nobody seems to do real work. Even *Coronation Street* lacks realism in this respect. As one viewer said of Mike Baldwin's factory: 'There aren't enough machinists, to start with. There are only four of them and they're making jeans for half the population of England' (p. 16).

People are, therefore, involved in television but simultaneously aware of their involvement and able to criticize and analyse all kinds of programme. This combination of involvement and detachment is intimately connected with the relationship of television to everyday life. For Taylor and Mullan, television is *used* by audiences to make sense of their everyday lives. The function of conversations about television is to interpret events on television so that they relate to everyday lives. People will, therefore, talk about characters in *Coronation Street* as if they were real characters because that is how the link with their everyday lives is forged. Audiences do not respond to television programmes passively; they actively use them for their own ends.

Summary

1 People nowadays have more time, and rather more money, for leisure, which is defined in terms of non-work.

2 There are gender, life-cycle and class differences in leisure patterns.

3 The great bulk of leisure time is spent in the home, especially in watching television.

4 Some sociologists have argued that commercial, popular culture and leisure produces an uncritical audience but they are mistaken. Even television watching, an apparently passive activity, engages an active and creative audience.

Related topics

For further discussion of the way that different members of the family are sociable inside and outside the home, see chapter 6, section 6.6. The way in which youth culture is organized around leisure is discussed in the next section, 10.4.

10.4 Youth Culture

The 1950s saw the birth of commercialized youth cultures, working-class teenagers possessed the necessary spending power. Financial independence led to cultural independence, and the leisure industries began to recognize youth as a distinct market . . . During the 1960s, London became internationally renowned for its swinging scene, with young people leading the action. By then they had become the undisputed pioneers in fashion. Their tastes dictated general trends in dress, coiffure and music. Young people set the pace, and adults followed.

Roberts (1983)

In modern Britain, youth has become a focus of attention, even a problem. It is assumed that being young is somehow special – it is a state that requires public notice from the middle-aged and the old. Obviously, a wide variety of attitudes are expressed towards the young, including envy, fear, dislike and, even, sympathy. Whatever the attitude, however, the young are seen as *different* as the cartoon strip in figure 10.6 illustrates.

This is a new phenomenon. Young people were not always treated as a problem or a special category. There have not always been well-marked characteristics of appearance or tastes in music, films or books special to the young; there has not always, in other words, been a distinctive *youth culture*. This suggests that youth cultures are not biologically determined by the facts of aging but are, rather, social constructions. Different societies treat aging in different ways. It would after all, be possible for British society to become especially aware of some other age-group and for a culture appropriate to that group to develop. There are signs that that may be happening for the middle-aged and, perhaps, also for the elderly.

What social factors account, then, for the creation of youth cultures and the identification of youth as a separate social category and a distinctive phase of life? The most general reason for this change is that the transitional period from dependent childhood to independent adulthood has been greatly lengthened in modern industrial societies. This change has been promoted by attitudes and policies towards education and work. With the separation of home and work, children no longer slip imperceptibly from childhood into the world of work. The gradual rise in the school-leaving age and the apparent insistence on educational qualifications for many jobs, lengthens the period in which young people cannot go out to work. Lastly, young people in the post-war period are better-off than those before the war, whether they are in full-time education or at work. The young have, therefore, become a market for records, clothes and books that can be commercially exploited. For example, in a relatively early study of the teenage consumer, Abrams (1959) calculated that, compared with 1938, the real earnings of teenagers in 1958 had increased by 50 per cent (twice as much as their parents' increase) and their real discretionary spending power (that is the money left over after necessities have been paid for) had almost doubled in the same period.

Public attention often concentrates on the extraordinary or spectacular aspects of youth culture and, partly as a result, sociologists also focus their research on the exotic, on skinheads or punks, for example. Yet it is reasonable to argue that all young people participate in a youth culture which has three important features. First, it is a culture of *leisure* rather than work. While the culture of the middle-aged, for example, revolves around work and social relationships at work, it is leisure time that provides the best means of self-expression for young people. Second, the

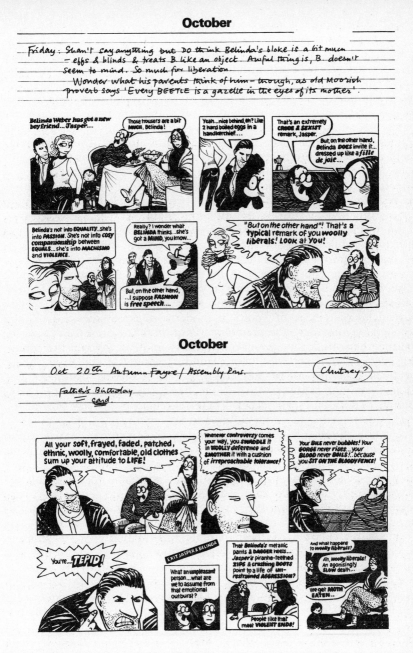

Figure 10.6
Source: Posy Simmonds. Reprinted by permission of A.D. Peters and Co. Ltd

social relationships of youth cultures are organized around the *peer group*; they are as much collective as individual. This contrasts with the adult orientation to families or individual friends. Lastly, youth groups are characterized by a strong interest in *style*.

Each distinct youth culture has its own style, a blend of special tastes in music, clothes or language. Different styles separate one culture from another, give members an identity, and enable them to recognize themselves and others. It is this emphasis on style that enables us to talk simultaneously about youth culture and youth cultu*res*. There are many youth cultures, each differentiated from the others by its own distinctive style. However, it is also possible to speak of a youth culture that is differentiated from other age-cultures in our society by the three features we have just mentioned. In this sense, all young people belong to a youth culture although, obviously, not all adopt the more spectacular styles.

Youth cultures are, then, characterized by leisure interests, peer groups and style. Adult groups of various kinds also have these characteristics but they are not so marked. The *culture* of any social group represents a way of defining and coping with the world and making some coherent sense of everyday experiences; they are 'maps of meaning'. Youth cultures represent ways of dealing with and giving meaning to the particular experiences of youth in modern industrial societies. Young people have to manage the period of transition that we referred to earlier and they have to acquire a sense of identity and control over their lives. However, in whatever ways youth cultures succeed in performing these functions, they are not isolated from the rest of society. Youth cultures relate to parent cultures, on the one hand, and the wider, dominant cultures of society, on the other. These relationships provide part of the reason for referring to youth cultures as *sub*-cultures.

If young people relate to the culture of their parents, and if parent cultures differ from one another, then so too will youth cultures. Growing up is not a similar experience for everyone and young people from different social groups will have different problems to face and will construct different maps of meaning. To a very large extent, these differences will depend on the parent culture. For example, middle-class parents have different experiences and cultures from working-class parents. The children of these parents will, similarly, have different experiences from each other and different youth cultures will result. This point is nicely illustrated in a small-scale way in a study by Kitwood (1980). He found that class and gender differences determine the content of negotiations between teenagers and their parents over going out. Middle-class children have to show that their school work will not suffer, while working-class boys have to convince their parents that they will not get into any kind of trouble with authority. Girls of both classes have, in addition, to persuade their parents that they are not at any sexual risk. They are also likely to have their leisure time limited by parental anxieties and domestic responsibilities at home. Clearly then, experiences of youth differ and the remainder of this section will be devoted to exploring these differences.

Working-class youth cultures

A great deal of sociological research has concentrated on working-class youth. This may be partly because many working-class youth cultures are publicly flamboyant and defiant, as the photographs in figure 10.7 demonstrate. Indeed, the *point* of these sub-cultural styles seems to be defiance. They are *spectacular*, constructed so that they can be seen. This, however, raises the question why working-class youth culture appears to be more flamboyant and defiant than its middle-class counterpart. Sociological answers to this question are heavily influenced by Hall and Jefferson (1976). They argue that there are certain problems faced by working-class youth because of their class position that are intensified by their age. They lack power and authority, have few material resources and cannot expect rewarding employment. Their adult life does not hold out much hope for them. In these circumstances, the adoption of a sub-cultural style gives other rewards of status and approval, an identity and a place in a world circumscribed by fellow participants, and a sense of being in control of at least some part of life. The adoption of a youth culture of this kind is, therefore, a symbolic resistance to society's definition of working-class life. It is symbolic because it takes over conventional images and gives them new, unusual and, perhaps, surprising meanings. Skinheads, for example, in wearing jeans, braces and boots all the time, transform the meaning of working-class work-clothes. These clothes are aggressively worn rather than carried, almost shamefully, as the badge of a manual worker.

This view, that working-class youth cultures represent a form of resistance to the conditions of working-class life, has to cope with the objection that there are large differences between youth cultures. Mods, for example, cultivate a neat and, sometimes, sharply dressed image, while skinheads aggressively assert what are assumed to be qualities of working-class life. There may, furthermore, be equally large differences between any of the more obvious youth cultures and 'conforming' youth. To some extent, these diversities may be 'merely' a question of the choice of one style rather than another. However, as we show in chapter 3, section 3.4, the working class is not homogeneous, but internally differentiated. Mods and skinheads may, therefore, be drawn from separate sections of the working class (or lower-middle class) and have dissimilar experiences that are reflected in the adoption of their distinctive styles.

The argument is, then, that working-class youth cultures are a form of symbolic resistance against a dominant culture which assigns working-class life a subordinate place. On this view, it is impossible to see these youth cultures independently of that dominant culture or, for that matter,

Figure 10.7   Youth Cultures
Source: Melanie Friend/Format; Homer Sykes/Camera Press; Geoff Franklin/Network (2); Network; Raissa Page/Format.

the culture of parents that provides many of the experiences on which youth cultures are based. However, resistance of this kind is not necessarily effective, although it is obviously true that the behaviour and style of young people can excite considerable adult fury. This lack of effectiveness derives, partly, from the fact that any individual's participation in a youth culture is short-lived and, partly, from the very fact that resistance is symbolic not 'real'.

There are also certain paradoxes in the resistance offered by working-class youth cultures. For example, a study by Willis (1977), described in more detail in chapter 8, section 8.3, gives an account of a group of working-class boys who defy the authority of the school but, in so doing, condemn themselves to dead-end jobs through lack of qualifications. Resistance, in this case, leads to subordination.

The defiance of working-class youth cultures and, especially, their delinquency, is, of course, one of the things frequently picked up in the mass media. All the youth culture styles of the post-war years in Britain – rockers, teds, mods, skinheads and punks – have been regularly reviled in the press. What is, perhaps, striking about the response of adult Britain (or older opinion-leaders at any rate) is the way that it repeats history. The same things are said about each style, chiefly that young people form gangs which are threatening and aggressive, they are immoral, work-shy and unable to engage in what their elders regard as constructive pursuits. A 'family doctor' writing in a newspaper in the 1950s could speak for many of his successors who comment on other youth cultures:

Teddy boys . . . are all of unsound mind in the sense that they are all suffering from a form of psychosis. Apart from the birch or the rope, depending on the gravity of their crimes, what they need is rehabilitation in a psychopathic institution. . . Because they have not the mental stamina to be individualists they had to huddle together in gangs. (Quoted in Brake, 1980)

The paradoxes of youth cultures are nicely illustrated by skinhead culture. On the one hand, skinheads are defiant of society and perhaps of their parents' generation. On the other hand, their activities seem to celebrate some traditional working-class values. Skinhead behaviour, chiefly their attacks on other people, frequently get them into trouble with authority. They are aggressive and violent with people they think of as outsiders – black people, students and anybody who looks 'odd'. At the same time, as Clarke (1976) suggests, skinhead culture also represents their parent, working-class, culture; it is a 'magical recovery of community', a reassertion of the virtues of collective solidarity that once held working-class communities together but no longer do so. For Clarke, the skinhead insistence on territory, their dislike of anybody different, and the antipathy to authority are all elements of working-class life.

Youth cultures and other social groups

The middle classes

The middle classes do, of course, participate to a limited extent in the more spectacular youth cultures especially, recently, in punk. In general, though, they are more conforming. The exception, of course, is the upsurge in youthful and largely middle-class protest in the 1960s. This was the time of the counter-culture, of hippies and of alternative life-styles. It was also a time of political involvement by middle-class youth in student protest and in the peace movement. We described youth culture, in general, earlier as a function of a concentration on leisure and the peer-group and an expression of style. Middle-class youth cultures, although they have these three features, differ from their working-class counter-parts in the emphasis placed on certain characteristics. For example, there is a more individualized response; more emphasis is placed on 'doing your own thing'. More importantly, middle-class youth cultures of this kind are more political; they are concerned with alternative social structures. The result is that they revolve less around the use of leisure time and the expression of style. We have to repeat the warning that we have already given in the analysis of spectacular working-class youth cultures. Political middle-class youth cultures almost certainly also only represent a small proportion of middle-class youth. The youth culture of the 'ordinary' majority may be altogether less one of resistance.

Girls and youth culture

There are two important questions to ask when investigating the relationship between gender and youth cultures: Do girls participate in the 'working'-class youth cultures that we have described? Or do girls have youth cultures of their own, that are distinctively feminine? (McRobbie, 1978). Girls do join in youth cultures. There are female skinheads or mods, for instance. However, the rate of participation by girls is very much lower; skinhead and mod cultures are predominantly male. Girls are much more tightly controlled by parents and local community. There is the ever-present fear of getting into trouble, especially sexual trouble. The result is that girls have less of a public, street, life and are more confined to home. To the extent that girls can go out, their participation in particular sub-cultures is marginal. They are not at the centre of a group but become supporters or helpers to the boys. It is true that there are exceptions to this marginal participation in predominantly male youth cultures. As McRobbie (1978) points out, more girls participate in mod groups than in other sub-cultural styles. This may be for a number of reasons. Mod boys, for example, cultivate a more feminine style of dress and behaviour which may exclude girls less. There is, also, the growing acceptability of unisex styles, which again is partly promoted by male rock stars adopting a more feminine public presentation.

McRobbie answers the second question about the existence of distinctively female youth cultures by again pointing to the marginality and subordination of women in modern Britain. It is true that young girls do create a 'teenybopper' culture of their own, based in their homes and organized around records, rock stars and fan magazines, and this culture can, to some extent, allow girls to 'negotiate a space of their own'. It can act to create groupings of girls that exclude boys. However, at the same time, the teenybopper culture also *subordinates* girls, for it is essentially oriented to marriage and the family as the only desirable goals, and it prepares girls for the role of girlfriend as a kind of hanger-on to a boy.

Ethnic groups and youth culture

If the involvement, or non-involvement, of girls in sub-cultures does not seem to imply resistance to the dominant culture of our society, the same cannot be said of ethnic sub-cultures. Young black people form sub-cultures as defiant as punks or skins. One of the most significant of these is Rastafarianism, which can be seen as a reaction to the dominance of white society, for Rastafarians rejoice in being black, believing that they are the lost tribe of Israel, while they see white society as corrupt and immoral. Rastafarianism is an essentially cultural and religious response that effectively means a withdrawal from society rather than a confrontation with it. It does have the same sub-cultural emphasis on style that we have noted in youth cultures, although it may also involve larger numbers of older people in a way that punks, for example, do not. Rastafarians may wear dreadlocks or dress in certain colours. It cannot be said, however, that black youth wholeheartedly and inevitably follow Rastafarian precepts of withdrawal from white society, as the riots of 1981 and subsequent years have demonstrated.

Summary

1 The post-war period in Britain has seen an emphasis on young people as a specific social category. There is a general culture of youth which is distinct from that of other age-groups.

2 There are many varieties of youth culture, often based in class, gender or ethnicity. Each adopts particular styles that differentiate them from other youth cultures.

3 Many youth cultures have an uneasy relationship with their parent cultures, borrowing certain features, but often otherwise being defiant of prevailing opinions or beliefs.

Related topics

The previous section, 10.3, pursues the question of leisure, which is such a marked characteristic of youth cultures. Chapter 8, section 8.3, discusses the relationship of youth culture to the school environment.

10.5   Religion

> In general, there can be little doubt about the decline in church-going, church-membership, sustained religious commitment, and the general standing of the Church in society. It is evident that institutionally the Church remains favourably placed, and that its agencies are well-entrenched in many respects. . . But even these facilities have more the appearance of power than the reality of it.
>
> Wilson (1966)

> The Moonies we had met at the camp were robots, glassy eyed and mindless, programmed as soldiers in this vast fund-raising army with no goals or ideals, except as followers of the half-baked ravings of Moon, who lived in splendour while his followers lived in forced penury.
>
> *Daily Mail* quoted in Barker (1984)

One of the main themes running through this chapter is the relationship between dominant cultures and subordinate ones. One of the questions that informed the discussion in the previous section was in what way youth cultures can be seen as opposing the dominant culture. The same question crops up in sociological analysis of religion in Britain.

In many ways, religion is a very powerful force in Britain. Churchmen are listened to and their pronouncements can stir up a good deal of public debate; recently, for example, a Church of England report effectively criticized government policy on poverty in the inner city. Religious worship is compulsory in schools. There is a strong religious component to many of our public ceremonies – coronations, for example. The same goes for private ceremonies – weddings in church or baptisms, for instance, are still much favoured. In these senses, then, Britain is a religious society. Furthermore, there is one form of Christianity that is dominant, namely the Church of England, which appears to define what we take to be religious experience or behaviour.

At the same time, two trends seem to point in a different direction. First, there has been something of a decline in *individual* adherence to Christian religious belief, as measured, for example, by the numbers of people who regularly go to church. Second, there is growth in newer religious movements which are often not Christian. They are frequently 'sectarian' and 'communitarian' in their social organization. This means that worshippers are organized into small groups in which everybody knows each other and is very committed to their religion. These new religious movements are often seen as alternatives to the dominant religious bodies (the Church of England or the Roman Catholic Church) and, occasionally, as dangerous and threatening. In the remaining part of this section we consider these two issues in more detail.

The Christian churches and secularization

Tables 10.4 and 10.5 give some idea of the changes in the membership of various religious faiths in the period 1970–85. Table 10.4 shows that there has been a steady decline in most of the Christian churches. In 1985, only one in seven of the adult population of Britain was a member of a Christian church. There were, however, significant differences between different parts of Britain. In England, for example, only 11 per cent of the adult population were church members, while in Northern Ireland the corresponding figure was 70 per cent. There was a certain vigour, however, in the smaller Christian churches and in some of the non-Christian faiths. As table 10.5 shows, membership of all non-Christian religions except Judaism grew in the period 1975–85.

Table 10.4   Membership in thousands of Christian churches

	1970	1975	1980	1985
Anglican	2,548	2,268	2,154	1,984
Presbyterian	1,807	1,646	1,509	1,389
Methodist	658	596	536	465
Baptist	296	270	240	236
Other Protestant	530	539	533	572
Total Protestant	5,839	5,289	4,972	4,646
Catholic	2,680	2,536	2,335	2,162
Orthodox	103	106	108	117
Total Christian	8,622	7,931	7,415	6,925
% of adult population	20.5	18.5	16.2	15.1

Source: MARC Europe, *UK Christian Handbook, 1987/88.* Reproduced with permission.

It has to be pointed out that, although the Christian churches lost some 1.3 million members between 1970 and 1985, Christianity is still very much larger than the other faiths. However, *membership* in a church may be an unreliable guide to the numbers of people who take their religion seriously. Membership figures may be inflated because they do not adequately reflect turnover, that is, they include people who have effectively lapsed from membership. Furthermore, people who are members of churches may not attend acts of worship particularly

Table 10.5 Membership in thousands of small Christian groups and non-Christian religions

	1970	1975	1980	1985
Non-Christian				
Muslims	250	400	600	853
Sikhs	75	115	150	80
Hindus	50	100	120	130
Jews	113	111	111	109
Other	50	88	154	196
Small Christian groups				
Mormons	88	80	91	81
Jehovah's Witnesses	62	80	84	101
Spiritualists	45	57	52	49
Other	86	98	100	114

Source: MARC Europe, *UK Christian Handbook 1987/88.* Reproduced with permission.

frequently. Thus, although 1 in 7 adults in Britain is a member of a Christian church, only 1 in 10 goes to church at all regularly.

There has been a gradual decline in participation in Christian churches – a process of *secularization*. There are many ways in which secularization can be measured. It is convenient to distinguish active participation in religious activities from attendance at one or two rituals that happen to be religiously solemnized. An example of the first would be regular attendance at church and, of the second, marriage in church. The point is that secularization is more marked for the first than the second. Thus, in the mid-nineteenth century, probably some 40 per cent of the population attended church on Sunday. The corresponding figure in the mid-1980s is around 10 per cent. Other activities that indicate a degree of commitment have also declined significantly. Both church membership and participation in Sunday schools, for example, have declined sharply. Involvement in the major rituals that mark out an individual's life – baptism, marriage and burial – have also declined over the past century but not by so much. For example, some 70 per cent of the population are married in some form of religious ceremony while at the turn of the century it was about 75 per cent.

So far, we have argued that there has been a decline in the rate at which the population of Britain participates in formal religious institutions; fewer people are members of churches and acts of worship and other religious ceremonies are less frequently attended. There are a number of reasons for this decline in what we can call *institutional adherence*. The state has grown in power and the Church is less involved in the political process – the Church has less political power. Science and the institutions of scientific work have grown in importance and claim to effectively solve problems, like those of health for example, which previously were in the province of religious institutions. Many of the welfare and charitable functions of the church are now also performed by other agencies.

The decline in institutional adherence does not, however, necessarily mean that Christianity – or religion in general – is a spent force in Britain. There are two further issues that have to be considered: civic rituals and privatized religion.

Civic rituals

We have already referred to the way in which the Church of England is integrated into the national culture. There are a whole series of national events – or *civic rituals* – that have a religious component. The Archbishop of Canterbury, for example, presides at coronations, royal weddings and services of thanksgiving. Children are brought up in a religious culture at school and there are many schools administered and controlled by religious bodies in which religious instruction is taken seriously. The Christian churches, in short, still have a considerable amount of power and influence.

Church influence does not only operate at the national level however. Major events in the lives of ordinary people are often commemorated in religious settings. As we have pointed out, the majority of people still prefer to have their births, marriages and deaths solemnized in church or chapel. One can, of course, argue that civic rituals or the religious sanctification of births, marriages and deaths does not have any particular *meaning* for the majority of the population. However, these forms of participation do indicate that the Church still carries considerable *institutional* weight.

Meaning

The second issue that must be considered in this connection concerns the question of meaning. It may well be that institutional adherence to the Church has declined but that does not imply that people are not privately religious. Berger (1969) for example, argues that religion in modern societies is pushed increasingly into the sphere of the family or even the individual. Religion becomes a question of private feeling rather than of public worship or even public morality. There is some evidence that, in Britain, religion does flourish in the private sphere, even when its public significance is in decline. For example, when asked in sample surveys, a large number of people declare religious beliefs of some kind even if they do not attend acts of worship. Again, respondents will admit to having had spiritual experiences which they had, significantly, not communicated to anyone else for fear of being laughed at. Another study, investigating private beliefs of various kinds, found that over three-quarters of their sample believed in God and almost 40 per cent often prayed in private (Abercrombie et al., 1970). The same study also found a large reservoir of beliefs which, if not precisely religious, are at least non-scientific or spiritual. A considerable proportion of respondents engaged in super-stitions or luck-bringing practices, like touching wood or throwing salt over the shoulder. About 20 per cent took astrological predictions seriously. As the authors say: 'It seems that for many people, probably the great majority, religious beliefs and practices merge almost indistin-guishably with superstitions of all sorts, to be summoned only in special situations and crisis and anxiety' (p. 113).

The continuing, if muted, significance of civic ritual and the apparent importance of private, as distinct from institutional religion, are reasons for moderating *extreme* theories of secularization that might be based solely on the decline of institutional adherence. On balance, though, the case for the existence of a process of secularization in *Christianity* is very strong. However, *some* religions have expanded, as table 10.5 shows. Since the 1960s, there has been a religious revival in more exotic religions, deriving either from the East or from a much-altered Christianity. Some of these have attracted a great deal of, usually unfavourable, press comment, as the quotation about Moonies at the beginning of this section shows.

New religious movements

There are a very large number of what have been called new religious movements. Among those that have appeared regularly in the press are: the Unification Church (the Moonies), the Hare Krishna movement, Transcendental Meditation and Scientology. In addition, certain Christian denominations, such as Mormons or Pentecostalists, have also been increasing in membership. There is a temptation to believe that these movements are all the same; they are undoubtedly new and religious and, above all, seem to inspire their believers with a degree of commitment and dedication missing in many church-goers let alone the bulk of the population. However, in fact, new religious movements are diverse. In a recent book, Wallis (1984) proposes a typology of new religious movements (NRMs). He suggests that there are two popular types – world rejecting and world affirming – which, as their names suggest, have opposite characteristics. Both of these can, in turn, be contrasted with a third type which he calls world-accommodating. These relationships are shown in the figure 10.8.

Figure 10.8 is an ideal-type characterization and many types of NRM actually fall at various points between the extremes. *World-rejecting movements* can be characterized as follows. They tend to be exclusive, being based on the importance of the community as against the individual. Converts are expected to renounce their past lives and

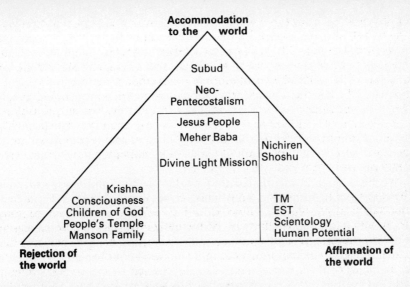

Figure 10.8 Types of new religious movements

Source: Wallis (1984) *The Elementary Forms of the New Religious Life* (London, Routledge and Kegan Paul), figure 1, p. 6. Reproduced with permission.

emotional ties, including those of their family, and the outside world is seen as threatening. The virtues of sharing money, clothes and affection are emphasized in contrast to the individual possession of these things. The submerging of personal identity is sometimes reflected in the similarity of appearance or dress or in the way in which converts may take new names.

World-affirming movements, on the other hand, may see the prevailing social order as having certain virtues. Mankind is seen not as essentially evil but, rather, as perfectible and having powers that can be released by participation in the given NRM. These may well be part-time movements without acts of collective worship or precise theologies. In contrast to the collective orientations of world-rejecting movements, world-affirming NRMs are individualistic, aiming to unlock the hidden powers latent in each person. The sources of unhappiness, in other words, do not lie in the society outside but rather within oneself. There is no rejection of the world involved but rather an attempt to relate to the world more effectively.

The method and pattern of recruitment of the two types of movement differs substantially. Conversion to the world-rejecting movements tend to be more sudden, involving a sharp break with the convert's previous life. Because world-affirming NRMs do not cut themselves off from the outer world so much, recruitment can be a more gradual process and one that uses existing networks of friends and relatives. Similarly, different types of people are attracted to the different NRMs. World-rejecting movements recruit relatively young people in their early or mid-twenties, who are of disproportionately middle-class origins and highly educated. Wallis (1984) suggests that these recruits are, in addition, socially *marginal* in some way, perhaps in having dropped out of higher education. By contrast, world-affirming movements recruit from socially *integrated* people, not necessarily middle class, with an average age of about 35 and who may be successful in life. On this account, therefore, world-rejecting NRMs appeal to those who have found no satisfaction in the conventional world; world-affirming movements recruit from those who are successful (and perhaps upwardly mobile) but who could be more so.

We have already mentioned that world-rejecting and world-affirming movements are pure types and many, if not most, NRMs are, in fact, found between the extremes. A third type – *world-accommodating* – contrasts with both the other two. For world-accommodating movements, religious experience is not social or collective but is, instead, personal and individual. It is the importance of individual religious *experience* which is at the heart of these movements, like the charismatic renewal movement within Christianity. Acts of worship are enthusiastic and vital, giving participants a spiritual element to their lives which they feel is lacking in the more orthodox Christian churches.

Becoming a Moonie: a case-study

Further light is thrown on the recruitment to world-rejecting movements by Barker's (1984) study of the Unification Church, members of which are usually called Moonies after the leader of the church, the Reverend Moon. Two main problems are addressed in this study. First, there is the problem of how people are recruited into the movement. Second, is the need to explain who is recruited, and why.

The Moonies have often been accused of brainwashing their converts, as the quotation at the beginning of this section illustrates. The assumption in much public discussion is that nobody could join a movement like that *unless* they were brainwashed. Critics of the Unification Church argue that the methods of recruitment practised by the church are very similar to techniques allegedly used in the Korean, or more recently Vietnam, wars. Barker describes the steps in the process of becoming a Moonie as follows. There is, first, an initial contact which may be through the personal networks of existing members, but is more likely to involve casual meetings in the street or in the course of everyday life. What follows is an invitation to a Unification Church centre where the potential convert may be offered a meal. A friendly and welcoming atmosphere prevails and there may eventually be discussion of serious personal and religious questions. Those who visit a centre will be invited to go to Unification Church workshops of varying lengths, from a weekend to three weeks. These workshops consist mainly of courses of lectures. Having been to advanced workshops and 'graduated', the recruit becomes a member of the Unification Church.

This process of recruitment is clearly rigorous and it has also been claimed that it deprives the potential recruits of the power of choice by subjecting them to a barrage of propaganda, depriving them of proper sleep and nourishment while at the workshops, or by giving them too *much* love and attention. However, Barker's research shows that the process of recruitment is actually very *inefficient*. Nothing is known about

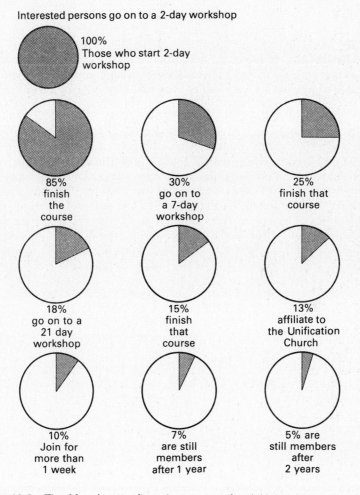

Figure 10.9 The Moonie recruitment process, after initial visit to a Unification Church Centre

Source: From Barker (1984) *The Making of a Moonie* (Oxford, Basil Blackwell), p. 146, with permission of the author.

how many of the people initially contacted actually get to a centre but, since many of these contacts are in the street, it seems unlikely that it is a particularly large proportion. However, Barker estimates that of those who go to a centre only 1 in 10 go on to any kind of workshop. Thereafter, as figure 10.9 illustrates, recruits drop out at every stage of the process. Only 5 per cent of those who start on the workshop stage of recruitment are still in the movement after two years. If one takes as the starting point a visit to a Unification centre, only 0.005 per cent of recruits are still members of the Unification Church after two years.

This very low rate of recruitment does strongly suggest that *particular* kinds of people become Moonies; it is not the case that all people are equally likely to become members of the Unification Church. Barker hypothesizes that it is not the recruitment methods that make a convert but, rather, the prior experiences that potential converts bring with them to the first meeting with a Moonie. The first step in testing this hypothesis was to compare Moonies with the population as a whole. The conclusions were that Moonies are younger (with an average age of 26), from more middle-class family backgrounds, better educated and disproportionately male (two-thirds are male). More precise conclusions were made possible by a comparison with a control group matched for age, gender social class, education and religious characteristics. One might expect this comparison to yield some indications of what is different about the Moonies. Barker concludes that Moonies are not inadequate or drifting personalities. They come from families as happy and secure as those of the control group. But Barker did find some important differences.

Moonies tend to come from more conventional and 'respectable' homes, in which traditional values of family life, morality and decency are prized. Perhaps related to this kind of family background, Barker also found that many Moonie recruits had encountered the problems of life relatively late on and were ill-prepared to meet them. Before meeting members of the Unification Church, they may well have experienced an 'emotional dip' which the warm family atmosphere of the Moonies helped them to cope with.

More important still, although the Moonie group and the control group were, of course, both drawn from the middle class, the parents of Moonies were less likely to be in jobs concerned with making money and more likely to have occupations 'usually associated with the values of duty or service, either to individuals (e.g. doctors, nurses, teachers) or to their country (e.g. the armed services, police, colonial service)' (p. 211). This parental background may well have given the Moonie recruits a particular set of values and attitudes that has been described as 'seekership'. Many of the Moonies were seeking something, some spiritual not material experience, but they were unclear what it was precisely. The Unification Church met that need.

Many of the new religious movements are very small in membership.

Figure 10.10   Open day celebrations at Bhaktivedana Manor in Hertfordshire –
the British headquarters of the Hari Krishna sect
Source: Dick Mikowski/Camera Press.

Barker (1984) estimates that in 1982 there were 700 Moonies, 200 followers each of Transcendental Meditation and the Bhagwan Rajneesh and 500 members of the Krishna movement. The small size of these cults makes it very difficult to understand the power and ferocity of public reaction to them. Of course, societies do sometimes react violently to the presence of strange and unfamiliar groups in their midst. Furthermore, that reaction is likely to vary with what Beckford (1985) has called the 'mode of insertion' of cults into society. Those cults that are world-affirming and are more integrated with the wider society will attract less controversy than do the world-rejecting NRMs. One possible explanation for societal reaction to world-rejecting movements such as the Moonies, lies in the centrality of family life in modern societies. The accusations of brainwashing stem from the sudden and apparently inexplicable way that people are converted and move away from their families. This sudden cessation of 'normal' family ties seems unnatural and perverse and, not surprisingly, the relatives of Moonie converts often become extremely upset about it. Ultimately, societal reaction is determined by the definition of a certain pattern of family relations as natural, right and proper; deviations from this norm are considered abnormal or even downright wicked (see also chapter 6).

In conclusion, we return to the question raised at the beginning of this section on new religious movements, concerning the relationship of these movements to the process of secularization. The new religions have recruited people who are not satisfied by the religious experience offered by the declining Christian churches. Where traditional religion remains a powerful force, as in Ireland, the new religions do not make much headway. Elsewhere, however, they appeal only to certain very small sections of the population, disproportionately young and middle class, who are likely to spend only a small part of their lives in the movement. In no sense, therefore, do the new religious movements in Britain compensate for the decline of the traditional religions or counteract the process of secularization.

Summary

1   There has been a process of secularization over the last century in Britain, at least as far as active participation in the Christian churches is concerned.

2   Although there has been, and is, such a process, it is still the case that a number of national events are organized around the church and significant numbers of people participate in religious, life-cycle rituals and hold beliefs privately that might be characterized as religious.

3   Although the main Christian churches are in decline, there has been a growth in a number of non-Christian sects and in newer branches of

Christianity. However, these groupings still only command the allegiance of a small proportion of the population.

4 New religious movements are very different from one another, having different outlooks, constituencies and methods of recruitment.

Further Reading

The best introductions to the study of the mass media come in the form of collections of articles. Two good recent readers are Curran et al. (1977) and Gurevitch et al. (1982). Leisure studies is a growing area but there is a shortage of basic textbooks. Parker (1976) is now rather old. A more deliberately argumentative book is Clarke and Critcher (1985). Sport is dealt with in the readings collected by Hargreaves (1982) and popular culture in Bennett et al. (1981).

Brake (1980) and Frith (1984) are good surveys of the whole field of youth culture, while Mungham and Pearson (1976) present a collection of articles on working-class youth culture. Wallis (1984) is a good introduction to the topic of religious secularization. Wilson (1981) is a collection of essays on new religious movements.

11 Deviance, Crime and Control

Today, institutions fundamental to the British system of government are under attack: the public schools, the House of Lords, the Church of England, the holy institution of marriage, and even our magnificent police force are no longer safe from those who would undermine our society. And it's about time we said 'enough is enough' and saw a return to the traditional British values of discipline, obedience, morality and freedom – freedom from the reds and the blacks and the criminals, prostitutes, pansies and punks, football hooligans, juvenile delinquents, lesbians and left-wing scum; freedom from the niggers, and the pakis and the unions, freedom from the gypsies and the Jews, freedom from the long-haired layabouts and students – freedom from the likes of you.

Tom Robinson Band, *Power in the Darkness*

11.1 Introduction

Social problems are inherently political phenomena. Social problems, in general, and deviant behaviour, in particular, are not objective 'givens' of social life, but are identified and shaped in an ongoing political process. We do not all agree on what is deviant behaviour. What is regarded as a problem by one group may not be seen in this way by another group in society. We are, therefore, engaged in a political process in which the values and interests of various groups are frequently in direct or indirect opposition to each other. The task – or perhaps the trick – of one group is to try to convince others that conditions which challenge their values or threaten their interests are objectively harmful and need to be corrected. In this sense, deviancy is created or socially constructed.

Police action against the travelling convoy of people wanting to hold a summer solstice festival at Stonehenge has received considerable media coverage in recent years. This is just one example of conflicting interests of landowners and travellers. Tim Greene, a London solicitor acting for many travellers charged after the police crackdown at Stonehenge, complained of the contrasting attitude of the Dorset police toward farmers and travellers: 'There is a one-sided view. Whatever the farmers do, whether it be carrying offensive weapons or threatening breaches of the peace, the police don't take action against them. . . But the minute members of the convoy – who have been very peaceful here today – take one step out of line they are arrested' (The *Guardian*, 2 June 1986). Certainly, those groups who command relatively greater power resources stand a much greater chance of seeing their particular definitions of deviance accepted widely and of having their favoured solutions or strategies put into practice.

A 'revolution' has taken place in the sociology of deviance since the 1960s. This has involved the rejection of absolutist definitions of deviant behaviour (which assume that everyone agrees about what is deviant) in favour of an approach that sees such behaviour as that which is defined or labelled in a particular way. This approach does not endear sociologists to those in power, for power-holders are in the business of trying to make their own definitions of deviance hold. It is not in their interests for the idea to get around that deviance is a relative concept and that there may be alternative versions of reality.

The two major insights regarding deviance that sociologists have recognized since the 1960s are, *first*, that the explanation of crime and deviance is logically bound up with the explanation of social control and, *second*, that we need to re-establish the links between crime and the political, which orthodox criminology totally neglected. So, instead of focusing exclusively on the controlled (the criminal, the delinquent, the mentally ill, the mentally retarded and so on), sociologists are now as much concerned – if not more so – with the controllers (the police, judiciary, medical profession, etc.).

However, it was recognized by sociologists that this was still too narrow an area of analysis. In short, the links between crime and the political became more explicitly drawn into sociological analysis with the advent of the 'new criminology' that emerged in the 1970s. The appreciation of the theoretical and empirical links between deviance and control, which was certainly the hallmark of the work of the American sociologists, Becker (1963), Matza (1964) and Lemert (1967), was challenged in the 1970s by a group of radical young British sociologists. This was the first time that theoretical ideas about deviance had been exported from Britain to the USA instead of the other way round. The emergence of radical or critical criminology, associated most closely with Taylor, Walton and Young (1973, 1975), called for an even greater theoretical and empirical widening of scope and, by implication, for a more radical politics. To use an analogy, traditional criminology tends to look at the animals in the zoo; the 1970s saw the development of an interest in those who controlled the animals (the police, the judiciary and so on), while more recently there has been a resurgence of interest in who exactly owns the zoo! Box 25 illustrates the links between the deviant, social-control agencies and the victim; recent work has stressed that we cannot afford to overlook the political context in which these interactions take place.

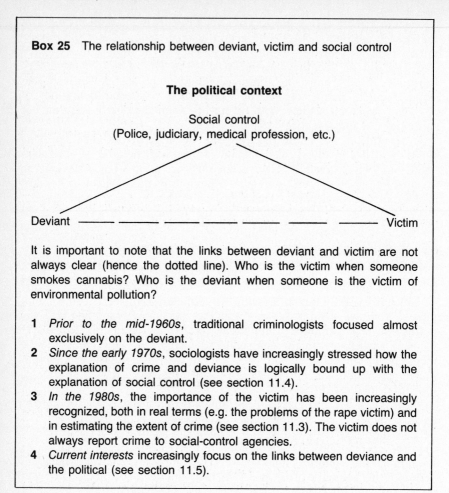

Box 25   The relationship between deviant, victim and social control

The political context

Social control
(Police, judiciary, medical profession, etc.)

Deviant ———— ———— ———— ———— ———— ———— ———— Victim

It is important to note that the links between deviant and victim are not always clear (hence the dotted line). Who is the victim when someone smokes cannabis? Who is the deviant when someone is the victim of environmental pollution?

1 *Prior to the mid-1960s*, traditional criminologists focused almost exclusively on the deviant.
2 *Since the early 1970s*, sociologists have increasingly stressed how the explanation of crime and deviance is logically bound up with the explanation of social control (see section 11.4).
3 *In the 1980s*, the importance of the victim has been increasingly recognized, both in real terms (e.g. the problems of the rape victim) and in estimating the extent of crime (see section 11.3). The victim does not always report crime to social-control agencies.
4 *Current interests* increasingly focus on the links between deviance and the political (see section 11.5).

Despite some differences in approach among sociologists, there is a growing tendency to stress the political nature of deviance and to structure empirical investigations around this emphasis. However, while all deviance may be *essentially* political, some deviance may *appear* to be more or less so in the eyes of observers, whether they be sociologists or lay persons: there is a variation in the degree of the *overt* political emphasis that may be observed in particular cases. At any given point in time, some issues excite considerable disagreement, while others seem to command a basic consensus.

11.2 Varieties of Deviance

A Canadian criminologist, Hagan (1984), has developed a framework that identifies the varieties of deviance. From the starting point of defining deviance as a variation from a social norm, he argues that we should think of deviance as a continuous variable. Quite simply, there is an obvious difference between multiple murder and adolescent marijuana use. He suggests that most deviant acts can be located empirically on a continuum of seriousness between these two extremes. Hogan identifies three measures of seriousness:

1 *The degree of agreement about the wrongfulness of the act*. This assessment can vary from confusion and apathy, through high levels of disagreement, to conditions of general agreement.
2 *The severity of the social reponse elicited by the act*. Social penalties can, of course, vary from life imprisonment to polite avoidance.
3 *Societal evaluation of the harm inflicted by the act*. Here the concern is with the degree of victimization and the personal and social harm a set of acts may involve.

Hagan argues that, in most modern societies, these three measures of seriousness are closely connected. So, what he is saying is that the more serious acts of deviance are those likely to evoke broad agreement about their wrongfulness, a severe social response, and an evaluation of the act as being very harmful. This approach provides insights but is also contentious. Hagan portrays the situation in visual terms as a pyramid, with the less-serious forms of deviance at the base and the more-serious forms of deviance at the peak (see figure 11.1). This is an interesting notion, for the form of a pyramid suggests that the most serious acts of deviance in a society tend also to be less frequent while less serious acts may be quite common. However, Hagan's framework provides a useful basis from which to consider the current British situation.

Hagan's major division is between criminal and non-criminal forms of deviance. In fact, he argues that 'the most serious forms of deviance are defined by law as criminal'. This can certainly be challenged, for one of the arguments of the radical criminologists is that the powerful manage to avoid some of *their* more dangerous activities either being proscribed (that is, forbidden) by criminal law or, if included, the sanctions are ludicrously light (such as small fines). For example, environmental pollution, health and safety in factories and unethical business practices, can adversely affect vast numbers in the population. However, the criminal law is either not operative in these areas or is not enforced to any significant degree.

What are generally regarded as *consensus crimes* – murder, rape,

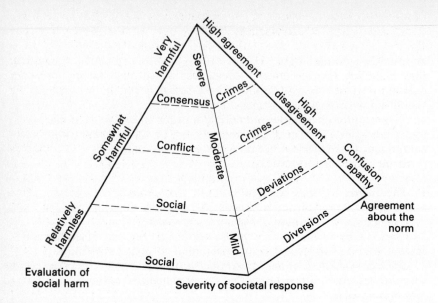

Figure 11.1   Varieties of deviance
Source: From *The Disreputable Pleasures* by John Hagan, p. 111. Copyright © McGraw-Hill Ryerson Limited 1984. Reproduced with permission.

robbery, etc. – are those that outrage and scare the public. One of the effects of the women's movement has been to make us all much more aware of the seriousness of the offence of rape, so that many people now – not just women – think the problem of rape should be tackled much more seriously and, where appropriate, offenders should be punished much more severely than they are at present.

Conflict crimes are activities about which public opinion is more divided. Social class and various interest groups may well be the source of such conflict. With these offences, there are examples of how the criminal law can be used by one class or interest group to the disadvantage of another.

There are a whole range of conflict crimes. Hagan includes public disorder offences (e.g. vagrancy, creating a public disturbance), chemical offences (e.g. alcohol and drug offences), political crimes (e.g. espionage, terrorism and conspiracy), minor property offences (e.g. petty theft, vandalism) and the 'rights-to-life' offences (e.g. abortion, euthanasia). In many ways, these contain the most interesting varieties of deviance for, as Hagan stresses, the feature that unites these offences is the public debate that surrounds them. In short, 'we lack societal consensus on the dimensions of public disorder, the use of comforting chemicals, permissible politics, the protection of private property and the limits of life' (p. 16). While Hagan applies his framework to Canada, it is equally, if not more, true of contemporary British society. In the second half of the 1980s, we are in the midst of debates at varying levels about all these areas. The miners' strike, the Campaign for Nuclear Disarmament, Greenham Common women, the Irish question, drug addiction, abortion, and so on, have all raised issues about the use and appropriateness of the criminal law as a weapon in social conflict.

One important point that should be recognized is that persons involved in conflict crimes are less likely than those who commit consensus crimes to differ in significant ways from the general population. In brief, there is probably nothing distinctive about political criminals apart from the fact that they happen to have been identified as current or potential political threats. While those in power often try to give pejorative labels to those who oppose their policies – 'troublemakers', 'mad', 'wicked', 'evil', and so on – this is simply part of the political game of defining deviance. In contrast, a person who kills his or her mother – a consensus but, fortunately, rare crime – is much more likely to suffer from some form of psychiatric disorder that makes him or her differ in significant ways from the general population. In short, a psychological explanation is much more likely to be useful for this type of crime, while the political context is likely to be much more important than personality in considering political crime.

Criminal forms of deviance depend for their definition on the *formal* processes of control – police, courts, prisons, etc. – while non-criminal forms of deviance depend for their definition on the *informal* processes of social control, such as the family, peer groups and other community groups.

Hagan considers two types of non-criminal forms of deviance, which he terms *social deviations* and *social diversions*. The distinction is not precise, but examples of *social deviations* would be psycho-social disturbances, the violation of trust and various adolescent pranks. The crucial point is that these activities and experiences are not considered criminal but are, nonetheless, disreputable. In contrast, *social diversions* tend to be frequent and faddish activities but which are not always looked upon favourably. Certain symbolic diversions (styles of dress, speech and mannerisms) are sometimes used in the development of stereotypes as indicators of more serious forms of deviance but, in themselves, are usually harmless.

Changes in definitions of deviant behaviour

Before leaving Hagan's pyramid, it is important to underline one point. As it stands, the pyramid, like the pyramids of Egypt, looks rather static. In studying deviance, however, it is crucial to recognize that there are significant shifts in what holds the centre of the stage of political debate. As Hagan stresses, probably the most important change that can occur in the societal evaluation of an act involves the movement of that act from criminal to non-criminal status. In the 1960s and early 1970s, there was much debate about and some action in decriminalizing certain activities. The so-called 'victimless' crimes were the main focus of this change, in particular, abortion, homosexuality and soft-drug use. Changes in the law have undoubtedly made some difference here. Abortion is now available in a much wider range of situations than prior to the 1967 Abortion Act; homosexuality – while still more restricted by law than heterosexual activity – is no longer outlawed in the way prior to the passing of the 1967 Sexual Offences Act; while the penalties for the possession of soft drugs have considerably reduced since the mid-1960s. Nevertheless, a cursory glance at newspapers or even a brief listen to neighbourhood gossip hardly suggests that such activities are totally acceptable. Having an abortion, declaring yourself homosexual or even smoking pot can still be personally hazardous.

The focus on mugging and football hooliganism in the 1970s illustrates how interest seems to shift. One needs to ask whether the nature of deviance or the focus of attention has changed. Like all such questions, there is no easy answer to this.

Patterns of deviance can change *and* shifts of focus can take place, but neither happens as drastically as we are sometimes led to believe. The developing interest in historical criminology is important in this respect. Historical research can indicate that a supposedly 'new' moral panic such as football hooliganism is not a startlingly new phenomenon. A study by Pearson (1983) has exploded the myth that street crime and hooliganism are the product of a permissive society or evidence of rapid moral decline from the stable traditions of the past. Pearson stresses the violent realities of street life in the past. He shows that successive generations have voiced identical fears of social breakdown and moral degeneration. In his lively and fascinating study, we can begin to identify the parallels between the 'garotters' and the original 'Hooligan' gangs of late Victorian London with the 'muggers' of contemporary urban streets. Pearson discovered that the word 'hooligan' made an abrupt entrance into common English usage, as a term to describe gangs of rowdy youths, during the hot summer of 1898. However, as figure 11.2 shows, there was clearly considerable unease about what was happening fifty years earlier, in the 1850s.

In the 1970s, 'new' kinds of deviance were identified. For example, baby-battering, wife-battering, even granny-bashing, have had their media coverage but one suspects that the 'newness' of these activities is more a feature of their becoming noticed. Nonetheless, there is no doubt that a focus on a specific activity, particularly by the media, can have the outcome of changing the phenomenon.

Currently, in the 1980s, there has been much more concern about the increasing criminalization of activities that were previously considered to be legitimate forms of dissent. We return later to this aspect when we consider legislation affecting public order.

Figure 11.2 'A Briton in time of peace', a cartoon from *Punch*, 1856
Source: Punch.

Summary

1 There are varieties of deviance. The major division is between criminal and non-criminal forms of deviance.

2 Crimes divide into consensus crimes (which outrage and scare the public) and conflict crimes (where public opinion is much more divided about the appropriate status of such crimes). Non-criminal forms of deviance are divided into social deviations and social diversions.

3 There are significant shifts in definitions of deviance over time. The most important shift involves the movement from criminal to non-criminal status. Historical research often indicates that a supposedly 'new' moral panic, such as football hooliganism, is not necessarily a startlingly new phenomenon.

11.3   Crime Statistics

There are a whole set of problems in studying official rates of deviance. Crime figures may well tell you more about the organizations that produce the figures than the actual occurrence of crime and deviance.

Sociologists have warned (and to some extent the message has got through) of the dangers of reading too much into the official crime figures. However, the general elections of 1979 and 1983 both had the backcloth of a 'law-and-order' campaign and even a cursory glance at the newspapers today suggests that the media will back politicians in continuing to make rising crime-rates a major issue.

Sociologists have somewhat diverse views on the value of official statistics in resolving debates about the extent of deviance and the social origins of deviants. Some continue to stress that official crime statistics are seriously misleading, owing to the vast numbers of crimes that are not reported to the police (known as the 'dark figure'). Other criminologists think that some of the criticisms of the official statistics have been exaggerated, arguing that crime statistics do reflect a reality. After all, they argue, what is so surprising about a disproportionate number of working-class people appearing in the crime statistics? Radical sociologists tend to believe that the law is essentially a 'class law' (that is, operating against the interests of the working class), so, of course, one would expect this to be the case.

The intricacies of the construction of official crime statistics are dealt with quite adequately in several texts (e.g. Box, 1981), but we still need to face basic questions such as the extent of crime, who is at risk and how we should handle the fear of crime. Hough and Mayhew (1983) indicate the interrelationship of these factors (p. 22):

> Increasingly it is being said that fear of crime in Britain is becoming as great a problem as crime itself. Criminologists suggest that preoccupation with crime is out of all proportion to the risks; that fear is needlessly reducing the quality of people's lives; and that fear of crime can itself lead to crime – by turning cities at night into empty, forbidding places.

The British Crime Surveys

A major development in the 1980s which enables us to probe more accurately some of these issues was the decision by the Conservative government in mid-1981 to carry out the first national survey of crime victimization. Surveys of victimization involve asking samples of the general population about crimes (whether or not reported to the police) that may have been committed against them in some preceding period (usually a year). They provide a measure of crime much closer to reality than the statistics of offences recorded by the police.

Two British Crime Surveys (Hough and Mayhew, 1983, 1985) have now been carried out. In the early part of 1982 and 1984, one person aged 16 and over was interviewed in each of about 11,000 households in England and Wales (in 1982, 5,000 households in Scotland were also included). They were asked whether they had been victims of various offences during the previous year – 1981 for the first survey and 1983 for the second. These surveys bring us much closer to assessing the real rate of any increase (or decrease) in the level of crime. Until the arrival of the British Crime Survey, we had to rely on police and court statistics which are published annually under the title *Criminal Statistics*. In truth, these provide a useful index of the workload of the police and a record of the working of the court system, but are not a reliable indicator of crime levels.

The value of the British Crime Surveys is that they yield estimates of the extent of various crimes that include incidents unreported to the police. They cover violence against the person, theft of, and damage to, private property. Figure 11.3 shows British Crime Survey estimates of the number of criminal incidents in 1983, by crime type.

What becomes quite evident from figure 11.3 is that the vast majority of crimes do not involve violence against the person but are offences against *property*. Together, crimes of violence and common assault comprised 17 per cent of the total. The message that emerges from this is that, while serious crimes of violence certainly occurred, in numerical terms they were overshadowed by the large number of comparatively trivial offences, particularly involving motor vehicles. In most thefts – whether or not they involved motor vehicles – losses were relatively low, exceeding £50 in only about a quarter of cases. Both the British Crime Surveys showed an inverse relationship between the severity and the frequency of incidents. This last finding, of course, gives some support for Hagan's use of the pyramid structure in considering varieties of deviance (figure 11.1).

In a fascinating manner, the British Crime Survey enables us to probe the dark figure of unreported and unrecorded crime. Figure 11.4 shows unreported incidents, those that were reported but not recorded, and those that found their way into police records. The interesting feature is the varying ratio of recorded and unrecorded crime. Except for thefts of motor vehicles, a large proportion of incidents went unreported for all types of crime. The survey indicated twice as many burglaries as were actually recorded by the police; three times as much theft from motor vehicles; and thirteen times as much vandalism.

There is no doubt that the British Crime Surveys are a tremendous advance in helping us to understand the extent and other dimensions of crime. However, we still need to recognize some of their possible limitations or at least where we need to exercise caution. For example, the surveys have had considerable difficulty in probing the number of offences against women – 'wife battering', indecent assault, attempted

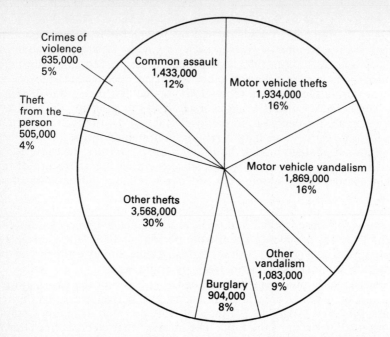

Figure 11.3 Offences in England and Wales, 1983, British Crime Survey estimates

Note: *'Crimes of violence' comprise wounding, robbery and sexual offences. (Unlike common assault, these are all 'notifiable' offences.) 'Motor-vehicle thefts' include attempted thefts. 'Other thefts' comprise personal thefts not involving contact with an offender, together with thefts in a dwelling, bicycle thefts and other household thefts not involving vehicles.*

Source: Hough and Mayhew (1985), p. 10.

rape and actual rape. In the first survey, the number of sexual offences was clearly an underestimate for at least two kinds of reason. Respondents may be reluctant to relive a painful or embarrassing experience for the benefit of a survey interviewer. Furthermore, with domestic violence, their assailant may be in the same room at the time of the interview. The questions about sexual attack were changed for the second British Crime Survey, but it still seems unlikely that it probed this area very accurately. The estimate for rape, for example, remained remarkably low – each survey uncovered only one attempted rape amongst its respondents.

In contrast, studies conducted by the women's movement show much more disturbing figures. A survey directed by Hall (1985) indicated that more than one in six women questioned in the survey claimed to have been the victim of a rape. In fact, this survey claims that nearly 1 in 3

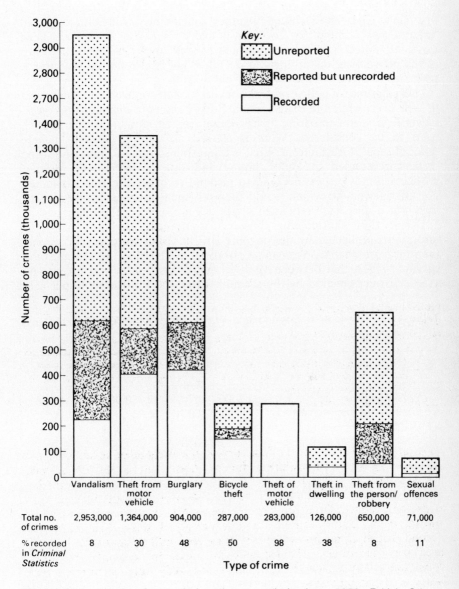

Figure 11.4 Levels of recorded and unrecorded crime, 1983, British Crime Survey estimates

women had been sexually assaulted, 1 in 5 had survived an attempted rape, and nearly 1 in every 100 had been raped by a gang or more than one man. The figures taken together – including legally unrecognized 'marital rape' – show that 2 women in every 5 said they had experienced rape, attempted rape or sexual assault at least once. The reporting rates to the police were disturbingly low. Only 8 per cent reported rape to the police and 18 per cent reported sexual assault.

Hall's figures, of course, refer to sexual assaults on women *at any point in their lives*, while the British Crime Survey refers to *one particular year*. Nevertheless, in comparing figures there are considerable dangers which need to be considered. What is classed as 'rape'? Does it include 'marital rape', for example? What is the response rate? 62 per cent of the women responded in Hall's survey and one needs to ask whether particular kinds of persons tend to respond to questionnaires. If women are interviewed, to whom would they tell such intimate details of their lives which may have remained secret but are never forgotten?

Despite these shortcomings, however, there is considerable value in the information collected by the ongoing British Crime Surveys, for we can then measure change. We can see from table 11.1 that the victimization surveys suggest that between 1981 (when the first survey was taken) and 1983 (the year covered by the second), there was an overall 10 per cent

Table 11.1 Offences in England and Wales, 1981 and 1983, British Crime Survey estimates

	1981	1983	% change
1 Vandalism	2,714,000	2,953,000	+ 9
2 Theft from motor vehicle	1,272,000	1,364,000	+ 7
3 Burglary in a dwelling	745,000	904,000	+ 21
4 Theft of a motor vehicle	283,000	283,000	—
5 Bicycle theft	214,000	287,000	+ 34
6 Theft in a dwelling	124,000	126,000	+ 2
7 Other household thefts	1,535,000	1,671,000	+ 9
8 Assault	1,909,000	1,852,000	− 3
9 Theft from person/robbery	596,000	650,000	+ 9
10 Sexual offences	33,000	71,000	[+115][a]
11 Other personal thefts	1,559,000	1,770,000	+ 14
All household offences (1–7 above)	6,887,000	7,588,000	+ 10
All personal offences (8–11 above)	4,097,000	4,343,000	+ 6

Note: [a] Due to questionnaire changes.
Source: Hough and Mayhew (1985), p. 14. Crown copyright.

rise in the number of household offences, while offences against the person rose by 6 per cent. The various offence categories show quite a range of shifts between 1981 and 1983.

The 21 per cent increase in burglary reflects a rapid rise in the number of burglary *attempts*; when these are excluded, there is then a much smaller increase, of 11 per cent. The increase in bicycle theft could be partly the result of increased ownership for, as the authors of the British Crime Survey point out, the vogue for BMX bikes only emerged after 1981. However, it needs to be stressed that the apparent increase in sexual offences is unreliable for, as mentioned previously, there were deliberate changes in the questionnaire that make direct comparisons between the surveys somewhat suspect.

Fears of crime

While the surveys tell us nothing about the psychological effect of being a victim, they do locate various fears about crime. For example, one in nine women under 30 thought it very or fairly likely that they would be raped in the next year. Nearly one out of six people felt themselves likely to be a victim of mugging. In general, the survey found that fear of crime was widespread and intruded into people's routine behaviour. Fear of crime may make people alter their lives. They may decide to remain indoors at night. They may also stay away from certain streets or areas after dark. In fact, the results from the surveys help to explain what has been a curious outcome of previous studies – that *those who are the most fearful are the least victimized*. Part of the explanation for this apparent anomaly is, of course, that fear leads many people to avoid risky situations and thereby to minimize their chances of being a victim.

In reality, the biggest single area of risk of crime is with motor vehicles. In 1983, one in five owners experienced some form of vehicle crime. 94 per cent of those who had valuables taken from their cars never got the property back, but 70 per cent of the vehicles stolen were recovered. The interpretation of such figures is, of course, hazardous. Fear is not simply about frequency. For example, being the victim of one vehicle crime a year is perhaps little more than a nuisance, while being raped once in a lifetime is a traumatic event that will never be forgotten.

Hidden 'crime'

It is crucial to remember that what criminologists and politicians pay attention to is not necessarily the most serious kinds of deviance. In the 1950s and 1960s, criminologists paid enormous attention to youth gangs, but this interest cannot be explained completely by the actual seriousness of gang delinquency and its extent relative to other kinds of delinquency. In the 1970s, mugging and football hooliganism occupied a disproportionate amount of media attention. While it would be foolish to deny that

Box 26   Some findings from the British Crime Survey on the extent and sources of fear of crime

* Women, the elderly and those in inner cities registered most anxiety about walking alone in their neighbourhood after dark. Fear of falling victim to robbery or 'mugging' plays a large part here, though more diffuse and unfocused anxieties appear to be implicated too.

* Asked how worried they were about different crimes, women expressed most fear of rape. Four out of ten women under 30 said they were 'very worried'. Aside from the alarming nature of the offence, exaggerated estimates of its likelihood may underpin some of this worry.

* Burglary causes widespread anxiety, in particular among women. The degree of worry in different areas tracks actual burglary risks, suggesting that most people have some grasp of the *relative* likelihood of break-ins. On the poorest council estates, where risks were highest – 19 attempted and actual break-ins per 100 homes in 1983 – four out of ten residents said they were 'very worried' about burglary.

* Even so, people in all areas tended to exaggerate the risks of burglary. Over half of respondents saw it as the most common crime in their area. Overestimation of actual risks is highest in areas where burglary is relatively infrequent, and those who overestimate most express most anxiety.

* Worry about becoming the victim of 'mugging' is as widespread among women as worry about burglary, though relative to other age-groups neither elderly men nor women appeared disproportionately worried. Again, people overestimated the risks of mugging: nearly one in six people thought they were very or fairly likely to be a victim in the next year.

* Fear of crime restricts people's behaviour. Half the women in the sample, for instance, said they avoided going out unaccompanied after dark; in high-crime areas one person in 25 said they *never* went out after dark wholly or in part because of fear of crime. The figure for the elderly in these localities was 18%.

* Across the country as a whole, crime and vandalism are outranked as the worst problems of local areas by other social and environmental factors. However, crime and vandalism takes the lead in multi-racial areas and in the poorest council estates. Crime levels and fear of crime were also highest in these areas. (Hough and Mayhew, 1985, p. 41. Crown copyright.)

these problems exist, they may not be so widespread as the media and the politicians tend to suggest. Indeed, there are other hazards for the community that do not figure in the criminal statistics but are potentially much more serious and widespread in their effects.

Environmental pollution, health and safety in factories, and even unethical business practices, may be much more crucial to the survival and well-being of the community than many of the issues highlighted by the media and the politicians. However, it is difficult to find such activities recorded in *Criminal Statistics* and those who design victimization surveys usually fail to consider these kinds of problems. More importantly, though – and this illustrates the most serious drawback of victimization surveys – what happens if people are not even aware that they are victims? For example, environmental pollution may be affecting everyone, but if no one notices, then there can be no record. To do something about deviance, one must know that it exists. However, is visibility the only issue?

There are increasing challenges to the commonly accepted notion that the job of the criminal law is to protect *all* the members of society. Questions about who makes the law and who really benefits from it have led to the view that, in fact, the criminal law does not serve the interests of the majority in society, but only appears to do so. It is suggested that the criminal law is virtually dictated by small and powerful groups in society and, as a result, serves the interests of these groups and works against the interests of larger but much less-powerful ones. Certainly, much of the activity of large, powerful organizations, such as companies and corporations, is potentially very dangerous, but it is not covered by the harsh rigours of the criminal law. We need to recognize the ability of transnational corporations to shape new legislation relating to their corporate activities. This clearly enables corporations to prevent some of the avoidable deaths, injuries and economic deprivation they sometimes cause from being included in the criminal law and, as a consequence, in crime statistics. In this sense, then, crime statistics and victimization surveys provide evidence of the extent of only a *particular* kind of deviance and, certainly, not necessarily the most dangerous and destructive behaviour.

Summary

1 Official crime statistics may indicate more about the work of the organizations producing the figures than the actual occurrence of crime and deviance.

2 Surveys of crime victimization show an inverse relationship between the severity and the frequency of incidents of crime. The vast majority of crimes do *not* involve violence against the person but are offences against property.

3 There is a varying ratio of recorded and unrecorded crime ('the dark figure'). The British Crime Surveys indicate twice as many burglaries as were actually recorded by the police; three times as much theft from motor vehicles; and thirteen times as much vandalism.

4 The occurence of offences against women – 'wife battering', indecent assault and rape – is very difficult to estimate accurately.

5 Those who are most fearful of crime are the least victimized. Part of the explanation is that fear leads many people to avoid risky situations and, thereby, to minimize their chances of becoming victims.

6 Official statistics and victimization surveys only provide evidence of particular kinds of deviance. Other, corporate, activity that is potentially dangerous may not be covered by the harsh rigours of the criminal law.

11.4 Law Enforcement

Social-control agencies

Since the 1970s, there has been a new interest in the societal response to acts and persons labelled deviant. There are a wide range of agencies involved in formal social control, ranging from the police, judiciary and prison service to other agencies less obviously part of the control framework, namely social workers and the medical profession. The focus has largely been on the decision-making activities of agencies of social control. There has been increasing concern about structurally generated injustices, reflected in class prejudice, racism and sexism. Questions have been raised about the assumed prejudice of decision-makers and there has been an increasing recognition – though not by government – of the limited access of socially disadvantaged persons to resources for their protection.

It is important, first of all, to identify a typical sequence of agency responses to deviance, starting with initial detection and going through to the final outcome. An important contribution of sociologists has been to indicate the processes by which social control itself can play a considerable part in transforming a 'normal' person into a 'deviant'. Box (1981) usefully summarizes much of the work that identifies the bureaucratic and social processes through which an individual becomes officially registered as deviant.

Figure 11.5 identifies the major stages in becoming deviant as well as – and most importantly – routes *out* of deviance. Sociologists have become known for suggesting that social control may well lead to further deviance, but it would be foolish to think this was an inevitable process. Nevertheless, the crucial point remains that, as each cycle of offence → detection → punishment → stigmatization is completed

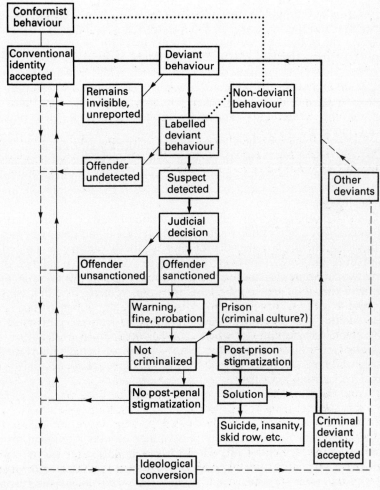

Figure 11.5 The bureaucratic and social process of becoming an official deviant

Source: Box (1981) *Deviance, Reality and Society*, 2nd edn (London, Cassell), p. 21. Reproduced with permission.

(follow the thick black line in figure 11.5), the chances of the next cycle are increased.

In terms of criminal deviance the two most important 'gatekeepers' are the police and the judiciary. In the Western world, there has been much work on the police as guardians of 'public morality', particularly on what happens during the 'on-the-street' encounters with suspects or suspicious persons. Box (1981) points out that it is when the policeman is in the community that *his* discretion is widest. Backing up the police as guardians of moral boundaries are 'judges and magistrates who have considerable discretionary space to display enough of their personal, social and political sympathies when arriving at verdicts and dispensing sentences for us to glimpse a disturbing truth beyond our proud myths about fair justice' (p. 178). In general terms, Box's concern is that '*when processing individuals who have behaved similarly*, the judicial system will discriminate against some, particularly the poor, the unemployed, and the ethnically oppressed' (p. 180).

There is nothing new in this phenomenon. In other words, the poor, the unemployed and ethnic minorities always get a bad deal, whether one is focusing on the last decades of the twentieth century or indeed any other time or place. However, we wish to consider two related issues. Some would argue that these are making the situation worse, while others maintain that they provide the basis for improvement. The first concerns policing in Britain, which is said to be undergoing its biggest change for half a century. The second focuses on whether we have embarked on a progressive programme in which non-custodial measures, rather than imprisonment, have become the central plank of penal policy. In both cases, optimists are encouraged by the changes, while pessimists view them with serious concern.

The police

In the sense that deviance can only be understood as a political process, then, of course, any form of policing becomes political. The notion that the police may be serving a political function rather than occupying an independent role between conflicting groups has been the focus of considerable public debate in the 1980s. No longer can the government of the day expect us to accept without question the idea that the police are necessarily acting for the general welfare of the community. There has been much controversy over the role of the police in recent riot situations and, even more problematic, in some industrial disputes. Certainly, the police have been, quite literally, in the middle of disputes between various sections of the community in ways not previously experienced in post-war Britain. Furthermore, because of the presence of television in virtually every home, these encounters between police and protesters have been witnessed by a much wider audience than ever before. In some situations, the police have been accused of simply being the agents of the government, helping to impose a particular industrial and economic strategy upon the nation. Such accusations have deeply concerned some members of the police force, who do not regard their task as helping to carry out the political will of the government in this way. There is quite widespread concern that the police are being drawn into the political arena.

The police have shifted quite dramatically since the 1970s from having a comparatively low profile in society to being a high-profile occupation. The riots of 1981, followed by the Scarman Report (1981) and the controversial policing of the 1984 miners' strike, produced examples of police action that indicate that police rule in contemporary society is in need of reappraisal. The police themselves have increasingly proclaimed their own particular views in public debates about social control in ways which would previously have been unthought of.

The two major issues that underpin debates on changing police behaviour are the growth of professionalism within the police and whether there has been a shift from consensus policing (that is, policing by consent) to something much more akin to military policing. Even more dramatically, some commentators are asking whether Britain is turning into a police state.

The development of 'professional' policing

Much of the discussion about increased professionalization of the police stems from the appointment of Sir Robert Mark as Commissioner of the Metropolitan Police in the early 1970s. Mark claimed the support of a 'long tradition of constitutional freedom from political interference in our operational role . . . the police are not servants of government at any level. We do not act at the behest of a minister or any political party, not even the party in government. We act on behalf of the people as a whole' (quoted in Reiner, 1985, p. 1).

One of the crucial, indeed defining, characteristics of a profession is that it is a body that can claim significant autonomy in the ordering of its own affairs. The reclaiming of police status and authority under the banner of professionalism has helped to free chief constables from the constraints of their local police authority. As a result, this has allowed the formulation and implementation of policing policies with virtually no public consultation. Some chief constables have handled controversial situations, such as riots and the policing of certain industrial disputes, particularly the miners' strike of 1984, in such a way that they have been challenged by local police authorities concerned about the lack of control over the actions of their chief constables.

So, whether by design or as an unintended consequence, professionalization has led the police away from public control and influence towards an increasingly political role. However, as Holdaway (1983) has pointed out, public control of the police has always been less than has been generally assumed.

Inside the British police; a case-study

In recent years there have been quite dramatic changes in the nature of policing and Holdaway's (1983) work captures many of these developments. This is essentially an ethnography of an urban police sub-division at work. It is an attempt to map out police organization, laying bare the assumptions that police officers make about their routine work.

The police, like the prison service, are a disciplined force similar in structure to the military. Holdaway has argued that the traditional militaristic style of command in the police has changed quite dramatically to one of 'management'. More specifically, he identifies the shift to one of 'managerial professionalism'. While discipline in the force has remained paramount, it is now maintained more by persuasion, consultation and encouragement than by enforcing blind obedience to authoritative commands.

There has been greater specialization in the police force and the importance of the growth of technology should not be underestimated. However, what Holdaway highlights as perhaps the most striking feature of his participant observation study of policing was the continuing dominance of the occupational values of the lower ranks. Curiously, the occupational culture of policing maintained by the lower ranks – the 'cop culture' – had clearly survived the various changes associated with the introduction of professional policing.

Holdaway relates a whole series of police anecdotes, stories and jokes that feed and sustain this occupational culture. They may be true; they may sometimes be false – accuracy is not the point of the humour and the numerous tales that are told. The task is to ensure that the perspective of the lower ranks survives despite various onslaughts. Holdaway regards the questioning of prisoners as one of the areas of police work where there is a clear separation between the 'working practices' of certain officers and the requirements of formal policy and law, and this provides fodder for humour and narrative (pp. 148–9):

> After his annual appraisal interview with the Chief Superintendent, a constable returns to duty in the station. A colleague asks: 'How did you get on?'
>
> *PC:* Fine, fine. 'Enthusiastic' I am, you know.
>
> Both officers laugh.
>
> *Colleague:* Yes, really enthusiastic.
>
> *Officer interviewed:* Professional ability, nil. Appearance, nil, grotesque. Yes, but he can't half hit prisoners.

Both laugh.

Holdaway's message is that there have been both continuities and changes in the police service. More specifically, he maintains that the development of professional policing has resulted in a greater freedom for all ranks of the force. Chief and senior officers articulate and implement policies appropriate to managerial professionalism and this, in turn, frees them from significant public constraint. More perniciously, however, the old views and practices of the rank-and-file police officers – though often in opposition to the publicly stated intentions of managerial policy – can actually persist in greater comfort by hiding under the powerful symbolic cloak of professionalism.

Thus, Holdaway points to the potential resistance of the lower ranks in the police service as a greater stumbling block to reform than is generally appreciated. In other words, the lower ranks are still able to undermine any new systems that are introduced by modifying them so that their own interpretations of police work remain dominant.

Consensus policing versus military policing

At the time Holdaway was completing his fieldwork in the late 1970s, it was unlikely that he could have envisaged some of the conditions under which police officers were to be called to work in the mid-1980s. Reiner (1985) to whom we will return later, has argued that, since the 1981 riots, there has been a significant redirection of police thinking and strategy. There is evidence of attempts by some sections of the police to be seen as less overtly political. However, with the effects of Conservative government policy becoming more apparent, particularly following the 1983 election, the chances of any redirection of police thinking being recognized as a shift towards a lower profile have been slim. Several commentators, far from recognizing any shift of emphasis from the strident tones of the 1970s, have come close to suggesting that the police were actively encouraging and welcoming the tougher approach of the Conservative government and, in certain respects, this seemed to resemble the growth of a police state.

Paradoxically, while Holdaway has argued that the militaristic style of command traditionally associated with police structures has over recent years shifted quite dramatically to one of 'managerial professionalism', others have noted what Lea and Young (1985) describe as a drift to military policing. However, it is important to distinguish between the nature of the police command structure, which may well be less militaristic than formerly, and the military style of policing practice, which some argue has become prevalent in certain areas.

Lea and Young stress that the harrassment of the public, or at least sections of it (particularly the black community) is a major political issue in Britain today. The enquiry carried out by Lord Scarman characterized the Brixton riots of 1981 as 'a spontaneous act of defiant aggression by young men who felt themselves hunted by a hostile police force'. It went on to note that 'the weight of criticism and complaint against the police is so considerable that it alone must give grave cause for concern' (quoted in Lea and Young, 1985, p. 65).

In an attempt to identify what has been happening to policing, particularly in the inner-city areas, and in areas with a high concentration of ethnic minorities, Lea and Young contrast two general types or styles of policing – consensus and military policing. They identify three major differences between these contrasting styles of policing, in terms of the support of the community, the flow of information, and the role of stereotypes. These contrasts are set out in box 27.

Box 27   Consensus and military policing

Consensus policing

1 Policing with the *support* of the community. The community supports the police because it sees them as doing a socially useful job. They are protecting the community against crime and crime is something that the community recognizes as harmful to its well-being.

2 Because of the support, there is a reasonably *high flow of information* concerning crime. People do come forward with information.

3 All policing involves the use of *stereotypes* to some degree. The more information is provided, however, the more the police can begin their investigations following actual leads and the *less* recourse there is to stereotypes as the basis for starting investigations.

Military policing

1 Policing *without* consent. Here the community does not support the police because it sees them as a socially or politically oppressive force in no way fulfilling any protective functions.

2 The flow of information to the police concerning 'crime' can be expected to *approach zero*. Hence, instead of 'certainty of detection', much police activity will consist of random harassment. The community may develop a type of surrogate policing, such as vigilante squads, which may operate clandestinely.

3 *Maximal use of stereotypes*, for example, beliefs develop that 'all blacks are criminal'.

Consensus and military policing in their pure forms are polar extremes: policing in most situations falls between these two extremes. It is fair to say that, in certain inner-city areas, consensus policing may never have existed in anything like its pure form. Nevertheless, Lea and Young are suggesting that policing practices in the inner city are moving away from something that was closer to consensus policing. There have always been areas the police have regarded as being more crime-prone than others. But recent policing practices in these areas have moved closer to the model of military policing. The kinds of police actions that encourage the view that such a shift is taking place include random stopping and searching, raids on youth clubs and houses and operations that involve the use of the more explicitly 'military' sections of the police, such as the Special Patrol Groups.

Causes of changes in policing

Lea and Young (1985) next focus on why these kinds of changes have been taking place. They note that the obvious explanation would be to point to the generalized recession of the capitalist economy, the emergence of long-term structural unemployment among youth in general and black youth, in particular. It could be argued that there is no longer a willingness to acquiesce to poverty, discrimination and lives of despair, and that young people today have been conditioned through the mass media and the education system to expect something better from life. From this point of view, the move towards military policing in inner cities is part of a general move in state policy towards the 'pole of coercion' in the control of a new generation of unemployed and disillusioned, and so the drift towards military policing is a development to keep down new forms of struggle against the capitalist crisis.

Lea and Young find difficulty with this explanation on at least two grounds. First, they feel that it leads to an exaggerated concentration upon the initiatives of the centralized state apparatus, as if they were consciously formulated. Second, they suggest that this leads to the other simplistic view that military policing is keeping the lid on a progressive struggle for emancipation by those suffering the consequences of economic crisis. In truth, however, much of crime is the poor robbing the poor and is not really part of a struggle for emancipation.

Lea and Young, instead, attribute the shift they see towards military policing in certain areas to three closely related factors:

1   A combination of rising rates of street crime with a lessened public disapproval of *petty* crime. Both of these result from unemployment and deprivation. Large numbers of young people hanging around on the streets begin to take on a life-style associated, in the eyes of the police, with petty crime. This encourages the police to stereotype a whole community as 'crime-people'.

2   Racial prejudice within the police force enables a smooth transition in the mind of the police officer from the proposition that certain areas with a high black population also have a high crime-rate, to a proposition that

all blacks are potential criminals. Lea and Young argue that such thinking, in turn, smoothes the path for the transition to military policing.
3   The changes in policing methods following the introduction of modern technology and communications has aggravated the situation by making normal, day-to-day, peaceful contact with the public a low priority. A former chief constable, John Alderson, has described the move to the 'technological cop':

> The impact of science and technology on the police over the thirteen years from 1966 to 1979 was very considerable . . . it had a profound effect on police methods, public image and reputation, to say nothing of police psychology. The police have been helped considerably, even crucially, by technology . . . Stemming from the universal introduction of personal pocket radio . . . together with the availability of cheap motor vehicles and later on expensive computerized command and control systems, what was basically a preventive foot-patrolling force has become a basically reactive patrolling force. (Lea and Young, 1984, p. 181)

Lea and Young argue that once the move in the direction of military policing is established, then a vicious circle is set in motion so that this drift becomes self-reinforcing (see figure 11.6). They describe this vicious circle, talking in particular about relations between the black community and the police, as follows (p. 193):

> Initial moves in the direction of military policing result in antagonizing the older generation of blacks, and in a further reduction of the flow of information; the weakening of effectiveness of other institutions of social integration result in more youngsters spending more time on the streets and in contact with the police, which reinforces the processes of stereotyping the community as a whole as crime-prone; and the propensity to collective resistance to arrest, when unchecked, threatens to make any attempt at policing a major military operation in the literal sense of the term.

Lea and Young's 'vicious circle' underlines the point that policing is changing. Their analysis is concerned largely with inner cities but, even so, military policing would only be one aspect towards the development of a 'police state' – a spectre that already concerns many civil libertarians.

Towards a police state?

In Reiner's (1985) view, a 'police state' results from five associated trends in policing, which he identifies as centralization, increasing police powers, militarization, pervasiveness and de-democratization. We have already dealt with militarization and de-democratization (that is, the lack of account-ability developed under the guise of professionalism). What of the others?

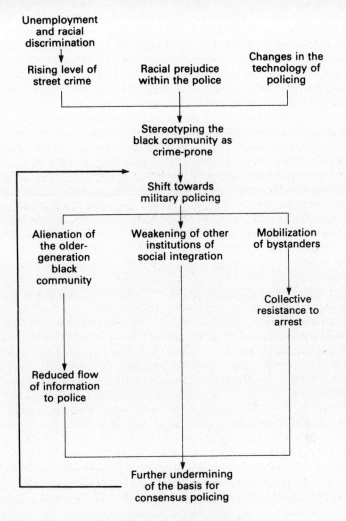

Figure 11.6 The self-reinforcement of military policing

Source: Lea and Young (1984), *What is to be Done about Law and Order? Crisis in the eighties* (Harmondsworth, Penguin), p. 194. © John Lea and Jack Young 1984. Reproduced by permission of Penguin Books Ltd.

The increase in the *centralization* of policing cannot be disputed. Amalgamations have reduced the number of police forces in England and Wales from the pre-war total of 183 to the present 43. Furthermore, police increasingly perceive themselves as a national force rather than as a local force serving a particular town or locality as was shown in the policing of the 1984–5 miners' strike.

In considering the *growth of police powers*, Reiner distinguishes between an increase in police resources, on the one hand, and a strengthening of their legal powers, on the other. There is no doubt about the substantial increase of police manpower. In 1961, as Reiner notes, there was only one police officer for every 602 people in Britain that, by 1982, this had increased to one per 394. Furthermore, expenditure on 'law and order' more than doubled in the five years from the Conservatives taking office in 1979.

Whether the legal powers of the police have, however, been extended is a much more contentious issue. One of the main planks of the Conservative government's law-and-order policy was the 1984 Police and Criminal Evidence Act. As a result of this Act, from 1 January 1986, sweeping reforms of police powers and practices, coupled with a new code of rights for citizens, came into force. The changes have provoked criticism from all sides. Civil libertarians see the legislation essentially as a strengthening of police powers (such as those to stop and search, arrest, enter, search and seize), with only 'illusory' safeguards for suspects. The police, for their part, fear that their investigations will be hampered by the need to adhere to detailed codes of practice (such as the first statutory scheme of rules for detention and questioning in police stations). So, in theory at least, the extension of police powers is hemmed in by wide-ranging safeguards.

Reiner (1985) has pointed out that many critics of the 1984 Act have overstated the extension of police powers by understating the previous powers held by them. In fact, while its safeguards regarding the abuse of power may be inadequate, in some respects the Act still represents a move away from a certain arbitrariness and absence of legal limits. In the final analysis, of course, it will be some time before it becomes clear whether the Act has improved police practice and whether breaches of the codes are the exception rather than the norm.

Finally, Reiner's notion of *pervasiveness* refers to the process whereby the police begin to penetrate and take over other social agencies. In this way, the police becomes the dominant state apparatus and there is a subtle redefinition of social and political issues as mere policing problems. The concern about the general extension of formal social control is a theme which will occupy us in our next two sections.

Prisons and punishment

There are many and varied relationships between forms of punishment and the society within which they are exercised. Methods of punishment are historically specific, different ones being employed under different economic, social and, indeed, religious conditions. Changes in these conditions make it possible, desirable and, in some cases even necessary, to abandon certain methods of punishment in favour of others.

Since the 1970s, there has been much discussion about decarceration, deinstitutionalization and diversion. Thorpe et al. (1980) note that the term decarceration' is really shorthand for a state-sponsored policy of closing down asylums, prisons and reformatories and replacing them with 'a range of facilities which will enable (delinquents) to be supported in the community'. Thorpe et al. focus on delinquents, but discussion about decarceration also encompasses areas of mental health (use of mental hospitals), gerontology (old-people's homes), and so on.

In general, the various community-control schemes for criminals that are being introduced are presented as enlightened reforms. Of course, few would deny that schemes that enable criminals to be dealt with in the community rather than being sent into custody should be applauded. However, the situation is rather more complex than it at first appears. Certainly, community controls are being set up but, at the same time, we are experiencing the biggest prison-building programme since the turn of the century. Some fear that there is no liberalization in the new method but, rather, a deepening and increasing repression of dissent. As imprisonment is no less used, perhaps it is simply that a wider framework of formal social control is being developed.

Most of the discussion about decarceration programmes concerns the USA which is now third in the world (behind the Soviet Union and South Africa) in its rate of imprisonment. Similarly, Britain, where there has been much recent talk of deinstitutionalization programmes, still has one of the highest imprisonment rates in Europe. Of course, one explanation of the massive increase in the numbers of people controlled by the criminal-justice system is that it is simply a response to increased crime. Let us consider these developments in a more systematic way.

Community control

Cohen (1985) has been influential in exposing some of the illusions of the community-control movement. For example, it is by no means clear that decarceration (that is, dealing with offenders in the community rather than in institutions such as prisons, detention centres, etc.) has been taking place particularly rapidly. The establishment of various supposed alternatives to incarceration does not necessarily decrease imprisonment rates, nor have beneficial effects on the rest of the system. In fact, there is so much investment in the 'delinquency business' that some see crime and delinquency having a definite function – delinquents keep the courts busy and provide legal-aid work for laywers; the crime problem helps to justify the employment of more policemen; delinquency management generates an expanding range of penal and social responses, drawing in more and more agencies and providing a range of services and intervention right across the delinquent and criminal career spectrum. In short, there is an enormous vested interest in the continuation of the crime and delinquency business.

Cohen (1985) and others have argued that, when new and extensive forms of intervention do result, these new forms may actually be quite hard to distinguish from the old institutions and may produce *in* the community the very practices they were designed to replace. Cohen expands on the various problems of community control and we will mention two aspects as examples here – what he calls (a) blurring and (b) widening.

Blurring: This refers to the increasing invisibility of the boundaries of the social-control apparatus. Prisons – segregated and insulated from the community – made the boundaries of control obvious enough. In today's world of community control, such boundaries are no longer as clear. There is, we are sometimes told, a 'correctional continuum' or a 'correctional spectrum'. Eventually, perhaps, we will all have a place on this 'correctional continuum'! The danger from the civil-liberties standpoint, is that the same treatment is sometimes used for those who have actually committed an offence and those who are thought to be 'at risk' of committing one. Certain legal niceties about the difference between guilt and innocence are therefore, sometimes blurred.

Widening: On the surface, one of the ideological thrusts behind the new movements towards 'community' and 'alternatives' was that the state should do less, rather than more. It is ironic, then, that one of the major results of the new network of social control has been to increase, rather than decrease, the *amount* of intervention directed at many groups of offenders; and to increase, rather than decrease, the *total* number of offenders who get into the system in the first place.

In other words the 'alternatives' have become not alternative at all, but *new* programmes that supplement the existing system or expand that system by attracting new populations – the net of social control, is thus, widened. In the next section, we note the various ways in which recent legislation (e.g. trade-union laws) and proposed legislation (e.g. the Public Order Bill) dramatically increases the numbers and kinds of criminal deviants in our midst.

While Cohen (1985) points to some of the dangers in the new movement, he also stresses that to be aware of these dangers is not to defend the old system. Undoubtedly, some programmes of community treatment or diversion are genuine alternatives – they are more humane and less intrusive. However, this should not allow us to obscure what social control is all about. For Cohen, at least, what is more striking are the continuities (rather than the discontinuities) with the system that established state control of crime in Britain two centuries ago. Certainly, the move to community entails more subtle calibrations of care, control, welfare, punishment and treatment. New categories and subcategories of deviants are being created before our very eyes. Cohen concludes that 'community' only exists for middle-class, white, healthy, middle-aged, socially powerful males. The rest have all been classified by them as various kinds of deviants who are only appropriate to live in ghettos which are patrolled as open prisons in the community. Sadly, the lyrics from the Tom Robinson Band's song, *Power in the Darkness*, which headed this chapter, begin to have an authentic ring about them.

Summary

1 Social control can play a considerable part in transforming a normal person into a deviant.

2 In terms of criminal deviance, the two most important 'gatekeepers' are the police and the judiciary.

3 Over the past decade, the police have shifted quite dramatically from having a low profile in society to being a high-profile occupation.

4 The two major issues involving the police are the growth of professionalism within the force and the shift some observers have identified from consensus policing (that is, policing by consent) to something more akin to military policing.

5 Lea and Young (1985) identify three major differences between the contrasting styles of consensus and military policing, in terms of the support of the community, the flow of information, and the role of stereotypes.

6 Lea and Young identify a shift towards military policing in certain areas as the consequence of unemployment and deprivation, racial prejudice within the police force, and changes in policing methods following the introduction of modern technology and communications.

7 Reiner suggests that a 'police state' results from five associated trends in policing – centralization, increasing police powers, militarization, pervasiveness, and de-democratization.

8 With the increase in community controls and the continued high use of imprisonment, a wider framework of formal social control is being developed. Two problems of community control are identified by Cohen (1985) as *blurring* and *widening* of boundaries.

Related topics

Chapter 5, section 5.4, deals with the relationship between ethnic minorities and the police. Crimes against women are discussed in chapter 4, in section 4.5.

Further Reading

A recent book which highlights some of the central social and political issues in the area of crime and deviance is Lea and Young (1985). Box

(1981) gives an excellent overview of the theoretical issues on deviance and is particularly helpful in discussing the social construction of official statistics. Box's (1983) more recent book has some excellent chapters on corporate crime, police crime, rape and sexual assaults on females and the question of female crime.

12 Politics

12.1 Introduction

There is a sense in which all of this book could be seen as being about
'politics'. When we consider the relationship between one social class and
another, or the character of gender relations, we are in a way dealing
with matters that are 'political'. In order, then, to be clearer about what
we shall be discussing in this chapter, it is necessary to distinguish
between two senses of the word 'political'. On the one hand, 'politics' can
be taken to refer to all aspects of social life where there is some inequality
of power between two or more people and where there are attempts to
sustain or to change that unequal relationship. In that sense, politics is
everywhere: all social life, all social institutions, are political. As the
contemporary women's movement argues, the 'personal is political',
which means that even people's closest personal relationships, with their
mothers or fathers, brothers and sisters, wives and husbands, friends and
colleagues, are all in some sense political because they involve
inequalities of power and attempts to sustain or to change those
inequalities. On the other hand 'politics' can be taken to refer to the main
social institutions that are concerned with organizing and regulating
society. This is often called 'the state'. The relevant social institutions in
Britain here consist of Parliament, which makes laws; the civil service and
local government, which implement laws and organize a wide range of
legally regulated public services; the legal institutions including the
police, which ensure obedience to the law; and the army which protects
the citizens of Britain against attack.

There is another distinction worth making. If we were to accept that
the second sense of politics is of great importance, what is the connection
between the state and the political organizations that operate within it
(such as political parties, political movements like the Campaign for
Nuclear Disarmament and pressure groups like the National Farmers
Union), and the rest of society? Is politics here independent, a set of
institutions separate from the rest of society? Can politics be studied on
its own? Or, when we consider Parliament, the civil service, political

parties, political movements and pressure groups, do these in fact reflect the social divisions, such as those of social class, that are found within the wider society? If the state and politics are part of society, exactly how does society affect them?

These questions involve complex issues, which we will consider shortly. For the present, there are two further points to note. First that we can talk of the 'state' on the one hand, and 'society' on the other, is the result of a revolution in people's thinking, which occurred particularly in the eighteenth and nineteenth centuries. Before then, the state and society were viewed as one – the state was society and it was impossible to think that there was something called society which might significantly 'cause' the state to have a particular form.

Second, the present arrangements between the 'state' and 'society' in Britain are the result of a long process of historical development, particularly involving the reduction in powers of the monarchy. In the nineteenth century, power came to reside much more with the House of Commons. There were substantial extensions of the franchise (those entitled to vote in elections), and the boundaries of different constituencies were changed so that they became rather more similar in size. Political parties also began to develop in the House of Commons and pressure groups, like the Anti-Corn Law League, first emerged to try to put pressure on Parliament to initiate or to amend legislation. It also became normal for the person chosen to be Prime Minister to have a majority of supporters in the House of Commons.

Elections, therefore, greatly increased in importance and, hence, so did a need to contact voters through well-organized political parties based on mass membership. People increasingly voted for such political parties and the parties developed 'programmes' of competing policies. Once elected, a party was expected to implement its programme and this, in turn, centralized power in the hands of the party leaders, especially the Cabinet, which had become the key element in the state by 1900. This was also reinforced by further extensions to the franchise, especially to women, so that, by 1928, all adults over 21 had the vote. Twentieth-century British politics has thus come to centre on the mobilization, organization, and control of mass public opinion, particularly as this is expressed in support for different national political parties and their leaders. Modern British politics appears in part to be a competition between two or three individuals, between the Prime Minister of the time and the leaders of the main opposition party or parties.

At the same time, there have been enormous developments in the size, range and power of the modern state. First, the modern state has at its disposal greatly enhanced powers of observing, recording, and repressing the population. Second, the British state provides a huge range of social services administered by large bureaucracies (both the civil service and local authorities). It has gradually become accepted that the state should plan and act on behalf of society as a whole and that, if matters were left to each individual, many people would suffer inequality and deprivation. During the twentieth century, there have been a number of major expansions in the expenditure and activities of the state, as it has intervened in pursuit of 'collective' goals and against purely individual interests. This was best seen in the development of an extensive welfare state in the period 1945–50, after a Labour government was elected at the end of the Second World War. Much contemporary politics is based upon divisions caused by this development: while modern Conservatism has attempted to reduce the size of the welfare state and to lower the taxation and rates to pay for it, the Labour Party has been committed to maintaining aspects of a welfare-state system. There are, likewise, a wide range of social groups that seek to restrict the size of the state (e.g. ratepayers associations) and others that endeavour to maintain or extend the present welfare state (e.g. the Child Poverty Action Group).

In the following section, we consider the question of elections, by analysing the factors that appear to influence the way people in Britain vote in general elections. What is the significance of social class, age, gender, ethnicity and where you live, on voting patterns? In section 12.3, we try to determine how power is organized in modern Britain – is it widely distributed or concentrated? If it is concentrated which groups have power? In section 12.4, we consider the state directly, particularly its source of power, internal organization and recent changes in its relations with other social forces in society. The chapter will be concluded with an assessment of current changes in British politics, particularly in the area of social policy.

12.2 Voting Behaviour

There is no simple sociological explanation of why people vote the way they do. There has always been some statistical relationship between a voter's social characteristics (occupation, religion, ethnic group, etc.) and choice between parties at elections. Usually, though, this 'correlation' has been fairly weak. 30 years ago, in the 1950s, if a voter came from a manual household, the odds were 2:1 that he or she would vote Labour; if the voter was from a non-manual household, the odds were about 3.5:1 in favour of the Conservatives. By present-day standards, though, voting in the 1950s was quite predictable. That decade saw the height of class alignment in British elections. The possibility of predicting a person's vote on the basis of occupational class (or any other social variable) has fallen since then.

There are a number of reasons why voting behaviour is difficult to predict sociologically. Most importantly, the political circumstances in which people choose, change. Since the Second World War, general elections have occurred in Britain on average at intervals of three to four years. Much may change over such a period: new political issues arise;

the programmes and policies of parties may alter. It has been an important feature of political change in Britain since the late 1960s that the parties between which the voter is permitted to choose have themselves changed. Moreover, voters are also passing judgement at elections on how satisfied they are with the out-going government, and how likely other parties are to perform better. In fact, knowing a person's opinion about a given party's past performance and position on important political issues is probably the best guide to voting intention. In this way, changing features of the political environment affect voting behaviour.

Consider, for example, the 1983 general election. A range of distinctive political circumstances contributed to a dramatic result. The Labour Party was remarkably disorganized, partly because of internal disputes which two years earlier had led to the defection of a group of Labour MPs to form the Social Democratic Party. This new party formed the Alliance with the Liberal Party, which significantly enlarged electoral choice. The Conservative Party, despite the dismal performance of the economy, increased its parliamentary majority, in part because of the personal qualities of its leader and the support for her arising from the Falklands War in 1982. Such political events, which undoubtedly affected the result of the election, may not happen again. Nevertheless, the individual voter's social attributes, and underlying social trends, also affect elections. The most frequently observed trend is a process of *dealignment*.

Dealignment

Dealignment refers to the breaking down of the patterns of voters' choice that characterized the period 1945–66. It has two aspects, which are not necessarily directly related to one another. First, voters have become unwilling to vote regularly for the two major parties. Second, a person's occupational class gives an increasingly poorer guide to his or her party choice. These aspects are called *partisan dealignment* and *class dealignment*. Since dealignment is a process, we must look at change over time, at a number of consecutive elections, making a comparison with the patterns of the 1950s.

It is generally agreed that between 1950 and 1964, voting preferences had two stable elements. First, individual voters identified with, and regularly voted for, one of the two major parties, that is either the Conservative Party or the Labour Party. Second, they tended to vote Conservative if they lived in a white-collar household, and Labour if the head of the household was a manual worker. These were, by no means, laws of voting behaviour: people did change party between elections; and other social factors besides social class were related to party choice – age, region and religious affiliation affected voting and cut across class divisions. Nevertheless, in the early 1960s, roughly four people in five who considered themselves middle class identified with and voted for the

Conservative Party, and two in three of the working class identified with the Labour Party. Such behaviour was explained in terms of class interest: the Labour Party, with its partly socialist tradition, was thought of as more likely to promote the interests of the working class, and the Conservative Party was seen as likely to favour the middle classes.

Partisan dealignment

A partisan is someone who feels a sense of identity with, or loyalty to, a political party. Whether people are partisan is usually measured by asking them whether they consider themselves to be supporters of a particular party, and how strong their attachment to that party is. The assumption is that partisans will usually vote for the party with which they identify, though they will not always do so. All things being equal, the higher the extent and intensity of partisanship among the electorate, the more voters will regularly vote for the same party at each general election. Three different kinds of evidence suggest that partisanship is declining.

1   If we look at general election results, it becomes apparent that, after 1970, the British voter began to desert the two major parties. In the elections between 1950 and 1970, on average 92 per cent of the poll (i.e. those who turned out to vote) was shared between the two major parties – Conservative and Labour. In the four elections following, those between February 1974 and 1983, the same average, called 'the two-party share of the poll', had fallen to 75 per cent. This is shown graphically in figure 12.1. The proportion of voters choosing another party rose sharply in 1974, partly as a result of nationalist parties gaining ground. In February 1974, for example, the Scottish Nationalist Party obtained 2 per cent of all votes in Britain, which amounted to 21.9 per cent of voters in Scottish constituencies. Plaid Cymru obtained 10.8 per cent of the vote in Wales. In Northern Ireland, neither of the 'two major parties' was represented at all after the 1970 election, votes there being cast for one of several Unionist parties or for the Social Democratic Labour Party or Sinn Fein. The Liberal Party, with 19.4 per cent throughout Britain in February 1974, got most of the rest of the votes cast for 'other' parties. In subsequent elections, the share of votes taken by the Scottish and Welsh nationalist parties declined. The share for the Liberal Party tended to increase, especially after forming the Alliance with the new Social Democratic Party to fight the 1983 election. The improving fortunes of the Liberal Party are shown in figure 12.2, which shows that the Liberals made substantial gains in 1964, 1974 and 1983, with a tendency for its share to subside in the intervening elections. The patterns for the two major parties are also shown in figure 12.2. Since 1970, 'other' parties have increased their support at the expense of the Labour and Conservative Parties.

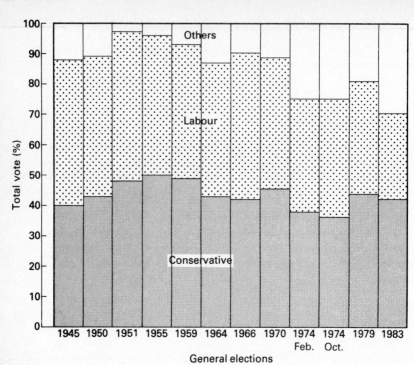

Figure 12.1 Parties' share of the poll in general elections, 1945–83 (Conservative, Labour, other)
Source: Butler and Sloman (1980), pp. 208–10.

2   While some of the increased support for 'other', or third, parties may have come from people who would otherwise have abstained, most was taken from the two major parties. This reduced the likelihood of electors regularly voting Labour or Conservative, but only slightly. It might not have reduced partisanship overall if people had instead, become attached to the nationalist parties or the Liberals. As a matter of fact, however, there is little sign of people becoming Liberal or SDP partisans. Liberal supporters appear to be fickle voters, rarely supporting the party at two consecutive elections. Thus, one study (Sarlvik and Crewe, 1983) showed that, in both the 1960s and 1970s, only 30 per cent of people who shifted their votes from a major party to the Liberals at one election voted Liberal again at the next. A significantly larger proportion, 45 per cent, returned to the party they had voted for previously. The generally increased support for the Liberal Party, and in 1983 for the Alliance, has meant that a lot of people are shifting votes between elections. However, the degree of such shifting, often called the degree of 'volatility', does not seem to have increased substantially since 1964. When there were

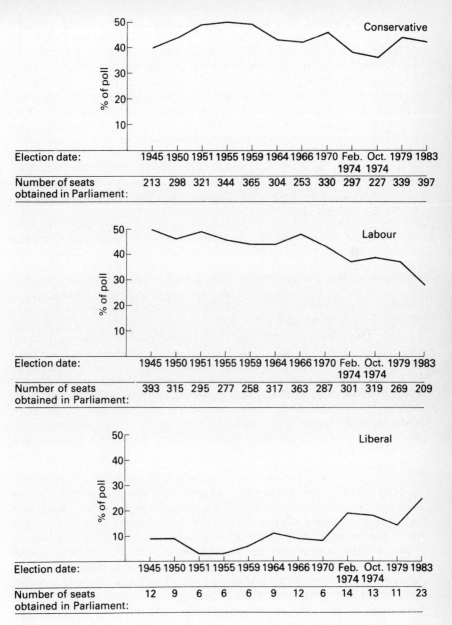

Figure 12.2   Parties' share of the poll in general elections 1945–83 (Conservative, Labour, Liberal*)

Note: *The Liberal figure for 1983 includes votes for their partners in the Alliance, the Social Democratic Party.

Source: Butler and Sloman (1980), pp. 208–10.

basically only two parties to choose between, many voters swopped from Conservative to Labour, and *vice versa*, from one election to the next.
3   A further body of evidence concerning partisan dealignment has been obtained by asking people whether they identify with a particular party and, if so, how strongly they are attached to that party. The number of electors who feel some attachment to a party seems to remain fairly constant: in 1979, 86 per cent of voters volunteered that they considered themselves supporters of a party. The intensity of their attachment has declined, though. In the 1979 election survey, 21 per cent of voters said their sense of identification was very strong, 46 per cent fairly strong, and 25 per cent not very strong (Sarlvik and Crewe, 1983). In the 1960s, around 40 per cent of voters had very strong identifications. (Unsurprisingly, the stronger the party identification, the more likely an individual is to vote for that party.)

The reason for the decline in intensity of identification is disputed. Several factors may be relevant.

1   There is some disillusionment with the major parties because of their failures when in government. This may have reduced commitment to them. It might also account for a slight tendency for absentions (non-voting) to have increased.
2   Voters may be becoming more instrumental, choosing between parties on the basis of which they think will best satisfy their personal interests. Identification and loyalty to a party would, then, become less relevant.
3   Voters may now be more concerned with political issues. Before, stability of identification was the result of political socialization, party identity being passed on from parents to children and rarely being abandoned thereafter. In such circumstances, it would make no difference to voters what their favourite party intended to do if it won power. The erosion of Labour Party support over the last five elections has been explained in these terms.

Crewe (1981), for example, argues that the Labour Party has increasingly offered policies to the electorate which its own supporters and identifiers dislike. Certainly, in 1979, more people were in favour of the Conservative than the Labour position on many issues. (Heath et al., 1985, however suggest that this was less the case in 1983.) Crewe implies that the Labour Party is unpopular because it offers traditional, socialist policies, including support for trade unionism, nationalization of industry, and the expansion of public-welfare services. He considers such appeals less successful now that people are no longer voting along class lines. This brings us to class dealignment.

Class dealignment

Class dealignment refers to the declining probability that any individual will vote for the party associated with his or her social class. Whereas we would have been moderately successful in predicting how a person would vote in the 1964 election, merely by knowing whether the head of the household was a white-collar or a blue-collar worker, this is no longer possible. Using conventional statistical measures, the correlation between occupational class position and voting has fallen. This occurred in two stages. Between 1964 and 1974 it was due to an increase in white-collar support for the Labour Party. This support seems to have come from people working in the public sector, and particularly from those in welfare services. In that period, there was no perceptible trend in voting preference among manual workers. Since 1974, however, there has been a steady decline in the proportion of manual workers, especially skilled workers, voting for the Labour Party. This particularly benefited the Conservative Party in 1979, but favoured the Liberal/SDP Alliance in 1983 (see figure 12.3).

As can be seen from table 12.1, in the 1983 election only slightly more than half of white-collar workers voted Conservative, and much less than half of all manual workers voted for the Labour Party. This is obviously, in part, the result of such a large number of people voting for the Liberal/SDP Alliance. If we only consider the vote for the two major parties, a class effect is apparent: the higher the occupational grade, the more likely a voter was to choose the Conservatives, the pattern being reversed for the Labour party. At the same time, though, a larger proportion of skilled manual workers voted Conservative (38 per cent) than voted Labour (34 per cent). This result was consistent with the trend towards dealignment that had begun in the late 1960s.

Another way of looking at the relationship between class and party is to examine the class composition of the supporters of each party. The

Table 12.1 Voting in June 1983 election by social grade – see box 28 (percentages)

Social grade	Conservative	Labour	Liberal	Other	Total %	Total number
White collar						
AB	60.8	12.0	26.1	1.1	100.0	781
C1	54.7	20.5	23.7	1.0	99.9	939
Manual retired, etc.						
C2	38.1	34.1	26.2	1.6	100.0	1,164
DE	27.9	42.5	27.1	2.3	99.8	1,230

Source: Gallup Report No. 275, July 1983, p. 4.

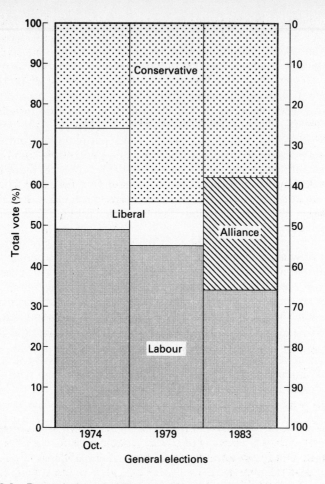

Figure 12.3 Party choice of skilled manual workers, 1974–83
Source: From Dunleavy (1983) and *Gallup Report No. 275*, July 1983.

results of such an examination of the 1983 election is in table 12.2. This shows that the Labour Party remained very heavily dependent upon the support of manual workers and those without employment: well over 75 per cent of Labour voters were from households from social grades, C2, D and E. This may create problems of electoral support for the Labour Party in the future, for one of the most important occupational changes is the declining proportion of manual employment. The Conservative Party drew a disproportionate amount of its support from white-collar workers, especially from grades AB but, nevertheless, obtained considerable manual support. The support of the Alliance, interestingly, was an almost perfect reflection of the occupational distribution. For example, 19 per cent of the British labour force is in grades AB and 19.1 per cent of Alliance support came from such people. This, as we shall see later, is an important reason why the Alliance won few seats in the 1983 election.

Table 12.2 Social composition of the support for Labour, Conservative and Alliance parties in 1983 general election by social grade – see box 28 (percentages)

Social grade	Conservative	Labour	Alliance	All of the electorate
White collar				
AB	26.7	7.8	19.1	19.0
C1	29.0	15.9	20.9	22.8
Manual retired etc.				
C2	25.0	32.9	28.6	28.3
DE	19.3	43.4	31.3	29.9
Total %	100.0	99.8	99.9	100.0
Total number	1,775	1,206	1,065	4,111

Source: Calculated from *Gallup Report No. 275*, July 1983, p. 4.

Interpreting dealignment

Some authors deny that class dealignment is occurring, a false impression being given because most studies use inappropriate class categories. Heath et al. (1985), in an important study of the 1983 election, suggest that the class-dealignment thesis grossly exaggerates the degree of change in voting behaviour. They argue that what is important is change in the class structure, and political change. They maintain that advocates of the class-dealignment thesis have used inappropriate class categories (see box 28).

Heath et al. (1985) show that self-employed manual workers and manual workers in supervisory positions systematically vote in a different fashion from the mass of manual workers. Looking at the mass of manual workers only, their behaviour was no different in 1983 from what it was in 1964: manual workers without authority voted Labour in the same proportions as before. Two other things have occurred, however. First, this group is smaller in size than it used to be. Second, the Labour Party was politically unpopular in 1983, a claim supported by the fact that fewer middle-class people voted for Labour then than at earlier elections. In other words, once we take into account changes in the class structure and

Box 28   Voting by class in the 1983 general election: comparison of different measures of class

In table 12.1, class voting was estimated using *social grade* as a measure. Social grade was designed for use in advertising, but is regularly and conventionally used in British election studies. Heath et al. (1985) used, instead, categories based on more sociological measures, distinguishing five categories:

1   salariat (i.e. professionals and managers);
2   routine white-collar workers;
3   *petite bourgeoisie* (i.e. the self-employed);
4   foremen and technicians; and
5   working class (manual workers).

(For a further discussion of class categories see chapter 3, sections 3.4 and 3.5.) The results from Heath et al.'s (1985) sample survey of voters in the 1983 election, calculating percentage of votes from each class for each party, were as follows:

Class and vote in 1983: the political distinctiveness of the classes (percentages)

	Conservative	Labour	Alliance	Others	Total number
Salariat	54	14	31	1	867
Routine non-manual	46	25	27	2	749
Petite bourgeoisie	71	12	17	0	245
Foremen and technicians	48	26	25	1	220
Working class	30	49	20	1	992

Source: Heath et al. (1985) *How Britain Votes* (Oxford, Pergamon Press), table 2.3, p. 20. Reproduced with permission.

This table gives a rather different impression to that in table 12.1. The working class quite strongly favoured the Labour Party – 49 per cent voted Labour. The distinctive support of the self-employed for the Conservative Party stands out – 71 per cent of the *petite bourgeoisie* voted Conservative. And the similarity of the voting behaviour of routine white-collar workers on the one hand and foremen and technicians, on the other, is marked.

continues

Box 28   *continued*

Using these class categories, Heath et al. (1985) also measured the proportions of voters for each party from each class. The results, which should be compared with table 12.2 are presented below:

Class and vote in 1983: the class distinctiveness of the parties

	Conservative	Labour	Alliance	Others
Salariat	34	14	35	24
Routine non-manual	25	21	26	37
Petite bourgeoisie	12	3	5	2
Foremen and technician	8	6	7	5
Working class	21	55	26	32
Total number	1,388	881	762	41

Source: Heath et al. (1985) *How Britain Votes* (Oxford, Pergamon Press), table 2.4, p. 21. Reproduced with permission.

This shows the extent to which the Labour Party relied on the manual working class for its support, and the extent to which the Alliance was supported by professional and managerial workers. It is also worth noting the great similarities between the profiles of support for the Conservative Party and the Alliance.

Finally, in interpreting these tables, each should be compared with the class composition of the electorate as a whole. One final table from Heath et al. (1985) shows the class composition of the electorate in 1983 (and compares it with 1964).

Class composition of the electorate: 1964 and 1983

	1964	1983
Salariat	18	27
Routine non-manual	18	24
Petite bourgeoisie	7	8
Foremen and technicians	10	7
Working class	47	34
Total number	1,475	3,790

Source: Heath et al. (1985) *How Britain Votes* (Oxford, Pergamon Press), table 3.3, p. 36. Reproduced with permission.

continues

Box 28 *continued*

On the basis of this transformation of the class structure Heath et al. (1985, p. 36) observe:

> The impact of these changes upon the electoral fortunes of the parties has probably been far greater than that of any class dealignment which may or may not have occurred. There is little evidence that class differences have withered away or that the classes have changed their character, but there can be no question that the *shape* of the class structure has been gradually changing throughout the postwar period.

Source: Heath, Jowell and Curtice (1985).

the political climate in 1983, the argument for class dealignment falls. In the view of Health et al. (1985), then, class position remains the major influence on an individual's voting behaviour.

Other authors acknowledge class dealignment, but disagree about its significance. But if class is no longer the basis of electoral choice, what, if anything, disposes people to choose between parties? Has some other social factor emerged to take its place? It seems not. There are other social characteristics correlated with voting. Members of trade unions still tend to vote disproportionately for the Labour Party, as do council-house tenants and immigrants. People who own houses, do not have trade-union members in the family, and who are in the highest income brackets, tend to vote Conservative. But none of these factors, alone or together, seems to account for very much of the pattern of voting. Nor are patterns much affected by gender or age. There is, therefore, considerable debate about how to interpret the available evidence.

Core-classes

It should not be entirely surprising (given what we know about changes in the labour process (see chapter 2, section 2.4), gender divisions (chapter 4), and change in the occupational structure (chapter 3, section 3.2) that occupational class, defined by a contrast between white-collar and blue-collar heads of household, does not explain electoral choice very well. Some writers have, therefore, suggested a modified model of class voting, based upon a wider interpretation of class. Rose (1974) defines 'ideal-types' of working-class and middle-class people. The attributes of these 'typical' persons are shown in figure 12.4. He suggests that the more of these 'class' traits people have, the more likely they are to vote for their 'natural' class party. Evidence from the 1979 election gives some support for this kind of explanation. In 78 per cent of cases, votes went to the Labour Party where the head of the household was a manual worker, in the manufacturing or mining sectors, a member of a trade union, and lived in a council house. This group of people, however, was no more than 9 per cent of the electorate. In contrast, in 81 per cent of cases, non-manual, owner-occupiers, without trade-union connections, and with a high standard of living, cast their vote for the Conservative Party. The voting choice of people with a mixture of these ideal, typical, class traits will be less predictable. The biggest problem with this approach is that very few people have all these traits, the behaviour of the rest being uncertain. (Though it does seem that the closer people are to a core class the more likely they are to vote for the 'core-class' party.) A second problem is whether it is acceptable to call a combination of factors which include housing and union membership a measure of *class*.

	Working class	Middle class
1 Occupation	Manual	Non-manual
2 Unionization	Trade-union member	Non-member
3 Housing	Council-house tenant	Owner-occupier
4 Education	Minimum length of time in school	Post-minimum education
5 Subjective social class	Self-identification with working class	Self-identification with middle class

Figure 12.4 'Core classes': ideal types of middle-class and working-class voters
Source: Constructed from Rose (1974).

Issues, attitudes and opinions

The failure to obtain strong correlations with social variables has led some psephologists (psephology is the study of voting behaviour) to turn their attention to electors' political opinions and attitudes. Asking people questions like 'Which party do you think will govern best?', gives some fair indication of how they will vote. The electorate's judgement of which is the best party is influenced by both their evaluation of the party's policies and their assessment of how well the parties have been performing in the recent past. This might seem unsurprising, since people may be expected to use their political knowledge and judgement when deciding how to vote. But many earlier studies suggested that people had very limited political knowledge; voters were unable to distinguish the policies of one party from another, for example. Wider knowledge may have made issues and policies more important. If this is so, it, becomes necessary to understand how people develop opinions and arrive at judgements. Workmates, friends and neighbours are all important in this process; so too is the mass media, whose predominantly conservative bias is significant, but it is very hard to isolate the effects of media exposure on voting.

Geographical change

One of the strongest recent trends has been increasing regional differences in voting behaviour. This was very marked in the 1983 election. Excluding the two big conurbations of London and the West Midlands, Labour won only three seats south of Derbyshire. The Alliance won four. The Conservatives won all the rest. The Labour Party won almost all its seats in the inner-city areas of the largest conurbations and in the mining and manufacturing areas of Scotland, Wales and the North of England. Labour support was concentrated in particular types of constituency in distinctive geographical areas. Indeed, support for both the Labour Party and the Conservative Party has steadily become more geographically concentrated since 1955. The Labour Party has increasingly obtained its support from urban and northern constituencies, whilst the Conservatives have got support from rural and southern constituencies. Each party has consolidated its support in different types of constituencies. This has several consequences for British elections. First, it reduces the number of marginal constituencies, as each major party has cumulatively increased its support in those types of constituencies it habitually wins. Second, the nationalist parties have benefited from regional variations because their potential support is inevitably geographically concentrated. Liberal and SDP votes, by comparison, are very evenly dispersed across the country. Thus it was that in 1983 the Alliance could get over 25 per cent of all votes while winning only 3 per cent of seats. To the supporters of the Alliance this was merely unfair, and proved the case for proportional representation. The same fact is, however, consistent with the observation that safe seats have become safer. The Alliance had no regional base in 1983; neither, as we have seen from table 12.2, did it have a class base. Without either it is difficult to win seats under the British 'first-past-the-post' electoral system.

The evidence concerning geographical variation in voting requires explanation. What could cause constituencies to become more and more safe for the two major parties? Psephologists long ago noted a neighbourhood effect: it has often been shown that if you are a white-collar worker and live in a manual-working-class district of a town, then you are more likely to vote Labour than if you lived in a predominantly white-collar neighbourhood. This is attributed to a process whereby social contact tends to produce consensus: if you associate with people who mostly intend to vote for one party then you are likely to be persuaded to vote for that party also. Interestingly, this effect, which typically exaggerated class voting, has not declined. It is an interesting paradox that, while an individual's occupational grade is not much guide to voting behaviour, the class composition of a constituency as a whole is a sound predictor of the success of the major parties. The implication of this seems to be that there still are class-based, local, networks for political communication, and that class remains important in voting behaviour, though in a much more complex way than used to be imagined.

Summary

We have seen that the interpretation of voting behaviour is controversial. However, a number of features stand out.

1 Partisan dealignment has occurred, support for the two major parties having declined since 1970.

2 Occupation predicts an individual's vote less well than it used to. However, it is still the variable that gives the most powerful prediction, though union membership and housing tenure are now almost as good.

3 Geographical concentration of support for the two major parties has occurred and this seems to be related to the social-class composition of different places.

12.3 Power and Politics in Britain

In this section, we step back somewhat from elections and voting patterns and consider the underlying distribution of power in Britain. There are three models of how power is distributed: the pluralist, elite and ruling-class analyses. We show that each model highlights certain aspects of contemporary politics but that none of them fully explains how politics is organized in modern Britain.

The pluralist approach

Pluralists argue that political power in Britain is dispersed and frag-mented, that there are a very large number of different groups and interests that seek to influence policy, and that no particular group is able to control the state or influence policy on a large number of different issues. In other words, different groups influence policy on different issues and, in many cases, the outcomes result from pressure from a large number of separate groups. Individuals are seen as free to join groups and attempt to influence policy. Any particular individual will be likely to have more than one interest, such that the individual's concerns will pull in different directions at different times on different issues – he or she will be 'cross-pressured'.

Pluralists, further, maintain both that all interests may be represented and may influence policy and that no particular interest, such as trade unions or the employers, is dominant within the state. The resources available to different groups are widely dispersed and are not cumulative. New issues come on to the political agenda and new groups can be favoured. Politics is always a matter of negotiation and competition for ideas and votes. The state is open to influence and it is not systematically biased towards any particular interest or another. The role of the state is two-fold: first, to maintain the rules of the game by which this competition between different groups takes place – to be in effect a referee; and, second, to implement appropriate policies through respond-ing to the balance of political forces on each relatively separate issue.

The main evidence supporting a pluralist view of Britain is as follows.

1   *There are many different groups attempting to influence policy* – groups that both support a sectional interest, such as the National Union of Teachers, and those that promote particular causes, such as the Campaign for Nuclear Disarmament. In general, such pressure-group activity is *not* as extensive as in the USA but it is both widespread and growing. We have already noted (in chapter 7, section 7.4) that in the 1970s there were over 4,000 groups attempting to influence political decisions in Birmingham alone. Furthermore, of the 350 groups listed in the 1980 *Guardian Directory of Pressure Groups and Representative Associations*, over half had been formed in the 1960s and 1970s. Many of the most effective groups are those that are relatively hidden from view and the very well-known ones are often those that do not have ready access to the organs of power. Also very many people are members of interest groups – for example, in 1984, 11 million people in Britain were members of trade unions, nearly 4 million were members of Christian churches – and many will be members of, or at least sympathetic to, more than one interest group.

2   In a study of British politics in the 1970s, it was found that *groups are generally involved in only one major political issue or at most two*. Very few were involved in a large number of issues. There were many conflicts

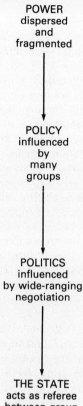

POWER
dispersed
and
fragmented

POLICY
influenced
by
many
groups

POLITICS
influenced
by wide-ranging
negotiation

THE STATE
acts as referee
between group
pressures

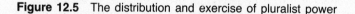

Figure 12.5   The distribution and exercise of pluralist power

where the sides changed from issue to issue. Moreover, groups involved
in policy-making enjoyed both victories and defeats and, indeed, no one
group appears to have been generally successful in getting its way. This
pattern varied considerably between different issues. While very few
groups were consistently involved in foreign-policy decisions, in all other
areas there was a plurality of groups. The influence of government bodies
themselves varied – again in foreign policy they were very powerful. On
other issues – social policy, transport, environment – they were less
effective. Conflicts also occur between different parts of the state,
between those ministries concerned to expand expenditure (on new
schools, roads etc.) and the economic ministries (especially the Treasury)
that seek to reduce public expenditure.

The elite approach

The *elite* view of British politics is based on challenging much of the pluralist account. In particular, it emphasizes how some topics are prevented from becoming issues for political resolution at all, how it is only *some* interests that are organized, and how there is a systematic bias in the political system, which favours certain groups rather than others over the long term. Although many people are members of organized groups in Britain, many others are not. For example, only half the working population are members of trade unions. Moreover, many groups themselves are generally undemocratically organized and lack participation by their membership. They are often run by 'self-perpetuating oligarchies'. Many interests are not represented by organizations (for example, young people or pensioners), or are represented very poorly (for example, women members of trade unions), while some other interests (for example the City of London) are very well-represented (through the Treasury, the Bank of England and the financial institutions themselves). These powerful elites tend to be relatively invisible, working beind the scenes in every sphere of social life. The main evidence put forward to substantiate the claim that there are powerful elites in modern Britain is as follows (see also chapter 2, section 2.2 and chapter 3, section 3.6).

1 *There are a number of key social institutions in British life* (Parliament, civil service, judiciary, church, the armed forces, business, finance, press, universities, etc.); *each of these is run by an elite, and each of these elites is recruited in approximately similar fashion*. In other words, it is argued that most elite members are white males who received private, rather than state, school education, went to Oxford or Cambridge Universities (Oxbridge), frequent similar London clubs, and who are connected to each other through kinship, friendship and overlapping elite membership. Thus, for example, a study in the early 1970s showed that 80 per cent of the directors of large banks, insurance companies, pension funds, etc. had been to fee-paying schools, 87 per cent had been to Oxbridge, 46 per cent were members of London's prestigious clubs. Nearly all these major institutions were linked to each other through 'interlocking directorships'. Likewise, two-thirds of the directors of industrial companies and of judges had been to fee-paying schools and Oxbridge; 85 per cent of Anglican bishops had a similar background (Coates, 1984). Until recently, not a single senior army officer, Anglican bishop, or High-Court judge, had a manual worker as their father; none were black and almost none were female. There is also considerable interchange between these various elite groups. It is common for ex-MPs to become directors of private companies. Conservative MPs hold, on average, two chairmanships and four directorships of companies. One study suggested that three-quarters of elite members in government, the civil service, private companies, the armed forces, the judiciary, the media, and the

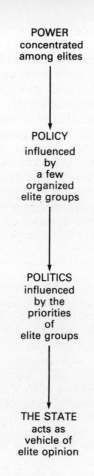

POWER
concentrated
among elites

POLICY

influenced
by
a few
organized
elite groups

POLITICS
influenced
by the
priorities
of
elite groups

THE STATE
acts as
vehicle of
elite opinion

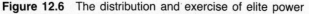

Figure 12.6 The distribution and exercise of elite power

aristocracy, all belonged to a small number of exclusive London clubs.
2 *These elites in these various institutions substantially control the
political process.* This is so, in the sense that they have prevented certain
issues from coming on to the political agenda. Thus, the main political
debate in recent years on economic issues has been between Keynesians
(followers of the economist J. M. Keynes) and monetarists. The former
argue that public expenditure and, especially, investment should be
increased in order to expand employment and, hence, that unemployment can be significantly lowered. The latter argue that too much public
expenditure and too large a supply of money cause high inflation and that
this increase in prices and in wages means unemployment is higher than it
need be. The debate between these two groups – Keynesians and
monetarists – has structured thinking on economic policy. The Labour

Party, the Alliance and so-called moderates or 'wets' in the Conservative Party are Keynesian, while the present Conservative leadership and much Conservative opinion is monetarist. What this means is that other kinds of economic policy have not really come on to the political agenda – the conflict between these particular elite groups has prevented other economic policies from being considered.

3   Elite theorists also show that *decisions made tend to favour the interests of the elite groups*. Thus, fee-paying schools are still thriving and providing an educational route straight into many elite occupations. Oxford and Cambridge are the two most financially favoured universities in Britain. Relatively little change has occurred in the distributions of income and wealth. When tax rates on high incomes appear to be put up too high, ways are found of minimizing tax liabilities and, in time, the tax rates get reduced (after the election of the 1979 Conservative Government, for example).

The ruling-class approach

The *ruling-class* analysis of British politics maintains that there is a centrally significant class structure in Britain, of capitalist employers and propertyless workers, and that politics and the state reflect this structure. It argues that elite theorists, although correct in criticizing pluralism, inadequately analyse this most fundamental feature of British society. It is not, the ruling-class model asserts, merely a question of there being a number of elites in a variety of social institutions. Rather, it is the class structure that lies at the very heart of British society and the state is, to a considerable extent, the 'instrument' of the capitalist employing class. Much contemporary politics, including voting patterns, is viewed as relatively unimportant compared with this more fundamental set of relationships. It is the civil service rather than Parliament that is significant, since it has the ability to implement decisions that sustain the economy, based on the private ownership of the means of production. Parliamentary politics is more significant 'ideologically' giving the false impression that people *can* exercise real political choices. Ruling-class theorists assert that all the major political parties are 'capitalist'. They all are concerned to run the capitalist economy as efficiently as possible and hence to maximize the rewards accruing to the capitalist class. The evidence to support this thesis is as follows.

1   *No elected government in Britain in the twentieth century has seriously sought to abolish the capitalist economy based on private ownership.* The most radical Labour Government was in power from 1945 to 1950 and then there was considerable nationalization but this mainly consisted of industries that were unprofitable in private hands (for example, railways, coal). Nor has any government seriously tried to reorganize industry so that it is run either by the workers themselves or at least in conjunction with the employers. Nor has any government in Britain extended the welfare services so that they provide adequate provision for all the

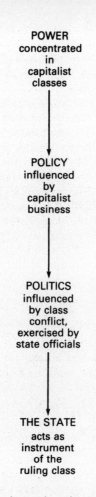

Figure 12.7   The distribution and exercise of power by the ruling classes

population from the 'cradle to the grave'. The Conservative Party obviously represents the interests of capitalist employers; the Alliance and the Labour Party, at the most, seek merely some modest reforms of that system.

2   *Business interests are not merely one elite group amongst a number, but they are the most significant and, in a way, the best organized elite.* Business interests are the wealthiest of all groups and were able, for example in the early 1970s, to mount extensive newspaper campaigns against the nationalization of the banks in Britain. They were also able to derive support from most MPs, very many of whom are actually employed by private companies. Many Cabinet ministers are previous company directors. The state is, moreover, dependent upon private

industry to provide both employment and taxation revenue. Radical governments, in particular, would not be able to finance large increases in public expenditure unless private industry continued to employ most of the working population, to pay them reasonable taxable salaries, and to provide some taxation themselves.

3   *The most well-organized group in Britain has been the institutions in the City of London*, that is, the commerical banks (such as Nat West), merchant banks (Hill Samuel), insurance companies (Guardian Royal Exchange), pension funds, finance houses, the Stock Exchange, foreign-currency dealers, and so on. These institutions have been exceptionally important in the British economy, providing what are known as high levels of invisible exports. Much British economic policy has been devoted to protecting these particular institutions through, for example, maintaining a strong value of the pound sterling, through enabling these institutions to invest abroad on a massive scale, and through ensuring that foreign confidence in the city of London is maintained by the pursuit of policies of a more deflationary rather than of an expansionary nature.

Summary

1   There are three well-known models of the distribution of political power in Britain.

2   *Pluralists* argue that political power is fragmented and dispersed among many different groups, which all influence policy on different issues. No one group or interest is dominant.

3   *Elite theorists* argue that power tends to be concentrated in the hands of the few – the leaderships of organized groups and people at the top of key institutions. These elites control political processes and political decisions tend to favour their interests.

4   *Ruling-class* theorists believe that politics reflects the class structure, which consists fundamentally of capitalist employers and propertyless workers. The political process works to the advantage of the former, who dominate political institutions.

12.4 The British State

In this section we will turn to consider the state directly, both in terms of its internal organization and of some of the policies it attempts to carry out.

The state and its powers

We define the state as consisting of that set of social institutions concerned with the passing of laws, implementing and administering those laws, and providing a legal machinery to enforce compliance with them. All these institutions rest upon the fact that the state enjoys a monopoly of legitimate force within a given territory and, as a result, it can ensure that most of the time the laws are upheld. All those activities we take to be part of the state ultimately rest upon the threat of legitimate force by the state. In Britain, the state comprises an extraordinary diversity of social institutions: the Prime Minister, Cabinet, Parliament, political parties, civil service, judiciary, police and army, local government, schools, colleges, universities, National Health System, supply of gas, water, electricity, post office, National Coal Board, British Nuclear Fuels, BBC, and so on.

By contrast with most countries, the powers of many of these different social institutions are not formally specified in a written constitution. Rather, in Britain, the constitution of the country is substantially unwritten but, nevertheless, binding. The partly unwritten character of the constitution means that changes can more easily occur in many of the social institutions that make up the state. For example, the power of the civil service has increased in recent years and that of Parliament has declined. In other words, there has been a *restructuring* of the state made possible by the substantially unwritten constitution. This, further, means that the powers of the government in Britain are extremely far-reaching, since they are not circumscribed by a written constitution that protects individual rights. Provided the government has appropriate authority to make and enforce certain laws, the judiciary will generally uphold them and ensure compliance. For example, in 1972, the Home Secretary introduced a bill in the House of Commons that retrospectively legalized various actions of the British Army in Northern Ireland, actions which the Northern Ireland High Court had determined were illegal. That bill was approved by both the Houses of Commons and Lords on the *same* day it was introduced.

Thus, the first power of the state is the almost unlimited ability to make and enforce laws. Some of these laws delegate authority to ministers to make what are, in effect, further laws (statutory instruments) without the necessity of bringing a whole new Act to Parliament. No other social institution possesses such powers. No private company, however powerful, is able to compel all British citizens to act in particular ways that are justified as being in accordance with the 'rule of law'. People in Britain generally obey the directives of the state, not because these directives are particularly popular, or just, or even necessarily sensible, but because they are the *law*. The levels of sanction necessary to enforce compliance are less marked in Britain than in other countries. There are proportionately fewer policemen in Britain. Northern Ireland aside, the police do not generally carry weapons, there is no large paramilitary force to enforce public order, and the army is generally kept out of policing work.

The second major power of the state is its ability to raise very large sums of money. In early 1985, taxation took over one-fifth of all the income received by people in Britain. However, this ability to raise taxes is not unlimited. If the government tries to raise taxes to very high levels, then this may reduce the size of the national income because it will lessen the amount of business activity in the country. As a result, the actual take from taxes would be lower than if there had not been an attempt to increase taxes in the first place. There is, thus, some restriction on the ability of governments to raise revenue through taxation, although there is much dispute as to where this limit actually lies. The Conservatives believe that taxes are already too high in Britain and that this is un-necessarily stifling initiative and entrepreneurship. By contrast, both Labour and the Alliance think that there are considerable opportunities for increasing taxes further, in order to provide improved transport, communications, hospitals or schools, and that this will, itself, enlarge the national income and, hence, future tax rates will not have to be so high. In their view, tax increases largely pay for themselves.

The third power of the state is the ability to employ large numbers of people. In wartime, for example, most of the male population were conscripted into the armed forces or organized into war-related civilian employment. In peacetime in recent years, about one-third of the labour force has been employed by the state, particular in providing services in education and the health service, providing benefits through DHSS offices, and producing goods and services in the nationalized industries (gas, electricity, coal etc.).

The fourth power of the state consists of its control over land. It is in its own right a major landowner; it can acquire land through compulsory purchase on favourable terms; it regulates the use of land through planning legislation, it can alter the relative value of privately owned land (through building a new motorway, for example), and it can establish wholly new uses for existing land (by establishing new towns like Milton Keynes).

The fifth set of powers consists of various instruments of economic policy. The state is a major investor in, and producer of, many commodities (British Leyland cars. British Aerospace planes, gas, electricity, ICL computers and British Telecom, have all been part of the public sector); it exercises some control over the exchange rate between sterling and other major currencies and, hence, affects the relative price of exports and imports; it has a certain degree of control over interest rates and the supply of money; and, through taxation and public borrowing, it affects the general level of economic activity in Britain – the national income, level of output, pattern of price increases, and the rate of unemployment.

So far, then, we have seen that the state is a particularly powerful set of interdependent social institutions. The British state has the power to pass and implement laws, to raise taxes, to employ people, to control land, and to regulate the economy. No set of private institutions possesses such

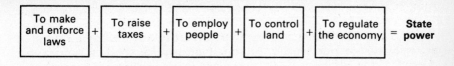

Figure 12.8 The powers of the state

a range of powers. Before considering some of these in more detail, we will briefly consider the organization of the British state.

The organization of the British state

The first point to note is that the British state is part of various international state organizations. It plays a subordinate role in the American military defence system, as evidenced by the siting of American-owned and -controlled cruise missiles on British territory. Britain is part of the International Monetary Fund which, especially in the 1960s and 1970s, dictated deflationary economic policy to a succession of British governments. Britain is also part of the European Economic Community, which enjoys legal authority over the British state. European laws take precedence over British laws where they conflict and it is possible for the actions of the British government to be declared illegal. In some cases, Conservative British laws such as those on

Table 12.3 Expenditure by various local authorities on secondary schools, 1985

Local education authority	Spending per pupil (£)	
	Books	Equipment
ILEA	18.87	88.71
Berkshire	15.82	25.54
Haringey	14.30	46.16
Walsall	12.31	32.62
Wigan	10.00	37.90
Kent	8.95	30.78
Lancashire	8.10	28.58
Sunderland	6.26	23.95

Source: Educational Publishers Council.

immigration, or very weak British laws such as on sex discrimination at work, have been declared illegal by the European Court at The Hague.

The British state is also divided internally into different levels – national, regional and local. There has been a steady reduction in the powers of the local level of government, both in the range of services provided through local authorities and in the degree of autonomy that they enjoy. This is of importance because this is the one level of government that is still relatively open to popular representation and accountability. Thus, local authorities spend greatly differing amounts on different services (e.g. on education per child), which suggests that they still possess *some* ability to decide matters on a partly local basis. Three processes have reduced the powers of local authorities:

1 the growth of new controls by central government, particularly over the level of rates;
2 the growth of a new level of government, what Dearlove and Saunders (1984) call the 'regional state' from the 1930s onwards; and
3 the increased importance of representation in the state on a 'functional' rather than on a 'territorial' basis.

On the first of these, the Conservative system of rate-capping enables central government to limit by *law* any rate increase proposed by a local council. This policy partly resulted from the way in which some local councils had been voted to power to substantially increase the range of local-authority provision of services (e.g. cheap fares and increased council housing, as in the Greater London Council, Liverpool, Sheffield, and South Yorkshire). In turn, this policy of rate-capping has added further fuel to the sense of *local* grievance and opposition to central government.

The second change is linked to the first. As some services have been taken out of local government since the 1930s, they have been administered instead by *regional* state institutions, like gas and electricity boards. These are all run by regional bodies which are non-elected, are directed by technical experts who are not really accountable to anyone, and generally do not resist central government. The relative growth in the importance of these bodies represents a considerable reorganization of the state to non-elected, undemocratic bodies. Local authorities are elected, regional bodies are not.

Finally, there has been some growth in the importance of the representation of functional groups like consumers, trade unions, professions, social workers, business and so on. At the same time, there has been a corresponding reduction in the importance of representation based on territory, as in the case of local government.

We will now consider three further issues concerning the British state: Is it a capitalist state; a corporate state; and a secret state?

Is Britain a capitalist state?

Does the British state basically work in the interests of private capitalist employers? Does it act as the ruling-class model, described in section 12.3, would suggest?

The first point to note here has been the way in which, from the 1930s until the later 1970s, there was an increasing involvement of the state in the management of the British economy. This took a number of different forms:

1 growth of extensive welfare provision;
2 attempts to regulate demand in the economy to ensure fairly low levels of unemployment and a reasonably healthy balance of trade with the rest of the world;
3 some experiments with planning the output levels of different industrial sectors;
4 various policies designed to regulate income and price increases; and
5 the nationalization of, and support for, various companies and industries that were economically unprofitable.

Since 1979, there has been a concerted effort to reverse many of these policies. This has been partly successful in that, for example, many nationalized industries have been 'privatized', there is no policy to control incomes in the private sector, and the inflation of wages and prices has been checked. However, the *attempt* to reduce state intervention has not brought about the revitalization of the British economy that was expected. Also, it has been more difficult to reduce government expenditure than was anticipated. Indeed, the total government expenditure as a proportion of national income leapt from 44 per cent to a massive 47.6 per cent between 1979 and 1980, in the first year of Conservative rule. There has, however, been some change in the distribution of state expenditure under the Conservatives. Expenditure on defence, law and order, and social-security payments have all increased greatly, while that on education, housing and overseas aid have remained constant or been reduced.

Although some changes have occurred in the past few years, the British state continues to be heavily involved in economic policy. However, perhaps the most significant fact about this is that most British economic policy has been unsuccessful and that the long-term decline of the British economy has not been halted. There are a number of reasons for this.

1 The British economy has always been heavily dependent on the state of the world economy. Crises occurring within the latter, such as the quadrupling of oil prices in 1973, affect the British economy and cause it to be highly unstable.
2 Although the British state appears highly centralized with strong

political parties, an effective civil service, and widespread popular support, it is, in fact, rather weak. It has not developed strong ties with industrial companies or developed the capacity for detailed support, planning and subsidy of industry that has occurred in other countries. The British state has not developed a close working relationship with industry.

3   In contrast, financial interests (the City of London) have been highly integrated into the British state. The Treasury and the Bank of England are both part of the state and, at the same time, are institutions of financial capital. Dearlove and Saunders (1984, p. 296) summarize the effects of this domination of the British state by finance: home-based industry would seem to have been sacrificed in the interests of the City of London; free trade has allowed foreign imports to undercut domestic producers; an over-valued pound has priced British exports out of foreign markets; the flood of capital overseas has starved home industry of new investment; and support of the balance of payments . . . has necessitated deflationary measures which have brought a halt to the growth of demand for industry's products.

So far, a ruling-class account of the distribution of power in modern Britain would seem convincing, given that this dominant class is seen to consist of essentially financial interests (sometimes termed 'finance capital'). However, although this is an extremely influential class, there is no justification for seeing the British state as the simple 'instrument' of such finance capital. This is for three reasons.

1   Economic policy in Britain has never been fully able to overcome major contradictions between different objectives, such as full employment, stable prices, a healthy balance of trade, rising productivity and output. All economic policy has been, in a way, unsuccessful and has failed to meet the interests of the major social classes and groups. However, this is also because the state operates partly separately from individual groups of employers. It makes a more general attempt to provide at least some of the conditions required for continued capitalist production and investment, conditions that would and could not be provided by individual employers. Examples of such conditions include a national motorway network, a comprehensive educational system, a system of unemployment benefit, and so on. A crucial reason why the state seeks to ensure some of the conditions necessary for continued production is because the state is, itself, dependent upon the success of the economy to provide a base for raising sufficient taxation revenue to pay for its multitudinous activities.

2   The state carries out a wide range of different policies and although some of these may reflect the interests of finance-capital, others will relate to other dominant interests, especially those of men and of whites. There is no question that the British state is not only 'capitalist' but also 'patriarchal' and 'racist'. Examples of how the British state is patriarchal

include the failure of the police and courts to protect women from sexual harassment, rape and, especially, 'domestic violence' within the family; the ways in which the social-security system works to treat women as necessarily dependent upon a male 'breadwinner'; and the overwhelmingly male composition of the upper levels of the state institutions.

That the British state is racist can be seen most clearly in the Immigration Acts of 1962, 1968, 1971 and 1982. After the 1971 Act, the status of Commonwealth immigrants was dramatically changed to being that of black migrant workers who might or might not be granted citizenship after a four-year period of probation. As Hall et al. (1978, p. 299) argue, it is from the time of this Act that we find 'The really tough "hassling" of the immigrant communities – the police "fishing expeditions" for illegal immigrants, the inspection of passports and documents, the routine "moving on" of groups of black youths, the heavy surveillance of ghetto areas, the raids on black social centres.'

3   The peculiar character of every advanced capitalist economy is that it is based on the generalization of market relationships. This means that there are countless individuals, groups and classes who are differently located in relationship to these complex market relationships. These make up a highly fragmented structure with all sorts of individuals, groups and classes seeking to maintain or improve their market position by various sorts of actions. Examples of such actions include organizing against other workers, forming trade unions, organizing with those of the same gender or ethnic group, taking industrial action, forming a professional group, and so on. In particular, the capitalist economy creates a mass of propertyless wage-labourers – the working class – which is forced to attempt to preserve itself by struggling against the employing class. One feature of the British state's recent development has been the expansion of its size and range of activities in the post-war period, partly brought about by pressure from this working class, expressed through the Labour Party. This, in turn, reflected a significant change in working-class politics that occurred in the inter-war period. This was the way in which working class leaders, especially in the trade unions, began to see the key to establishing a gradual advance to socialism as lying in the massive expansion of state-provided and centralized social-welfare facilities. This expansion was found particularly during the 1945–50 Labour government.

Is Britain a corporatist state?

If the ruling-class theory does not altogether fit, what about the pluralist and elite theories? In recent years, there has been considerable debate about the plausibility of an approach that combines pluralist and elite approaches, namely corporatism. What is argued here is that, in the early days of British capitalism, the role of the state was minimal, and was concerned with enforcing a legal structure necessary for trade to flourish. This changed after the First World War with heightened international competition, increased size of firms, the growth of monopolies, the development of well-organized trade unions, rapid technological change and mass unemployment. As a result, social conflicts became heightened and new ways were sought to reorder British society. Large and powerful interest groups came together to coordinate entire economic sectors. In exchange for controlling their members, groups of employers, on the one hand, and trade unionists, on the other, began increasingly to participate in government. The pluralist pattern became less significant as two massively powerful interest groups – employers and unions – came almost into the state itself. They provided the social order which the market could not deliver. As long as they controlled their members, they could continue to get a share in the fruits of government: the employers received state expenditure on social infrastructure and some level of subsidy; and trade unions received extensions of social-welfare provision in exchange for engaging in only modest levels of industrial action and disruption.

However, although some societies do exhibit such a pronounced 'corporate bias', the British state cannot be said to be completely corporatist. This is for the following reasons.

1   Trade unions have often not been able to control their members and prevent strikes. Trade-union leaders have only infrequently been taken 'into' the state.
2   Employers' associations have also not been part of the state for long periods. The most important, organization representing industrial employers – the CBI – was only formed in the 1960s. Before then, industrial capital had no fully representative association.
3   Corporatist arrangements are unlikely during times of high un-employment and recession, since there is less need to buy off workers with promises of a 'social contract'. Increased differences of interest between workers also make policies to control incomes almost impossible to sustain over any period.
4   Even if corporatist arrangements are established (as in 1974–6, for example) this partly encourages the politicization of other social groups outside of the corporatist bargain: women, blacks, pensioners, con-sumers, environmental groups, community-action groups, anti-nuclear protest, etc. The emergence of a radical politics formed around these new social movements makes 'corporatism' only a partial account of recent developments in British politics and the state.

To some degree, these new political forces have supplanted the working class as the major source of opposition in modern Britain. They are particularly strong in some of the major cities in Britain and, indeed, have influenced the politics of local Labour Parties. The Greater London Council (GLC), before its disappearance, most enthusiastically embraced the demands of many of these groups. For example, it subsidized many feminist groups, it declared London a nuclear-free zone, it tried to protect the environment by encouraging the use of public rather than the private transport, and it supported many local community groups.

The politics of these new social movements challenge the existing politics of social class in three important ways.

1 They assert that there are a wide range of groups discriminated against in society and not just the 'working class'.
2 They argue for new political forms that are democratic, anti-hierarchical, small-scale, and relatively decentralized. CND, for example, consists of well over one thousand different local groups, each with a considerable degree of autonomy from the central organization.
3 They maintain that the state is by no means a benevolent body that can simply redress injustices in the wider society. Rather, the state is itself to be fought against. It is the problem rather than the solution. The new social movements are fundamentally 'anti-statist' and are especially opposed to the secrecy of the British state.

The secret state in Britain

Parts of the British state are democratic and open but there is also an extremely powerful secret state. This consists of those state institutions that are non-elected, that enjoy considerable autonomy from Parliament and from the government of the day, and that tend to be closed and secretive in the manner in which they exercise their extensive powers. The nationalized industries (coal, railways, gas, Bank of England, for instance), the legal system, police, security services and the armed forces, make up the 'secret state' in Britain (see Dearlove and Saunders, 1984, chapter 5).

There are two points to note about this aspect of the state.

1 There is the fact of secrecy itself. Civil servants rarely appear in public to explain or justify their actions and to be subjected to questioning or investigation. Judges maintain that their deliberations are secret and they never have to explain why particular judgments are made. The police are not really accountable to anyone apart from the Home Secretary. This is particularly true of the most powerful force, the Metropolitan Police, which does not even have a local police authority or committee to whom it is minimally responsible but answers directly to the Home Secretary. The security services are the most secretive of all. The three most important are MI5, which is not established by statute or recognized in law, MI6, which does not officially exist, and the Government Communications Headquarters (GCHQ) at Cheltenham, which is at the centre of a worldwide network of spying, eavesdropping and communications. These bodies operate almost entirely outside the law, since there are few, if any, laws that relate to their work. All are protected by

Section 2 of the 1911 Official Secrets Act, which makes it a crime for anyone employed by any of these bodies to disclose any significant information learnt in the course of his or her job. It is also an offence to receive such information. Likewise the Defence, Press and Broadcasting Committee 'advises' the press not to publish what are meant to be sensitive matters of information relating to state actions and policies.

2   This secret state is extremely powerful. For example, although, in theory, ministers control their departments of state, in fact, the permanent civil servants exercise a great deal of control *over* ministers. This is well-shown in the BBC television programme '*Yes, Minister*', which illustrates how permanent civil servants can undermine the reforming intentions of new ministers. Among the nationalized industries in Britain, the most powerful is the Bank of England, which is in some cases more or less able to determine government economic policy. The 'advice' given by its Governor carries great weight in questions of government policy determination. This is, particularly, because only those in the Bank, the Treasury and the Cabinet know what that advice happens to be and no one outside can, therefore, put forward counter-arguments. Leading judges, who in theory are bound by the laws made by Parliament are, in fact, actively engaged in making the law. This is because they are continuously involved in interpreting the existing law; and this process of interpretation, particularly through the establishment of 'precedents', itself, in a sense, creates the law. But as Dearlove and Saunders (1984, p. 137) note, 'judicial rule-making is inherently undemocratic'. Likewise, although the social background of the police is very different from these other groups being considered here (being working class, non-public school and non-university background), it similarly attempts to limit its accountability, particularly to local-authority representatives. The police are powerful because they have the scope to exercise discretion. Amongst millions of law-breakers, the police decide who to stop on suspicion, and they do so in terms of a number of crude stereotypes of who looks like a criminal. The security services also enjoy a very high degree of autonomy in their operations and operate largely outside the law. The elected parts of the state have little idea of what security services do, or of the scale of their operations.

Summary

A number of conclusions can be drawn from the discussion in the last two sections (12.3 and 12.4).

1   The *pluralist* account is by and large incorrect, except in pointing out the wide and increasing variety of interest and promotional groups attempting to influence the state, especially at the local level.

2   As the *elite* view maintains, the central and regional levels of the state,

Figure 12.9 Special Branch officers load material removed from BBC offices in Glasgow, in a move to prevent the broadcasting of the controversial *Secret Society* series (February 1987)

Source: Stephen Gibson.

and many pressure groups, are undemocratically organized, often maintaining exceptional levels of secrecy.

3 As the *ruling-class* analysis maintains, British financial interests have been extremely powerful in sustaining central aspects of British economic policy. But, since this has not obviously been in the wider interests of producing a growing and prospering economy, a ruling-class analysis is not altogether correct.

4 The state is fundamentally patriarchal and racist in its composition and in its policies.

Related topics

Much of the discussion in chapter 3 on class is relevant to theories of the state, especially section 3.6 on the upper class. Questions of racism and sexism in politics and state policy are discussed in chapters 4 and 5.

12.5 Political Change and Social Welfare

Other than to discuss changes in voting behaviour we have said little in this chapter about party politics. This serves to emphasize that politics is not just a matter of party leaders, parliamentary debates and cabinet decisions. Nevertheless, parties are of importance in understanding social and political change. The 1980s have seen the consolidation of certain trends in the political system. A period of 'consensus politics' characterized the years after the Second World War. The two major parties, which attracted almost everybody's vote, pursued similar objectives and policies. The basis of consensus was eroded in the 1970s, as the two parties began to pursue different solutions to Britain's political problems, especially those of economic management. A Labour Government that had pursued a corporatist strategy, was replaced at the 1979 election by a government, led by Mrs Thatcher, committed to the philosophy and policies of 'neo-Conservatism'. Thatcher's government altered the course of economic and social-welfare policies. At the same time that the content of party politics was changing, the nature of mass political activity was also shifting towards involvement in unconventional protest, through what have come to be called 'the new social movements'. These developments can be interpreted as a shift from an old, consensus, politics to a 'new politics'.

The 30 years after the end of the Second World War are often referred to as the period of consensus politics. During this period, there was considerable agreement between the two major parties about broad strategic objectives in the spheres of economic and social policy.

Economic policy revolved around obtaining high levels of economic growth in a mixed economy. (A mixed economy is one in which the state owns a significant proportion of industrial enterprise, though the majority of production occurs in the private, capitalist sector.) The pursuit of economic growth entailed high degrees of state intervention and planning. The state tried to regulate the behaviour of the multitude of economic agents – firms, unions and individuals – by means of policies for prices and incomes, selective incentives to firms, changing the values of the currency, imposing foreign-exchange controls, establishing training schemes for workers, and by developing long-term, strategic, economic plans. The state also exercised control through the nationalized industries (coal, electricity, telecommunications, railways, etc.), to which direct instructions could be given. In addition, the state had control over enormous spending power and, in allocating public expenditure, it could also affect the general economic climate.

One principal area of public expenditure is in the sphere of social welfare. Expenditure on welfare has increased greatly during the twentieth century, indicating an expansion of the public provision of services, the quality and quantity of which are determined by political decision and implemented by state officials (see table 12.4). The social functions of welfare are many. Among other things, welfare policies control the behaviour of people receiving benefits; they encourage loyalty to a state that guarantees material security; and they provide a way of regulating the distribution of resources between social classes, between men and women, and between workers and those without work. A second major plank of consensus politics was a commitment to expanding and improving welfare services, i.e. housing, health, education, social security and personal social services.

Table 12.4 Social expenditure 1910–51

| | % of GNP at factor cost | | | | | | |
	1910	1921	1937	1951	1961	1971	1975
All social services	4.2	10.1	10.9	16.1	17.6	23.8	28.8
Total state expenditure	12.7	29.4	25.7	44.9	42.1	50.3	57.9

Source: Abrams and Brown (1984) *UK Society: work, urbanism and inequality* (London, Weidenfeld and Nicolson Ltd), p. 312. Reproduced with permission.

The bases of consensus politics were: economic growth; the coexistence of capitalist and state enterprises; economic planning; muted conflict between capital and labour; and expanded welfare services that offered both material security and greater equality of treatment and opportunity to all citizens. In many respects, consensus politics represented a political compromise between two parties acting as representatives of the interests of social classes. The mixed economy/welfare state was a basis for class equilibrium, though a balance subject to constant negotiation between capital and labour.

This political compromise collapsed during the 1970s. A difficult situation arose, sometimes called the 'fiscal crisis' of the state, and sometimes the problem of 'overload'. This problem was the failure to achieve levels of economic growth sufficient to fund continued extension of state intervention in the economy and the provision of welfare services. Faced with contracting resources, but without reduction in the expectations or demands of groups for more state spending, governments had to seek new policies to deal with the situation. In these circumstances, the two parties grew apart, developing different approaches to the social and economic problems. New parties emerged; consensus disappeared, challenged most fundamentally by the neo-Conservatism of the governments of Margaret Thatcher.

Neo-Conservative policies since 1979

The policies and pronouncements of the governments of Mrs Thatcher, elected in 1979 and re-elected in 1983, mark the burial of consensus politics and a shift away from the political compromise of the welfare state. In the economic sphere, these governments have been concerned to reduce the size of the state sector, by selling profitable parts of the nationalized industries to private investors (e.g. British Telecom, British Shipbuilders, Jaguar Cars) and by inducing the remaining state-owned enterprises to cut costs and reduce staffing (e.g. the National Coal Board, civil service, universities). This corresponds to the neo-Conservative ideological conviction that the market mechanism is the most effective and efficient means for determining what should be produced and how the product should be distributed. The more transactions are undertaken in the market, the less room there is for economic planning and regulation, which is not to say that the government's policies have had no effect on economic performance – the operation of the market has entailed very high levels of unemployment, for instance. Other aspects of legislation, especially regarding trade unions, have also had economic effects but the intention is, nonetheless, to reduce state intervention in economic affairs.

In the realm of social policy, the same ideology of the market has played a part in restructuring services. The central issue is one of cost, of state expenditure. A variety of means have been employed in order to reduce expenditure on education, housing, etc. In a very few cases, services have simply been discontinued. Otherwise, three approaches have been followed.

1   Savings may come from *reducing the range or quality of the service to the client*. The rules of eligibility can be altered so that fewer people are entitled to receive the service. Alternatively, the quality of the service may decline: less money for school text-books and the faster turnover of beds in maternity hospitals, are examples of this. Another possibility is to

What we need now is a far greater degree of personal responsibility and decision, far more independence from the government and a comparative reduction in the role of government.

Mrs Margaret Thatcher, Conservative Political Centre lecture, October 1968

The first requirement for progress in social policy is that lip-service to equality be supplanted by an effective universal minimum standard. Since the essential pre-condition of acceptable standards in food, shelter, warmth and the rest is adequacy of income, the government's duty is not to supply goods or services to everyone, but to direct financial support to the minority with inadequate incomes. State education and the NHS are *supply* responses to a deficiency of *demand*.

R. Harris and A. Seldon, *Over-Ruled on Welfare*, 1979

It must be remembered that independent providers ... are nearer to public demand than local authorities can ever be ... their perpetual search for profitability ... stimulates them to discover and produce what the consumer wants ... In this sense the market sector is more genuinely democratic than the public sector, involving the decisions of far more individuals and at much more frequent intervals.

The Omega File, 1983–4

It has become abundantly clear in the period [the 1970s] that Governments themselves cannot ensure high employment, so that it would be misleading to present the change of emphasis in objectives as 'ending the post-war commitment to high employment'. Governments can create the conditions in which it can be achieved, but whether it is achieved depends on the responses of management and labour.

Treasury memorandum to the Treasury and Civil Service Committee of the House of Commons, June 1980

One other myth too must be laid to rest: that is the notion that our approach to Britain's social and economic problems has its origins in the University of Chicago or even the Free Trade Hall of Manchester. It does not. But let me for my part assert that the Conservative tradition is too rich and vital to be hijacked by the advocates of paternalistic interference. The aristocratic tradition of paternal Toryism has a place, and an honourable one. But the Prime Minister's Grantham and my Port Talbot, and the values and traditions which they bred, are just as much the cornerstone of what today's Conservatives believe. Thrift, hard work, independence, the desire to succeed – not just for oneself but for one's family and country too – are and always have been the moral bulwark of the Conservative creed.

Sir Geoffrey Howe, Chancellor of the Exchequer, speech at Hemel Hempstead, 30 March 1983

Figure 12.10 Neo-Conservative policies since 1979

increase charges to the client: increased dental and prescription charges, or higher council-house rents fall into this category.

2   The *organization and working practice involved in delivering the service may be changed.* There are cases where technical change (computerization, for example) or changes in administration (centraliz- ation of services, as in the 1974 reorganization of the National Health Service), may reduce costs. But, since most welfare services are labour- intensive, savings usually come from reducing the number of people employed to deliver the service. There are now fewer school teachers, university lecturers and social-security officials per client than there were in 1980. By and large, this means that workers in welfare services have had to work harder and deal with more cases.

3   Savings may come from *altering the way the service is provided.* The government can encourage private agencies to provide more services. Thus the supply of, and demand for, private-school places and private health care signifies a shift from state provision to market-based provision. This is partly a knock-on effect from the other two changes: as service workers become more hurried and the quality of the service to the client, therefore, deteriorates, many of those who can afford to, turn to the private (market) sector, buying medical insurance and education. Another shift in the mode of the provision of services is signified by the policy of community care, which returns some forms of caring from the state to families. The policy of 'deinstitutionalizing' mental care, returning patients to 'normal living in the community', is appealing in the sense that mental hospitals are often unpleasant places. The problem is, though, that 'caring communities' scarcely exist. In fact, care outside institutions (for the infirm and the elderly as well as the mentally ill) is largely provided by kin, overwhelmingly by *female* relatives. In the absence of satisfactory, but also expensive, back-up services – day-centres and mobile welfare workers – community care means either poor care or care by women. A third important change has been in the realm of housing, where council-house building has largely ceased and the existing stocks have been sold at attractive prices to tenants. Again, the state has withdrawn its involvement and the private sphere has increased, though not sufficiently to fill the gap.

These changes in the provision of welfare services are significant. They undoubtedly have some deleterious effects both on clients and workers in the services concerned. Clients suffer hardship, misery, inconvenience; workers are reported to be demoralized, more prone to absenteeism, and dissatisfied with the service being given to the client. These changes are consistent with the general political values of neo-Conservatism, as well as being a response to the crisis of public expenditure. In fact, public expenditure on welfare has not fallen, though it has been redistributed, to some degree, between different services. As table 12.5 shows, while spending on housing has fallen dramatically, social-security payments have increased, largely due to high levels of unemployment. Cost reductions in other major services – education and health – have not been very great. The welfare state is, thus, being restructured, rather than abandoned, which perhaps bears out Offe's (1984, p. 153) claim about the key contradiction of the welfare state: 'while capitalism cannot co-exist *with* the welfare state, neither can it exist *without* the welfare state'.

Table 12.5 Shares of public expenditure, 1976–7 to 1983–4 (percentages)

	1976–7	1978–9	Planned 1979–80	1980–1	1982–3	1983–4
Defence	11.3	11.4	12.0	12.0	12.2	12.8
Law and order	3.1	3.1	3.3	3.4	3.6	3.7
Education	12.7	12.3	12.1	12.2	11.1	10.4
Health and personal social services	10.9	11.3	11.5	12.2	11.8	11.9
Housing	7.0	5.6	6.1	5.0	3.0	2.2
Social security	21.2	24.9	25.1	25.1	27.8	27.6

Source: Abrams and Brown (1984) *UK Society: work, urbanism and inequality* (London, Weidenfeld and Nicolson Ltd), p. 318. Reproduced with permission.

Party politics is, then, changing to some degree. The old consensus between the two major parties has dissolved as the Labour Party has become increasingly critical of the economic and welfare policies pursued by Conservative governments since 1979. At the same time, new types of political action have become important.

New social movements

The term 'new social movements' refers to groups of people affiliated to loosely linked campaigns for social and political change. The most important in Britain are the women's liberation movement, the peace movement – of which the Campaign for Nuclear Disarmament (CND) is best known – and the environmental movement (the 'Greens' are, though, more popular and influential on the continent). It is now frequently argued that these movements signify the emergence of a new kind of politics.

Issues and values

The new social movements each concentrate on a single set of themes: the establishment of equality and autonomy for women, the preservation of peace, and the preservation of the environment. They are primarily

Figure 12.11   A demonstration of the movement for peace: the CND rally, Hyde Park, 1983
Source: Jenny Matthews/Format.

protest movements, reacting against the main thrust of established party politics and state policies. Each stands for greater *control* for the mass of people over the conditions of everyday life. Control is more important than money or material wealth. Self-management and personal autonomy are key values. Indeed, both the peace and the environmental movements see materialist values and mass political apathy as major threats to the very survival of the human race. Nuclear war or ecological imbalance (radiation poisoning, pollution, the exhaustion or mismanagement of the world's natural resources) threaten human extinction. A sense of human identity and dignity, along with moral outrage, inspires the belief that ordinary people must become involved to protest against the irrational, undisciplined and uncontrolled tendencies of the established political system. Such values are universalistic rather than class-based: nuclear fall-out respects neither class distinctions nor national boundaries – *all* human beings are at risk.

Organization of action

Internally, the new social movements are made up of supporters of campaigns around particular issues. Becoming a member is not considered especially important; rather, people are supporters or sympathizers who act together for the duration of a particular campaign, often at the local level. The absence of high levels of central organization is a feature that corresponds to the values of self-management and democratic control. The women's liberation movement is the clearest example, refusing to set up a substantial, national, central organization and rejecting hierarchy (there are no leaders), because it is both undemocratic and typical of masculine forms of behaviour, to which the movement is opposed. Instead, it works on the basis of small, egalitarian groups (the 'consciousness-raising group' is the basic unit) without any formal membership. The movement acts together by engaging in particular campaigns around specifically gender issues, for example, on abortion legislation, for equal pay and opportunities, against male violence, and against nuclear weapons at the Greenham Common women's camp. Thus, action is organized around immediate, single-issue campaigns, rather than on a platform of policies with an ideological base, as with political parties. Nor is there regular negotiation, consultation and bargaining, as with pressure groups and trade unions. The sporadic nature of involvement in temporary campaigns causes some difficulties in the coordination of action, but is consistent with the anti-centralist values of the movement.

Looseness of organization also influences the tactics of these movements, the way in which they operate with respect to outside agencies. The march, public demonstration, petition and civil disobedience (intentional, non-violent, law-breaking) are among the main ways in which movements express protest and try to influence the public and the politicians. Such tactics are relatively unconventional and designed to express opposition. The formal channels of representative party politics are generally avoided, indicating some disillusionment with the effectiveness of parliamentary, democratic procedures.

Social actors

The people involved in these movements are far from being a cross-section of British society. The most prominent group are the so-called 'new middle class' – professional and technical-scientific workers, highly educated and, often, in state employment. However, they do not act as a *class* and this feature generally distinguishes 'new' from 'old' politics. Rather, they tend to act on behalf of other kinds of collectivities; youth, ethnic group, women and humanity are collectivities defined without reference to achievement, mobility, property ownership or occupation (which are defining attributes of class). Significantly, another main category of participants are not in paid employment at all – housewives and students, especially. The most notable absentees from the new social movements are the principal classes of capitalist society – the bourgeoisie and the proletariat – neither of which participate to any significant degree. It is this last feature that has led to speculation about the end of class politics. Perhaps the new social movements embody a new and

modern politics of social change, indifferent to older concerns with
economic growth, material inequality and social security. Alternatively,
these movements can be interpreted as negative expressions of moral
protest that are largely irrelevant to the centres of political power –
governments, classes and the organs of the state. Whichever of these is
true, the new movements do indicate some change in British political
culture and are part of a shift from a stable, two-party system with a

		'Old' politics	'New' politics
Issues and values		Economic growth and management; social security; material distribution	Preservation of peace and the environment; establishment of equal human rights
		Security; equal opportunity; personal consumption and material improvement	Opposition to centralized, bureaucratic or state control. In search of personal autonomy and democratic self-management
The organization of action	Internal organization	Formal organization and large representative associations (e.g. parties, pressure groups)	Informal, spontaneous, egalitarian, impermanent groups of campaigners
	Channels of interest	Interest-group bargaining; competitive party politics	Protest based on demands, formulated in negative terms about single issues, using unconventional tactics
Social bases of participants		Classes and occupational groups acting in their own group interests, especially with respect to material rewards	Certain socio-economic groups (especially the 'new middle class') acting not in own interests but on behalf of other ascriptive collectivities (e.g. women, youth, humankind)
Axis of politics		Class interest	Moral concern

Figure 12.12   The distinctiveness of the new social movements: a summary
Source: Adapted from Offe (1985), p. 832.

generally passive population, to more volatile, active and shifting political involvement.

Summary

1 Consensus politics, which entailed a stable two-party system, broad agreement over policies for running a mixed-economy/welfare state, and a politically passive population, has now disappeared.

2 The political idea underpinning the economic policies and welfare service provision by the Conservative governments since 1979 have altered the ideological climate of British politics.

3 The new social movements have increased their support, encouraging unconventional political action around issues which have little to do with class politics.

Related topics

Chapter 7, section 7.4 presents a discussion of new social movements in an urban context. Section 12.2 gives an account of voting and the two-party system. Comparisons with the social bases of new religious movements (chapter 10, section 10.5) can be instructive.

Further Reading

On voting behaviour, the classic work on Britain is Butler and Stokes (1974). Some of the themes of change are pursued in a recent book which takes in the 1983 election, Heath, Jowell and Curtice (1985). A recent short restatement of the dealignment thesis can be found in Crewe (1984). The most useful single book on the British state is Dearlove and Saunders (1984). Other useful sources are Coates (1984) and Drucker et al. (1984).

Bibliography

Aaronovitch, S. and Sawyer, M. (1975) *Big Business* London, Macmillan.

Abercrombie, N. and Urry, J. R. (1983) *Capital, Labour and the Middle Classes* London, George Allen and Unwin.

Abercrombie, N., Baker, J., Brett, S. and Foster, J. (1970) Superstition and religion: the God of the gaps, *Sociological Yearbook of Religion in Britain* 3: 93–129.

Abrams, M. (1959) *The Teenage Consumer* London Press Exchange Papers, No. 5.

Abrams, P. and Brown R. (eds) (1984) *UK Society: work, urbanism and inequality* London, Weidenfeld and Nicolson.

Allan, G. A. (1979) *A Sociology of Friendship and Kinship* London, George Allen and Unwin.

Allan, G. (1985) *Family Life* Oxford, Basil Blackwell.

Anderson, M. (1971) *Family Structure in Nineteenth Century Lancashire* Cambridge, Cambridge University Press.

Anwar, M. (1979) *The Myth of Return* London, Heinemann.

Anyon, J. (1980) Social class and the hidden curriculum of work, *Journal of Education* 162(1): 67–92.

Atkinson, A. B. and Harrison, A. J. (1978) *Distribution of Personal Wealth in Britain* Cambridge, Cambridge University Press.

Atkinson, A. B. and Harrison, A. J. (1980) Trends in the distribution of wealth in Britain, in Atkinson A. B. (ed) *Wealth Income and Inequality* Oxford, Oxford University Press.

Atkinson, A. B. (ed.) (1980) *Wealth, Income and Inequality* Oxford, Oxford University Press.

Bain, G. S. (ed.) (1983) *Industrial Relations in Britain* Oxford, Basil Blackwell.

Bain, G. S. and Elsheikh, F. (1976) *Union Growth and the Business Cycle* Oxford, Basil Blackwell.

Ball, M. (1983) *Housing Policy and Economic Power* London, Methuen.

Ball, S. J. (1981) *Beachside Comprehensive: a case study of secondary schooling* Cambridge, Cambridge University Press.

Banks, O. (1976) *The Sociology of Education* 3rd edn, London, Batsford.

Barker, E. (1984) *The Making of a Moonie* Oxford, Basil Blackwell.

Baron, S. et al. (1981) *Unpopular Education: schooling and social democracy since 1944* London, Hutchinson.

Barr, A. and York, P. (1982) *The Official Sloane Ranger Handbook* London, Ebury Press.

Barrett, M. (1980) *Women's Oppression Today* London, Verso.

Barrett, M. and McIntosh, M. (1982) *The anti-Social Family* London, Verso.

Barron, R. D. and Norris, G. M. (1976) Sexual divisions, and the dual labour market, in Diana Leonard Barker and Sheila Allen (eds) *Dependence and Exploitation in Work and Marriage* Harlow, Longman.

Bechofer, F. and Elliott, B. (1968) An approach to a study of small shopkeepers and the class structure, *European Journal of Sociology* 9:2.

Becker, H. (1963) *Outsiders: studies in the sociology of deviance* New York, Free Press.

Beckford, J. (1985) *Cult Controversies* London, Tavistock.

Beechey, V. (1978) Women and production: a critical analysis of some sociological theories of women's work, in A. Kuhn and A. M. Wolpe (eds) *Feminism and Materialism* London, Routledge and Kegan Paul.

Beechey, V. and Whitelegg, E. (eds) (1986) *Women in Britain Today* Milton Keynes, Open University Press.

Bennett, T., Boyd-Bowman, S., Mercer, C. and Woollacott, J. (eds) (1981) *Popular Television and Film* London, BFI/Open University Press.

Berger, P. (1968) *The Social Reality of Religion* London, Faber and Faber.

Berle, A. A. and Means, G. C. (1932) *The Modern Corporation and Private Property* New York, Macmillan.

Bernstein, B. (1971) *Class, Codes and Control* London, Routledge and Kegan Paul, vol. 1 *Theoretical Studies Towards a Sociology of Language*.

Berman, M. (1983) *All That Is Solid Melts Into Air: the experience of modernity* London, Verso.

Beynon, H. (1973) *Working for Ford* London, Allen Lane.

Beynon, H., Hudson, R. and Sadler, D. (1986) The growth and internationalisation of Teesside's chemicals industry, Durham, Working Paper No. 3, Middlesborough Locality Study.

Beynon, H. and Wainwright, H. (1979) *The Workers Report on Vickers* London, Pluto.

Beveridge Report (1942) *Social Insurance and Allied Services* London, HMSO.

Black Report (1980) *Inequalities in Health: report on a research working group*, London, DHSS.

Blau, P. and Duncan, O. (1967) *The American Occupational Structure* New York, Wiley.

Blumler, J. G. and McQuail, D. (1968) *Television in Politics: its uses and influence* London, Faber and Faber.

Bowles, S. and Gintis, H. (1976) *Schooling in Capitalist America* London, Routledge and Kegan Paul.

Boyd, D. (1973) *Elites and their Education* Slough, NFER Publishing Co.

Box, S. (1981) *Deviance, Reality and Society* 2nd edn, London, Cassell.

Box, S. (1983) *Power, Crime and Mystification* London, Tavistock.

Brake, M. (1980) *The Sociology of Youth Culture and Youth Subcultures* London, Routledge and Kegan Paul.

Braverman, H. (1974) *Labor and Monopoly Capital: the degradation of work in the twentieth century* New York, Monthly Review Press.

Brenner, M. H. (1977) Health costs and benefits of economic policy, *International Journals of Health Services* 7(4): 581–623.

Brown, C. (1984) *Black and White Britain* London, Heinemann.

Brown, R., Curran, M. and Cousins, J. (1983) *Changing Attitudes to Employment?* Department of Employment, Research Paper No. 40, London, HMSO.

Burgess, R. (1986) *Sociology Education and Schools: an introduction to the sociology of education* London, Batsford.

Burgoyne, J. and Clark, D. (1982) Reconstituted families, in R. N. Rapoport, M. P. Fogarty and R. Rapoport (eds) *Families in Britain* London, Routledge and Kegan Paul.

Burns, T. and Stalker, J. (1961) *The Management of Innovation* London, Tavistock.

Burns, T. (1977) *The BBC: Public Institution and Private World* London, Macmillan.

Butler, D. and Sloman, A. (1980) *British Political Facts 1900–79* 5th edn, London, Macmillan.

Butler, D. and Stokes, D. (1974) *Political Change in Britain: the evolution of electoral choice* 2nd edn, London, Macmillan.

Campbell, M. (1981) *Capitalism in the UK* London, Croom Helm.

Cashmore, E. and Troyna, B. (1983) *Introduction to Race Relations* London, Routledge and Kegan Paul.

Centre for Contemporary Cultural Studies (1982) *The Empire Strikes Back* London, Hutchinson.

Child, J. (1972) Organizational structure, environment and performance: the role of strategic choice, *Sociology* 6(1).

Civil Service Department (1984) *Civil Service Statistics* London, HMSO.

Clarke, I. M. (1982) The changing international division of labour within ICI, in M. Taylor and N. Thrift (eds) *The Geography of Multinationals: studies in the spatial development and economic consequences of multinational corporations* London, Croom Helm.

Clarke, J. (1976) Style, in S. Hall and T. Jefferson (eds) *Resistance through Rituals* London, Hutchinson.

Clarke, J. and Critcher, C. (1985) *The Devil Makes Work: Leisure in capitalist Britain* London, Macmillan.

Coates, D. (1984) *The Context of British Politics* London, Hutchinson.

Cockburn, C. (1983) *Brothers: male dominance and technological change* London, Pluto.

Cohen, S. (1972) *Folk Devils and Moral Panics* Oxford, Martin Robertson.

Cohen, S. (1985) *Visions of Social Control* Cambridge, Polity.

Commission on the Poor Law (1909).

Compton, J. M. (1968) Open competition and the Indian civil service, 1854–1876, *English Historical Review* 83: 265–84.

Crewe, I. (1981) The Labour Party and the electorate, in D. Kavanagh (ed.), *The Politics of the Labour Party* London, George Allen and Unwin.

Crewe, I. (1984) The electorate: partisan dealignment ten years on, in H. Berrington (ed.), *Change in British Politics* London, Cass.

Crompton, R. and Jones, G. (1981) Clerical 'proletarianization': myth or reality, British Sociological Association Annual Conference.

Crompton, R. and Jones, G. (1984) *White-Collar Proletariat: deskilling and gender in clerical work* London, Macmillan and Philadelphia, Temple University Press.

Curran, J., Gurevitch, M. and Woollacott, J. (1977) (eds) *Mass Communication and Society* London, Edward Arnold.

Daniel, W. W. and Millward, N. (1983) *Workplace Industrial Relations in Britain: the DE/PSI/SSRC survey* London, Heinemann.

Davis, D. (1977) Where comprehensives score, *Times Educational Supplement* 25 March 1977, quoted in Rutter et al. (1979) *Fifteen Thousand Hours: secondary schools and their effects on children* London, Open Books.

Deane, P. and Cole, W. A. (1967) *British Economic Growth 1688–1959: trends and structure* 2nd edn, Cambridge, Cambridge University Press.

Dearlove, J. and Saunders, P. (1984) *Introduction to British Politics* Cambridge, Polity.

Deem, R. (1985) Women and leisure, paper delivered at the University of Lancaster.

Department of Education and Science (1978a) *Comprehensive Education* London, HMSO.

Department of Education and Science (1978b) *Statistics of Education 1978* London, HMSO.

Department of Education and Science (1985) *Statistics of Schools* London, HMSO.

Department of Education and Science (1986) *Statistics of Education: Schools 1985* London, HMSO.

Department of Employment (1981) *New Earnings Survey 1981* London, HMSO.

DHSS (1984) *The Health Service in England: Annual Report* London, HMSO.

Diamond Commission (1975) *Report No.2* London, HMSO.

Donnison, D. and Soto, P. (1980) *The Good City: a study of urban development and policy in Britain* London, Heinemann.

Downing, H. (1980) Word processors and the oppression of women, in T. Forrester (ed.) *The Microelectronics Revolution* Oxford, Blackwell.

Doyal, L. (1979) *The Political Economy of Health* London, Pluto.

Drucker, D., Dunleavy, P., Gamble, A. and Peele, G. (eds) (1984) *Developments in British Politics* revised edn, London, Macmillan.

Dunleavy, P. (1977) Protest and quiescence in Urban Politics: a critique of some pluralist and structuralist myths, *International Journal of Urban and Regional Research* 1(2): 193–218.

Dunleavy, P. (1983) Voting and the electorate, in H. Drucker (ed.) *Developments in British Politics* London, Macmillan.

EEC Labour Force Survey London, OPCS, biannually.

Edgell, S. (1980) *Middle-Class Couples* London, George Allen and Unwin.

Employment Gazette Department of Employment, monthly.

Engels, F. (1969) *The Condition of the Working Class in England* London, Panther.

Engels, F. W. (1972) *The Origin of the Family, Private Property and the State* London, Lawrence and Wishart.

Equal Opportunities Commission (1985) *Women and Men in Britain: a statistical profile* London, EOC.

Erickson, C. (1959) *British Industrialists: Steel and Hosiery 1850–1950* Cambridge, Cambridge University Press.

Evans, M. (ed.) (1982) *The Woman Question: readings on the subordination of women* 3rd edn, London, Fontana.

Fagin, L. (1984) *The Forsaken Families: the effects of unemployment on family life* Harmondsworth, Penguin.

Family Expenditure Survey London, HMSO, annually.

Family Policy Studies Centre (1984) *An Ageing Population* London, Family Policy Studies Centre.

Finch, A. and Scrimshaw, P. (eds) *Standards, Schooling and Education* London, Hodder and Stoughton, 1980.

Finer Report (1974) *Report of Committee on One-Parent Families* London, HMSO.

Frankenberg, R. (1966) *Communities in Britain* Harmondsworth, Penguin.

Fraser, R. (ed.) (1968) *Work* vol. 1, London, Penguin/New Left Books.

Frith, S. (1984) *the Sociology of Youth* Ormskirk, Causeway.

Fothergill, S. and Gudgin, G. (1979) Regional employment change: a subregional explanation, *Progress in Planning* 12; 155–219.

Fothergill, S. and Gudgin, G. (1982) *Unequal Growth: urban and regional employment change in the UK* London, Heinemann Educational Books.

Gallagher, E. B. (1976) Lines of reconstruction and extension in the Parsonian sociology of illness, *Social Science and Medicine* 10; 207–18.

Gallie, D. (1978) *In Search of the New Working Class: automation and social integration within the capitalist enterprise* Cambridge, Cambridge University Press.

Gallie, D. (1983) *Social Inequality and Class Radicalism in France and Britain* Cambridge, Cambridge University Press.

Gallup Political Index Reports, Social Surveys (Gallup Polls), London, periodic.

General Household Survey OPCS, annually.

Gershuny, J. (1978) *After Industrial Society* London, Macmillan.

Gershuny, J. (1983) *Social Innovation and the Division of Labour* Oxford, Oxford University Press.

Giddens, A. (1973) *The Class Structure of Advanced Societies* London, Hutchinson.

Giddens, A. (1980) *The Class Structure of the Advanced Societies* 2nd edn, London, Hutchinson.

Glasgow University Media Group (1976) *Bad News* London, Routledge and Kegan Paul.

Glasgow University Media Group (1980) *More Bad News* London, Routledge and Kegan Paul.

Goldthorpe, J. H., Llewellyn, C. and Payne, C. (1980) *Social Mobility and Class Structure in Modern Britain* Oxford, Oxford University Press.

Goldthorpe, J. H., Lockwood, D., Bechhofer, F. and Platt, J. (1968a) *The Affluent Worker: industrial attitudes and behaviour* Cambridge, Cambridge University Press.

Goldthorpe, J. H., Lockwood, D., Bechofer, F. and Platt, J. (1968b) *The Affluent Worker: political attitudes and behaviour* Cambridge, Cambridge University Press.

Goldthorpe, J. H., Lockwood, D., Bechhofer, F. and Platt, J. (1969) *The Affluent Worker in the Class Structure* Cambridge, Cambridge University Press.

Gorz, A. (1985) *Paths to Paradise: on the liberation from work* London, Pluto.

Gray, A. (1982) Inequalities in Health. The Black Report: a summary and comment, *International Journal of Health Services* 12: 3.

Gurevitch, M., Bennett, T., Curran, J. and Woollacott, J. (eds) (1982) *Culture, Society and the Media* London, Methuen.

Hagan, J. (1984) *The Disreputable Pleasures* Toronto, McGraw-Hill.

Hakim, C. (1979) *Occupational Segregation: comparative study of the degree and pattern of differentiation between men and women's work* Department of Employment research paper 9.

Hakim, C. (1982) The social consequences of high unemployment, *Journal of Social Policy* 11(4); 433–67.

Hales, C. P. (1986) What do managers do? A critical review of the evidence, *Journal of Management Studies* 23(1): 88–115.

Hales, M. (1980) *Living Thinkwork* London, CSE Books.

Hall, P. (1975) *Urban and Regional Planning* Harmondsworth, Penguin.

Hall, R. (1985) *Ask any Woman* London, Falling Wall Press.

Hall, S., Critcher, C., Jefferson, T., Clarke, J. and Roberts, B. (1978) *Policing the Crisis* London, Macmillan.

Hall, S. and Jefferson, T. (eds) (1976) *Resistance through Rituals* London, Hutchinson.

Halsey, A. H., Floud, J. and Anderson, C. A. (eds) (1961) *Education, Economy and Society: a reader in the sociology of education* New York, Free Press.

Halsey, A. H., Heath, A. F. and Ridge, J. M. (1980) *Origins and Destinations: family, class and education in modern Britain* Oxford, Clarendon Press.

Hanmer, J. and Saunders, S. (1984) *Well Founded Fear* London, Hutchinson.

Hannah, L. (1976) *The Rise of the Corporate Economy* London, Methuen.

Harbury, C. D. and Hitchens, D. M. W. N. (1979) *Inheritance and Wealth Inequality in Britain* London, George Allen and Unwin.

Hargreaves, D. H. (1982) *The Challenge for the Comprehensive School: culture, curriculum and community* London, Routledge and Kegan Paul.

Hargreaves, J. (ed.) (1982) *Sport, Culture and Ideology* London, Routledge and Kegan Paul.

Harrison, A. and Gretton, J. (eds) (1984) *Health Care UK 1984: an economic, social and policy audit* London, Chartered Institute for Public Finance and Accountancy.

Harrison, A. and Gretton, J. (eds) (1985) *Health Care UK 1985: an economic, social and policy audit* London, Chartered Institute of Public Finance and Accountancy.

Harrison, P. (1983) *Inside the Inner City: life under the cutting edge* Harmondsworth, Penguin.

Hartmann, H. (1979) Capitalism, patriarchy and job segregation by sex, in Z. Eisenstein (ed.) *Capitalist Patriarchy* New York, Monthly Review Press.

Heath, A. (1980) Class and meritocracy in British education, in A. Finch and P. Scrimshaw (eds) *Standards, Schooling and Education* London, Hodder and Stoughton.

Heath, A. (1981) *Social Mobility* London, Collins.

Heath, A., Jowell, R. and Curtice, J. (1985) *How Britain Votes* Oxford, Pergamon.

Hill, S. (1976) *The Dockers: class and tradition in London* London, Heinemann.

Hill, S. (1981) *Competition and Control at Work: the new industrial sociology* London, Heinemann.

Holdway, S. (1983) *Inside the British Police* Oxford, Basil Blackwell.

Hole, W. V. and Pountney, M. T. (1971) *Trends in Population Housing, and Occupancy Rates 1861–1961* Department of the Environment Building Research Station, HMSO.

Hough, M. and Mayhew, P. (1983) *The British Crime Survey: first report* London, HMSO.

Hough, M. and Mayhew, P. (1985) *Taking Account of Crime: key findings from the second British Crime Survey* London, HMSO.

Hunt, A. (1978) *The Elderly at Home* London, HMSO.

Husband, C. (ed.) (1982) *'Race' In Britain* London, Hutchinson.

Hyman, R. and Price, R. (eds) (1983) *The new working class? White collar workers and their organizations: a reader* London, Macmillan.

Jencks (1972) *Inequality: a reassessment of the effect of family and schooling in America* New York, Basic Books.

Johnson, J. H. (1972) *Urban Geography* Oxford, Pergamon.

Jowell, R. and Airey, C. (1984) *British Social Attitudes* London, Gower.

Kelly, M. P. (1980) *White Collar Proletariat* London, Routledge and Kegan Paul.

Kelman, S. (1975) The social nature of the definition problem in health, *International Journal of Health Services* 5 (4): 625–42.

Kelsall, R. K. (1974) Recruitment to the higher civil service: how has the pattern changed?, in Stanworth, P. and Giddens, A. (eds) *Elites and Power in British Society* Cambridge, Cambridge Univesity Press.

King, R. and Raynor, J. (1981) *The Middle Class* Harlow, Longman.

Kitwood, T. (1980) *Disclosures to a Stranger* London, Routledge and Kegan Paul.

Klein, R. (1983) Is the NHS really in crisis, *New Society* 3 November.

Kumar, K. (1975) Holding the middle ground: the BBC, the public and the professional broadcaster, *Sociology* 9 (3).

Kumar, K. (1978) *Prophecy and Progress: the sociology of industrial and post-industrial societies* Harmondsworth, Penguin.

Lane, T. and Roberts, K. (1971) *Strike at Pilkingtons* London, Fontana.

Laslett, P. (1965) *The World we have Lost* London, Methuen.

Lea, J. and Young, J. (eds) (1984) *What is to be Done about Law and Order? Crisis in the eighties* Harmondsworth, Penguin.

Leach, E. (1968) The Cereal Packet Norm, The *Guardian* 29 January 1968.

Lee, C. H. (1984) The service sector, regional specialisation, and economic growth in the Victorian economy, *Journal of Historical Geography* 10(2): 139–55.

Lee, R. M. (1979) Communes as alternative families, MPhil thesis, North East London Polytechnic.

Leete, R. (1977) Changing patterns of marriage and remarriage, in R. Chester and J. Peel (eds) *Equalities and Inequalities in Family Life* London, Academic Press.

Leggatt, T. (1970) Teaching as a profession, in J. A. Jackson (ed.) *Professions and Professionalization* Cambridge, Cambridge University Press.

Leichter, H. (1980) *A Comparative Approach to Policy Analysis: health care policy in four nations* Cambridge, Cambridge University Press.

Lemert, E. (1967) *Human Deviance, Social Problems, and Social Control* Englewood Cliffs, Prentice-Hall.

Littler, C. R. (1982) *The Development of the Labour Process in Capitalist Societies: a comparative study of the transformation of work organization in Britain, Japan and the USA* London, Heinemann.

Lockwood, D. (1958) *The Blackcoated Worker* London, George Allen and Unwin.

Lockwood, D. (1966) Sources of variation in working class images of society, *Sociological Review* 14(3): 249–67.

Mack, J. and Lansley, S. (1985) *Poor Britain* London, George Allen and Unwin.

Matza, D. (1964) *Delinquency and Drift* Chichester, Wiley.

McCulloch, A. (1982) Alternative households in R. N. Rapoport, M. P. Fogarty and R. Rapoport (eds) *Families in Britain* London, Routledge and Kegan Paul.

McNally, J. (1979) *Women for Hire: a study of the female office worker* London, Macmillan.

McNaught, A. (1984) *Race and Health Care in the United Kingdom* London, Centre for Health Service Management Studies, Polytechnic of South Bank.

McQuail, D. (1977) The influence and effects of mass media, in J. Curran et al. (eds) *Mass Communications and Society* London, Edward Arnold.

McRobbie, A. (1978) Working class girls and the culture of femininity, in Birmingham University Centre for Contemporary Cultural Studies, Women's Studies Group *Women Take Issue: aspects of women's subordination* London, Hutchinson.

Martin, J. and Roberts, C. (1984) *Women and Employment: a lifetime perspective; the report of the 1980 DE/OPCS women and employment survey* London, HMSO.

Massey, D. (1984) *Spatial Divisions of Labour: social structures and the geography of production* London, Macmillan.

Massey, D. and Meegan, R. (1982) *The Anatomy of Job Loss: the how, why and where of employment decline* London, Methuen.

Mellor, J. R. (1977) *Urban Sociology in an Urbanized Society* London, Routledge and Kegan Paul.

Michels, R. (1915) *Political Parties: a sociological study of the oligarchical tendencies of modern democracy* Illinois, Free Press of Glencoe.

Mitchell, J. (1984) *What is to be Done about Illness and health* Harmondsworth, Penguin.

Moorhouse, H. F. (1976) Attitudes to class and class relations in Britain, *Sociology* 10(3): 469–96.

Morgan, D. H. J. (1969) The Social and educational background of Anglican bishops – continuities and changes, *British Journal of Sociology* 20: 295–310.

Morley, D. (1980) *The 'Nationwide Audience'* London, BFI.

Mungham, G. and Pearson, G. (eds) (1976) *Working Class Youth Culture* London, Routledge and Kegan Paul.

Murdock, G. (1982) Large corporations and the control of the communications industries, in J. Curran et al. (eds) *Mass Communications and Society* London, Edward Arnold.

Nakase, R. (1981) Some characteristics of Japanese-type multinational enterprises today, *Capital and Class* 13: 61–98.

New Earnings Survey Department of Employment, annually.

Newby, H., Bell, C., Rose, D., and Saunders P. (1978) *Property, Paternalism and Power* London, Hutchinson.

Newby, H. (1979) *The Deferential Worker: a study of farm workers in East Anglia* Harmondsworth, Penguin.

Newby, H. (1980) *Green and Pleasant Land?* Harmondsworth, Penguin.

Newton, K. (1976) *Second City Politics: democratic processes and decision making in Birmingham* Oxford, Oxford University Press.

Nichols, T. and Beynon, H. (1977) *Living with Capitalism: class relations and the modern factory* London, Routledge and Kegan Paul.

Nyman, S. and Gilbertson, A. (1978) The ownership and control of industry, *Oxford Economic Papers* 3(1).

Oakley, A. (1974) *The Sociology of Housework* Oxford, Martin Robertson.

Oakley, A. (1982) *Subject Women* London, Fontana.

Offe, C. (1984) *Contradictions of the Welfare State* trans. J. Keane, London, Hutchinson.

Offe, C. (1985) New social movements: challenging the boundaries of institutional politics, *Social Research*, 52(4): 817–68.

Office of Population Censuses and Surveys (1980) *Classification of Occupations, 1980* London, HMSO.

Open University (1977), DE 353: Mass Communication and Society, Unit 10, Patterns of ownership; question of control, by G. Murdock, Open University Press.

Otley, C. B. (1970) The social origins of British army officers, *Sociological Review* 18: 213–39.

Otley, C. B. (1973) The educational background of British army officers, *Sociology* 7.

Pahl, R. (1984) *Divisions of Labour* Oxford, Basil Blackwell.

Pahl, R. E. and Wallace, C. (1985) Household work strategies in the recession, in N. Redclift and E. Mingione (eds) *Beyond Employment* Oxford, Basil Blackwell.

Parker, R. (1982) Family and social policy: an overview, in R. N. Rapoport, M. P. Fogarty and R. Rapoport, *Families in Britain* London, Routledge and Kegan Paul.

Parker, S. (1976) *The Sociology of Leisure* London, George Allen and Unwin.

Parkin, F. (1971) *Class Inequality and Political Order*, London, MacGibbon and Kee.

Parry, N. and Parry, J. (1976) *The Rise of the Medical Profession* London, Croom Helm.

Parsons, T. (1956) The American Family: its relations to personality and to the social structure, in T. Parsons and R. F. Bales (eds) *Family, Socialization and Interaction Process* London, Routledge and Kegan Paul.

Pearson, G. (1983) *Hooligan: a history of respectable fears* London, Macmillan.

Poole, M., Mansfield, R., Blyton, P. and Frost, P. (1981) *Managers in Focus: the British Manager in the early 1980s* Aldershot, Gower.

Popay, J., Rimmer, L. and Rossiter, C. (1983) *One Parent Families, Parents, Children and Public Policy*, London, Study Commission on the Family.

Price, R. and Bain, G. S. (1983) Union growth in Britain: retrospect and prospect, *British Journal of Industrial Relations* 21(1): 46–67.

Rapoport, R. N., Fogarty, M. P. and Rapoport, R. (eds) (1982) *Families in Britain* London, Routledge and Kegan Paul.

Razzell, P. E. (1963) Social origins of officers in the Indian and British home army, *British Journal of Sociology* 14: 248–60.

Reiner, R. (1985) *The Politics of the Police* Brighton, Wheatsheaf.

Rex, J. and Tomlinson, S. (1979) *Colonial Immigration in a British City* London, Routledge and Kegan Paul.

Rex, J. and Moore, R. (1967) *Race, Community and Conflict* Oxford, Oxford University Press.

Richardson, J. and Lambert, J. (1985) *The Sociology of Race* Ormskirk, Causeway Press.

Roberts, J. M. (1976) *The Hutchinson History of the World* London, Hutchinson

Roberts, K. (1978) *The Working Class* London, Longman.

Roberts, K. (1983) *Youth and Leisure* London, George Allen and Unwin.

Roberts, K., Cook, F. G., Clark, S. C., and Semeonoff, E. (1977) *The Fragmentary Class Structure* London, Heinemann.

Robson, B. T. (1971) *Urban Analysis: a study of city structure* Cambridge, Cambridge University Press.

Rose, R. (1974) Britain: simple abstractions and complex realities, in R. Rose (ed.) *Electoral Behaviour* New York, Free Press.

Rose, R. (1980) Class does not equal party, University of Strathclyde, Centre for Study of Public Policy, *Occasional Paper* 74.

Routh, G. (1980) *Occupation and Pay in Great Britain* London, Macmillan.

Rowthorn, B. (1986) Deindustrialisation in Britain, in R. Martin and B. Rowthorn (eds) *The Geography of Deindustrialisation* London, Macmillan.

Royal Commission on the Distribution of Income and Wealth (1979) London, HMSO *Report No. 7.*

Runciman, W. G. (1983) *A Treatise on Social Theory* Cambridge, Cambridge University Press, vol. 1, *The Methodology of Social Theory.*

Rutter, M., Maughan, B., Mortimore, P. and Ouston, J. (1979) *Fifteen Thousand Hours: secondary schools and their effects on children* London, Open Books.

Sarlvik, B. and Crewe, I. (1983) *Decade of Dealignment: the Conservative victory of 1979 and electoral trends in the 1970s* Cambridge, Cambridge University Press.

Saunders, P. (1979) *Urban Politics: a sociological interpretation* London, Hutchinson.

Saunders, P. (1981) *Social Theory and the Urban Question* London, Hutchinson.

Scarman Report (1981) *The Brixton Disorders 10–12 April 1981* London, HMSO.

Scott, J. (1979) *Corporations, Classes and Capitalism* London, Hutchinson.

Scott, J. (1982) *The Upper Classes: Property and Privilege in Britain* London, Macmillan.

Scott, J. (1985) The British upper class, in Coates, D., Johnston, G. and Bush, R. (eds) *A Socialist Anatomy of Britain*, Cambridge, Polity.

Scott, J. and Griff, C. (1984) *Directors of Industry* Cambridge, Polity.

Seabrook, J. (1978) *What Went Wrong?: working people and the ideals of the labour movement* London, Gollancz.

Sharpe, S. (1976) *'Just Like a Girl': how girls learn to be women* Harmondsworth, Penguin.

Sinfield, A. (1981) *What Unemployment Means* Oxford, Martin Robertson.

Skelton, R. (ed.) (1964) *Poetry of the Thirties* Harmondsworth, Penguin.

Smith, D. J. (1977) *Racial Disadvantage in Britain* Harmondsworth, Penguin.

Social Trends, London, HMSO, annually.

Stacey, M. (1978) The Sociology of health and illness: its present state, future prospects and potential for health research, *Sociology* 12(2): 281–307.

Stanworth, P. and Giddens, A. (1974) An economic elite: a demographic profile of company chairmen, in Stanworth, P. and Giddens (eds) *Elites and Power in British Society* Cambridge, Cambridge University Press.

Stanworth, M. (1983) *Gender and Schooling: a study of sexual divisions in the classroom* London, Hutchinson.

Stark, E. (1977) The epidemic as a social event, *International Journal of Health Services* 7(4):691–705.

Stewart, A., Prandy, K., and Blackburn, R. M. (1980) *Social Stratifications and Occupations* London, Macmillan.

Taylor, L. and Mullan, B. (1986) *Uninvited Guests* London, Chatto and Windus.

Taylor, L., Walton, P. and Young, J. (1973) *The New Criminology* London, Routledge and Kegan Paul.

Taylor, L., Walton, P. and Young, J. (eds) (1975) *Critical Criminology*, London, Routledge and Kegan Paul.

Thompson, K. (1974) Church of England bishops as an elite, in Stanworth, P. and

Giddens, A. (eds) *Elites and Power in British Society* Cambridge, Cambridge University Press.

Thompson, P. (1983) *The Nature of Work: an introduction to debates on the labour process* London, Macmillan.

Thornes, B. and Collard, J. (1979) *Who Divorces?* London, Routledge and Kegan Paul.

Thorpe, D., Smith, D., Green., C. J. and Paley, J. H. *Out of Care* London, George Allen and Unwin.

Townsend, P. (1979) *Poverty in the United Kingdom* Harmondsworth, Penguin.

Townsend, P. and Davidson, N. (1982) *Inequalities in Health* Harmondsworth, Penguin.

Turner, B.S. (1985) Knowledge, skill and occupational strategy: the professionalisation of paramedical groups, *Community Health Studies* 9(1): 38–47.

UCCA (1984) *Report 1984, Statistical Supplement* Cheltenham, UCCA.

University Grants Commission (1984) *University Statistics 1983/4* London, HMSO, vol.1.

Wallis, R. (1984) *The Elementary Forms of the New Religious Life* London, Routledge and Kegan Paul.

Weber, M. (1968) *Economy and Society* Berkeley, University of California Press.

Westwood, S. (1984) *All Day, Every Day: factory and family in the making of women's lives* London, Pluto.

Whitelegg, E. et al. (1982) *The Changing Experience of Women* Oxford, Martin Robertson.

Willis, P. (1977) *Learning to Labour* London, Saxon House.

Wilson, B. (1966) *Religion in Secular Society* London, C. A. Watts.

Wilson, B. (ed.) (1981) *The Social Impact of New Religious Movements* New York, Rose of Sharon Press.

Winship, J. (1978) A woman's world: woman – an ideology of feminity, in Women's Studies Group, Centre for Contemporary Cultural Studies, *Women Take Issue: aspects of women's subordination*, London, Hutchinson.

Women's Studies Group, Centre for Contemporary Cultural Studies, University of Birmingham (1978) *Women Take Issue: aspects of women's subordination* London, Hutchinson.

Young, M. and Willmott, P. (1957) *Family and Kinship in East London*, London, Routledge and Kegan Paul.

Young, M. and Willmott, P. (1973) *The Symmetrical Family* London, Routledge and Kegan Paul.

Index

Index by Elizabeth Clutton